Inside the Offertory

Inside the Offertory

ASPECTS OF CHRONOLOGY AND TRANSMISSION

Rebecca Maloy

OXFORD

UNIVERSITY PRESS

2010

OXFORD
UNIVERSITY PRESS

Oxford University Press, Inc., publishes works that further
Oxford University's objective of excellence
in research, scholarship, and education.

Oxford   New York
Auckland   Cape Town   Dar es Salaam   Hong Kong   Karachi
Kuala Lumpur   Madrid   Melbourne   Mexico City   Nairobi
New Delhi   Shanghai   Taipei   Toronto

With offices in
Argentina   Austria   Brazil   Chile   Czech Republic   France   Greece
Guatemala   Hungary   Italy   Japan   Poland   Portugal   Singapore
South Korea   Switzerland   Thailand   Turkey   Ukraine   Vietnam

Published by Oxford University Press, Inc.
198 Madison Avenue, New York, New York 10016

Publication of this book was supported by the Manfred Bukofzer Publication
Endowment Fund of the American Musicological Society

www.oup.com

Oxford is a registered trademark of Oxford University Press.

Library of Congress Cataloging-in-Publication Data
Maloy, Rebecca.
Inside the offertory : aspects of chronology and transmission /
Rebecca Maloy.
Includes bibliographical references and index.
ISBN: 978-0-19-531517-2
1. Offertories (Music)—History and criticism.   2. Gregorian chants—History and criticism.   I. Title.
ML3082.M36 2009
782.32′35—dc22   2008006685

Companion Web site is available online at www.oup.com/us/insidetheoffertory
Access with username Music4 and password Book2497

9 8 7 6 5 4 3 2 1
Printed in the United States of America
on acid-free paper

For CK and my parents

ACKNOWLEDGMENTS

This project has benefited from the advice of many. I am especially indebted to Edward Nowacki, who first opened my eyes to the richness of chant studies and supervised my early efforts in the field. I have learned much from the following colleagues, who read and commented on parts of the manuscript, shared invaluable work in advance of its publication, or offered expert advice on particular questions: Terence Bailey, Calvin Bower, Steven Bruns, Carlo Caballero, Daniel DiCenso, Joseph Dyer, James Grier, Elissa Guralnick, Roman Hankeln, Emma Hornby, Jay Keister, Lori Kruckenberg, Luisa Nardini, Andreas Pfisterer, Carl Serpa, Jeremy Smith, Ruth Steiner, Richard Valantasis, and the anonymous reviewers for Oxford University Press. The participants in the offertory symposium organized by Roman Hankeln in Trondheim in 2004 have provided much food for thought, as have the members of the International Musicological Society study group "Cantus Planus." Feedback in earlier stages of writing was given by the students in my Fall 2005 seminar: Ross Hagen, Spencer Hutchings, Chad Hamill, JoãoJunquiera, Rebecca Mindock, Robin Ethridge Pentland, and Richard von Foester. I am grateful for the expert guidance of the editorial staff at Oxford University Press, especially Suzanne Ryan, Norm Hirschy, and copyeditor Martha Ramsey, who guided the project through its various stages with enthusiasm and aplomb. For much needed technical support I thank Sean Brady, David Bugher, John Drumheller, and Claire Miller.

The project was supported by a Research Grant from the University of Colorado Graduate Committee on the Arts and Humanities and by an American Musicological Society Subvention for Publication. I am grateful to my colleagues in the College of Music for their support, especially chairs Jeremy Smith, Tom Riis, Brenda Romero, and Dean Dan Sher. Release time from teaching duties in the spring of 2006 greatly helped me to see the project to completion. For far more than I can name, I am indebted to my family and friends, especially to Cynthia Katsarelis and my parents, Janette and John Maloy, whose support has made everything possible.

ABOUT THE COMPANION WEB SITE

At the companion Web site for this volume, www.oup.com/us/insidetheoffertory, readers may download PDF files for each of the ninety-four offertories in the edition. The required user name and password for the site may be found on the copyright page.

CONTENTS

Inside the Offertory

1

INTRODUCTION

In November of 753, Pope Stephen II began a long journey across the Alps to seal an alliance with the Frankish kingdom. Pepin had ascended to the Frankish throne in 751 with the approval of Stephen's predecessor Zacharias, marking the end of Merovingian rule. In an earlier exchange of envoys and correspondence, Stephen had sought Pepin's protection against invasions from the Lombard King Aistulf. Stephen's journey to Francia followed a failed diplomatic visit to Pavia and a final entreaty to Aistulf to abandon occupied Roman lands. Upon Aistulf's refusal, Stephen and his entourage proceeded to Pepin's villa at Ponthion. In the events that followed Stephen's arrival in January 754, Pepin took an oath to restore the lost territories of the Papal Republic; he and his two sons were titled Patricii Romanorum, and their descendants given exclusive rights to the Frankish throne.[1] The alliance with Rome initiated a new role for the Frankish kings, now invested with temporal and spiritual power.

It is doubtful that Stephen's visit occasioned the Franks' first exposure to Roman liturgy and chant. Beginning in the early seventh century, Roman practices had been brought to England and subsequently transmitted to Gaul by English missionaries.[2] In the early decades of the eighth century, however, Boniface's

---

1. The circumstances surrounding the Frankish-Papal alliance have been recounted in numerous places. For a Roman perspective, see especially Thomas F. X. Noble, *The Republic of St. Peter: The Birth of the Papal State, 680–725* (Philadelphia: University of Pennsylvania Press, 1984), 61–98. For studies focusing on the adoption of Roman liturgy in Francia see N. Netzer, *L'introduction de la messe romaine en France sous les Carolingiens* (Paris: Picard, 1901); Theodor Klauser, "Die liturgischen Austauschbeziegungen zwischen der römischen und der fränkisch-deutschen Kirche vom achten bis zum elften Jahrhundert," *Historisches Jahrbuch* 55 (1933): 169–77; Gerald Ellard, *Magister Alcuin, Liturgist* (Chicago: Loyola University Press, 1956); Cyrille Vogel, "Les échanges liturgiques entre Rome et les pays Francs jusqu'a l'époque de Charlemagne," in *Settimane de studi del centro italiano di studi sull'alto medio evo VII* (Spoleto: Presso la Sede del Centro, 1960), 185–295; Rosamund McKitterick, *The Frankish Church and the Carolingian Reforms, 789–895* (London: Royal Historical Society, 1977); J. M. Wallace-Hadrill, *The Frankish Church* (Oxford: Clarendon Press, 1983). For a thorough look at Frankish-Roman relations during the Merovingian period, see Fritz Beisel, *Studien zu den fränkisch-römischen Beziehungen: Von ihren Anfängen bis zum Ausgang des 6. Jahrhunderts* (Idstein, Germany: Ullrich–Schulz-Kirchner, 1987). For the Merovingian cultural picture, see Yitzhak Hen, *Culture and Religion in Merovingian Gaul, A.D. 481–751* (New York: Brill, 1995).
2. See Yitzhak Hen, "Rome, Anglo-Saxon England and the Formation of the Frankish Liturgy," *Revue Bénédictine* 112 (2002): 301–22l; and Catherine Cubitt, "Unity and Diversity in the Early Anglo-Saxon Liturgy," in *Unity and Diversity in the Church*, ed. Robert Swanson (Oxford: Blackwell, 1996),

---

attempts to spread further Roman influence in Francia had met with resistance from the Frankish nobility. It was through Stephen's visit and the resultant political and spiritual alliance that the Roman liturgy and chant were fully adopted throughout the Frankish kingdom.

After Pepin's death in 768, efforts toward Romanization were continued by his son Charlemagne, who sought from Pope Hadrian an authentic copy of the Gregorian sacramentary, usually referred to as the Hadrianum.[3] His *Admonitio generalis* of 789 provided an official mandate that the Franks should conform to the liturgical and musical practices of Rome.[4] A unified, Roman use throughout the kingdom would serve as a powerful symbol of the Carolingians' authority and unity with Rome. As primary documents attest, however, the adoption of Roman liturgy in the north did not proceed smoothly.[5] Although eighth-century liturgical practices were largely compatible throughout the region, they were far from uniform in their details.[6]

If Pepin and Charlemagne's vision of unified liturgical practice was difficult to realize, that of musical uniformity must have seemed even more elusive. Liturgical conformity to Rome was facilitated by the Carolingian emphasis on literacy and the many written documents that made their way through the kingdom.[7] The liturgy's

---

45–59. The nature of Roman liturgical and musical influences on seventh-century England remains sketchy; the prevailing practice was likely a combination of Roman and Anglo-Saxon liturgy. Recent scholarship has explored the possible transmission of the Old Gelasian Sacramentary to Gaul via England. See Yitzhak Hen, "The Liturgy of St. Willibrord," *Anglo-Saxon England* 26 (1997): 41–62; and Donald A. Bullough, *Alcuin: Achievement and Reputation* (Leiden: Brill, 2004), 176–217. James McKinnon suggests that the practice described by Bede reflects Roman monasteries rather than the *schola cantorum*. James McKinnon, *The Advent Project: The Later-Seventh-Century Creation of the Roman Mass Proper* (Berkeley: University of California Press, 2000), 909–8. See also Peter Jeffery, "Rome and Jerusalem: From Oral Tradition to Written Repertory in Two Ancient Liturgical Centers," in *Essays on Medieval Music in Honor of David G. Hughes*, ed. Graeme M. Boone (Cambridge, Mass.: Harvard University Press, 1995), 227–29. Further details of the influence of English missionaries on Gaul were presented by Jeffery at the annual meeting of the American Musicological Society, 2003.

3. As is well known, the Hadrianum was anything but a "pure Gregorian" sacramentary. For a summary of relevant sources, see Cyrille Vogel, *Medieval Liturgy: An Introduction to the Sources* (Washington, D.C.: Pastoral Press, 1986): 80–85.

4. *Monumenta germaniae historica Capitularia regum francorum*, ed. Alfred Boretius (Hannover: Hahn, 1883), 1:53–54.

5. Various accounts of the discrepancies between Frankish and Roman practice are given by John the Deacon, Notker, and others (see notes 10, 11, and 12).

6. Rosamund McKitterick, "Unity and Diversity in the Carolingian Church," in Swanson, *Unity and Diversity*, 59–82; Rosamund McKitterick, review of *Gregorian Chant and the Carolingians*, by Kenneth Levy, *Early Music History* 19 (2000): 283–85. "Although a remarkable degree of consistency may have been achieved by the tenth century, parallel liturgical and textual evidence would suggest that harmony rather than uniformity prevailed before that" (284). A thesis in progress by Daniel J. DiCenso of Magdalene College, Cambridge, promises to further challenge the view of liturgical uniformity in the Carolingian era. DiCenso's work finds much variety among the sacramentaries attached to the graduals indexed in Hesbert's *Antiphonale Missarum Sextuplex*. DiCenso presented preliminary results at the annual meeting of the American Musicological Society, Quebec, November 1, 2007.

7. For perspectives on the cultural context of literacy in the Carolingian era, see especially François Louis Ganshof, "The Use of the Written Word in Charlemagne's Administration," in *The*

significance as a token of unity with Rome extended to its music as well. The symbolic weight of the liturgical music was embodied in the very term that came to designate it, "Gregorian chant." The legend that Gregory the Great had received the chant directly from the Holy Spirit invested the melodies themselves with a certain authority. In the eighth century, however, the Frankish cantors had only their unnotated chant books and aural memories to aid them in the momentous task of learning the melodies.[8]

By the late ninth century, the time of the earliest notated witnesses to the Frankish-Gregorian repertory, the melodic tradition had achieved a certain degree of consistency.[9] The decades between the Frankish reception of Roman chant and its preservation in notation, however, have left us with scores of unresolved questions. Did the Frankish cantors intend to reproduce the Roman chant verbatim, following Charlemagne's mandate, or did they deliberately modify the melodies to conform to their own sensibilities? And if complete faithfulness to the Roman tradition was the goal, could it be achieved through memory alone?

Carolingians and the Frankish Monarchy, trans. Janet Sondheimer (Ithaca, N.Y.: Cornell University Press, 1971), 125–42; Rosamund McKitterick, *The Carolingians and the Written Word* (Cambridge: Cambridge University Press, 1989), and *The Uses of Literacy in Medieval Europe* (Cambridge: Cambridge University Press, 1990). The importance of the written word in the Carolingian era has played an important role in the debate on the origins of chant notation. See especially Leo Treitler, "Reading and Singing: On the Genesis of Occidental Music Writing," and Charles Atkinson, *"De Accentibus Toni Oritur Nota Quae Dicitur Neuma:* Prosodic Accents, the Accent Theory, and the Paleofrankish Script," in Boone, *Essays on Medieval Music in Honor of David G. Hughes*, 227–29. The significance of literacy in the Frankish adoption of Roman chant is addressed especially in Susan Rankin, "Carolingian Music," in *Carolingian Culture: Emulation and Innovation*, ed. Rosamond McKitterick (Cambridge: Cambridge University Press, 1994), 274–316.

8. The earliest proposed date for a written archetype of the Gregorian repertory is Kenneth Levy's of c. 800, in "Charlemagne's Archetype of Gregorian Chant," *Journal of the American Musicological Society* 40 (1987): 1–30; this theory was further developed in Levy's "Abbot Helisachar's Antiphoner," *Journal of the American Musicological Society* 48 (1995): 171–86. The existence of an early neumed version has also been argued by James Grier, "Adémar de Chabannes, Carolingian Musical Practices, and *Nota Romana*," *Journal of the American Musicological Society* 56 (2003): 43–98. This theory has not received universal acceptance. For critiques see Leo Treitler, "Communication," *Journal of the American Musicological Society* 41 (1988): 566–75; Marcel A. Zijlstra. "On 'Abbot Helisachar's Antiphoner' by Kenneth Levy, Summer 1995," *Journal of the American Musicological Society* 50 (1997): 238–52; Emma Hornby, *Gregorian and Old Roman Eighth-Mode Tracts: A Case Study in the Transmission of Western Chant* (Aldershot, England: Ashgate, 2002), 129–34, and especially "The Transmission of Western Chant in the Eighth and Ninth Centuries: Evaluating Kenneth Levy's Reading of the Evidence," *Journal of Musicology* 21 (2004): 418–57.

9. The relative uniformity of the early chant manuscripts vis-à-vis later books has been demonstrated by David Hughes, "Evidence for the Traditional View of the Transmission of Gregorian Chant," *Journal of the American Musicological Society* 40 (1987): 377–404; and further developed in "The Alleliuas *Dies sanctificatus* and *Vidimus stellam* as Examples of Late Chant Transmission," *Plainsong and Medieval Music* 7 (1998): 101–25. Hughes discerned the early uniformity, however, on the basis of adiastematic sources. Hornby has appropriately characterized the situation as one of "compatibility" rather than uniformity. See Hornby, "Transmission of Western Chant," Also see Hendrick van der Werf, "Communication," *Journal of the American Musicological Society* 42 (1989): 432–34. Hornby and Pfisterer, however, do present evidence that many variants entered the tradition at a later date. See Hornby, *Gregorian and Roman Eighth Mode Tracts*, 15–54; and Andreas Pfisterer, *Cantilena Romana: Untersuchungen zur Überlieferung des gregorianischen Chorals* (Tützing: Hans Schneider, 2002): 10–76.

These questions, as posited and probed by modern chant scholars, point to a more fundamental one: is the melodic tradition recorded in the late ninth century as "Gregorian chant" the same one the Franks first heard the Romans sing some fourteen decades earlier? The well-known anecdotes suggest that it was not. Amalar of Metz and Helisachar, abbot of St. Riquier, express concern about inconsistencies between Frankish and Roman practice.[10] From a Roman perspective, John the Deacon tells us that the Franks failed to appreciate the subtleties of Roman chant and mixed elements of their own melodies with the Roman ones.[11] John's remarks are often taken as evidence that Roman melodies underwent substantial change in the hands of the Frankish cantors. Another colorful testimony, traditionally attributed to Notker of St. Gall, blames the discrepancies on the Romans. Because the Roman singers wished to keep their chant for themselves, he writes, they made every effort to confuse the Franks, teaching different versions of the melodies in various regions of the kingdom.[12] These stories are heavily laden with political overtones, and in modern retellings, John's account has fared better than Notker's; a willful deception on the part of the Roman singers somehow rings false to modern ears. If there is a kernel of truth in Notker's story, however, it may point to a lack of uniformity in the Romans' performance of their chant.

These eighth- and ninth-century accounts of inconsistencies between the Frankish and Roman singing of chant present a puzzle for modern scholars. If the reasons for the discrepancies eluded contemporary observers, how can we hope to solve the problem so many centuries later? A possible key lies in the survival of five manuscripts from Rome, copied between the eleventh and thirteenth centuries. As is well known, these books preserve a local, Roman dialect of chant, traditionally called Old Roman, that differs substantially from the international Gregorian one. The origins of the melodic dialect presented in these sources have been hotly debated since the 1950s, when the question first received wide attention from scholars. Bruno Stäblein and the liturgical historian S. J. P. van Dijk believed that both melodic traditions existed simultaneously in Rome, with Gregorian chant

10. *Prologus antiphonarii a se compositi, Amalarii episcopi opera liturgica omnia*, Studi e testi, ed. J. M. Hanssens (Rome, 1948). For the letter of Helisachar, see *Monumenta Germaniae Historica, Epistolarum*, 5:307–9. For a translation see Levy, "Abbot Helisachar's Antiphoner," 177–84.
11. "Huius modulationis dulcedinem inter alias Europae gentes Germani seu Galli discere crebroque rediscere insigniter potuerunt, incorruptam vero tam levitate animi, quia nonnulla de proprio Gregorianis cantibus miscuerunt, quam feritate quoque naturali servare minime potuerunt," John the Deacon, *Sancti Gregorii Magni Vita*, in *Patrologia Latina* 75 (Paris: J. P. Migne, 1884), columns 90–91. For a translation see James McKinnon, ed., *The Early Christian Period and the Latin Middle Ages*, vol. 2, *Source Readings in Music History*, rev. ed., ed. Leo Treitler (New York: Norton, 1998), 178–80.
12. *Gesta Karoli Magni Imperatoris*, ed. Hans Haefele, in *Monumenta germaniae historica*, scriptores rerum germanicarum 12 (Berlin, 1959), 12–13, translated in McKinnon, *Source Readings in Music History*, 181–83.

reserved for the papal liturgy and Old Roman for the urban churches.[13] Support for this view has since faded in favor of Helmut Hucke's argument that Gregorian chant represents a Frankish redaction of the eighth-century Roman chant adopted under Pepin and Charlemagne, a position solidly supported by the historical evidence.[14] Despite widespread accord on this basic point, however, the relative proportion of Frankish and Roman contributions to the Gregorian melodies remains a topic of debate. Many have argued that the Old Roman (hereafter "Roman") versions, with their tendency toward formulaicism, accurately represent the eighth-century tradition, even though they were not committed to notation until three centuries later.[15] Others propose that the Gregorian melodies more closely reflect the eighth-century Roman chant, notwithstanding their reception into a very different, Frankish, cultural milieu.[16]

This book examines these larger questions about the origins of the Gregorian melodies through the lens of one genre, the offertory. An integrated examination of musical, textual, and liturgical evidence will shed new light on questions surrounding the origins, transmission, and chronology of the genre. The study consists of two parts, a monograph and an edition, the latter published in electronic format at the companion Web site. The monograph revolves around three central questions. The first is the relationship between the Gregorian and Roman versions of the offertories and which dialect more closely resembles the eighth-century prototype.

13. Bruno Stäblein, "Zur Entstehung der gregorianischen Melodien," *Kirchenmusikalisches Jahrbuch* 35 (1951): 5–9; and *Die Gesänge des altrömischen Graduale, Monumenta Monodica Medii Aevi* 2 (Kassel: Bärenreiter, 1970); S. J. P. van Dijk, "The Urban and Papal Rites in Seventh- and Eighth-Century Rome," *Sacris Erudiri* 12 (1961): 411–87, and "The Papal Schola versus Charlemagne," in *Organicae Voces: Festschrift Joseph Smits van Waesberghe angeboten anlässlich seines 60. Geburtstag* (Amsterdam: Instituut voor Middeleeiwse Muziekwetenschap, 1963), 21–30.

14. Helmut Hucke, "Die Einführung des gregorianischen Gesanges in Frankreich," *Römische Quartalschrift* 49 (1954): 172–87. Although the Frankish-redaction theory has received wide acceptance, Pfisterer has recently offered a critique of it. See Pfisterer, *Cantilena*, 178–94. Hucke, however, did not rule out the possibility of change in the Roman tradition subsequent to its separation from the Gregorian. See especially "Gregorianischer Gesang in fränkischer und altrömischer Überlieferung," *Archiv für Musikwissenschaft* 12 (1955): 74–87; and commentary by Edward Nowacki, "Chant Research at the Turn of the Century and the Analytical Programme of Helmut Hucke," *Plainsong and Medieval Music* 7 (1998): 47–71.

15. Thomas Connolly, "Introits and Archetypes: Some Archaisms of the Old Roman Chant," *Journal of the American Musicological Society* 25 (1972): 157–74; Joseph Dyer, "'Tropis semper variantibus': Compositional Strategies in the Offertories of the Old Roman Chant," *Early Music History* 17 (1998): 1–59; Philippe Bernard, *Du chant romain au chant grégorien (IVe–xIIIe siècle)* (Paris: Cerf, 1996); and Max Haas, *Mündliche Überlieferung und altrömisher Choral: Historische und analytische computergestützte Untersuchungen* (Bern: Peter Lang, 1997).

16. This view was first articulated by Walter Lipphardt, "Gregor der Grosse und sein Anteil am Römischen Antiphonar," *Actes du congrés internationale de musique sacrée* (1950): 248–54; and explored again by Paul Cutter, "The Old-Roman Chant Tradition: Oral or Written?" *Journal of the American Musicological Society* 20 (1967): 167–81; and Edward Nowacki, "The Gregorian Office Antiphons and the Comparative Method," *Journal of Musicology* 4 (1985): 243–75. More recently, the possibility of extensive change in the Roman tradition after its separation from the Gregorian has been proposed by McKinnon, *Advent Project*, 375–403; Brad Maiani, "Approaching the Communion Melodies," *Journal of the American Musicological Society* 53 (2000): 283–84; and Pfisterer, *Cantilena*, 178–93.

The second issue concerns the implications of the musical and textual evidence for the genre's origin and chronology. Finally, I consider the origins of the offertory's solo verses, long a topic of debate. The evidence relevant to these questions is presented in chapters 2, 3, and 4. A close analysis of the offertory's verbal texts, their origin and structure, forms the focus of chapter 2. Turning to melodic analysis in chapter 3, I illustrate the central differences between the Gregorian and Roman melodies with representative examples. Chapter 4 incorporates the Milanese cognates of the melodies into the analytical picture. Chapter 5 offers a synthesis of the musical, textual, and liturgical evidence and its bearing on the main questions addressed in this study.

The edition at the companion Web site includes the ninety offertories that form the core repertory transmitted from Rome to Francia, as well as four additional pieces that are not part of the core repertory but are fully or partially shared by the two traditions.[17] The Gregorian and Roman versions of the melodies are presented on alternate pages, a format that allows for side-by-side viewing, with the Gregorian on the left and the Roman on the right. With this layout, one may easily read each version and compare the two. Each version is transcribed from a single manuscript, which serves as a base reading to which other sources have been compared. For each offertory, the results of the comparative transcriptions are summarized and analyzed in the commentary found in appendix 3. An overview of the sources employed, the criteria for selecting base versions, and the types of variants encountered in the manuscript tradition is given in chapter 6, which serves as an introduction to the edition. The remainder of this introductory chapter will be an overview of the evidence and strategies I employ to address the central questions of this study, followed by some liturgical and cultural background.

THE GREGORIAN AND ROMAN DIALECTS

There can be little doubt that the offertory formed a part of the core repertory transmitted from Rome to Francia in the eighth century. It is mentioned in *Ordo Romanus* I, which represents the Roman liturgy from around 700–750, indicating that it was an established tradition when the Franks received the Roman chant.[18] Further evidence of the offertory's presence in the core repertory lies in its verbal texts, liturgical assignments, and the division of responds and verses, which are

---

17. *Memor sit* (91), *Domine Iesu* (92), *Stetit angelus/In conspectu* (93), and *Beatus es Symon Petre* (94). I discuss the specific circumstances of these four additional pieces in the course of this study and in the commentary of appendix 3. *Memor sit*, for the ordination of a bishop, may have been a part of the core repertory, but due to its liturgical function it is not common in Gregorian manuscripts and has two distinct melodic traditions. I have not given a full accounting of variants for *Memor sit* or for the offertory for the Requiem Mass, *Domine Iesu*.

18. Michel Andrieu, *Les Ordines Romani du haut moyen âge*, (Louvain: Spicilegium Sacrum Lovaniense Bureaux, 1931), 2: 62–65.

generally the same in the Roman and Gregorian traditions.[19] Despite these indices
of an early origin, however, many offertories lack the musical resemblance between
the two traditions that has been demonstrated in other genres, particularly in their
solo verses.[20] The central difference between the two dialects is a pervasive
formulaicism in the eleventh-century Roman melodies that is not reflected in the
Gregorian tradition. The repertory of Gregorian offertory verses contains some of
the most magnificent melodies of the chant repertory, with expansive ranges,
lengthy melismas, and occasional examples of word painting. Many Roman verses,
by contrast, are based on standard formulas, with a persistent internal repetition.
These formulaic verse melodies typically show little or no similarity to the
Gregorian ones.

Perhaps because of these differences, the offertory has recently served as a
springboard for positing theories about the origins of Gregorian and Roman chant.
Joseph Dyer, for example, has argued that the formulaicism and repetitive structure
of the eleventh-century Roman versions represents the eighth-century tradition
and that the Franks replaced the formulaic passages of the Roman melodies with
new material. These conclusions are based primarily on analysis of the Roman
versions.[21] Kenneth Levy has maintained the view that Roman formulas represent
the original state of affairs but has proposed a radical alternative for the origins of
the Gregorian melodies. With Levy's hypothesis, the Franks replaced the Roman
melodies with preexisting Gallican ones; these Gallican melodies with Roman texts
eventually made their way to Rome, where they were partially incorporated into
the Roman dialect.[22] Levy's theory challenges a historically grounded assumption

19. On the basis of textual variants between the two dialects in one offertory, however, Hucke argued that the Romans used Frankish sources in copying their manuscripts. Helmut Hucke, "Die Texte der Offertorien," in *Speculum Musicae Artis: Festgabe für Heinrich Husmann zum 60 Geburtstag,* ed. Heinz Becker and Reinhard Gerlach (Munich: W. Fink, 1970), 193–97. Other small discrepancies in the text tradition involve the occasional shortening or omission of verses in the Old Roman sources.
20. For studies of other genres, see Hucke, "Gregorianischer Gesang in fränkischer und altrömischer Überlieferung," and the commentary by Nowacki, "Chant Research at the Turn of the Century"; Joseph Michael Murphy, "The Communions of the Old-Roman Chant" (Ph.D. diss., University of Pennsylvania, 1971); Thomas Connolly, "The Introits of the Old Roman Chant" (Ph.D diss., Harvard University, 1972); Nancy van Deusen, "A Historic and Stylistic Comparison of the Graduals of Gregorian and Old Roman Chant" (Ph.D. diss., Indiana University, 1972); Hornby, "Gregorian and Old Roman Eighth-Mode Tracts"; and Alberto Turco, *Les Antienns d'introït du chant romain comparées a celles du grégorien et de l'ambrosiem* (Solesmes, France: 1993). In addition to these genre studies, partial comparisons are made in a number of places, including Hendrik van der Werf, *The Emergence of Gregorian Chant* (Rochester, N.Y., 1983), Theodore Karp, *Aspects of Orality and Formularity in Gregorian Chant* (Evanston, Ill.: Northwestern University Press, 1998): 365–424; McKinnon, *Advent Project*; and Pfisterer, *Cantilena.* Although each of these studies highlights and focuses on differences between the Gregorian and Roman versions, none of these genres exhibits the nearly absolute breach of affinity between the two dialects as do the offertory verses in the later liturgical seasons.
21. Dyer, "'Tropis semper variantibus.'"
22. Kenneth Levy, "A New Look at Old Roman Chant I," *Early Music History* 19 (2000): 81–104, "A New Look at Old Roman Chant II," *Early Music History* 20 (2001): 173–98, "Gregorian

that has guided most work on the origins of the Gregorian melodies, namely that they reflect Frankish redactions—not replacements—of the melodies received from Rome in the eighth century.[23]

The centrality of the offertory in these recent theories about the origins of the Gregorian melodies invites a closer analysis of its music. The premise that melodic analysis can shed light on questions about the origins of the Gregorian and Roman dialects will be substantiated as the study unfolds.[24] I do not accept either theory as an exclusive model to explain the origins of the Gregorian and Roman dialects; certainly both melodic traditions underwent change after their separation. In many cases, however, close readings of the music pose a challenge to the view that the Roman formulas more closely resemble the eighth-century prototypes. Central to this argument are some fundamental differences between Roman formulas and the corresponding Gregorian versions, manifest not only in surface detail but also in their underlying approaches to making melodies. In the Roman formulas, the cantors respond in systematic and predictable ways to verbal conditions, such as the length and accent pattern of a clause. The close relationship between words and music suggests that the Roman singers adhered to a complex system of syntactical rules that determined the underlying structure and surface detail of the melodies. Gregorian offertories lack this consistent correlation between words and music. Their singers were evidently guided by a broader set of constraints, such as mode and tonal structure, more general principles of text declamation, and genre.

These general differences between the two dialects inform my examination of individual Gregorian and Roman cognate melodies. The repertory exhibits a prominent trend that plays a central role in evaluating theories about the origins of the two dialects: Roman melodies with distinctive musical profiles often resemble their Gregorian counterparts quite closely, whereas Roman melodies based on formulas show only occasional melodic correspondence to their Gregorian counterparts. This pattern invites two possible explanations. The first is that the Franks received the offertories in the formulaic state we see in the eleventh-century Roman melodies. In this scenario, the Franks retained some structural characteristics of the Roman melodies but modified certain details of the formulaic melodies to produce a more varied melodic tradition. This view, however, becomes problematic if we accept the evidence that the Franks intended to reproduce the Roman chant faithfully. In many Gregorian and Roman cognate pairs, the two versions are

Chant and the Romans," *Journal of the American Musicological Society* 56 (2003): 5–42, and "*Tollite Portas* Revisited: An Ante-Evangelium Reclaimed?" in *Western Plainchant in the First Millennium: Studies in the Medieval Liturgy and Its Music*, ed. Sean Gallagher et al. (Aldershot, England: Ashgate, 2003), 231–42.

23. I examine the recent challenges to this long-standing assumption on the basis of psalter evidence in chapter 2.

24. The epistemological questions surrounding the value of musical evidence are more explicitly explored in chapter 5.

dissimilar precisely in the passages where the Roman singers adopt formulas. Isolated nonformulaic details of the Roman reading, by contrast, are often similar to the corresponding passage in the Gregorian reading. In view of this evidence, the premise that the Roman formulas represent the melodic state of the offertory in the eighth century requires us to view the Frankish reception of Roman chant as a selective revision process, in which the Frankish singers retained isolated, unique details of some Roman melodies but eliminated their formulas, precisely their most salient characteristic. Given the difficulties of learning such a large repertory, I find this scenario implausible. Reliance on a system of melodic formulas would have facilitated the Franks' assimilation of the Roman repertory.

A second possibility is that the Gregorian offertories more closely resemble the eighth-century prototypes, and that the melodic tradition in Rome underwent further development in the centuries following the separation of the two dialects. In this scenario, the eleventh-century Roman formulas and their underlying system of rules arose through a process of progressive melodic homogenization that took place in the Roman tradition after its separation from the Gregorian. Melodies with only broad structural similarities became stereotyped into homogeneous formulas that were easily recalled and reproduced. I favor this explanation in many cases because it is more consistent with evidence that the Roman chant was transmitted in a purely oral tradition for much longer than the Gregorian was.[25] In the reconstructive processes I propose, the general set of constraints that guided the composition and transmission of the melodies, such as the conventions of mode and text declamation, grew increasingly rigorous, exerting a pervasive control on the musical surface. Supporting this hypothesis with close readings of the music, I conclude that progressive homogenization in the Roman dialect is often the more probable scenario.

The offertory's verbal texts and their melodic treatment also come into play in considering the Gregorian and Roman question. In most offertories, the scriptural source is modified in some way to form a "libretto."[26] As illustrated in chapter 3, Frankish singers often set these texts in ways that emphasized their rhetorical content, calling attention to specific words or phrases with melismas or contrasts in range. In the Roman tradition, by contrast, many of these centonized texts are set to repeated statements of formulas. The more cursory Roman approach seems to contradict the great care taken in the creation of the texts, casting further doubt on the theory that the formulas reflect the eighth-century state of the melodies.

25. See especially John Boe, "Chant Notation in Eleventh-Century Roman Manuscripts," in Boone, *Essays on Medieval Music in Honor of David G. Hughes*, 43–58, and "Music Notation in Archivio San Pietro C 105 and in the Farfa Breviary, Chigi C. VI. 177," *Early Music History* 18 (1999): 1–45.
26. The word "libretto" is borrowed from Kenneth Levy's work on the nonpsalmic offertories in "Toledo, Rome, and the Legacy of Gaul," *Early Music History* 4 (1984): 499–9. The prominence of text centonization in the psalmic offertories was demonstrated in McKinnon, *Advent Project*, 309–14, and is further analyzed in chapter 2 here.

While the comparative analysis suggests that the Roman melodies became increasingly uniform between the eighth and eleventh centuries, questions remain about what types of change occurred on the Frankish side. Noting the stylistic similarities among Roman, Milanese, and Beneventan chant, some have argued that the more ornate, oscillating style of Roman chant is a native Italian trait, a property of the eighth-century Roman dialect that Frankish cantors minimized.[27] In chapter 4, I consider the question of Italianate style by examining some offertories common to the Roman, Gregorian, and Milanese traditions. In their structural traits, the Milanese readings correspond more closely to the Gregorian versions than to the Roman, consistent with studies of other genres.[28] In surface style, however, they exhibit the "Italianate" ornateness and share melodic vocabulary and turns of phrase with the Roman dialect. In isolated passages, moreover, the Milanese versions more closely resemble the Roman ones. These trends suggest that the Milanese cantors learned the melodies in a form that had the structural traits of the Gregorian version but certain stylistic features of the Roman dialect. The compelling similarities between the Roman and Milanese versions in style and melodic vocabulary ultimately support the hypothesis that these were native traits, present in the Roman prototypes of these melodies. The Milanese versions reinforce the evidence that both the Gregorian and the Roman dialects changed in the centuries following the reception of the tradition in Francia and offer some insight into the probable nature of that change.

ORIGIN AND CHRONOLOGY

Another question this study addresses is the origin and chronology of the offertory. As mentioned, the first witness to the offertory of the papal liturgy is *Ordo Romanus* I, representing the liturgy of 700–750. The verbal and musical traits of the genre have given rise to several hypotheses that focus on a possible non-Roman origin. Kenneth Levy proposed a Gallican origin for most Gregorian offertories with nonpsalmic texts, several of which have counterparts in the Roman tradition.[29] James McKinnon, by contrast, maintained that the nonpsalmic offertories are Roman in origin, citing their seamless thematic consistency with the offertory and communion cycles to which they belong.[30] Andreas Pfisterer has recently

27. Joseph Dyer, 'Tropis semper variantibus,' and review of *The Advent Project: The Later-Seventh-Century Creation of the Roman Mass Proper*, by James McKinnon, *Early Music History* 20 (2001): 307; and David Hiley, *Western Plainchant: A Handbook* (Oxford: Clarendon Press, 1993), 547–49, 562.
28. See especially Helmut Hucke, "Die Gregorianische Gradualeweise des 2. Tons und ihre ambrosianischen Parallelen: Ein Beitrag zur Erforschung des Ambrosianischen Gesangs," *Archiv für Musikwissenschaft* 13 (1956): 285–314; and Michel Huglo, *Fonti e paleografia del canto ambrosiano* (Milan: Archivio Ambrosiano, 1956), 127–37.
29. Levy, "Toledo, Rome."
30. McKinnon, *Advent Project*, 318–21.

suggested a widespread non-Roman influence on the psalmic offertories, based on the psalter readings they employ. Examining a handful of offertories that depart from the Roman psalter, he posits Gaul and North Africa as more probable places of origin.[31]

Chapter 2 approaches the question of non-Roman origin from several different directions. Taking Pfisterer's recent work as a point of departure, I begin with an examination of the psalter readings employed in the psalmic offertories. Substantial differences from the Roman psalter are evident in approximately a quarter of the repertory, with another two-dozen exhibiting traces of other psalter readings. Although I have reservations about this methodology as a basis for establishing the origins of specific chants, a non-Roman origin is indeed plausible in some cases. Turning to the nonpsalmic offertories, I consider their thematic characteristics, their position in the Roman-Gregorian, Old Hispanic, and Milanese cycles, and their use of Old Latin translations rather than the Vulgate. This evidence reinforces the impression that the nonpsalmic offertories are more at home among the non-Roman repertories, particularly the Old Hispanic.

The verbal and melodic characteristics of the offertory also have potential implications for questions of chronology. The musical traits of the offertories correlate with their placement in the liturgical calendar, a trend especially evident in the verses of the Roman offertories. Roman verses assigned to Advent and Christmas are similar in many respects to their Gregorian counterparts, with expansive ranges and lengthy melismas. The Roman Lenten and Paschaltide offertories, however, are marked by an increasing use of formulas, especially in their verses; many of these verses consist of little besides repeated statements of formulas. A parallel trend is that the relationship between Gregorian and Roman melodies becomes increasingly weak during the course of the liturgical year, especially among verses. Verses assigned to the Advent and Christmas seasons often show some resemblance between the two versions. The Gregorian and Roman Lenten and Paschaltide verses, by contrast, often show no traces of a common origin.

In chapter 5, I explore the potential chronological implications of the findings presented in this study. In considering their significance, I am informed by two contrasting theories about the origins of the Mass Proper put forth in recent scholarship, namely those of James W. McKinnon and Andreas Pfisterer. The relation between melodic traits and liturgical assignments brings to mind the Advent Project theory of the origins of the Mass Proper recently proposed by McKinnon. Contrary to the traditional view that the repertory evolved gradually

---

31. Pfisterer, "Remarks on Roman and Non-Roman Offertories," *Plainsong and Medieval Music* 14 (2005): 169–81, and *"Super flumina Babylonis:* On the Prehistory of a Roman Offertory," in *The Offertory and Its Verses: Research, Past, Present, and Future,* ed. Roman Hankeln (Trondheim: Tapir Academic Press, 2007), 41–56.

during the fourth, fifth, and sixth centuries, McKinnon argues that it took shape in the later seventh century, in a concentrated effort by the Roman *schola cantorum* to create proper chants for each day of the year. He proposes that the *schola* began with chants assigned to Advent and proceeded through the liturgical year season by season. This theory turns on a critical examination of patristic sources, liturgical documents, patterns of liturgical assignment, and the texts and music of the repertory itself.[32]

Since the publication of McKinnon's book, various aspects of this theory have met with skepticism. Peter Jeffery, for example, questions McKinnon's identification of text centonization and nonpsalmic texts as indices of lateness and argues that centonized texts existed long before the seventh century.[33] The most substantial challenges to the Advent Project theory have come from Pfisterer, whose alternative chronological model rests not only on the types of evidence McKinnon employed but also on the biblical translations that serve as the basis of the chant texts. Pfisterer argues for a gradual expansion of the repertory based on the solemnity of feasts rather than calendrical order. He places the creation of the earlier Mass Proper chants in the fifth and sixth centuries and the later layers in the early seventh century.[34]

Chapter 5 proceeds from a critique of McKinnon's and Pfisterer's arguments to a reflection on the patterns that have emerged in the analysis. While some aspects of the musical and textual picture would appear to support the Advent Project thesis, the multiplicity of psalter readings in the offertories contradicts this theory: if the entire repertory were created in Rome within a short time span, one would expect its psalters to be more consistent in their conformity to the Roman psalter. While the majority of nonpsalmic offertories are assigned to more recent layers of the liturgical year, such as Easter Week and the Post-Pentecost Sundays, a majority use Old Latin translations, suggesting an origin earlier than McKinnon's late seventh-century date. The verbal traits, however, do not provide sufficient evidence for a precise chronology of the repertory or a secure date for its earlier layers. While the Old Latin basis of the nonpsalmic offertories would not be expected with a late seventh-century origin, it need not suggest an origin as early as the fifth or early sixth centuries, as Pfisterer and Christoph Tietze have proposed for the introits based on the Vetus Latina (VL).[35] Work on the history of Vulgate in Italy has shown that the

32. McKinnon, *Advent Project*.
33. Peter Jeffery, review of *The Advent Project: The Later-Seventh-Century Creation of the Roman Mass Proper*, by James McKinnon, *Journal of the American Musicological Society* 56 (2003): 168–79. For additional caveats, see the reviews by Joseph Dyer in *Early Music History* 20 (2001): 279–309, and by Susan Rankin in *Plainsong and Medieval Music* 11 (2002): 73–82. Rankin cites Margot Fassler's evidence that Advent existed theologically and conceptually—if not liturgically—long before the seventh century. Moreover, Dyer has questioned the significance of Advent as a vehicle for the creation of new chants.
34. Andreas Pfisterer, *Cantilena*, and "James McKinnon und die Datierung des gregorianischen Chorals," *Kirchenmusikalisches Jahrbuch* 85 (2001): 31–53.
35. Christoph Tietze, *Hymn Introits for the Liturgical Year* (Chicago: Hillenbrand Books, 2005), 41–98.

transition from the VL to the Vulgate was a gradual process, with both translations in simultaneous use until at least the later sixth century.[36]

The musical picture adds yet another layer of complexity to the questions of origins and chronology. Offertories with "non-Roman" verbal characteristics span the full stylistic spectrum of the genre, lacking any special features that would distinguish them from those based on the Roman psalter. Offertories with different psalter origins, in fact, occasionally even share melodic material. If the creation of the Roman offertory repertory was a product of assimilation as much as composition, this pattern has several possible explanations. One possibility is that foreign melodies incorporated into the Roman repertory underwent assimilation to native style before they were transmitted to the Franks and that the question of non-Roman origin is ultimately one of words rather than melodies. Another is that the melodic style of the offertories is fundamentally "non-Roman." The latter hypothesis receives some support in chapter 5 from an examination of several offertories that lie outside of the core Roman-Gregorian repertory.

THE OFFERTORY VERSE

A third question I take up concerns the origins of the offertory's solo verses, long a topic of debate. These elaborate solo melodies, which fell out of use in the twelfth and thirteenth centuries, remain among the least familiar genres of the Gregorian repertory.[37] Despite the shared textual basis of the Gregorian and Roman versions, the verse melodies were once thought to be ninth-century Frankish additions to the repertory. Willi Apel proposed that they were originally sung to psalm tones that were later replaced with Frankish melodies.[38] The psalm-tone theory was based in part on an ambiguous remark by Aurelian of Réôme that seemed to suggest an origin in antiphonal psalmody.[39] The theory of antiphonal origin held

36. See especially Jean Gribomont, "L'Église et les versions bibliques," *La Maison-Dieu* 62 (1960): 41–48, and "La transmission des textes bibliques in Italie," in *La cultura in Italia fra tardo antico e alto medioevo: Atti del convegno tenuto a Roma, Consiglio Nazionale delle Ricerche, dal 12 al 16 novembre 1979*, 2 vols. (Rome: Herder, 1981), 2:731–41, and "Le texte bibliques de Grégoire," in *Grégoire le Grand (Colloque de Chantilly, 182)*, ed. Jacques Fontaine et al. (Paris: CNRS, 1986), 467–75. Most of the biblical passages that serve as sources for the nonpsalmic offertories are not a part of the lectionary.

37. For the presence of offertory verses in some isolated later sources, see Jean-François Goudesenne, "Un missel de Noyon avec versets d'offertoire (XIVe siècle): Réévaluation d'une prétendue 'décadence' du chant grégorien," forthcoming in the proceedings of Cantus Planus Niederaltaich (Budapest: Hungarian Academy of Arts and Sciences Institute for Musicology).

38. Willi Apel, *Gregorian Chant* (Bloomington: Indiana University Press, 1954), 512. The antiphonal origin of the offertory was also held by Peter Wagner, *Einführung in die gregorianischem Melodien* (Leipzig: Breitkopf und Härtel, 1911), 1:108.

39. The passage in question is "Quod versus offertoriarum per tonos in ipsis intromittantur, cantor nemo qui dubitet." *Aureliani Reomensis Musica disciplina*, ed. Lawrence Gushee, Corpus scriptorum de musica 21 ([Rome]: American Insititute of Musicology, 1975). The interpretation of

that the elaborate verse melodies of the Gregorian offertories were later, Frankish additions. Dyer's investigation into the liturgical history of the offertory, however, has demonstrated beyond a doubt that it could not have originated as an antiphonal chant. A fundamental premise behind the antiphonal hypothesis was an analogy between the offertory and other "processional" chants such as the introit. Through examination of contemporary liturgical documents, art, and architecture, however, Dyer showed that the Roman papal liturgy included no offertory procession or offering for ordinary laity, customs that subsequently developed in the north. The offertory rite described in *Ordo Romanus* I belongs solely to the nobility. In examining references to the offertory chant in the *Ordines Romani*, moreover, Dyer determined that they have little in common with descriptions of antiphonal psalmody.[40] Certain stylistic traits of the offertory also played a role in Apel's hypothesis of ninth-century origin. He viewed the melismas with repeat structures and "unusual tonal progressions," for example, as late characteristics. Ruth Steiner, however, showed that Apel's assessment of style was based primarily on the unreliable edition of Karl Ott.[41]

Although Dyer's conclusive demonstration of the offertory's responsorial origins leaves little historical basis on which to posit a Frankish origin for the elaborate verse melodies, many questions remain. The exceptional traits of Gregorian offertories, such as expansive ranges, are present in the Roman tradition, but to a far lesser extent. Gregorian and Roman verses evince a weaker melodic affinity between the two traditions than their responds do. Differences are especially evident in the final verses. In many Gregorian offertories, each successive verse is increasingly expansive in range and melismatic density. Final verses of plagal offertories are often in the corresponding authentic mode, creating a striking climactic effect. In most Roman offertories, by contrast, each successive verse relies increasingly on melodic formulas. As a result, final verses of the two traditions are often utterly dissimilar.

this passage as a reference to an antiphonal origin for offertory verses was also argued in Joseph Perry Ponte, "*Aureliani Reomensis Musica disciplina:* A Revised Text, Translation, and Commentary" (Ph.D. diss., Brandeis University, 1961), 5–6. Dyer's more convincing reading of the passage is that "tone" refers to "finalis" and not to "psalmodic formula." See Dyer, "The Offertory Chant of the Roman Liturgy and Its Musical Form," *Studi Musicali* 11 (1982): 20.

40. Dyer, "The Offertories of Old-Roman Chant: A Musico-Liturgical Investigation" (Ph.D. diss., Boston University, 1971), 70–71, 85–113, and "Offertory Chant of the Roman Liturgy." A similar view regarding lay participation was articulated in Alan Clark, "The Function of the Offertory Rite in the Mass," *Ephemerides Liturgicae* 64 (1950): 309–44. Clark, however, did not undertake an extensive examination of primary sources.

41. Ruth Steiner, "Some Questions about the Offertories and Their Verses," *Journal of the American Musicological Society* 19 (1966): 162–81. The edition in question is Karl Ott, *Offertoriale sive versus offertoriorum* (Paris: 1935), reprinted in *Offertoriale triplex cum versiculis* (Solesmes, France: 1985). Ott's edition, based primarily on the Dijon tonary, was intended for practical use, not scholarly study. As Steiner showed, it often contains anomalous tonal progressions, such as leaps of a seventh, that are not found in any known manuscript source, including the Dijon tonary.

The lack of resemblance between Gregorian and Roman verses indicates that verse melodies underwent further development, in one dialect or both, after their separation. While I argue that greater part of the melodic change occurred on the Roman side, the variant readings in the manuscript tradition point to isolated points of instability on the Gregorian side. On the whole, the early Gregorian manuscripts show a tradition that is stable with respect to melodic contour. Certain points of melodic and modal variance, however, suggest that the tradition was subject to some variation in performance. I do not attribute this instability to different origins or dates for verses and responds. In many cases, the verbal characteristics of the offertories suggest that they were created to be sung with verses. As my examination of the texts in chapter 2 will show, the body of the offertory respond and the section chosen for the repetendum are often taken from different parts of the psalm. The structure of the texts suggests that the repetendum was carefully selected to provide an appropriate summary or concluding thought for the themes treated in the verses. The great care taken by the compilers of these texts in selecting repetenda suggests that the responds were created to fit the form of verses with repetenda and that the verses were, in many cases, part of the offertories' original conception. Some possible reasons for the apparent melodic instability of offertory verses may lie in the history of the offertory rite.

THE EARLY HISTORY OF THE OFFERTORY RITE AND ITS CHANT

The origin of the offertory chant is closely tied to the questions about the origin of its liturgy, which have been thoroughly explored by Dyer. Much of the following summary draws on his exhaustive readings of the liturgical sources. My objective in reexamining the liturgy here is not to present new information, but to provide context for the issues I will explore in subsequent chapters. The following reexamination of the sources, then, will focus primarily on the aspects of the liturgy relevant for the origin and performance context of the offertory and its verses. I shall briefly examine the earliest witnesses to the rite in Gaul and North Africa, proceed to a consideration of Roman and Frankish evidence, and propose a hypothesis about its implications for performance.

The date of the earliest offertory rites cannot be established with certainty. Liturgical historians once assumed that the earliest Christian liturgies included an offertory procession of the laity.[42] If such a ceremony existed in the early church, it might well have had musical accompaniment. A lay offering during the liturgy of the early church, however, cannot be substantiated. While Early Christian writers

---

42. See, for example, Theodor Klauser, *A Short History of the Western Liturgy*, trans. John Halliburton (New York: Oxford University Press, 1979), 45; additional references in Dyer, "The Roman Offertory: An Introduction and Some Hypotheses," in Hankeln, *Offertory and Its Verses*, 15–40.

do admonish the laity to offer gifts, their offering probably took place before the service. The *Testamentum domini*, a Syrian document perhaps from the fifth century, directs the deacons to receive offerings in a room on the right side of the church set aside for that purpose, clearly indicating that the offering was not part of the service.[43] Jerome refers to the custom of deacons announcing the names of those who had offered the bread and wine during Mass.[44] A similar tradition is witnessed in a letter of Pope Innocent I, who recommends that these prayers be incorporated into the Eucharistic rite.[45] As Dyer argues, if the laity offered during the service, there would be no need to announce their names.[46]

The first witness to a lay offering during Mass comes from the rich Christian culture that flourished in fourth-century North Africa. While certain remarks of Tertullian and Cyprian concerning offerings do not clearly establish the existence of an offertory procession, Augustine's writings do suggest that the laity approached the altar to present their offerings.[47] He expresses regret, for example, that a woman captured by barbarians could not make her offering at the altar.[48] Despite these clear references to a lay offering, it is unclear whether Augustine's often-cited mention of "hymns from the book of Psalms . . . before the oblation" refers to offertory chants. The passage, from a summary of the lost polemic *Contra Hilarum*, details the attack of an opponent named Hilary on this new practice at Carthage.[49] While it was once believed that "hymni ante oblationem" referred to offertory chants, subsequent work has cast doubt on that interpretation.[50] Much of the ambiguity surrounding this passage lies in the meaning of "oblatio," which may refer either to the Mass as a whole or to the sacrificial part of the Mass.[51] Hilary also objected to a psalm sung "while what is offered is distributed to the people." As Dyer has argued, it is unlikely that Hilary would object to a psalm sung during the

43. Jungmann, *Mass of the Roman Rite* (New York: Benziger, 1951), 2:5. For a summary of scholarship on the origins of this text, see Paul E. Bradshaw, *The Search for the Origins of Christian Worship* (New York: Oxford University Press, 2002), 73–87.

44. Commentary on Ezekiel 6.18, in *Patrologia latina* 25, column 175.

45. Robert Cabié, *La lettre du pape Innocent Ier à Décentius de Gubbio (19 mars 416): Texte critique, traduction et commentaire*, Bibliothèque de le Revue d'Histoire Ecclésiastique 58 (1973): 22, cited in Dyer, "Roman Offertory," 19.

46. Dyer, "Roman Offertory," 16–18.

47. Jungmann interpreted remarks of Tertullian and Cyprian as witnesses to an offering of the faithful, but Dyer sees them more plausibly as figurative references. See Jungmann, *Mass of the Roman Rite*, 2:1–4; and Joseph Dyer, "Augustine and the 'hymni ante oblationem': The Earliest Offertory Chants?" *Revue des études augustiniennes* 27 (1981): 88–91.

48. See references in Dyer, "Augustine and the 'hymni ante oblationem,'" 90.

49. The passage reads: "Inter haec Hilarus quidam uir tribunitius laicus catholicus nescio unde aduersus dei ministros—ut fieri assolet—inritatus morem, qui tunc esse apud Carthaginem coeperat, ut hymni ad altare dicerentur de Psalmorum libro, siue ante oblationem siue cum distribueretur populo quod fuisset oblatum, maledica reprehensione ubicumque poterat lacerabat, asserens fieri non oportere." *Sancti Aurelii Augustini Retractationum libri 2*, ed. Almut Mutzenbecher, in Corpus Christianorum: Series Latina (Turnhout: Brepols, 1984), 57:98, lines 1–8.

50. See Jungman, *The Mass of the Roman Rite*, 2:6; and Dyer, "Augustine and the 'hymni ante oblationem.'"

51. Dyer, "Augustine and the 'hymni ante oblationem,'" 91–95.

distribution of Communion, already an established custom in many places. In his earlier work, Dyer cautiously hypothesized that Hilary's objection was to the singing of psalms during the distribution of *eulogia*, blessed bread given to catechumens at the end of the service.[52]

Augustine's "ante oblationem" is reminiscent of the famous passage of the *Liber pontificalis* attributing the introduction of a psalm "ante sacrificium" to Pope Celestine I.[53] "Sacrificium" was traditionally thought to refer to the Mass as a whole, leading Amalar of Metz and many modern scholars to the conclusion that Celestine I introduced the introit into the Mass.[54] Like "oblationem," however, "sacrificium" is ambiguous to modern readers. Peter Jeffery has argued brilliantly that "sacrificium" here refers to the sacrificial part of the Mass, the Eucharist, and that Celestine is thus credited with introducing the responsorial Fore-Mass psalm, the antecedent of the gradual. Dyer's recent examination of other uses of the word "sacrificium," however, offers some support for the traditional interpretation of the passage as a reference to the introit.[55] Recently the *Liber pontificalis* passage has played a role in the debate over the interpretation of Augustine's liturgical descriptions. Reading Augustine's "ante oblationem" in light of Jeffery's work on the *Liber pontificalis* reference, McKinnon concludes that "oblationem" refers to the sacrificial rite of the Eucharist, and that "hymni ante oblationem" is thus the Fore-Mass psalm. Even if "oblatio" is taken literally to mean "offering," he argues, Augustine's remark refers to a psalm sung before the oblation, not during it. Taking the argument a step further, McKinnon views Augustine's descriptions of the Fore-Mass and Communion psalms as all-encompassing references to Mass psalmody that preclude the existence of an offertory chant in North Africa.[56] Given the lack of context for Augustine's references, this reading is not the only conceivable interpretation of the passage. Noting that the psalms to which Hilary objected were sung "ad altare," Dyer points to the arrangement of North African churches. The altar was in the middle of the nave, far from the podium where the readings were delivered, making it highly unlikely that the gradual was sung near the altar.[57] Dyer's argument freshly underscores the ambiguity of Augustine's psalmody, for "ad altare" clearly precludes an interpretation of the passage as a reference to the introit and calls into question the analogy to the *Liber pontificalis*

52. Ibid., 97–98.
53. Louis Duchesne, *Le Liber Pontificalis: Texte, introduction, et commentaire* (Paris: Boccard, 1957), 1:230.
54. Amalarius Metensis, *Liber officialis* 3.5.2, in *Amalarii episcopi opera liturgica omnia*, ed. Jean-Michael Hanssens (Vatican City: Biblioteca Apostolica Vaticana, 1950), 2:272.
55. Peter Jeffery, "The Introduction of Psalmody into the Roman Mass by Pope Celestine I (422–32): Reinterpreting a Passage from the *Liber Pontificalis*," *Archiv für Liturgiewissenschaft* 26 (1984): 147–65; Dyer, review of McKinnon, *Advent Project*. Dyer shows that "sacrificium" refers in most early Christian Latin to the Mass as a whole.
56. McKinnon, *Advent Project*, 299–301.
57. Dyer, review of McKinnon, *Advent Project*, 289–90.

reference. In short, the meaning of this tantalizing reference is unclear. Though it seems unlikely that the innovation to which Hilary objected was an offertory chant, I am hesitant to completely exclude the possibility.

The Gallican offertory rite was modeled on the Great Entrance of the Eastern Church. As described by Gregory of Tours and the *Expositio brevis* of Pseudo-Germanus, it consists of a solemn procession in which elements to be consecrated are brought into the church. In this description, the bread is brought forth in a *turris* (tower), probably a tower-shaped vessel, that lent itself to rich allegorical interpretation by the author of the *Expositio brevis*.[58] The *Expositio* describes a *sonus* sung during the rite that closed with a threefold alleluia. Despite the hypothesis that many of the Roman-Gregorian offertory chants were imported from Gaul, little can be discerned from this description about the nature of the Gallican offertory chant. In a characteristic metaphor, the *Expositio* ties the *sonus* to the silver trumpets Moses created for the Levites to play as the victim was being offered.[59] This sacrificial imagery from the Pentateuch immediately brings to mind the Old Hispanic offertory chants, called sacrificia, which often draw their themes of offering and sacrifice from the Hebrew scriptures; the imagery, in fact, would seem to offer circumstantial support for Levy's theory that Gallican *soni* had characteristics reflected in some nonpsalmic Roman offertories. Others, however, have argued that the Gallican rite did not have a proper series of offertories. On the basis of the quoted text and other references, Johannes Quasten has proposed that the *sonus* is an adaptation of the Byzantine Cheroubikon.[60] What seems clear is that the laity did not participate in the rite.[61] While the necessity of offering is

58. "Corpus vero domini ideo defertur in turribus, quia monumentum domini in similitudinum turris fuit scissum in petra." *Expositio brevis*, in *Patrologia latina* 72, column 92; and Edward Ratcliff, *Expositio antiquae liturgiae Gallicanae* (London: Henry Bradshaw Society, 1971), 7. See also Gregory of Tours, *Liber miraculorum* I, in *Patrologia latina* 71, columns 781–82 Terence Bailey provides support for the interpretation of *turris* as a tower-shaped vessel in a forthcoming study of the Ambrosian offerendae, citing R. E. Latham, *Revised Medieval Word-List* (Oxford, 1965).

59. "Sonum autem, quod canetur quando procedit oblatio hinc traxit exordium. Praecepit dominus Moysi ut faceret tubas argenteas, quas levitae clangerent quando offerebatur hostia, et hoc esset signum per quod intelligeret populus qua hora inferebatur oblatio, et omnes incurvati adorarent dominum donec veniret columna ignis aut nubes qui benediceret sacrificium. . . . Nunc autem procedentem ad altarium corpus Christi non jam tubis inrepraehensibilibus, sed spiritalibus vocibus praeclara Christi magnalia dulci melodia psallet Ecclesia. Corpus vero domini ideo defertur in turribus, quia monumentum domini in similitudinem turris fuit scissum in petra, et intus lectum ubi pausavit corpus dominicum unde surrexit Rex gloriae in triumphum. Sanguis vero Christi ideo specialiter offertur in calice, quia in tale vasum consecratum fuit mysterium eucha-ristiae pridiem quam pateretur dominus ipso dicente, Hic est calix sanguinis mei." *Expositio brevis*, 92. One of the many ambiguities in this description is the implication that the bread being brought forth has already been consecrated ("corpus vero domini"). In his forthcoming study, Bailey argues for a less literal reading of the passage, i.e., "the approach of [what will become] the Body of Christ." Dyer suggests that a small amount of previously consecrated bread was mixed with the bread to be consecrated. "Offertories of Old-Roman Chant," 61.

60. Johannes Quasten, "Oriental Influence in the Gallican Liturgy," *Traditio* 1 (1943): 70–71.

61. Gregory of Tours tells of a widow who offered the best wine at daily Masses for her deceased husband. Receiving communion one day, she discovered that the deacon had exchanged her

emphasized by Caesarius of Arles and the Council of Macon (585), the lay offering clearly took place before the service.[62]

THE BEGINNINGS OF THE OFFERTORY IN ROME

The offertory rite in the papal liturgy makes its first appearance in *Ordo Romanus* I, which describes the liturgy celebrated in the various stational churches around 700–750. It is not known when the rite was introduced in Rome. Emphasizing the extraneous nature of the ceremony to the liturgy as a whole, Dyer has hypothesized that the offertory rite did not exist in Rome before the second half of the seventh century. Noting that the rite is not mentioned in Gregory the Great's liturgical references or in any sources of the papal liturgy prior to *Ordo Romanus* I, Dyer has linked its emergence to social and cultural conditions in later seventh-century Rome. The repeated sacking of the city by the Lombards, the resulting decline in population, and the breakdown of secular institutions led to a more important role for the church in securing a grain supply for the city and feeding the poor. By the late sixth century, the senate had ceased to meet, and most of the aristocratic class had abandoned the city. Military personnel formed the new aristocracy, and this new upper class, Dyer argues, was called on to provide bread for the poor in the elaborate offertory rite described in *Ordo Romanus* I.[63] An alliance between the church and this new upper class provided a means of securing grain supply. The offering within the liturgy could in no way provide enough bread to meet the needs of the city's poor, but the newly instituted lay participation in the Mass would have encouraged further lay assistance in providing for their needs, possibly by means of the "reliquas oblationes" referenced in *Ordo Romanus* I, which were gathered by a bishop after the pope had received the bread and wine.[64] Dyer's contextual argument places the offertory among the later core genres of the Mass Proper, perhaps followed only by the alleluia.

Although *Ordo Romanus* I is the first witness to an offertory rite in the Roman papal Mass, an offering by the ordinary laity in the context of urban liturgy is mentioned in the Old Gelasian sacramentary, dated approximately between 628–715.[65] Dyer has speculated that this urban offering of the *plebs* may have

---

offering for wine of a lesser quality before the service. *De gloria confessorum*, in Patrologia latina 81, columns 875–76. Cited in Dyer, "Offertories of Old-Roman Chant," 63.

62. *Sermo in parochiis necessarius*, ed. Germain Morin, in Corpus Christianorum: Series Latina (Turnholt: Brepols, 1970), 103:65, and *Concilium Matisconense*, ed. Charles de Clercq, in Corpus Christianorum: Series Latina (Turnholt: Brepols, 1963), 148a:240–41.

63. Dyer, "Roman Offertory."

64. Ibid.

65. "Post haec offert plebs, et confitiuntur sacramenta." Cunibert Mohlberg et al., eds., *Liber sacramentorum Romanae aeclessiae ordinis anni circuli*, Rerum Ecclesiasticarum Documenta (Rome: Herder, 1960), 59.

emerged in imitation of the papal rite or that the passage might reflect a Frankish interpolation.[66] We do not know whether music accompanied this offering in the urban rite, nor can we completely rule out a monastic origin for the offertory chant.[67] Given the elaborate style of the chant, however, it seems likely that its emergence in its present form is associated with the highly trained and organized body of clerical singers referenced in *Ordo Romanus I*, the *schola cantorum*. The date and details of the *schola*'s institution remain a topic of debate. The earliest explicit reference to it is from the reign of Pope Adeodatus (672–76), when Sergius I received his training in the *schola*.[68] The existence of highly trained singers in mid-seventh-century Rome, moreover, is attested by the presence of one such singer in England. As Bede recounts, John, archcantor of St. Peter's, was sent to teach the Anglo-Saxon monks the Roman method of singing, including a yearly cycle of chants, as done at St. Peter's.[69]

The legend of the founding of the *schola* by Gregory the Great begins nearly three centuries after Gregory's death, with John the Deacon's biography of him. Hucke, Joseph Smits von Waeseberghe, Dyer, and McKinnon have argued against its existence at the time of Gregory.[70] McKinnon suggests that Gregory's well-established favoring of monastics over secular clergy seems incompatible with the foundation of a highly organized clerical institution.[71] Dyer cites Gregory's reference to the responsorial performance of the Kyrie by clergy and people ("a clericus dicitur, a populis respondetur"). In *Ordo Romanus* I, the role of the people in the Kyrie is replaced by the prior of the *schola*.[72] The case for a seventh-century establishment of the *schola* is nevertheless circumstantial, depending mainly on the lack of earlier references to it. Philippe Bernard has argued for an earlier origin.[73] Pfisterer, moreover, notes that a reference to responsorial singing in the *Agnus dei* by "clerius et populo," similar to Gregory the Great's reference to the Kyrie, is made in the *Liber Pontificalis* biography of Pope Sergius, contemporaneous

66. Dyer, "Roman Offertory."
67. For the influence of monasticism on the development of the Roman repertory, see Peter Jeffery, "Monastic Reading and the Emerging Roman Repertory," in Gallagher et al., *Western Plainchant*, 45–103. For particular relevance for the offertory, see especially 67–68. Jeffery notes that Psalm 138, the source of the offertory *Mihi autem*, for Peter and Paul, is associated with St. Peter in the writings of Arnobius.
68. Louis Duchesne, *Le Liber Pontificalis: Texte, introduction, et commentaire* (Paris: Boccard, 1957), 2:92.
69. *Historia ecclesiastica gentis anglorum* IV, ed. J. E. King (Cambridge, Mass.: Harvard University Press, 1963).
70. See Joseph Smits von Waeseberghe, "Neues über die Schola Cantorum zu Rom," in *Zweiter Internationaler Kongreß für Kirchenmusik* (Vienna, 1955), 111–19; and Helmut Hucke, "Zu einigen Problemen der Choralforschung," *Die Musikforschung* 11 (1958): 400.
71. McKinnon, *Advent Project*, 86–89.
72. See Joseph Dyer, "The *Schola cantorum* and Its Roman Milieu in the Early Middle Ages," in *De musica et cantu: Studien zur Geschichte der Kirchenmusik und Oper, Helmut Hucke zum 60. Geburtstag*, ed. Peter Cahn and Ann-Katrin Heimer (Hildesheim: Georg Olms Verlag, 1993), 32.
73. Bernard, *Du chant romain*, 385–439.

with the mention of the *schola* in *Ordo Romanus* I.[74] Thus the congregational
singing of Mass Ordinary chants does not preclude the existence of the *schola*.

In the absence of further sources, a date for the institution of the Roman
offertory and its chant will remain speculative. Dyer's grounding of the rite in the
context of seventh-century Roman social conditions is appealing in many respects,
and it places the beginning of the offertory rite at a time when the *schola cantorum*
is clearly documented.[75] The argument for an origin in the later seventh century,
however, is in part an *ex silentio* argument, based on a lack of earlier references to a
Roman offertory. A later seventh-century origin, moreover, conflicts with Pfisterer's plausible hypothesis that most of the Mass Proper repertory was in place by
the beginning of the seventh century.[76] Without being able to offer a better reason
for the incorporation of the offertory into the Roman rite, then, I would cautiously
suggest a date somewhat earlier than Dyer's later seventh-century spectrum. The
chronological issues raised by this conflicting evidence are further examined in
chapter 5.

THE *ORDINES ROMANI*

In this description of *Ordo Romanus* I, the pope, accompanied by *primicerii* of the
notaries and the defensors and followed by the archdeacon, processes to various
parts of the church to receive offerings from laity of high social standing. He
receives the offerings from the men in the *senatorium*, those of chief notary and the
chief defensor in the *confessio*, and those of the women in the *pars mulierium*. He
then returns to his seat and washes his hands. After the archdeacon and subdeacon
prepare the oblations on the altar, the pontiff ceremoniously receives them. Then,
bowing slightly toward the altar, he indicates to the *schola* that they should be
silent. ("Et pontifex, inclinans se paululum ad altare, respicit scolam et annuit ut
sileat.")[77]

Although *Ordo Romanus* I does not mention the beginning of the offertory
chant, the instructions to cease singing indicate that the actions it describes were
accompanied by singing. The length of the rite and the music required to
accommodate it is difficult to determine. The pope processes to various parts of
the church to collect offerings from selected laity of high social standing. Members
of the laity who present offerings are gathered in two places: the *senatorium* and the
pars mulierum. In addition, the pope receives the offerings of the accompanying

---

74. Pfisterer, *Cantilena*, 232–34.
75. The social conditions are documented in T. S. Brown, *Gentlemen and Officers: Imperial Adminis-
    tration and Aristocratic Power in Byzantine Italy, A.D. 554–800* (Hertford: British School at Rome,
    1984), 101–8. For further sources, see Dyer, "Roman Offertory," 31.
76. See Pfisterer, "Cantilena," 217–34.
77. Michel Andrieu, *Les Ordines Romani*, 2:95.

dignitaries in the *confessio*. Dyer has addressed the meaning of these terms and their location in Roman churches. In general, the *confessio*, where the *primicerii* present their offerings, was a repository under the altar that held relics. *Senatorium* refers to an area on the right side of the altar reserved for lay men of high social standing ("principum") who present offerings in the order of their rank ("per ordinem archium"). The same is done in the *pars mulierum*, on the left side of the altar. *Ordo Romanus* I is modeled on the Easter Mass as celebrated at Santa Maria Maggiore, and presumably the exact location of these places and the resulting movements of the pope and dignitaries would depend on the arrangement of the stational church in question. In some churches, both sections may have been at the rear of the apse, on respective sides.[78] After the pontiff collects the offerings in each section, he gives them to the archdeacon, who transfers the wine from the containers the laity have brought into a large chalice held by the subdeacon, who in turn empties it into a *sciffus*, a large vessel held by an acolyte. Since it is likely that the chant mentioned at the conclusion of the offertory accompanied the collection and preparation of the gifts, it was evidently a performance of some length, to be concluded only at the signal of the pope.

The papal nod instructing the *schola* to stop singing in *Ordo Romanus* I recalls its description of the introit and communion. The account of the entrance rite in *Ordo Romanus* I mentions the introit antiphon, which is begun by the prior of the *schola*. At the conclusion of the entrance, the pope cues the *schola* to proceed immediately to the end of the chant by singing the *gloria patri*.[79] In the performance of the communion, the *schola* likewise begins the antiphon at the distribution of communion, sings until the people have received, and begins the doxology on a signal from the pope.[80] The resemblance of offertory's description to that of the introit and communion is perplexing on first glance. In the case of the introit and communion, references to the doxology and the term "antiphona" clearly attest to their antiphonal structure. Chants consisting of an antiphon with psalm verses could easily be modified to adapt to the length of the liturgical action. The reference to the conclusion of the offertory chant, however, does not mention a doxology. As Dyer has argued, the lack of reference to a doxology in *Ordo Romanus* I and in subsequent ordines clearly supports the view that the offertory was not an antiphonal chant.[81] The surviving repertory, moreover, certainly shows no vestiges of an antiphonal structure. For McKinnon, the papal nod to conclude the offertory poses an insurmountable difficulty. He suggests that the elaborate melodies in the

---

78. Dyer, "Offertory Chant of the Roman Liturgy," 3–7.
79. "Et respiciens ad priorem scolae annuit ei ut dicat Gloriam; et prior scolae inclinat se pontifici et inponit." Andrieu, *Ordines Romani*, 2:83.
80. "Nam, mox ut pontifex coeperit in senatorio communicare, statim scola incipit antiphonam ad communionem <per vices cum subdiaconibus> et psallunt usquedum communicato omni populo, annuat pontifex ut dicant *Gloria patri*; et tunc repetito versu quiescunt." Ibid., 105.
81. Dyer, "Offertory Chant of the Roman Liturgy," 15, and "Offertories of Old-Roman Chant," 71–72.

surviving sources were unlikely to be concluded abruptly, in the manner of the antiphonal introit and communion. McKinnon proposes an alternative explanation of the passage: that the reference to the papal nod in *Ordo Romanus I* is a mere instance of archaic language, a relic of an earlier time when the offertory was a psalm of variable length.[82]

Despite its seeming incompatibility with the responsorial format and elaborate nature of the offertory chant, the papal nod to the *schola* is echoed in several later ordines adapted for Frankish use, *Ordines IV, V,* and *VI.* Although they borrow extensively from *Ordo I,* these *ordines* incorporate northern liturgical customs. The offertory rite of *Ordo IV,* from St. Amand and dating from 770–790, is derived largely from that of *Ordo I* but mentions the beginning of the chant and an offering of the ordinary laity.[83] As in *Ordo I,* the bishop takes up offerings from the people, first from the men's section and then from the women's section. After the gifts have been prepared by the archdeacon, the pope ceremoniously receives them. He then indicates to the *schola* that they should conclude.[84]

Ordo V reflects a hybridization of Frankish and Roman practice dating from 850–900. Compiled largely from *Ordo I* and the writings of Amalar of Metz, it bears witness to further adaptations of the Roman rite to northern custom. Here the entire congregation makes an offering of bread and wine, first the men, then the women.[85] The reference to the beginning of the offertory chant now specifically mentions its verses.[86] The author refers several times to the continued singing of offertories with verses during the description of the ceremony. The bishop receives the bread, first from the men and then from the women, and then the archdeacon receives the wine, "interim cantant cantores offertorium cum versibus." The bishop returns to his seat and washes his hands while the archdeacon prepares the bread on the altar, "cantantibus adhuc cantoribus."[87] The author shows particular concern that the singing should continue throughout the ceremony. Although these verses were undoubtedly the elaborate sort handed down to us in Gregorian sources, the author of *Ordo V* nevertheless instructs that offertory chant is to be concluded with a signal from the bishop: "Et pontifex, inclinans se paululum ad altare, respicit scolam et annuit ut sileat."[88]

Like much of *Ordo V,* this remark is copied verbatim from *Ordo I.* It is doubtful, however, that the compilers of *Ordines IV* and *V* adopted the instruction merely out of slavish adherence to received wording. It is far more likely that they believed

82. McKinnon, *Advent Project,* 301–2.
83. "Deinde descendit pontifex ad suscipiendum oblationes a populo et annuit archdiaconus scholae ut dicatur offertorium." Andrieu, *Ordines Romani,* 2:161.
84. "Et annuit pontifex scola, ut faciant finem, et revertitur scola subtus tabula." Ibid., 163.
85. "Et offerunt cum fanonibus candidis masculi, deinde feminae." Ibid., 218–29. Andrieu notes the dependency of these details on the writings of Amalar. See ibid., 202.
86. "Tunc canitur offertorium cum versibus." Ibid., 218.
87. Ibid., 218–20.
88. Ibid., 220.

it to be an accurate description of the papal liturgy, and that this practice was adopted in some parts of the north. In these *ordines, Ordo I* is not reproduced without changes but is adapted to the needs and liturgical customs of Francia. The participation of the ordinary laity in the offertory ceremony, a custom not practiced in the papal liturgy, is one of many changes.[89] It thus seems plausible that the bishop's signal to end the offertory is not a mere instance of archaic language but reflects Roman and early Frankish practice, at least in some institutions. *Ordo V* was widely distributed in the north after it was incorporated into the Romano-German pontifical.[90]

While the other *ordines* representing the adaptation of the Roman liturgy in Francia do not indicate that the offertory is concluded with a signal from the celebrant, many *ordines* mention a reception of lay offerings. An offering of the entire congregation was widespread in areas north of the Alps.[91] *Ordo XVII*, the work of a Frankish monk at the end of the eighth century, specifically refers to customs that varied according to whether members of the laity were present. If "populus vel feminis" were permitted to enter, the priest descended from his chair with the deacons and received their offerings, placed them in a *lentea* held by an acolyte, and returned to his seat and washed his hands. When members of the laity were not present, the first priest washed his hands while the others collected the offerings. The length of the rite was clearly variable. Like *Ordo V, Ordo XVII* refers to the continued singing of the offertory during the ceremony.[92]

The details of the lay offering evidently varied from place to place, sometimes differentiating between men and women. Haito of Basel's remarks, for example, indicate that the men were permitted to approach the altar while the women remained in the chancel and presented their offerings there.[93] Theodulf of Orleans reports that the women stand in their place while the priest receives their offerings.[94] Because the lay offering during the service had not been a part of the Gallican liturgy, its development after the reception of the Roman liturgy is probably best seen as an adaptation of the principles of *Ordo I* to the specific needs of northern congregations.

---

89. See ibid., 141–54 and 193–206. Many changes involve differences in the architecture of Frankish churches and the omission of specifically Roman titles (153).
90. For a summary of the contents and distribution, see Vogel, *Medieval Liturgy*, 235–40.
91. See Jungmann, *Mass of the Roman Rite*, 315–25; and Georg Nickl, *Der Anteil des Volkes an der Messliturgie im Frankenreich* (Innsbruck: F. Rausch, 1930), 41–47.
92. "Inde vero in monasterio, ubi populus vel feminis licitum est introire, discendens sacerdos a sede sua cum diaconibus et accepit oblationes a populo. Et ponet sacerdos ipsas oblationes in lentea quas acoletus ante pectus suum tenere videtur. . . . Acceptas autem ipsas oblationes, revertentur ad sedem suam. Et iterum lavet manus. In monastirio [sic] ubi non ingrediuntur femine, postquam primitus sacerdos laveret manus, ingrediuntur sacerdotes dum levitas in sacrario et accipient oblationes. Et procedant de sacrario. Et offerentur super altare, canentibus interim fratribus offertoria." Andrieu, *Ordines Romani*, 3:180–81.
93. Cited in Nickl, *Anteil des Volkes*, 47.
94. Ibid.

IMPLICATIONS FOR PERFORMANCE

These witnesses to Roman and Frankish practice form a context for some of the musical and textual evidence I will consider in subsequent chapters. The description of *Ordo Romanus I* and the Frankish witnesses derived from it suggest that the length of the chant varied according to the time required for the ceremony. The duration of the ceremony, in turn, would depend on how many members of the laity were offering and where they were situated in the church. As noted, McKinnon attributes the reference to the papal nod in *Ordo Romanus I* to a time when the offertory was sung as a simple psalm. The repertory handed down to us, however, presents no textual or musical evidence that this was ever the case. As Hucke has demonstrated, the texts show very few traces of traditional psalmody, antiphonal or responsorial.[95] In chapter 2, moreover, I argue that the offertory was a highly formalized chant, sung with verses in responsorial format from its beginning.

The papal instruction to stop singing need not be dismissed simply because there was no lay procession or because the offertory was not antiphonal. The form of the offertory with two or three verses is in fact quite suited to the varying length of the ceremony as described in *Ordo Romanus I* and elsewhere. The description of the introit and communion in these *ordines* can perhaps serve as a clue to reading this passage. For these chants, the author of *Ordo Romanus I* indicates that the *schola* begins the doxology at the cue from the pontiff. Applying a similar principle to the offertory, the passage describing the papal nod would suggest that singing did not stop immediately with the papal signal but the soloist concluded the current verse and the *schola* followed with the repetendum. This singing would accompany the movement of the regional subdeacons to a position behind the altar, as described in *Ordo Romanus I*.[96] The responsorial format of the offertory is consistent with liturgical witnesses indicating a varying length.

The flexibility provided by the respond-verse-repetendum format of the Roman offertory would have successfully accommodated the development of a lay procession when the rite and chant were adopted in Francia. The references to singing inserted throughout the description of the ceremony in *Ordo V* lend support to the hypothesis that the chant was of variable length. As noted, the compiler shows a special concern that the singing accompany the entire rite, and it is concluded with a nod from the bishop. With the participation of the entire congregation, the length of the ceremony and the music required to accommodate it would be variable. In some locations, the entire offertory with verses was undoubtedly sung, even when the ceremony did not require it. An ambiguous instruction in *Ordo XXII*, a description of the Lenten liturgy from 795–800, says: "Concerning the offertory

---

95. Hucke, "Texte."
96. Andrieu, *Ordines Romani* 2: 95.

and its verse, it is sung with two alternations [duobus vicibus] at one papal mass."[97] Some witnesses to liturgical practices in the north, however, suggest that the length of the chant continued to vary according to the duration of the offering, or that not all verses were sung at every Mass. The Bamberg codex of the *Musica Enchiriadis* (*tractatulus de cantu*), for example, mentions a practice of singing alternate verses on different days of the week:

> Let it be observed . . . that on Sundays all verses of the offertory are sung, likewise when a special service takes place. Then on Monday likewise the offertory, on Tuesday the first verse, on Wednesday the following verse, on Thursday the offertory, on Friday one verse, on Saturday the following verse. If on any weekday whatever, the verse of the day [versus suus] is not sung because of [the observance] of a saint's day, still, on the following day no verse is sung other than the one for that day.[98]

Some witnesses suggest that the length of the ceremony and the chant continued to vary in some locations until the singing of solo verses declined. The eleventh-century customary of Uldaric of Cluny, for example, remarks: "About offertory verses I know nothing further to relate, except that the cantor intones [them] according to what seem appropriate to him, at times one, at times all, principally depending on [the number of] those offering." He indicates that all verses are sung on Sundays.[99] That verses were seen as a functional accompaniment to the liturgy is also reflected in their eventual disappearance, attributed by Durand to the decline in lay participation in the offertory.[100]

These witnesses to the variable length of the offertory chant in Rome and Francia suggest that the usual two or three verses given in most manuscripts were not consistently performed. Although conclusions about the impact of these

---

97. "De offertorio seu et versu ipsius duobus vicibus ad unam missam domni pape cantatur." Ibid., 262. The meaning of "duobus vicibus" is unclear. It may refer simply to two alternations of verse and repetendum. In other words, both verses were performed at Papal Masses. Dyer suggests it might refer to a special treatment of verses in the presence of the pope. See Dyer, "Offertory Chant of the Roman Liturgy," 16. *Ordo XXII* was composed in Francia with the aid of Roman documents.

98. "Observandum est . . . ut dominicis diebus versus offertorii omnes canantur, similiter ubi speciale officium evenit. Porro II feria similiter offertorius, ferius III prior versus, feria IIII secundus, item feria V offertorius, feria VI unus versus, feria VII secundus versus. Si in feria qualibet propter sanctorum natalica: versus suus non canitur, non tamen feria sequente alius quam suus versus canatur." In Hans Schmid, ed., *Musica et scolica Enchiriadis una cum aliquibus tractatulis adiunctis* (Munich: Bayerische Akademie der Wissenschaften, 1981), 220.

99. "De versibus offerendis nihil aliud referre novi, nisi praecentor secundum quod sibi videtur imponit, nunc unum, nunc omnes, maxime propter offerentes." *Antiquiores consuetudines Cluniacensis monasterii*, in *Patrologia Latina* 149, column 652.

100. "Et attende quod offertorii versus cum multa diligentia ab antiquis patribus inventi, hodie plerisque locis omittuntur, tum brevitatis causa, ut tam ministri quam populus oblationibus, orationi et sacramento altaris liberius vacent." Guillaume Durand, *Rationale Divinorum Officiorum* IV, ed. G. H. Buijssen (Assen: Van Gorcum, 1983) 27, 4.

performance circumstances on the melodies must remain tentative, the performance context offers a possible key to the lack of similarity between the Gregorian and Roman verses. The frequent absence of melodic resemblance between the two dialects suggests that the verse melodies underwent change, in one tradition or both, between their separation in the eighth century and the time they were recorded in notation. The possibility of extensive change in either dialect becomes compelling in view of the verses' liturgical context. If verses were inconsistently used in the liturgy, the members of the Roman *schola cantorum* might have been less inclined to devote the same effort to maintaining the melodic tradition that they dedicated to other Mass proper chants. Without repeated rehearsal and performance, the melodies would be unlikely to survive centuries of oral transmission in Rome. In the north, inconsistency of performance, perhaps coupled with a variable or unstable melodic tradition received from Rome, may have led the Franks to take greater liberty with the verses than they did with the standard repertory, at least in the early, oral transmission. The development of an offertory rite that included members of the ordinary laity, with its expanded duration, would have provided Frankish singers with ample incentive for further development of the verse tradition. The liturgical history is consistent with the musical evidence I will present in chapter 3 that both traditions changed in the course of oral transmission.

2

THE TEXTS OF THE OFFERTORIES

The verbal texts of the chant repertory have played an important role in the recent debates on its origins. Kenneth Levy and James McKinnon have focused on structural aspects, emphasizing centonization or text adjustment, the modification of biblical passages to create a coherent lyric. Levy has pointed to the centonization in the nonpsalmic offertories as evidence that they were imported from Gaul, while McKinnon has brought to light the widespread use of centonization in much of the psalmic Mass Proper repertory, including the offertory.[1] He views departures from traditional antiphonal and responsorial structures as evidence of a chant's late integration into the tradition. As Peter Jeffery has recently suggested, however, centonization is a common feature of early sermons, liturgies, and monastic writing; it is not necessarily a meaningful chronological index.[2]

The biblical translations employed in the chant repertory have also played a role in debates on its origins and chronology, particularly in the work of Andreas Pfisterer. Noting that many of the nonpsalmic chants use Old Latin translations rather than the Vulgate, Pfisterer argues that the repertory originated long before McKinnon's proposed seventh-century date, a line of reasoning also pursued in Christoph Tietze's recent study of the introit.[3] Pfisterer's work also touches on the question of non-Roman origin. Based on the numerous departures from the Roman psalter (PsR), he argues that some offertories were imported into Rome from Gaul and North Africa long before the tradition was transmitted to the Franks.[4]

1. Kenneth Levy, "Toledo, Rome, and the Legacy of Gaul," *Early Music History* 4 (1984): 49–99; James McKinnon, *The Advent Project: The Later-Seventh-Century Creation of the Roman Mass Proper* (Berkeley: University of California Press, 2001), 13–14; 103–4, 310, 312–14, 237–38; 215–20; 368–69; for discussion of centonization, see also Thomas Connolly, "The *Graduale* of St. Cecilia in Trastevere and the Old Roman Tradition," *Journal of the American Musicological Society* 23 (1975): 428.

2. Peter Jeffery, review of *The Advent Project: The Later-Seventh-Century Creation of the Roman Mass Proper*, by James McKinnon, *Journal of the American Musicological Society* 56 (2003): 168–79.

3. Andreas Pfisterer, *Cantilena Romana: Untersuchungen zur Überlieferung des gregorianischen Chorals* (Tützing: Hans Schneider, 2002): 127–35; 221–34, and "James McKinnon und die Datierung des gregorianischen Chorals," *Kirchenmusikalisches Jahrbuch* 85 (2001): 31–53; Christoph Tietze, *Hymn Introits for the Liturgical Year* (Chicago: Hillenbrand Books, 2005), 41–98.

4. Andreas Pfisterer, "Remarks on Roman and Non-Roman Offertories," *Plainsong and Medieval Music* 14 (2005): 169–81, and "*Super flumina Babylonis*: On the Prehistory of a Roman Offertory," in *The*

The role of verbal characteristics in these theories about the repertory's origins calls for a comprehensive examination of the offertory's words and a reconsideration of their implications for origin and chronology. Building on the work of Pfisterer and Dyer, I begin by examining the textual tradition and verbal structure of the psalmic offertories. Although departures from the Roman psalter may be found in more than half of the repertory, the paucity of extant psalter manuscripts and the complexity of the psalter's textual transmission make it difficult to pinpoint the origin of specific variants. From the textual tradition, I turn to the structural aspects of the psalmic offertories. A comparison of selected offertories with their biblical sources indicates that biblical passages were selected and arranged specifically for a musical setting. For this reason, I often refer to the offertory texts as "lyrics." In many cases, they are structured to correspond to the musical form of the offertory, with verses and repetenda. Finally, I examine the nonpsalmic offertories and the question of non-Roman origin, beginning with a critique of Levy's Gallican hypothesis, placing these offertories in their Old Hispanic and Milanese contexts, and considering the chronological implications of the translations they employ.

PSALTER SOURCES

The psalter translations in the chant repertory have emerged as an important issue in recent scholarship for the insight they might yield into its origins and transmission. Because the repertory was long assumed to have originated in Rome, early studies of the texts focused on their resemblance to the PsR. In a preliminary study, for example, Bruno Stäblein established their general concordance with the PsR, a pattern further illustrated by Dyer.[5] Although his work revealed numerous departures from PsR witnesses, Dyer nevertheless argued that the offertories were of "purely Roman origin," a conclusion reaffirmed in his subsequent look at the Lenten Mass Proper repertory.[6] In recent studies, however, Pfisterer has given greater emphasis to the offertories' differences from the PsR. On this basis, he challenges the long-standing consensus that the bulk of the repertory originated in Rome.[7]

These divergent conclusions of Dyer and Pfisterer, based on essentially the same evidence, invite another examination of the textual variants and their implications for the repertory's origin. Pfisterer's work in particular raises questions

Offertory and Its Verses: Research, Past, Present, and Future, ed. Roman Hankeln (Trondheim: Tapir Academic Press, 2007), 41–56.

5. Bruno Stäblein, "Nochmals zur angeblichen des gregorianischen Chorals in Frankenreich," *Archiv für Musikwissenschaft* 27 (1970): 110–21; Joseph Dyer, "The Offertories of Old-Roman Chant: A Musico-Liturgical Investigation" (Ph.D. diss., Boston University, 1971), 131–46.

6. Joseph Dyer, "Latin Psalters, Old Roman and Gregorian Chants," *Kirchenmusikalisches Jahrbuch* 68 (1984): 11–30.

7. Pfisterer, "Remarks," and *"Super Flumina."*

for further investigation and reflection. To what extent are the "non-Roman" verbal characteristics, demonstrated by Pfisterer in a handful of offertories, found among the offertory repertory as a whole? Do the surviving psalters form a body of evidence sufficient for establishing a plausible theory of origin? The following pages are devoted to exploring these questions. I begin with a brief overview of the various branches of the Old Latin psalter, followed by an illustration of the tradition's deviations from the PsR. The numerous departures from the PsR do perhaps suggest a substantial non-Roman influence on the repertory, as Pfisterer has argued. Because of the rarity of extant psalter witnesses and the complexity of the textual variants, however, the psalter evidence does not often yield clear, compelling conclusions about the origins of specific chants. While the presence of non-PsR readings is consistent with a non-Roman origin in some cases, the evidence is not always conclusive enough to warrant a departure from the long-standing assumption of Roman origin.

The psalters employed in the chant texts are branches of the Old Latin psalter, a family of translations from the Greek Septuagint.[8] The most pervasive Old Latin influence on the textual tradition of the chant repertory as a whole is the PsR, which enjoyed widespread use in Rome and southern Italy for much of the Middle Ages. Its traditional designation "Roman" arose only in ninth-century Gaul, where it was so labeled to distinguish it from other psalters in common use.[9] In assessing the chant tradition's correspondence to early versions of the PsR, the surviving sources present something of an obstacle. The earliest examples are from eighth-century England, reflecting the PsR's introduction into England by Roman missionaries under Gregory the Great. The PsR served as the preferred psalter in England until the Norman Conquest.[10] The earliest Italian PsR manuscripts date from the eleventh and twelfth centuries. No sources, then, survive from the period of the chant repertory's formation, and the earliest Italian manuscripts postdate the chant repertory by at least four centuries. The extant PsR witnesses, moreover, are far from uniform. The variants within the tradition are shown in Robert Weber's edition, based on the best manuscripts representing the English and Italian branches.[11] While the PsR

---

8. Dyer's "Latin Psalters" remains the classic introduction to this topic for chant scholars. For an excellent recent overview of the Old Latin psalter branches, sources, scholarship, and editions, see Pierre-Maurice Bogaert, "Le psautier latin des origines au douzième siècle: Essai d'histoire," in *Der Septuaginta-Psalter and seine Tocherübersetzungen: Symposium in Göttingen 1997* (Göttingen: Vandenhoeck und Ruprecht, 2000), 51–81.

9. A long-discredited view held that the PsR was first the recension made by Jerome, a correction of earlier psalters made according to the Greek text, but the PsR cannot be convincingly tied to Jerome. See Donatien De Bruyne, "Le problème du psautier romain," *Revue Bénédictine* 42 (1930): 101–26.

10. Mechthild Gretsch, "The Roman Psalter, Its Old English Glosses, and the English Benedictine Reform," in *The Liturgy of the Late Anglo-Saxon Church*, ed. Helen Gittos and M. Bradford Bedingfield (London: Boydell Press, 2005), 13–28.

11. Robert Weber, *Le Psautier Romain et les autres anciens psautiers latins* (Rome: Abbaye Saint-Jérôme, 1953).

presented in Weber's edition is undoubtedly similar to the one used in Rome centuries earlier, we lack an exact picture of its development.

The Gallican Psalter (PsG), more appropriately called the hexaplaric psalter, is Jerome's revision of an older Latin psalter, made according to Origen's Greek hexapla. Jerome's hexaplaric psalter was intended not as a text for practical use but as a scholarly edition. It was the preferred liturgical text in Ireland, and its initial introduction into Gaul was probably made by Irish missionaries in the fifth century. The influence of the PsG on the textual tradition in Gaul is evident in a fragmentary psalter from Lyon dating to 500, known by Weber's siglum η, which mixes the PsG with psalter traditions previously used in Gaul.[12] The hexaplaric psalter became the favored text in Gaul, however, only in Carolingian times, under the influence of Alcuin's scriptorium at Tours.[13] The prevailing traditions in pre-Carolingian Gaul are reflected in a group of Old Latin sources loosely termed "gaulois."

The designation "Gallican" for the hexaplaric psalter dates from the ninth century, a period marked by efforts toward textual uniformity. Bonifatius Fischer has shown that more than half of the mistakes in the Carolingian psalters descend from a single exemplar; he places the exemplar text to 770–90 and the roots of the hexaplaric psalter's adoption in Francia to 750–60.[14] Efforts to spread the hexaplaric psalter in Francia, then, are contemporaneous with the beginnings of Roman chant reception. The reasons for the hexaplaric psalter's preferred status in a culture that claimed to look to Rome for its liturgical practices are unclear. In view of the prior Irish influence, some previous familiarity with the text may have been a factor.[15] Replacing a familiar liturgical text, however, is rarely a simple matter. The PsG was mixed with gaulois traditions from pre-Carolingian Gaul, whose influence is the primary source of mistakes in the exemplar.[16]

The influence of the PsG on the chant repertory has been the focus of several studies. Thomas Connolly has argued that the PsG readings in the Roman introits point to a Gregorian influence on the Roman tradition, a position further argued by Philippe Bernard and, more recently, Kenneth Levy.[17] Dyer, however, has shown

---

12. Bonifatius Fischer, "Zur Überlieferung altlateinischer Bibeltexte im Mittelalter," *Nederlands Archief voor Kerkgeschiedenis* 56 (1975): 19–33.

13. McKitterick, however, has argued that the Alcuinian Bibles exerted less influence on the Carolingian tradition than previously believed. Rosamond McKitterick, "Carolingian Bible Production: The Tours Anomaly," in *The Early Medieval Bible: Its Production, Decoration, and Use* (Cambridge: Cambridge University Press, 1994), 63–77.

14. Fischer, "Zur Überlieferung," 25, and "Die Texte," in *Der Stuttgarter Bilderpsalter Bibl. fol. 23 Württembergische Landesbibliothek Stuttgart* (Stuttgart: E. Schreiber Graphische Kunstanstalten, 1968): 2:223–88.

15. Fischer, "Zur Überlieferung," 23–25.

16. For examples, see Donatien De Bruyne, "La Reconstitution du Psautier Hexaplaire Latin," *Revue Bénédictine* 41 (1929): 297–324.

17. Connolly, "*Graduale* of S. Cecilia," *Journal of the American Musicological Society* 413–58; Philippe Bernard, "Les variantes textuelles entre "vieux-romain" et "grégorien"—quelques résultants," in *Requirentes modos musicos: Mélanges offerts à Dom Jean Claire à l'occasion de son 75e anniversaire, de*

that a great majority of purported PsG readings in the chant repertory are also concordant with various Old Latin traditions. The variants between the Gregorian and Roman versions of the texts, he argues, are consistent with variants between the psalters themselves and can be explained without supposing the influence of the Gregorian tradition on the Roman.[18] Only in a few isolated cases, in fact, does a chant text have a PsG concordance that is not also found in at least one branch of the Old Latin tradition, such as the gaulois sources. When the PsG readings occur in Old Latin sources, Dyer and Pfisterer have sensibly given priority to the Old Latin readings.

The designation "gaulois" is traditionally given to a group of related Old Latin manuscripts representing traditions used in Gaul before the adoption of the PsG. The gaulois witnesses may be divided into two groups, the first associated with Lyonnaise Gaul and the second with Narbonnaise Gaul. Among the first group are several important witnesses, customarily designated with Weber's sigla: the Psalter of St. Germain, γ, probably copied in the north of Italy in the sixth century; the triple psalter of Corbie, δ, copied in Corbie in the eighth century; a closely related tenth-century source from Chartres; and a manuscript now in Reichenau, probably copied in Francia at the end of the sixth century. The Narbonnaise group, closer to Visigothic Spain, includes the seventh-century Psalter of Coislin, ϵ, and a different psalter from Reichenau, λ. Psalters that combine characteristics of various traditions include the palimpsest Psalter of Verona, ζ, copied in the seventh or eighth century, which mixes readings from both gaulois branches; and the previously mentioned Psalter of Lyon, η, which mixes the gaulois tradition and the PsG. As I will show, several offertory texts present readings close to those of γ, δ, η, and, in one case, ϵ.

The psalter quoted by Augustine has played an important role in Pfisterer's recent work. The tradition is preserved in two fragmentary North African witnesses and two European sources: another Verona psalter, a, copied in northern Italy in the sixth or seventh century, and the closely related St. Gall palimpsest psalter, β, also from northern Italy, copied in the ninth century. This tradition shows some correspondence to that quoted by Ambrose and probably originated in northern Italy before it was taken to North Africa by Augustine.[19] Pfisterer has argued for a North African influence on offertories exhibiting concordances with a on the basis

ses 50 ans de profession monastique, et de ses 25 ans comme maître de choeur à Solesmes, ed. Jean Claire et al. (Sablé-sur-Sarthe: Abbaye Saint-Pierre de Solesmes, 1995), 62–82. PsG concordances have recently been cited by Levy to support a theory that the Gregorian offertories are pre-existing Gallican melodies with Roman texts, circumventing Dyer's explanation for this phenomenon. While acknowledging the limits of the psalter evidence, Levy argues that these melodies were transported back to Rome and partially incorporated into the Roman chant tradition, leaving their mark on the texts of the Old Roman manuscripts. Levy also suggests that PsG readings are consistent with a pre-Carolingian, "Gallican origin," even though the PsG was not the prevailing tradition in Gaul until the Carolingian era. See Levy, "A New Look at Old Roman Chant I," *Early Music History* 19 (2000): 93–94.

18. Dyer, "Latin Psalters," 17.
19. Alberto Vaccari, "I salteri de S. Girolamo e di S. Agostino," in *Scritti di erudizione e di filologia* (Rome: Edizioni di storia e letteratura, 1952), 207–55.

of *a*'s known liturgical use in Hippo. These concordances, however, could also point to Northern Italian influences.

THE TEXTUAL TRADITION OF THE OFFERTORIES

As the studies of Dyer and Pfisterer have shown, the offertories exhibit numerous textual departures from the PsR tradition represented in Weber's edition, often corresponding to other Old Latin traditions such as the Verona psalter *a* or the gaulois sources *γ* and *δ*. Dyer's systematic investigation, based on the manuscripts representing the Roman dialect, demonstrated departures from the PsR in well over half of the core offertory repertory. In most cases, the chant text was matched in another Old Latin psalter.[20] Appendix 1 provides my own list of textual variants, intended to complement Dyer's by incorporating several early Gregorian sources and listing variants within and between the Gregorian and Roman manuscripts. Column 2 gives the PsR reading of the variant passage; column 3 gives the reading of the passage in the Roman chant manuscripts, and column 4 presents the readings in a group of early sources representing the Gregorian tradition. In columns 3 and 4, the chant manuscripts with the indicated reading are given in parentheses. Blank spaces indicate that the passage in question corresponds to the PsR. The first time a given variant occurs, either in column 3 or 4, it is followed by a list of concordances from the psalter traditions, designated with Weber's sigla. The Greek letters refer to other Old Latin psalter traditions; the capital Roman letters to the earliest PsR witnesses, many of English origin; and the lowercase letters to late Italian PsR sources. I have omitted the most obvious cases of text adjustment and variants that can be easily explained as errors occurring only in one source.

For a well-rounded picture of the early Gregorian traditions, I have incorporated both notated and unnotated sources, including four of the manuscripts in *Antiphonale missarum sextuplex*. Of these unnotated sources, only Compiègne (Co) gives the complete texts of the offertories and verses. Corbie (Cr) normally has complete texts of the responds and incipits for verses; Mont-Blandin (Bl) and Rheinau (Rh) are inconsistent in their indications of full texts or incipits.[21] I have also considered a sampling of geographically diverse early notated sources: Laon 239 (La 239), Chartres 47 (Cha 47), and Einsiedeln 121 (Ei 121),

---

20. Dyer, "Offertories of Old-Roman Chant," 138–42.
21. Rheinau presents unique readings in several passages and contains two significant variants that are not included in appendix 1 because they are not related to the different psalter traditions. The respond *Iubilate deo omnis* (11) lacks text repetition, hence matching the Roman version. The respond *Eripe me . . . deus* (42) has a longer text, the end of which reads "ab insurgentibus me a viro iniquo eripias me domine." Mont-Blandin has a different incipit for the second verse of *De profundis* (69). Also noteworthy are cases where Rheinau is the only source to concord with the PsR, such as "providebam dominum" in *Benedicam*, "extendisti" in *Si ambulavero*, and "Libani" in *Iustus ut palma*. These variants among the earliest sources may be significant enough to challenge

along with Benevento 34 (Ben 34), which serves as the main source for the edition. As appendix 1 shows, Beneventan manuscripts often lack the textual departures from the PsR that are found in the northern manuscripts, reflecting in part a southern Italian preference for the PsR.[22] For the Roman text I have incorporated the two manuscripts with verses, Bodmer 74 and Rome Vat 5319. The latter has several variants that are not found in the former; many of these are probably simple errors.

Appendix 1 serves several functions: it demonstrates where the Gregorian and Roman texts differ, shows variants within the Gregorian and Roman groups of manuscripts, and indicates where each version of the chant differs from the PsR and corresponds to other psalters. Some of the offertories listed in Appendix 1 are essentially consistent with the PsR tradition. In *Exaltabo te* (17), for example, the omission of PsR's "et bona" in the Gregorian manuscripts is probably best viewed as an adaptation to the PsG. (The numbers in parentheses refer to the number of the piece in the edition, tables, and appendix 1.) The text as a whole presents no evidence that its source is anything other than the PsR. The information summarized in appendix 1 is consistent with Dyer's and Pfisterer's observations that the offertories often concord with the manuscripts α, γ, and δ. The conclusions to be drawn from these variants, however, are far from clear. Many of the offertories are extensively centonized, a process I will examine later in this chapter. In a culture that knew the psalter by heart, moreover, it is probable that memory played a role in the creation of these lyrics. Centonized texts may be characterized as "quasi original composition[s] created by the author from remembered biblical fragments, rather than a conscious adaptation of a specific scriptural passage."[23] Alteration of the biblical source can arise out of a conscious attempt to create a coherent lyric or a more ad hoc approach, in which bits of the psalm are recalled from memory and stitched together; the latter process is well known to students of monastic literature. Both processes appear to be at work in the offertories.

To take an example of possible oral influence, *Benedictus es . . . et ne / non tradas* (43) is one of several Lenten offertories centonized from Psalm 118. The Gregorian version is given in the right-hand column of table 2.5 (in conjunction with a more detailed discussion later in this chapter), the corresponding passages from the PsR in the left-hand column. The text shows two concordances with the Psalter of Lyon, η: "calumniantibus" instead of "persequentibus" and "appropinquaverunt" instead of "adpropiaverunt." Of particular interest here are the words "et revereantur" at the end of the second verse, which do not occur in Psalm 118.

---

the assumption that there was a single textual archetype transmitted from Rome to the Franks. A full examination of variants particular to these traditions merits a separate study in its own right.

22. This correspondence to the PsR in Beneventan manuscripts is cited as evidence for the early arrival of Gregorian chant in southern Italy in Thomas Forrest Kelly, *The Beneventan Chant* (Cambridge: Cambridge University Press, 1989), 19.

23. McKinnon, *Advent Project*, 103.

The phrase "confundantur et revereantur," however, does occur several other times in the psalter, in Psalms 34, 39, and 69. The word "confundantur" evidently prompted the lyricist to recall these psalms in the process of creating a centonized chant primarily from Psalm 118. Such a conflation would be especially likely when the lyricist was creating a piece from memory.

The textual adjustment found throughout the repertory makes it difficult in some cases to determine whether a given reading reflects the influence of another psalter tradition, a deliberate alteration of the psalm, or a memory slip. *Iubilate deo omnis* (11), for example, has one departure from the PsR. In the passage "quia dominus ipse est deus," (Ps. 99:3) the PsR has "quod" instead of "quia." "Quia" matches the gaulois source γ, the Psalter of St. Germain. Yet this passage has a textual adjustment: the psalm reads "scitote quod dominus ipse est deus." In the process of omitting "scitote," the compiler of the text may have changed "quod" to "quia." Because the gaulois influence is absent in the rest of the text, it is unclear whether this variant is best viewed as an example of text adjustment or a sign of gaulois influence. Tracing the psalter source can become difficult when the text has been altered from the biblical source, as it has in the majority of offertories.

Another problem inherent in interpreting the evidence concerns the presence of gaulois readings. As noted, the traditions represented in δ and γ seem particularly influential. Pfisterer interprets concordances with these manuscripts as archaisms, evidence of a pre-Carolingian Gallican origin. When a chant text matches a gaulois source against the PsR, he gives chronological priority to the gaulois reading. Although efforts to spread the PsG in Francia can be traced to the mid-eighth century–precisely when the Roman liturgy and chant were being adopted–it is nevertheless extremely doubtful that the transition from the gaulois traditions to the PsG took place overnight. The early PsG manuscripts demonstrate the continuing influence of older psalters on the textual tradition of the PsG in Francia.[24] It is probable, then, that the psalter tradition was still in a transitional state when the Franks received the Roman chant. Pfisterer is certainly correct to give preference to gaulois readings in many cases, particularly when they are found in the Roman manuscripts. The historical situation, however, raises the possibility that a gaulois concordance that is found in early Gregorian sources but not in the Roman tradition reflects a local adaptation to a familiar gaulois tradition.[25]

Not all departures from the PsR indicated in appendix 1 can be equally regarded as indices of non-Roman textual influence. Before turning to some of the more compelling examples and the criteria for selecting them, I would like to consider some of the variables that enter into evaluating the evidence. First, the

---

24. See notes 15 and 16.
25. There are several possible examples of this phenomenon in appendix 1, such as the reading "iusticiam meam" in *Expectans* (35) in some Gregorian sources.

influence of traditions other than the PsR is more extensive in some offertories than in others. In this respect, the summary format of appendix 1 omits some information that is central to judging the importance of a given variant. Although it indicates where the offertories correspond to other Old Latin psalters, it does not show where a given offertory matches the PsR against these psalters. Second, some variants are more significant aurally than others. Third, some variants are found consistently in early Gregorian sources, whereas others are limited to a specific area or group of sources. The following two examples illustrate various ways the evidence can be interpreted and the problems inherent in attempting to pinpoint the textual influences.

Some offertories show only one or two minor variants from the majority of PsR sources. In *Benedixisti* (3) for the Third Sunday of Advent, for example, the three manuscripts of the Roman dialect correspond fully to the PsR; several early Gregorian sources, however, exhibit one departure, in the passage "remisisti iniquitatem plebis tuae" (Ps. 84:3). Rheinau, Corbie, and Einsiedeln 121 match the Roman chant text and the PsR here, whereas Compiègne, Chartres, and Laon have "plebi" instead of "plebis." Among early psalter manuscripts, "plebi" is found only twice, in α and in one tenth-century PsR witness, B. However, α has several aurally significant departures from the PsR that are found neither in the Gregorian nor the Roman chant text, most conspicuously "sedasti" instead of "mitigasti" and the insertion of "deus" in the respond. I am hesitant to attribute priority to α on the basis of one variant, "plebis/plebi," particularly when Gregorian sources that transmit this variant are limited to one geographic region. It is unclear how the variant reading "plebi" entered these sources. Because it is unlikely that the transmission of Roman chant to the Franks was made with a single Roman archetype, "plebi" could reflect either a lack of uniformity in the Roman tradition itself or a psalter tradition, no longer extant, that was known in this region before the PsG was adopted there.

Of the many offertories with departures from the PsR, only a few correspond fully to a known Old Latin tradition. *Exaudi deus* (30), for example, has one significant variant, "deum" instead of "dominum" in verse 2. "Deum" corresponds to the manuscripts α and γ and one early PsR witness, H. However, α and γ have readings not reflected in the chant text, such as "precem" instead of "deprecationem" in α (54:2) and "iniquitatem" instead of "peccatorum" in γ (54:4). Does the lyric descend from a non-Roman psalter related to α and γ? If so, are the passages that match the PsR against these texts assimilations to the PsR? Did the compiler of the text simply know a version of the PsR with "deum" instead of "dominum"? Or was he recalling the text from memory, conflating Psalm 54 with another psalm? We can only speculate. In this case, centonization further complicates the matter. Although this section of the offertory respond replicates the psalm without gaps, elsewhere the text is highly adjusted, raising the possibility that the lyrist deliberately or inadvertently changed the psalm.

TABLE 2.1 Offertories with Textual Traditions Other Than the PsR

Alpha	Gaulois	Mixtures
Tollite portas	Iubilate deo	Benedicite gentes γεα
Reges tharsis	universa δ	Populum humilem
Meditabor	Benedictus es . . . non tradas	αβδη
Benedicam	η	Eripe me . . . deus (med)
Super flumina	Miserere mihi δ	Intonuit αβδ
Illumina oculos (β)	Expectans γ (λ)	Eripe me . . . domine α, med
	Improperium ε (δ)	Mirabilis αβγδε
	Portas caeli γ	
	Iustus ut palma γδ	
	Inveni δ	
	Confirma (γδ)	
	Constitues eos δ	
	*Ascendit η	
	*Offerentur δγ	
	*Confitebor tibi γ	

The textual tradition of the offertories confirms the impression that the psalter tradition is multifaceted and complex, and that the surviving psalter manuscripts give us a limited picture of that tradition. Several offertories have readings that correspond to no extant psalter manuscript, a phenomenon illustrated by Dyer. These unknown readings are indicated with the symbol "–" in appendix 1. In several cases, I have found corresponding readings in the VL database of patristic citations, and these instances are mentioned in the footnotes to appendix 1.[26] Because many other offertories present a set of variables similar to those of *Benedixisti* and *Exaudi deus*, determining the most compelling cases of other psalters' influence requires a careful evaluation of these factors in each individual offertory. On this basis, I have extracted some of the more compelling departures from the PsR; these are listed in table 2.1. Borderline cases are indicated with an asterisk.

I have adopted several interacting criteria in determining which departures from the PsR are most significant, which are questionable, and which should not be listed in table 2.1 at all. When a variant found only in the Gregorian tradition can be explained as an adaptation to the PsG, I have given priority to this explanation, except in cases where Old Latin readings are prominent elsewhere in the text. *Exaltabo* (17), *Perfice* (15), and *Bonum est* (14) are examples of this phenomenon:

26. *Vetus latina Database: The Bible Versions of the Latin Fathers* (Turnhout: Brepols, 2003).

departures from the PsR that can be traced to psalter MSS are found only in the
Gregorian tradition, and each of these variants concords with the PsG. Although
the Gregorian readings also correspond to other Old Latin psalters, these other
psalters often have significant variants that are not found in the chant text,
strengthening the impression that the Gregorian readings are PsG adaptations.
These cases are not included in table 2.1.

In determining the more compelling cases of non-PsR influence, I have also
considered the number of times a given lyric differs from Weber's primary PsR
edition together with the number of times that the lyric matches the PsR against
other psalters. I have omitted cases such as *Benedixisti*—with only one or two
minor departures from the PsR, especially when they are found only in localized
Gregorian traditions—and *Exaudi deus*, where the other Old Latin sources present
major variants that are not found in the chant lyric. A third criterion I have
considered is the aural significance of the variant in question. Pfisterer adopts a
sensible premise in weighing the significance of the variants: variants and corruptions would be more likely to enter into the tradition where they could
be accomplished with minimal change to the melody. In the opening of *Portas
caeli* (51), an example Pfisterer discusses, the PsR has "ianuas" instead of "portas."
Not only would the two words be difficult to confuse but also their different
syllable count would result in at least a minor melodic change. A less aurally
significant variant, such as "plebis/plebi" in *Benedixisti*, would require no melodic
changes; the aural similarities between the two words might subject them to
conflation in the memory of the singer and assimilation to a more familiar psalter
reading. Finally, I have considered the degree to which a departure from Weber's
edition is found among other PsR witnesses, particularly the older ones. *Scapulis suis*
(19) is essentially consistent with the PsR, as both versions of its variants, "obum-
bravit/bit" and "speravit/bit," are found among PsR witnesses. In this case, the
variants may merely reflect inconsistency within the PsR tradition itself. A similar
picture is evident in *Factus est dominus* (38), *Domine in auxilium* (27), and several
others.

A few additional examples will illustrate how the criteria interact in determining
the most significant departures from the PsR. I have listed *Miserere mihi* (26) in
table 2.1 as a probable case of δ influence. Its opening, "miserere mihi domine," is
aurally distinct from the PsR reading "miserere mei deus." This particular reading,
moreover, is found only in δ; it is lacking in all PsR manuscripts and the PsG. Aside
from very minor variants, such as "delectum" instead of "delictum," the chant is in
concordance with δ. Following the criteria I have established, then, a version
closely related to δ seems a plausible source for the text. *Benedicam* (25) has one
significant variant in Gregorian sources, "fecisti mihi" rather than "mihi fecisti," that
is found only in α; α has one variant, "delectatio/delectationes," that is not found in
the chant text. Because the α reading "fecisti mihi" is the more aurally significant
variant, however, I have given priority to α and listed *Benedicam* in the table.

Offertories for which the evidence for a non-PsR source is inconclusive are omitted from table 2.1. *Emitte spiritum* (59), for example, is a possible case of δ influence. The Gregorian and Roman versions show some correspondence with δ, each in different passages. The two concordances with δ in the Gregorian version, however, also match the PsG and can thus be explained as PsG adaptations. Two of the correspondences between the Roman chant text and δ, moreover, are also shared with at least five early PsR witnesses, plausibly reflecting variants within the PsR tradition. In this case, a look at the δ text itself does not clarify the source for the chant: δ has only one variant not matched in the chant, "decore" instead of "decorem" (Ps. 103:1), which is not aurally significant. Because the evidence lends itself to a particularly wide range of interpretations, I have not included *Emitte spiritum* in the table.

Some offertories with a correspondence to α are given in the first column of table 2.1. The list includes the two pieces identified by Pfisterer as corresponding to α: *Super flumina* (66) and *Meditabor (22)*. To these we may add *Illumina oculos* (28) and *Tollite portas* (6). *Illumina oculos* has several readings that correspond to β, a psalter closely related to α, and its reading "nequando" is matched in a psalter manuscript from Montecassino that represents in part an African tradition.[27] The respond of *Tollite portas* shows one correspondence to η, "vestras." In the verses, however, the Roman text corresponds fully to α, and only α. Where the Gregorian manuscripts differ, the variants may be regarded either as adaptations to the PsG or, in the case of the Beneventan source, to the PsR.[28] Levy has tied *Tollite portas* to a series of North Italian chants on the same text with various liturgical uses.[29] The offertory respond shares its text with a Milanese *responsorium cum infantibus*, a Mantuan *ante-evangelium*, and a chant of unknown liturgical use from a Florentine theoretical manuscript. Levy proposes that the ultimate origin of these chants is Gallican and points to a "high-G" modality as a musical thread that connects the offertory to the Milanese and Florentine chants. I would not characterize the modal structure of the offertory as primarily *tetrardus*. In a majority of sources examined for this study, it closes on D. The versions with a G final follow a transposed second-mode profile and move to G, very suddenly, at the end of the

27. See Ambrogio Amelli, *Liber psalmorum iuxta antiquissimam latinam versionem nunc primum ex Casinensi cod. 557 in lucem profertur* (Rome: F. Pustet, 1912); and B. Capelle, "L'élément africain dans le Psalterium Casinense," *Revue Bénédictine* 32 (1920): 113–31.
28. The PsG takes "orbis" as the subject in 23:1 and hence uses masculine pronouns throughout verses 1 and 2.
29. Kenneth Levy, "*Tollite Portas*: An Ante-Evangelium Reclaimed?" in *Western Plainchant in the First Millennium: Studies in the Medieval Liturgy and Its Music*, ed. Sean Gallagher et al. (Aldershot, England: Ashgate, 2003), 231–41. The three northern Italian chants, consisting only of Ps. 23:7, present a divergent textual tradition according to Levy's transcriptions and reproductions. The Mantuan and Florentine chants have "adtollite," which is found only in the PsG, perhaps indicating an origin or influence from the Carolingian or post-Carolingian era, when the PsG was in use. The Milanese version has "principis vestri," corresponding to the Milanese psalter. The α influence, manifest only in the verses of the offertory, is absent in these texts.

closing melisma. Most manuscripts with a G final indicate a b-flat, thereby retaining *protus* characteristics.[30] Levy's comparison of the G-mode version of the offertory to the Florentine version nevertheless reveals some compelling similarities in contour and range. The use of the α text, then, may reinforce the impression of a North Italian origin. Although Pfisterer has argued for a North African origin for the chants with α influence on the basis of that psalter's liturgical use in Africa, the α text is known to have originated in northern Italy and is related to the text quoted by Ambrose.[31]

Offertories that show some probable influence of the gaulois traditions are listed in column 2 of table 2.1. These include *Miserere mihi* (26), *Expectans expectavi* (35), *Improperium* (44), *Iubilate deo universa* (12), *Iustus ut palma* (71), and *Portas caeli* (51), examined by Pfisterer. The source that corresponds most often with the offertories is δ.

Listed in column 3 are offertories with important departures from the PsR that cannot be traced to a particular psalter. In several cases, the variants show concordances with a number of different manuscripts, and a more specific influence is not possible to determine. *Populum humilem* (37), for example, resembles δ, η, and β, a close relative of the Verona psalter α, in its omission of "dominus" and "et" in the second verse. Because these manuscripts are concordant in the other passages, it is not possible to narrow down a more specific influence. Included in this group is *Mirabilis*, only psalmic offertory with a partial cognate in the Old Hispanic sacrificium repertory, perhaps reinforcing the impression of non-Roman origin. This chant has one significant variant that corresponds to several different psalters. *Benedicite gentes* (36) presents far more complex mixture of influences, with variants that match ε in the respond and α or γ in the verses. This mixture probably does not indicate separate influences of α and γ on the chant text; it is even less likely that it reflects different origins for the respond and verses. More plausibly, the chant descends from a source no longer extant. These cases point to the limitations of psalter evidence as a basis for positing a chant's origin.

To summarize, the twenty-five offertories listed in table 2.1 have variants from the surviving PsR witnesses that seem significant enough to suggest that the source is a psalter other than the PsR. This influence, then, is discernable in more than a quarter of the core Roman-Gregorian offertories. Traces of possible non-PsR influence are in evidence in some two dozen other offertories, bringing the total to more than two-thirds of the repertory. As I have shown, however, the

30. See the commentary on *Tollite* in appendix 3. See also the remarks in Hubert Sidler, "Studien zu den alten Offertorien mit ihren Versen" (Ph.D. diss. University of Fribourg, 1939); and *Die Offertoriumsprosuln Der Aquitanischen Handschrift: Voruntersuchungen Zur Edition Des Aquitanischen Offertoriumscorpus und Seiner Erweiterungen*, 3 vols. (Tutzing: Hans Schneider, 1996), 1:97–101. In the versions ending on G, the ending is an aural surprise, and these readings employ a b-flat, a *protus* characteristic.
31. Most of the Ambrose quotations in *Vetus latina Database* have "fundavit eam," the reading of the PsR, and "preparavit eam," the reading of α.

meaning of these variants is difficult to ascertain. Having chosen some of the more compelling cases for non-Roman origin, I return to a point made previously: there are a number of ways to interpret the evidence. Observing the frequent correspondence of the offertories' textual tradition to α, γ, and δ, Dyer nevertheless concludes that the PsR was the dominant influence and that the tradition as a whole is consistent with the Roman origin of the repertory. Attributing greater significance to these non-Roman readings, Pfisterer argues for a North African or Gallican origin in several cases.

These contradictory conclusions of Dyer and Pfisterer are rooted not so much in the body of evidence examined but in different methods and fundamentally divergent interpretative approaches. Dyer employs the Roman manuscripts as his primary basis for comparing the chant to the psalters. His presentation of variants indicates which Roman departures from the PsR are also found in the Gregorian versions, but he does not consider departures from the PsR that are found only in Gregorian sources. Pfisterer, by contrast, gives priority to the early Gregorian sources, with the premise that they may provide a more direct path to recovering the original text. The crux of the different conclusions, however, resides in the significance attributed to the variants. Although Dyer's primary objective was to propose an alternative to Connolly's hypothesis of PsG influence at Rome, his conclusion that the tradition is based on the PsR appears to give greater weight to the common origin of the Old Latin branches, the absence of early Roman witnesses, and the lack of uniformity in the PsR tradition itself. Although the surviving PsR sources present a consistent picture, they are far from uniform; to different degrees, they correspond to the other Old Latin psalters with which they share origins. In view of this variety, a lyric that mixes PsR readings with other Old Latin psalters can be seen as generally consistent with the PsR, perhaps deriving from a lost PsR witness. Pfisterer, on the other hand, views departures from the PsR as significant indicators of non-Roman origin. When a given chant shows an influence of both the PsR and another Old Latin psalter, he gives chronological priority to the Old Latin reading. In receiving a chant with an unfamiliar psalter translation, he reasons, the Roman and Frankish cantors would be expected to assimilate the text to a more familiar psalter, respectively the PsR or PsG, especially when the familiar textual tradition was compatible with the existing melody. In a mixed PsR and gaulois text, then, he views the gaulois tradition as the primary influence and the PsR readings as secondary—assimilations to the PsR made by Roman singers when they adopted that particular chant into their repertory.[32]

Underlying Pfisterer's reading of the evidence, it seems, are several important premises. The first is that the only viable source for the compilation of chant texts in Rome is the PsR; in creating a psalmic text for a melodic setting, a singer would not seek a psalter manuscript from a library but would turn instead to the psalter he

32. Pfisterer, *Cantilena*, 127–36.

or she knew best, the one in current liturgical use. A second premise is that the surviving witnesses to the PsR can give us an accurate picture of the psalter of the sixth- or seventh-century Roman *schola cantorum*, even though the earliest English witnesses postdate that tradition by more than a century. I find the first premise valid, with the caveat that centonization and oral tradition could result in deliberate or accidental changes to the psalmic text. The second premise, however, must be approached with some caution. Our understanding of the PsR tradition is based on the limited sampling of sixteen manuscripts employed by Weber, and these manuscripts do not present a uniform tradition. As I have shown, the offertories include many variants that are not found in any psalter manuscript or citation, reinforcing the impression that the psalter tradition was more complex and varied than surviving witnesses suggest. The PsR itself, moreover, descends from the same tradition as the other Old Latin psalters and is viewed by scholars as being closely related to them.[33] We should not be surprised, then, to find certain concordances with other Old Latin branches in a tradition that primarily employs the PsR. Although the PsR was well established in Italy in the fourth century, biblical scholars have hypothesized that variety rather than uniformity prevailed in the Italian tradition of the psalter before the eighth century, even in Rome.[34] Jean Gribomont, for example, demonstrates the textual variety of citations in the Rule of the Master and the Rule of Benedict. Despite a strong preference for the PsR in the Rule of Benedict, his study yields variants whose meaning is difficult to ascertain because of the frequency of paraphrase and the lack of contemporaneous psalters.[35] Arnobius the Younger, a Roman monk writing in the later fifth century, cites many passages from memory in his commentary on the psalms, sometimes paraphrasing. His citations correspond at times to the PsR, at times to the PsG, and at times to no known tradition.[36] The verbal tradition of the offertories in the Roman manuscripts also shows an occasional lack of uniformity, suggesting an inconsistency in the PsR tradition as it was practiced at Rome.

The paucity of surviving sources and the common origin of the traditions allow the evidence to be read in a number of ways. Pfisterer's example of the Easter Week offertory *Portas caeli* (51) is a case in point. On the basis of its correspondence to γ, he argues that the origin of this chant is to be sought in Gaul. As shown in table 2.2,

33. For a penetrating illustration of the common origin, see Jean Gribomont's work on the citations of Rufinus. He divides the very early sources into two groups, one close to α and the other closer to the PsR, the parent of γ, δ, moz, and med. See Francesca Merlo and Jean Gribomont, *Il Salterio di Rufino* (Rome: Abbey of St. Girolamo, 1972); and the summary in Bogaert, "Le Psautier latin," 67.
34. See especially Jean Gribomont, "La règle et la Bible," in *Atti de 7 congresso internazionale di studi sull'alto Medioevo* (Spoleto: Presso la sede del Centro studi, 1982), 380.
35. Ibid., 379–81.
36. Klaus Daur, "Einleiting," in *Arnobii Iunoris Commentarii in Psalmos* (Turnholt: Brepols, 1990), xxxiii–xxxv. For the significance of Arnobius's exegesis for Roman chant, see Peter Jeffery, "Monastic Reading and the Emerging Roman Chant Repertory," in Gallagher et al., *Western Plainchant*, 63–69.

TABLE 2.2 Textual Variants in *Portas caeli*

Gregorian Lyrics	*γ*	*PsR*
Portas caeli aperuit dominus Et pluit illis **manna ut ederent panem** caeli dedit **illis** panem angelorum manducavit homo alleluia.	**Portas** caeli aperuit et pluit illis **mannam ad manducandum et panem** caeli dedit **illis** panem angelorum manducavit homo.	**Ianuas** caeli aperuit Et pluit illis **manna manducare panem** caeli dedit **eis** panem angelorum manducavit homo
v. 1 **Adtendite popule** meus **in legem meam** inclinate **aurem vestram** in verba oris mei	v. 1 **Intendite popule** meus **in legem meam** inclinate **aures vestras** in verba oris mei	v. 1 **Adtendite populus** meus **legem meam** inclinate **aurem vestram** in verba oris mei
v. 2 Aperiam in parabolis os meum **loquar propositiones** ab initio seculi	v. 2 Aperiam in parabolis os meum **eloquar propositionem** meam ab initio seculi	v. 2 Aperiam in parabolis os meum **loquar propositiones** ab initio seculi

the text corresponds partially to γ and partially to the PsR. "Ut ederent," a departure from the more common readings "manducare" and "ad manducandum," is not found in the psalter manuscripts, but does occur in a citation from a collection of fifth- and sixth-century sermons known as the "Eusebius Gallicanus" collection.[37] This work of numerous authors, intended for the use of Gallican clergy, was widely circulated and extensively plagiarized in late antiquity and the Middle Ages.[38] Another aurally significant variant is "portas/ianuas," two different translations of the Greek "thyras." "Ianuas" is the reading of all known PsR witnesses, whereas "portas" is found in γ, α, and the Mozarabic psalter (moz). The chant text has one other variant that uniquely corresponds to γ, "illis" instead of "eis." "Popule" is found in γ, moz, the Milanese psalter, and in several PsR witnesses. Pfisterer gives priority to "portas/ianuas" and the other variants shared with γ. Because the lyric does not completely correspond to γ, however, he concludes that it is based on a version no longer extant that was close to γ and that the origin of the chant text is to be sought in Gaul.[39]

Although I find this argument plausible, it is not a foregone conclusion. In the eleven places where the γ text and the PsR differ, the Gregorian text corresponds to the PsR in six cases: "manna/mannam," "et panem/panem," "attendite/ intendite," "aurem vestram/aures vestras," "loquar/eloquar," and "propositiones/ propositionem meam"; and to γ in four cases, "portas/ianuas," "popule/populus,"

37. *Vetus latina Database.*
38. See the recent study of the collection by Lisa Bailey, "Preaching and Pastoral Care in Late Antique Gaul: The Eusebius Gallicanus Sermon Collection" (Ph.D diss., Princeton University, 2004).
39. Pfisterer, "Remarks," 180–81.

"illis/eis," and "in legem/legem." The Roman lyric is identical to the Gregorian except for "legem," possibly an assimilation to the PsR. Pfisterer's methodology would view all PsR correspondences as assimilations that took place when the chant was adopted into the Roman repertory. In some respects, the nature of the variants supports Pfisterer's conclusion: several of the correspondences to the PsR in this text are aurally insignificant, whereas one correspondence to γ, "ianuas/portas" is an aurally significant variant that is not found in any PsR witness. The unique citation of "ut ederent" in the Eusebius Gallicanus collection further bolsters the argument. On the whole, this chant is among the more compelling cases for non-Roman origin that can be made on the basis of the psalter evidence. Yet some doubt remains. Given the paucity of surviving sources, can we assume that "portas" and "ut ederent" were limited to Gaul? Some alternative explanations, though perhaps less plausible, are that the PsR is the dominant influence on this text and that differences from known PsR witnesses are to be expected, given the lack of uniformity within the PsR tradition and the common origin of the PsR and other Old Latin psalters; or that the variants in common with γ and Eusebius Gallicanus emerged through the influence of memory and oral tradition, and that the correspondence of the chant lyric to these texts is fortuitous.

More problematic than *Portas caeli* are those cases listed as questionable in table 2.1. *Confitebor tibi* (39), for example, has one significant variant from the PsR, "vultum" instead of "faciem," which matches α and γ. Because α has many aurally conspicuous variants that are not found in the offertory, it can be eliminated as the source. The text corresponds to γ except for one aurally significant variant: γ has "ad utilitatem" instead of "in avaritia." The chant, then, shows an equal degree of correspondence to γ and to the PsR. Is one variant, "faciem/vultum" sufficient evidence for a non-Roman argument? The structure of the lyric further complicates the matter: it is highly centonized, raising the possibility that a lyricist paraphrasing the psalm and recalling it from memory simply replaced "faciem" with "vultum."

Perhaps the most compelling instances of non-PsR influence are those few offertories that are fully concordant with a specific manuscript. *Improperium* (44), for example, corresponds to ϵ, the Psalter of Coislin. For most of its departures from the PsR, concordances are found only in Spain and Narbonnaise Gaul.[40] *Iustus ut palma* (71) corresponds fully to δ. These most plausible cases, however, are rare. One alternative reading of the evidence I have presented in the case of *Portas caeli*, on the basis of a possible reading in a lost source, is an *ex silentio* argument, and certainly cannot be proved or disproved. It is also pernicious, however, to assume that the surviving sources of the PsR and gaulois traditions give us a picture of the early medieval texts that is sufficiently complete to serve as the foundation for a theory of origin.

---

40. Its reading "esca mea," for example, is cited in the *Liber comicus* and by Isidore, but not found elsewhere. See *Vetus latina Database*.

In summary, attempting to localize the origin of a chant on the basis of its textual tradition can be a tenuous proposition, particularly when the lyric in question also has many readings in common with the PsR. Too little is known about the textual state of the psalter in sixth- and seventh-century Rome and elsewhere. In some cases, moreover, a literal reading of the lyrics as derivations from specific psalter translations gives too little consideration to the role of memory and paraphrase. While word-for-word, *ad verba* memorization was certainly valued, especially as it pertained to the psalter, memorization *ad res*, of concepts, also plays an important role in Medieval treatises on memory.[41]

Despite the problems inherent in pinpointing non-Roman influences in specific offertories, however, the total number of departures from the PsR renders plausible an influence of other psalter traditions. The hypothesis seems feasible particularly when the psalter evidence is considered in conjunction with the nonpsalmic offertories, to be considered next. The variety of textual readings, moreover, has some implications for questions of chronology. It appears to pose a challenge to McKinnon's theory that the repertory was all created by the Roman *schola cantorum* in the same time and place. If so, we might expect the chants to exhibit a more unified psalter tradition. The variety of the textual tradition is more consistent with a scenario of gradual compilation, with the probable incorporation of some non-Roman repertory.

The tantalizing possibility that traces of lost Gallican or North African repertories survive under a Roman guise raises the question of whether the offertories with "non-Roman" verbal characteristics exhibit any distinctive musical features. As I will show, many of the more plausible cases of non-PsR influence share stylistic traits and even melodic substance with offertories that correspond solely to the PsR, a pattern demonstrable in both the Gregorian and Roman melodic dialects. If these items were imported into the Roman repertory from Gaul or northern Italy, I see several possible explanations: that their melodies underwent a process of assimilation to native Roman style; that the question of non-Roman origin concerns only the words and not the melodies; that their style did not differ significantly from that of Roman chant to begin with; or that the style of the genre as a whole is "non-Roman." I explore each possibility in chapter 5.

FRANKISH ADDITIONS TO THE PSALMIC REPERTORY

This overview of psalter traditions provides a context for ascertaining the extent to which new offertories and verses were added by the Franks. The early Gregorian

---

41. See Mary Carruthers, *The Book of Memory: A Study of Memory in Medieval Culture* (Cambridge: Cambridge University Press, 1990), 160–61; and Anna Maria Busse Berger, *Medieval Music and the Art of Memory* (Berkeley: University of California Press, 2005), 53.

sources indexed by Hesbert in *Antiphonale Missarum Sextuplex* transmit twelve
offertories that are lacking in the Roman manuscripts, four psalmic and eight
nonpsalmic. Three of the psalmic offertories, *Posuisti, In omnem terram,* and
Exsultabunt, are contrafacts of others from the core repertory, and have long
been viewed as Frankish additions.[42] *In omnem terram, Exsultabunt,* and the fourth
psalmic offertory, *Domine ad adiuvandum,* show a palpable PsG influence, consistent with a Frankish origin.

Several Gregorian psalmic offertories have more verses than their Roman
counterparts do. Most of these verses match the PsR against the PsG, suggesting
that they were once part of the Roman repertory but fell out of use before the
Roman manuscripts were copied.[43] In three cases, the situation is more complex.
The Roman versions of *Offerentur, Diffusa est,* and *Filiae regum* have the same
verses, in text and melody: *Eructavit* and *Specie tua.* In most Gregorian manuscripts,
these offertories have different sets of verses: *Offerentur* (minor) has *Eructavit* and
Adducentur; Filiae regum has *Eructavit* (with a different melody) and *Virga recta;*
and *Diffusa* has only *Specie.* One of these Gregorian verses, *Virga recta,* is lacking in
Roman manuscripts. A few early Gregorian sources, however, present these
offertories with the same set of verses we find in Rome. In the Mont-Blandin
Gradual, for example, *Filiae regum* and *Offerentur* (minor) have incipits for the
verses *Eructavit* and *Specie.* In Compiègne and Corbie, *Diffusa* also has *Eructavit* as
a verse, as in Rome. These examples suggest that the verse tradition of these
offertories was subject to some revision in Francia.

Finally, the multiplicity of verse traditions found among a small handful
of offertories suggests an independent circulation of responds and verses. *Eripe
me...domine* (Ps. 142:9–10) for Monday of Holy Week has only one verse,
Exaudi me, in the earliest Gregorian sources and in many later manuscripts. The
Roman and Beneventan manuscripts have a second verse, *In factis* (Ps. 142:1–2),
which may be related to a Milanese offerenda; some Aquitanian manuscripts have
Expandi manus (Ps. 142:6–7) as a second verse, and Montpellier 159 has yet a
different second verse. For Tuesday of Holy Week's *Custodi me* (Ps. 139:5) the
Roman manuscripts lack the verse *Eripe me* (Ps. 139:2), which circulates in most
Gregorian sources, but have another verse, *Domine virtus* (Ps. 139:8, 13), that is not
found in the Gregorian tradition.[44] The Post-Pentecost offertory *De profundis* also

42. *Exsultabunt* is a contrafact of *Offerentur* maior, *Posuisti* of *Angelus domini,* and *In omnem terram* of
Dextera domini. See Peter Wagner, *Einführung in die gregorianischen Melodien: Ein Handbuch der
Choralwissenschaft,* 3:419–21; Ruth Steiner, "Some Questions about the Gregorian Offertories and
Their Verses," *Journal of the American Musicological Society* 19 (1966): 173–76. Nonpsalmic
contrafacts are discussed below.
43. This is the case, for example, with *In virtute, Desiderium,* and *Expectans.*
44. The textual variants in these verses are described in more depth in the notes in appendix 3. The
Gregorian version of *Tu exurgens,* a verse of *Domine exaudi,* matches the PsG and is probably a
Frankish addition, with a separately added Roman version. The verses *Quia oblitus* and *Eripe me,*
however, match the PsR against the PsG.

lacks verses in the Roman manuscripts. The Gregorian verses match the PsR against the PsG, suggesting that the verses once existed in Rome. The Mont-Blandin Gradual, however, has a unique incipit for the second verse, one I have not found in any other source.[45] These examples suggest that in rare cases, verses were transmitted and added independently of their responds, a situation more common among nonpsalmic offertories.

STRUCTURE OF THE PSALMIC TEXTS

The structural traits of the psalmic offertories also have potential to shed light on their origins. In their analyses of the offertory's verbal traits, Helmut Hucke and James McKinnon have shown that the offertories and their verses demonstrate little connection to antiphonal and responsorial psalmody. Thus it is unlikely that the repertory grew out of traditional psalmodic practices. Hucke examined the offertories' verbal texts for structural formats reminiscent of antiphonal and direct psalmody. In the antiphonal format, the choral part of the chant is excerpted from the internal part of a psalm, whereas the solo verses begin with the first verse of the psalm and proceed through the verses in numerical order. In direct psalmody, the respond begins with the first verse of the psalm, and the chant progresses through the psalm verses with no alterations or omission. Most offertories are of the type Hucke termed "responsorial," freely chosen from various parts of the psalm.[46] Hucke's work thus supports Dyer's thesis that the offertory did not originate as an antiphonal chant.[47]

Although Hucke demonstrated that the offertory lyrics are not compatible with an antiphonal origin, McKinnon argued that they have little in common with traditional responsorial psalmody. Gradual responds typically consist of a single psalm verse or portion of a verse that would be suitable as a congregational refrain. To McKinnon, this structure suggests continuity, at least in character, with ancient responsorial psalmody. In comparison to the gradual and alleluia, he notes, the offertory texts exhibit a "formal contrivance": the responds are longer than those of the gradual and often employ text adjustment; only the repetendum functions as a refrain. Although the musical structure of the offertory is clearly associated with that of responsorial psalmody, its verses are rarely the integral psalm verses one would expect in responsorial psalmody.[48]

---

45. The verse incipit reads "Quia apud te qui propiciato est"; Ps. 129:4.
46. Helmut Hucke, "Die Texte der Offertorien," in *Speculum Musicae Artis: Festgabe für Heinrich Husmann zum 60 Geburtstag,* ed. Heinz Becker and Reinhard Gerlach (Munich: W. Fink, 1970), 193–207.
47. Dyer, "Offertories of Old-Roman Chant," and "Offertory Chant of the Roman Liturgy."
48. McKinnon, *Advent Project,* 303–5. It is worth noting, however, that similar textual arrangements are also found in some office responsories. See James Grier, "The Divine Office of St. Martial in

The work of Hucke and McKinnon clearly demonstrates the offertory's lack of foundation in traditional psalmody. The structural characteristics of the texts, however, have further implications for the origin of the genre. In many cases, the psalmic excerpts seem to have been chosen and arranged to fit the musical form of the offertory with verses and repetenda. Although verses could occasionally circulate independently of their responds, the parallels between the verbal structure and the musical form suggest that many responds were created to be sung with verses.

McKinnon's examination of the words focused on their lack of what he termed "plausible verses," musical verses that are formed from discrete and complete psalm verses. Only twelve offertories have musical verses that consist entirely of discrete psalm verses. Eight of these are of Hucke's "antiphonal" text type: *Tollite portas* (6) and *Laetentur caeli* (7) for Christmas; the Lenten offertories *Domine fac mecum* (31) and *Domine convertere* (40); the Easter and Pentecost offertories *Portas caeli* (51), *Ascendit deus* (58), and *Emitte spiritum* (59); and the Post-Pentecost offertory *Immittet Angelus* (62). In *Tollite portas*, for example, the respond is formed from Psalm 23:7; the verses are discrete psalm verses consisting of 23:1 and 23:2.

This straightforward verbal structure is exceptional among the offertories. In most cases, the offertory texts are lyrics, carefully crafted verbal compositions characterized by thematic and structural coherence. The responds often close with a small passage of text that would serve as an appropriate repetendum, to be sung as a refrain after each verse. An example is *Intende voci*, presented in table 2.3. In the left-hand column the parts of the psalm chosen for the offertory text are highlighted in boldface. The right-hand column provides the offertory text, with the single added word in italics. Of central interest here is the respond text, which reveals the lyricist's concern for choosing an appropriate repetendum. The respond is formed from Psalm 5:3 and the first half of Psalm 5:4. The repetendum, beginning at "rex meus," draws from both psalm verses. The significance of this repetendum is reflected in the choice of text for the verses. Verse 1, a centonized lyric, consists of the complete verse 5:2, followed by a paraphrased excerpt from 5:4. The second person "et exaudies vocem meam," the end of 5:4, is abbreviated and changed to the imperative "et exaudi me," presumably to match the two imperatives already in the verse and adapt to the repetendum that follows, "rex meus et deus meus quoniam ad te orabo domine." The concern for the cogency of the lyric is reflected in the passage selected for the repetendum and the ways verses are crafted to correspond to it. Portions of the psalm were chosen, rearranged, and altered to suit the musical form of an offertory with verses and repetenda.

The concern for thematic coherence and structural unity is especially evident in centonized lyrics. Minor changes to the psalm include the addition of the vocative "domine"; in rare cases, additional phrases such as "miserere mihi"; and changes

---

the Early Eleventh Century," in *The Divine Office in the Latin Middle Ages*, ed. Margot Fassler and Rebecca Baltzer (New York: Oxford University Press, 2000), 186–89.

TABLE 2.3 *Intende voci*

Psalm 5 Excerpts (PsR)	Gregorian Offertory
5:3	Respond
Intende voci orationis meae	Intende voci orationis meae (repetendum)
rex meus et deus meus	rex meus et deus meus
5:4	
Quoniam ad te orabo domine mane et exaudies vocem meam	quoniam ad te orabo domine
5:2	Verse 1
Verba mea auribus percipe domine intellege clamorem meum	Verba mea auribus percipe domine intellege clamorem meum
5:4	
Quoniam ad te orabo domine mane et **exaudies vocem meam**	et exaudi me
5:9	Verse 2
Deduc me domine in tua iustitia propter inimicos meos **dirige in conspectu tuo viam meam**	Dirige in conspectu tuo viam meam
5:12	
Et laetentur omnes qui sperant in te in aeternum	et laetentur omnes qui sperant in te domine in aeternum
Exsultabunt et inhabitabis in eis et **gloriabuntur in te omnes qui diligunt nomen tuum**	gloriabuntur qui diligunt nomen tuum, *domine*

from "a me" to "a plebe tua." Text repetition, a feature seemingly unique to the offertories, is typically underscored with melodic repetition, sometimes varied, as in *Iubilate deo omnis terra, Iubilate deo universa terra, Benedictus es . . . in labiis*, and *Domine exaudi*. Many offertories are extensively centonized, stitched together from various parts of a psalm. In rare cases, moreover, the lyrics reach beyond centonization to present a paraphrase of the biblical source. A few examples will illustrate the nature of the changes and shed light on possible reasons for text adjustment.

Centonization typically serves to abbreviate a psalm excerpt, reducing it to a central theme and eliminating elaborative or descriptive material. In many cases, the psalm seems to have been modified with the verse-repetendum form of the offertory in mind. Gaps in the psalm often occur just before the repetendum, suggesting that the repetendum text was selected expressly for its role as a refrain in the musical form. In the Christmas offertory *Laetentur caeli* (6), for example, the respond begins with

TABLE 2.4 *Iustitiae*

Psalm 18 excerpts (PsR)	Gregorian offertory
18:9	Respond
Iusticiae domini rectae letificantes corda preceptum domini lucidum inluminans oculos	Iusticiae domini rectae letificantes corda
18:10	
timor domini sanctus permanet in saeculum saeculi iudicia dei vera iustificata in semetipsa	
18:11	
desiderabilia super aurum et lapidem pretiosum multum et dulciora super mel et favum	et dulciora super mel et favum
18:12	
nam et servus tuus custodiet ea in custodiendo illa retributio multa	nam et servus tuus custodiet ea
18:9	Verse 1
Iusticie domini rectae letificantes corda preceptum domini lucidum inluminans oculos	Preceptum domini lucidum illuminans oculos
18:10	
Timor domini sanctus permanet in saeculum saeculi iudicia dei vera iustificata in semetipsa	timor dei sanctus permanens in saeculum saeculi iudicia domini vera
18:15	Verse 2
Et erunt ut conplaceant eloquia oris mei et meditatio cordis mei in conspectu tuo semper domine adivtor meus et redemptor meus	Et erunt ut complaceant eloquia oris mei et meditatio cordis mei in conspectu tuo semper

the first half of Psalm 95:11. For the repetendum, the lyricist skips to the beginning of 95:13, "ante faciem domini quoniam venit." This repetendum, which is sung three times, emphasizes Christ's arrival, the central theme of the season, and forms an appropriate conclusion to the verses "cantate domino canticum novum, cantate domino omnis terra." In adapting the psalm for the musical setting, the compilers seem to have had in mind the specific form of the offertory with verses.

The Lenten offertory *Iustitiae* (29) reveals similar formal characteristics, as shown in table 2.4. The respond combines two brief excerpts from a longer descriptive passage extolling the precepts and commandments of the Lord (Psalm 18:9–12). In the psalm, the passage closes with the summary "nam et servus tuus custodiet ea" (verse 12). The entire passage of the psalm is given in the left-hand column of table 2.4, the offertory text in the right-hand column. The respond begins with the first half of verse 9 and proceeds directly to the end of verse 11, incorporating only a brief passage of description ("dulciora super mel et favum") before the concluding statement of verse 12.

The first verse musical verse of the offertory, however, is based on the same psalm verse as the respond. Drawing from verses 9 and 10, it incorporates much of the descriptive material that was omitted in the respond. The repetendum may begin at either "et dulciora" or "nam et." In either case, it is an appropriate refrain, functioning as a summarizing thought and conclusion to the descriptive passages in the respond and first verse. In the first verse and repetendum, moreover, the material is presented in an order that approximates that of the psalm. Taken together, the respond, verses, and repetenda form a unified whole.

Extensive centonization is perhaps most evident in a group of Lenten offertories based on Psalm 118: short excerpts from the entire psalm are chosen for their thematic emphasis and combined to create a unified lyric. Although the overriding theme of Psalm 118 is law and justice, *Benedictus es . . . et non tradas*, for Saturday of Passion Week, combines various passages of the psalm that focus on the speaker's enemies, as shown in table 2.5. In a departure from usual practice, the psalmic excerpts are presented out of order. The repetendum, for example, combines the second half of verse 121 and the first half of verse 42. The first verse of the offertory consists of excerpts from verses 158 and 84; the second verse combines excerpts from verses 150 and 78. The resulting lyric forms a unified whole focused on the speaker's enemies, a theme expressed in the repetendum: "et respondebo exprobantibus mihi verbum."

The selection and arrangement of psalmic passages often creates a structural as well as a thematic unity. The respond *Sperent in te* (table 2.6) for example, concludes with excerpts from Psalm 9:12 and 13. The repetendum, beginning either at "psallite" or "quoniam," emphasizes the Lord's concern for the poor. The closing passage of each verse articulates the same theme, producing a parallel structure among the three sections of the offertory. At the end of the second verse, the lyricist skips from verse 19 to verse 38 for "desiderium pauperum exaudivit deus." This passage rephrases the theme of the repetendum that follows, "quoniam non est oblitus orationes pauperum." The closing passage of the verse is chosen for its thematic relationship to the repetendum, betokening a concern for cogency and structural unity. Similar features are manifest in many other offertories.

My analysis of these examples yields several points about the origins of the offertory. First, to echo the conclusions of Hucke and McKinnon, the offertory texts show no resemblance to those of traditional psalmody, responsorial or

TABLE 2.5 *Benedictus es ... et non tradas*

Psalm 118 excerpts (PsR)	Gregorian offertory
118:12	Respond
Benedictus es domine doce me iustificationes tuas	Benedictus es domine doce me iustificationes tuas[1]
118:121	(repetendum)
feci iudicium et iustitiam ne tradas me persequentibus me	et non tradas calumniantibus me superbis
118:42	
et respondebo exprobantibus mihi verbum quia speravi in sermonibus tuis	et respondebo exprobantibus mihi verbum
118:158	Verse 1
Vidi non servantes pactum et tabescebam quia eloquia tua non custodierunt	Vidi non servantes pactum et tabescebam domine
118:84	
quot sunt dies servi tui?	
Quando facies de persequentibus me iudicium?	Quando facies de persequentibus me iudicium?
118:150	Verse 2
Adpropiaverunt persequentes me iniqui a lege autem tua longe facti sunt	Appropinquaverunt persequentes me iniqui
118:78	
Confundantur superbi quia iniuste iniquitatem fecerunt in me ego autem exercebor in mandatis tuis	Confundatur et revereantur quia iniuste iniquitatem fecerunt in me

1. This line is repeated in the Roman version.

antiphonal. On the contrary, they are carefully crafted verbal compositions. Furthermore, many were structured as lyrics for the specific verse-repetendum form of the offertory. In their choice of psalmic excerpt, responds often reveal a concern for the selection of an appropriate repetendum, implying that they were meant to be sung with verses. The structure of these texts suggests that verses, at least in many cases, were part of these offertories' original conception.

In view of the varied psalter tradition I have shown, the structural analysis raises the question of whether the particular psalter readings correlate with the structural features of specific offertories. I was unable to find any pattern of correlation. The eight offertories that adopt antiphonal formats, for example, show various

TABLE 2.6 *Sperent in te*

Psalm 9	Gregorian Offertory
9:11	Respond:
et sperent in te omnes qui noverunt nomen tuum quoniam non derelinques quaerentes te domine	Sperent in te omnes qui noverunt nomen tuum domine quoniam non derelinquis quaerentes te.
9:12	
psallite domino qui habitat in Sion adnuntiate inter gentes mirabilia eius	psallite domino qui habitat in Sion
9:13	(repetendum)
quoniam requirens sanguinem eorum memoratus est et	Quoniam
non est oblitus orationem pauperum	non est oblitus orationem pauperum
9:5	Verse 1
Quoniam fecisti iudicium meum et causam meam	
sedes super thronum qui iudicas aequitatem	Sedes super thronum qui iudicas aequitatem.
9:6	
Increpasti gentes et periit impius nomen eorum delisti in aeternum et in saeculum saeculi	increpasti gentes et periit impius.
9:9	
et ipse iudicabit orbem terrae in aequitate	
iudicabit populos cum iustitia	iudicare populum cum iustitia.
9:10	
et factus est dominus refugium pauperum adiutor in oportunitatibus in tribulatione	et factus est refugium pauperum
9:17	Verse 2
Cognoscitur Dominus iudicia faciens in operibus manuum suarum conprehensus est peccator.	Cognoscetur dominus iudicia faciens
9:19	
Quoniam non in finem oblivio erit pauperum patientia pauperum non peribit in finem	quoniam patientia pauperum non peribit in finem
9:38	
Desiderium pauperum exaudivit dominus desideria cordis eorum exaudivit auris tua	Desiderium pauperum exaudivit deus

influences on their textual tradition: *Tollite portas* (6) is among the most compelling examples of α influence; two examples, *Portas caeli* (51) and *Ascendit deus* (58),
have readings associated with psalters from pre-Carolingian Gaul, γ and η, and the
rest are PsR-based. A similar variety is evident in the centonized, highly structured
lyrics. *Sperent in te*, for example, is fully consistent with the PsR, whereas another
centonized text, *Benedicite gentes* (36), exhibits a complex mixture of other
Old Latin traditions.

A comparison of text types with the liturgical assignments of the offertories
reveals a pattern noted by McKinnon: text centonization is far more frequent
and extensive among Lenten offertories than those of any other season.[49] Five of
the seven psalmic offertories assigned to Advent and Christmas employ centonization. In four of these offertories, however, the centonization is limited to one
section of the offertory. Only one of these, *Tui sunt caeli* (9), undertakes an
extensive modification and rearrangement of the psalm in the respond and
all verses. Among Lenten offertories, text centonization is far more common and
extensive. Of the thirty offertories assigned to the period between Septuagesima
and Palm Sunday, twenty-three employ centonization. In many of these, the
omission and rearrangement of the biblical text is extensive. Beginning with
the Palm Sunday offertory *Improperium* (44), however, modification of the
biblical texts becomes far less frequent. Of the three Holy Week offertories, only
one, *Domine exaudi* (47), modifies the psalm, and only by adding a repetition of
one line of text. The Paschaltide and Post-Pentecost seasons include a total
of fourteen psalmic offertories. Of their forty-seven responds and verses, only
four alter the biblical text. Several of the offertories with an antiphonal format,
moreover, are concentrated in these later liturgical seasons.

The distribution of textual traits in particular seasons of the liturgical year
brings to mind a pattern to be demonstrated in chapter 3: melodic resemblance
between the Gregorian and Roman offertories becomes increasingly weak in the
course of the liturgical year, especially among verses. In a related trend, the Roman
offertories rely ever more on melodic formulas in the later liturgical seasons. In my
earlier thinking on the subject, these two trends seemed to bolster an aspect of
McKinnon's Advent Project theory, namely that the repertory for each season of
the year reflects a different compositional layer. McKinnon argued that the
Paschaltide and Post-Pentecost seasons are marked by a paucity of new repertory
and an increased borrowing of offertories previously assigned to other feasts,
concluding that the Romans experienced creative exhaustion and failed to complete the project of composing new offertories for each day of the year.[50]
A majority of Lenten offertories are carefully crafted verbal compositions, evidently

49. McKinnon, *Advent Project*, 303–25.
50. Ibid., 309–22.

written to suit the musical form of the offertory. Those of the later seasons, by contrast, exhibit a minimal alteration of the psalmic sources. These patterns strengthen the impression that the Lenten and Paschaltide offertories are separate layers of the repertory. Furthermore, the approach to making texts in the psalmic Paschaltide and Post-Pentecost offertories has an air of expediency that seems to reinforce the Advent Project hypothesis. As they progressed through the liturgical year, the Romans approached the composition of lyrics with increasing care and artfulness, culminating in the highly centonized Lenten ones. On reaching Palm Sunday, however, they reverted to taking psalmic texts directly from the source, with minimal modification. With this view, the lack of centonization and presence of the antiphonal format in the later liturgical seasons can be seen as a symptom of McKinnon's "creative exhaustion," with the nonpsalmic Post-Pentecost offertories as a final burst of creative activity.

Despite the undeniable attractions of this narrative, several problems emerge on closer reflection. Pfisterer has proposed equally plausible ways of reading the liturgical sources, resulting in very different conclusions about the formation of the liturgical year and the creation of the chant repertory. His chronology, which roughly matches the addition of feasts and liturgical seasons, places the Sundays of Advent, the ferias of Easter Week, and the common Sundays as the latest strata of the repertory.[51] As noted, much of McKinnon's hypothesis rests on the premise that traditional psalmodic formats imply continuity with the antiphonal and responsorial practices of the early church, and that centonized pieces arose later. But antiphonal text types in the offertory are a rarity. Whether or not McKinnon's premise is valid more generally, it is unlikely that these exceptional cases have great chronological import for the offertory, which seems to have been a highly formalized genre from its inception. My own examination of the Old Hispanic sacrificia, moreover, has raised reservations about some of the assumptions that underlie McKinnon's theory, such as the use of thematic evidence to posit discrete layers of the repertory and the relevance of centonization and nonpsalmic texts as chronological markers. I shall consider both issues in the examination of nonpsalmic texts that follows.

NONPSALMIC OFFERTORIES

The nonpsalmic Gregorian offertories are listed in table 2.7, along with their text sources and primary liturgical assignments. The offertories are divided into three categories according to their repertorial status. Listed first are the core

---

51. See especially Pfisterer, "James McKinnon und die Datierung."

TABLE 2.7 *Nonpsalmic Gregorian Offertories*

1. Core Roman/Gregorian Offertories	Liturgical Assignments
Confortamini M, OH	Ember Wed. Advent
Exsulta satis	Ember Sat. Advent
Ave Maria	Ember Wed./Annunciation
Angelus domini (Matt. 28: 2, 5–6) M, Old Beneventan	Easter Monday
In die sollemnitatis (Exod. 13) M	Easter Thursday
Erit vobis (Exod. 12.24) M, OH	Easter Friday
Precatus est Moyses (Exod. 32:11–15) M	Pent XII
Oravi deum (Dan. 8:4–19) OH	Pent. XVII
Sanctificavit Moyses (Exod. 24:4–5) OH, M	Pent. XVIII
Vir erat (Job 1:2, 7)	Pent. XXI
Recordare mei (Esther 14:12–13)	Pent. XXII
Domine deus in simp. (1 Chron. 29:17–18) [OH]	Dedication
Oratio mea (Job 16:18–21) M	Vigil of St. Lawrence
2. Common Gregorian offertories in early sources	
Stetit Angelus [OH, M]	Michael
Sicut in holocausto (Daniel 3)	Dom. VII p. Pent.
Viri Galilei (Acts 1:11)	Ascension (vigil, octave)
Elegerunt (Acts 6) OH	Stephen
Benedictus sit (Tob. 12)	Trinity
3. Rare Gregorian offertories in early sources:	
Factus est repente (Acts 2) [OH]	Pentecost
Audi Israhel M responsory	Fifth Sunday before Christmas, Ember Friday
Ingressus est Zacharias (Luke)	St. John the Baptist

Roman-Gregorian offertories. Those in the second group are absent in the Roman tradition but appear in the early Gregorian sources (*Antiphonale Missarum Sextuplex*) and remain part of the standard Gregorian repertory. Listed in the third row are items that are not part of the standard Gregorian repertory; they appear only in isolated early sources and later manuscripts.

Many of the core Roman-Gregorian offertories with nonpsalmic texts are assigned to festivals of later institution, such as the Dedication, the ferias of Easter

Week, and the Post-Pentecost Sundays.[52] Exceptions to this trend, however, include *Oratio mea*, for the Vigil of Lawrence, and possibly *Ave Maria*, which has a dual assignment to the Annunciation and Ember Wednesday of Advent. While most scholars have assumed that *Ave Maria* was newly composed for the late seventh-century Annunciation festival, placing it among the latest additions to the repertory, Pfisterer gives priority to the Ember Week assignment, suggesting an earlier origin.[53]

The Gregorian nonpsalmic offertories outside of the core repertory are assigned to a mixture of later and earlier festivals. Probable Frankish assignments include *Sicut in holocausto* for the seventh Sunday after Pentecost, *vacat* in the Roman calendar, and *Benedictus sit* for Trinity, a Frankish instituted feast. Other offertories in this group are assigned to important festivals in earlier manuscripts and later displaced to lesser occasions. *Viri Galilei*, for example, is assigned to the Ascension in Mont-Blandin and Rheinau, but to the vigil or octave in later manuscripts. Two of these offertories, *Elegerunt* and *Benedictus sit*, make a somewhat later appearance than the others, occurring for the first time in the ninth-century Senlis gradual. All of these offertories have been viewed as probable Gallican survivals, an issue I shall consider presently.

The presence of some nonpsalmic offertories in the Old Hispanic and Milanese repertories has played an important role in the argument for Gallican origin. Table 2.7 shows the offertories with Old Hispanic and Milanese cognates (indicated by the abbreviations OH and M). As Levy, Giacomo Baroffio, and Jordi Pinell have demonstrated, these offertories exhibit different degrees of verbal and musical similarity between the Gregorian, Roman, Old Hispanic, and Milanese traditions.[54] *Oravi deum*, for example, has different second verses in the Gregorian and Old Hispanic traditions. Despite these differences, the verbal and musical similarities to the Gregorian versions suggest that most of the

---

52. Some indices of late "properization" of the Post Pentecost Sundays include their absence in the Old Gelasian sacramentary and the Hadrianum, as well as the borrowing of chants for many Sundays from earlier festivals. For summaries see McKinnon, *Advent Project*, 104–7; and Pfisterer, "Remarks," 175–77. The Dedication is widely viewed as the last feast with proper chants added to the calendar. See Peter Jeffery, "Rome and Jerusalem: From Oral Tradition to Written Repertory in Two Ancient Liturgical Centers," in *Essays on Medieval Music in Honor of David G. Hughes*, ed. Graeme M. Boone (Cambridge, Mass.: Harvard University Press, 1995), 214–19. A date of 609 may be established on the basis of a *Liber Pontificalis* report on Boniface IV's rededication of the Pantheon to Mary and the martyrs. McKinnon argues for a later date for the festival's institution and proper chants. *Advent Project*, 155–56, 187–90.

53. See Hesbert, *Antiphonale Missarum Sextuplex*, xxxviii–xxxix; McKinnon, *Advent Project*, 182–84; Pfisterer, *Cantilena*, 121–22.

54. Levy, "Toledo, Rome"; Jordi Pinell, "Repertorio del 'sacrificium' (canto ofertorial del rito hispánico) para el ciclo dominical 'de quotidiano,'" *Ecclesia orans* 1 (1984): 57–111; Giacomo Baroffio, "Die Offertorien der ambrosianischen Kirche: Vorstudie zur kritischen Aufgabe der mailändischen Gesänge" (Ph.D. diss., University of Cologne, 1964), 31, and "Die mailändische Überlieferung des Offertoriums Sanctificavit," in *Festschrift Bruno Stäblein zum 70. Geburtstag*, ed. Martin Ruhnke (Kassel: Bärenreiter, 1967), 1–8.

shared offertories are cognates. For *Stetit angelus, Factus est repente*, and *Domine deus in simplicitate*, however, a cognate relationship between the Old Hispanic and Gregorian versions is tenuous. These doubtful cases are indicated with brackets enclosing the abbreviations.

In his study of nonpsalmic Mass Proper chants, Petrus Pietschmann demonstrated the use of centonization in the nonpsalmic offertories and showed that the majority stem from VL translations rather than the Vulgate.[55] Subsequent scholarship has focused on their probable Gallican origin. As discussed in chapter 1, little is known about the Gallican offertory chant called a sonus, except that it ended with a threefold alleluia. Huglo and Gastoué proposed a Gallican origin for several of the nonpsalmic offertories outside of the core repertory, including *Factus est repente, Elegerunt*, and *Benedictus sit deus*.[56] Levy has expanded the sphere of Gallican influence to include all nonpsalmic offertories except the two for Ember days of Advent, and Pfisterer has raised the possibility of a non-Roman origin for these as well.[57] McKinnon, by contrast, has placed the core nonpsalmic offertories among the later layers of the Roman Mass Proper repertory.[58]

In the following pages I will explore various aspects of these offertories, beginning with a critique of Levy's argument, proceeding to a consideration of some Gregorian and Roman nonpsalmic offertories in their Old Hispanic and Milanese contexts, and finally examining the chronological implications of their use of VL translations. Although it is difficult to prove a Gallican origin for these offertories, I do see it as plausible in many cases. While I do not find Levy's argument from textual evidence fully convincing, a look at these items in their international context strengthens the impression of a non-Roman origin. The employment of the VL in the majority of nonpsalmic offertories, moreover, renders unlikely both a late seventh-century Roman origin and an eighth-century Frankish origin.

Levy's argument forms a sensible point of departure for exploring the question of non-Roman origin. He points to two traits of the nonpsalmic offertories that seem to distinguish them from the rest of the repertory: their nonpsalmic texts and the presence of text centonization. The texts are not taken directly from the Bible but are modified in some way to form a "libretto." In his exhaustive examination of the Mass Proper, however, McKinnon determined that nonpsalmic texts and centonization are widespread. Nearly half of the chants of the Mass Proper modify the biblical source in some way, often extensively.[59] As I have shown, centonization

---

55. Petrus Pietschmann, "Die nicht aus dem Psalter entnommenen Meßgesangstücke auf ihre Textgestalt untersucht," *Jahrbuch für Liturgiewissenschaft* 12 (1932): 114–30.
56. Michel Huglo, "Altgallikanische Liturgie," in *Geschichte der katholischen Kirchenmusik, Von den Anfängen bis zum Tridentinum*, ed. Karl Gustav Fellerer (Kassel: Bärenreiter, 1972), 219–33, reprinted as chapter 8 in *Les anciens répertories de plain-chant* (Aldershot, England: Ashgate, 2005).
57. Levy, "Toledo, Rome"; Pfisterer, *Cantilena*, 226–27, 231–32.
58. McKinnon, *Advent Project*, 316–25.
59. Ibid., 14–15.

is quite prominent among the Roman psalmic offertories, so it is not a distinguishing feature of the nonpsalmic offertories. The Romans, moreover, did evidently turn to nonpsalmic sources in creating chants for other genres, especially communions and responsories.

Levy's case for Gallican origin begins with a group of eighteen nonpsalmic offertories transmitted in early Gregorian sources. Most of these circulate in at least one other chant tradition, be it Roman, Old Hispanic, or Milanese. The crux of the argument that they originated in pre-Carolingian Gaul resides in a complex network of verbal variants and similarities between the Gregorian, Roman, Old Hispanic, and Milanese traditions. The relationships between these verbal texts are diverse and complex. Some offertories, for example, have an Old Hispanic or Milanese version whose lyrics are closely related to the Gregorian. In other cases, the cognate relationship between these traditions is questionable. Despite this variegated picture, Levy bases his analyses on the premise that all nonpsalmic offertories have a common origin. Presupposing that a "lost" tradition underlies all of the offertories under consideration, he rejects any hypothesis that does not account for every example.[60]

Some of these conclusions rest on assumptions that are not easily substantiated. In the case of *Erit vobis*, for example, the Gregorian, Old Hispanic, and Milanese readings show only minor verbal variants in the passages they share. Because the Milanese tradition lacks the second verse, however, Levy concludes that it cannot be the source for the other two versions. This conclusion is based on a premise that underlies much of his textual analysis: that the shorter version of an offertory must derive from the longer one.[61]

The circulation of two related texts of differing lengths can have several plausible explanations, depending on one's starting assumptions about the origins of the chants in question. By way of illustration, consider some other examples from the offertory repertory. In many of the nonpsalmic offertories Levy cites, the missing section of the offertory forms a discrete verse. As I have shown, a similar phenomenon is evident in a few psalmic offertories common to the Gregorian and Roman traditions: the Roman version of an offertory lacks one or more of the verses that circulate with it in the Gregorian tradition. How one interprets this evidence depends on where one places the origins of these offertories. If we accept the traditional model of Roman-to-Frankish transmission, we may draw one of two conclusions: either these offertories originally circulated with fewer verses in

60. For example, "And though the close relationship between MOZ and MED for *Stetit angelus* suggests a direct dependency, that is poorly supported by our other examples, where MOZ and GREG are 'musically' related while MED is a corner. In short, there is every reason to continue looking beyond MOZ, MED, and GREG." Levy, "Toledo, Rome," 77.

61. "Still, the MED *Erit* is not likely to be the source for the MOZ-GREG *Erit*, since it lacks their second verse. Thus MED may turn out to be a textual-musical derivative of MOZ or GREG, yet it is not likely to be the lost branch we spoke of earlier." Ibid., 67.

the Roman tradition and the verses were later added by the Franks, or the verses once existed in Rome but fell out of use there before the Old Roman sources were copied in the late eleventh and twelfth centuries. In many cases, the missing verse is based on the PsR, suggesting that it once existed in the Roman tradition. The absence of a full array of verses in some Roman offertories may be rooted simply in a desire to shorten them. By the late eleventh century, when the Roman sources were copied, offertory verses were beginning to fall out of use in some locations. In rare cases, however, the Franks to seem to have added verses to existing offertories. These examples suggest that responds were occasionally transmitted without a full set of verses and that verses were subsequently added. Levy's preferred explanation, that the shorter Roman form of the text must derive from a longer Gregorian/ Gallican one, would be valid only with the premise that a piece can be shortened but never lengthened.

Returning now to Levy's example of *Erit vobis*, its lack of a second verse in the Milanese tradition is by no means unique. The Milanese offerendae exhibit a tendency toward reduced length, often lacking the verses that appear in the corresponding Roman-Gregorian or Old Hispanic versions. In some cases, Roman-Gregorian verses are transmitted as offerendae in Milan, independently of their responds. A division of verses and responds into separate pieces is evident in the earliest complete unnotated Milanese sources, dating from the eleventh century.[62] While it is probable that the Milanese offerendae shared with the Gregorian, Roman, and Old Hispanic traditions are imports, the lack of a second verse in the Milanese *Erit vobis* cannot in itself prove that it derives from another tradition. In this respect, Levy's reasoning is circular: he bases his text analyses on the premise that a lost tradition underlies the various readings, yet the existence of this lost tradition is precisely what he intends to prove.

Similar problems arise with another premise that underlies Levy's argument. He examines the verbal texts with the premise that two variant versions must be the offspring of a common source that lies behind both. The evidence of textual variants can be of great assistance in tracing transmission patterns of specific chants and determining the relationship between manuscripts, as it often has in the case of tropes and sequences. When used to determine the origin of a chant, however, the assumptions inherent in such arguments can become problematic. With the nonpsalmic offertories, the argumentative strategy is cogent in some cases but less so in others. Levy shows that the Old Hispanic *Isti sunt* and the Milanese *Haec dicit*, for example, are undeniably related verbally in ways that suggest a direct dependency, and he reasonably argues that a third tradition must underlie the two

---

62. Marco Magistretti, ed., *Manuale Ambrosianum ex codice saec. xi olim in usum canonicae Vallis Travaliae* (Milan: U. Hoepli, 1904–5). Baroffio shows that this division seems to have occurred even among offerendae with no counterparts in other traditions. Baroffio, "Offertorien," 34–35.

versions.[63] Neither of these offertories circulates in the Old Roman tradition, and it quite conceivable that they descend from a common Gallican prototype as Levy argues. It is also possible, however, that the text originated in one of the two traditions and was subsequently modified on its adoption into the other tradition. Without knowing the origins of the chant, it is difficult to know precisely how to interpret the textual variants.

In other cases, this line of reasoning is less persuasive. Levy shows that the Gregorian and Old Hispanic versions of *Oravi deum*'s respond have nearly identical verbal texts, centonized from the Book of Daniel. Each tradition, however, has a different text for the verse. The Gregorian and Old Hispanic verses are centonizations of the same passage from Daniel, the one that immediately follows the source of the respond. Because the two texts show no direct relationship, Levy concludes that a third source must lie behind them. The two verses, however, can also be explained as separate centonizations of the same passage. The verses are lacking in the Roman manuscripts, raising the possibility that *Oravi deum* circulated without verses in some places. With this hypothesis, the Gregorian and Old Hispanic traditions independently added verses to the respond, each drawing its text from the most logical source, the next passage of Daniel. The evidence for either theory is circumstantial, and it seems the two possibilities must be weighed simply on the basis of probability. Levy would reject the second possibility, however, because it does not explain the transmission of the other nonpsalmic offertories. Levy's reading of this evidence is dependent on the aforementioned premise that nonpsalmic offertories form a discrete, unified group. If this assumption is set aside, it becomes difficult to posit convincing theories about the origin of these offertories on textual evidence alone.

The most persuasive aspect of Levy's argument is the liturgical assignments of the offertories in the various regional repertories. *Factus est repente*, for example, serves as the Pentecost offertory in some early sources, and Levy argues that it was the Gallican Pentecost offertory, later to be displaced by the Roman Pentecost offertory *Confirma hoc*. A similar argument can be made in the case of *Viri Galilei*, which serves as the Ascension offertory in some earlier manuscripts and is later assigned to the Ascension Vigil. Given the lack of these items in the Roman repertory, a Gallican origin seems likely. Levy, however, makes the same argument in the case of two offertories with Roman cognates, *Erit vobis* for Friday of Easter Week and *Angelus domini* for Monday Easter Week. In Milan, *Erit vobis* is assigned to Pentecost and *Angelus domini* to Easter Sunday. As Levy argues, it seems unlikely that the Milanese would borrow offertories for such major celebrations from dates

63. "The differences between the verses, which are to some extent mutually exclusive, suggest that the verses circulated independently of the refrains, and that the whole historical situation was more complicated. In effect, we must be dealing with at least one other branch of our textual-musical offertory tree, a lost branch that was closer than either MOZ or GREG to the trunk of that tree." Levy, "Toledo, Rome," 66.

of lesser significance. *Angelus domini* is also assigned to Easter Sunday in the Beneventan liturgy. Although the Old Beneventan version shows little melodic correspondence to the Gregorian, Roman, or Milanese, the nearly identical centonized lyrics suggest that the four versions share a textual origin.

While the argument from liturgical assignments is powerful, the extent to which "properization" prevailed in the Gallican liturgy is an open question. In examining witnesses to pre-Carolingian liturgical practice in Gaul, McKinnon has drawn a distinction between "lector chant" and "schola chant." Schola chant is associated with the practice of properization, the assignment of chants to specific liturgical occasions, whereas lector chant involves a smaller body of existing chants for general use that were subject to ad hoc selection. McKinnon hypothesizes that the period preceding the adoption of the Roman liturgy in Gaul was one of lector chant. In the seventh-century writing of Caesarius of Arles, the psalm of the Mass is still referred to as a reading, and the descriptions of Gregory of Tours indicate a lack of specific liturgical assignments.[64] Any hypothesis about a "Gallican repertory," moreover, must be informed by the prevalence of regional variation in the Gallican liturgy. Although the liturgy was consistent in essentials such as the types of chants sung, heterogeneity in prayers, readings, and the commemoration of saints is well documented.[65] The various Gallican lectionaries, for example, list different sets of readings.[66] It is highly doubtful, then, that a single, "properized" Gallican chant repertory existed. Michel Huglo has suggested that it is more appropriate to speak of Gallican liturgies, in the plural.[67] In speculating on the degree of properization in Gaul, we might distinguish between thematically specific offertories and those with more general themes. *Viri Galilei* and *Factus est repente*, for example, are so specific to Ascension and Pentecost that they are unlikely to have been used on unrelated days. Other offertories are associated with liturgical seasons in a more general way. *Audi Israhel*, for example, adopts a prophetic theme suitable for any day of Advent. Still others, such as those of the Roman-Gregorian Post-Pentecost Sundays, lack thematic specificity and were probably for general use.

64. McKinnon, "Lector Chant versus Schola Chant: A Question of Historical Plausibility," in *Laborare fratres in unum: Festschrift Laszlo Dobszay zum 60. Geburtstag*, ed. Janka Szendrei and David Hiley (Hildesheim: Olms, 1995): 201–11. Further skepticism about the existence of a fully developed Gallican repertory is expressed by Jane Bellingham in "Gallican Chant," in *New Grove Dictionary of Music and Musicians*, 2nd ed. (New York: Grove, 2001).

65. Yitzhak Hen, *Culture and Religion in Merovingian Gaul 481–751* (Leiden: Brill, 1995), 70–71, and "Unity in Diversity: The Liturgy of Frankish Gaul before the Carolingians," in *Unity and Diversity in the Church: Papers Read at the 1994 Summer Meeting, and the 1995 Winter Meeting of the Ecclesiastical History Society*, ed. Robert Swanson (Oxford: Blackwell, 1996), 19–30; and Els Rose, "Liturgical Commeration of the Saints in the *Missale Gothicum* (vat. reg. lat. 317): New Approaches to the Liturgy of Early Medieval Gaul," *Vigiliae Christianae* 58 (2004): 75–97.

66. See the comparison in Pierre Salmon, ed., *Le Lectionnaire de Luxeuil (Paris, ms. lat. 9427)*, Collectanea Biblica Latina 7 (Rome: Abbaye Saint-Jérôme, 1944), CIV–CXXIII.

67. Huglo, "Altgallikanische Liturgie," 220.

Although I am not fully convinced by Levy's use of textual evidence in the Gallican argument, the presence of some offertories in the Old Hispanic liturgy does bolster a circumstantial case for Gallican origin. The purported affinity between Gallican and Old Hispanic chant, often cited in chant scholarship, has relied primarily on liturgical similarities between them. The two liturgies are indeed identical in certain respects, such as the Canon of the Mass.[68] Other evidence attests to a strong connection between Spanish and Narbonnaise practice in the fifth century.[69] In an often-cited anecdote, Charles the Bald invited Spanish priests to celebrate Mass at his court so that he could experience the liturgy of his forefathers. An edict of the Council of Toledo in 633, moreover, prescribes a single order of worship for all of Spain and Gaul. The heterogeneity of Gallican practice and the repertorial differences between branches of the Old Hispanic rite nevertheless cast tremendous doubt on a reading of this passage as a reference to a single repertory of chant. Although much of the Old Hispanic repertory was in place by the early seventh century, attested by its presence in the Verona orational, further repertorial developments are documented in the course of the seventh century, under the influence of clerics and bishops such as Leander, John of Saragossa, and Conantius of Palencia.[70] The extent to which these innovations spread through Gaul is unknown. Despite the implausibility of repertorial unity, however, the liturgical connections between Spain and Gaul do raise the possibility of non-Roman origin for those offertories with Old Hispanic cognates, and, perhaps by extension, the others that are similar in character to the Old Hispanic sacrificia. The presence of some Roman-Gregorian nonpsalmic offertories in the Milanese repertory is less persuasive as evidence for Gallican origin simply because the Milanese borrowed many psalmic Roman-Gregorian offertories, probably during a period of extensive Carolingian influence in the eighth and ninth centuries.[71] The nonpsalmic offertories could have entered Milan in this context.

On the basis of their thematic unity and context in the Roman repertory, McKinnon has placed the nonpsalmic Post-Pentecost offertories among the later layers of the Roman repertory. He observes that the five nonpsalmic Post-Pentecost offertories, the communions assigned to the corresponding Sundays,

---

68. Thus the well-known borrowing of Isidore's *De ecclesiasticis officiis* from the *Expositio* of Pseudo-Germanus. See the comparison in Ismael Fernández de la Cuesta, "El canto viejo-hispánico y el canto viejo-galicano," *Revista de musicología* 16 (1993): 477–90. On the direction of borrowing, see A. van der Mensbrugghe, "Pseudo-Germanus Reconsidered," *Studia Patristica* 5 (1962): 172–84.

69. See the summaries in Archdale King, *Liturgies of the Primatial Sees* (London: Longmans, 1957), 480–81.

70. W. S. Porter, "Studies in the Mozarabic Office," *Journal of Theological Studies* 35 (1934): 266–86; J. Vives, ed., *Oracional visigótico*, Monumenta hispaniae sacra, Serie litúrgica, 1 (Barcelona: Consejo Superior de Investigaciones Científicas, Escuela de Estudios Medievales, Sección de Barcelona, Balmesiana: Biblioteca Balmes, 1946). For summary of seventh-century developments and references, see King, *Liturgies*, 485–94.

71. These issues are discussed in chapter 4.

and the psalmic offertories of the other Post-Pentecost Sundays are united by
themes of harvest, sacrifice, and justice. The thematic unity, he argues, could hardly
be coincidental; rather, it suggests that the Post-Pentecost offertory and communion cycles are products of the same Roman effort.[72] The concentration of the
other temporal items in the later liturgical seasons suggests to McKinnon that they
were late Roman chants. A thematic argument for Roman origin can also be made
for *Recordare mei*, which has a dual tradition as an offertory and responsory. Brad
Maiani has tied this responsory to eighth-century revisions to the Roman night
office lectionary.[73]

The value of thematic evidence in positing theories of origin and chronology
has recently come into question.[74] The phenomenon of thematic unity within
particular repertories or liturgical seasons can have a number of possible explanations. While McKinnon hypothesizes that the repertory in question forms a
discrete layer, it is also possible that preexisting pieces were borrowed precisely
because of their thematic compatibility with the liturgical occasion in question or
with a repertory already in place. A case in point is the offertory for the first Sunday
of Advent, *Ad te domine levavi*, which is also assigned to Wednesday of the second
week in Lent. On the basis of its thematic appropriateness for Advent, McKinnon
assumes that Advent was its original assignment. Pfisterer, however, gives priority
to the Lenten ferial assignment for the same reason: an Advent borrowing from a
Lenten feria for reasons of thematic appropriateness is plausible, whereas a
seemingly arbitrary Lenten ferial borrowing from Advent would have no discernable explanation.[75] If the nonpsalmic offertories originated outside of Rome, they
may have been borrowed by the Romans because they were thematically appropriate for the occasion or consistent with a repertorial cycle already in place.

Despite these well-founded reservations about the value of thematic
evidence in hypotheses of origin and chronology, the thematic and contextual
argument for Roman origin invites an examination of the nonpsalmic offertories
in their international contexts, particularly among the Old Hispanic offertory
chants, called sacrificia. Although the "non-Roman" character of the Roman and
Gregorian nonpsalmic offertories has been emphasized, their place in the Old
Hispanic and Milanese liturgies remains to be fully explored. The number of core

72. McKinnon, *Advent Project*, 318–22; 369–70.
73. Brad Maiani, "The Responsory-Communions: Toward a Chronology of Selected Proper Chants"
    (Ph.D. diss., University of North Carolina, Chapel Hill, 1996), 175–222, and "Readings and
    Responsories: The Eighth-Century Night Office Lectionary and the *Responsoria Prolixa*," *Journal
    of Musicology* 16 (1998): 125–281. On its dual use as a responsory see *Aureliani Reomensis Musica
    disciplina*, ed. Lawrence Gushee ([Rome]: American Institute of Musicology, 1975). On the two
    different melodic traditions, see Dean Richard Justmann, "Mode-One Offertories: A Critical
    Edition with Analysis" (Ph.D. diss., Northwestern University, 1980), 126–29; and Ruth Steiner,
    "The Offertory-Responsory *Recordare mei Domine*," in Hankeln, *The Offertory and Its Verses*,
    57–66.
74. See Jeffery, review of McKinnon, *Advent Project*, and Pfisterer, "James McKinnon."
75. Pfisterer, "James McKinnon," 43, and "Remarks," 175–76.

Roman-Gregorian offertories with cognates in the Old Hispanic tradition is relatively small, as shown in table 2.7: *Confortamini* for Ember Wednesday of Advent, *Erit vobis* for Thursday of Easter Week, the Post-Pentecost offertory *Sanctificavit*, and, in part, the Post-Pentecost *Oravi deum* and the psalmic sanctoral offertory *Mirabilis*. The Gregorian repertory has one additional piece in common with the Old Hispanic, *Elegerunt*, for St. Stephen, as well as a few others of questionable cognate status. While the Roman nonpsalmic Post-Pentecost offertories are indeed thematically unified to the other Roman offertories and communions of the same season, several of them fit equally seamlessly into their respective Old Hispanic context, with a similar character and thematic emphasis. While a look at the international picture cannot conclusively resolve the question of Roman or Gallican origin, it strengthens the impression that the nonpsalmic Roman offertories are more at home among the other repertories. I begin with a brief overview of each repertory, and then I consider the place of these offertories in the Old Hispanic and Milanese repertories.

THE OLD HISPANIC AND MILANESE REPERTORIES

The Old Hispanic sacrificia and Milanese offerendae are similar to the Roman-Gregorian offertories in certain aspects of style. All four traditions share a concept of the offertory chant as a responsorial form with solo verses. The long melismas that characterize the Roman-Gregorian offertories, moreover, are also found in the Old Hispanic and Milanese traditions. The various branches of the Old Hispanic rite transmit a total of 116 sacrificia, with repertorial differences between each branch.[76] Most are lengthy pieces with two or three verses. In their preference for nonpsalmic texts, the sacrificia contrast markedly with the majority of Gregorian and Roman offertories. Only twelve sacrificia have psalmic texts, whereas seventy-seven of the ninety offertories that form the core Roman-Gregorian repertory are based on the psalms. The sacrificia show a particular predilection for Old Testament narratives: twenty-three are from the Pentateuch and twenty-six from the prophets. Others are from historical books or hagiographical texts. The Gospels are also well represented, in fifteen sacrificia. In these respects, there is little doubt that certain nonpsalmic Roman-Gregorian offertories resemble the sacrificia.

The Old Hispanic repertory exhibits evidence of thematic unity and "compositional planning" similar to that so often observed among the Roman introits and communions. In many cases, textual sources for the sacrificia were carefully chosen to reflect relevant liturgical themes or the genre's liturgical function, with a

---

76. Almost all of these are listed in Don Randel, *An Index to Chants of the Mozarabic Rite* (Princeton, N.J.: Princeton University Press, 1973). Two additional sacrificia are listed in Pinell, "Repertorio del 'sacrificium.'"

prominent focus on offering and sacrifice. Many sacrificia have a similar verbal structure: the respond describes an erection of an altar or a sacrifice, and the verses recount various events of salvation history that led to that offering. The adoption of narrative from the Hebrew scriptures for the sacrificia reflects a fundamental principle of Christian exegesis: all events are presented within a Christian framework wherein Christ's life, death, and resurrection is the ultimate fulfillment of God's covenant with Israel. In the context of the offertory rite, the sacrificia would have served as a powerful reinforcement of this exegesis for participants in the liturgy, explicitly tying the offerings of the Hebrew scriptures to the sacrifice of Christ about to be reenacted in the Eucharist. In the Roman-Gregorian offertories, the offering theme is found far less frequently, even among nonpsalmic texts. It is explicitly manifest in only three of the nonpsalmic offertories: the core Roman-Gregorian offertory *Sanctificavit* and the Gregorian *Stetit angelus* and *Sicut in holocausto;* and occasionally in psalmic offertories such as *Confirma hoc, Reges tharsis,* and *Iubilate deo universa.*

In comparison to the parallel Roman-Gregorian and Hispanic repertories, the Milanese is small. Baroffio identified eighty pieces designated as responds or verses of offerendae in the Milanese manuscripts.[77] Nearly half of these are probable borrowings from the Gregorian or Roman tradition, and a handful have Old Hispanic cognates. The offerendae of probable Milanese origin are variously assigned: the first, third, and sixth Sundays of Advent; Christmas Day and the first Sunday and eighth day of Christmas; two Lenten Sundays and one Lenten feria; three ferias of the Easter octave; and several saints' days, including Holy Innocents, Agatha, John the Baptist, and the Invention of the Cross. The *Commune sanctorum* and *Commune dominicale,* by contrast, employ probable borrowings from Francia or Rome. Like the Old Hispanic sacrificia, the native Milanese offerendae show a propensity for nonpsalmic texts. Four are from the Pentateuch, six from the prophets or historical books, two from the New Testament, several from unknown sources, and only a handful from the psalms. These offertories are typically shorter than those of the Mozarabic and Roman liturgies, with only one or no verses. An offering theme is also found, with less frequency, among several of the native Milanese offerendae.

THE POST-PENTECOST COGNATES

In considering the place of the Gregorian and Roman nonpsalmic offertories in the Old Hispanic and Milanese repertories, I will begin with the Post-Pentecost

---

77. Baroffio, "Offertorien," 16–17. The larger number in the modern edition can be attributed to the addition of new offerendae, many of which are contrafacts of earlier offerendae or borrowings from other genres.

offertories *Oravi deum* and *Sanctificavit*. The latter piece serves a similar dominical role in the Old Hispanic repertory; the former is assigned to St. Jerome. *Sanctificavit* is especially consistent in character and thematic emphasis with the Old Hispanic repertory. The sacrificium belongs to the cycle of nonfestal, "quotidiano" Sundays, a repertory characterized by thematic unity and arrangement in an ascending numerical series.[78] In the Toledo A rite, for example, the first seven sacrificia of the quotidiano Sundays are narrative pieces from Genesis and Exodus, commencing with the creation story from Genesis, *Formavit Dominus hominem*. Passages from two books are selected in order that they occur. Beginning with *Aedificavit Noe* for the second Sunday, the sacrificia draw their texts from passages referring to offering and sacrifice. Focusing on subjects' personal encounters with God, the verses typically incorporate dialogue, with a repetendum that returns to the offering theme of the respond. *Aedificavit Noe*, for example, begins with Noah's offering of animals after the Flood (Gen. 8:20–21). The first verse (Gen. 8:15–16) recounts God's instruction to Noah to bring his family and animals out from the ark, and the second continues with God's instruction to be fruitful and multiply. The repetendum that follows each verse returns to the theme of offering. The subsequent sacrificia of the set are similar thematically and structurally: the respond recounts a story of offering or sacrifice and the verses narrate an encounter with God.

Sanctificavit is similar to the other Old Hispanic sacrificia of the quotidiano cycle, not only in thematic emphasis but also in structure. The respond (Exod. 24:4–5) tells of the offering Moses made to God after the exodus from Egypt and reception of the law. The verses recount subsequent events: Moses asking for forgiveness on Mount Sinai (Exod. 34) and God's order that his face not be seen (Exod. 33). The repetendum returns to the theme of offering. Whereas its narration, dialogue, and offering theme distinguish it from the majority of Roman offertories, *Sanctificavit* is an apparently seamless fit into the Old Hispanic quotidiano cycle. The other Roman-Gregorian Post-Pentecost offertories cannot be as convincingly tied to the Old Hispanic sacrificia for the common Sundays. Of these, *Precatus est Moyses* is perhaps most reminiscent of the Old Hispanic sacrificia. Although it lacks the offering theme, its lengthy narrative and dialogue text perhaps add weight to a circumstantial case for a non-Roman origin.

THE EASTER WEEK CYCLE

Three Roman-Gregorian nonpsalmic offertories have Easter Week assignments: Monday's *Angelus domini*, Friday's *Erit vobis*, and Thursday's *In die sollemnitatis*.

---

78. Pinell, "Repertorio del 'sacrificium.'"

TABLE 2.8 *Easter Week Offertory Chants*

Assignment	Old Hispanic	Roman/Gregorian	Milanese
Sun.	Alleluia temporibus Mt. 28 Vulgate	Terra tremuit (Ps. 75)	**Angelus domini** (Mt.28)
Mn.	In pascha domini (Num. 28) Vulgate	**Angelus domini** (Mt. 28)	Celebraverunt (Lev. 23: 5–6)
Tu.	Ecce agnus (Jn., Ps 106)	Intonuit (Ps. 17)	Alleluia Steterunt (II Par 35, Lev. 23)
Wd.	Sollemnem habeatis (Num 28) VL	Portas caeli (Ps. 27)	Isti sunt dies quos nulla (Esth. 9, 28)Vulgate
Th.		**In die sollemnitatis** (Exod. 13)	Ego audivi (Esth. 9)
Fri.	**Erit hic vobis** (Exod. 12, 14, 34) VL	**Erit vobis hic** (Exod. 12, 14, 34) VL	Resurrexit Ps. 77
Sat.	Haec dixit dom. Apoc. Alleluia quasi carmen (Ez. 33: 32, 47: 12) Isti sunt dies festi (Lev. 23, 36, Deut. 27)	Benedictus qui Ps. 117	**In die sollemnitatis** (Exod. 13)
Oct.	Omnis populus adoraverunt Macc. 4, 13	Benedictus qui Ps. 117	Preparatum II Par. 35

The parallel offertory chants in the Old Hispanic and Milanese liturgies are listed in table 2.8. Cognate items are shown in boldface. *Angelus domini* and *In die* are found at Milan, where *Angelus* serves as the Easter Sunday offertory and *In die* is assigned to Saturday of Easter Week. *Erit* has an identical assignment, Easter Friday, in the Old Hispanic tradition but is assigned to Pentecost at Milan. Although the Old Hispanic and Milanese Easter Week cycles share no repertory, many of their offertories are unified by a Passover-festival theme, a trait also found the Roman-Gregorian *Erit* and *In die*.

Among the branches of the Old Hispanic rite, only León has proper sacrificia for Easter Week. In addition to the ubiquitous offering and sacrifice theme, five sacrificia of the Easter week cycle are unified around a festival theme. Some sacrificia in the León cycle specifically reference the seven-day period of the Passover celebration, linking it to the continuous celebration of Easter during the octave. Monday's *In Pascha domini*, for example, paraphrases Numbers 28:16–18, expressly mentioning the first day of the seven-day celebration: "In pascha domini erit vobis sollemnitas septem diebus quarum dies prima venerabilis." In addition to its Monday assignment, this sacrificium may be sung on any day within Easter Octave. References to a seven-day festal period, with the added theme of offering, are also found in Wednesday's *Sollemnem habeatis* ("Sollemnem habeatis istum diem festum domino et offeretis septem diebus fructum holocausti in odorem suavitatis domino") and Saturday's *Isti sunt dies festi* ("offeretis domino septem diebus odorem suavitatis preter holocaustum sempiternum altissimo facies litationes eius et dies primus sanctus erit vobis in sempiternum."). *Omnis populus adoraverunt*, from 1 Maccabees 4, continues the festal theme, alluding to the eight-day period of celebration and offering that followed the rebuilding of the temple altar after its destruction by Antiochus Epiphanes and Antiochus's defeat by Judas Maccabaeus. Each of these sacrificia ties Easter to Old Testament acts of salvation, reinforcing the exegetical link between God's covenant with Israel and the ultimate fulfillment of that covenant in Easter.

Although the other sacrificia for the Easter Octave lack the festal theme, they may be linked to specific liturgical events of the week. Tuesday's *Ecce agnus* derives its verses from Psalm 106, "Let them say who were redeemed by the Lord, redeemed from the hand of the enemy, brought together from the lands by the rising and setting of the sun and the sea," perhaps a reference to the newly baptized, whose white robes were removed after Mass on that day.[79] *Alleluia Quasi Carmen musicum*, one of three sacrificia for Saturday, celebrates the return of the alleluia during Paschaltide. Saturday's *Haec dixit dominus* is centonized from various passages of the Apocalypse, which was read in the Old Hispanic lectionary during the Easter Octave.

The Milanese offerendae of Easter Octave show a preference for nonpsalmic texts that broadly links them to the Old Hispanic cycle. Several of these offerendae, moreover, echo the León cycle in their adoption of the Passover/festival theme. As Baroffio has argued, is likely that some separate items of this cycle once belonged together as single offertories, *Celebraverunt* with *Alleluia steterunt* and *Isti sunt dies quos nulla* with *Ego audivi*.[80] *Isti sunt dies quos nulla* draws its respond text from the deuterocanonical chapters of Esther, the instructions to celebrate the feast of Purim; *Ego audivi*, at one time its probable verse, recounts some events leading to this celebration. The thematic emphasis of respond and verse is similar to that of many Old Hispanic sacrificia. *Celebraverunt* and *Alleluia steterunt* consist of the instructions to celebrate Passover from Leviticus 23, but are probably not cognate with the Old Hispanic *Isti sunt dies festi*, based on some of the same passages. The two pieces appear to be separate centonizations.

---

79. See King, *Liturgies*, 491. King cites the Liber sacramentorum: "Missa in die tertia feria paschae quando et baptizatis infantibus albae tolluntur."
80. Baroffo, "Offertorien," 34.

These thematic parallels between the Old Hispanic and Milanese cycles suggest that the two liturgies had a common conception of Easter Week offertory chants. In the Roman-Gregorian offertories, however, the Passover/festival theme of the Milanese and Old Hispanic repertories is manifest only in two of the three nonpsalmic offertories, *Erit* and *In die*. *Portas caeli* refers to the tradition of the open doors of heaven throughout Easter Week; *Benedictus qui venit* adopts as its verses Psalm 117, the traditional psalm employed in the week's graduals, "Haec dies quam fecit dominus." In short, two of the three nonpsalmic Roman-Gregorian Easter Week offertories in the Roman-Gregorian repertory, *Erit vobis* and *In die*, seem more at home among the non-Roman repertories.

This examination of the Old Hispanic context may have implications for the intended liturgical use of *Erit*, which is assigned to Pentecost at Milan. Levy has proposed that *Erit* was originally the Pentecost or Easter Sunday offertory in the Gallican liturgy, on the basis of its more important assignment at Milan and its text, which, he argues, suggests that it was intended for a major feast. Giving priority to the more important feast seems sensible at face value: it is unlikely, as Levy suggests, that the Milanese would borrow an offertory for a major festival. As previously argued, however, it is probable that the Gallican sonus lacked fixed liturgical assignments. The Milanese repertory, moreover, is small; many of its offertories for important festivals, such as *Angelus domini* for Easter Sunday, are shared with other traditions and may indeed be borrowings. In the case of *Erit*, an equally compelling argument can be made for an original Easter Week assignment. In its Old Hispanic context, the focus on the events surrounding Passover strongly links *Erit* to the other sacrificia of Easter Week. Although the specific reference to the exodus from Egypt comes only in the second verse, which the Milanese tradition lacks, the entire lyric is taken from the passages of Exodus that refer to Passover, more appropriate for Easter than for Pentecost. As for its reference to a single day of solemnity, one could make a similar argument in the case of Easter Saturday's *Sollemnem habeatis istum diem* or, for that matter, "Haec dies quam fecit dominus," the psalm verse used throughout Easter Week in the Roman liturgy. The single day is consistent with the treatment of Easter Week as one continuous celebration. Given the probable lack of properization in Gaul, however, it may have been customary to sing this piece on both occasions, Easter and Pentecost.

ADVENT

The Old Hispanic, Milanese, and Gallican rites had a five- or six-week Advent, which is reflected in the five-week Advent of the Rheinau gradual. For Advent sacrificia, the León and Rioja rites adopt passages from Isaiah, Zechariah, and

Daniel, with a prophetic theme also reflected in the Old Hispanic lectionary.[81] The Milanese Advent repertory contains a number of proper offerendae on a similar theme.[82] In the Roman-Gregorian repertory, by contrast, psalmic offertories are assigned to the first three Advent Sundays, with the fourth *vacat*. Ember Wednesday and Saturday, however, have the nonpsalmic offertories *Confortamini* and *Exsulta satis*, thematically linked to the Old Hispanic Advent repertory through the adoption of prophetic passages from Isaiah. In addition to its Advent assignment at Milan, *Confortamini* is found in the Old Hispanic *Missale Mixtum* and, as Pfisterer has argued, was probably a traditional part of the Old Hispanic repertory.[83] On the basis of the Old Hispanic presence of *Confortamini* and the use of Old Latin texts in *Confortamini* and *Exsulta satis*, Pfisterer has proposed that both offertories are Gallican or possibly North African borrowings. *Audi Israhel*, assigned to the first Sunday of a five-week Advent in Rheinau and to Ember Friday in a few Italian and Aquitanian sources, also exhibits this prophetic theme. Three of the six Advent Sundays in Milan have offerendae that are unique to that tradition, one based on the psalms and two based on prophetic passages from Joel. Thematically, then, the Roman-Gregorian Advent offertories *Confortamini*, *Exsulta satis*, and the rare *Audi Israhel* are more at home among the non-Roman Advent repertories.

To summarize, my examination of the Roman-Gregorian nonpsalmic offertories in their international contexts adds some weight to a circumstantial case that some of them originated outside Rome. As noted, McKinnon argued for a Roman origin for the Post-Pentecost nonpsalmic offertories on the basis of their thematic compatibility with other offertories and communions assigned to that season. Post-Pentecost items of both genres are unified by an emphasis on harvest, justice, and sacrifice. In the case of several offertories I have examined, however, a thematic argument might lead more convincingly to Spain than Rome. The offering themes of *Sanctificavit* and *Stetit* are far more typical of the Old Hispanic sacrificia. *Erit vobis* and *In die*, with their Old Testament festal emphasis, are similar in character and theme to the Old Hispanic and Milanese Easter Week offertories, and the prophetic lyrics of *Confortamini* and *Exsulta satis* are thematically close to those of the Advent sacrificia.

CHRONOLOGY AND BIBLICAL VERSIONS

While it is generally agreed that nonpsalmic offertories of Easter Week and the Post-Pentecost Sundays are among the latest layers of the repertory, the date of

---

81. Germain Morin, *Liber comicus, sive Lectionarius missae quo Toletana Ecclesia ante annos mille et ducentos utebatur* (Maredsol: In Monasterio S. Benedicti, 1987).
82. These features are discussed in a forthcoming study by Terence Bailey. I am thankful to Professor Bailey for sharing this work in advance of its publication.
83. Pfisterer, *Cantilena*, 226–27.

their addition to the Roman repertory has been a topic of debate. By arranging the offertories according to the dates feasts were added to the calendar and positing probable original assignments, Pfisterer has proposed that the composition of the offertory repertory came to a conclusion around the year 600.[84] As noted, however, McKinnon places these offertories among the later layers of a repertory that arose primarily in the later seventh century.[85]

The biblical translations employed in the nonpsalmic offertories can be of some help in resolving the question. As Petrus Pietschmann has shown, a majority of nonpsalmic offertories in the Gregorian repertory depart substantially from the Hebrew-based Vulgate and derive instead from VL translations made from the Greek Septuagint. No complete version of the VL survives; patristic citations have served as our primary witnesses. For several of the nonpsalmic offertories, no VL version of the source texts exists. Pietschmann's study demonstrates a VL basis for *Sanctificavit, Precatus est Moyses, Exsulta satis, Confortamini, Erit vobis, In die, Oravi Deum,* and *Oratio mea.*[86] Though a specific origin cannot be traced, *Recordare mei* is also VL based.[87] The Vulgate, by contrast, is the source for *Domine deus in simplicitate, Vir erat,* and *Sicut in holocausto.* For New Testament pieces, determining whether the chant in question is based on the Vulgate or the VL is more difficult. Both were translations from the Greek, and Jerome used existing translations in his preparation of the Vulgate New Testament. Among the New Testament–based offertories, a VL basis can be established for *Elegerunt* and *Stetit angelus,* whereas the source of the others is uncertain.[88]

The use of the VL in the Roman repertory has played an important role in Pfisterer's hypothesis that the bulk of it arose before the sixth century, an argument echoed in Tietze's recent study of the introit.[89] Pfisterer's work has focused on Isaiah chants. The crux of his argument for a fifth- or sixth-century origin lies in two forms of evidence: the liturgical placement of chants based on the Vulgate vis-à-vis those that use the VL and the time of transition from the VL to the Vulgate. Pfisterer demonstrates that the Vulgate-based Isaiah chants are concentrated in Advent, whereas the VL-based ones, with a few exceptions, are placed outside of Advent. Advent was the final season added to the calendar, between Gregory the Great and the Leonine Sacramentary (650). The distribution of Vulgate texts in Advent and VL texts outside of Advent, Pfisterer argues, suggests that the proper chants for other seasons were in place before the seventh-century addition of

---

84. Pfisterer, "Remarks," 178.

85. McKinnon, *Advent Project*, 316–23.

86. Pietschmann, "Die nicht aus dem Psalter entnommenen," 114–30.

87. This offertory's lack of correspondence to the Vulgate has been discussed by Pothier; Jean-Claude Haelewyck has identified it as a translation of the LXX, as cited in Steiner, "Offertory-Responsory *Recordare.*"

88. Pietschmann identified a VL source for *Elegerunt.* "Die nicht dem Psalter," 129–30. The VL basis of *Stetit angelus* is demonstrated below.

89. Tietze, *Hymn Introits.*

Advent.[90] Tietze's study confirms a general trend toward use of the Vulgate among introits assigned to later feasts.[91]

Attempts to define the time of transition from the VL to the Vulgate have relied primarily on the evidence of citations. In identifying the time of transition for Isaiah in southern Italy, Pfisterer notes that Leo I cites the VL, whereas Gregory the Great cites the Vulgate. The lauds canticles Pfisterer examines, cited in the Rule of Benedict, use partially Vulgate and partially VL. Thus, Pfisterer concludes, the Vulgate was already in use for new Isaiah chants in Rome in the beginning of the sixth century. The use of the VL in a majority of Isaiah chants thus suggests they were completed before the turn of the sixth century.[92]

If an analogy can be made from Pfisterer's argument, based on Isaiah, to the other books of the Bible, the prominence of the VL may suggest a similarly early origin for some of the nonpsalmic offertories. Since books of the Bible circulated separately or in small collections, however, the date of transition becomes a separate question for each book. Gribomont demonstrates an increasing preference for the Vulgate in citations from the fifth and sixth centuries and places the later stages of its adoption in Rome later than Pfisterer does, between 550–590, with Gregory the Great as a pivotal figure.[93] The prominence of the Vulgate in seventh-century Rome is further attested by its use in the Würzburg epistolary, whose prototype dates to the seventh century or perhaps earlier.[94] In view of this evidence, an origin as late as the end of the seventh century for the VL-based nonpsalmic offertories seems unlikely.

Can the time of transition from VL to Vulgate help to establish a terminus ante quem for the nonpsalmic offertories? Because the transition between the two texts occurred at different times in different places, the answer depends partially on where the origin of these chants is sought. If the nonpsalmic offertories are indeed of Gallican origin, their use of the VL might point to a very early date of creation. The transition occurred earlier in Gaul than in Italy, propagated by students of Pelagius in the fifth century.[95] For most books, citations from the north in the later fifth and early sixth centuries refer to the Vulgate, sometimes mixed with elements of the VL. A palimpsest source from Wolfenbüttel, dating from the beginning of the sixth century, employs the Vulgate for the Pentateuch, the source for several of

90. Pfisterer, *Cantilena*, 221–32.
91. Tietze, *Hymn Introits*, 54–81.
92. Pfisterer, *Cantilena*, 230–31.
93. Gribomont, "La règle et la Bible," 383.
94. Gribomont, "L'eglise et les versions bibliques," *La maison-dieu* 62 (1960): 41–68.
    See *Comes Romanus Wirziburgensis: Facsimile edition of Codex M.p.th.f. 62 of the University Library of Würzburg* (Graz: Akademische Druck-u. Verlagsanstalt, 1968). On the date of Würzburg, see Cyrille Vogel, *Medieval Liturgy: An Introduction to the Sources* (Washington, D.C.: Pastoral Press, 1981), 339–40; and McKinnon, *Advent Project*, 116.
95. See the summary in Raphael Loewe, "The Medieval History of the Latin Vulgate," in *Cambridge History of the Bible* 2:120–25.

our nonpsalmic offertories.[96] From Rome and southern Italy, fifth- and sixth-century citations from the Pentateuch and Job are unfortunately sparse. The evidence we have, however, supports an early date of transition. The Rule of Benedict, for example, employs the Vulgate in its citations of Genesis.[97]

Although these circumstantial factors suggest that the nonpsalmic offertories with VL texts were created before the late seventh century, I do not think that the choice of translation can give us a precise terminus ante quem. The central issue is whether the time of transition from the VL to the Vulgate can be pinpointed as precisely as Pfisterer proposes. Underlying his argument, it seems, is a premise that the transition was a one-time event, and that once the Vulgate was introduced, a lyricist would no longer turn to the older translation in creating a chant text. Work on the history of the Vulgate, however, has shown that the transition between the two texts was gradual, complex, and multifaceted. The Vulgate was introduced, met with resistance, and was mixed with the VL.[98] While it shows an increasing influence of the Vulgate during the fifth and sixth centuries, Gribomont's compilation of citations presents a picture of a gradual transition.[99] In many places, the Vulgate and the VL were in simultaneous use, and the two versions were mixed. Pfisterer presents just such an example of a mixed text from Isaiah in the Benedictine lauds canticles.[100] At the end of the sixth century, the transitional period defined by Gribomont, Gregory the Great nearly always cites the Vulgate, sometimes with VL corruptions.[101] In the preface to his commentary on Job, however, Gregory remarks that both translations are still in use in the apostolic see. While announcing that he will use the "novam translationem" as the basis for his commentary, he states that he will sometimes refer to the "veterem" when it better suits his purposes.[102] These statements clearly suggest that the transition from the VL to the Vulgate for Job was not yet a fait accompli in Gregory's time and, more important, that the two were in simultaneous use. Rosamond McKitterick

---

96. Gribomont, "L'église," 51–53.
97. Ibid.
98. Summaries of this situation are provided in numerous places. See Fischer, "Zur Überlieferung," 20–21. ("In den meisten Fällen entschied man sich nicht radikal für den alten oder den neuen Text. Wenn man auch den Wert des Neuen anerkannte, wollte man doch andererseits nicht das Alte, an das man gewöhnt war, ganz aufgeben. So entstanden schon in der Zeit der Einführung Mischtexte.") See also Gribomont, "Les plus anciennes traductions latins," in Le monde latin antique et la Bible, ed. Jacques Fontaine and Charles Pietri (Paris: 1985), 56–57; Bogaert, "La Bible latine des origines au moyen âge," Revue théologique de Louvain 19 (1988): 293–95; and Richard Marsden, The Text of the Old Testament in Anglo-Saxon England (Cambridge: Cambridge University Press, 1995), 5–11.
99. Gribomont, "La règle et la Bible," 383, "Le texte biblique de Grégoire," in Grégoire le Grand (Colloque de Chantilly, 1982) (Paris: 1986), 467–75, and "L'eglise," 41–68.
100. Pfisterer, Cantilena, 230.
101. Gribomont, "Le texte biblique de Grégoire."
102. "Novam vero translationem dissero; sed cum probationis causa me exigit, nunc novam nunc veterem per testimonia adsumo, ut, quia sedes apostolica cui Deo auctore praesideo utraque utitur, mei quoque labor studii ex utraque fulciatur." Moralia in Iob, ed. Marci Adriaen, in Corpus Christianorum: Series Latina 143 (Turnholt: Brepols, 1979), 7.

emphasizes the variety of biblical texts that circulated even during Carolingian times, citing Bruce Metzger's identification of fourteen manuscripts dating from late eighth century that transmit VL texts of the New Testament.[103] Although these manuscripts were probably copied for scholarly reference and preservation rather than practical use, we cannot be sure. In short, the use of the VL as a source for chant texts in the later seventh century, though unlikely, is not impossible.

To summarize, the use of the VL renders implausible a late seventh-century Rome origin for a majority of the nonpsalmic offertories but does not absolutely preclude it. Pfisterer's work clearly demonstrates a concentration of Vulgate Isaiah chants in Advent; his argument that the bulk of the Lenten Isaiah chants were already in place by that time is cogent. At the same time, the complexity of the Bible's textual history suggests that this evidence should be employed with some caution as a means of dating specific chants and the repertory as a whole.

The evidence of biblical sources also bears on the chronology of the Old Hispanic sacrificia and their relationship to the Roman-Gregorian nonpsalmic offertories. Although the sacrificia exhibit a mixture of VL and Vulgate translations, the preference is for the Vulgate among the Advent, Easter, and dominical cycles I have examined. Of the thirty-three quotidiano sacrificia that circulate in the various branches of the Old Hispanic rite, I was able to determine a textual source for seventeen. Eleven are drawn from the Vulgate and two from apparent mixed translations. Only four, including *Sanctificavit*, are purely VL. This variety is found even among sacrificia drawn from the same book. Of the five based on Genesis, for example, three are from the Vulgate, one from the VL, and one is a mixed text.[104] The Easter Week cycle exhibits a similar variety, as shown in table 2.8. The sacrificia for Easter Sunday and Monday are Vulgate-based, whereas those for Wednesday and Friday use the VL. This prominence of the Vulgate among the sacrificia is no surprise. The Vulgate was introduced in Spain in the fifth century. Spanish Bibles transmit the Vulgate for most books, with characteristic Spanish Old Latin corruptions either written into the margins or incorporated into the main text.[105] Aside from the psalter, no pure VL manuscript from Spain survives.[106]

---

103. McKitterick, "Carolingian Bible Production," 69–70. Bruce M. Metzger, *The Early Versions of the New Testament: Their Origin, Transmission, and Limitations* (Oxford: Clarendon Press, 1977), 293–301.

104. *Formavit dominus hominem, Aedificavit Abraham,* and *In temporibus illis* are Vulgate texts; *Aedificavit Noe* is from the European tradition of the VL, and *Melchisedech* appears to be a mixture of the Vulgate and the European VL.

105. The palimpsest León 15 has the VL of several books, including Maccabees, Judith, Esther, II Paralimpoma, and Tobias. These are among the books preserved in VL long after the transition was complete for others. See Gribomont, "Les plus anciennes traductions," 56; and Bogaert, "La Bible latine des origines au moyen âge," 293–95.

106. See the overview in Loewe, "The Medieval History of the Latin Vulgate," 120–25; and Donatien De Bruyne, "Études sur les origines de la Vulgate en Espagne," *Revue Bénédictine* 31 (1914): 373–401.

The mixture of translations employed in the sacrificia has important implications, both for the history of the Old Hispanic repertory, a topic that merits a full
study in its own right, and for the methodologies employed in examining chant
repertories. The thematic unity and signs of "compositional planning" we have
observed among dominical and Easter Week sacrificia give these repertories the
appearance of unified cycle. The variety of biblical translations employed, however,
suggests that these cycles are chronologically stratified products of gradual assimilation.[107] The scenario of composition over a lengthy period is consistent with the
gradual development of the Old Hispanic liturgy. A fifth-century origin has been
proposed for much of the liturgy, including formularies for the quotidiano Masses,
while further additions have been documented in the seventh century.[108] The
shared thematic emphasis within these sacrificia, then, has little, if any, chronological import. Newer sacrificia were evidently written to complement existing ones,
with a similar thematic emphasis. The numerical ordering of the quotidiano
sacrificia is clearly a later imposition of structure on a preexisting repertory.

The Old Hispanic sacrificia considered here exhibit no correlation between
choice of translation and the presence or absence of verbal centonization. This lack
of correlation suggests that centonization has little chronological significance in the
Old Hispanic repertory, at least among the nonpsalmic chants that form the great
majority of sacrificia. In the quotidiano cycle, for example, the four VL-based
sacrificia are extensively centonized, whereas the Vulgate ones are mixed, some
taken directly from the Bible and others with textual adjustment.[109] The variety of
translations, moreover, reinforces the sense that the creation of the sacrificia, at
least in many cases, preceded their assignment to specific feasts: their composition
and properization occurred in separate stages. The León Easter Week sacrificia are
a case in point. If their assignments were contemporaneous with their creation, we
might expect to find a more ancient, VL-based sacrificium assigned to Easter
Sunday, when in fact the VL sacrificia of the group are assigned to Wednesday
and Friday. The simplest explanation is that the Easter Week sacrificia were
selected from a fund of general chants for the week, or perhaps for Paschaltide
as a whole, that were only later given specific assignments at León. This impression
of separate composition and properization is strengthened by the inconsistency of
repertory and assignments among the branches of the Old Hispanic rite.

To return to the Roman-Gregorian nonpsalmic offertories, I have shown that
several of those with Old Hispanic cognates, including *Confortamini*, *Stetit angelus*,
Sanctificavit, and *Erit*, are consistent in character and thematic emphasis with the

---

107. Pinell's assertion that the verses of these sacrificia were tenth-century additions inspired by the
    Gregorian repertory does not withstand an examination of the verses' texts, since the verses rely
    on the same translations as the responds do. Pinell, "Repertorio del 'sacrificium,'" 82–83.
108. See the summary in King, *Liturgies*, 479–94.
109. Examples of sacrificia with little centonization include *Formavit dominus hominem* and *Sacertotes
    domini offerent*.

Old Hispanic cycles they belong to. While the nonpsalmic narratives and sacrificial themes link these offertories to the sacrificia used in Spain, however, their use of the VL distinguishes them from the majority of Old Hispanic sacrificia. The early adoption of the Vulgate in Spain suggests that either these lyrics are very early compositions or that their origins lie elsewhere. The preference for the VL among the Roman-Gregorian nonpsalmic offertories is, in fact, an important distinguishing feature of these offertories in their international context. In cases where a source can be established, all nonpsalmic Roman-Gregorian offertories with Old Hispanic or Milanese cognates use the VL, whereas the two Vulgate-based offertories of the core Roman-Gregorian repertory, *Domine deus in simplicitate* and *Vir erat*, are not found in the Old Hispanic or Milanese tradition. While the Milanese offerendae exhibit a mixture of translations, the Vulgate also predominates there. These trends raise the possibility that the offertory chants that circulate internationally are part of a small core of older repertory, to which chants with similar traits were later added locally.

SUMMARY OF NONPSALMIC CORE OFFERTORIES

My examination of the translations, along with the Old Hispanic and Milanese contexts, supports a theory of non-Roman origin for some nonpsalmic offertories of the core Roman-Gregorian repertory. The use of the VL texts, moreover, suggests that they originated before the seventh century. The differing translations among the nonpsalmic offertories and sacrificia I have examined, however, should caution against searching for the origins of all nonpsalmic offertories in the same time and place. Nonpsalmic sacrificia and offertories with a similar character and thematic emphasis were undoubtedly composed over a long period of time and, most likely, in different places.

If the nonpsalmic offertories originated outside of Rome, their thematic compatibility with other Roman chants is best explained by a scenario of borrowing or proper assignment made precisely for that reason. Brad Maiani, for example, has argued that *Recordare mei*, which has a dual use as a responsory and offertory, became part of the night office during revisions to the Esther reading cycle in the late eighth century.[110] As I have shown, use of the VL for a new chant in the eighth century, while not impossible, is unlikely. *Recordare mei's* VL basis, then, suggests that it was incorporated into matins as a preexisting piece. The use of the VL supports Steiner's argument that it originated as an offertory and was later adopted as a responsory, leading eventually to the creation of a second melody for the

---

110. Maiani, "Responsory-Communions," 175–222, and "Readings and Responsories: The Eighth-Century Night Office Lectionary and the Responsoria Prolixa," *Journal of Musicology* 16 (1998): 254–82.

offertory.[111] Similarly, the nonpsalmic Post-Pentecost offertories may have been borrowed because their thematic emphasis is consistent with that of other Post-Pentecost offertories and communions.

While many factors suggest an origin outside of Rome, I would be hesitant to rule out a Roman origin for all nonpsalmic offertories simply because they are rare in Rome and common elsewhere. *Domine deus in simplicitate* for the Dedication, a seventh-century festival, shares substantial melodic material with the core psalmic offertory *Domine in auxilium* and may very well be of Roman origin. While *Domine deus*'s use of the Vulgate does not answer the question of Roman or non-Roman origin, it is at least consistent with the festival's seventh-century institution. Although *Vir erat* has a narrative lyric that broadly links it to the other nonpsalmic offertories, its use of the Vulgate suggests that it may be a later addition. As Steiner has recently suggested, "it may be that each of these chants has a history of its own."[112]

Wherever the ultimate origin of each offertory lies, Pfisterer is certainly correct to place the nonpsalmic offertories of the core Roman-Gregorian repertory among the items transmitted from Rome to the Franks. If the Roman versions are imports from Gaul or elsewhere, their adoption into the Roman repertory took place prior to the repertory's transmission north. Observing that chants for several of the Lenten Thursdays, added to the calendar by 730, were taken over from the Post-Pentecost Sundays as sets, Pfisterer notes that the nonpsalmic offertory *Precatus est Moyses* is among these, with its dual assignment to Thursday of the second week in Lent and the twelfth Sunday after Pentecost. The placement of *Precatus* in this group of chants suggests that its Post-Pentecost assignment in the Roman liturgy was in place by the time the Lenten Thursdays were added. If *Precatus* was part of the Roman repertory before its transmission to the Franks, he argues, there is no reason to suspect a Carolingian-era Frankish-to-Roman transmission for the other nonpsalmic offertories. Indeed, examples of Gregorian chant taken over by the Romans between the eighth and eleventh centuries are isolated, localized phenomena.[113] The textual variants further support the argument that these offertories were a part of the Roman repertory adopted by the Franks. In *Sanctificavit* and *Erit* in particular, the Gregorian texts correspond more closely to the Roman than to the Old Hispanic and Milanese, a pattern I will consider further in chapter 4.[114] While pre-Carolingian Gaul may have known these pieces in a form like that of the

111. Steiner, "Offertory-Responsory *Recordare*."
112. Ibid.
113. Pfisterer, "Remarks," 169–72. Some of these cases are briefly surveyed in chapter 5.
114. To summarize the differences in *Sanctificavit*: Roman and Gregorian have "immolans" instead of the Old Hispanic "inferens," in v. 1 "surgens" instead of "audiens" and "deus," omitted in the Old Hispanic text. In v. 2 the Old Hispanic and Milanese have a phrase that is lacking in the Roman and Gregorian, "non poteris videre faciem meam." There are, however, some textual differences between the Roman and Gregorian versions, as is evident in the transcriptions provided.

Old Hispanic versions, the textual variants suggest that the Gregorian version was adopted from Rome, consistent with the Carolingian mandate to conform to Roman practice.

GREGORIAN OFFERTORIES OUTSIDE THE CORE REPERTORY: "GALLICAN" OR "CAROLINGIAN"?

As noted, the graduals of Hesbert's *Antiphonale Missarum Sextuplex* transmit eight nonpsalmic offertories that are not found in Roman manuscripts. Five of these are part of the standard Gregorian repertory; the other three are found only rarely (see table 2.7). The Vulgate-based *Benedictus sit*, for the Frankish-instituted Trinity Sunday, is a contrafact of the core Roman-Gregorian offertory *Constitues eos*. With its basis in an earlier melody, *Benedictus sit* is analogous to several newly added Frankish psalmic offertories. As shown in table 2.1, however, *Constitues eos* itself may be a non-Roman chant, since it exhibits textual variants that correspond to δ, a psalter used in pre-Carolingian Gaul. Similarly, *Viri Galilei* and *Stetit angelus*, chants of possible Gallican origin, share melodic material.[115] *Sicut in holocausto* is for the seventh Sunday after Pentecost, *vacat* in the Roman liturgy; it shares this assignment with the introit *Omnes gentes* and communion *Inclina aurem*, probable new Frankish compositions.[116] Although this Vulgate-based offertory has the offering theme so prominent among the Old Hispanic sacrificia, it is unclear whether its origin is Carolingian or pre-Carolingian.

For several of these offertories, various types of circumstantial evidence point to a pre-Carolingian origin. Three have the distinction of circulating only in Mont-Blandin (*Factus est repente* and *Ingressus est*) or Rheinau (*Audi Israhel*) and a very small number of later manuscripts, primarily of northern or central Italian or Beneventan origin.[117] Several factors suggest that these are not new compositions, including their far-reaching geographical presence and their virtual disappearance from later sources. In some cases, an important liturgical assignment in early sources further suggests a pre-Carolingian origin, as Levy has argued. *Factus est*, for example, is given in Mont-Blandin and the Prüm gradual as an *alia* offertory for Pentecost, whereas in the later Italian manuscripts it is displaced to Pentecost Thursday. *Viri Galilei* is assigned to the Ascension in Mont-Blandin and to the Vigil

---

115. I address this sharing of material among probable pre-Carolingian offertories in chapter 5.
116. A Roman version of *Omnes gentes* appears in the Bodmer manuscript. Pfisterer's argument that this is a case of reverse, Frankish-to-Roman transmission, however, is compelling. See *Cantilena Romana*, 110.
117. On *Factus est*, see René-Jean Hesbert, "Un antique offertoire de la Pentecôte: 'Factus est repente,'" in *Organicae voces: Festschrift Joseph Smits van Waesberghe* (Amsterdam: Instituut voor Middeleeuwse Muziekwetenschap, 1963); and Kenneth Levy, "Charlemagne's Archetype of Gregorian Chant," *Journal of the American Musicological Society*. On *Ingressus est*, see Hesbert, *Antiphonale Missarum Sextuplex*, 107; on *Audi Israhel*, ibid., 36, and Pfisterer, *Cantilena*, 122.

or Octave in later manuscripts. It seems unlikely that the Franks would create new offertories for such major feasts after the reception of Roman chant. Finally, recall that *Audi Israhel*, assigned to Ember Friday of Advent in some Italian sources, is thematically consistent with the Advent offertories of the Old Hispanic and Milanese traditions, perhaps a circumstantial factor in favor of pre-Carolingian origin. As Levy has shown, a piece with the same text circulates as a Milanese responsory.[118] With the caveat that translation evidence should be used with caution, a pre-Carolingian case can be made for *Elegerunt*, which uses a pre-Vulgate translation and is long thought to be a Gallican survival. *Ingressus est* has several passages that differ from the Vulgate and may also be based on a VL source.[119]

Stetit angelus, clearly based on a pre-Vulgate source, is a special case among the Gregorian offertories. Related texts are found in chants of diverse genres and in different regional traditions, complicating the question of its origin. Levy noted the partial verbal correspondence to an Old Hispanic sacrificium and Milanese offerenda. This sacrificium/offerenda, assigned to the third Sunday after Easter in Spain (perhaps to complement the reading from the Apocalypse on Paschaltide Sundays) and to John the Evangelist in Milan, has lengthy verses, also taken from the Apocalypse, that are lacking in the Gregorian *Stetit angelus*.[120] Closer verbal correspondences, however, are found in the Roman and Gregorian repertories. A related text, for example, serves as the basis for antiphons in the Roman St. Michael office.[121] Lyrics nearly identical to those of *Stetit angelus* are employed for a responsory found in the Hartker antiphoner and in many later Gregorian manuscripts. The verse text of *Stetit angelus*, based on Psalm 137, is very similar to the respond of the Roman St. Michael offertory, *In conspectu angelorum*.

Using the Vulgate as the basis for comparing the Gregorian and Old Hispanic *Stetit angelus*, Levy concluded that both were highly centonized and based on a common source.[122] The Old Hispanic/Milanese *Stetit*, however, is so different from the Gregorian that a cognate relationship of the two pieces is far from certain. The recent publication of the VL of the Apocalypse allows for closer examination of the two texts and their possible sources. The Old Hispanic respond may be

---

118. Levy, "Toledo, Rome," 88–89. Unfortunately, however, its textual characteristics give few clues to its origins. The respond cannot be compellingly tied to any scriptural passage, and the psalmic verse is consistent with the PsR, but also psalters such as δ, the Psalter of Corbie used in pre-Carolingian Gaul.

119. I was unable to find corresponding readings in *Vetus latina Database*.

120. Terence Bailey attributes the assignment to St. John in Milan to the traditional attribution of the Apocalypse to John.

121. The text appears in San Pietro B 79 as three successive antiphons. The first is "Stetit angelus iuxta aram templi habens turibulum aureum in manu sua alleluia." The second differs from the Gregorian offertory in the italicized passage: "Data sunt ei incensa multa ut *daret orationibus sanctorum alleluia.*" The third is "Ascendit fumus aromatum in conspectu domini *de manu angeli alleluia.*"

122. Levy, "Toledo, Rome," 75–77.

TABLE 2.9 *Stetit angelus* and Its Concordances

Vulgate: Apoc. 8:3	Old Hispanic Stetit	Gregorian Stetit	Roman In conspectu angeloum (Respond)
Et alius angelus venit et stetit ante altare habens turibulum aureum	(**Stetit angelus**) *{**super**}* {**aram**} *dei* habens turabulum aureum	(**Stetit angelus**) [**iuxta**]{*super*} {**aram**} ^**templi**^ habens thuribulum aureum ^**in manu sua**^	
et data sunt illi incensa multa	et ^**date**^ sunt *ei* **supplicationes multe***	et data sunt *ei* incensa multa	
ut daret orationibus sanctorum omnium super altare aureum quod est ante tronum	ut daret de orationibus sanctorum* *ad* altare **coram domino** quod est ante tronum		
et ascendit fumus	et ascendit fumus	et ascendit fumus	
incensorum de orationibus sanctorum de manu angeli coram deo	*supplicationum* de manu angeli {in conspectu dei} alleluia	^**aromatum**^ {in conspectu dei} alleluia. Verse:	
		In conspectu angelorum psallam tibi *domine et* adorabo in templum sanctum tuum et confitebor *tibi domine*	In conspectu angelorum psallam tibi *et* adorabo in templum sanctum tuum et confitebor nomini tuo *domine*

**C
{}s
[]I
^^G
()D (another mixed tradition)
Gregorian sources vary in their use of "super" or "iuxta." "Iuxta" is the majority version, but "super" is found in a few MSS included in the sampling, including RoV 52

compared with the Gregorian in table 2.9. Departures from the Vulgate are shown in boldface.[123] Among the branches of the VL Apocalypse text defined by the editor, Roger Gryson, those of greatest relevance for the chant lyric are the African

123. There are variants within the Gregorian tradition at "iuxta/super": SG 339 and Ein 121 have "super," whereas Laon 239, Chartres 47, and Ben 34 have "iuxta."

text C, witnessed in the commentaries of Primasius; the text of Tyconius, S; the European Type I, and a mixed VL/Vulgate text, G.[124] These influences are represented by symbols enclosing the word or phrases in question.

An examination of the two responds yields several observations. First, each is based closely on a biblical source. Most departures from the Vulgate are matched in at least one VL witness. The influence of the African text C is especially discernable in the Old Hispanic version, which is identical to C (and partially to the Vulgate) at "ei supplicationes multe ut daret de orationibus sanctorum." The Gregorian's "in manu sua," though rare, is found in G, a mixed text that originated in northern Italy.[125] Although the lyrics reflect gaps in the biblical text, particularly on the Gregorian side, they exhibit little evidence of extensive modification or paraphrase. Second, neither offertory corresponds fully to any of the principal VL witnesses; rather, each is based on a VL text with a mixture of characteristics, corresponding in various passages to C, S, I, and G. The Old Hispanic verses, not shown in the table, exhibit a similar mixture of traits, with a notable influence of the Tyconian Type S, a text that is mixed with the Vulgate both in the Old Hispanic liturgy and in the writings of Caesarius of Arles.[126] Third, the word variants between the two chant texts can be explained by variants among the VL witnesses: each corresponds to a different VL tradition in these passages.

On this basis, a direct relationship between the Gregorian and Old Hispanic responds is not possible to establish. The two texts share no features that are distinct from the biblical text. Where the Gregorian and Old Hispanic pieces differ in word choice, the Old Hispanic is often closer to the African text C and the Gregorian to G and the Vulgate (which also corresponds in many passages to the European type I). It is possible that the Gregorian piece is derived from a source close to that of the Old Hispanic and that the word differences reflect assimilations to a biblical text more familiar in certain parts of Gaul. The two pieces, however, are perhaps better explained as separate derivations from different VL traditions. A case for separate origin is strengthened by a look at the melodies. The Milanese melody is similar to the Old Hispanic, at least in distribution of neumatic passages and melismas. The Gregorian and Milanese pieces, however, show no discernable melodic resemblance, a situation very unusual among Gregorian-Milanese pairs. Given the thematic suitability of this passage for the censing of the altar during the offertory, it is possible that the lyricists of each tradition independently selected it for an offertory. While the use of a pre-Vulgate translation all but preludes the possibility that the Gregorian *Stetit angelus* is a new Carolingian composition, then, its origin is uncertain.

---

124. *Apocalypsis Iohannis.* Vol. 26, 2, Vetus Latina: Die Reste der Altlateinischen Bible Volume 26, part 2, ed. Roger Gryson (Freiburg: Herder, 2000), 81–96.
125. Ibid., 18, 359.
126. Ibid., 87–88.

Also unresolved is the apparent relationship between *Stetit angelus* and the Roman St. Michael offertory, *In conspectu angelorum*. As noted, the respond text of this Roman offertory is similar verbally to the verse of the Gregorian *Stetit angelus*, as shown in column 4 of table 2.9. The Roman offertory, with two verses, is found in only one Gregorian manuscript known to me, the Mont-Blandin gradual. All other Gregorian manuscripts give *Stetit angelus* as the St. Michael offertory. Both texts are based closely on the psalm verse; departures from the psalter are indicated by italics in the table. Although the two pieces are not identical, they do depart from the psalter in two of the same places; the word "et" and the "domine" at the end, present in both versions, are lacking in the psalm.[127] While these similarities suggest that Roman offertory and Gregorian verse may be cognates, the evidence is inconclusive. The presence of *In conspectu* in Mont-Blandin and in the Roman manuscripts suggests that it was the St. Michael offertory in the eighth-century Roman liturgy, an impression strengthened by its textual tradition, which matches the PsR. For unknown reasons, *In conspectu* was either inconsistently transmitted to Francia or replaced early on by *Stetit angelus*.

Finally, two other nonpsalmic offertories outside the core repertory warrant consideration because of their relevance for the Roman repertory. *Felix namque*, for Marian festivals, is based on a prayer text that also serves as an office responsory. This piece is absent from the *Antiphonale Missarum Sextuplex* graduals but found in Aquitaine, Benevento, and northern Italy. In its Aquitanian context, examined by Steiner, *Felix namque* circulates with two different verse texts and no less than four different melodies. Collectively, the melodies incorporate some new material but also share melodic substance with standard offertories such as *Factus est dominus, Stetit angelus,* and *Angelus domini*.[128] An offertory with an identical respond text and a different verse is found in northern Italian sources, and Beneventan sources transmit still a different verse.[129] Although it is not part of the core Roman-Gregorian repertory, *Felix namque*, without a verse, is written into the Roman manuscript F 22 in a different and probably later hand from the rest of the manuscript. This Roman version, part of a Votive Mass for the Virgin, adopts Formula B, one of the two common melodic formulas in the Roman repertory, as its melody. This example illustrates that foreign pieces occasionally found their way into Roman practice in the period after the tradition was transmitted to the Franks.

---

127. The Gregorian reading "confitebor tibi" rather than "confitebor nomini tuo" is not found in the psalters included in Weber's *Le psautier romain*.

128. See Ruth Steiner, "*Holocausta medullata*: An Offertory for St. Saturnius," in *De Musica et Cantu, Studien zur Geschichte der Kirchenmusik und der Oper: Helmut Hucke zum 60. Geburstag*, ed. Peter Kahn and Anne-Katrin Heimer (Hildesheim: Georg Olms Verlag, 1993), 263–74; Joseph Pothier, "L'offertoire 'Felix namque es,'" *Revue du chant grégorien* 15 (1907): 105–14, and "Offertoire 'Beata es,'" *Revue du chant grégorien* 7 (1898): 17–20.

129. On the Bolognese version, see Giampaolo Ropa, "Il culto della vergine a Bologna nel Medioevo," in *Codex Angelicus 123: Studi sul graduale-tropario Bolognese del secolo XI e sui manoscritti collegati*, ed. Maria Teresa Rosa-Barezzani and Giampaolo Ropa (Cremona: Una cosa rara, 1996), 24–26.

The Roman repertory includes one nonpsalmic offertory, *Beatus es Simon Petre*, most likely composed after the transmission of the tradition to the Franks. This chant is assigned to the Octave of Peter and Paul, which has different Mass formularies in Gregorian and Old Roman manuscripts and was most likely *vacat* in the Roman calendar when the tradition was transmitted to the Franks. The Roman formulary includes an offertory and communion that are not found in the standard Gregorian repertory. Both chants, however, circulate in Beneventan sources. *Beatus es*, with a different melody, is also found in the Bolognese RoA 123. The Roman and Beneventan melodies are borrowed from the respective versions of *Angelus domini*, a melody that also serves as the basis for several neo-Beneventan offertories.[130] The Bolognese version appears to be a contrafact of *Ave Maria*. Apart from their basis in two versions of the same chant, *Angelus domini*, the Roman and Beneventan melodies have little in common.

To summarize, several types of evidence, verbal, liturgical, and repertorial, suggest that the majority of Gregorian nonpsalmic offertories outside of the core repertory are of pre-Carolingian origin. A more thorough study of regional repertories might yield more pre-Carolingian repertory. Many of the local Aquitanian offertories studied by Steiner, Olivier Cullin, and Roman Hankeln are melodically modeled on more common pieces. While the contrafact status may suggest a Carolingian origin, the offertories most frequently used as source melodies are *Angelus domini*, *Stetit angelus*, and *Constitues eos*, all pieces of possible Gallican origin.[131] Another rich repertory of local offertories may be found in northern Italian manuscripts such as RoA 123.

The nonpsalmic offertories outside the core repertory contrast with the core offertories in some important ways. *Elegerunt*, for example, exhibits a melodic instability that is unknown among the core offertories, existing in several distinct versions.[132] Some of these offertories are inconsistent in the transmission of their verse texts. *Factus est repente*, for example, is known in northern and Beneventan versions. The northern version is witnessed in Mont-Blandin and, as Levy notes, in a gradual from Prüm dating from around 1000. Although the Prüm version is closely related melodically to the Beneventan in its respond, the two versions have different verses; even where the verses share a short passage of text, their melodies

130. See Luisa Nardini, "Il Repertorio Neo-Gregoriano del *Proprium Missae* in Area Beneventana" (Ph.D. diss, Università degli Studi di Roma, 2001), 204–21. In Beneventan manuscripts, the Gregorian melody for *Angelus domini* has an additional verse that is not found elsewhere, possibly a "neo-Gregorian" addition. I examine the Roman and Beneventan versions of *Beatus es* in chapter 3.

131. See Steiner, "*Holocausta medullata*"; Olivier Cullin, "Une pièce Gallicane conservée par la liturgie de Galliac. L'Offertoire Salvator Mundi pour les défunts," *Cahiers de fanjaeux* 17 (1982): 287–96; and Roman Hankeln, *Die Offertoriumsprosuln der aquitanischen Handschriften: Voruntersuchungen zur Edition des aquitanischen Offertoriumscorpus und seiner Erweiterungen* (Tutzing: Hans Schneider, 1996), 2:65–70.

132. Levy, "On Gregorian Orality," *Journal of the American Musicological Society* 43 (1990): 193–207.

are dissimilar.[133] Steiner has shown that the verses of *Elegerunt* vary in text as well as melody, usually according to regional tradition. Despite their different melodic traditions, most regional versions of the respond are broadly related in modal and melodic substance.[134]

These factors suggest that in the pre-Carolingian period, responds and verses sometimes circulated separately and that verses were added independently in various regions. A similar picture is evident in the Old Hispanic and Milanese versions of several offertories from the core repertory: *Oravi deum*, *Mirabilis*, and *Stetit angelus* (if it can be considered a cognate) have different verses in the Old Hispanic tradition, and *Oratio mea* has an additional verse at Milan. In the core Roman-Gregorian psalmic repertory, by contrast, there are only two instances of verses that vary by regional tradition. The differences in regional transmission among the international nonpsalmic offertories confirm the sense that the ideal of unity so prevalent in Carolingian times did not exist in the pre-Carolingian period. Moreover, the different versions of *Elegerunt* suggest that when the desire for unity did arise, it did not necessarily apply to pieces outside the core Roman-Gregorian repertory. *Elegerunt*'s various verse traditions continue to be transmitted into the twelfth century.

My examination of the offertory texts in this chapter has provided some confirmation of Levy's and Pfisterer's arguments that the offertory repertory incorporates some pieces of non-Roman origin. While the observations made thus far are limited to the texts and prehistory of these pieces, they raise pressing questions about melodic style. As noted, certain stylistic features of the Gregorian offertories, such as the long melismas with repeat structures, are also found among the Old Hispanic sacrificia and Milanese offerendae. If the Romans incorporated foreign pieces into their repertory, did they adopt the foreign melodies as well, or were the texts fully assimilated to Roman melodic style? To the musical questions I now turn.

133. *Factus est repente* has played an important role in Levy's hypothesis that a notated archetype of Gregorian chant existed at the turn of the ninth century. See Levy, "Charlemagne's Archetype," 11–25; Pfisterer, *Cantilena*, 79; Leo Treitler, "Communication," *Journal of the American Musicological Society* 41 (1988): 569; and Emma Hornby, "The Transmission of Western Chant in the Eighth and Ninth Centuries: Evaluating Kenneth Levy's Reading of the Evidence," *Journal of Musicology* 21 (2004): 450–51. The different verse texts of the two traditions would seem to cast doubt on the theory that the Beneventan version was copied from the same written archetype as the Prüm version.

134. Ruth Steiner, "On the Verses of the Offertory Elegerunt," in *The Study of Medieval Chant: Paths and Bridges, East and West: In Honor of Kenneth Levy*, ed. Peter Jeffery (Woodbridge, England: Boydell and Brewer, 2001), 283–303.

3

THE GREGORIAN AND ROMAN OFFERTORIES

Note to the reader: The melodic analyses in this chapter refer to the transcriptions available at the companion Web site to this volume, www.oup.com/us/insidetheoffertory. The username and password may be found on the copyright page. Each offertory is referenced by its incipit and number in the edition. The PDF files present the Gregorian and Roman versions on alternate pages, odd-numbered for the Gregorian version and even-numbered for the Roman. The two versions are best viewed in side-by-side format. Readers will especially need the following PDF files: 2, 4, 12, 19, 21, 26, 27, 30, 31, 36, 37, 49, 64, 67, 70, 89, and 94.

The sharp differences between the Gregorian offertories and their eleventh-century Roman counterparts present a perplexing problem that goes to the heart of the melodies' origins. The central distinction between the two traditions is a pervasive formulaicism in the Roman melodies that is lacking in the Gregorian. The Gregorian repertory includes some of the most elaborate melodies of medieval chant. With their verses, Gregorian offertories often span a combined plagal and authentic ambitus. Final verses are often marked by a heightening of range and one or more lengthy melismas. Similar characteristics may be found in some Roman melodies, but to a far lesser extent. These differences between the two traditions are especially striking in the Lenten and Paschaltide offertories, indicating that these melodies underwent change, in one dialect or both, after their separation.

This chapter employs musical analysis as a means of addressing the questions surrounding the origins of the two dialects. The basis for the comparative analysis lies not primarily in the stylistic characteristics of the two traditions but in their structural traits, such as range, melodic contour, and placement of melismas—criteria to be fully illustrated in the course of the chapter. I shall consider not only the relationship between individual Gregorian and Roman melodies but also the compositional principles that underlie each dialect. As the analysis will show, the Roman singers responded in consistent ways to verbal conditions. The close correlation between words and music suggests that the singers were guided by a complex system of syntactical rules and verbal cues that determined the structure and surface details of the melodies. The Gregorian melodies exhibit only traces of these syntactical rules. The Frankish singers were evidently guided by a broader set of constraints, such as conventions of mode, text declamation, and genre. While these constraints determine many general features of the melodies, such as modal structure, they permit far more variability in melodic detail than the Roman formulas do. Following a separate consideration of each dialect, this chapter explores some important trends that define the Gregorian and Roman cognate pairs as a whole. I will take up the significance of these patterns in chapter 5, evaluating various theories about the origins of the two dialects in the light of the musical, textual, and liturgical evidence.

THE ROMAN OFFERTORIES

The Roman offertories are stylistically diverse, particularly in their verses. Roman Advent and Christmas verses are often similar to their Gregorian counterparts, with expansive ranges, lengthy melismas, and minimal use of melodic formulas. Typical Lenten and Paschaltide verses, by contrast, exhibit an extreme melodic economy, consisting of little besides repeated statements of formulas. As I will show, the degree of resemblance between the Gregorian and Roman melodies correlates with the melodic characteristics of the Roman version. Nonformulaic Roman melodies often correspond quite closely to their Gregorian counterparts, whereas those based on formulas typically lack any resemblance to the Gregorian version. Because this trend will play a significant role in my consideration of the relationship between the two dialects, the distinction between formulaic and nonformulaic Roman melodies warrants illustration and discussion.

I begin with a close examination of some representative formulas. The tendency toward melodic stereotyping and formulaicism in the Roman offertories has been extensively illustrated by Joseph Dyer and Inge Kähmer.[1] In the work of Leo Treitler, Helmut Hucke, and Max Haas, moreover, certain Roman offertories have been presented as ideal examples of formulaic melodies operating in oral tradition.[2]

---

1. Joseph Dyer, "The Offertories of Old-Roman Chant: A Musico-Liturgical Investigation" (Ph.D. diss., Boston University, 1971), "The Offertory Chant of the Roman Liturgy and Its Musical Form," *Studi Musicali* 11 (1982): 3–20, and "*'Tropis semper variantibus:'* Compositional Strategies in the Offertories of the Old Roman Chant," *Early Music History* 17 (1998): 1–59; and Inge Kähmer, "Die Offertoriums-Überlieferung in Rom vat. lat. 5319" (Ph.D. diss., University of Cologne, 1971). Kähmer's dissertation is the first thorough demonstration known to me of the significance of text declamation in Old Roman chant. This significant contribution is referenced in very few subsequent studies.
2. Helmut Hucke, "Zur Aufzeichnung der altrömischen Offertorien," in *Ut Mens Concordet Voce: Festschrift Eugene Cardine*, ed. J. B. Göschl (St Ottilien, Germany: EOS Verlag, 1980), 296–313; Leo Treitler, "Oral, Written, and Literate Process in the Transmission of Medieval Music," *Speculum* 56 (1981): 476–80, and "Orality and Literacy in the Music of the Middle Ages," in *The Oral and Literate in Music*, ed. Tokumaru Yosihiko and Yamaguti Osamu (Tokyo: Academia Music, 1986), 40–44, and "The 'Unwritten' and 'Written Transmission' of Medieval Chant and the Startup of Musical Notation," *Journal of Musicology* 10 (1992): 139–45; and Haas, *Mündliche Überlieferung und altrömischer Choral: Historische und analytische computergestützte Untersuchungen* (Bern: Peter Lang, 1997), 82–100. Hucke's and Treitler's analyses of the formulas focus primarily on *Factus est dominus*, which is quite anomalous in its employment of Formula B.

What I hope to add to the established knowledge of the Roman formulas is the extent of their correlation between words and music, as manifest in the underlying syntactical rules that determine the word-music relationship. The analysis reveals not only where formulas and standard melodic material are employed but also the underlying processes that determine the melodic details. The consistent correlation between verbal conditions and melodic detail allows us to extract general principles from the examples and to draw inferences about the process of making the melodies. The analysis will serve as a basis for developing a model of oral transmission for the formulas and comparing the Roman melodies to their Gregorian counterparts.

DEFINING FORMULAICISM

Although many studies of the eleventh-century Roman dialect have emphasized its tendency toward melodic uniformity, illustrations of formulaicism in chant studies have often relied on an intuitive understanding of "formula," without a more precise definition. Because all chant melodies, Gregorian and Roman, rely on common tonal structures and standard turns of phrase, the more extensive use of formulas in the Roman dialect can be better illustrated by a more precise definition of terminology. In his early work on the oral transmission of chant, Treitler distinguished between "formula" and "formulaic system." Formulaic system refers to the "system of constraints of a melody or a phrase."[3] These constraints include the underlying tonal characteristics of a melody, such as its typical range and emphasized pitches. Other elements of a formulaic system may include principles of text declamation and the stylistic or formal traits of a particular genre, such as the order of standard phrases in a family of graduals or tracts. In Treitler's conception, these elements of the tradition serve as a framework through which it is learned and transmitted.[4] Treitler defined formulas as "standard passages," stereotyped realizations of the underlying formulaic system.[5]

Treitler's definition of "formula" is broadly applicable to many chant genres, including the offertory. In this study, however, I have adopted a more limited use of the word, one based in particular characteristics of the Roman offertories. All passages labeled as formulas here constitute a musical phrase, a unit with a beginning, middle, and end that normally comprises one sense unit of the text.

3. Leo Treitler, "Homer and Gregory: The Transmission of Epic Poetry and Plainchant," *Musical Quarterly* 60 (1972): 352.
4. "A formulaic system can be transmitted only through melodies, but that is not to say that the singer can only learn it as a melody. He learns one melody and he imitates its pattern in inventing another like it. At some point his inventions do not refer back to the models of concrete melodies but are based on his internalized sense of pattern." Ibid., 360.
5. Ibid., 352.

A formula is defined simply as a standard phrase that occurs, with some variation, in more than one offertory. As I will show, a formula consists of a series of small melodic segments that occur in a predictable order. In addition to complete statements of formulas, the Roman offertories also incorporate standard melismas, cadential patterns, or turns of phrase that occur independently of the full formulas. I refer to this freer use of stereotyped material simply as "standard material."

The two most common formulas in the Roman offertories are exemplified in the verses of *Domine fac mecum* (31) and *Benedic anima* (23). Following Dyer's labeling, I shall call them Formulas A and B.[6] In *Domine fac mecum*, complete statements of Formula A occur in phrases 5 ("Quia hos peccatoris") and 12 ("Pro eo ut . . .").[7] The central feature of Formula A is the torculus b-c-a (E-F-D in the lower transposition). Phrases 5 and 12 show two different ways of opening the formula: directly with the torculus, as in phrase 12, or with the opening element a/bacba, as in phrase 5. As *Domine fac mecum* illustrates, partial statements of the formula are also common. Phrases 4, 6, and 7, for example, begin with the Formula A material but continue with a different cadential pattern. Undoubtedly because of its focus on E or b, this formula is heavily concentrated in offertories of the third and fourth modes. A few examples of it, however, may also be found among eighth-mode offertories, such as *Confitebuntur* (82), and in the second-mode offertories *Expectans expectavi* (35) and *Exaudi deus* (30).

Formula B, exemplified by *Qui propitiatur*, the first verse of the second-mode offertory *Benedic anima* (ex. 3.1), occurs in offertories of all modes. The formula is tonally focused on F, as evident in the repeated F-G pes. In fifth- and eighth-mode offertories, such as *Reges tharsis* (10) and *Emitte spiritum* (59), it is written a fifth higher. Example 3.1 illustrates several characteristics of formulaic Roman offertories. First, the entire verse consists of repeated statements of Formula B, resulting in an extreme economy of melodic material. Second, each statement of the formula comprises a verbal sense unit. The melodic figure at the end of each statement, G-F-E-F-G (or the longer version in phrase 2), serves as a kind of half cadence, marking the end of the musical phrase and dividing the text into syntactical units: "Qui propitiatur omnibus iniquitatibus tuis / et redimet de interitu vitam tuam / qui coronat te in miseratione et misericordie."

In addition to Formulas A and B, the Roman offertories include a set of formulas associated with specific modes. First-mode offertories, for example,

6. Dyer, "Offertories of Old-Roman Chant," "Offertory Chant of the Roman Liturgy and Its Musical Form," and "'*Tropis semper variantibus.*'" These two formulas are also discussed in Kähmer, "Die Offertoriums-Überlieferung in Rom vat. lat. 5319," where they are labeled "Singweise 1" and "Singweise 2."

7. The cadence at the ends of these phrases is the standard one for Formula A. The torculus of Formula A is also used in combination with other standard cadential material, as in the opening phrases of verses 1 and 2 (e.g. v. 1, "tacueris"). This cadence pattern is more common in eighth-mode offertories. This freer combination of standard material, common in the repertory, has been more thoroughly demonstrated by Dyer, "'*Tropis semper variantibus.*'"

EXAMPLE 3.1 *Benedic anima* v. 1

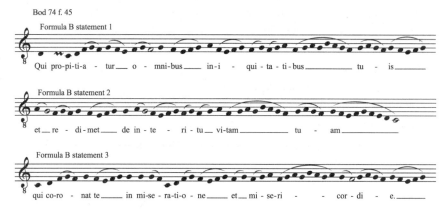

employ one recurring formula, as found in the verses of *Deus deus meus* (55) for the second Sunday of Easter and *Super flumina* (66) for the nineteenth Sunday after Pentecost. Some formulas occur in offertories of different modes. A very similar set of formulas, at different pitch levels, is employed in offertories of modes 2 and 8, and the same formulas occur a few times in fifth-mode offertories.[8] Since the formation of the repertory preceded the modal theory that was later applied to it, the figural and gestural similarity between different modes is not surprising.[9] I will discuss and illustrate several of these additional formulas in the course of this chapter.

FORMULAIC MELODIES AND SYNTACTICAL RULES

Perhaps the most salient characteristic of the Roman offertory formulas is their rigorous correlation between words and music. An illustration of this phenomenon requires a bit of detailed analysis. Returning briefly to the verse *Qui propitiatur* (ex. 3.1): it consists of three statements of Formula B. Despite the melodic economy of this verse, these three statements are not identical. The first statement, for example, begins on D; the second statement begins on a. These variants in the use of the formula are often attributable to verbal differences. In this respect, Formula B exemplifies a fundamental principle of all Roman offertory formulas: the singers respond in consistent ways to verbal conditions such as clause length and accent

8. Compare, for example, the verses of *Veritas mea* (76) and *Bonum est* (14), which close on D, to those of *Confitebor domino* (57) and the second and third verses of *Improperium* (44), which close on G, and those of the fifth-mode *Inveni* (73) and *Intende* (32), which close on F. Since the finals of these offertories do not correlate with their melodic characteristics in the Roman tradition, it is not surprising that the Gregorian readings often close on different finals (*Confitebor domino*, for example, on F, and *Inveni* on G).
9. See especially Edward Nowacki, "Reading the Melodies of the Old Roman Mass Proper: A Hypothesis Defended," in *Western Plainchant in the First Millenium: Studies in the Medieval Liturgy and Its Music*, ed. Sean Gallagher et al. (Aldershot, England: Ashgate, 2003), 319–30.

pattern. This close correlation between words and music suggests that the singers relied on a system of syntactical rules that determined the structure and surface detail of the melodies.

The key to the syntactical rules of Formula B lies in the distribution of its melodic segments. Example 3.2 shows several different statements of the formula, here divided into small segments that comprise a syllable. The goal of the segmental analysis is to establish patterns of correlation with verbal characteristics such as word accent and position in the clause.[10] Each segment plays consistent roles in the melodic syntax and delivery of the words, as indicated by the Roman numeral headings at the top of each column. The function of each melodic segment is evident in its position in the clause and its relationship to the accents in the text. Function I is preaccentual; all segments in columns labeled I serve the role of accent preparation. Function II carries the accent; segments in columns labeled II fall on an accent. Function III is postaccentual; segments under this heading fall after the accent or on the final syllable of the word. Function IV (column 9) is accent-neutral recitation on the F-G pes. This neume occurs on both accented and unaccented syllables and is repeated as often as needed to accommodate syllables remaining before the cadential pattern. Function V is precadential and may occur on either an accented or unaccented syllable. Finally, functions VI, VII, and VIII are cadential, accommodating the final three or four syllables of the clause.

The small variations between statements of the formula can typically be traced to differences in the length and accent pattern of a clause. Although it is not possible to illustrate this principle fully here, a few examples will suffice to demonstrate the types of constraints that govern the word-music relationship. At the opening of a Formula B phrase, segments representing Functions I, II, and III work together as a unit to emphasize the initial accent of the clause. The melodic segments in column 1, under the heading I, occur before the first accent and show the ways the singers accommodate different numbers of preaccentual syllables. The first accent of the clause always falls on F, as indicated in column 2. In column 3, the segments labeled A and B accommodate the syllables after the accent and always fall on the last syllable of the word. If the word is a proparoxytone, as in line 1, a single F, bistropha, or G-F clivis is given to the intervening syllable between the accent and the final syllable. The treatment of postaccentual syllables in column 3 points to a concern for shaping individual words and indicating the divisions between them.

The segments under the headings I, II, and III occur in a number of different distributional patterns. Some segments are employed only in specific verbal

10. The segmental analysis presented here was developed along the lines of David Lidov, "Lamento di Tristano," in *Music before 1600*, ed. Mark Everist (Oxford: Blackwell, 1992), 93–113. A similar approach was implicit in the work of Treitler, Hucke, and Haas (see note 2).

EXAMPLE 3.2 Statements of Formula B

contexts; others alternate as free variants in the same context.[11] At the beginning of a phrase, for example, the two syllables before the accent are always carried with the pitches C and D. When the initial accent falls on the fourth or fifth syllable, however, the treatment of additional preaccentual syllables depends on the position of the clause within the verse. If the phrase is the initial clause of a verse, additional syllables are accommodated with repeated D's (not shown in the example). Internal clauses, however, often begin from above, with the pitches a and G, as in line 3. Accented syllables under the heading II may be carried by one of two segments, F-G or F-G-F, which alternate freely in the same context. The postaccentual segments A and B, under the heading III, perform the same function but occur under slightly different conditions. Segment A, with its dip down to E, is always followed by an accented syllable, as in lines 1 and 4. Segment B, less restricted, may be followed either by an accented or unaccented syllable.

Following the opening of the phrase, segments representing Functions I, II, and III are often repeated one or two times, depending on the length of the clause. As the singer approaches the end of the clause, syllables before the cadential pattern are accommodated with Function IV, accent-neutral repetition of the pes F-G (see col. 9). Function IV is prepared in a special way. The accent that precedes it, in column 8, is always represented by segment B, which here carries the accent. In this context, moreover, the accent is approached in a different way, from the pitch a (col. 7) rather than from C and D, as it often is earlier in the phrase. This consistent treatment of the syllables preceding the accent-neutral recitation serves to signal

11. This discussion of distributional patterns is informed in a general way by concepts of structuralist linguistics. The concepts of complementary distribution, contrastive distribution, and syntactical homonymity, however, are borrowed mainly as convenient analytical tools that aptly apply to the musical phenomena of the Old Roman formulas. I am not making the claim that the formulas work exactly like a language. A clear English-language introduction to these concepts is Terence Hawkes, *Structuralism and Semiotics* (Berkeley: University of California Press, 1977).

the approach of the end of the clause and the cadential pattern.[12] In this context, accents in two-syllable words are on occasion treated as unaccented syllables ("super," line 1). Although this sequence of events always occurs toward the end of a phrase, shorter clauses sometimes begin with this material, as shown in line 5. In this respect, the length of the clause is a further constraint in adapting Formula B to different words.

The cadential pattern of Formula B further attests to the fundamental role of accent in making the melodies. The cadence takes two specific forms, depending on the accent pattern of the final words in the clause. If the final accent falls on the penult, as in lines 1, 3, and 5, segments representing Functions VI, VII and VIII are placed on the last three syllables. If the final accent is on the antepenult, as in "domine," lines 2 and 4, the initial segment of Function VI is altered, and the antepenult is accommodated with an extra G-F clivis on the accent. In terms of surface detail, the version of the cadence in lines 1 and 5 is the most common. Other segments, however, may be used interchangeably to represent functions VII and VIII, such as the alternate version of VII in line 3 and the extended version of VIII in line 4.[13]

Some segments that comprise Formula B exhibit a principle of syntactical homonymity whereby the same segment may serve more than one role in the melodic syntax. These separate functions are clearly distinguished by position and context. The segment labeled B, for example, occurs in two contexts, as indicated in columns 3 and 8. At beginning of the phrase, in column 3, segment B follows an accent. At the end of the phrase, as in column 8, it carries the accent and is always followed by recitation on the F-G pes and the cadential pattern. The single note a, moreover, serves as a preaccentual segment toward the end of the phrase, as in column 7, and as the precadential element in column 10. The distinct functions of these segments are clear from their position in the phrase, the verbal context, and the melodic material that precedes and follows.

The consistent use of melodic segments in specific verbal contexts suggests that a complex series of constraints interacted in the making of an offertory verse based on Formula B. The fundamental role of clause length and accent pattern in these melodies allows us to speculate about the processes that underlie their learning and transmission. Because of their similarity in surface detail, the melodies would have been very difficult to learn solely by rote. In a learning process model based exclusively on the traditional understanding of "rote memorization," the soloists would have encountered difficulty in distinguishing the subtle differences in detail

---

12. Haas makes the same observation in *Mündliche Überlieferung*, 88–92.
13. In a discussion of *Factus est dominus*, Treitler suggests that to some degree, the specific form of the cadence pattern responds to verbal syntax, and that closings on the focal pitch F occur at the ends of complete sentences. See Treitler, "'Unwritten' and 'Written,'" 143–44. Although this principle appears to be at work in some isolated examples, I have found no consistently applied distinction in the function of these segments.

between each statement of the formula. The close correlation between words and music suggests a reconstructive process: the underlying syntactical rules and principles would have allowed the singers to adapt the melodies to different texts without relying solely on rote memorization. The Roman formulas are consistent with the model of oral transmission proposed by Treitler. Their systematic nature allows us to envision a transmission in which the stability of the tradition was established not through adherence to a fixed, mental "text" but through the singers' adherence to traditional rules and customs.[14] It is doubtful that the singers learned these rules through a conscious effort. More plausibly, they absorbed the principles of making formulaic melodies intuitively and nonverbally, in the process of rehearsing individual instances of the formulas. The reconstructive process I have proposed should not be viewed as excluding any role for a more conventional notion of rote learning, a point I shall explore presently. The rules and principles I have observed in the formulas, moreover, raise questions about the processes involved in making nonformulaic melodies, those that lack the surface uniformity and predictability of the formulas. I will return to this issue after some further illustration of formulaic processes.

In some offertories, verbal conditions influence not only the specific melodic decisions within a formula, but the choice of formulas themselves. As an illustration, I will consider a set of formulas specific to second-mode offertories, shown in example 3.3. To indicate their association with the second mode, these formulas are labeled with the number 2 (2.1, 2.2, etc.). After demonstrating the constraints that underlie these formulas, I will consider their use in one representative offertory. Lines 1–4 show four statements of Formula 2–1.[15] The melodic segments are labeled according to their functions in the melodic syntax, which are similar to those of Formula B. This formula, however, is not quite as uniform in detail or as systematic in principle as Formula B. For example, the first two syllables before the accent, under the heading I, are usually accommodated by the pitches C and D, but if there are three or four syllables before the accent, the first two are treated with some flexibility, as shown in lines 1 and 2. As in Formula B, the same function may be carried out by several different segments. The first accent in the clause, under the heading II, is accommodated with either D-F-G-F or just F-G-F; these segments are free variants that alternate under the same conditions. The interior part of the phrase consists of an embellished repetition of F that distinguishes between accented and unaccented syllables, with F-G-F on the accent. In

14. Treitler, "Homer and Gregory," "Transmission and the Study of Music History," in *International Musicological Society: Report, Berkeley 1977* (Kassel: Barenreiter, 1981), 202–11, "Oral, Written, and Literate," "Orality and Literacy," and "'Unwritten' and 'Written.'"

15. All examples are taken from Bodmer 74, with the exception of *Bonum est*, which is from Vat 5319. The three manuscripts are very similar in their use of the formulas, with small variants within or between manuscripts. This kind of variant is illustrated in example 2.3, with Formula 2–1, with a comparison of "eius" in *Benedic anima* and "meus" in *Ad te domine*. The first starts on E and the second starts on F.

EXAMPLE 3.3 Second-mode formulas

most cases, these recitational passages in the middle of the phrase mark word boundaries with a bistropha on the final syllable of each word.

The importance of accent is also evident in the different forms of the cadential pattern. Segments under the headings VI, VII, and VIII are given to the final syllables of the clause. The first cadential form occurs when the final accent falls on the antepenult, as in lines 1 and 4, which close with "dómine" and "dóminus." When the penultimate syllable of the clause is accented, as in lines 2 and 3, a longer segment, a slightly varied combination of VI and VII, is placed on the penult. The final cadential segment, under the heading VIII, may take the form of a simple D-E-F climacus, as in line 1, or the more elaborate form in lines 2, 3, and 4. These segments are used interchangeably.

Lines 5 and 6 show two statements of Formula 2–2. This formula occurs only under specific verbal conditions, namely in clauses that conclude with two

two-syllable paroxytones in succession. These clauses close with "vías túas" and "pédes méos." The opening preaccentual syllables are accommodated with pitches C and D. The repeated climacus under the heading IV accommodates all internal syllables; accented syllables are often distinguished by an oriscus on F. The last four segments form the cadential pattern.[16] Finally, lines 7 and 8 show two statements of Formula 2–3. This formula occurs in offertories of different modes and is also tied to specific verbal conditions: it is used primarily in clauses that close with a noun, usually a three-syllable proparoxytone, followed by a possessive adjective.[17] These two clauses conclude with "animam meam" and "populos meos." Formula 2–3 shares some melodic material with Formula B, but its distinguishing feature is its treatment of these final words, which often receive a similar setting elsewhere, independently of full statements of the formula. Once again, the singers set these final two words in a way that underscores the boundaries between them: the second, unaccented syllable of the first word is given a single F or bistropha, as in Formula B. The downward motion that accommodates the final syllable of the first words, "animam" and "populos," prepares for the upward motion that emphasizes the accents on "meam" and "meos."[18]

Having given an illustration of these formulas, I will now consider their context. *Benedicite gentes* (36) illustrates the types of constraint that interact in the making of an extended melody from formulas. The Roman melody often divides the text into shorter units than the Gregorian does; some phrases in the Roman version are subdivided in their labeling for the purpose of discussion (i.e., 1a and 1b). This offertory employs nonformulaic material in phrases 1a and 5b (on "qui non amovit"); phrase 7 consists of standard melismas that occur in many second-mode offertories. The rest of the respond consists of second-mode formulas, adopted according to verbal conditions. The primary constraint in the selection of formula is the accent pattern of the final words in the clause. Phrases 1b, 2, and 4b, for example, are sung to Formula 2–2, which occurs only in clauses that end with two two-syllable paroxytones in succession.[19] Since these phrases close with the words "déum nóstrum," "láudis éius," and "pédes méos," the conditions are appropriate for Formula 2–2. Phrase 5a, however, ends with the proparoxytone "dóminus," an accent pattern not associated with Formula 2–2. The singers respond to this change by employing Formula 2–1, which may be flexibly adapted to different accent patterns.

16. This formula is found primarily in two offertories, *Benedicite gentes* (36) and *Meditabor* (22).
17. I have found only two exceptions in the repertory. In *Benedicite gentes* and *Ascendit deus*, it occurs on the words "iubilate deo."
18. This formula is also found in offertories of other modes, such as the eighth-mode *Confitebor domino* (57) ("manus tua") and *Populum humilem* (37) (on "popule meus"). It occasionally occurs in conjunction with other verbal conditions. See note 17.
19. The version of Formula 2–2 in phrase 1b differs in its opening from the instances of the formula given an example 3.3. This variant of the formula occurs when the first syllable of the clause is accented (similar to Formula 2–1).

Phrase 3a employs Formula 2–3; this formula typically occurs when the end of the clause contains a noun followed by possessive adjective. Here the singers are clearly responding to the words "animam meam," and this statement of the formula is echoed with a partial recurrence in phrase 5b, on "deprecationem meam." In phrase 3, however, the use of the formula is somewhat irregular. In Formula 2–3, the melodic segments on words "animam meam" normally serve a cadential role, marking the end of a verbal clause. In this phrase, however, the same material is placed in the middle of a sense unit, where a caesura would not ordinarily occur. The result is that the verbal clause is divided into two phrases ("qui posuit animam meam / ad vitam"), labeled 3a and 3b. Here the singers respond in a customary way to an immediate verbal cue, "animam meam," rather than considering the verbal clause as a whole. The result is that the following clause, "ad vitam" has too few syllables to accommodate a full statement of a formula.

My examination of Formula B and *Benedicite gentes* illustrates the centrality of the words in making melodies from formulas. In Formula B melodies, nearly every aspect of the musical surface was guided by established customs for matching melody and lyric. The only real exceptions are places where various segments alternate as free variants in the same context, such as the final cadential segment, G-F-E-F-G, and the slightly longer version, G-F-E-F-G-F-E-D. In *Benedicite gentes*, I have shown that most internal clauses are set to formulas associated with the second mode, and that these formulas were chosen according to the accentual conditions at the end of the clause. Within each phrase, moreover, the singers treat accented syllables and word boundaries according to conventions of the tradition.

The reconstructive model I have defined for these formulas brings to mind a question Hucke posed years ago in a preliminary study of the Roman offertories: to what extent were the singers' decisions planned out in advance and to what extent made on the spur of the moment?[20] Although I cannot fully answer this question, the analytical observations offer a partial answer. To make a verse based on Formula B, the singer must have been intimately familiar with the lyric as a whole. In most cases, the text is divided into musical phrases that correspond to the verbal syntax. We can speculate, moreover, that a strong element of preconception was involved in adapting the formula to different verbal conditions. In order to properly sing the opening and internal syllables of each clause, the singers had to consider in advance the length and accent pattern of the complete clause. In this respect, the reconstructive model I have proposed is altogether distinct from "improvisation" as it is often informally understood, in the sense of "freedom" and "license."[21]

20. "Wie weit hat der Notator seine Aufzeichnung vorgeplant und wie weit hat er bei der Aufzeichnung improvisiert?" "Zur Aufzeichnung," 306.
21. Levy mischaracterizes the reconstructive model proposed by Treitler and Hucke as "improvisation," involving "freedom" and "license." See especially *Gregorian Chant and the Carolingians* (Princeton, N.J.; Princeton University Press, 1998), 141–48; 171–77. As Hornby has pointed out,

Despite the evidence for preconception in a great majority of formulaic melodies, however, the Roman tradition does show occasional lapses in attention to syntax. In phrase 3 of *Benedicite gentes*, for example, I have shown that a passage that normally marks a caesura is placed in the middle of a sense unit, contradicting the sense construction of the clause as a whole. Here the words "animam meam" seem to have served as an immediate aural cue, taking precedence over the concern for syntax normally evident in the melodies. Similar neglect of syntax is occasionally found elsewhere in the Roman repertory.[22] A great majority of these cases are demonstrable responses to verbal cues and present in all three Roman manuscripts.[23] It is tempting to think of them as spontaneous responses to verbal cues that became consistently incorporated into performances of the melodies. The association of particular melodic phrases with specific words occasionally superseded the attention usually given to verbal syntax. As interesting as this phenomenon is, however, it is relatively rare. On the whole, the correlation between melody and syntax suggests that preconception played a fundamental role in the creation and transmission of the formulas.

IDIOMELIC ROMAN MELODIES

My classification of certain Roman melodies as nonformulaic or idiomelic requires clarification. Most Gregorian and Roman melodies show some reliance on standard material, evident especially in cadential patterns and traditional ways of opening a phrase. For my purposes, the distinction between idiomelic and formulaic melodies concerns the use of standard material on a larger scale: idiomelic Roman melodies are defined simply as those that lack a complete statement of a formula. Although they may incorporate common cadential patterns or other standard material, they lack the rigorous order and predictability of the formulas.

The respond of *Deus tu convertens* (2) for the second Sunday of Advent may serve as an example of an idiomelic Roman melody. It is similar in tonal structure to others of the third mode, consisting primarily of oscillation between G and c.

---

this characterization has served as something of a straw man in many of Levy's essays on the subject. See Emma Hornby, "The Transmission of Western Chant in the Eighthand Ninth Centuries: Evaluating Kenneth Levy's Reading of the Evidence," *Journal of Musicology* 21 (2004): 418–57. The characterization obscures differences in the terminology and thinking of Treitler and Hucke: Hucke does use the term "free improvisation," but Treitler uses the term "improvisation" only with qualification. Levy and Treitler, in fact, share the view that the chant melodies were stabilized before they were written down.

22. See, for example, the discussion of *Desiderium* below. In Formula B melodies, there are several other instances. Unexpected divisions of the text occur twice—for example, in *In conspectu angelorum* (93) ("quoniam exaudisti omnia / verba oris mei" and "quoniam audierunt omnia / verba oris tui").

23. Another instance of the same phenomenon with Formula 2–3 occurs in the third verse of *Bonum est* (14), where the words "oculus tuus" occur in the middle of a sense unit.

Moreover, it incorporates several standard turns of phrase, like the cadential patterns on "te" (phrase 2) and "tuam" (phrase 3). The melodic segment that recurs on the first syllables of "convertens" and "vivificabis" (phrase 1) is a common element of the melodic vocabulary, and the segment on "plebs" (phrase 2) is a typical way of starting a phrase. On the whole, however, the surface details of the melody are distinctive. Although small melodic figures recur, they do not do so in a predictable, systematic series.

The presence of idiomelic material in the Roman melodies raises questions about its implications for the reconstructive theory I have proposed. The most persuasive illustrations of reconstructive models in chant scholarship have been based on formulaic melodies. Treitler demonstrates the processes with reference to second-mode graduals and Roman offertories.[24] The compatibility of the reconstructive paradigm with formulaic chants is further revealed in penetrating analyses of antiphons, tracts, and responsories by Edward Nowacki, Emma Hornby, and Kate Helsen. By examining particular instances of melodic types in relation to others of the same family, they show that variants between individual chants are often dependent on the texts or other controlling factors.[25] The nonformulaic Roman offertories, however, exhibit distinctive melodic details that cannot be predicted according to a discernable system of rules. The same holds in the Gregorian offertories and other nonformulaic genres. Understandably, these melodies have aroused skepticism toward reconstructive processes in chant transmission. Levy has gone so far as to propose entirely different memory processes for formulaic and nonformulaic melodies.[26] The stability of the written tradition on the Gregorian side has stimulated further resistance to a reconstructive paradigm.[27] Most scholars, in fact, agree that the melodies of the core repertory had gained a certain degree of stability by the time they were notated, and the Roman manuscripts are consistent with this view. The three sources transmit essentially the same melodies; significant variants between them, while present, are not the norm.[28]

It is clear that any theory to explain the oral transmission of chant must consider both the prominence of individual melodic detail and the stability of the written tradition. The idiomelic features of the chant melodies suggest that an

---

24. See notes 2 and 3.
25. Edward Nowacki, "Studies on the Office Antiphons of the Old Roman Manuscripts" (Ph.D. diss., Brandeis University, 1980), "The Gregorian Office Antiphons and the Comparative Method," *Journal of Musicology* 4 (1985): 243–75, and "Text Declamation as a Determinant of Melodic Form in the Old Roman Eighth-Mode Tracts," *Early Music History* 6 (1986): 193–255; Emma Hornby, *Gregorian and Old Roman Eighth-Mode Tracts: A Case Study in the Transmission of Western Chant* (Aldershot, England: Ashgate, 2002); Kate Eve Helsen, "The Great Responsories of the Divine Office: Aspects of Structure and Transmission," Ph.D. diss. Universität Regensburg, 2008.
26. Levy terms them "referential memory" and "associative memory." See *Gregorian Chant and the Carolingians* (Princeton, N.J.: Princeton University Press, 1998), 195–213.
27. See especially David Hughes, "Evidence for the Traditional View of the Transmission of Gregorian Chant," *Journal of the American Musicological Society* 40 (1987): 377–404.
28. See, for example, the critical notes for *Desiderium (89)* and *Scapulis suis (19)*.

element of rote learning came into play. Yet any sharp distinction between "rote learning" and "reconstruction" is an artificial one. In invoking rote learning to explain the transmission and stability of the idiomelic melodies, I do not mean that formulaic and nonformulaic melodies were learned and remembered by entirely different processes, nor do I intend to posit a model of "memorization" or "rote learning" that stands in opposition to "reconstruction." Cognitive psychologists have shown that all memory is reconstructive; memorization and reconstruction cannot be distinguished in any absolute sense.[29] In a less formal way, however, we can think of them as points on a spectrum. The continuity between memorization and reconstruction is evident in both formulaic and nonformulaic melodies. Although the singers may have employed "rote learning" in assimilating some individual details of nonformulaic melodies, we can assume that this process was supported by their knowledge of the chant tradition, their internalized sense of the way a melody in that tradition should properly proceed. Certain principles of tonal structure and text declamation are evident in both formulaic and nonformulaic melodies. The idiomelic *Deus tu convertens* (2), for example, shares some general traits with other third-mode melodies, such as a tendency to hover around the tenor c and remain primarily within the tetrachord G-c. Moreover, it employs standard cadential patterns associated with third- and eighth-mode offertories. In the second mode, nonformulaic melodies are similar to formulaic ones in tonal structure, focusing primarily on the third D-F. Furthermore, they often share broad principles of text declamation with the formulaic melodies. At the beginnings of phrases, the pitches C and D often serve the role of accent preparation, accented syllables fall on the tenor F, and longer melismas are usually placed on accented syllables. As I will show, these shared features are present in many Gregorian versions of these melodies.[30] These general principles of tonal structure and text declamation would have provided the singers with a framework for learning and remembering the distinctive melodic details of the tradition.

The stability of the written sources can perhaps be viewed as another index of the inseparability of memorization and reconstruction. The similarities between the two Roman manuscripts that transmit verses, Bod 74 and Vat 5319, extend to the ways they use the formulas. The two sources are often alike even at points were Formula B was subject to some flexibility, such as the selection of interchangeable melodic segments to represent certain functions. Although the two manuscripts do

---

29. In F. C. Bartlett's often-cited formulation, "Memorization is not the re-excitation of innumerable fixed, lifeless, and fragmentary traces. It is an imaginative reconstruction, or construction, built out of the relation of our attitude towards a whole active mass of organized past reactions and experiences, and to a little outstanding detail which commonly appears in image or in language form." F. C. Bartlett, *Remembering: A Study in Experimental and Social Psychology* (London: Cambridge University Press, 1932), 213. For a review of cognitive research since Bartlett, see David Rubin, *Memory in Oral Traditions: The Cognitive Psychology of Epics, Ballads, and Counting-Out Rhymes* (New York: Oxford University Press, 1995), 21–37.

30. See especially the discussion of the Gregorian version of *Benedicite gentes* later.

occasionally differ in certain details, such as their choice of cadential material, the extent of their correspondence suggests that either the tradition had attained some fixity by the time the manuscripts were written down or that the two manuscripts descend from a common written source—most likely, both. The reconstructive model I have proposed for the Roman formulas, then, certainly does not preclude an element of rote learning. By the same token, the idiomelic melodies are not entirely free from the types of constraints that govern the formulaic melodies. The difference between the formulaic and nonformulaic melodies lies not in sharply distinct approaches to creating and remembering them but simply in the degree of stereotyping present in their surface details.

GREGORIAN OFFERTORIES

Gregorian offertories exhibit a great stylistic diversity, ranging from neumatic items in a reiterative style, focused around F or c, to ornate and wide-ranging ones. The Gregorian melodies lack the melodic formulas found in their Roman counterparts; the melodies are so individual, in fact, that a complete assessment of their style would require a look at numerous individual examples. The general characteristics of the Gregorian offertories, however, have been introduced in several standard works of reference and need only be reviewed here.[31] My objective in summarizing these traits here is to draw attention to some important points of similarity and contrast with the Roman offertories. Although my primary criteria for investigating the relationship between the two dialects are structural rather than stylistic, the similarities and contrasts in style between the two traditions will form a context for examining their structural relationship in greater detail.

Gregorian responds and first verses show a preference for the plagal modes, with an expansion to the corresponding authentic mode in the final verse. The respond and first verse of *Tollite portas* (6), for example, are in a narrow plagal range, focusing on D and F, with a typically neumatic texture. The reiteration of F is a trait found in many offertories. This repercussive style, creating a tonal focus on F or c, is especially common in responds and first verses. The second verse of *Tollite portas*, which begins with phrase 6, expands into the corresponding authentic range; the opening leap from D to a and subsequent emphasis on the third a-c are typical of the first mode.[32] A similar modal expansion is evident in some Roman offertories,

31. For example, Willi Apel, *Gregorian Chant* (Bloomington: Indiana University Press, 1958), 363–74; and David Hiley, *Western Plainchant: A Handbook* (Oxford: Clarendon Press, 1993), 121–30.
32. Although the heightening of range in final verses is an important aesthetic attribute of the offertory, the issue of ambitus is more complex than it first appears. The offertories exhibit many variants in their notated pitch level, beginning with the earliest pitch-readable manuscripts. These variants are discussed in the preface to the edition and in the commentary of appendix 3. A compelling recent study dealing with this issue in the Aquitanian manuscripts is Roman Hankeln, *Die Offertoriumsprosuln der aquitanischen Handschriften: Voruntersuchungen zur Edition*

but to a far lesser extent. Roman offertories exhibit these characteristics primarily in the Advent and Christmas offertories, such as *Tollite portas*. Verses of the later seasons, by contrast, are based primarily on the melodic formulas I have examined.

In many final verses, the climactic effect of the heightened range is enhanced with one or more lengthy melismas, typically placed at the end of the final verse. A common feature of offertory melismas is the presence of various repeat structures. The AAB form in the closing melisma of *Deus tu convertens* (2), for example, is found in many other melismas (see phrase 10). The melismas are occasionally subject to variants in structure between manuscripts. In *Tollite portas*, for example, the final melisma of the second verse (phrase 7) has a threefold statement of its opening material in the Beneventan tradition, whereas in the majority of other sources, it has a more typical twofold statement. Offertory melismas often share melodic material with one another, and occasionally the same melisma circulates among two or more offertories.[33] Although similar melismas are found in some Roman offertories, they occur with less frequency and melodic variety. In the Gregorian, for example, the closing melisma of *Deus tu convertens* is found in one other offertory, *Domine exaudi* (47). In the Roman tradition, the corresponding melisma occurs here and in two additional offertories, each sung in close liturgical proximity to *Deus tu convertens* or *Domine exaudi*.[34]

Another characteristic of many Gregorian offertories that broadly links them to the Roman is repetition and reuse of melodic material. Although the tendency toward repetition often results in musical unity, repetition does not occur in a prescribed order or result in a set form. In the offertory *Confirma hoc* (60), for example, much of the third verse is a restatement of material from the first and second verses. In *Iubilate deo universa* (12), for the second Sunday of Epiphany, restatement and repetition serve to underscore another distinctive trait of the genre: the repetition of short passages of text. The most audible and effective instances of melodic restatement in this long, elaborate offertory occur at points of structural importance. The openings of the respond and final verse, for example, are melodically similar (compare phrases 1 and 10); the closing melismas of the two verses share their opening and closing material but vary in the middle (compare phrases 9 and 12).

des aquitanischen Offertoriumscorpus und seiner Erweiterungen (Tutzing: Hans Schneider, 1999). For earlier studies, see Hubert Sidler, "Studien zu den alten Offertorien mit ihren Versen" (Ph.D. diss., University of Fribourg, 1939); Grover Allen Pittman, "The Lenten Offertories of the Aquitainian Manuscripts" (Ph.D. diss., Catholic University of America, 1973); Cheryl Crawford Frasch, "Notation as a Guide to Modality in the Offertories of Paris, B.N. lat. 903" (Ph.D. diss., Ohio State University, 1986); Dean Richard Justmann, "Mode-One Offertories: A Critical Edition with Analysis" (Ph.D. diss., Northwestern University, 1988).

33. The melisma that closes the final verse of *Deus tu convertens*, for example, is also found in *Domine exaudi* (47), and *Laetamini* (79) and *Confitebor tibi* (39) share the melisma at the opening of the first verse.

34. See *Exulta satis* (5) for Ember Saturday and *Custodi me* (46) for Tuesday of Holy Week.

The many text repetitions in *Iubilate deo universa* are marked by melodic returns, varied and expanded to add rhetorical emphasis. In the respond, for example, the repeat of the opening words is given weight by the lengthy melisma on the second statement of "iubilate" (phrase 1). This melisma is unusual in its wide range, which consists of an octave plus a fourth. What follows on "deo universa terra," however, is a melodic return of the first statement of these words, with a melismatic expansion on "terra." A similar technique of expanded repetition is employed in each of the two verses, as evident in phrases 7–8 and 10–11. The tendency to set the same words to the same music is manifest throughout the repertory, a phenomenon I will explore more fully in the course of this chapter.

For the purpose of contrast with *Iubilate deo omnis*, I will examine a representative example of a less ornate offertory, a type often found in the Lenten repertory. With a few exceptions, Lenten responds and first verses are neumatic and narrow in range, and often in a reiterative style, with an extensive focus on c or F.[35] Although the Gregorian versions lack the surface uniformity that characterizes the Roman formulas, they exhibit their own sort of melodic economy, drawing on a vocabulary of small melodic segments and cadential patterns that are shared among different offertories. Their final verses, like those of most Gregorian offertories, are often marked by an expansion of range and a lengthy closing melisma.

As an example of these traits, consider the fourth-mode *Domine fac mecum* (31), for Wednesday of the third week in Lent, transposed in the Beneventan reading to end on b. The respond and first two verses have a narrow range defined primarily by the third a-c. The pitches b and c serve as the primary tonal focus. In a feature typical of many Lenten offertories, *Domine fac mecum* shows a tendency toward repetition and reuse of melodic material. The melodic material on the words "propter nomen tuum" in the respond (phrase 2), for example, is echoed (with small variants) at the end of the second verse (on "ego autem orabam," phrase 13). Much of the melodic substance of verse 1, moreover, recurs in verse 3. "Detrahebant michi" in verse 3 (phrase 12), for example, is very similar to "ne tacueris" in verse 1 (phrase 4). Gregorian Lenten offertories also exhibit a tendency to set the same words to the same music. In the respond of *Domine fac mecum*, for example, the words "misericordiam tuam" and "misericordia tua," in phrases 1 and 3, receive nearly identical settings of the last four syllables. This penchant for melodic repetition and word-music parallelism is also found in the Roman offertories, which attests to a broad similarity between the two dialects. Both phenomena, however, occur with far more frequency in the Roman tradition, a trend I shall consider in some depth.

Another feature of the Gregorian Lenten offertories that is reminiscent of the Roman tradition is their use of a fund of melodic material common to different

---

35. With the exception of third- and fourth-mode offertories, which adopt b as a focal pitch in the Beneventan tradition, reflecting the older preference for b as the third-mode reciting tone. This preference, for example, is evident in the Beneventan version of *Domine fac mecum*, discussed below.

offertories. Although the Gregorian Lenten offertories lack the formulas of their
Roman counterparts, many share a vocabulary of small melodic segments and
cadential patterns that articulate the narrow range of a third or fourth. Much of the
material in *Domine fac mecum*, for example, is found among other Lenten offertories. The opening passage of the respond is nearly identical to that of the third-
mode *Domine vivifica* (18), perhaps a response to the identical opening word. The
material that occurs on "miseri*cordiam tuam*" and "miseri*cordia tua*" (phrases 1 and
3) recurs in several other Lenten offertories of various modes and often has a
particular association with these words.[36] Finally, the recurring material on "propter nomen" (phrase 2), "quia os pecca[toris] (phrase 5), and "ego autem" (phrase
13) is a common way of opening a phrase. In a typical pattern, *Domine fac mecum*
has one verse, *Locuti sunt* (beginning with phrase 7), that presents a sharp contrast
in range and modal structure with the respond and other verses.[37] The opening of
the verse calls to mind many first-mode chants. As noted, this modal expansion and
contrast is lacking in a great majority of Roman Lenten and Paschaltide offertories.

To a certain extent, the stylistic traits of the Gregorian offertories vary by
liturgical season. While the neumatic, recitational style of *Domine fac mecum* is
typical of Lenten offertories, Advent, Christmas, and Paschaltide offertories are
often more elaborate, incorporating long melismas. The Lenten offertories, however, do include several melodies of this more elaborate sort, especially in the final
weeks of the season, including *Sperent in te* (41), and *Factus est dominus* (38),
Wednesday of Passion Week's *Eripe me . . . deus* (42), and Palm Sunday's *Improperium* (44). The stylistic distinction between the neumatic melodies with a narrow
range and the more elaborate ones with a wider range has potential importance in
considering the relationship and relative historical position of the Gregorian and
Roman dialects. Although the Gregorian offertories lack the formulas of the
Roman versions, some examples do share very general melodic characteristics
with the Roman formulas. As I will show, these shared characteristics are evident
primarily in the neumatic Gregorian melodies; the more elaborate Gregorian
offertories often contrast sharply with the Roman formulas.

DEFINING SIMILARITY AND DIFFERENCE

Some of the central observations in this study revolve around the degree of
similarity between the Gregorian and Roman versions. Defining similarity and
difference is, to some extent, a matter of judgment. When judgment serves as the

36. It occurs on the same words, for example, in *Miserere mihi* (26) in phrase 2 and *Domine vivifica*
    (18) in phrase 4. I discuss this passage and its importance further below.
37. The order of the verses *Locuti* and *Pro eo* is sometimes reversed in Gregorian sources. The order
    presented here reflects both the Roman and Beneventan traditions, as well as the Mont-Blandin
    Gradual.

basis for hypothesis and argument, it needs to rest on clearly defined and consistently followed criteria. My criteria for comparison are informed by the often-cited stylistic differences between the two dialects. As a general rule, the Roman version of a chant is more ornate than the Gregorian and tends toward stepwise motion. These stylistic preferences typically result in differences of surface detail between cognate pairs. Although surface similarities do occur, they are usually brief. Affinity between the two traditions is more often manifest in underlying structural traits: range, tonal structure, melodic contour, and the distribution of neumatic passages and melismas. Despite stylistic differences, then, the two versions can often be seen as different realizations of the same underlying musical structure, with the surface details of the melodies determined by dialectical preference.

For these reasons, it is the structural characteristics of the melodies, on a phrase-by-phrase basis, that serve as the principal criteria for evaluating the degree of resemblance between the two versions of a melody. I define tonal structure in terms of the pitches that are most consistently emphasized through repetition or embellishment, those adopted as cadential pitches, and the intervals that serve as a focal point of the melodic activity. A similarity of contour and placement of neumatic passages and melismas is taken as further evidence of continuity, allowing for the generally more ornate style of Roman chant.

A look at a few examples will help to clarify the distinction between structural and stylistic traits and the criteria for comparison. Let us return briefly to the respond of the Advent offertory *Deus tu convertens* (2). In the opening phrase ("deus tu convertens vivificabis nos"), the two versions show structural similarity. The focus of the melodic activity lies within the narrow range of the fourth G-c, with much embellished repetition of c. In their localized realizations of this underlying structure, however, the two versions are quite different. The differences are manifest on a syllable-by-syllable basis, as, for example, in the number of times they dip from c to G, and in the specific places they do so. To some extent, these differences are determined by dialectical preference: the Gregorian focuses more extensively on the tenor and the Roman more frequently dips down to a or G. In several passages of *Deus tu convertens*, the Roman also exhibits a typical tendency toward ornateness and stepwise motion, as on the standard cadential figure on "in te" (phrase 2), the melisma on "ostende" (phrase 3), and throughout phrases 3 and 4. Because these dialectical differences between the two versions are present in nearly every passage of every offertory, they offer no basis on which to posit meaningful degrees of similarity and difference. More significant criteria reside in the structural characteristics of the phrase as a whole. I consider the two versions of this opening phrase to be similar in tonal structure because both articulate the tetrachord G-c, consist largely of repetition or embellishment of c, and cadence on E. A further index of resemblance is the similarity in contour at the beginning of the melisma "nos." The four criteria for judging similarity—range, tonal structure, contour, and placement of melismas—interact in judging the two versions of the phrase as similar.

The application of the criteria for similarity on a phrase-by-phrase basis, rather than syllable-by-syllable, allows for passing differences between cognate pairs. I regard dissimilarities as passing when they comprise less than three or four syllables. At the opening of the second phrase of *Deus tu convertens*, "et plebs tua letabitur in te" (phrase 2), the two versions show a passing dissimilarity in range, where the Gregorian begins on E and the Roman on a. Here the Roman version adopts a standard phrase opening and shows a corresponding lack of similarity to the Gregorian version. On the whole, however, the two phrases are similar in their articulation of the tetrachord G-c and their placement of a melisma on the final syllable of "tua." Because the more ornate surface texture of the Roman version, manifest especially at the cadential figure on "te," is a stylistic trait found in nearly every cognate pair, it is not taken as a significant index of difference.

Certain passages of *Tollite portas* (6) illustrate what I view as significant differences between the two versions. In terms of melismatic density, the Roman version has several longer melismas that are completely lacking in the Gregorian: on the final syllables of "porte" and "eternales" (phrase 2) and on the penultimate syllable of "introibit" (phrase 3). The two readings, moreover, differ in range and contour on "porte," and on the final two syllables of "eternales," (phrase 2) where Roman articulates the tetrachord D-G and the Gregorian extends up to b (flat).

A comparative analysis of the repertory has yielded a number of patterns: resemblance between the two versions of a melody often correlates with its placement in the liturgical calendar, its status as a respond or verse, and the melodic characteristics of the Roman version. As a convenient way of illustrating these patterns in summary form, I place each respond and verse into one of five categories, depending on the degree of similarity between the Gregorian and Roman version. Responds and verses in category 1 display the closest relationship. The two versions correspond in range and contour on a phrase-by-phrase basis and occasionally resemble one another in surface detail. Although the Gregorian and Roman readings in category 1 are generally similar in neumatic density and placement of melismas, they do diverge at times, particularly at cadences, where the Roman tendency toward ornateness is especially prevalent.

Because category 1 is reserved for cognate pairs that show the closest resemblance, examples of it are relatively rare. *Deus tu convertens* is one of only eighteen offertory responds of the core repertory in this category.[38] Despite their dialectical differences on a syllable-by-syllable basis, the two readings show an unmistakable affinity. In both versions, for example, phrase 1 opens on G, moves to c, and ends on E. Moreover, both versions place longer melismas on "nos" (phrase 1) and "da" (phrase 4). As previously noted, the two readings also correspond in their internal

---

38. A nineteenth, *Domine Iesu* (92), was added to the Roman repertory after the transmission of the tradition to the Franks, and is not part of the core repertory.

cadences: the first phrase concludes with a cadence on E ("nos"), phase 2 with a cadence on G ("te"), and phrase 3 with a cadence on D ("tuam").

Melodies in category 2 also exhibit specific points of similarity between cognate pairs, but contain one or more longer passages that are dissimilar in range, contour, or placement of melismas. According to these criteria, I have shown that the two versions of the respond *Tollite portas* (6) diverge in phrases 2 and 3. In other passages, however, they display a noticeable resemblance according to all three criteria. In both versions, the melisma on "vestras" (phrase 1) spans from G downward to C or D, and the melisma on "elevamini" (phrase 2) spans from a downward to D. A similarity of contour is particularly evident in the melisma on "elevamini," where both versions ascend from F to a and descend to D by stepwise motion. The affinity between the two versions is also manifest in their second-mode tonal characteristics, articulating the third between D and F. In short, melodies assigned to category 2 show evidence of descent from a common tradition, but evidently underwent some change in their underlying structural characteristics subsequent to the separation of the two dialects.

Gregorian and Roman cognate pairs in category 3 exhibit a general similarity in range and tonal structure but show only traces of specific similarity. The two readings of the Lenten respond *Scapulis suis* (19), for example, share aspects of tonal structure despite their different finals, remaining mainly in the range of the fourth G-c. In most passages, however, they are quite divergent in contour and placement of melismas. In phrase 1, the Roman version is far more ornate than the Gregorian, and the two versions are sharply different in contour. The second syllable of "tibi," for example, is articulated with downward motion in the Gregorian version and upward motion in the Roman. Through "obumbravit," the Roman version is verbally and melodically identical to the Roman communion sung on the same day, *Scapulis suis*; the Gregorian melody differs from that of the corresponding Gregorian communion. The cadence of phrase 1 ("dominus"), along with the final cadence of the respond (phrase 3), falls on G in the Gregorian version and E in the Roman. The respond is in category 3 because the two versions show traces of a closer resemblance in phrases 2 and 3, with a similar contour on "eius sperabis" (where both have a cadence on b typical of the *deuterus* modes) and "scuto." The two versions of this respond may descend from a common melodic tradition, but if so, the melody underwent substantial change after the separation of the two dialects.

Gregorian and Roman melodies in category 4 share a broad tonal similarity but lack evidence of a more specific continuity. This category is exemplified by the Lenten respond *Miserere mihi* (26). Although the two readings close on different finals, both remain primarily within the range of the fourth G-c. Each version adopts a melodic vocabulary shared with other Lenten offertories in its own tradition, but the two show little or no specific correspondence and close on different finals. Although stylistic differences have not been employed as a criterion for categorization, it is worth noting that the typical stylistic distinctions between the two traditions are especially pronounced in this offertory: the Roman is far more ornate than the Gregorian, and the Gregorian exhibits more frequent repercussions on the tenor c.

Finally, verses and responds in category 5 lack even the broadest similarity in tonal structure. Most melodies assigned to this category are verses that exhibit a stark contrast between the two traditions, such as the third and final verse of the Lenten offertory *Benedicite gentes* (36), which begins in phrase 15. The Gregorian version begins as typical first-mode melody, with a range expanding from D to a and c. The Roman, by contrast, is based on repeated statements of Formula B. The two versions show no traces of a common origin.

Throughout this chapter, I will employ these categories as a way of conveniently illustrating patterns characteristic of the repertory as a whole. The categories themselves, of course, are not inherent properties of these melodies, and for this reason assigning the melodies to categories can hardly be an undertaking of absolute precision. My primary goal in the process of categorization has been to state the criteria clearly and to follow them consistently. It is unlikely that every reader will agree with every decision, and readers may make their own assessments using the side-by-side transcriptions provided. Since the melodies were not made to fit into these categories, there are bound to be gray areas between them. *Miserere mihi* is a case in point. I have assigned it to category 4, indicating that the two versions show only a general similarity in tonal structure and not a more specific similarity. Both versions, however, begin on G and move in stepwise motion to c on the second syllable. I have not judged this point of similarity as significant enough to move the melody to category 3, for two reasons. First, it is an isolated occurrence consisting of only a few notes; second, it is such a common way of opening a phrase in third- and eighth-mode chants that the two traditions could have arrived at this opening independently of one another. The remainder of the melody lacks sufficient resemblance to indicate that the two descend from a common tradition. Having illustrated the criteria for judging similarity and difference, I now turn to a closer comparative analysis.

GREGORIAN AND ROMAN MELODIES: AN OVERVIEW

The relationship between the Gregorian and Roman offertories is defined by important trends that emerge only on consideration of the repertory as a whole. To facilitate this overview, table 3.1 summarizes the degree of similarity between the Gregorian and Roman versions and the placement of formulas in the Roman repertory. Each respond and verse is placed in a separate column, with reference to the categories just illustrated. The melodic characteristics of the Roman reading are summarized by the parenthetical letters and numbers that follow each respond and

TABLE 3.1 Resemblance between Gregorian and Roman Versions

Liturgical Assignment	Category 1	Category 2	Category 3	Category 4	Category 5
1. Advent I	v 1. Dirige (NF)	Ad te domine (NF, 2) v 2 Respice (NF)			
2. Advent II	Deus tu Convertens (NF)	v 1 Benedixisti (NF) v 2 Misericordia (NF)			
3. Advent III		Benedixisti (NF) v 1 Operuisti (NF)	v 2 Ostende (NF)		
4. Ember Wednesday		Confortamini (NF) v 1 Tunc (NF) v 2 Audite (NF)			
5. Ember Saturday	Exsulta satis (NF)		v 1 Loquetur (NF) v 2 Quia (NF)		
6. Christmas Vigil		Tollite portas (NF) v 2 Ipse (NF)	v 1 Domini (NF, 2)		
7. Christmas I	Laetentur (NF)	v 1 Cantate (NF, A) v 2 Cantate (NF, A)			
8. Christmas II		Deus enim (NF)	v 1 Dominus (NF) v 2 Mirabilis (NF, 8)		

(continued)

TABLE 3.1 (continued)

Liturgical Assignment	Category 1	Category 2	Category 3	Category 4	Category 5
9. Christmas III	Tui sunt (NF, A)	v 3 Tu humiliasti (NF)	v 1 Magnus et metuendus (NF)	v 2 Misericordia (NF)	
10. Epiphany			Reges tharsis (NF, 2)	v 1 Deus (NF, 2)	v 2 Suscipiant (B) v 3 Orietur (B)
11. Epiphany I/II			Iubilate deo omnis (NF, 2)	v 1 Ipse fecit (2)	v 2 Laudate (B)
12. Epiphany I/II		Iubiliate deo universa (NF) v 1 Reddam (NF), v 2 Locuti (NF)			
13. Dominica III		Dextera domini (NF, 2)	v 1 In tribulatione (2)	v 2 Inpulsus (NF, 1)	
14. Septuagesima					Bonum est (NF, 2) v 1 Quam (2) v 2 Ecce (2) v 3 Exaltabitur (2)
15. Sextagesima		Perfice (NF, A)			v 1 Exaudi (A) v 2 Custodi (A) v 3 Ego (A)
16. Quinquagesima			Benedictus es . . . in labiis (NF)		v 1 Beati (NF) v 2 In via (NF) v 3 Viam (NF)
17. Wednesday		Exaltabo (NF, 2) v 1 Domine (NF, 2)			v 2 Ego (NF, 2)

18. Friday		Domine vivifica (NF)		v 1 Fac cum (8) v 2 Da mihi (8)	
19. Lent I		v 3 Super (NF) Levabo (NF)	Scapulis (NF)	v 1 Dicet (NF)	v 2 Quoniam (A)
20. Monday		v 1 Illumina (2, B)	v 1 Legem (8)	v 2 Veniant (8)	
21. Tuesday	In te speravi (NF)				v 2 Quam magna (B, NF)
22. Wednesday	Meditabor (NF, 2)			v 1 Pars mea (NF, 2)	v 2 Miserere (NF, 2)
23. Friday					Benedic anima (NF, 2) v 1 Qui propitiatur (B) v 2 Iusticia (B)
24. Lent II		Domine deus (NF) v 1 Inclina (8, A)			v 2 Factus (NF, A, 8)
25. Monday		Benedicam (NF)	v 1 Conserva (NF)	v 2 Notas (NF, 1)	
26. Tuesday				Miserere (NF) v 1 Quoniam (A)	v 2 Tibi (A)
27. Friday			Domine in auxilium (B, 6)	v 1 Avertantur (B, 6)	v 2 Expectans (B, 6)
28. Saturday		Illumina (NF)	v 1 Usquequo (NF)	v 2 Respice (NF)	
29. Lent III		Iustitiae (B, 6)		v 1 Preceptum (B, 6)	v 2 Et erunt (B, 6)
30. Monday	Exaudi deus (NF)		v 2 Ego (NF)		v 1 Conturbatus (A)

(continued)

TABLE 3.1 (continued)

Liturgical Assignment	Category 1	Category 2	Category 3	Category 4	Catgory 5
31. Wednesday		Domine fac (NF)	v 1 Deus (A, 8, NF)	v 3 Pro eo (A, 8, NF)	v 2 Locuti (A, 8, NF)
32. Friday		v 1 Verba (NF 8)	Intende voci (NF)	v 2 Dirige (8)	
33. Saturday		v 2 Cognovi (NF)	Gressus (NF) v 1 Declaratio (8, NF)		
34. Lent IV	Laudate (NF, 2)				v 1 Qui (B) v 2 Domine (B) v 3 Qui timetis (B)
35. Tuesday					Expectans (A) v 1 Multa (A) v 2 Domine (A)
36. Wednesday		Benedicite (2, NF)		v 1 Iubililate (2)	v 2 In multitudine (2) v 3 Venite (B)
37. Friday		Populum (NF)			v 1 Clamor (B) v 2 Liberator (B)
38. Saturday					Factus est (B, 6) v 1 Persequar (B, 6) v 2 Precinxisti (B, 6)
39. Lent V		Confitebor tibi[2] (NF) v Viam (NF, 1)			
40. Monday		Domine convertere			v 2 Miserere (B, 6)

41. Tuesday	(B, 6) v 1 Domine (B, 6)			Sperent (B, 6) v 2 Cognovi (B, 6)
42. Wednesday	Eripe me . . . deus (NF) v 1 Quia ecce (NF)	v 2 Quia factus (NF, 8)		
43. Friday		Benedictus es . . . non tradas (NF, 8) v 1 Vidi (A)		v 2. Appropin-quaverunt (A, 8)
44. Palm Sunday	Improperium (NF)		v 1 Salvum (NF) v 2 Adversus (NF, 8)	v 3 Ego vero (NF, 8)
45. Monday	Eripe . . . domine (NF)[3]			v 1 Exaudi (NF, A) v 2 In factis[4] (NF, A)
46. Tuesday	Custodi (NF)			v 1 Dixi (NF) v Qui cogitaverunt (A, NF)
47. Wednesday		Domine exaudi (NF) v 1 Ne avertas (NF)		v 2 Tu exurgens (A)
48. Easter		Terra tremuit (NF) v 2 Et factus (NF, A)	v 1 Notus (NF)	v 2 Ibi (NF, A)

(continued)

TABLE 3.1 (*continued*)

Liturgical Assignment	Category 1	Category 2	Category 3	Category 4	Category 5
49. Monday			Angelus (NF) v 2 Iesus (NF, 8) Intonuit (NF)	v 1 Euntes (NF, 8)	
50. Tuesday					v 1 Diligam (NF, A) v 2 Liberator (NF, A)
51. Wednesday		Portas (NF, 8)		v 1 Attendite (8, B)	v 2 Aperiam (B)
52. Thursday					In die (NF) v 1 Audi (B) v 2 Non (B)
53. Friday					Erit vobis (B, NF) v 1 Dixit (B) v 2 In mente (B)
54. Saturday				Benedictus qui venit (NF, 8) v 1 Haec (8) v 2 Lapidem (8, B)	
55. Easter II		Lauda anima (NF)	Deus deus (NF)	v 2 In matutinis (1)	v 1 Sitivit (1)
56. Easter III					v 1 Qui (A) v 2 Dominus (A)

57. Major litanies	Confitebor domino (NF)			v 1 Adiuva (8, NF) v 2 Qui insurgunt (8, NF)	
58. Ascension		Ascendit (NF)			v 1 Omnes (2) v 2 Subiecit (2) v 3 Quoniam (2)
59. Pentecost Vigil			Emitte spiritum (NF, 8)	v 1 Benedic (8)	v 1 Confessio (B) v 2 Extendes (B)
60. Pentecost			Confirma (NF)		v 1 Cantate (NF, A) v 2 In ecclesiis (NF, A) v 3 Regna (A, NF)
61. Dominica XI		Precatus (NF)	v Dixit Moyses (NF, 8)	v Dixit dominus (NF)	
62. Dominica XIII	Immittet angelus	v 1 Benedicam (8)		v 2 In domino (NF)	V 3 Accedite (B, NF)
63. Dominica XVI			Oravi deum (NF)[5]		
64. Dominica XVII			Sanctificavit (NF)	V 1 Locutus (NF) V 2 Oravit (NF)	
65. Dominica XVIII		Si ambulavero (NF)	v In quacumque (NF, 8) v Adorabo (NF, 8)		
66. Dominica XIX	Super flumina (NF)		v 1 In salicibus (NF, 1)	v 2 Si oblitus (1) v 3 Memento (1)	
67. Dominica XX		v 1 Utinam (2, NF) v 3 Quae (NF) v 4 Quoniam (NF)	Vir erat (NF) v 2 Numquid (NF)		

(continued)

TABLE 3.1   (continued)

Liturgical Assignment	Category 1	Category 2	Category 3	Category 4	Category 5
68. Dominica XXI		Recordare mei (NF)[6]			
69. Dominica XXII					De profundis[7] (8)
70. Stephen	In virtute (6, B)			v 1 Vitam (6, B)	v 2 Magna est gloria (6, B)
71. John Evangelist	Iustus ut (NF)		v 1 Bonum (NF, A) v 3 Plantatus (NF)		v 2 Ad annuntiandum (A, NF)
72. Holy Innocents			Anima nostra (NF, 2)	v 1 Nisi (NF, 2) v 1 Torrentem (NF, 2)	
73. Various		Inveni (NF)		v 1 Potens (NF, 8)	v 2 Et ponam (2)
74. Various		Offerentur (minor) (NF, 1)		v 2 Eructavit (NF, 8) v 3 Specie (NF, 8)	
75. Various	Gloria et honore (NF)	v 1 Domine (NF)			v 2 Quid est (6, B)
76. Various	Veritas mea (NF)	v 2 Misericordia (NF)	v 1 Posui (NF, 2)		
77. Peter and Paul et al.		Constitues (NF)		v 1 Eructavit (2)	v 2 Lingua (2) v 3 Propterea (B)
78. Various					Filiae regum (NF, B, 2)

79. Various	Laetamini (NF) v 1 Beati (NF, 1)		v 2 Pro hac (NF, 6)	
80. Purification	Diffusa est (NF, A, 8)			
81. Annunciation		v 2 Ideoque (NF)	Ave Maria (NF)	v 1 Misericordia (A) v 2 Quoniam (A)
82. George et al.		v 1 Quomodo (NF) Confitebuntur (NF, A)		Repleti (A) v 1 Domine (A) v 2 Priusquam (A)
83. Various				
84. Various		Mirabilis (NF, 8)	v 1 Exurgat (NF, 8) v 2 Pereant (8, B)	
85. Various			Gloriabuntur (6, B)	v 1 Verba (B) v 2 Quoniam (B)
86. Vigil of Peter		Mihi autem (NF)		v 1 Intellexisti (A) v 2 Ecce (A, NF)
87. Vigil of Lawrence		Oratio (NF, A)	v Probavit (NF)	
88. Lawrence et al.			Confessio (NF, A)[8]	
89. Various			Desiderium (6, B)	
90. Dedication			Domine Deus in simplicitate (6, B) v 1 Maiestas (6, B)	v 2 Fecit (6, B)

(continued)

TABLE 3.1 (continued)

Liturgical Assignment	Category 1	Category 2	Category 3	Category 4	Category 5
91. Ordination					Memor sit (6, B)
92. Requiem	Domine Iesu (NF)[9]				
	v Hostias (NF)				
93. Michael					Stetit angelus/In conspectu (NF, B)
94. Octave of Peter and Paul			Beatus es Simon	v Hiesus	

1. *Iubilate deo omnis* is one of the few offertories with different assignments in the Gregorian and Roman traditions. In the Gregorian MSS, it is assigned to the first Sunday, and *Iubilate deo universa* to the second. In the Roman manuscript, their order is reversed.

2. In the Roman tradition, *Confitebor tibi* circulates with only one verse, the lengthy *Viam veritatis*. Although the first verse of the Gregorian version, *Beati immaculati*, is lacking in the Old Roman sources, it shows a compelling musical similarity to the Roman reading of the verbally identical verse of the third-mode *Benedictus es . . . in labiis*.

3. The Roman tradition is missing the verse *Quia oblitus*, which normally circulates with this offertory in Gregorian sources.

4. The Gregorian and Roman sources differ in the second verse for this offertory. Only the Beneventan MSS transmit the text of the Roman verse *In factis*.

5. The Roman version has no verses.

6. There are two distinct versions in the Gregorian tradition. The Roman version is clearly related to the earlier of the two, as transmitted in Beneventan sources.

7. The Roman manuscripts have no verses.

8. In both dialects, *Confessio* borrows the verse *Cantate domino* from the Christmas offertory *Laetentur caeli*. Most sources notate only the incipit of this verse.

9. This offertory for the dead is a Frankish addition to the repertory, taken over into the Roman tradition with few changes.

verse. Idiomelic, nonformulaic melodies are indicated by the letters NF. Although these melodies may employ brief passages of standard material such as cadential patterns, they lack a complete statement of a formula. Letters A and B indicate Formulas A and B, and numbers refer to formulas associated with specific modes. For example, 2 indicates the use of second-mode formulas; 6 indicates standard melodic material associated with sixth-mode offertories.

The table shows several important trends. First, the degree of resemblance between the Gregorian and Roman versions corresponds to their placement in the liturgical calendar.[39] All Advent and Christmas responds are in category 1 or 2, indicating a relatively close relationship between cognate pairs. From Septuagesima through Holy Week, only four of the thirty-four responds are in category 1, with seventeen in category 2. A great majority of Paschaltide responds are in categories 3, 4, and 5, showing little or no resemblance between the two dialects.

The contrast between the liturgical seasons is even more pronounced among verses. Most Advent and Christmas verses exhibit some affinity between the two dialects, with a majority in categories 2 and 3. By contrast, more than half of the Lenten verses and a great majority of the Paschaltide ones are in category 5, showing no continuity between the two dialects. These patterns suggest that after the separation of the two traditions, the offertory verses were subject to increasing melodic change in the course of the liturgical year. With a few exceptions, the sanctorale offertories are similar to the Lenten and Paschaltide ones: the Roman verses are based on formulas and show little resemblance to the Gregorian reading. *Iustus ut Palma* (71) and *Veritas mea* (76), however, do stand out as exceptions.

A second, correlating trend is that formulaic and idiomelic melodies in the Roman offertories are distributed in patterns according to the liturgical season. Most Advent and Christmas responds and verses are idiomelic (indicated by the letters NF for nonformulaic), lacking extensive use of melodic formulas. These verses are similar to the Gregorian ones in certain aspects of style, with expansive ranges and lengthy melismas. Beginning with the Epiphany offertory *Reges tharsis* (10), however, formulas become increasingly prevalent in the Roman repertory, with a particular concentration in Lent and Paschaltide. Most final verses of the Lenten offertories and nearly all Paschaltide verses are based on formulas, a trend

---

39. The temporale offertories in the table are presented in the order of their placement in the liturgical calendar. In the case of multiple assignments in the temporale, I list the offertory according to chronological priority in cases where such knowledge is well established—omitting, for example, the Thursdays of Lent and giving preference to the other Lenten ferias over the Post-Pentecost Sundays. In cases where chronological information is not securely established, such as the First Sunday of Advent and a Lenten feria, I have simply listed the chant the first time it occurs. The Post-Pentecost assignments follow those of the Roman manuscripts. The sanctorale offertories are listed after those of the temporale. Most sanctorale offertories are assigned to more than one festival, and because their original assignments are subject to debate, they are simply listed here according to their order in most manuscripts. Those with probable unique assignments include *Oratio, Constitues eos, In conspectu,* and the Marian offertories *Ave Maria* and *Diffusa est.*

also evident in most offertories of the sanctorale. With the Post-Pentecostal offertories, however, we once again see some idiomelic material in the verses.

Finally, the degree of resemblance between the two traditions correlates with the melodic traits of the Roman reading. A great majority of nonformulaic Roman melodies are in categories 1, 2, and 3, showing some resemblance to the Gregorian versions. Most Roman melodies based on formulas, by contrast, are in categories 4 and 5. The continuity between the two dialects is particularly weak in cases where the Roman version employs Formulas A and B. Despite the pervasiveness of this trend, however, there are a few important exceptions. Category 3, for example, includes some idiomelic melodies that show only vestiges of continuity between the two dialects. Furthermore, some formulaic melodies do exhibit similarity to the Gregorian reading. A few Lenten melodies based on formulas of modes 2 and 8, for example, are in categories 1 and 2, including *Meditabor* (22), for Wednesday of the first week in Lent, and *Benedicite gentes* (36), for Wednesday of the fourth week. These examples will play an important role in evaluating theories about the origins of the two traditions.

Table 3.1 illustrates one further phenomenon of interest. Despite the prevalence of formulas in the Roman Lenten and Paschaltide verses, a few offertories present a striking exception to this trend. The verses of the Easter Sunday *Terra tremuit* (48), for example, employ a substantial amount of nonformulaic material, as do those for the Easter Monday *Angelus domini* (49). Although the exceptional stylistic traits of *Terra tremuit* could perhaps be attributed to the solemnity of its feast, similar characteristics are evident in the final verses of two isolated Lenten offertories, *Scapulis suis* (19), for the first Sunday, and *Exaudi deus* (30), for Monday of the third week. Both verses exhibit stylistic traits more commonly associated with Gregorian final verses: an expansion to the authentic range, lengthy melismas, and no traces of formulas. Not surprisingly, these verses also show some resemblance to their Gregorian counterparts.

Setting aside these stylistic departures for the moment, I can summarize the overriding trends as follows. Breaches of affinity between the two dialects are concentrated in the later seasons of the year, particularly among verses. In most of these cases, the Roman version relies on formulas. The resemblance between the Gregorian and Roman versions in the early seasons suggests that these offertories were relatively stable melodically, retaining evidence of their common melodic origin during several centuries of separate transmission. The lack of resemblance between the two dialects in the later seasons, however, evinces substantial melodic change, in one dialect or both, after their separation in the eighth century. I will address possible reasons for this instability from different perspectives in chapter 5, where I take up the question of the relative historical position of the two dialects. Put simply, which dialect more closely resembles the eighth-century prototypes? Does the pervasive formulaicism of the eleventh-century Roman offertories reflect the tradition the Franks learned from the Romans in the eighth century, or did the formulas emerge in the centuries following the Frankish reception?

The remainder of this chapter will focus on illustrating several specific trends that address this question. Of particular importance is the tendency for nonformulaic Roman melodies to resemble the Gregorian counterparts more closely than the formulaic melodies do. As I will show, this larger trend is also manifest on a local level, within individual melodies: the Gregorian version often departs from the Roman precisely in the places where the Roman singers rely on formulas or other conventions particular to their tradition. A similar pattern emerges in comparing the responds and verses of the same offertory: the idiomelic passages, primarily in responds, show a greater resemblance between the two traditions than the formulaic passages do.

The two versions of *Populum humilem* (37), for Friday of the fourth week in Lent, illustrate this trend. The respond is in category 2, with a discernable melodic resemblance between the two versions. The Roman reading lacks a complete statement of a formula, relying on standard material primarily at cadences (for example, on "superborum" and "humiliabis," phrase 2). In these passages, it exhibits a typical tendency toward ornateness and corresponding lack of resemblance to the Gregorian version. The two versions are also dissimilar in the opening passage, where the Gregorian features a sharply etched movement from F to c, contrasting with the typical repetitions of the trichord c-b-a in the Roman. In terms of underlying tonal structure, however, the Roman melody resembles the Gregorian version quite closely, particularly at the beginnings of phrases. At "salvum facies" (phrase 1), for example, both versions focus on the tenor c and ascend to e on the first syllable of "facies." At "et oculos superborum" (phrase 2), the Roman is similar to the Gregorian in its focus on a, and at the end of phrase 2 ("humiliabis") the two versions have a nearly identical ascent to c and place melismas on the accented syllable of "humila-bis." Despite their differences, the two readings show evidence of a common origin. More important, they are dissimilar precisely where the Roman version relies on the vocabulary and customs of its own tradition, primarily at cadences.

With the beginning of the first verse (phrase 4), the resemblance between the two versions of *Populum humilem* comes to an abrupt end. In the Roman tradition, both verses are formed from repeated statements of Formula B, whereas their Gregorian counterparts are elaborate, distinctive melodies. Although the Gregorian verses lack the modal contrast found in many offertories, they incorporate lengthy melismas on "clamor meus" (phrase 4), "[liberator] meus" (phrase 6), and "exaltabis" (phrase 9), perhaps in an effort to add rhetorical emphasis to these words and phrases. The final melisma on "exaltabis" spans nearly an octave and reaches several times to high e, resulting in a typical climactic effect. The Roman version lacks these lengthy melismas and rhetorical responses to the words. The two readings of the verses, in fact, show no traces of a common melodic origin.

Populum humilem illustrates the tendency for the two readings to diverge in places where the Roman version relies on formulas, typically in verses. In light of the traditional view that the two dialects share a common origin, this pattern invites several possible explanations. The first is that the Roman offertories more closely reflect the eighth-century state of the repertory. With this hypothesis, we would conclude that the Franks were selective in their assimilation of the Roman melodies. In the case of nonformulaic melodies, they often adopted the Roman version quite closely; when met with formulas, however, they replaced the Roman melodies with new ones, perhaps because the formulas were inimical to Frankish tastes.[40] This scenario would view elaborate verse melodies that have no counterpart in the Roman tradition, such as those of *Populum humilem* and many other Lenten offertories, as Frankish creations. An alternative explanation is that the Roman tradition underwent change after the separation of the two dialects, becoming increasingly uniform in response to the pressures of maintaining the melodies in a purely oral form.[41] The recent work of Levy raises yet a third possibility: that Gregorian offertories are Gallican melodies adapted to Roman texts.[42]

Although each of these hypotheses has an established place in chant studies, none has been thoroughly tested against a close analysis of the Gregorian and Roman offertories. While musical analysis cannot provide an empirically provable explanation for the discrepancies between the two traditions, it will allow us to rule out certain theories, thereby leading us closer to a plausible answer. To this end, I will consider several other important facets of the relationship between the two dialects, focusing in particular on the word-music relationship and the extent of continuity between the Gregorian melodies and Roman formulas.

WORD-MUSIC PARALLELISM

A tendency to set the same words to the same music is evident in both Gregorian and Roman offertories. In examining the Gregorian version of *Domine fac mecum*, for example, I noted that the two statements of the words "misericordiam tuam"

40. The view that the formulas represent the original state of the melodies was proposed in Thomas Connolly, "Introits and Archetypes: Some Archaisms of the Old Roman Chant," *Journal of the American Musicological Society* 25 (1972): 157–74; and more recently in Dyer, "'*Tropis semper variantibus*'"; Philippe Bernard, *Du chant romain au chant grégorien (IVe–XIIIe siècle)* (Paris: Cerf, 1996); and Haas, *Mündliche Überlieferung und altrömisher Choral.*
41. For evidence of a longer period of oral transmission in Rome, see especially John Boe, "Chant Notation in Eleventh-Century Roman Manuscripts," in *Essays on Medieval Music in Honor of David G. Hughes,* ed. Graeme Boone (Cambridge, Mass.: Harvard University Press, 1995), 43–58, and "Music Notation in Archivio San Pietro C 105 and in the Farfa Breviary, Chigi C. VI. 177," *Early Music History* 18 (1999): 1–45.
42. Kenneth Levy, "A New Look at Old Roman Chant I," *Early Music History* 19 (2000): 81–104, "A New Look at Old Roman Chant II," *Early Music History* 20 (2001): 173–98, "Gregorian Chant and the Romans," *Journal of the American Musicological Society* 56 (2003): 5–42, and "*Tollite Portas* Revisited: An Ante-Evangelium Reclaimed?" in Gallagher et al., *Western Plainchant,* 231–42.

are set to nearly identical music, and that these words receive a similar setting in other offertories. In the Roman tradition, these instances of word-music parallelism are far more common. Differences between the two versions, in fact, often occur precisely in places where the Roman responds to such verbal cues.

This pattern is evident in *In te speravi* (21), for Tuesday in the first week of Lent. In the first verse, *Illumina faciem*, the two versions are markedly dissimilar in some passages, such as phrase 4 and the first half of phrase 6;elsewhere they seem discernibly related, as in phrase 5 (beginning with "servum") and the second part of phrase 6 ("misericordiam tuam"). The most conspicuous breaches in continuity between the two readings occur where the Roman version adopts a customary response to the words that is not matched in the Gregorian. In phrase 4, for example, the Roman melody adopts Formula 2–3, typically used in phrases that end with a noun followed by a possessive adjective. Here the Roman singer is evidently responding to a verbal cue, "faciem tuam," and the melody departs noticeably from the Gregorian reading.

Another point of contrast between the two readings is on "propter" (phrase 6). The complete text of this phrase, "salvum me fac propter misericordiam tuam," also occurs at the close of the sixth-mode *Domine convertere* (40), for Monday of Passion Week. Although the verbal relationship to *Domine convertere* is reflected in both versions of *In te speravi*, the melodic response to the words is more extensive in the Roman melody. Parallel readings of the two passages are presented in example 3.4.

Lines 1 and 2 show the Roman and Gregorian readings of the passage in *Domine convertere;* lines 3 and 4 show the verbally identical passage in *In te speravi.* Beginning with "propter," the Roman version of *In te speravi* (line 3) departs from the Gregorian (line 4) and instead resembles the verbally identical passage from the Roman version of *Domine convertere* (line 1). In the Gregorian tradition, by contrast, the two offertories (lines 2 and 4) maintain distinctive melodic profiles until "misericordiam tuam," where they are nearly identical. This exceptional incorporation of sixth-mode material into a second-mode Gregorian offertory is clearly prompted by the verbal similarity to a sixth-mode offertory. Although *In te speravi* demonstrates the importance of verbal cues in both dialects, however, the Roman version manifests this dependency more extensively. The Gregorian and Roman readings of this verse are most dissimilar in places where the Roman version responds to verbal cues and the Gregorian does not: "faciem tuam" in phrase 4 and "propter" in phrase 6.

Formula 2–3 offers perhaps the most striking illustration of the prevalence of word-music parallelism in the Roman repertory. This formula occurs in Roman offertories of all modes, and in a great majority of cases it is prompted by specific verbal conditions: a noun, usually a three-syllable proparoxytone, followed by a possessive pronoun. Nearly every statement of this formula coincides with a breach

EXAMPLE 3.4 Parallel passages in *Domine convertere* and *In te speravi*

of melodic affinity with the Gregorian reading, even when the two versions are otherwise closely related. *In te speravi* offers the single exception: in the respond, the Roman version incorporates Formula 2–3 on the words "manibus tuis" (phrase 3). In this particular case, the corresponding Gregorian passage is similar in melodic shape on the word "manibus." In every other instance of Formula 2–3, the parallel passage in the Gregorian reading bears no melodic affinity with the Roman version.

On rare occasions, the Gregorian offertories exhibit word-music parallelism in passages where the Roman does not. In all of these cases, however, the corresponding Roman version is based on Formula A or B.[43] On the whole, parallelism is far more common in the Roman melodies.[44] This pattern suggests that verbal cues exerted a deeper influence in the Roman melodic tradition than in the Gregorian. With the premise that the two dialects are descendents of a common tradition, I see two possible explanations for this phenomenon. The first is that the eleventh- and twelfth-century Roman offertories, with their extensive dependency on verbal cues, represent the state of the repertory in the eighth century. With this hypothesis, we would conclude that Franks retained certain aspects of the Roman melodies but modified the specific passages that were influenced by verbal cues.[45] Another possibility is that verbal cues took on an increasing role in the Roman dialect after the eighth-century Frankish reception, as a means of retaining a large repertory without the aid of written notation. I shall consider the evidence for each view in chapter 5, in conjunction with the rest of the musical, verbal, and liturgical evidence.

ROMAN FORMULAS AND THE GREGORIAN MELODIES: IMPLICATIONS FOR THE GALLICAN QUESTION

The lack of formulas in the Gregorian offertories has led some scholars to the conclusion they are either newly created Frankish melodies or preexisting Gallican ones. Levy argues that the Franks replaced these formulas with preexisting Gallican melodies; these Gallican melodies with Roman texts found their way

---

43. I have found three examples. The first verses of *Gloria et honore* (75)and *Repleti sumus* (83) begin with the word "domine." The two Gregorian verses open with an identical melisma. A corresponding melisma is found in the Roman version of *Gloria et honore*, but not in *Repleti*, which is based on Formula A. Even this example, however, illustrates the tendency toward uniformity in the Roman tradition. The Roman melisma of *Gloria et honore* is found in the opening of each verse of *Laetamini* (79), whereas the Gregorian *Laetamini* uses different melismas here. The melodic relationships among this group of first-mode offertories, which also includes *Confitebor tibi* (39), is described briefly in the notes for individual offertories in appendix 3. For another example of word-music parallelism in the Gregorian tradition that is not found in the Roman, see the first verses of *Intende voci* (32) and *Gloriabuntur* (85). These verbally identical verses have the same melody in the Gregorian tradition but not in the Roman, where the *Gloriabuntur* verse uses Formula B. The final example occurs in *Benedictus es . . . et non tradas* (43). The words "confundantur and revereantur" (phrase 8) occur in *Domine in auxilium* (27), and in the Gregorian tradition the two passages are melodically identical (though notated at different positions). The corresponding Roman passage of *Benedictus es* employs Formula A.
44. For some additional examples, see *Gressus meos* (33), *Levabo oculos* (20), and *Domine vivifica* (18). In the Roman tradition, each of these passages has similar melodic material on "domine" (which occurs twice in *Gressus meos*). The Gregorian tradition has similar material in only two of these passages, the first verses of *Gressus* and *Levabo*. The pattern is also illustrated by *Scapulis suis* (19). As noted, the Roman version is verbally and musically identical to the communion sung on the same day. In the Gregorian tradition, the openings of the two chants share the same words but not the same music.
45. This view is proposed by Haas in *Mündliche Überlieferung und altrömischer Choral*. See especially 133–38.

back to Rome, where they were partially incorporated into the Roman dialect.[46]
I would like briefly to examine this hypothesis from a musical perspective. With a
theory of Frankish-to-Roman transmission, one would expect all Gregorian offertories to be utterly dissimilar to the Roman formulas. As I have shown, many
Gregorian melodies meet this expectation, departing sharply from the Roman
formulas especially in final verses of the later liturgical seasons. Certain Gregorian
offertories, however, do show traces of resemblance to the Roman formulas,
particularly among the neumatic and repetitive Lenten responds and first verses.
The similarities are typically manifest in a broad tonal affinity and a common
vocabulary of small melodic segments and cadential patterns. The two versions also
share principles of text declamation and similar responses to verbal cues, which
suggests that they are rooted in a common approach to singing. These instances of
similarity reinforce the traditional view that, wherever the offertories ultimately
originated, the Gregorian and Roman melodies are separate descendants of a
common, eighth-century Roman tradition. In view of the Gallican hypothesis,
they warrant some detailed illustration and discussion.

For an initial example of the shared vocabulary and principles, I turn once again
to the respond *Domine fac mecum* (31). As noted, "misericordiam tuam" and
"misericordia tua" (phrases 1 and 3) receive very similar musical settings in the
Gregorian version, especially on the last four syllables. The Roman version of this
passage resembles the Gregorian in contour, particularly on the last three syllables
of the second statement (phrase 3). In both dialects, these words receive a similar
setting in other offertories. The melodic material is not exclusively associated with
these words. In the Roman tradition, it is sometimes employed as a cadential
pattern in third- and fourth-mode offertories that use Formula A. In *Domine fac
mecum*, it also occurs at the end of verse 1, on "apertum est" (phrase 6). Closely
related material, however, appears often in conjunction with certain verbal conditions: a longer noun followed by a possessive adjective ("misericordiam tuam,"
"deprecationem meam," etc.). A similar passage is found, for example, in the two
versions of the respond *Exaudi deus* (30), for Monday in the third week of Lent, on
the words "deprecationem meam" (phrase 2).

The theory that the Gregorian melodies originated in Gaul holds that the
resemblance between the Roman and Gregorian traditions is attributable to an
importation of Gallican melodies into Rome. This particular standard passage,
however, evinces far more than a mere resemblance between the two individual
cognate pairs, *Domine fac mecum* and *Exaudi deus*. A look at the context of this
melodic material in each dialect shows that its use and its association with
particular words and phrases is deeply engrained in both traditions. The two
dialects, however, often employ this material in different places. In the Roman
tradition, the passage occurs in *Benedixisti* (3) (on "misericordiam tuam," phrase 6)

46. See note 42.

and, in varied form in the lower transposition, in *Perfice gressus* (15) ("iustitiam meam" and "orationem meam," phrases 5 and 7). Although the Gregorian tradition does not employ the same material in these places, it does so in two other offertories, in *Miserere mihi* (26) and *Domine vivifica* (18), both times on "misericordiam tuam"; and a few times in verbally dissimilar passages. (See, for example, *Laudate dominum* (34), where it occurs in the lower transposition on "saecula saeculorum," phrase 9).

If the presence of this melodic figure in Rome is attributable to a late importation of individual melodies from Gaul, wherein the imported Gallican melodies were mixed with the native formulas of the Roman melodies, we might imagine that the Romans overgeneralized in their adoption of this passage, forgetting where it was originally used and unconsciously incorporating it into other melodies. The alternative is to view the shared patterns of association between words and music as a token of descent from a common, eighth-century tradition. I see this explanation as far more plausible, particularly in view of the historical evidence supporting Roman-to-Frankish transmission. The association of this standard passage with particular verbal conditions suggests that the two traditions share certain underlying word-music associations that predate their separation.

Further evidence for the traditional view of Roman-to-Frankish transmission lies in certain underlying structural similarities between the Roman formulas and some corresponding Gregorian melodies. If the Franks completely replaced the Roman melodies with preexisting ones of their own, we would expect to find no affinity between the Roman formulas and the Gregorian melodies. Certain Gregorian second-mode melodies, however, show an unmistakable resemblance to the Roman second-mode formulas in tonal structure and principles of text declamation. As an example, I shall consider the Lenten offertory *Benedicite gentes* (36) in some depth. Examining the Roman version of the respond earlier in this chapter, I noted that it consists primarily of second-mode formulas, chosen in response to verbal conditions. Although the Gregorian reading lacks formulas, it is similar to the Roman in range, tonal structure, and aspects of its melodic vocabulary. More important, it shows traces of the syntactical rules I have demonstrated in the Roman formulas.

The two readings of the respond *Benedicite gentes*, in category 2, are clearly related in terms of range and tonal structure, each exhibiting typical second-mode traits. In both versions, most phrases remain in the narrow range of the primary structural interval, D-F. Expansions of range often occur in the same place in each reading: the third A-C in the opening and in phrase 5b ("amovet/amovit") and the third F-a in phrase 3 (on "animam"). A further point of affinity between the two versions of *Benedicite gentes* lies in their tendency toward melodic economy. Although the Gregorian version lacks the large-scale repetition of the Roman, much of the melody is formed from small melodic segments, usually comprising a syllable, that are repeated and reused throughout. These segments typically articulate the third D-F, further attesting to the tonal continuity between the two versions.

The recurring melodic segments in the Gregorian version are correlated, to some degree, with accent. In this respect, the melody reflects principles of text declamation similar to those of the Roman formulas. The pitches D and C, for example, often accommodate the syllables before the first accent in the clause, just as they do in many Roman formulas ("et obaudite," phrase 2, "et non dedit," phrase 4a, and "deprecationem," phrase 5b) preceding an accent that falls on F. As in the Roman Formula 2–1, accented syllables are often emphasized by a movement from C or D to F ("deum," phrase 1b, "vocem," phrase 2, "dedit," phrase 4a, and "commoveri," phrase 4b) or from F to G ("benedictus" and "dominus," phrase 5a). Accented syllables occasionally receive a brief excursion into the third F-a ("animam," phrase 3a, "suam," phrase 6). Finally, the Frankish singers distinguish boundaries between words in a way similar to that of the Roman Formula 2–1: repeated F's often fall after the accent or on the final syllable of the word ("animam" and "meam," phrase 3a). Although the two versions often employ this shared vocabulary in different places, its presence in both traditions nevertheless suggests that the two dialects are rooted in a common approach to singing. The broad similarities between the two readings in melodic vocabulary and declamation occasionally result in a more detailed resemblance between them. In both versions, for example, the segment D-F-G-F (or some variant of it, such as D-E-G-F or simply F-G-F) often falls on accented syllables, resulting in fleeting similarities of surface detail between them (for example "*do*minum," phrase 1b, and "non," phrase 5b).

To summarize, the two readings of *Benedicite gentes* share an underlying tonal structure, melodic vocabulary, and certain principles of text declamation, evident in a common approach to emphasizing accented syllables and shaping particular words. Their central difference is that the Gregorian melody lacks the uniformity and predictability of the Roman formulas. Similar points of affinity and difference between the Gregorian melodies and Roman formulas may be found in other Lenten offertories of modes 2 and 8.[47] These similarities in range, tonal structure, melodic vocabulary, and principles of text declamation are best explained by the traditional view: both versions descend from the common, eighth-century tradition transmitted from Rome to the Franks.

FORMULA A AND THE GREGORIAN MELODIES

The two most common Roman formulas, Formulas A and B, only rarely exhibit this broad continuity with the Gregorian tradition. Recall that in table 3.1, a great majority of Roman verses based on Formulas A and B are in category 5, indicating

47. See, for example, the responds and first verses of the eighth-mode *Gressus meos* (33) and *Levabo oculos* (20), along with the second-mode *Meditabor* (22) and *Laudate dominum* (34).

a complete lack of resemblance to their Gregorian counterparts. Affinity between the Gregorian and Roman offertories is particularly weak among Roman melodies that employ Formula A. Of the thirty-seven Roman responds and verses that make substantial use of this formula, only a few show any similarity to their Gregorian counterparts. In these cases, the resemblance is manifest in a very broad similarity of tonal structure. I have examined the Gregorian version of *Domine fac mecum* (31), for example, as an illustration of some typical features of Lenten offertories. In the Roman tradition, the verses of this offertory (beginning with phrase 4) combine Formula A with standard cadential material found in offertories of modes 3, 4, and 8. In its first and third verses, the Gregorian shows traces of similarity to the Roman in range and tonal structure. Like the Roman version, the Beneventan reading of the first verse focuses on b at the opening of the verse (phrase 4) and remains mainly within the third a-c. A similar sort of broad continuity between Formula A and the corresponding Gregorian melody is evident in the first verse of *Benedictus est . . . et non tradas* (43).

Although the affinity between the Gregorian and Roman readings in these two melodies is certainly not close at the level of surface detail, the nature of their relationship is inconsistent with the view that the Gregorian is a preexisting Gallican melody. It is far more plausible that the similarity between them in range and tonal structure reflects the origin they share in the eighth-century Roman prototype. The alternative is to imagine that the Franks, receiving the Roman verses in a formulaic state and observing the prominence of Formula A, searched through the Gallican repertory to find a few melodies with a broad resemblance to this formula. This hypothesis would suggest, moreover, that they did so only in a few isolated instances, for as I have shown, the great majority of Roman melodies based on this formula have utterly dissimilar Gregorian counterparts. I find this entire scenario implausible. The simpler and more compelling explanation is that the broad correspondence between Formula A and isolated Gregorian counterparts is a vestige of their common origin.

SIXTH-MODE OFFERTORIES: A PARALLEL MELODIC FAMILY

Because the Gregorian melodies are generally idiomelic, family resemblance between parallel groups of Gregorian and Roman melodies is rare. The sixth-mode offertories constitute the only such melodic family in the repertory. The responds and first verses of the Gregorian sixth-mode offertories share structural traits, melodic vocabulary, and to some extent, a set of syntactical principles for adapting the melodies to different texts; these traits are also found in the Roman versions of these offertories. Despite these general similarities between the two traditions, however, the shared vocabulary is employed very differently in each dialect, which often results in a lack of affinity between individual cognate pairs. Because of these traits, the sixth-mode offertories can shed further light on the reconstructive model proposed earlier in this chapter.

In the Roman tradition, there are ten sixth-mode offertories: *Domine in auxilium* (27), *Iustitiae* (29), *Factus est dominus* (38), *Domine convertere* (40), *Sperent in te* (41), *In virtute* (70), *Desiderium* (89), *Gloriabuntur* (85), *Domine deus in simplicitate* (90), and *In conspectu angelorum* (93). Although formed primarily from Formula B, these melodies exhibit certain characteristics that distinguish them from other Formula B melodies. For example, the Roman version of *Domine in auxilium* (27), for Friday of the second week of Lent, shares much of its melodic material with others of the sixth mode. The lengthy melisma that begins each verse and the truncated form of it that concludes the respond and two verses, for example, is found (with small variants) in all other members of this melodic family (compare phrases 6, 8, 9, and 11). The passage articulating the lower tetrachord C-F on "et revereantur" (phrase 2) is a common marker of internal cadences in Roman sixth-mode offertories, often serving to join together two parts of a dependent clause in the penultimate phrase. Brief expansions beyond the typical Formula B range occur in response to specific words. The figure articulating the third D-F on "domine" in the opening phrase, for example, occurs frequently on this word.[48] So does the expansion of range to c on the word "animam" (phrase 3).[49]

Most of these defining traits of the Roman sixth-mode offertories are also found among responds and first verses in the parallel family of Gregorian sixth-mode melodies. Reflecting the trend toward greater melodic variety in the Gregorian repertory, this group includes only six of the corresponding melodies: *Domine in auxilium* (27),[50] *Iustitiae* (29), *Domine convertere* (40), *In virtute* (70), *Desiderium* (89), and *Domine deus in simplicitate* (90). Like their Roman counterparts, the Gregorian sixth-mode responds and first verses focus extensively on F, with periodic internal cadences that articulate the lower tetrachord of the mode, F-C. In *Domine in auxilium*, the lower tetrachord passage occurs in the same place in each version, on "revereantur" (phrase 2). A second point of affinity lies in the melismas employed in each dialect; several Gregorian sixth-mode offertories incorporate melismas reminiscent of the one that circulates in the Roman versions. In the Gregorian melodies, however, the placement of this melisma often differs from its location in the corresponding Roman version. In the Gregorian version of *Domine in auxilium*, this melisma occurs on "retrorsum" and "erubescant"

---

48. For example, at the beginning of *Domine convertere* and in the respond *Sperent in te*.
49. See *Domine convertere* and *Desiderium*, for example.
50. The Beneventan version of *Domine in auxilium* is shorter than the Roman, lacking the repeat of the opening words at the end. As a consequence, the two versions end on different finals. A cue to repeat the opening words, however, is found in many Gregorian manuscripts, a summarized in the notes in appendix 3. *Iustitiae* has a varied ending, closing on either E or F. In the base reading of Pa 776, it closes on E. It is listed here in the group of sixth-mode offertories because its internal phrases are indistinguishable from those of the others in this group.

EXAMPLE 3.5　Cadential patterns in Gregorian sixth-mode offertories

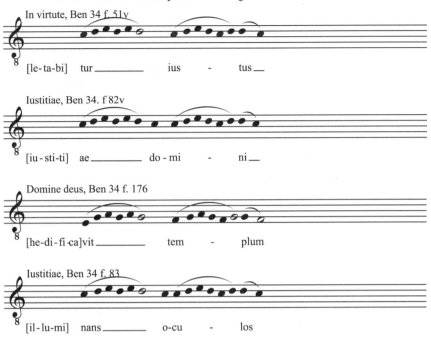

(phrase 7); the two melismas share their last thirteen or fourteen notes, and the same closing material is found in other Gregorian offertories.[51] This ending of the melisma shares material with the latter portion of the Roman melisma that occurs in phrase 6 and 9: a thrice-repeated F is approached from the lower fourth, and the last part of the melisma articulates the third F-a with stepwise motion. Other Gregorian melismas show similarity to the Roman one in beginning with movement from F to c. In *Domine in auxilium*, for example, the closing melisma of verse 1 (phrase 8, on "mala") is similar to the corresponding Roman one in range, opening with F-a-c, followed by a descent to low C.

Finally, the cadences in Gregorian sixth-mode offertories respond to accentual conditions of the final words in a way reminiscent of the Roman Formula B. A sampling of these cadences is given in example 3.5. Each cadential pattern consists of three melodic segments, placed on the last three or four syllables of the phrase. If the final accent of the phrase falls on the penult, the three segments are placed on the final three syllables, as in lines 1 and 3. If the antepenult is accented, a single note is placed on it, as in lines 2 and 4. Despite their lack of formulas, Gregorian offertories exhibit vestiges of Formula B's syntactical principles, reinforcing the traditional view that the Gregorian melodies and Roman formulas share a common origin.

51. This melisma occurs, for example, several times in *In virtute* (70) and in *Desiderium* (89).

The points of broad similarity between the Gregorian and Roman sixth-mode offertories suggest that the two dialects are descendants of a common tradition. In their use and distribution of this shared vocabulary, however, the two dialects differ greatly, reflecting the defining trends of each tradition. The general differences between the two dialects are, in fact, especially pronounced in the sixth-mode offertories, resulting in a weak correspondence between individual Gregorian and Roman pairs. Although the lengthy melismas of the two traditions share melodic material, these melismas rarely occur in the same places within individual cognate pairs. The Roman offertories are consistent in their placement of this melisma: it occurs at the opening of nearly every verse and, in shortened form, as a closing melisma for several verses and responds. In the Gregorian tradition, the use of this material is far less predictable. In the first verse of *In virtute* (70), for example, it functions as an important means of unity, occurring five times on the vowel e (see phrases 3–7). Here the melody is written at the affinal position, with a final of c. In *Desiderium* (89), by contrast, it functions as closing melisma (phrase 3). The passage that articulates the lower tetrachord is also employed very differently in each dialect. In the Roman offertories, it is usually placed in the penultimate phrase, serving to join together parts of a dependent clause. In the Gregorian versions, it can occur at any point within the melody. One additional example, *Desiderium* (89), will help to illustrate these differences and their implications for the reconstructive model.

The two readings of the respond *Desiderium* (89) are in category 4. In the Roman version of Vat 5319, this offertory is written a fifth above the normal pitch level for sixth-mode offertories, closing on c. To facilitate comparison, the Gregorian version of Pa 776 has been transcribed at the affinal position as well. Each version employs melodic vocabulary common to the two dialects, but the two show little or no direct correspondence. Many of the breaches in continuity between the two versions can be traced to the greater propensity for word-music parallelism in the Roman repertory. The Roman cantors respond to the words in ways that are not reflected in the Gregorian reading. This tendency is evident in the placement of the lower tetrachord passages. In the Roman version, the final statement of this passage, which articulates the tetrachord c-G in the higher transposition, is placed in its usual position, the penultimate phrase ("eius," phrase 4). Here it serves its typical role in the Roman tradition, functioning as a kind of half cadence that joins together dependent parts of a clause ("Desiderium animae eius / tribuisti ei"). In this particular offertory, however, the passage occurs two additional times, on the words "animae eius" (phrase 1) and "capite eius" (phrase 3), evidently a response to the similarities between these passages in assonance and accent pattern. In the Gregorian version of *Desiderium*, by contrast, the aural similarities between "animae eius" and "capite eius" are not reflected in the melody. Rather, the lower tetrachord passage occurs on "eum" (phrase 2), the end of the first complete sentence.

Another difference between the two versions of *Desiderium* is verbal: the Roman concludes with a repeat of its opening words that is lacking in the Gregorian. Here the Roman version is perhaps influenced by a close verbal relationship with the offertory *In virtute*.[52] Both texts are taken from Psalm 20, and the opening words of *Desiderium* are identical to the closing words of *In virtute*. These pieces were performed several times during the course of the liturgical year, and the musical and verbal similarities between them may have prompted the Roman soloists to repeat the final words of *Desiderium* by habit, resulting in an ending similar to that of *In virtute*.[53]

I have shown that the Roman melodies exhibit an occasional tendency to respond immediately to a verbal cue rather than considering the syntax of the phrase as a whole.[54] The opening passage of *Desiderium* illustrates this tendency; here the two versions differ in their division of the text. In the Gregorian version, a cadence occurs on "domine," the end of the verbal sense unit (phrase 1). In the Roman reading, however, a typical Formula B cadence occurs between "ei" and "domine," contradicting the verbal syntax. As Hucke suggested, the anomalous division of text in the Roman reading is probably a cursory response to the words, a result of the close relationship to *In virtute*: the final phrase of *In virtute* is identical verbally, except that it lacks the vocative "domine." [55] In these respects, *Desiderium* exemplifies the deeper influence of aural cues in the Roman tradition.

To summarize, the two versions of *Desiderium* share a melodic vocabulary and certain structural principles, but show little direct correspondence. Passing and probably fortuitous similarities between them are limited to the ascent to g on "voluntate" (phrase 2), the typical sixth-mode caesura that follows on "eius," and the melisma on "pretioso" (phrase 3). These patterns invite further reflection on the reconstructive model of transmission proposed earlier in this chapter. The differences between the Gregorian and Roman sixth-mode offertories illustrate a phenomenon that is exceptional among Gregorian offertories: they raise the possibility that these pieces were transmitted to Francia, at least in part, not as a series of distinct, individual melodies but as a melodic vocabulary and a set of principles for adapting this vocabulary to different texts. Edward Nowacki has presented compelling evidence for this hypothesis in the case of the office antiphons, and the marked differences between sixth-mode offertories of the two traditions in their use of common vocabulary would seem to support this hypothesis.[56]

52. The relationship between these offertories was discussed by Hucke in "Zur Aufzeichnung," 300–302.
53. *In virtute* opens with verse 2 of Psalm 20 and continues with the first half of verse 3; *Desiderium* consists of the first half of verse 3 and the second half of verse 4.
54. See the discussion of *Benedicite gentes* above.
55. Hucke, "Zur Aufzeichnung," 300.
56. Nowacki, "The Gregorian Office Antiphons and the Comparative Method," *Journal of Musicology* 4 (1985): 243–75. See especially the final example, pp. 273–275. Beside a group of antiphons

Individual melodic detail, however, also played an important role in the transmission of this melodic group, as is evident in another sixth-mode offertory, *In virtute (70)*. (Here both readings are also written at the affinal position, with the final of c.) On "Et super salutare" (phrase 2), the Roman version expands beyond the narrow range of Formula B, first embellishing pitch e, then moving to f as the focal pitch for the accented syllable on "salutare" and dipping down to a on "tuum." A clear departure from the sixth-mode formulas, this passage is similar to the Gregorian reading in contour. The final melisma of the respond ("ei," phrase 3) also shows some affinity between the two versions. The Roman closes not with the standard sixth-mode melisma but a related one found only in *In virtute* and a few other offertories; the Gregorian version resembles it quite closely. The Roman version is most similar to the Gregorian precisely in places where it employs idiomelic material, a trend I have observed throughout the repertory.

The sixth-mode offertories reaffirm the sense that the oral transmission of the offertories involved both distinct melodic details and a set of rules and principles. These two facets of melodic transmission in an oral milieu cannot be easily distinguished. The shared melodic vocabulary of the sixth-mode offertories, moreover, is found only among the responds and first verses in the Gregorian offertories. The final verses of the two dialects are utterly dissimilar: the Roman versions are formed from Formula B and other sixth-mode material; the Gregorian ones are idiomelic, with a typical expansion into the authentic range.[57] These verses cannot be viewed as separate realizations of shared principles.

THE SPECIAL CASE OF *BEATUS ES SIMON PETRE*

As briefly described in chapter 2, the Roman Mass formulary for the Octave of Peter and Paul was developed after the Roman repertory was transmitted to the Franks. The formulary included two new chants, the offertory *Beatus es Simon Petre* and the communion *Domine si tu es*. Although these pieces were never disseminated in Francia, both found their way into Beneventan manuscripts.[58]

---

consisting only of the word "alleluia," the Roman singer cues the text of antiphons of the same melodic type to prompt the memory of the manuscript's users. In terms of melodic detail, however, the notated alleluia antiphons differ from those that are cued, indicating that the scribe was thinking of the melody as a general type that could be realized in various ways.

57. Although the Gregorian versions are primarily idiomelic, there is a close melodic resemblance between the final verses of *Domine in auxilium* and *Domine deus in simplicitate*. The Roman version of *In virtute* lacks a second verse, and the Roman version of *Desiderium* lacks the two or three verses that circulate with it in the Gregorian tradition.

58. Both chants are discussed, along with another case of "direct transmission" from Rome to Benevento, in Luisa Nardini, "Written and Oral Transmission in Chant Repertories: Old-Roman 'Intruders' in Non-Roman Manuscripts" (forthcoming). I am grateful to Professor Nardini for sharing this work before publication and stimulating my own thinking on *Beatus es*. The companion communion is unfortunately only cued in Ben 35.

Because *Beatus es* reached Benevento independent of Frankish mediation, it can shed a special light on the different compositional processes that underlie the Roman dialect and the "Gregorian" tradition, specifically as it was practiced at Benevento.

The Beneventan and Roman versions of *Beatus es* (94) are based on the respective Gregorian and Roman versions of *Angelus domini* (49).[59] While it is not clear when these pieces were transmitted to Benevento, the basis of the Beneventan version in the Gregorian melody for *Angelus domini*, rather than the Old Beneventan one, indicates that *Beatus es* was adopted after the early or mid–ninth century, when Gregorian chant arrived in Benevento.[60] As Luisa Nardini has shown, several other Beneventan offertories for newly added festivals, such as the Assumption and its vigil, are also contrafacts of *Angelus domini.*[61]

Despite their bases in the two versions of the same chant, *Angelus domini,* the Beneventan and Roman melodies for *Beatus es* differ greatly in their degree of correspondence to their respective models. A comparison of the Beneventan *Beatus* to the Beneventan-Gregorian *Angelus* shows that it is a literal, line-by-line contrafact:"Beatus es Simon Petre" corresponds to "angelus domini descendit," "quia caro et sanguis" to "de caelo et dixit," and so on. The verse of *Beatus es* is based on the second verse of *Angelus domini.* Extra syllables, such as those on "quem dicunt homines," are accommodated with syllabic note repetitions.

The Roman *Beatus es* is shaped not only by *Angelus domini* but also by verbal cues, musical relationships to another offertory, and the ever-present Roman tendency toward formulaicism and repetition. Although the Roman version of *Angelus* draws heavily from standard eighth-mode material, it shows a particular affinity with the eighth-mode *Ave Maria* (81). *Angelus domini*'s melisma on "descendit" (phrase 1), for example, also occurs in the first phrase of *Ave Maria,* and the two offertories are very similar on the word "mulieribus."[62] These melodic similarities between *Angelus domini* and *Ave Maria* eventually influence the melodic course of *Beatus es.* The first phrase of *Beatus es* is formed from two parts of a longer section of *Angelus domini*'s opening material, "angelus" and "caelo." "Quia caro" (phrase 2) is based on "et dixit" of *Angelus domini.* In the following phrases, however, *Beatus es* departs from *Angelus domini* and the typical penchant for

59. *Beatus es* is also found in the Bolognese manuscript RoA 123, which lacks pitched notation but appears to be modeled on *Ave Maria.*
60. Gregorian chant probably reached Benevento before 838. The argument is made in Thomas Forrest Kelly, *The Beneventan Chant* (Cambridge: Cambridge University Press, 1989), 11–13, 27–28, and I summarize it in chapter 6.
61. Luisa Nardini, "Il Repertorio Neo-Gregoriano del *Proprium Missae* in Area Beneventana" (Ph.D. diss, Università degli Studi di Roma, 2001), 204–21.
62. The Gregorian *Angelus* is also related to Gregorian *Ave Maria,* on the words "dominus tecum," but this material is almost certainly a later addition. See the notes for *Ave Maria* in appendix 3. As discussed in chapter 5, this melisma also occurs in probable pre-Carolingian compositions such as *Factus est repente.*

repetition and economy takes over. Accounting for differences in number of syllables, the next passage, "et sanguis" (phrase 2) is a repetition of "quia caro." "Non revelavit tibi sed pater meus" is based on standard eighth-mode material; "qui est" is a varied restatement of material heard previously. The respond closes with a shorter version *of Angelus domini's* closing melisma.

Like the Beneventan verse, the Roman verse (phrase 4) begins in imitation of the second verse of *Angelus domini*. While the Beneventan melody follows the *Angelus domini* verse closely and literally, however, the Roman melody soon departs from it. In response to a verbal cue, the Roman singer draws the melody for "discipulis suis" from verse 1 of *Angelus*, "discipuli eius" (phrase 4). The same material also occurs several times in the Roman *Ave Maria*.[63] Following this verbal prompt, the verse loses all resemblance to the second verse of *Angelus domini*. Beginning with "filium hominis" (phrase 5), the verse is marked by a change of modal characteristics, incorporating standard *protus* material. The only other offertory in the Roman repertory to mix eighth-mode and first-mode material in this way is *Ave Maria*. At the end of the verse, *Beatus es* employs nonformulaic *protus* material that is also found, with slight variance, at the end of *Ave Maria's* second verse. The melodic similarities between *Beatus es* and *Ave Maria* earlier on in the melody evidently prompted the Roman singer to adopt the closing material of *Ave Maria* at the end of *Beatus es*.

To summarize, the Beneventan version of *Beatus es* is a close contrafact of *Angelus domini*. The Roman *Beatus es*, by contrast, begins like *Angelus domini* but is subsequently influenced by other factors, including verbal cues, *Ave Maria*, and the Roman penchant for repetition and economy. These different procedures result in melodies that are quite distinct. Specific similarities between the Roman and Beneventan versions of *Beatus es* are evident only at the opening of the respond and the opening of the verse. Noting these differences, Luisa Nardini has suggested that *Beatus es* was transmitted from Rome to Benevento without notation.[64] Her hypothesis is certainly supported by the rare use of notation in Rome before the eleventh century.[65] The question remains, however, whether the transmission of the piece from Rome to Benevento involved only the lyrics—in which case the Beneventan singers would simply have chosen the frequently used *Angelus domini* melody for it—or whether it also involved an orally transmitted melody. I consider it more probable that the transmission involved words and melody. In examining a similar case of direct transmission from Rome to Benevento, the communion *Sint lumbi vestri*, Nardini has shown that the Roman and Beneventan versions correspond much more closely, clearly suggesting a transmission of melody.[66] It is

63. See "dominus tecum," "gratia plena," etc.
64. Nardini makes this argument in "Written and Oral Transmission."
65. See John Boe, "Music Notation in Archivio San Pietro C 105 and in the Farfa Breviary, Chigi C. VI. 177," *Early Music History* 18 (1999): 1–45.
66. Nardin, "Written and Oral."

doubtful, moreover, that the correspondence of both versions of *Beatus es* to *Angelus domini* is mere coincidence. The Roman *Beatus es* may once have resembled *Angelus domini* more closely, later diverging from it under the influence of typical Roman compositional procedures. Another possibility is that the Beneventan singers, noticing the similarities in the openings of *Beatus es* and *Angelus domini*, simply created a more literal contrafact, modeled on other contrafacts such as *Assumpta est Maria* and *Beata es virgo Maria*.

While I do not know which scenario is more likely, it is clear that both versions of *Beatus es* originated in an oral milieu and that they demonstrate very different conceptions of oral composition. The Roman version, typical of its tradition, draws on a rich complex of verbal and musical associations that seem to affect the melody on an ad hoc, phrase-by-phrase basis. The status of the Beneventan as a literal contrafact, by contrast, implies that the Beneventan singers conceived the preexisting piece, *Angelus domini*, as a fixed entity, perhaps reflecting an encroaching influence of the Carolingian valuing of systemization and stabilization.

RHETORICAL TREATMENT OF THE WORDS

My analysis of verbal structure in chapter 2 demonstrated that many offertories, psalmic and nonpsalmic, are extensively centonized, modified from the biblical source to form a lyric suitable for a musical setting. In many cases, moreover, the lyrics were evidently created to fit the specific musical form of the offertory with verses and repetenda. The Frankish and Roman singers differ greatly in their treatment of these texts. I have shown that in the Roman formulas, the singers respond in consistent ways to aural or structural aspects of the words, such as length and accent pattern of each clause. In many cases, however, the Frankish cantors respond more explicitly to the content and meaning of the texts. In view of the frequent centonization, these differences have potential importance in determining the origins and relative historical position of the two dialects. Levy has noted that centonized texts seem to have been made explicitly for a musical setting of the elaborate sort reflected in the Gregorian offertories.[67] Verbal centonization, however, is most prominent among the psalmic offertories assigned to Lent, precisely the repertory that exhibits the most pervasive formulaicism in the Roman tradition. It must be asked, then, whether these centonized lyrics were made to be sung with the formulas of the eleventh-century Roman tradition. Did the Franks enhance these special texts with rhetorical emphasis, or were the

---

67. See especially Kenneth Levy, "Toledo, Rome, and the Legacy of Gaul," *Early Music History* 4 (1984): 49–99.

rhetorical aspects of the melodies present in the eighth-century Roman tradition and deemphasized in subsequent centuries?

Recent examinations of the relationship between words and music have enhanced our understanding of the differences between the Gregorian and Roman dialects. Susan Rankin demonstrates a sharper rhetorical outline in the Gregorian version of the introit *Ad te domine levavi* vis-à-vis the Roman version.[68] Emma Hornby shows that departures from the formulaic system in the second-mode tracts are far from random; rather, they are made to emphasize specific aspects of the words.[69] In many cases, the Gregorian offertories manifest a similar concern for the content and meaning of the text, shaping the melody in a way that highlights particular words or structural features of the text. There are several ways to achieve these rhetorical readings outside the confines of melodic formulas. One is through the use of range, a technique observed in certain communions.[70] As I have shown, many offertories remain primarily within a narrow range, focused within the tetrachords C-F or G-c, with an emphasis F or c as a referential pitch. Departures from these norms through a sudden heightening or lowering of range can create a sense of markedness, serving to draw attention to a particular word or phrase.[71] Sudden changes from the moderately neumatic stylistic norm can produce a similar effect.

The attention to verbal content and meaning in the Gregorian melodies is especially evident in the nonpsalmic offertories such as *Sanctificavit Moyses* (64), whose narrative and dialogue lend themselves so well to dramatic treatment. Centonized and paraphrased from Exodus, *Sanctificavit* adopts a sacrificial theme characteristic of many Old Hispanic sacrificia.[72] In the Gregorian reading, the fifth-mode range is divided into separate units that underscore the meaning of the text and mark shifts between narrative and quotation. The first verse, beginning in phrase 5, starts in the lower part of the fifth-mode range, articulating the fifth F-c. In phrase 6, however, the melody expands into the upper part of the range

68. Susan Rankin, "Carolingian Music," in *Carolingian Culture: Emulation and Innovation*, ed. Rosamund McKitterick (Cambridge: Cambridge University Press, 1994), 281–87.
69. Emma Hornby, "Reading the Bible: Rhetoric, and Exegesis in Gregorian Chant," in *Cantus Planus: Papers Read at the Twelfth Meeting, Lillafüred, 2004*, ed. László Dobszay (Budapest: Hungarian Academy of Sciences, 2006), 285–301, and "From Nativity to Resurrection: Musical and Exegetical Resonances in the Good Friday Chants *Domini audivi* and *Qui habitat*," presented at the International Medieval Congress, Leeds, 2005. I thank Dr. Hornby for sharing these works in advance of their publication.
70. Brad Maiani, "The Responsory-Communions: Toward a Chronology of Selected Proper Chants" (Ph.D. diss., University of North Carolina, Chapel Hill, 1996), 115–71, and "Approaching the Communion Melodies," *Journal of the American Musicological Society* 53 (2000): 250–86.
71. "Markedness" is borrowed from Robert Hatten's usage of the term in *Musical Meaning in Beethoven: Markedness, Correlation, Interpretation* (Bloomington: Indiana University Press, 1994), 34–39.
72. The words and their relationship to other sacrificia are discussed in chapter 2. Also see Giacomo Baroffio, "Die mailändischen Überliefering des Offertoriums *Sanctificavit*," in *Festschrift Bruno Stäblein zum 70. Geburtstag*, ed. Martin Ruhnke (Kassel: Barenreiter, 1967), 1–8.

beginning with the melisma on "ascende," which reaches high e. This apparent text painting also highlights the shift between the voice of the narrator and the voice of God. The word "ascendit" (phrase 8) is emphasized with further expansion of the range to f and g, and "descendit" (phrase 9) is marked by a return to the lower part of the range, another literal depiction of the text. The Roman melody lacks these rhetorical responses to the words. Carrying the words with a characteristic melodic economy, it consists primarily of three recurring phrases that are altered according to word accent and clause length.

Two offertories from the core repertory are based on prophetic passages from Isaiah, *Confortamini* (4) and *Exsulta satis* (5), both assigned to Ember Days of Advent. The Gregorian *Confortamini* provides a reading of the words through changes in texture and the use of range as a syntactical tool. In the respond, the alternation between two tonal areas that often characterize fourth-mode chants, D-F or C-F and E-G or E-a, helps to shape and distinguish syntactical units. In phrase 1, for example, "confortamini" lies primarily within the D-F area, with G as upper neighbor; the next unit, "et iam nolite timere," is distinguished from the first through articulation of the E-a interval, and "nolite" is given emphasis through a moderate melisma and expansion to the upper neighbor b (flat). These two areas remain the focus of the melody until the portion of the respond that serves as the repetendum, "ipse veniet et salvos nos faciet," (phrase 3) which emphasizes the central theme of Advent.[73] Musically these words are marked by a move into the G-c tetrachord more commonly associated with third-mode chants. This final phrase of the respond is distinguished from the others not merely by its expansion into the higher part of the range but also though its wider range overall. In view of the prophetic Advent theme of this chant, the most important word in the respond is "veniet." On this word, the melody transverses nearly the entire range of the respond, c to D. The melody seems to follow a long-range plan that reaches a climax on "veniet." As part of the repetendum, this striking passage was sung two or three times in the course of a complete performance.

The two verses of this offertory show a similar treatment of the words. The first verse is similar to the respond in its tonal plan. The first phrase expands to pitch a in a lengthy melisma that emphasizes the important word "aperientur" (phrase 4). Beginning with "et aures" (phrase 5), the range is expanded to b (flat, on "surdorum") and then to c on the word "ascendet" (phrase 6). The verse melody is shaped in a way that underscores distinctions between syntactical units and

73. As Pfisterer has emphasized, the Ember Days of Advent predate the incorporation of Advent as a liturgical season. The prevalence of Advent themes in the chants for Ember Days, however, certainly attests to its existence as a theological concept, even if it did not exist as a liturgical season. *Cantilena Romana: Untersuchungen zur Überlieferung des gregorianischen Chorals* (Paderborn: Schöningh, 2002), 231–32. Also see Margot Fassler, "Sermons, Sacramentaries, and Early Sources for the Office in the Latin West: The Example of Advent," in *The Divine Office in the Latin Middle Ages: Methology and Source Studies, Regional Developments, Hagiography*, ed. Margot E. Fassler and Rebecca A. Baltzer (New York: Oxford University Press, 2000), 15–47.

highlights important words, resulting in a gradual expansion of range leading to the climax on the word "ascendet." The first phrase of the second verse, which calls on the House of David to listen to the subsequent prophecy, traverses the range of a seventh, from D to c (phrase 8). The prophetic words that follow, "non pusillum vobis certamen praestare hominibus" (phrase 9), are marked by immediate contrast, evident in a sudden change to nearly syllabic recitation—highly unusual in offertories—and a lower, very narrow range. The exhortation to listen and the subsequent prophetic words are contrasted by an abrupt shift of range and a syllabic style in which the prophetic words are clearly proclaimed.

This rhetorical approach to text setting is reflected in the Roman version of *Confortamini* to a far lesser extent. The Roman version is notated a fifth higher than the Gregorian, closing on the affinal b. The respond has a range and melodic outline similar to that of the Gregorian version. Even its verses show a few points of similarity to the Gregorian reading, with only traces of the formulas that characterize the verses of Lent and Paschaltide. In the respond, the melismas and expanded range on "nolite" (phrase 1) and "veniet" (phrase 3) correspond to the Gregorian version. In the verses, however, the Roman is less explicit than the Gregorian version is in its reading of the words. The melisma on "aperientur" (phrase 4), for example, is shorter and narrower in range than the corresponding Gregorian melisma. More important, the Roman version is less explicit than the Gregorian in its use of range as a syntactical tool. It lacks, for example, the Gregorian reading's gradual expansion of range with each clause leading up to the climax on "ascendit" (*sic*; phrase 6). The Roman version, moreover, exhibits less concern for large-scale planning in terms of range, articulating the higher tetrachord c-f for "caecorum" (phrase 4) but returning once again to the lower register for the subsequent phrase. The second verse makes a similar impression: although the switch to syllabic declamation for "non pusillum . . . " (phrase 9) is present in the Roman version, the contrast of range between phrases 8 and 9 is less sharply etched than in the Gregorian melody. Similar characteristics of the Gregorian and Roman versions are evident in the other canticle offertory for Advent, *Exsulta satis*.[74]

The nonpsalmic offertories, with their prophecy and dialogue, offered the singers perhaps the most ripe opportunities for a dramatic musical reading of the text. A similar approach, however, is evident in many psalmic Gregorian offertories. A concern for depicting the content of the text is discernable, particularly when offertories depart from the neumatic, recitational style that characterizes the

---

74. In the Gregorian version of *Exsulta*, the rhetorical approach to the text is especially striking in the second verse, which introduces the Advent theme, "quia ecce venio et habitabo in medio tui." "Ecce" is highlighted with a long descending melisma that draws attention to the following clause, "et habitabo in medio," which is set syllabically and in a contrasting range. The descending motion can be viewed as a musical depiction of God's coming to dwell on the earth, and the syllabic setting draws attention to the prophetic words. In the Roman reading, the opening words of the verse lack this large-scale descending motion. The nearly syllabic setting of "et habitabo in medio" is present, but the use of range as a syntactic tool is not.

responds and first verses of most Lenten offertories. *Venite et videte* is the final verse of the second-mode offertory *Benedicite gentes* (36). In this highly centonized lyric, the psalmic excerpts that make up the respond and final verse were selected to create a structural and thematic unity. The text is clearly created specifically for a musical setting. In the Gregorian tradition, the final verse (beginning in phrase 15) has the traits of mode 1 in its opening, exhibiting a modal expansion and climactic effect typical of Gregorian final verses. Beginning with the words "ad ipsum ore meo clamavi" (phrase 17), a series of changes creates a sense of tonal markedness, distinguishing these words from the second-mode context of the respond and previous verses. The version of the base transcription, Pa 776, moves into the G-*protus* tonal area, with a b-flat.[75] Here melodic material normally associated with the second mode is projected a fourth higher, articulating the third G-b-flat and allowing G to be heard as a temporary final. The manuscripts incorporated into this study exhibit variants in pitch level at this point, as illustrated in the in the critical commentary of appendix 3. In some sources, this passage is written a tone higher, in a range more typical of the first mode. As I argue, it is likely that the G-*protus* version is the preferred one, the others emendations. The move into a different tonal area, I hypothesize, results in the introduction of the nondiatonic pitch E-flat on "mea." With this shift in range, the Gregorian version provides a reading of the words that highlights these words as a verbal and musical climax.

The Roman approach to setting these words is cursory by comparison. With a characteristic melodic economy, each clause is sung to Formula B. The two readings of this verse exhibit the sharpest contrast: the Frankish cantors exploit the dramatic possibilities inherent in the lyrics, whereas the Roman melody lacks the crafted individuality of the lyrics. Other Lenten offertories present a similar picture. In *Sperent in te* (41), for example, I noted that the psalmic excerpts are carefully chosen to create a thematically and structurally unified libretto. The Roman version of this offertory, a melody of mode 6, draws heavily on Formula B for its respond and both verses, and is nearly identical to the other sixth-mode offertories.

As illustrated in chapter 2, verbal centonization is most heavily concentrated among the psalmic offertories of Lent. Yet, as I have shown, it is precisely these Lenten offertories that exhibit such a marked formulaicism in the Roman tradition. The carefully constructed texts of the Roman Lenten offertories and the perfunctory formulaicism of their melodies are an apparent contradiction, raising the question of whether these texts were created for the formulaic melodies we see in the Roman sources of the eleventh and twelfth centuries. In considering this paradox, one further phenomenon warrants mention. Despite the overwhelming formulaicism of the Roman Lenten verses, I have shown that a very small number

---

75. A b-flat is indicated in the sources that distinguish between b-natural and b-flat. I discuss the "G-*protus*" tonal area and its importance in some manuscripts in chapter 6.

have distinctive melodic profiles, and that these often resemble their Gregorian counterparts. In two Roman Lenten offertories, *Scapulis suis* (19) and *Exaudi deus* (30), the final verses are individual melodies, exhibiting a modal expansion and climactic effect typical of the Gregorian tradition.

The text of the eighth-mode *Exaudi deus* (30) is highly centonized; the lyricist selects excerpts from the psalm to create an appropriate verse-repetenda form. In the final verse of *Exaudi deus*, beginning in phrase 8, the Gregorian version has the traits of mode 7, exhibiting a typical modal expansion. Its treatment of the text is comparable to that of *Venite et videte*, the final verse of *Benedicite gentes*. Through the use of range, the melody provides a reading of the text, highlighting "clamavi" with an expansion to f (phrase 8). "Libera" and "animam" (phrase 9) are emphasized in a similar way. In the final melisma of the verse, the expansion to g and aa creates a climactic effect. Although the Roman version of this verse differs greatly from the Gregorian in surface detail, it is similar in range, expanding to f on "clamavi" and remaining within the fourth c-f for much of the verse.

Scapulis suis (19), for Quadragesima Sunday, presents a similar picture. Its source text, Psalm 90, also provides the source for the day's other proper chants. Because the story of the temptation of Christ in the Gospel of Matthew alludes to this psalm, it became associated with the temptation and Christ's victory over the devil. In view of these associations, a particularly important passage from the psalm occurs in the second verse of the offertory, "conculcabis leonem et draconem," "you will trample upon the lion and the serpent." The imagery of the lion and serpent is vividly depicted in illuminated psalters from the later Middle Ages.[76] In both versions of *Scapulis suis*, these words are given special emphasis through expanded range and melismas, on "conculcabis" (phrase 10), which extends to g, and again on "draconem," where the Roman extends to aa. The melisma in the Gregorian version of "draconem" is found on the same word in the tract for the day, where the melody departs markedly from the formulaic system in order to emphasize this word.[77] In these isolated final verses of two Lenten offertories, *Scapulis suis* and *Exaudi deus*, the Roman melodies exhibit a rhetorical approach to text setting that is far more characteristic of Gregorian offertories. The melodic formulas so prominent throughout the Lenten verses are lacking here, and instead the melodies show a concern for individuality comparable to that of their lyrics.

Vir erat (67) offers perhaps the most striking example of rhetorical effect in the Gregorian offertories. The text repetitions in this extraordinary piece were cited by Amalar of Metz, who characterized them as expressions of Job's sickness and suffering.[78] The respond, in the voice of the narrator, is centonized from the

76. Hornby, "From Nativity to Resurrection."
77. Ibid.
78. "Interim occurrit mihi repetitio verborum quae est in versibus offertorii *Vir erat....* Verba Iob aegroti et dolentis continentur in versibus. Aegrotus cuius anhelitus non est sanus neque fortis, solet verba imperfecta saepius repetere. Officii auctor, ut affectanter nobis ad memoriam reduceret

opening of the Book of Job. The verses, in Job's voice, are centonized from chapters 6 and 7, Job's response to Eliphaz that his suffering is unwarranted. The repetitions of short passages comprising incomplete thoughts, such as "et calamitas" (phrase 11) and "quae est enim" (phrase 12), and their musical treatment were perhaps inspired by the opening of chapter 6, where Job compares his sorrowful speech to the involuntary braying of a hungry ass or lowing of a barren ox. The initial statement of each repeated passage remains within a narrow range, with many repeated F's. Subsequent statements of the words occur in varied melodic repetition, given rhetorical emphasis with melismatic expansion or wide leaps, as in the repetitions of "utinam appenderentur" in phrases 7 and 8, and "et calamitas" in phrase 11, whose distinctive F-b (flat) leaps, followed by downward motion, are echoed in the repetition of "quae est enim" in phrase 12.

Job's expressions of grief reach a dramatic climax in verse 4. His lament that his eyes will never again look on good things, one of the most stunningly expressive passages of the chant repertory, is set to nine successive statements of the words "ut videat/videam bona," underscored with varied repetition and expansion of range. The sources incorporated into this study are exceptionally diverse in their indication of pitch level here. The music examples included in appendix 3 present no less than eleven different readings, resulting, I hypothesize, from the use of nondiatonic pitches, the wide range, and a problematic transition to the repetendum. The reading of Pa 776 given in the base transcription spans nearly two octaves, from low B (flat) to high g. To an extent that is unique in the repertory, the Roman version of *Vir erat* mirrors the Gregorian in its rhetorical treatment of Job's words, with the distinctive fourth leaps on "calamitas" and "quae est enim," along with the same varied repetition and expansion of range in the fourth verse. The pitch-level profile of the Roman reading, is, in fact, very similar to that of Pa 776.

The occasional presence of dramatic text treatment and climactic modal expansion in the Roman verses indicates that the aesthetic principles that underlie the Gregorian verses were known to the Roman cantors. These examples of individualism, however, are extremely rare among the Roman verses in the later part of the liturgical year. Of the seventy-five Roman verses that have primary assignments from Septuagesima through Holy Week, only thirteen consist primarily of idiomelic material; of these, only four are final verses. On the whole, the Roman Lenten verses are highly formulaic. The expedient, cursory nature of their melodies seems incompatible with their highly crafted, individual lyrics. In chapter 5, this pattern will thus play a role in my argument that the melodies of the eleventh-century Roman dialect reflect not an archaic, eighth-century tradition but

---

aegrotantem Iob, repetivit saepius verba more aegrotantium." Amalarius Metensis, *Liber officialis* 39, in *Amalarii episcopi opera liturgica omnia*, ed. Jean-Michael Hanssens (Vatican City: Biblioteca Apostolica Vaticana, 1950), 2:373.

rather a trend toward progressive uniformity and homogenization during the three
centuries of purely oral transmission.

SUMMARY

The examples examined in this chapter have shown how the Roman melodies
depend more extensively on formulas and verbal cues than their Gregorian
counterparts do. While the Gregorian melodies show occasional vestiges of correspondence to the Roman formulas—evidence that the two dialects are rooted in a
common tradition—the Roman versions resemble the Gregorian most closely
precisely where they depart from the formulas and adopt idiomelic material.
I have also shown that breaches of affinity between the two dialects occur with
greatest frequency among verses of the later liturgical seasons, where the Roman
tradition shows a particular concentration of formulas. Resemblance between the
two traditions, moreover, often grows weaker with each successive verse. Finally,
the Gregorian melodies show a greater tendency to depict the content and
meaning of the text. In chapter 5, these patterns will serve a basis for evaluating
different theories about the origins of the two dialects. It is probable that both
dialects changed during their period of separate oral transmission. As I will argue,
however, the evidence presented in this chapter is difficult to reconcile with the
theory that the Roman formulas represent the archaic tradition of seventh- or
eighth-century Rome.

4

THE MILANESE MELODIC DIALECT AND THE
QUESTION OF "ITALIANATE" STYLE

The stylistic features of Italianate dialects have often been cited in the debate over the relationship between Gregorian and Old Roman chant and their relative historical position. Milanese, Roman, and Old Beneventan chant are unified by a tendency toward stepwise motion and ornateness. Joseph Dyer and David Hiley, among others, have argued that these Italianate features were present in the Roman chant transmitted to the Franks and that the melodies subsequently underwent assimilation to native Frankish style.[1] Because of their relatively late preservation in notation, however, Beneventan and Milanese chant raise questions very similar to those surrounding the Roman dialect. Beneventan liturgical practice developed during the Lombard period and flourished from the seventh to eighth centuries, but the chant was not preserved in notation until the late tenth century. The first notated manuscripts of Milanese chant date from the twelfth century. Do these late written sources reflect an earlier, archaic state of the melodies or developments that took place in the oral tradition between their creation and their preservation in writing?

The examination of the Gregorian and Roman melodies in chapter 3 focused primarily on their differences in melodic structure. The "Italianate argument," however, invites a more explicit examination of style and an incorporation of other dialects into the analytical picture. A comparative analysis of cognate melodies can throw some light on the origins of the Italianate style. Because the Old Beneventan repertory has very few offertories in common with the Roman-Gregorian, my primary vehicle for analysis will be offertories common to Rome, Francia, and Milan.[2] Nearly half of the Milanese offerendae are also found in the

---

1. Joseph Dyer, "'*Tropis semper variantibus*': Compositional Strategies in the Offertories of the Old Roman Chant," *Early Music History* 17 (1998): 1–59, and review of *The Advent Project: The Later-Seventh-Century Creation of the Roman Mass Proper*, by James McKinnon, *Early Music History* 20 (2001): 307; and David Hiley, *Western Plainchant: A Handbook* (Oxford: Clarendon Press, 1993), 547–49, 562.
2. The Milanese offertories are studied on their own terms in Giacomo Baroffio, "Die Offertorien der ambrosianischen Kirche: Vorstudie zur kritischen Ausgabe der mailändischen Gesänge" (Ph.D. diss., University of Cologne, 1964); See also the overview of the shared offertories in P. Odilo Heiming, "Vorgregorianisch-römische Offertorien in der mailändischen Liturgie," *Liturgisches Leben* 5 (1938): 72–79; Karl Ott, "I versetti ambrosiani e gregoriani dell'offertorio," *Rassegna Gregoriana* 10 (1911): 345–60; and Michel Huglo, *Fonti e paleografia del canto ambrosiano* (Milan: Archivio Ambrosiano, 1956), 127–37.

Franco-Roman repertory and have long been viewed as borrowings. Michel Huglo has noted that many of the Roman-Gregorian chants with Milanese counterparts correspond to the PsR rather than the Milanese psalter, suggesting an ultimate origin in Rome.[3] In assessing the implications of these borrowings for the questions of Gregorian and Roman chant, however, we encounter considerable uncertainty surrounding their path into Milan and time of importation. In separate studies, Huglo and Hucke proposed that the Romano-Frankish imports were late integrations into the Milanese repertory, borrowed from the Gregorian tradition rather than the Roman. Noting that the Milanese versions correspond more closely to the Gregorian than to the Roman, Hucke and Huglo argued that they were adopted into Milan directly from the Gregorian tradition, subsequently acquiring the ornate, "Italianate" surface style associated with Milanese chant.[4]

The liturgical history of Milan offers contextual support for a Carolingian influence on the repertory after the Frankish conquest of Milan in 774. Beginning in the late eighth century, the Milanese liturgy was permeated by Franco-Roman influence. The earliest Milanese sacramentaries, dating from the ninth and tenth centuries, reflect an amalgamation of Franco-Roman and Old Ambrosian elements, borrowing extensively from the eighth-century Gelasian and Gregorian sacramentaries. The influence of these books is evident even in festivals of Milanese origin, suggesting a late reworking along Franco-Roman lines.[5] The Milanese liturgical books incorporate the Marian festivals and the feast of the Holy Cross, practices attributed to Franco-Roman influence.[6] Additional markers of Carolingian influence include formularies for each Lenten feria, including the previously aliturgical Lenten Fridays,[7] and a set of votive Masses for the seven days of the week from Alcuin's *Liber sacramentorum* that probably entered Milan in the early ninth century.[8] While it is rarely possible to pinpoint the specific circumstances of these accretions, opportunities for liturgical exchange arose in numerous contexts: the travels of Paul the Deacon and Alcuin, contacts between Ambrosian and

3. Huglo, *Fonti e paleografia*, 127.
4. Helmut Hucke, "Die Gregorianische Gradualeweise des 2. Tons und ihre ambrosianischen Parallelen: Ein Beitrag zur Erforschung des Ambrosianischen Gesangs," *Archiv für Musikwissenschaft* 13 (1956): 285–314; Huglo, *Fonti e paleografia*, 134–36; see also Luigi Agustoni, "Ein Vergleich zwischen dem Gregorianischen und dem Ambrosianischen Choral-einige Aspekte," in *Cantando praedicare: Godejard Joppich zum 60. Geburtstag*, ed. Stefan Klöckner (Regensburg: Gustav Bosse, 1992), 13–28.
5. The Frankish influence is documented in most studies of the Ambrosian sacramentaries. For detailed documentation and references, see Judith Frei, *Das ambrosianische Sakramentar D 3-3 aus dem mailändischen Metropolitankapitel: Ein textkritische und redaktionsgeschichtliche Untersuchung der mailändischen Sakramentartradition* (Achendorff, Germany: Münster Westfalen, 1974).
6. Ibid., 144–46; 154–55; Pietro Borella, "Influssi carolingi e monastici sul Messale Ambrosiano," in *Miscellanea liturgica in honorem L. Cuniberti Mohlberg* (Rome: Edizioni Liturgiche, 1948), 1:78–93.
7. Frei, *Das ambrosianische Sakramentar*, 39–44.
8. Odilo Heiming, "Die Mailändischen sieben Votivemessen für die einzelnen Tage der Woche und der Liber Sacramentorum des sel. Alkuin," in *Miscellanea liturgica*, 2:317–39.

Frankish monasteries.[9] The first half of the ninth century also saw two Frankish archbishops in Milan, Angilbert I and II, who introduced Frankish customs into the cathedral office.[10]

In view of these Frankish liturgical influences, the Carolingian period may offer the best context for the reception of many offertories at Milan. Several of the borrowed offerendae are assigned to festivals that exhibit other Frankish influences. Frankish festivals such as the Marian festivals and Holy Cross, for example, have offerendae borrowed from the Romano-Frankish repertory.[11] In the Milanese sacramentary, the *commune sanctorum* and Post-Pentecost Sundays consist largely of Franco-Roman formularies, mixed with some Old Ambrosian elements.[12] The offerendae for these occasions likewise consist of a small body of Roman-Gregorian offertories.

Although these circumstantial factors support Huglo's and Hucke's hypothesis that the Milanese melodies were borrowed from the Gregorian tradition, some shared chants were evidently known in Milan prior to the reception of Roman chant in Francia. A palimpsest fragment from the seventh or early eighth century preserves a portion of the Milanese Mass for Easter Sunday, including a small fragment of *Angelus domini*, an offertory of probable non-Roman origin, and parts of the confractorium *Pascha nostrum*, which functions as the Easter Sunday communion in the Franco-Roman liturgy.[13] On balance, however, at least some borrowing of offertories can be safely placed in the Carolingian era. Terence Bailey argues persuasively for similar imports among both transitoria and offerendae.[14] He points to certain anachronistic features of the Milanese repertory as evidence that the borrowing of Franco-Roman chants came to a close after the first quarter of the ninth century.[15] Although the Milanese tradition has counterparts to untexted sequences, it lacks Carolingian innovations such as tropes and texted

9. Borella, "Influssi," 93–115.
10. Ibid., 98–99.
11. The offerenda for the Invention of the Cross is the Roman-Gregorian communion *Nos autem*.
12. Frei proposes the existence of a Common of Saints in the Old Milanese (i.e. pre-Carolingian) liturgy but demonstrates that the Common was substantially revised during the Carolingian period. Frei, *Ambrosianische Sakramentar*, 158–61.
13. Alban Dold, *Getilgte Paulus- und Psalmtexte unter getilgten Ambrosianischen Liturgiestücken aus cod. Sangall. 908*, Texte und Arbeiten 14 (Beuron, Germany: Kunstschule der Erzabtei, 1928). I thank Andreas Pfisterer for this reference. Although the fragment preserves only half a word from *Angelus domini*, the identification seems secure in view of the other Easter chants in its context. Dold places the fragment in the seventh century; Huglo places it in the eighth. See Huglo, *Fonti e paleografia*, 5–6.
14. Terence Bailey, *The Transitoria of the Ambrosian Mass: Compositional Process in Ecclesiastical Chant* (Ottawa: Institute of Mediaeval Music, 2003), and a forthcoming study of offerendae.
15. Terence Bailey, "Ambrosian Chant," in *Revised New Grove Dictionary of Music and Musicians*, and "The Development and Chronology of the Ambrosian Sanctorale: The Evidence of the Antiphon Texts," in *The Divine Office in the Latin Middle Ages*, ed. Margot E. Fassler and Rebecca A. Baltzer (New York: Oxford University Press, 2000), 257–76.

sequences.[16] Its paucity of office repertory and alleluia melodies—there are only ten—further attest to its conservatism.[17] Bailey thus hypothesizes that Milan was not open to repertorial expansion after the early ninth century.

In the case of the offertories, a third possibility arises for transmission into Milan. Among the offertories common to Milan, Francia, and Rome are several of possible non-Roman origin. Milan lay at a crossroads between Rome and the North, Spain and the Byzantine East. Comparative studies of its liturgy and chant have demonstrated a rich blend of pre-Carolingian influences, evident in repertorial sharing with Gaul, Lombard northern Italy, Benevento, and the Byzantine East.[18] Some offertories, then, may have reached Milan independently of Frankish or Roman influence. In this scenario, the Milanese and Roman-Gregorian versions would be separate descendants of a common, non-Roman archetype. In sum, it is probable that the Milanese borrowed their offerendae from different sources. While some Roman and possibly Gallican offertories were likely known in Milan before the Carolingian period, a circumstantial case for transmission through Frankish channels can be made for many pieces, particularly those of the *commune dominicarum* and the *commune sanctorum*.

In this chapter, I undertake comparative analysis with these myriad possibilities in mind. With a working hypothesis that the Milanese melodies are based on the same Gregorian melodies that were preserved in writing a century later, they would have little relevance for the questions surrounding Gregorian and Roman chant. Their ornate surface style would appear to be a secondary, superficial assimilation to Milanese stylistic preferences. Frankish chant in the later eighth century, however, is marked by documented discrepancies with Roman practice and continued efforts toward unification. The state of the Gregorian repertory at this time remains an open question. Whether the melodies were received through Roman, Gallican, or eighth-century Frankish channels, the Milanese tradition

16. Terence Bailey, "Milanese Melodic Tropes," *Journal of the Plainsong and Medieval Music Society* 11 (1988): 1–12.
17. See Terence Bailey, *The Ambrosian Alleluias* (Englefield Green, England: Plainsong and Mediaeval Music Society, 1983).
18. Kenneth Levy, "The Byzantine Sanctus and Its Modal Tradition in East and West," *Annales musicologiques* 6 (1958–63): 7–67, "The Italian Neophytes' Chants," *Journal of the American Musicological Society* 23 (1970): 181–227, and "Toledo, Rome"; Terence Bailey, "Ambrosian Chant in Southern Italy," *Journal of the Plainsong and Mediaeval Music Society* 6 (1983): 173–95; James Borders, "The Northern Italian Antiphons *ante evangelium* and the Gallican Connection," *Journal of Musicological Research* 8 (1988): 1–53; Thomas Forrest Kelly, "Beneventan and Milanese Chant," *Journal of the Royal Musical Association* 62 (1987): 173–95, "Non-Gregorian Music in an Antiphoner of Benevento," *Journal of Musicology* 4 (1987): 478–97, and *The Beneventan Chant* (Cambridge: Cambridge University Press, 1989), 181–201; Bailey, *Ambrosian Alleluias*; Daniele Sabaino, "Reminiscenze ambrosiane nella creatività liturgica di Angelica 123? Elementi e ipotesi di rilettura," in *Codex Angelicus 123: Studi sul graduale-tropario Bolognese del secolo XI e sui manoscritti collegati* (Cremona: Una cosa rara, 1996), 67–116; and Luisa Nardini, "Aliens in Disguise: Byzantine and Gallican Chants in the Latin Liturgy," *Plainsong and Medieval Music* 13 (2007): 145–72.

becomes an important witness in formulating hypotheses about the state of the melodic prototypes and the origins of the Italianate style.

In many cases, a comparative study of offertories will confirm Hucke's and Huglo's observations. The offerendae do correspond more closely to the Gregorian melodies than to the Roman ones, especially in their structural traits such as range, contour, and placement of melismas. Most conspicuously, they lack the formulas that pervade many of the Roman offertories. Occasionally, however, the Milanese versions depart from the Gregorian readings in structure and show an unmistakable resemblance to the Roman. With a theory that the offerendae were taken over directly from fully formed Gregorian melodies, these correspondences with Roman chant would be difficult to explain. Despite their greater structural resemblance to the Gregorian versions, moreover, the Milanese melodies share some melodic vocabulary and aspects of their style with the Roman dialect. These patterns suggest the Milanese cantors worked from models that had characteristics of both the Gregorian and Roman versions, but were closer to the Gregorian. After illustrating these patterns, I consider the implications of the comparative study for the origins of the Italianate style and the melodic changes that occurred in each tradition.

REPERTORIAL OVERVIEW AND TEXTUAL VARIANTS

A list of Milanese offerendae that also serve as Gregorian and Roman offertories is given in table 4.1, in the order of their liturgical assignments at Milan. The table shows the liturgical assignments in both liturgies (column 3), textual traits and variants (column 4), and an assessment of musical resemblance to the Gregorian and Roman versions (column 5).[19] The rows are numbered for purposes of reference. Most of the offerendae listed in the table are present in the *Manuale*, the earliest complete witness to the Milanese chant repertory.[20] Most offerendae in the table show evidence of a common origin with the Gregorian and Roman versions, manifest in verbal and melodic similarities. The verbal evidence is especially compelling among lyrics that are centonized or otherwise altered from the biblical source. Because the verbal text is nearly identical in the Milanese, Gregorian, and Roman traditions, the cognate status of the three versions would be demonstrable even in the absence of melodic resemblance.

The offerendae show a tendency toward brevity, often lacking the verses of the Gregorian and Roman versions. Certain Roman-Gregorian offertory verses,

---

19. As table 4.1 shows, a few of these offerendae have dual assignments. *Benedixisti*, without the verse, is part of the *commune dominicarum*, but Bailey, in a forthcoming study, argues for an original assignment of Advent.

20. Marco Magistretti, ed., *Manuale Ambrosianum ex codice saec. xi olim in usum canonicae Vallis Travaliae* (Milan: U Hoepli, 1904–5).

TABLE 4.1 Milanese Offerendae Found in Francia and Rome

Offerenda	Counterpart in Gr/R	Liturgical Assignments	Textual Traits and Variants	Melodic Correspondence
1. Sperent in te	Sperent in te	M: Advent II G/R: Tues. of Lent V	PsR orationes (R)	To G
2. Benedixisti v. Ostende	Benedixisti v. 2 Ostende	M: Advent IV, Com. dom. G/R: Advent III	PsR	No
3. Confortamini v. Audite	Confortamini v. 2 Audite	M: Advent VI V G/R: Ember Wed. of Adv.	Isaiah VL M verse has longer text	To G and R
4. Orietur	Verse of Reges tharsis	M: Epiphany G/R Epiphany		No
5. Iubilate . . . universa	Iubilate . . . universa	G/R: I/II Epiphany, Easter IV M: Sextagesima, Easter II	δ M: Iubilate *domino* deo (med)	To G and R
6. Scapulis suis v. Super	Scapulis suis v. Super	M: Lent I G/R Lent I	Possibly PsR M: obumbravit, *speravit* (R, some G sources)	To G and R
7. Precatus est v. Et placatus	Precatus est	M: Lent I; Sabb. G/R: 12th Sunday after Pentecost	Exodus VL	To G
8. Dixit dominus ad Moysen v. Et placatus	First verse of Precatus+ Repetendum of Precatus	M: Lent III. Saturday of Lent III G/R: 12th Sun. after Pent.	Exodus VL	To G, less so to R
9. Dixit Moyses	Second verse of Precatus	M: Lent II IV G/R: 12th Sun. after Pent.	Exodus VL	To G, less so to R
10. Eripe v. In factis	Eripe v. In factis (Roman and Beneventan MSS only)	M: D Oliv G/R: Monday of Holy Week v. In factis	M: Missing ad te confugi M: domine de inimicis meis M: tu es deus meus (med)	Slightly to G In factis: lacks correspondence to R and Ben.

11. Angelus v. Euntes v. Hiesus	Angelus v. Euntes v. Hiesus	M: Easter Sunday G/R: Monday of Easter Week	Matthew	To G, slightly to R
12. In die	In die	M: Saturday of Easter Week G/R Thursday of Easter Week	Exodus VL	To G
13. Erit vobis v. Dixit	Erit vobis v. Dixit	M: Pentecost G/R: Friday of Easter Week OH: Friday of Easter Week	Exodus VL M: Erit *hic* vobis (OH) M: v. begins with alleluia (OH)	To G
14. Exaltabo v. Ego autem	Exaltabo v. Ego autem	M: Com. Dom. G/R: Wed after Quinquagesima	M: in voluntate (bona omitted) (G, med)	Respond: To G; less so to R v: to G
15. Exaudi domine	v. 1 of Perfice^{+} repetendum of Perfice	M: Com. Dom. G/R: Sextagesima	PsR M has shortened text	To G
16. Perfice	Perfice	M: Com. Dom. G/R: Sextagesima	PsR	To G, less so to R
17. Super flumina	Super flumina	M: Com. Dom.	α	To G and R
18. Si oblitus fuero	2nd verse of Super flumina	M: Com. Dom. G/R: 20th Sunday after Pentecost	α M matches G not R	To G
19. Dominus regnavit	1st verse of Deus enim	M: Com. Dom., Ascension G/R: Christmas	Possibly α M: virtu*tem* (R, med)	To G and R

(continued)

TABLE 4.1 (continued)

Offerenda	Counterpart in Gr/R	Liturgical Assignments	Textual Traits and Variants	Melodic Correspondence
20. Deus enim	Deus enim	M: Com. Dom. G/R: Christmas	Possibly α	To G and R
21. Domine convertere v. Miserere	Domine convertere v. Miserere	M: Com. Dom. G/R: Monday of Lent V	PsR	Respond to G and R v. To G, slightly to R
22. Exaudita v. Probavit v. Liberavi	Oratio mea v. Probavit- not found	M: St. Lawrence G/R Vigil of St. Lawrence	Job VL M: exaudita est (not in R, G) M: domine (not in R, G) M: v. 2 (not in R, G)	To G, less to R
23. In virtute	In virtute	M: Com. San. G/R: various	PsR M: exaltavit (R)	To G, slightly to R
24. Desiderium	Desiderium	M: Com. San. G/R: various	PsR	To G
25. Gloriabuntur	Gloriabuntur	M: Com. San. G/R: various	PsR M: iustum (R, med)	To G
26. Quoniam ad te	2nd verse of Gloriabuntur + repetendum	M: Com. San. G/R: various	PsR	To G
27. Veritas mea	Veritas mea	M: Com. San. G/R: various	PsR	To G and R

28. Afferentur	Offerentur "maior" (G only)	M: Com. San. G: various	δ M: *af*ferentur (med) M: afferentur (PsR)	Yes
29. Inveni	Inveni	M: Ambrose G/R: various	δγ *et in* oleo (G)	To G and R
30. Oravit Moyses v. Dum pertransiero	Verse of Sanctificavit	M: Dedication G/R: 18th Sunday after Pentecost OH: Quotidiano	Exodus VL M: non poteris videre faciem meam (not in G, R, but in OH)	To G
31. Stetit angelus		M: John Evangelist [G: St. Michael]	Apoc. VL Cognate with OH	No

moreover, circulate as offerendae in Milan, independently of their responds, a relationship summarized in column 2 of table 4.1. These abbreviations are especially evident in the *Commune dominicarum. Dominus regnavit* (row 19), for example, serves as the first verse of the Christmas offertory *Deus enim firmavit* in the Gregorian and Roman traditions, and parts of the lengthy nonpsalmic offertory *Precatus est Moyses* are transmitted as three separate offerendae in Milan, assigned to successive Sundays in Lent (rows 7, 8, and 9). The offerendae *Ego autem, Quoniam ad te, Si oblitus,* and *Exaudi domine* are also verses of Gregorian and Roman offertories. In many cases, these excerpted verses close with the repetendum of the original offertory, probably to compensate for their modal incompleteness. *Dominus regnavit,* for example, closes with repetendum ("ex tunc a seculo tu es") of *Deus enim firmavit,* the offertory with which it was originally sung. Like many offertory verses, *Dominus regnavit* does not close on the final; appending the repetendum to the verse gives it the modal coherence that would be lacking without it.

With only one exception, offerendae for the *commune dominicarum, commune sanctorum,* and Post-Pentecost Sundays are borrowed from the Romano-Frankish liturgy.[21] For the *commune dominicarum,* shown in rows 14–21, the Milanese adopted the responds and one verse of six different offertories, assigning a total of eleven borrowed pieces to separate Sundays.[22] Most of these items serve similarly general functions in the Franco-Roman liturgy, with multiple sanctorale assignments or double assignments to Lenten ferias and Post-Pentecost Sundays. Among offerendae with specific assignments, many have identical or very close functions in the Franco-Roman liturgy, such as *Scapulis suis* for the first Sunday in Lent and *Exaudita est oratio mea* for St. Lawrence.

The textual tradition of the shared offertories can help to posit possible directions of borrowing. Of particular interest is whether the pieces in question correspond to PsR or other Old Latin traditions; whether the Milanese versions show any particular influence of the Milanese psalter, a close relative of the PsR; and the textual variants between the Gregorian, Roman, and Milanese versions. The textual traits of the Milanese version are summarized in column 4 of table 4.1. The overall source of the text is given first, followed by differences from the Roman and Gregorian version and correspondences to the Roman chant (R), Gregorian chant (G), Old Hispanic chant (OH), and Milanese psalter (med).

21. The exception is *Portio mea,* which does not appear to be cognate with the Roman-Gregorian verse *Pars mea.* This Milanese offertory lacks a discernable melodic resemblance to the Gregorian and Roman verse based on the same text, and includes some centonized text that is not present in the Roman-Gregorian verse ("dum dilatares cor meum," Ps. 118:32). The textual differences between the two versions, moreover, indicate that they are drawn from different psalters. As Pfisterer has shown, the Gregorian and Roman texts are drawn primarily from α. The Milanese text, by contrast, matches the Roman and Mozarabic psalters (often against the Milanese psalter). See Andreas Pfisterer, "Remarks on Roman and Non-Roman Offertories," *Plainsong and Medieval Music* 14 (2005): 161–81.
22. Only one respond-verse pair, *Domine convertere* and *Miserere,* occur together as respond and verse in the Milanese commons.

As the table shows, the majority of psalmic offertories shared with the Gregorian and Roman traditions are consistent with the PsR, including the *commune* pieces *In virtute, Desiderium, Domine convertere, Exaltabo, Veritas mea, Sperent in te, Perfice,* and *Gloriabuntur*. In the absence of evidence to the contrary, it seems reasonable to assume that these offertories are Roman in origin, as Huglo and Bailey have argued. In most cases, the Milanese texts match the PsR, with few signs of assimilation to the closely related Milanese psalter. The textual bases of *Scapulis suis, Deus enim,* and *Dominus regnavit* are inconclusive; their texts are generally consistent with the PsR but also with other psalter traditions.

A few of the shared psalmic offerendae show the influence of other psalters, as illustrated in chapter 2 and summarized in appendix 1. *Super flumina* and its verse *Si oblitus* (rows 17 and 18), for example, exhibit a strong verbal influence of α, the northern Italian/North African psalter cited by Augustine. As Pfisterer has argued, an ultimate non-Roman origin for the lyric seems plausible.[23] In the case of *Si oblitus*, the Gregorian and Roman texts differ significantly, and the Milanese matches the Gregorian. Other candidates for non-Roman origin include *Iubilate deo universa* and *Inveni*, which correspond to the *gaulois* psalter δ. While these offertories may have come to Milan through a Roman or Gregorian path, it is also possible that they reached Milan independently of Franco-Roman influence. The unique assignment of *Inveni* (row 29) to Ambrose, contrasting with its more general use in the Roman-Gregorian liturgy, is of particular interest. *Inveni* is the only borrowed psalmic offerenda with a unique sanctorale assignment; the others are assigned to multiple dates or to the *commune sanctorum*. These factors may suggest a pre-Carolingian presence of *Inveni* in Milan. Another piece that may have taken a non-Carolingian path to Milan is *In factis*, a verse of *Eripe me* (row 10). Although this verse is lacking in most Gregorian sources, a verse with a partial correspondence is found at Benevento and Rome, perhaps suggesting an Italian origin.

Several of the shared psalmic offertories exhibit textual variants between the Roman and Gregorian versions, as summarized in appendix 1. These verbal differences are addressed in column 4 of table 4.1, using the *Manuale* as the source for the Milanese text. M indicates a variant found in the Milanese text, and the abbreviations G, R, and OH indicate correspondence to the Gregorian, Roman, or Old Hispanic chant text. In most cases, however, the textual variants do not answer the question of whether the Milanese versions were adopted from the Roman or Gregorian tradition, though a look at borrowed chants of other genres might help to resolve the question. It is often unclear whether the variant between the Roman and Gregorian version is attributable to a Frankish adaptation to the PsG or a

23. Andreas Pfisterer, "*Super flumina Babylonis*: On the Prehistory of a Roman Offertory," in *The Offertory and Its Verses: Research, Past, Present, and Future*, ed. Roman Hankeln (Trondheim: Tapir Academic Press, 2007), 41–56.

Roman assimilation to the PsR, made subsequent to the repertory's exportation to the north. In Milan, assimilation to the Milanese psalter is also possible. Some examples will briefly illustrate these problems. In *Gloriabuntur* (row 25), the Milanese reading "ius*tum*" matches the Roman chant text and the PsR, as against the early Gregorian sources examined, which have the PsG reading "ius*to.*" Although it is tempting to see this pattern as evidence that the Milanese version was received from Rome, "iustum" is also the reading of the Milanese psalter, raising the possibility that the lyric was assimilated to the psalter more familiar in Milan. In *Exaltabo te* (row 14) by contrast, the Milanese lyric matches the Gregorian sources and the PsG at "in voluntate" (Ps. 29:8), whereas the Roman version, following the PsR, has "in bona voluntate." "In voluntate," however, is also the reading of the Milanese psalter. *Afferentur* (row 28) is cognate with the Gregorian *Offerentur (maior)*. This piece is lacking in the Roman tradition, suggesting that the Milanese version is a Frankish borrowing.

The Milanese tradition transmits parts of several nonpsalmic Roman-Gregorian offertories, including *Sanctificavit, Stetit angelus, Erit vobis, Oratio mea, Precatus, Confortamini,* and *In die.* In the first three cases, the Milanese verbal tradition is more closely allied with the Old Hispanic version than the Roman or Gregorian, suggesting that these pieces reached Milan independently of Rome or Francia. As illustrated in chapter 2, the Gregorian and Old Hispanic *Stetit angelus* have very different lyrics in the Gregorian and Old Hispanic traditions, calling their cognate status into question. The Milanese text adheres closely to the Old Hispanic. The same is true of the offerenda *Oravit Moyses,* which circulates in the Gregorian and Old Hispanic traditions as the second verse of *Sanctificavit Moyses.* While the three versions are clearly cognates, the Milanese *Oravit* is closer verbally to the Old Hispanic. It is probable, then, that *Stetit* and *Oravit* reached Milan through a Gallican or Spanish path. *Erit hic vobis* presents a similar picture: though it lacks the second verse, the Milanese text conforms more closely to the Old Hispanic. Although it has no Old Hispanic cognate, *Exaudita est oratio mea* is another possible example of independent reception in Milan because of verbal differences from the Romano-Frankish cognate *Oratio mea.*[24]

Finally, the Milanese repertory includes four offerendae that share a partial text with Roman-Gregorian offertories, but their cognate status is questionable because of significant textual differences and a lack of melodic resemblance. The Epiphany offerenda *Orietur in diebus* (not shown in table 4.1) shares some text with a verse of the Roman-Gregorian offertory *Reges tharsis.* Melodically, however, it is utterly distinct from the Gregorian and the Roman versions, and some of its verbal

---

24. The Milanese respond and first verse have the same text as the Gregorian version, except for the opening words "exaudita est" and an addition of the word "domine." The Milanese version has a second verse not found in Rome or Francia. In his forthcoming study, Bailey points to the general theme of almsgiving as a relevant one for St. Lawrence and proposes that this second verse was added to make the text more proper for St. Lawrence.

differences are attributable to a dependency on the Milanese psalter. Psalm 71 has a long association with the Epiphany, raising the possibility that the Milanese liturgists adopted the text for this feast independently of the Roman liturgy. *Benedixisti* (row 2) and *Portio mea* (not shown in the table) make a similar impression, with a partially shared text and no discernable melodic resemblance.

MELODIC VARIANTS

Despite the probability that the cognate offerendae originated at different places and took different routes into Milan, the melodic comparisons yield a largely unified picture. With only a few exceptions, the offerendae exhibit similar relationships between the Gregorian, Roman, and Milanese versions. In melodic structure, the Milanese versions are more akin to the Gregorian melodies, utterly lacking the formulas that are so prevalent in the Roman offertories. The Milanese melodies, in fact, are most dissimilar to the Roman ones in the passages where the Roman version relies on formulas. In surface style, however, the Milanese versions show a typical "Italianate" preference for ornateness and stepwise motion. Some aspects of the Milanese melodic vocabulary, in fact, are strikingly reminiscent of the Roman dialect. The respond *Perfice gressus*, example 4.1, exemplifies some typical similarities and differences between Gregorian, Roman, and Milanese counterparts. All three versions are fourth-mode melodies and share a basic tonal structure. Faint traces of closer resemblance between them, such as the move to the third F-a on the final syllable of "vestigia" (box 1) and the cadence on G at "tuas" (box 2), suggest that they descend from a common melodic tradition. In terms of style and melodic vocabulary, however, each version of *Perfice* realizes the underlying tonal structure in a distinct way, consistent with dialectical preference. Certain passages of the Gregorian version exhibit a reiterative, *tritus* style, with frequent repercussions on the tenor F, as in box 3.[25] The Milanese reading is more ornate than the Gregorian and shows a tendency toward stepwise motion, as evident in boxes 4, 5, and 6. In the Roman version, the D-F interval often takes the form of the torculus, the most prominent feature of Formula A.

In melodic structure, the Milanese version adheres much more closely to the Gregorian than to the Roman. The Gregorian and Milanese have a similar contour in several passages, including the opening, "inclina aurem tuam," "mirifica misericordias tuas" (box 7) and "qui salvos" (box 6). The Roman version is most divergent from the other two when it adopts the standard vocabulary of its own tradition. Full or partial statements of Formula A, for example, occur in most

25. The term "tritus style" was coined by David Hughes, "Guido's tritus: An Aspect of Chant Style," in *The Study of Medieval Chant: Paths and Bridges, East and West: In Honor of Kenneth Levy*, ed. Peter Jeffery (Woodbridge, England: Boydell and Brewer, 2001), 211–26.

EXAMPLE 4.1A Gregorian, Milanese, and Roman versions of *Perfice*

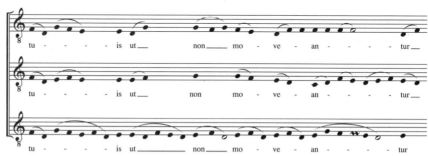

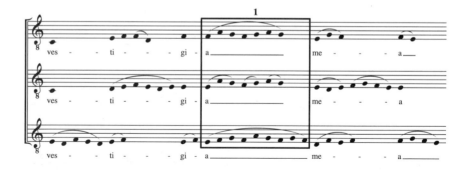

internal phrases. Another typically Roman aspect of this version is its opening gesture, with its turn figure and repeating pes. Here the Roman is utterly different from the Gregorian and Milanese in range and contour. The most conspicuous difference between the Roman and Milanese versions, then, is the lack of Formula A in the Milanese reading. The same pattern is evident among the offertories that employ Formula B in the Roman tradition. The Milanese tradition transmits the responds of *Desiderium, In virtute,* and *Gloriabuntur,* along with the respond and first verse of *Domine convertere.* These offerendae differ most from the Roman in the exact passages where the Roman employs formulas.

Despite its clear structural similarity to the Gregorian version, the Milanese version of *Perfice* is evocative of the Roman dialect in certain aspects of its style.

EXAMPLE 4.1B (*continued*)

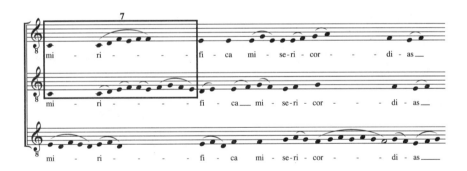

The underlying contour, for example, is realized with a more ornate surface texture in the Milanese, as at "inclina" and "mirifica" (boxes 4 and 7). The circular, stepwise ornamentation of certain pitches, moreover, results in a striking aural similarity to Roman chant, as exemplified by the rotation around G and closing torculus in box 4. A very similar melodic figure, in fact, occurs on the previous syllable in the Roman version, and a similar gesture is employed as a precadential element in first-mode Roman offertories.[26] Other instances include the rotation

---

26. The figure F-G-F-E-F-D is found in the cadences of the first-mode formula that occurs in the verses of *Super flumina, Laetamini,* and *Benedicam.*

EXAMPLE 4.1c *(continued)*

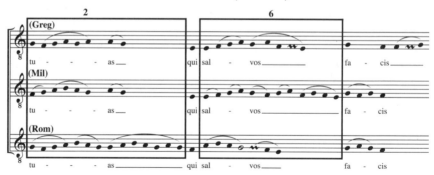

around F and E on the last syllable of "verba" (box 5) and G and F on "salvos" (box 6). As these examples show, the Milanese version is also similar to Roman chant in its tendency to adorn the final syllables of words with ornate figuration. Notably absent from the Milanese version is any trace of the Gregorian's repercussive, *tritus* style. In short, the Milanese version of *Perfice* resembles the Gregorian in terms of contour and melodic structure but departs substantially from it in surface style.

Perfice is consistent with the findings of Hucke and Huglo, namely that the Milanese versions are closer to the Gregorian melodies than to the Roman. A similar trend is evident in a majority of offerendae common to the three traditions. In a few passages, however, the Milanese versions depart from the Gregorian ones and show a closer structural correspondence to the Roman, as illustrated in an excerpt from *Dominus regnavit* (ex. 4.2). In the Gregorian and Roman traditions, this offerenda circulates as the second verse of the Christmas offertory *Deus enim firmavit. Dominus regnavit* provides a special opportunity to compare the three versions. Most of the shared offertories are assigned to the later liturgical seasons in the Franco-Roman liturgy and show a corresponding lack of melodic affinity between the Gregorian and Roman versions. As a verse assigned to the early part of the liturgical year, however, the Roman *Dominus regnavit* exhibits a minimal use of formulas and an exuberant style more akin to Gregorian verses. The

EXAMPLE 4.2 *Dominus regnavit*, excerpt

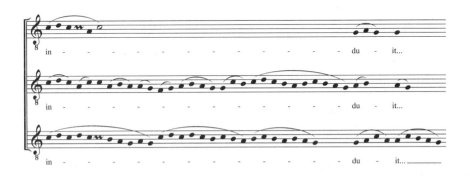

Milanese version differs from the other two in several passages, most notably its opening melisma (not shown in the example), which has a distinctive repeat structure and is substantially longer than the corresponding Gregorian and Roman melismas. In some passages, however, the Milanese version resembles the Roman melody. In considering which types of structural resemblance are most indicative of a common origin, I give particular weight to the placement of long melismas. Conceivably, two melodic traditions setting the same text could independently arrive at the same contour, whereas the same placement of melismas implies more than an accidental connection. In this passage of *Deus enim firmavit*, the Gregorian version (in line 1) places a long melisma on the last syllable of "decorem." In the Milanese and Roman, lines 2 and 3, the melisma occurs on the first syllable of "induit." In this case, the Milanese version has characteristics in common with both the Gregorian and the Roman, and cannot be securely traced to either. *Veritas mea* and *Inveni*, discussed below, present a similar picture.

Before looking more closely at the stylistic tendencies of the three dialects, I would like to reflect on the trends illustrated thus far and the questions they raise. *Perfice* and *Dominus regnavit* exemplify several broad trends. In their structural traits, such as range, cadential pitches, and placement of melismas, the Milanese versions generally correspond more closely to the Gregorian. Stylistically, however, they are reminiscent of the Roman dialect in their ornateness, their melodic vocabulary, their tendency to encircle pitches with stepwise motion, and the absence of the repercussive style that characterizes many Gregorian melodies. As *Dominus regnavit* has illustrated, moreover, the offerendae occasionally show a structural similarity to the corresponding Roman version rather than the Gregorian.

These patterns indicate that the melodies the Milanese singers learned were closer to the eighth-century Gregorian tradition than to the eleventh-century Roman tradition. The broader conclusions to be drawn from the Milanese evidence, however, depend in part on assumptions about the Gregorian-Roman problem and the reception of these pieces into Milan. With the premise that the Roman melody reflects an archaic, eighth-century tradition, we might conclude that the Milanese singers learned the melodies directly from the Franks. If so, we could attribute the more ornate style in Milan to a subsequent assimilation to native stylistic traits. Hucke reached precisely this conclusion in his examination of graduals common to the three traditions.[27] This hypothesis, however, does not explain the isolated places where the Milanese version corresponds to the Roman and not to the Gregorian. Although these passages are rare, I am hesitant to dismiss them as coincidence. With the premise that the pieces reached Milan through a seventh-century Roman path, by contrast, we might conclude that the tradition underwent a substantial change in Rome between the eighth and eleventh centuries and that the Gregorian melodies are thus closer to this seventh-century prototype.

To escape the perils of this circularity, we may acknowledge the probability that all three versions reflect changes that occurred in the course of oral transmission and focus on the probable directions of change. Because each version realizes the underlying melodic structure with a characteristic vocabulary and surface style, the question of which dialect's melodic vocabulary is closest to the "original" melody in its earliest performances is unlikely to be resolved. Comparative study, however, does allow us to formulate some general hypotheses about the types of change that took place in each dialect. Points of similarity common to all three versions, we may speculate, reflect stable features of the melodies that were consistently present in early performances. Affinity between the Milanese and Gregorian versions, with a divergent Roman reading, could suggest either a transmission through Frankish channels or a development in the Roman dialect subsequent to the repertory's exportation to the north. A close likeness between the Roman and Gregorian versions, with a markedly dissimilar Milanese reading, would suggest that the greater melodic change took place in Milan, whereas resemblance between the Milanese and Roman versions might point to changes on the Frankish side.

What can that reasoning tell us about the state of the common prototype and the changes that took place in the Gregorian and Roman traditions? First, there is the question of style and melodic vocabulary. I have shown that the central

27. Hucke, "Gregorianische Gradualeweise."

difference between the Milanese and the Gregorian versions resides in the degree and nature of the surface elaboration. There is little doubt that Beneventan chant shares some characteristics with the Roman dialect, an issue I shall explore presently. On this basis, we may speculate that early performances of these melodies had "Italianate" stylistic traits akin to the Roman and Milanese readings but structural traits more like those of the Gregorian. Given the marked aural similarities between Milanese and Roman chant, this reasoning seems cogent. It is also possible, however, that the Milanese style merely reflects a localized assimilation of foreign melodies to native style. Bailey points to the prolonged period of oral tradition in Rome and Milan as fertile ground for progressive elaboration: "The filling-in of intervals which produced this smoothness, like the decoration with inserted melismas, is probably the result of a change of fashion in ecclesiastical music—a stylistic change that was unimpeded in an oral tradition but constrained (as in Gregorian regions) where the melodies had been fixed forever by notation."[28]

In considering these two alternatives it will be fruitful to compare the Milanese and Roman ornamentation in greater detail, to see whether the two versions are elaborate on the same words and syllables. If the bulk of the elaboration took place after the separation of the three branches, we would expect the Roman and Milanese versions to be quite different in the details of elaboration. The musical picture is often consistent with this expectation, but not always. In the opening of *Veritas mea* (Example 4.3), the Milanese and Roman versions share several characteristics that are absent in the Gregorian, most notably a long melisma on the first syllable of "mea." The Roman and Milanese melismas have very similar endings. The Milanese version is perhaps most evocative of Roman chant, however, in its repeated figuration on the final syllables of "misericordia" and "mea." As I have shown, a similar penchant for repetition is a hallmark feature of the Roman dialect. In the corresponding passage of the Roman version, however, this repetition is not present. The opening of *Inveni* (ex. 4.4) presents a very similar picture. At the cadence on "meum" (box 1) each version adopts its own typical cadential material; the Roman is much more ornate than the Milanese, especially on the final syllable. In certain other passages, however, the Roman and Milanese versions are elaborate in the same places, contrasting with Gregorian reading. On the final syllables of "servum" (box 2), the two have similar stepwise melodic motion between a and c, and on "eum" (box 3), both have a melisma that is lacking in the Gregorian version. In short, their styles of elaboration are similar in some passages and different in others.

The patterns observed thus far invite several preliminary conclusions. First, if the melodies of the *commune sanctorum*, such as *Veritas mea*, are Frankish

---

28. Bailey, "Ambrosian Chant," in *Revised New Grove Dictionary of Music and Musicians* (New York: Grove, 2001).

EXAMPLE 4.3 *Veritas mea,* opening

borrowings, as seems likely, their occasional correspondence to the Roman versions casts doubt on the notion that the "Gregorian" melodies transmitted to Milan were identical to those later preserved in notation. Rather, it gives weight to the probability that all three versions changed in the course of oral transmission. Second, the ornate, repetitive, and stepwise style observed in Milanese and Roman chant supports the view that these stylistic traits were native Italian features, neglected or deemphasized by the Franks. The less likely alternative is that a very similar melodic vocabulary emerged independently in Rome and Milan between the time the melodies were received in Milan and the eleventh and twelfth centuries, when the Roman and Milanese dialects were preserved in notation.

The patterns I have observed suggest that earlier versions of these melodies had a structure and contour very similar to that of the Gregorian and Milanese versions, but with certain stylistic traits typically associated with Italianate dialects. At the same time, the differences between the Roman and Milanese versions are consistent with Bailey's hypothesis of increasing elaboration. The stylistic tendencies of the three versions are suggestive of types of melodic change occurring in each dialect: in Milan, a tendency toward further melodic elaboration. In the hands of the Franks, we might suppose, a less ornate style emerged, with a tendency toward

EXAMPLE 4.4 *Inveni,* opening

greater tonal focus on F and c, manifest in the repercussive style that characterizes so many Gregorian offertories.[29]

A comparison of the three traditions suggests that the long melismas found in many offertory verses were a point of change, perhaps even subject to variable treatment in performance. In the Milanese and Gregorian cognate pairs, melismas usually occur in the same places, indicating that they are a long-standing tradition. The two dialects, however, sometimes differ greatly in the melodic details of the

29. McKinnon has made the same argument for the emergence of a greater tonal focus in the Gregorian melodies. McKinnon, *The Advent Project: The Later-Seventh-Century Creation of the Roman Mass Proper* (Berkeley: University of California Press, 2001), 399–403.

168 INSIDE THE OFFERTORY

melismas, with the Milanese often exceeding the Gregorian ones in prolixity. Very lengthy melismas with repeat structures abound in the native Milanese repertory, raising the possibility that the lengthier melismas in Milan represent, in part, assimilation to native style. In comparison to their Gregorian counterparts, the Milanese melismas are often more elaborate in their repeat structures. The Milanese *Si oblitus*, for example, has a melisma with 179 notes and the form AAA[1]A[1]BBCCDDE. The corresponding melisma in the Gregorian melody is much shorter, and in the Roman version the melisma is lacking altogether. The differences between the three dialects in the treatment of melismas raise the possibility that these soloistic displays of musical exuberance were subject to some flexibility, at least in the earlier stages of their adoption in Francia and Milan. The addition of melismas to office responsories offers a precedent for such a practice.[30] There is little evidence of such flexibility, however, from the time the Gregorian manuscripts were copied.[31] A few exceptions aside, the Carolingian desire for liturgical unity evidently brought the melismas into uniformity or at least a broad conformity before the melodies were committed to notation.

Finally, the relationship between the Gregorian, Roman, and Milanese versions has implications for the emergence of the Roman formulas. As I have shown, the Milanese melodies lack all traces of the two most common Roman formulas, A and B; the Roman versions, in fact, particularly diverge from the Gregorian and Milanese in passages where they adopt formulas. Either the Franks eliminated all traces of the Roman formulas before passing the melodies on to Milanese cantors or the formulas developed in the centuries following the transmission of the repertory to the North. In considering these two alternatives, it is helpful to examine some offertories of probable non-Roman origin. The Gregorian, Roman, and Milanese versions of these pieces exhibit same stylistic and structural tendencies I have observed in those of probable Roman origin. The Roman version of *Si oblitus*, a verse of *Super flumina*, is formed from repeated statements of a formula common to mode-one offertories, whereas the Gregorian is a typical elaborate, distinctive melody. The Milanese *Si oblitus* is far more closely aligned with the Gregorian. The nonpsalmic offertories present a similar picture: the Roman versions are stylistically indistinguishable from other Roman offertories. Their verses are made of standard formulas and show a pervasive internal repetition, traits consistent with their placement in the later seasons of the year. *In die* and *Erit vobis*, for example, have verses based largely on Formula B; *Precatus est,*

30. Paul Cutter, "Oral Transmission of the Old Roman Responsories?" *Musical Quarterly* 62 (1976): 182–94; and Ruth Steiner, "Some Melismas for Office Responsories," *Journal of the American Musicological Society* 26 (1973): 108–31.
31. Exceptions occur most frequently in Beneventan sources, attesting to the independence of the Benventan tradition. These are discussed summarily in chapter 6 and in greater detail in the notes for individual offertories.

Oravi deum, and *Oratio mea* are a mixture of idiomelic material and formulas, and the verses of *Sanctificavit,* as illustrated in chapter 3, behave very much like the formulas, with an extreme economy of melodic material and predicable adaptation to aural features such as word accent. The Milanese versions of the nonpsalmic offertories, by contrast, are distinctive melodies and, with the exception of *Stetit angelus,* similar to the Gregorian in many aspects of range, contour, and placement of melismas.

It is likely that the Gregorian versions of these offertories were part of the core repertory transmitted from Rome to the Franks, as Pfisterer has argued from liturgical evidence.[32] As noted in chapter 2, the textual variants confirm this impression: the Gregorian offertories with Roman and Old Hispanic cognates, *Sanctificavit* and *Erit,* are closer to the Roman versions than to the Old Hispanic. The Milanese versions, however, are verbally much closer to the Old Hispanic tradition than to the Gregorian.[33] It is unlikely that these offerendae reached Milan through a Frankish or Roman path. Either the Milanese adopted them from the Old Hispanic version or the Old Hispanic and Milanese versions descend from a third, common tradition, as Levy has argued.[34]

With the premise that these offerendae were independently adopted into the Milanese and Roman-Gregorian traditions, a look at the melodic relationships among the different versions can shed further light on questions of style, melodic origin, and change. In two cases, *Sanctificavit* and *Erit,* we can incorporate Old Hispanic versions into the analytical picture. Given the pattern of textual variants, one might expect melodic analysis to reveal close ties between Milan and Spain on the one hand and Rome and Francia on the other. Nonpsalmic offertories, however, are no exception to the trends observed in chapter 3: melodic correspondence between Gregorian and Roman verses of the later liturgical seasons is rare. To the extent that melodic affinity can be determined on the basis of adiastematic neumes, the Gregorian versions of *Sanctificavit* and *Erit* show a closer melodic affinity with the Old Hispanic. This trend, already observed by Levy, deserves some further illustration and reflection.[35]

In chapter 3, I examined the Gregorian and Roman versions of *Sanctificavit* and one of its verses as an illustration of the two dialects' different approaches to text treatment. With a typical melodic economy, the Roman cantors respond to aural features of the text, such as accent pattern. The Gregorian version, by contrast, presents a rhetorical reading of the words, responding to their content and meaning and employing range to distinguish the voices of the dialogue. Certain words, such as "ascendit" and "descendit," are emphasized with lengthy ascending

32. Pfisterer, "Remarks," 169–72.
33. Ott and Baroffio illustrate the pattern with reference to *Sanctificavit.* See Ott, "I versetti," 354; and Baroffio, "Die mailändische Überlieferung des Offertoriums Sanctificavit," in *Festschrift Bruno Stäblein zum 70. Geburtstag,* ed. Martin Ruhnke (Kassel: Bärenreiter, 1967): 1–8.
34. Levy, "Toledo, Rome."
35. Ibid.

and descending melismas, an apparent text painting that is lacking in the Roman version. The Old Hispanic neumes imply a similar expression of the words, with lengthy melismas on "ascendit" and "descendit." The Gregorian version, in fact, is often similar to the Old Hispanic in its placement of longer melismas.

The Milanese tradition transmits two parts of *Sanctificavit*, its verse *Oravit Moyses* (divided into respond and verse at "dum pertransiero") and repetendum. A lengthy excerpt with the four readings is shown in example 4.5. In the Gregorian tradition, this offertory is especially subject to variants in pitch level. Some are attributable to nondiatonic pitches; others may reflect different performance traditions. The version of Benevento 39 in example 4.5 reflects the preferred, "unemended" reading in most passages. Here it is presented a fifth above its written pitch level to facilitate comparison to the Milanese melody.[36]

Oravit exemplifies the general stylistic affinity between offertory chants of the four traditions. At the melismas on "dicens" and "meam," for example, the Old Hispanic neumes imply an AA^1B repeat structure similar to that found in many Gregorian and Milanese melismas and, less frequently, in the Roman tradition. On "meam," the corresponding Milanese melisma has a similar repeat structure. A common foundation of the Gregorian, Milanese, and Old Hispanic versions of *Oravit* is suggested by the placement of longer melismas on "dicens," on "transiero," and at other points not shown in the example.[37] The three versions, however, exhibit some divergence. Despite the closer verbal relationship between the Milanese and Old Hispanic—the Gregorian and Roman lack the phrase "non poteris videre faciem meam"—the Milanese and Gregorian have several melismas that are lacking in the Old Hispanic, as in the opening word "oravit" and on "ip sum" and "mani *fes* te." These patterns may support Levy's hypothesis that a third version underlies the three. Particularly striking is the Roman version's divergence from the others. Formed primarily from a set of melodic phrases that occur elsewhere in this offertory, it exhibits the melodic economy that characterizes nearly all Roman offertory verses in the later liturgical seasons. In this respect, the musical and verbal evidence are contradictory. While the verbal text suggests a close link between the Gregorian and Roman versions, the Gregorian is melodically much closer to the Milanese and Old Hispanic.

---

36. To some extent, the pitch-level problems are reflected in the divergence between the Milanese and Gregorian readings. The Milanese reading differs from Ben 39 in range in two places, "te ipsum manifeste" and "dum pertransiero," but otherwise follows it closely. According to the hypothesis I present in the critical notes (in appendix 3), the preferred Gregorian reading is a fifth below the Milanese in range until "dum pertransiero." The Milanese range at "te ipsum manifeste" has no equivalent in the Gregorian sources examined for this study. The Milanese version also differs from Ben 39 at "donec pertranseam." The Milanese use of c as the recitational pitch here is consistent with most Gregorian sources. The reasons for this variant are explained in the critical notes in appendix 3.
37. Especially at "terra," toward the end of the verse.

EXAMPLE 4.5 *Oravit*, excerpt

EXAMPLE 4.5 (*continued*)

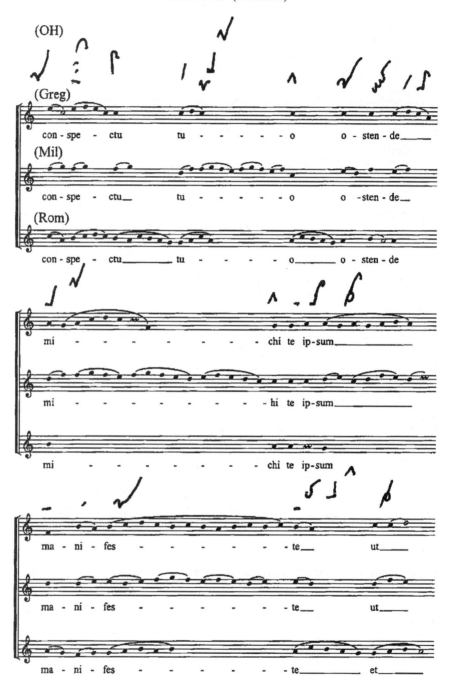

EXAMPLE 4.5 (*continued*)

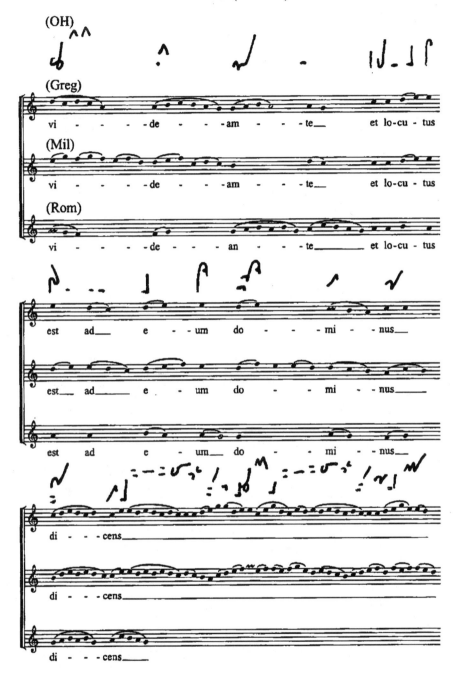

EXAMPLE 4.5 (*continued*)

(OH)

(Greg)

(Mil)

non po - - te - ris_____ vi - de - re__ fa - - ci - em

(Rom)

me - am_____

non__ e - nim vi - de - - bit me ho - - - - -mo____ et__

non e - nim vi - de - - -bit me__ho - - - - -mo____ et__

non___ e - nim vi - de - - bit__me ho - - - - mo____ et__

EXAMPLE 4.5 (*continued*)

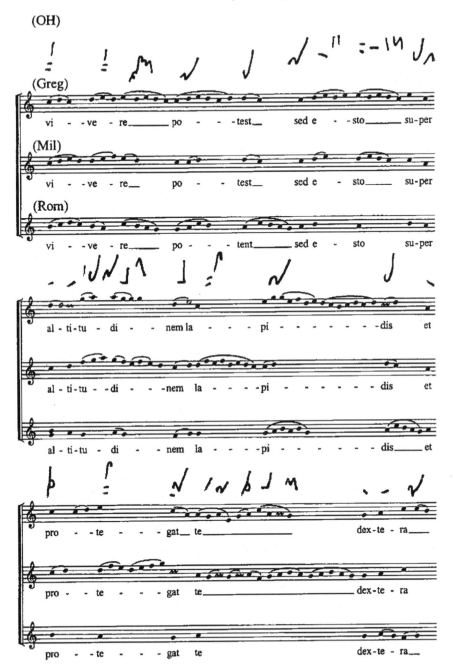

EXAMPLE 4.5 (*continued*)

Erit [hic] vobis, the other offertory common to the four traditions, presents a very similar picture. The verbal evidence indicates a close relationship between the Milanese and Old Hispanic on one side and the Gregorian and Roman on the other side. Melodically, however, the Gregorian and Roman show very few traces of a common origin. The Roman reading is distinct from the other three in its repetition of Formula B, and in these passages it exhibits the usual divergence from the Gregorian and Milanese readings. The Gregorian, Old Hispanic, and Milanese versions are similar in their distribution of neumatic passages and longer melismas, with a divergent Roman reading.

The incorporation of Old Hispanic versions into the analytical picture allows for further reflections on the dialectal differences and the probable types of change that occurred in each tradition. Like the psalmic offertories, *Sanctificavit* lends some circumstantial support to Bailey's hypothesis of increasing elaboration in the Milanese tradition. The Milanese has several shorter melismas that do not occur in the other readings, as on "inveni" and "gratiam" (enclosed in boxes), each characterized by a typical circular, stepwise motion. The Old Hispanic version, by contrast, is even less ornate than the Gregorian in many passages. *Sanctificavit* exemplifies several other stylistic trends I have observed. In the Gregorian version, for example, typical repercussions of c occur in the melisma on "dicens," whereas they are lacking in the Milanese version. The neumes of the Old Hispanic version suggest that this "tritus" feature was less pronounced than it was in the Gregorian version, with fewer instances of repeated notes. These patterns, also evident in *Erit vobis*, imply changes toward surface elaboration in Milan, increasing tonal focus on c and F in Frankish regions, and melodic homogenization at Rome.

The probability that *Erit* and *Sanctificavit* originated outside Rome has implications for the relative historical position of the Gregorian and Roman melodies, a question I will fully explore in the next chapter. If the Franks learned these melodies from the Romans in a formulaic form similar to that reflected in the eleventh-century Roman versions, how can we explain the greater melodic correspondence to the Milanese and Old Hispanic readings? One possibility is that the Franks had a preexisting knowledge of both items as part of their native Gallican liturgy. When they received the Roman versions, they "corrected" the words according to a Roman manuscript but retained the Gallican melody. Another possibility is that the eighth-century Roman tradition had melodies for these offertories that were similar to the Gregorian versions but much of the Roman melodic tradition was lost between the eighth and eleventh centuries. I find the latter explanation more plausible: if the Franks took the trouble to make textual changes to conform to the Roman version, why not adopt the Roman melody as well? While neither hypothesis is empirically provable, the evidence clearly points to a tendency for idiomelic melodies, especially verses, to become increasingly repetitive and formulaic in the Roman tradition. Like the *Veterem hominem* antiphons, these examples point to convergent tendencies at Rome.[38] Whether the changes took place before or after the eighth-century transmission to the Franks, comparison of the offertories in four traditions indicates that the melodies underwent the greatest change in Rome, acquiring the formulaic and repetitive characteristics of the other Roman offertories.

BROADER IMPLICATIONS FOR ROMAN FORMULAICISM

The demonstrable process of convergent change in the Roman dialect among imported melodies bears on the question of Roman formulaicism in general. I find it unlikely that the trend toward melodic homogenization applied only to imported chants and not to those of Roman origin. The singers who performed these melodies in the centuries following their reception in Rome were not musicologists; it is doubtful that they were aware of the diverse origins of specific chants in their repertory. If melodies from elsewhere were subject to processes of increasing formulaicism, it is sensible to suspect that native melodies could undergo the same kinds of changes. In pondering Roman formulaicism more broadly, however, another bit of Italian evidence warrants consideration: the parallels between Roman and Old Beneventan chant. The Old Beneventan conception of offertory chants is very different from that of Rome, both textually and thematically. Most Old Beneventan offertories are based on nonscriptural texts. In length and style, they are similar to office antiphons and communions, lacking verses and lengthy melismas. In several cases, their texts do in fact double as Old Beneventan communions or serve as antiphons in the Gregorian, Roman, or Milanese tradition.[39] Despite these differences, some Old Beneventan melodies exhibit compelling melodic similarities to the Roman offertory formulas: narrow range, melodic economy, and penchant for internal repetition. The Old Beneventan offertory of the second Holy Cross formulary, *Miraculo de tam miro* (ex. 4.6), is evocative of the Roman offertories in its melodic economy.[40] The melody consists largely of standard melodic material, formed from a series of melodic segments found in other Beneventan melodies. The stereotyping at cadences can be readily seen in a comparison of "omnes terrerentur," "signum sanctae crucis," and "fulgore resplendere." *Miraculo de tam miro* also exhibits a large-scale varied repetition reminiscent of the Roman formulas. The third phrase, beginning with "in caelo," is a varied repetition of phrase 2 (beginning at "respicientes"). Perhaps

---

38. Edward Nowacki, "Constantinople-Aachen-Rome: The Transmission of *Veterem hominem*," in *De Musica et Cantu: Studien zur Geschichte der Kirchenmusik und der Oper: Helmut Hucke zum 60. Geburstag*, ed. Peter Kahn and Anne-Katrin Heimer (Hildesheim: Georg Olms Verlag, 1993), 95–115.

39. See Kelly, "Beneventan and Milanese Chant," and *Beneventan Chant*, 77–78.

40. The base pitch level, not indicated with a clef in Old Beneventan chant, was determined with reference to Kelly's work on the melodic formulas and their pitch level. Each Beneventan chant closes either on G or a. See *Beneventan Chant*, 97–109; 153–56.

EXAMPLE 4.6 *Miraculo de tam miro*

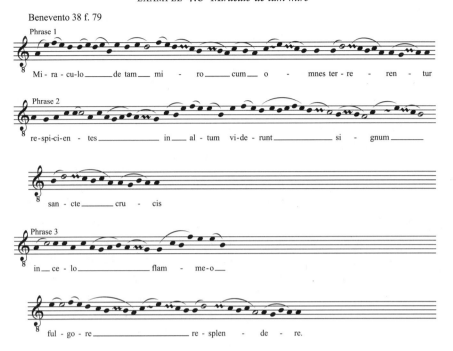

Benevento 38 f. 79

the most striking similarity to the Roman dialect lies in the melodic vocabulary. The precadential segment d-c-b-c-a on "ter *re* rentur," "sanct *ae*" and "re *splen* dere," for example, serves a very similar role in Roman offertories of mode 1.[41] Other Beneventan melodies employ the repeating pes, a defining feature of Formula B.

The similarities between Old Beneventan chant and the Roman offertory formulas could support an argument that formulaicism and internal repetition were native properties of southern Italian chant. We might speculate that a formulaic southern Italian style of offertory chants existed in opposition to the exuberant style that characterized offertories in Gaul, Spain, and Milan, and that the offertories imported into Rome were assimilated to this style. Aspects of the musical picture, however, raise reservations about this hypothesis. Clearly not all Roman and Beneventan chant consisted of melodic formulas. Nonformulaic chants, including offertories, exist side by side with the formulas both in Rome and in Benevento. Given that Roman and Beneventan melodies flourished in oral tradition for several centuries before they were preserved in notation, it is possible that their melodic economy developed during this time. Were Beneventan melodies subject to processes of melodic homogenization similar to those of the

41. At the lower transposition, G-F-E-F-D. See, for example, the verses of *Deus deus meus* (55), on the final syllables of "caro," "virtutem," gloriam," etc.

nonpsalmic offertories at Rome? Considering some probable borrowings in the Beneventan tradition can help to answer the question.

In comparing melodies common to the Milanese and Beneventan traditions, Thomas Forrest Kelly has pointed to the more repetitive, economic style of the Beneventan versions. He sees it as unlikely that the Beneventan singers would create repetition where none existed previously and more plausible that the Milanese singers varied chants that were originally formulaic and repetitive. Thus, he concludes, the Beneventan melody is in some cases closer to the original.[42] The same characteristic economy, however, is discernable in Beneventan melodies whose lyrics probably originated elsewhere. The offertories *Omnes qui in Christo* for Holy Saturday and *Angelus domini* for Easter Sunday, for example, share material with one another and with other Beneventan melodies. It is doubtful that the text for either chant is of Beneventan origin. Levy has brought to light a series of settings of *Omnes qui in Christo* in the Franco-Roman, Ravennate, and Byzantine liturgies.[43] Although these settings show significant melodic differences, they exhibit possible vestiges of a common melodic substance in their underlying modal structure. *Angelus domini* serves as the Easter Sunday offertory at Milan and the Easter Monday offertory in the Franco-Roman liturgy. Although the Beneventan melody bears no discernable resemblance to the others, the common origin of the lyrics is evident in the similarities between their centonized texts.

Despite their probably different origins, the Beneventan versions of *Omnes qui in Christo* and *Angelus domini* are substantially absorbed into the Beneventan style and share melodic material with other Beneventan chants.[44] As Levy has remarked, "chant dialects impose their own style on whatever materials they contain."[45] The two offertories, moreover, have nearly identical opening phrases, adjusted for differences in length. In this respect, they exhibit a pattern also observed in Nowacki's study of the Roman office antiphons: chants tend to acquire the characteristics of others sung in close liturgical proximity.[46] This phenomenon, much more apparent in the Roman antiphons than in their Gregorian counterparts, is best explained in the context of oral tradition and "thrift." To repeat a melody sung on the previous day was, in Nowacki's characterization, "the path of least resistance" in an oral tradition.[47] It is more expeditious to recreate a melody fresh from recent performance than to create a new one. Like the Roman melodies, then, the Beneventan dialect exhibits evidence of convergent developments in its melodic tradition.

---

42. Kelly, "Beneventan and Milanese Chant," 189, and *Beneventan Chant*, 170–71; 178–81; 188.
43. Levy, "Italian Neophytes' Chants."
44. The two melodies can be compared in Kelly, *Beneventan Chant*, 103–4.
45. Levy, "The Italian Neophytes' Chants," 210.
46. Edward Nowacki, "Studies on the Antiphons of the Old Roman Manuscripts" (Ph.D. diss., Brandeis University, 1980), and "The Gregorian Office Antiphons and the Comparative Method," *Journal of Musicology* 4 (1985): 243–75.
47. Edward Nowacki, "Text Declamation as a Determinant of Melodic Form in the Old Roman Eighth-Mode Tracts," *Early Music History* 6 (1986): 224.

These common traits of the Roman and Beneventan traditions raise the question of whether their melodic homogeneity is best regarded as an archaic feature or whether it betokens a later, convergent development. I doubt the answer is a simple matter of one or the other. While the evidence of imported chants points toward convergent change as a plausible explanation for formulaicism, it is unlikely that the repetitive style and melodic vocabulary common to Rome and Benevento emerged ex nihilo, from a melodic language that was previously very different. It would be imprudent to attribute all Roman and Beneventan characteristics, including melodic thrift, to later development. As the comparisons of Roman, Gregorian, and Milanese offertories suggest, the same argument may be made in the case of the Italianate style. While the audible surface similarities between the Roman and Milanese renditions of the melodies suggest that the common stylistic traits were innate features, their differences imply that the style matured like fine wine in the course of oral transmission.

5

ORIGIN AND CHRONOLOGY

In previous chapters, I have examined characteristics of offertory with potential implications for questions of origin and chronology. The look at psalmic offertories in chapter 2 confirmed that they often deviate from the Roman psalter, showing various degrees of correspondence to other Old Latin psalters. Further trends illustrated in chapter 2 include the extensive verbal centonization of the psalmic offertories and the prominence of Old Latin texts among the nonpsalmic offertories. Turning to musical questions in chapters 3 and 4, I illustrated the sharp contrasts between the Gregorian and Roman versions of the melodies, especially among verses assigned to Lent and Paschaltide. The differences between the two traditions, evident both in surface details and in underlying compositional procedures, are most conspicuous in passages where the Roman versions rely on formulas. The Milanese cognates correspond more consistently to the Gregorian readings in structural traits such as range and contour but show compelling resemblance to Roman chant in surface style and melodic vocabulary.

These musical and verbal characteristics of the offertory raise several questions for further reflection. If substantial portions of the repertory originated elsewhere, when were they incorporated into the Roman liturgy, and what are the implications for melodic style? These questions are closely tied to the relationship between the Gregorian and Roman offertories, the characteristics of the common tradition that underlies them, and the types of the melodic change that occurred in each tradition. This chapter is devoted to these issues. I begin with the origins of the genre itself and proceed to a consideration of the Gregorian and Roman question.

THE COMPILATION OF THE ROMAN REPERTORY

Documentary evidence—reviewed in chapter 1—for an offertory rite in the Roman Mass begins only in the seventh century, with the Old Gelasian sacramentary and the detailed description in *Ordo Romanus I*. To pinpoint a more precise time span for repertory's compilation, it is helpful to consider the chronology of the Mass Proper as a whole, beginning with the recently proposed theories of McKinnon and Pfisterer. McKinnon holds that the bulk of the repertory emerged in the later seventh century in an attempt by the *schola cantorum* to create proper chants for each day of the year. The *schola*, he argues, began with Advent chants and progressed through the liturgical year, season by season.[1] Pfisterer, by contrast, proposes that the Mass Proper is a product of gradual accumulation, beginning in the late fifth or early sixth century, proceeding according to the solemnity of festivals and the evolution of the liturgical year, and reaching completion around the year 600.[2] These divergent conclusions arise partially from different starting assumptions and evidence examined. More fundamentally, McKinnon and Pfisterer differ in their ways of employing the liturgical sources and constructing a historical narrative that connects the gaps between them. Because of their relevance for the subject at hand, I will briefly summarize and explore their arguments.

McKinnon and Pfisterer base their respective hypotheses on a traditional approach to establishing a date for the repertory's completion. The first step is to ascertain the most plausible dates for the addition of each festival to the calendar, based on the liturgical sources and the *Liber pontificalis*; the next is to determine which festivals have uniquely assigned chants and which employ chants already in existence. The date of the last festival with newly composed chants serves as the terminus ad quem for the repertory. McKinnon's theory of late seventh-century origin begins with the observation that indices of "compositional planning," such as thematic appropriateness and uniquely assigned chants for each day, are present more consistently in Advent than in other seasons. These characteristics, he argues, point to a project to create individual chants for each day of the year. Because these signs of planning become less pronounced in the later seasons, he concludes that the project started with Advent; the singers progressed through the year, season by season, but failed to complete the project. The seventh-century date rests on McKinnon's dating of specific festivals, coupled with patterns of unique and borrowed chants. In contrast with earlier writers, he places the Dedication and Marian festivals, the last with newly created chants, in the papacy of Sergius (687–701).[3]

Pfisterer's argument for an earlier date of completion resides partly in a different approach to reading the evidence of liturgical sources. McKinnon arranges witnesses to the sacramentary, evangelary, and epistolary in chronological order and employs them as a basis to establish dates of institution for particular festivals. His proposed date for each festival rests on the absence of a feast in one

1. James McKinnon, *The Advent Project: The Later-Seventh-Century Creation of the Roman Mass Proper* (Berkeley: University of California Press, 2000).
2. Andreas Pfisterer, *Cantilena Romana: Untersuchungen zur Überlieferung des gregorianischen Chorals* (Tützing: Hans Schneider, 2002). See especially pp. 217–34.
3. The traditional date of 609 is established on the basis of a *Liber Pontificalis* report on Boniface IV's rededication of the Pantheon to Mary and the martyrs. See Peter Jeffery, "Rome and Jerusalem: From Oral Tradition to Written Repertory in Two Ancient Liturgical Centers," in *Essays on Medieval Music in Honor of David G. Hughes*, ed. Graeme M. Boone (Cambridge, Mass.: Harvard University Press, 1995), 214–19. I address McKinnon's argument for a later date for the festival's institution and proper chants in note 9.

layer and its presence in the next. Pfisterer does not view these different types of
liturgical sources as a linear trajectory on which a single Roman liturgy can be
reconstructed. Discrepancies between liturgical books, he maintains, are normal.
The lack of a feast in a particular book does not mean that it was never celebrated
in Rome. In these doubtful cases, he views a positive piece of evidence in one
source as more compelling than negative evidence from other sources.[4] In keeping
with this reasoning, Peter Jeffery has emphasized the lack of a single, unified
Roman calendar before the thirteenth century. Because the Roman books in
question come from different institutions, different calendars are to be expected.[5]

   A further methodological difference resides in the sources used to establish the
original assignments of chants. McKinnon views the Roman gradual Vat 5319 as a
reflection of the eighth-century Roman calendar, whereas Pfisterer looks to the
early Gregorian sources as a more accurate index of eighth-century Roman
practice. These two approaches produce sharply distinct results. McKinnon, for
example, sees uniquely assigned chants for festivals added at the time of Sergius
I and attributes the bulk of the activity to this period. Pfisterer, however, notes the
inconsistent treatment of these festivals in early Gregorian sources. The Annunciation formulary, for example, appears in Mont-Blandin but not in Monza, and such
variations among later festivals are common. If proper chants for these feasts were
established at the time of Sergius, one would expect them to have consistently
assigned chants in early Gregorian sources. Pfisterer thus concludes that the
antiphoner was completed before the time of Sergius. He presents similar indices
that place the Mass Proper at an increasingly early date. The eighth Sunday after
Pentecost, for example, shares the introit *Suscepimus* with the Purification, a festival
Pfisterer places at the time of Pope Theodore I (642–49). Because the introit is
thematically suited to the Purification, Pfisterer argues that the Purification is the
borrower rather than the lender. The reuse of a thematically appropriate chant
from a Post-Pentecost Sunday for Purification, he reasons, is more probable than
an arbitrary borrowing of a Purification chant for a thematically neutral Sunday.
Thus, he argues, the numerical series of Post-Pentecost introits was in place by the
mid–seventh century.[6] On the basis of similar evidence and argument, he concludes that the later layers of the Mass proper originated in the early seventh
century.

   The most important point of divergence between McKinnon and Pfisterer lies
in the dates they establish for the earlier layers of the repertory. As I have shown,
Pfisterer's fifth-century date rests on the distinction between the VL and the
Vulgate, a form of textual evidence McKinnon does not consider. Focusing

4. Pfisterer, "James McKinnon und die Datierung des gregorianischen Chorals," *Kirchenmusikalisches Jahrbuch* 85 (2002): 35–36.
5. Jeffery, review of *The Advent Project: The Later-Seventh-Century Creation of the Roman Mass Proper,* by James McKinnon, *Journal of the American Musicological Society* 56 (2003): 171–72.
6. Pfisterer, "James McKinnon," 39–40.

particularly on the Isaiah chants, Pfisterer notes that those of Advent, the last season added to the calendar, employ the Vulgate, whereas those outside of Advent are VL based. On the evidence of citations, he proposes an early sixth-century date for the transition from the VL to the Vulgate and concludes that the repertory for the earliest liturgical festivals was in place before this time.[7]

In considering which hypothesis is more consistent with the evidence examined here, I can note that McKinnon's theory complements aspects of the musical picture. Resemblance between Gregorian and Roman offertories becomes increasingly weak in the later seasons of the liturgical year, especially among verses. Using McKinnon's scenario of season-by-season composition, the verses of the later seasons could be viewed as later compositions, less firmly fixed in memory than the earlier Advent and Christmas layer. McKinnon's hypothesis also concords with Dyer's theory that the offertory rite arose in Rome in the mid–seventh century. One could envision an importation of chants and creation of new chants beginning in the mid–seventh century and continuing through the later seventh century, when the offertory was "properized."

On reflection, however, Pfisterer's use of liturgical sources to establish an early seventh-century terminus ad quem for completion of the repertory emerges as the more persuasive hypothesis. I remain skeptical of Pfisterer's dating of the earlier repertorial layers. The hypothesis rests on a precisely pinpointed date for the transition from the VL to the Vulgate. As I argued in chapter 2, I am not convinced that the shift ought to be viewed in such a linear way. A gradual transition between the two texts is supported by large body of scholarship documenting the emergence of mixed texts and an occasional use of the VL even at the time of Gregory the Great.[8] For this reason, the use of the VL as the basis for a chant after the Vulgate's introduction is not inconceivable. Although the Vulgate/VL evidence is problematic on the earlier side, however, it does reinforce the liturgical evidence for a completion of the repertory in the early seventh century. Pfisterer demonstrates that chants based on the VL are concentrated among earlier festivals, whereas most Vulgate chants are assigned to Advent. With the assumption that Vulgate chants are generally newer than VL chants, this pattern indeed implies that most of the repertory was in place by the early seventh century, when Advent was added to the calendar. The most probable scenario for the formation of the liturgical year places the last festival with a proper offertory, the Dedication, in the first decades of the seventh century; thus, it seems, the composition of new offertories came to

---

7. Pfisterer, "James McKinnon," 50–51, and Pfisterer, *Cantilena*, 221–32.

8. See the discussion in chapter 2. Also see Bonifatius Fischer, "Zur Überlieferung altlateinischer Bibeltexte im Mittelalter," *Nederlands Archief voor Kerkgeschiedenis* 56 (1975): 20–21; Jean Gribomont, "Les plus anciennes traductions latins," in *Le monde latin antique et la Bible*, ed. Jacques Fontaine and Charles Pietri (Paris: 1985), 56–57; Bogaert, "La Bible latine des origines au moyen âge," *Revue théologique de Louvain* 19 (1988): 293–95.

completion around this time.[9] While dating of the earliest layers of the repertory must remain a matter of speculation, the evidence points to a terminus ad quem in the earlier seventh century.

Another question that arises from the textual and musical evidence is the nature of the possible imports into Rome and their relationship to a presumably native repertory. My examination of the psalter traditions in chapter 2 pointed to the problems inherent in using psalter evidence to establish a chant's origin. The number of departures from the PsR, coupled with the evidence of nonpsalmic offertories, nevertheless raises the possibility that some offertories originated outside Rome. At the very least, the hypothesis needs to play a role in any speculations about the repertory's origins. Noting the presence of possible non-Roman items in all layers of his chronology, Pfisterer proposes that foreign offertories were assimilated into the repertory at different points, suggesting periods of long contact and repertorial exchange.[10] With this scenario, "non-Roman" offertory chants emerge as a repertory of great diversity. Despite the paucity of psalmic offertories in the Old Hispanic repertory—they comprise only about 10 percent of the sacrificia—in chapter 2 I demonstrated a consistent "non-Roman" textual tradition in twenty-five of the Roman-Gregorian psalmic offertories and possible traces of non-PsR influence in at least two dozen others. Because of their psalmic basis, most of these texts are quite distinct in character from those of the nonpsalmic sacrificia, lacking their narrative element and—with some notable exceptions such as *Confirma hoc* and *Iubilate deo universa*—their offering theme. Some non-Roman pieces may have originated as chants with other liturgical uses. Studies on the Italic repertories have shown that the same lyric could serve more than one liturgical function, either within a liturgical tradition or between different traditions.[11] Levy, in fact, has demonstrated that a group of pieces possibly related to *Tollite portas*, without verses, served multiple roles.[12] If they are indeed Gallican or northern Italian in origin, however, these chants call

---

9. The Dedication is traditionally dated in 609. McKinnon's argument for a later date for the festival's institution and proper chants is based on two pieces of circumstantial evidence: the absence of the festival in certain liturgical sources that postdate the *Liber pontificalis* reference and the absence of Marian references in the festival's proper chants (in view of the fact that the Pantheon was dedicated to Mary). On the basis of the latter evidence, McKinnon suggests that the Dedication's proper chants were composed only after the Marian festivals were in existence. When all the evidence is taken into consideration, however, I do not find this argument fully convincing. See *Advent Project*, 155–56, 187–90.

10. Andreas Pfisterer, "Remarks on Roman and Non-Roman Offertories," *Plainsong and Medieval Music* 14 (2005): 169–81.

11. Kenneth Levy, "The Italian Neophytes' Chants," *Journal of the American Musicological Society* 23 (1970): 181–227; James Borders, "The Northern Italian Antiphons *ante evangelium* and the Gallican Connection," *Journal of Musicological Research* 8 (1988): 1–53. Thomas Forrest Kelly, "Beneventan and Milanese Chant," *Journal of the Royal Musical Association* 62 (1987): 173–95.

12. Kenneth Levy, "*Tollite portas*: An Ante-Evangelium Reclaimed?" in *Western Plainchant in the First Millennium: Studies in the Medieval Liturgy and Its Music*, ed. Sean Gallagher et al. (Aldershot, England: Ashgate, 2003), 231–41.

into question a sharp qualitative and thematic distinction between "Roman" and "non-Roman" offertories. Although the nonpsalmic pieces are more at home among the Old Hispanic sacrificia, the same cannot be said for the psalmic offertories with "non-Roman" verbal characteristics.

The hypothesis that many offertories originated outside of Rome raises questions about the musical style of the offertories. If the formation of an offertory repertory in Rome involved borrowings, what are the musical implications? Can "Roman" and "non-Roman" characteristics be defined and differentiated? The question can be approached from several perspectives. First, we might ask whether the verbal characteristics of the offertories correlate with their musical traits— whether offertories that depart from the PsR exhibit any stylistic traits that distinguish them from those that do not. The short answer to this question is no. Whether one takes the Gregorian or Roman versions as a basis for comparison, the offertories with "foreign" verbal traits are musically indistinguishable from the repertory as a whole. The Christmas offertory *Tollite portas* is a case in point. In chapter 2, I presented it as one of the more compelling cases of non-PsR influence, with many variants matching the northern Italian/North African psalter *α*. In chapter 3, however, the Gregorian version of *Tollite* served to illustrate some typical characteristics of Gregorian offertories: a moderately neumatic style with occasional long melismas, a final verse in the corresponding authentic range, and a long closing melisma in the last verse. Consistent with its Christmas assignment, the Roman version exhibits similar characteristics.

The psalmic offertories of possible non-Roman origin span the full stylistic spectrum of the genre. Perhaps the greatest point of stylistic diversity in the Gregorian offertories resides in their range and use of musical space, as illustrated in chapter 3. The responds and first verses of *Benedicite gentes, Miserere mihi*, and *Domine fac mecum* lie within a narrow range, whereas others, such as *Terra tremuit, Si ambulavero, Eripe me . . . deus*, and *Iubilate deo universa*, are more active in range, often traversing a sixth or an octave within a phrase or partial phrase. These two range types correlate, to some extent, with other stylistic traits. Offertories in the first group are often characterized by repetition of small motives, a repercussive, "tritus" style, and a tonal focus on F or c (b for the fourth mode), traits especially evident in responds and first verses of Lenten offertories. Offertories with a wider range are often more melismatic.

Pieces with "non-Roman" verbal traits lie at both ends of this spectrum, with a greater concentration among the more elaborate melodies. Some of the most ornate and virtuosic offertories of the repertory, such as *Iustus ut palma, Super flumina, Improperium*, and *Intonuit*, have textual readings that depart from the PsR. There are, however, some notable exceptions to this tendency. Two of the more compelling instances of non-PsR influence, *Miserere mihi* and *Benedicite gentes*, exemplify the neumatic, recitational style typical of many Lenten offertories. As illustrated in chapter 3, *Miserere mihi* shares melodic material with *Domine fac mecum*, an offertory consistent with the PsR. Among the Gregorian melodies, then, it is not possible to define "Roman" and "non-Roman" styles. If one takes the Roman versions as a basis for comparison, the homogeneity of offertories with different verbal traits stands out even more clearly. Some of the more compelling cases of offertories with a non-Roman verbal tradition, such as *Expectans, Portas caeli*, and *Intonuit*, make extensive use of Formulas A and B, a trait also found in several nonpsalmic offertories.

My examination of Gregorian, Roman, Milanese, and Beneventan chants in chapter 4 demonstrated the tendency for imported pieces to become absorbed into the melodic language of the new dialect. In view of this trend, the lack of musical distinction between "Roman" and "non-Roman" offertories suggests that the question of non-Roman origin may ultimately be a matter of lyrics rather than melodies. As I have shown, however, the melodic style of the Gregorian offertories is, to some extent, an international phenomenon. The Old Hispanic sacrificia share with the Roman-Gregorian offertories a conception of the genre as a lengthy piece sung in responsorial format, with solo verses and long melismas. Similar pieces may be found among the Milanese offerendae. In their narrow range, repetition, and extreme melodic economy, the formulaic Roman melodies stand in stark contrast to the elaborate style of offertory chants found in Francia, Spain, and, to some extent, Milan.

The international presence of these traits raises the possibility that the melodic style of the offertories is fundamentally non-Roman—a hypothesis proposed by Levy—or that it is at least influenced by non-Roman styles.[13] Placing the interaction between Rome and Gaul in the Carolingian period, Levy has explained some of these trends with a theory of reverse, Frankish-to-Roman transmission. The Franks, he argues, received the bulk of their repertory from the Romans but replaced the Roman melodies with preexisting Gallican ones. The Gallican melodies with Roman texts then made their way back to Rome and were partially incorporated into the existing Roman dialect.[14]

While I do not think this theory is the most plausible explanation for the situation as it stands, the notion that Gregorian offertories are stylistically "non-Roman" warrants further consideration. As illustrated in chapter 2, the Gregorian repertory incorporates several nonpsalmic offertories that lack Roman counterparts. On the basis of Old Latin texts or important liturgical assignments, a case for pre-Carolingian origin can be made for *Stetit angelus, Elegerunt, Factus est repente, Audi Israhel*, and *Ingressus est Zacharias*. Because the latter three pieces are found only in Mont-Blandin or Rheinau and in isolated later sources, they are especially

---

13. Kenneth Levy, "A New Look at Old Roman Chant I," *Early Music History* 19 (2000): 81–104, "A New Look at Old Roman Chant II," *Early Music History* 20 (2001): 173–98, "Gregorian Chant and the Romans," *Journal of the American Musicological Society* 56 (2003): 5–42, and "*Tollite Portas*."
14. Levy, "New Look at Old Roman Chant I,"; "New Look at Old Roman Chant II," and "Gregorian Chant and the Romans."

plausible as cases of pre-Carolingian survival. The wide geographic distribution of these pieces, which were known both north and south of the Alps, precludes their categorization among local repertories that emerged in the Carolingian period. Their rarity in manuscripts and their important liturgical assignments, moreover, distinguish them from universally known Frankish chants such as those for Frankish-instituted festivals or the *Omnes gentes* Mass. With the caveat that their melodies are witnessed only in much later sources, these pieces may bring us as close as we can come to defining a "pre-Carolingian" style for offertory chants.

Although they are diverse in some respects, these five offertories from outside the core Roman-Gregorian repertory are stylistically indistinguishable from the standard Gregorian offertories. Each has a moderately neumatic style broken by lengthy melismas, a defining feature of the Gregorian offertories. Several of them show a penchant for internal repetition and reuse of melodic material.[15] The stylistic continuity between the pre-Carolingian offertories and the Gregorian repertory is perhaps best illustrated with *Audi Israhel* and *Ingressus est*. *Audi Israhel* (ex. 5.1) is assigned in the Rheinau gradual to the first Sunday of a five-week Advent and in a handful of eleventh- and twelfth-century sources to Ember Friday of Advent. Although these later manuscripts are primarily of northern Italian origin, the chant is also found in Paris 780, an eleventh-century gradual from Toulouse, in a version melodically similar to the Italian one. This eighth-mode offertory shares several features with the standard Gregorian offertories, such as the varied repetition in the melismas on "absolvo" and "plebis" and the tonal contrast and expansion of range at the beginning of the verse. A similar movement into the authentic range, with a tonal focus on d and f, characterizes final verses of many Gregorian eighth-mode offertories, including *Scapulis suis*, *Miserere mihi*, and *Exaudi deus*. The repeat structure of the melisma on "Israhel" is another feature of the core offertories, also found in the Old Hispanic, Milanese, and, to a lesser extent, Roman offertories. Also typical of Gregorian offertories is *Audi's* rhetorical treatment of its words. The melody draws attention to the opening exhortation, "audi Israhel ecce," by traversing the range of an octave on "audi." The melodic line comes to a climax on "ecce" and then recedes. At the beginning of the verse, "Israhel" is chosen as the point of rhetorical emphasis, with the leaps up to high f and down to G. In this rhetorical treatment, *Audi Israhel* is reminiscent of the canticle offertories for the other Ember Days of Advent, *Confortamini*, examined in chapter 3, and *Exsulta satis*.

---

15. For a discussion of these traits in *Factus* and *Elegerunt*, see René-Jean Hesbert, "Un antique offertoire de la Pentecôte: 'Factus est repente,'" in *Organicae voces: Festschrift Joseph Smits van Waesberghe* (Amsterdam: Instituut voor Middeleeuwse Muziekwetenschap, 1963), 59–69; Kenneth Levy, "On Gregorian Orality," *Journal of the American Musicological Society* 43 (1990): 193–207; and Ruth Steiner, "On the Verses of the Offertory *Elegerunt*," in *The Study of Medieval Chant: Paths and Bridges, East and West: In Honor of Kenneth Levy*, ed. Peter Jeffery (Woodbridge, England: Boydell and Brewer, 2001), 283–303.

EXAMPLE 5.1 *Audi Israhel*

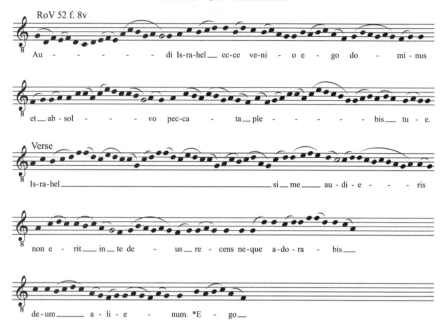

Ingressus, a lengthy piece assigned to John the Baptist in Mont-Blandin and found in a few Beneventan sources, exhibits many of the same characteristics. Excerpts of this G-mode piece are presented in example 5.2. In its treatment of the verbal dialogue, *Ingressus* brings to mind several nonpsalmic offertories of the core repertory. The opening narrative remains in the lower part of the range, not reaching above c until just before the quotation beginning with "ne timeas." "Dixit ad eum angelus," which sets up the quotation, is declaimed with recitation and a standard cadential pattern on c. In this melodic context, the expansion of range to f at the beginning of the quotation pointedly highlights the angel's words that foretell John's birth. The contrast between narrative and dialogue is similarly underscored in *Sanctificavit,* as demonstrated in chapter 3, and in *Precatus est Moyses.* The verse of *Ingressus* closes with a final melisma that is typical of many Gregorian offertories in its repeat structure and in emphasizing the fourth between G and c with typical figuration.

Further melodic links between core Roman-Gregorian offertories and pre-Carolingian ones lie in a network of melodic relationships between Gregorian offertories. The Gregorian version of *Angelus domini* shares melodic material with several other offertories, some of probable non-Roman origin, including *Factus est repente.*[16] Brief passages of *Angelus*'s material are also found in *Precatus est, Si*

16. Hesbert, "Antique offertoire."

EXAMPLE 5.2 *Ingressus est Zacharias*, opening and final melisma

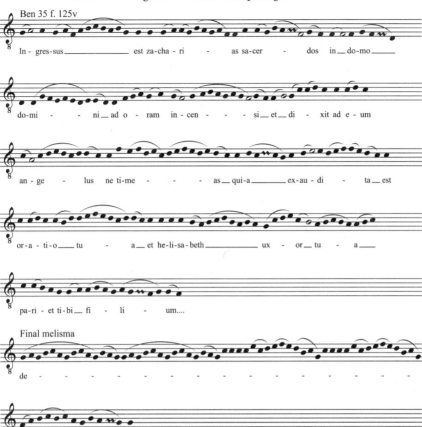

ambulavero, and *Ave Maria*.[17] Along with another offertory of possible non-Roman origin, *Constitues eos*, and one of certain non-Roman origin, *Stetit angelus*, *Angelus domini* serves as a source melody for several other offertories, many of local circulation. The final melisma of *Gressus meos* offers yet another connection between the Gregorian offertories and pre-Carolingian chants, occurring as a texted and untexted sequence in Beneventan, northern Italian, and Aquitanian sources.[18] A corresponding melisma is also found in the Roman version of *Gressus meos*, with a typical Roman melodic style.

17. See the discussion in chapter 2 and Ruth Steiner, "*Holocausta medullata*: An Offertory for St. Saturnius," in *De Musica et Cantu: Studien zur Geschichte der Kirchenmusik und der Oper: Helmut Hucke zum 60. Geburstag*, ed. Peter Kahn and Anne-Katrin Heimer (Hildesheim: Georg Olms Verlag, 1993), 263–74; and Luisa Nardini, "Il Repertorio Neo-Gregoriano del *Proprium Missae* in Area Beneventana" (Ph.D. diss., Università degli Studi di Roma, 2001), 204–21.
18. Kenneth Levy, "*Lux de Luce*: The Origin of an Italian Sequence," *Musical Quarterly* 57 (1971): 40–61.

These connections between pre-Carolingian offertories and the standard Gregorian repertory add weight to the verbal evidence that the Roman-Gregorian offertories were influenced by an international tradition, incorporating certain stylistic features common to Spain, Gaul, and northern Italy. Perhaps the best explanation lies in Pfisterer's theory that foreign pieces were imported into Rome at several stages during the Roman repertory's formation, long before its transmission to the Franks. If so, what did the Romans contribute to the repertory? I have shown that many of the psalmic offertories correspond to the PsR, and that these offertories are stylistically indistinguishable from those based on other psalters. A correspondence between a chant lyric and the PsR, of course, does not prove Roman origin of the chant in question. The stylistic consistency of the repertory, however, raises at least the possibility that the Romans composed their own chants in a similar vein. But how can such a hypothesis account for the melodic dialect of eleventh-century Rome? As I have shown, the Roman offertories exhibit ·a peculiar mixture of traits. Some have the expansive ranges and long melismas found in the Gregorian, Old Hispanic, and Milanese offertories; others consist of repeated statements of formulas found nowhere north of the Alps. In the international context, these formulas are patent exceptions.

As illustrated in chapter 4, the repetitive and formulaic style of the formulas finds a parallel among many Old Beneventan chants, suggesting that these were inherent Italianate traits. Perhaps the stylistic diversity of the Roman melodies, then, arose from an encounter between an exuberant Gallican/Old Hispanic style and a plainer, economical native style. In chapter 4, I illustrated the tendency for imported chants to become absorbed into Roman and Beneventan stylistic milieux and proposed that native chants could be subject to the same processes of homogenization. While melodic economy and ornateness were undoubtedly innate features of the Roman and Beneventan dialects, it is likely that these features became more pronounced in the course of oral transmission. I believe it is exactly these processes that transpired in the Roman offertories, either before or after the eighth-century transmission of the melodies to the Franks. The question of when the greater part of the melodic change occurred touches on a central issue of this study: the relative historical position of the Gregorian and Roman dialects.

GREGORIAN AND ROMAN CHANT

Until recently, the prevailing view of the Gregorian-Roman question was that the eleventh-century Roman dialect was closer to the tradition of eighth-century Rome. Adherents to this view have included Levy, Thomas Connolly, Joseph

Dyer, Philippe Bernard, Max Haas, and recently John Boe.[19] This hypothesis holds that the Roman melodies underwent a substantial revision in the hands of Frankish cantors. The possibility of extensive change in the Roman tradition after its separation from the Gregorian was first articulated by Walter Lipphardt.[20] More recently, it has been given extensive consideration by Nowacki, McKinnon, and Pfisterer.[21] Levy's theory that the Franks replaced Roman melodies with preexisting Gallican ones, later transmitted back to Rome, offers a third alternative.

I believe that the musical evidence examined in chapters 3 and 4 is of great value in addressing these questions. While the musical picture cannot offer empirical proof of one theory or another, it does point in clear directions of probability. By way of illustration, I will begin with Levy's hypothesis of Frankish-to-Roman transmission in the Carolingian period. The notion that the Franks modified the chant they learned from the Romans, incorporating some elements of their own, is nothing new. As contemporaneous anecdotal evidence suggests, the adoption of Roman chant was an enormous task for the Franks, and it is doubtful that they accomplished it with absolute accuracy.[22] Even as scholars have debated the relative proportion of Frankish and Roman contributions to the melodies, however, they have generally accepted the traditional wisdom that both dialects descend from the tradition of eighth-century Rome. This assumption is supported by historical documents mandating the adoption of Roman liturgy and chant in Francia, the widespread circulation of Roman liturgical books in the North, and other liturgical sources attesting to the use of a Roman liturgy mixed with Frankish elements. The liturgical evidence nevertheless offers some support for a later transmission of Franco-Roman practice back to Rome. In the late tenth century, mixed Gregorian sacramentaries and the Romano-Germanic pontifical were

19. Levy, "New Look at Old Roman Chant I"; Thomas Connolly, "Introits and Archetypes: Some Archaisms of the Old Roman Chant," *Journal of the American Musicological Society* 25 (1972): 157–74; Joseph Dyer, "'*Tropis semper variantibus*': Compositional Strategies in the Offertories of the Old Roman Chant," *Early Music History* 17 (1998): 1–59; Philippe Bernard, *Du chant romain au chant grégorien (IVe–XIIIe siècle)* (Paris: Cerf, 1996); Max Haas, *Mündliche Überlieferung und altrömisher Choral: Historische und analytische computergestützte Untersuchungen* (Bern: Peter Lang, 1997); and John Boe, "Deus Israel and Roman Introits," *Plainsong and Medieval Music* 14 (2005): 125–67.

20. Walter Lipphardt, "Gregor der Grosse und sein Anteil am Römischen Antiphonar," *Actes du congrés internationale de musique sacrée* (1950): 248–54.

21. Edward Nowacki, "The Gregorian Office Antiphons and the Comparative Method," *Journal of Musicology* 4 (1985): 243–75; McKinnon, *Advent Project*, 375–403; Pfisterer, *Cantilena*, 178–93. See also Paul Cutter, "The Old-Roman Chant Tradition: Oral or Written?" *Journal of the American Musicological Society* 20 (1967): 167–81; and Brad Maiani, "Approaching the Communion Melodies," *Journal of the American Musicological Society* 53 (2000): 283–84.

22. For example, the often-cited comment of John the Deacon: "Huius modulationis dulcedinem inter alias Europae gentes Germani seu Galli discere crebroque rediscere insigniter potuerunt, incorruptam vero tam levitate animi, quia nonnulla de proprio Gregorianis cantibus miscuerunt, quam feritate quoque naturali servare minime potuerunt," John the Deacon, *Sancti Gregorii Magni Vita*, in *Patrologia Latina* 75 (Paris: J. P. Migne, 1862), columns 90–91. For a translation see James McKinnon, ed., *The Early Christian Period and the Latin Middle Ages*, vol. 2, *Source Readings in Music History*, 2nd ed., ed. Leo Treitler (New York: Norton, 1998), 179.

adopted in Rome.[23] The Cluniac reform of monasteries near Rome, also in the tenth century, provides a further context for the reception of northern liturgical practice in Rome.[24] The Roman repertory, moreover, does transmit a few Gregorian pieces, including the Easter Vigil canticle tracts, which are purely Gregorian in style. Other imported items, such as the *Veterem hominem* antiphons and the Noah responsories, are absorbed into Roman style.[25] These borrowings, however, are generally regarded as isolated, special cases. The work of McKinnon and Pfisterer demonstrates that there was little such "seepage." As Pfisterer has shown, festivals that lacked a series of proper chants in the eighth century are given different Mass formularies in Frankish and Roman manuscripts.[26] Clearly the Romans made no comprehensive effort to conform to Frankish practice. With its proposal of large-scale Frankish-to-Roman transmission in the Carolingian period, then, Levy's hypothesis would fundamentally change the contextual framework that has guided most work on the early history of chant.

In view of the musical evidence presented in chapter 3, Levy's theory has several advantages. First, it would help to explain the wide stylistic diversity within the Roman repertory, the presence of formulaic melodies alongside the highly elaborate, idiomelic ones. With Levy's scenario, idiomelic Roman melodies could be seen as imports from the North, the formulas as remnants of an earlier Roman layer. The reverse-transmission theory would also account for the relatively strong correspondence between the idiomelic Roman melodies and their Gregorian counterparts, vis-à-vis the lack of the formulas in the Gregorian tradition. The similarities I have observed between core Gregorian offertories and pre-Carolingian offertories, moreover, could perhaps support the theory that the Franks replaced the Roman offertory melodies with preexisting melodies of their own.

Despite certain attractions of this theory, it emerges as problematic in the light of other trends I have observed. While Levy's attention to the Roman formulas is

23. See the summary in Cyrille Vogel, *Medieval Liturgy: An Introduction to the Sources* (Washington, D.C.: Pastoral Press, 1986), 104–5, 237–47.
24. Most notably Farfa. See Guy Ferrari, *Early Roman Monasteries: Notes for the History of Monasteries at Rome from the Fifth through the Tenth Century* (Vatican City: Pontifico Istituto de Archeologia Christiana, 1957); and Susan Boynton, *Liturgy and History at the Imperial Abbey of Farfa* (Ithaca, N.Y.: Cornell University Press, 2006). The possible impact of this reform in musical practice is considered in John Boe, "Chant Notation in Eleventh-Century Roman Manuscripts," in *Essays on Medieval Music: In Honor of David G. Hughes*, ed. Graeme Boone (Cambridge, Mass.: Harvard University Press, 1995), 43–57. Boe suggests it was in these monasteries that Gregorian chant first made its way to Rome. Roman repertorial borrowings from Benevento are also well known. Thomas Forest Kelly, "A Beneventan Borrowing in the Saint Cecilia Gradual," in *Max Lutolf zum 60. Geburtstag: Festschrift*, ed. Bernard Hangartner and Urs Fischer (Basel: Wiese, 1994), 11–20; and Alejandro Planchart, "Proses in the Sources of Old Roman Chant, and Their Alleluias," in *The Study of Medieval Chant: Paths and Bridges, East and West: In Honour of Kenneth Levy*, ed. Peter Jeffery (Cambridge: Boydell and Brewer, 2001), 313–39.
25. The Noah responsories have been convincingly posited as Frankish borrowings in Thomas Forrest Kelly, "Old-Roman Chant and the Responsories of Noah," *Early Music History* 26 (2007): 91–120.
26. Pfisterer, *Cantilena*, 119–36.

focused primarily on Formulas A and B, I have shown that Roman repertory incorporates numerous other formulas, such as those associated with modes 1, 2, and 8. Levy does not address the presence of these formulas in the repertory, and it is unclear whether he believes them to be original to Rome or Gallican melodies assimilated into a Roman oral milieu. As demonstrated in chapter 3, however, these formulas are based on syntactical principles similar to those of Formulas A and B; their melodic segments occur in a predictable series and play consistent roles in the delivery of the words. In the absence of historical evidence supporting a Frankish-to-Roman transmission, I see no reason to posit a non-Roman origin for these formulas.

If the eighth-century Roman prototypes were purely formulaic and the Franks replaced them with preexisting Gallican melodies, we would expect the Gregorian melodies to show no traces of continuity with the Roman formulas. As the examples in chapter 3 illustrate, however, the Gregorian melodies do show some similarity to the Roman formulas, particularly in offertories of modes 2, 6, and 8. Among several of these offertories, I have shown that the Roman formulas resemble the Gregorian readings in tonal structure, melodic vocabulary, and a tendency toward repetition, occasionally showing even brief points of more detailed similarity. These examples, evident primarily among responds and first verses, cast doubt on the theory that the Franks replaced them wholesale with preexisting Gallican melodies. This scenario would suggest that the Franks consciously sought isolated Gallican melodies with points of broad tonal similarity to the Roman formulas, perhaps so that the repertory would retain an appearance of Roman origin. I find this explanation untenable. With a preponderance of historical evidence supporting a Roman-to-Frankish transmission, the instances of resemblance between the Gregorian melodies and Roman formulas are more plausibly viewed as tokens of a common melodic vocabulary that predates the separation of the two branches.

While I ultimately resist Levy's theory of late reverse transmission, the relationship between the Gregorian and Roman offertories remains to be accounted for, and here we return to the traditional positions on the relationship between the Gregorian and Roman dialects. To help ascertain which theory is more consistent with the evidence presented here, I will review the historical framework established thus far. By the early seventh century, a full repertory of offertories had been assembled in Rome, most likely arising from some combination of non-Roman items and native compositions. The repertory was transmitted to the Franks in the middle and later eighth century. While the continuity between Frankish and Roman manuscripts in liturgical assignment indicates a Frankish intention to at least appear to conform to Roman practice, we see substantial differences between Gregorian and Roman melodies, particularly in places where the Roman version relies on formulas. How are Roman formulas to be understood within this framework? Does the combination of formulas and idiomelic material in the eleventh-century Roman offertories represent the melodic tradition of eighth-century Rome, altered by the Franks, or does it reflect developments that took place after the Frankish reception of Roman chant?

It would be imprudent to accept either theory as an exclusive model to explain the differences between the Gregorian and Roman dialects. Since it is unlikely that the Franks were able to reproduce the Roman melodies with absolute accuracy, Gregorian chant is undoubtedly in part a creative reconstruction of what the Franks heard the Romans sing. There is every likelihood that they brought something of their native tradition to the chant received from the Romans. The patterns illustrated in chapters 3 and 4, however, pose a substantial challenge to the view that the Roman formulas purely reflect the original state of affairs. As I have shown, resemblance between the two dialects is most consistently present when the Roman reading is idiomelic, with a minimal use of formulas and other standard material. With the assumption that the Roman versions represent the eighth-century state of the melodies, we would conclude that the Frankish singers were selective in their assimilation of the Roman repertory, absorbing the majority of nonformulaic Roman melodies into their tradition, but modifying or altogether eliminating the formulas.

An insurmountable difficulty with this theory arises if we accept the traditional wisdom that the Franks took seriously the mandate to sing Roman chant. Certainly they would have managed to assimilate the formulas with some accuracy. Relying on formulas, had they been available to the Franks, would have eased the burden of memory. Consider the trend observed in chapter 3 among certain cognate pairs such as *In virtute* and *In te speravi*: although the Gregorian reading lacks the formulas of the Roman version, it resembles the Roman melody in isolated, nonformulaic details. With this evidence, the theory that the formulas represent the eighth-century state of the repertory requires us to view the Frankish reception of Roman chant as a selective revision process in which Franks absorbed isolated, idiomelic passages of the Roman melodies but rejected precisely the passages that would have been easiest to remember. Given that learning a new repertory must have posed an enormous challenge to the Franks, I find this scenario improbable.

An alternative possibility is that the Roman melodies were once more varied in melodic detail but became increasingly formulaic during the three centuries in which they were transmitted in primarily oral form. My examination of two nonpsalmic offertories in chapter 4 demonstrated a process of convergent melodic change in melodies imported into the Roman tradition. It is doubtful that the Roman singers of subsequent generations were aware of the diverse origins of the chants they sang. Thus, I argued, native melodies were probably subject to the same types of change.

A more widespread application of the model of convergent change in Rome would attribute much of the formulaicism in the eleventh-century Roman versions to progressive homogenization in the Roman tradition between the eighth and eleventh centuries, the prolonged period of oral transmission that followed the Frankish reception. Certain melodies I have examined offer much to recommend this hypothesis. As illustrated in chapter 3, some Gregorian melodies show a broad similarity to the Roman formulas in tonal structure, a phenomenon evident especially in Lenten responds and first verses of the second, sixth, and eighth modes. These melodies, moreover, are generally similar to the Roman formulas in their narrow range, neumatic style, and repetitive surface structure. Although these Gregorian melodies lack the systematic repetition of the Roman versions, they draw on a similar vocabulary of small melodic segments that are repeated and reused throughout. Many Gregorian melodies, moreover, are highly repetitive on a structural level. In *Benedicite gentes*, for example, we noted that each internal phrase is based on embellished repetition of F or oscillation between D and F. *Domine in auxilium, Desiderium,* and *In virtute* are representative examples of the Gregorian family of sixth-mode offertories. These offertories share a tonal focus on F and a vocabulary of standard cadential patterns and melismas. Turning to their Roman counterparts, I showed that the shared material was employed in a more systematic way, producing a more uniform melodic surface. Since the underlying similarity in tonal structure between phrases is present in both the Gregorian and Roman versions, we may assume that it was a feature of the eighth-century prototype. The structural similarities between phrases would have allowed a more uniform, repetitive version of the melody to emerge without changes in its overall structure.

The differences between the two traditions in their underlying approach to making melodies further argue in favor of convergent change on the Roman side. In creating formulaic melodies, Roman singers relied on a complex system of verbal cues and syntactical rules that would have allowed them to reconstruct the melodies without learning each one individually. The Frankish singers, by contrast, appear to have placed greater value on retaining the individual details of each melody. Gregorian offertories show only vestiges of the Roman syntactical rules, evident in broader principles of text declamation and correlation between melodic segments and word accent. These syntactical principles, however, would have lent themselves to further development under the conditions of reconstructive oral processes.

In chapter 3, I suggested that processes of oral transmission may fall on different points along a spectrum, between "reconstruction" and "rote learning." These two models cannot be distinguished in any absolute sense, and to different degrees, each plays a role in the transmission of formulaic and nonformulaic melodies. The Roman and Beneventan versions of *Beatus es Simon Petre*, examined in chapter 3, illustrate different points on this spectrum. The Beneventan melody is a literal contrafact of the source chant, *Angelus domini*, reflecting an understanding of that melody as a fixed entity. The Roman *Beatus es*, by contrast, demonstrates a typical penchant for melodic repetition and a dependency on verbal and musical cues that is lacking in the Beneventan version. These different compositional procedures are perhaps most evident in the way the singers accommodate the verbal differences between *Beatus es* and *Angelus domini*. Roman singers employ standard eighth- and first-mode material, applying the usual syntactical rules. Beneventan singers, by contrast, simply accommodate extra syllables with syllabic repetition of D or G, exhibiting few signs of the dynamic oral processes that underlie the Roman melody. Applying these observations more widely, it seems that the reconstructive type of oral process exerted a deeper influence in the Roman melodies than it did in their Gregorian counterparts, both because oral tradition continued for longer in Rome and, perhaps more important, because the Carolingians placed such a great value on systematization and stabilization.

In view of the historical evidence, the model of convergent change in Rome after the mid-eighth century has several advantages. It is compatible with the evidence that the Roman tradition was transmitted by purely oral means for two centuries longer than the Gregorian was.[27] It is also consistent with the Frankish mandate to learn Roman chant and with the Frankish tendency toward systematization. In terms of the musical picture, the progressive-homogenization hypothesis is compelling particularly in cases where the Gregorian melodies show an underlying similarity to the Roman formulas. It is less satisfactory, however, in the many instances where the Gregorian melodies show no affinity with the Roman formulas—an issue I shall explore presently.

Finally, the phenomenon of word-music parallelism warrants consideration in weighing the possibilities of melodic change in Rome and Francia. Although both dialects show a tendency to set the same words to the same music, this phenomenon occurs far more frequently in the Roman offertories. As I have shown, the differences between the two dialects are often most pronounced in passages where the Roman singers respond habitually to the words. This pattern suggests two possible scenarios. The first is that the close correlation between words and music in the Roman melodies reflects their eighth-century state. With this premise, we would conclude that the Franks neglected to assimilate the particular passages of the Roman melodies that most clearly manifest this dependency, perhaps because they failed to grasp the verbal parallelism that underlies these passages.[28] This explanation seems improbable, for several reasons. The examples of word-music parallelism I have observed in the Gregorian offertories indicate that the Frankish singers were well aware of the phenomenon. The importance of the words to

27. Boe, "Chant Notation in Eleventh-Century Roman Manuscripts," and "Music Notation in Archivio San Pietro C 105 and in the Farfa Breviary, Chigi C. VI. 177," *Early Music History* 18 (1999): 1–45.
28. In stating the case for Gallican origin, Levy argues that these instances of "doubles," cases of word-music parallelism, rule out a Roman-to-Frankish transmission. See "Gregorian Chant and the Romans," 18–35. This line of reasoning, however, is dependent on the assumption that the Roman reading reflects the eighth-century melodic state.

Frankish singers, moreover, is manifest in the rhetorical emphasis given to certain words and the use of range as a syntactical tool to underscore the meaning of the text, evidently features of certain pre-Carolingian melodies such as *Audi* and *Ingressus*.[29] Given their sensitivity to the words and their meaning, it is unlikely that the Franks would fail to notice instances of word-music parallelism in the Roman melodies. Finally, if the Roman melodies reflect the eighth-century state of the repertory, the patterns I have observed would suggest that the Franks eliminated the specific parts of the Roman melodies that were prompted by verbal cues but retained their more distinctive, idiomelic passages. With this last point, I return to the argument of thrift: the consistent association of certain words with particular melodic phrases would have served as a powerful memory aid, facilitating the Frankish efforts to learn the Roman melodies. The cognitive psychologist David Rubin has discussed the role of rhyme and assonance as memory cues in oral traditions: "The repetition of sound is an aid to memory. When a sound repeats, the first occurrence of a sound limits the choices for the second occurrence and provides a cue for it."[30] It is improbable that the Franks would selectively and systematically eliminate instances of word-music parallelism in the Roman melodies while keeping idiomelic passages that were more difficult to remember.

With this last argument, an alternative hypothesis emerges to explain the greater frequency of word-music parallelism in the Roman offertories, namely that during the centuries following the Frankish reception, the Roman singers became increasingly dependent on the words as an aid to remembering the melodies. Once again, this theory is consistent with the mandate that the Frankish singers reproduce Roman chant faithfully and with the evidence that the Roman tradition relied on purely oral transmission for a much longer period than the Gregorian did. Although both dialects have their origins in oral tradition, we might expect the Roman offertories to exhibit more discernable signs of a dynamic, reconstructive oral tradition. The dependency on melodic formulas and verbal cues in Roman offertories is consistent with this expectation; both factors would have aided Roman singers in learning and remembering the melodies in the absence of notation.

The evidence for change in the Roman dialect having been presented, the argument requires further clarification, particularly in the method of reasoning.

29. Also see Susan Rankin, "Carolingian Music," in *Carolingian Culture: Emulation and Innovation*, ed. Rosamond McKitterick (Cambridge: Cambridge University Press, 1994), 281–90.
30. David Rubin, *Memory in Oral Traditions: The Cognitive Psychology of Epics, Ballads, and Counting-Out Rhymes* (New York: Oxford University Press, 1995), 75. Rubin does not analyze the relationship between words and music specifically, but discusses the role of sound as a cue to memory throughout his study. See especially 65–89; and the analyses of counting–out rhymes and North Carolina ballads, 227–98. Emma Hornby has drawn compellingly on Rubin's theories in presenting a model of transmission for the Gregorian and Roman eighth-mode tracts. See Emma Hornby, "The Origins of the Eighth-Mode Tracts: What Kept the Oral Transmission Stable?" *Études grégoriennes* 26 (1998): 135–62.

The Roman repertory was created orally and transmitted without notation for at least a century—perhaps much longer—before it reached the Franks. There is certainly no inherent reason that the Roman singers of the eleventh century would have more trouble remembering the melodies than would those of the seventh and eighth centuries. It is possible that all of the pervasive formulaicism in the Roman melodies emerged during this initial period of oral transmission, before the repertory was exported north. When the Gregorian melodies and their relationship to the Roman ones are taken into account, however, this hypothesis emerges as an unlikely one.

The argument for progressive stereotyping is inductive, based on observation of the situation as it stands in the available historical and musical sources. The core of the argument lies in four premises. The first is that the Roman tradition was transmitted in purely oral form for far longer than the Gregorian was. This broad consensus among scholars is reinforced in Boe's survey of known Roman manuscripts. Boe concludes that notation reached central Italy in the late ninth century but was used only "tentatively and occasionally" in Rome between the ninth and eleventh centuries.[31] The second premise, demonstrated in chapter 3, is that the eleventh-century Roman melodies are much more formulaic than their Gregorian counterparts. The third premise, supported with argument in chapter 3, is that the formulaic melodies would have been easy to recall and reproduce. The melodic economy and syntactical rules of the formulas allow for adaptation of the material to different texts without rote memorization of numerous individual chants.

The fourth premise is that the Franks intended to reproduce the Roman melodies faithfully, and it is this premise that is least likely to find consensus among scholars. Before discussing its role in the argument and its potential problems, however, I will clarify the relationship between the first two premises. The formulaicism of the Roman melodies does not by itself prove a deeper influence of oral tradition in Rome. The presence of formulaic and nonformulaic melodies side by side in core plainsong genres indicates that there is no inherent correlation between formulas and oral tradition, or between nonformulaic melodies and written tradition. Both types of melodies arose in an oral tradition, both are possible within the confines of oral transmission, and both persisted after the melodies were written down.

Rather than attempting to prove through melodic analysis that solely oral tradition continued for longer in Rome, I take it as a given on the basis of the manuscript evidence. The hypothesis of late progressive homogenization in the Roman tradition ties the premise of a longer oral transmission in Rome together with the formulaicism and reconstructive processes observed in the melodies by a process of causal inference, a causal connection based on the conditions of the occurrence of an effect. I suggest that the formulas developed during the prolonged

31. Boe, "Music Notation in Archivio San Pietro C 105," 1–45.

period of oral transmission that followed the Frankish reception. This inference is supported by my analysis of the formulas, which suggests that they were both easily recalled and reproduced by reconstructive processes, by the greater prominence of individual melodic detail in the Gregorian melodies, and by features of the Gregorian melodies that would have lent themselves to further stereotyping under the conditions of oral transmission. This inductive reasoning does not prove the conclusion but rather supports it by establishing a direction of probability.

Now to the fourth premise, the Franks' intention of adherence to Roman tradition, which is an important element of the hypothesis that the bulk of structural changes to the melodies occurred on the Roman side. The eleventh-century Roman formulas, with their extreme economy of melodic material, would have been easy for the Franks to recall and reproduce. If the Franks intended to reproduce the Roman melodies faithfully, they could not have failed to absorb the melodic substance of the formulas. In the surviving witnesses to the Frankish tradition, however, we see only faint vestiges of the formulas' melodic substance. It is therefore doubtful that the formulas of the eleventh-century Roman tradition represent the eighth-century prototype.

The premise of Frankish intentions to sing Roman chant is certainly supported by Carolingian mandate to do so. The well-rehearsed anecdotal evidence from the time nevertheless suggests that the Franks did not gain full mastery of the Roman melodies.[32] To counter the assumption that the Franks tried to learn Roman chant, Levy emphasizes the political overtones in the accounts of John the Deacon and Notker. As different as their stories are, however, both authors present Roman chant as the tradition to be emulated and the discrepancies between Frankish and Roman practice as a shortcoming. With McKinnon, I am inclined to attribute the lack of full conformity to Roman melodies not to a lack of *intention* but rather to the difficulties of learning the new repertory—thousands of Mass and Office chants—without musical notation. The traditional wisdom that the Franks intended to learn Roman chant faithfully is borne out by the near uniformity between the two traditions in liturgical assignments. In cases where repertories and assignments differ, Pfisterer has argued persuasively that the greater change occurred on the Roman side.[33] Further support for the premise resides in other core chant genres, which exhibit a much more consistent similarity between the Gregorian and Roman traditions than the offertory verses do.[34] Finally, the

32. See the often-cited comments of John the Deacon, Amalar of Metz, and Helisacher, abbot of St. Riquier (cited in chapter 1).
33. Pfisterer, *Cantilena*, 119–36.
34. For studies of single genres, see Helmut Hucke, "Gregorianischer Gesang in fränkischer und altrömischer Überlieferung," *Archiv für Musikwissenschaft* 12 (1955): 74–87; Joseph Michael Murphy, "The Communions of the Old-Roman Chant (Ph.D. diss., University of Pennsylvania, 1971); Thomas Connolly, "The Introits of the Old Roman Chant" (Ph.D. diss., Harvard University, 1972), and "Introits and Archetypes"; Nancy van Deusen, "A Historic and Stylistic

traditional view that the Franks intended to sing Roman chant is supported by the liturgy's status as a symbol of Franco-Roman alliance, eventually resulting in the late ninth-century attribution of the melodies to Gregory the Great. While some variability in the tradition was inevitable, the position of the liturgical song as a token of conformity to Roman practice seems incompatible with the view that the Franks played fast and loose with the Roman melodies.

Against this evidence for intended faithfulness to Rome, one could argue that the offertories are exceptional. Some of them may have been known to the Frankish singers previously, as part of their native repertory. If so, the Franks may have been more resistant to learning the Roman melodies than they were with other genres. For this reason and several others, I believe that change on the Frankish side warrants a place in any efforts to explain the discrepancies between the two traditions. In some respects, however, the musical picture presented in chapter 3 is difficult to reconcile with the theory that the Franks deliberately and selectively altered the Roman melodies. I have shown that the Gregorian melodies do show traces of similarity to the Roman formulas in some cases, whereas in other cases they are utterly dissimilar to the Roman formulas. With the scenario that all changes to the tradition took place in Francia, we would conclude that the Franks absorbed the basic melodic structure of the nonformulaic sections of the Roman offertories and undertook a stylistic revision, giving the melodies the greater sense of tonal focus and "directionality" so often associated with the Gregorian dialect. When faced with formulaic Roman melodies, however, the Franks responded in various ways. In some cases, they retained the tonal structure of the formulas and aspects of their melodic vocabulary but changed their melodic details to produce a more varied musical surface. In many other instances, they eliminated the formulas altogether. The varied musical picture casts doubt on the scenario of selective revision: if the Franks replaced the formulas in some cases, why retain traces of them in others?

Despite these arguments in its favor, the premise of the Franks' intended faithfulness to Rome is not universally accepted, and the lack of consensus on this matter brings us to the heart of a debate that is ultimately circular. In short, the premise that the eleventh-century Roman melodies represent the eighth-century prototype is incompatible with the premise that the Franks intended to reproduce the Roman melodies faithfully: if both were true, we would see more traces of the

Comparison of the Graduals of Gregorian and Old Roman Chant (Ph.D. diss., Indiana University, 1972); Albert Turco, *Les Antienns d'introït du chant romain comparées a celles du grégorien et de l'ambrosiem* (Solesmes, 1993); and Hornby, "Study of the Eighth-Mode Tracts." In addition to these studies, partial comparisons are made in numerous places, including Hendrik van der Werf, *The Emergence of Gregorian Chant* (Rochester, N.Y.: 1983); Theodore Karp, *Aspects of Orality and Formularity in Gregorian Chant* (Evanston, Ill.: Northwestern University Press, 1998): 365–424; Brad Maiani, "The Responsory-Communions: Toward a Chronology of Selected Proper Chants" (Ph.D. diss., University of North Carolina, Chapel Hill, 1996), and "Approaching the Communion Melodies"; McKinnon, *Advent Project*; and Pfisterer, *Cantilena*.

Roman formulas in the Gregorian melodies. Whichever premise one accepts may be ultimately a matter of scholarly temperament and epistemological orientation. Some scholars, most notably Dyer and Levy, reject the premise of the Frankish singers' intended faithfulness to Roman tradition on the basis of the musical picture: if the Franks intended to reproduce Roman chant faithfully, we would expect to see a greater similarity between the two dialects, and certainly more traces of the Roman formulaicism in the Gregorian offertories. From the lack of similarity between the two traditions, they conclude that the Franks deliberately altered the Roman melodies. Often underlying this reasoning is yet another premise, particularly evident in Levy's arguments, that formulas are a sign of archaism.[35] I find the arguments for Frankish intentions to adhere to the Roman tradition far more compelling than the view that formulas are an inherent index of archaism. For these reasons, a hypothesis of convergent change on the Roman side emerges as more consistent with the musical and historical picture than the alternatives are. The lack of consensus on this premise, coupled with the inductive nature of the argument, means that progressive stereotyping is unlikely to move from hypothesis to established fact. What I hope to have shown is that convergent change on the Roman side between the eighth and eleventh centuries is highly likely. At the very least, it is untenable to view the eleventh-century Roman chant uncritically as a reflection of the eighth-century Roman melodies.

The offertories' lyrics offer some circumstantial support for the theory of a later melodic homogenization at Rome. As shown in chapter 2, most offertories have a highly stylized verbal structure. In particular, the Lenten psalmic offertories are marked by extensive centonization, with a concern for structure and thematic unity. Parts of the psalm were chosen and rearranged to create a lyric for the musical form of the offertory with verses and repetenda. Turning to the treatment of these words in chapter 3, we saw that the Gregorian offertories often exploit dramatic possibilities of the text through the use of range or changes in neumatic density. Similar responses to the text are evident in some Roman nonformulaic melodies, but to a far lesser extent. The eleventh-century Roman formulaic verses appear cursory by comparison. The Roman singers respond to certain key structural features of the text, such as clause length and accent pattern, whereas the Frankish singers respond to its content and meaning. Given the care that went into the creation of the texts, it seems unlikely that they were created to be sung with the formulas of eleventh-century Rome.

If the Roman dialect became increasingly formulaic between the eighth and eleventh centuries, what types of change occurred on the Frankish side? The Milanese versions examined in chapter 4 suggest a hypothesis. Although these

---

35. For example, "ROM-11's still simple, improvisational-formulaic stance suggests that between it and its ROM-8 forerunner there was little in the way of change." Levy, "New Look at Old Roman Chant I," 96.

melodies normally resemble the Gregorian versions in structure, lacking the Roman formulas, they nevertheless show an occasional structural resemblance to the Roman version rather than the Gregorian. The Roman and Milanese dialects, moreover, share an ornate, stepwise style, along with certain aspects of melodic vocabulary and turns of phrase. The similarities in surface style between the Roman and Milanese versions support the hypothesis, proposed by Dyer and others, that these are native Italianate traits. It is likely, then, that the Roman melodies had something of the ornate texture and melodic vocabulary shared with the Milanese and Old Beneventan traditions, as well as some tendency toward melodic thrift. If so, we may hypothesize that the melodies underwent a stylistic transformation in the hands of the Franks, becoming less ornate and gaining a greater tonal focus on F and c. At the same time, the differences in melodic detail between the Roman and Milanese versions suggest that the Italianate traits become more pronounced over time.

In the light of the patterns I have observed, progressive homogenization in the Roman tradition between the eighth and eleventh centuries emerges as a plausible explanation for many of the differences between the Gregorian and Roman versions. It is especially compelling in cases where the Gregorian melodies show an underlying structural similarity to the Roman formulas. While convergent, incremental change on the Roman side plays an important role in explaining the differences between the two dialects, however, it is not a satisfactory explanation for melodies that lack any resemblance between the two versions. With a model of convergent change, we would expect to see some vestige of the common melodic tradition that underlies the two dialects. Many Gregorian and Roman verses of the later liturgical seasons, however, lack all traces of a common melodic origin. Considered in the context of other chant genres, these verses stand out as exceptions. A much more consistent similarity between the two traditions is found among graduals, tracts, and communions.

In pondering the reasons for the utter lack of melodic resemblance among these Lenten and Paschaltide verses, some isolated exceptions warrant consideration. Two Roman Lenten offertories examined in chapter 3, *Exaudi deus* and *Scapulis suis*, have elaborate, nonformulaic final verses in the corresponding authentic range. We find similar examples of nonformulaic Roman final verses in sanctoral offertories such as *Iustus ut palma* and *Veritas mea*, and in the incomparable Post-Pentecost offertory *Vir erat*. These isolated idiomelic verses exhibit a much closer continuity with the Gregorian tradition than the formulaic verses do, indicating that the aesthetic principles that underlie the Gregorian verses were known to Roman singers. The remaining elaborate Gregorian verses were either created by the Franks or lost in the Roman tradition during centuries of oral transmission.

Each possibility raises difficult questions. If the Franks undertook a complete recomposition of many Roman verses, focusing on the formulaic melodies of Lent and Paschaltide, why would they retain the tonal characteristics and melodic contour of most responds and many first verses, even those that are repetitive and formulaic? If on the other hand a well-established tradition of elaborate Lenten and Paschaltide verses existed in eighth-century Rome, would these melodies simply vanish, leaving so few traces of their existence in the Roman tradition of the eleventh and twelfth centuries? Even with a convergent dynamic, the diversity of the Roman verse repertory is puzzling. The vivid depictions of the suffering Job's repeated cries in *Vir erat* contrast markedly with the many cursory verses based on Formulas A and B.

This sharp stylistic contrast within the Roman repertory and the corresponding breaches of affinity with the Gregorian verses may be best explained by a partial disruption of the solo verse tradition in Rome. As indicated in *Ordo Romanus I*, the offertory chant was concluded with a signal from the pope when the rite had come to an end, whether or not all verses had been performed. Second and third verses, then, may have been sung less frequently than responds and first verses. If so, perhaps the *schola cantorum* gave minimal attention to maintaining their melodic tradition. This context provides a possible clue to the melodic differences between successive verses. As I have shown, many Roman offertories exhibit an increasing reliance on formulas with each successive verse, coupled with a decline in resemblance to the Gregorian reading. Without repeated rehearsal and performance, these verse melodies would be unlikely to survive centuries of oral transmission. The Frankish addition of a lay offering, moreover, raises the possibility that the verse tradition underwent further development in the North. The increased time required for the rite may have served as an impetus for renewed concentration on verse melodies.

These speculations bring to mind a primary unanswered question in chant research: to what extent were the melodies "fixed" in their transmission to the Franks? Did the Frankish singers receive a stable, invariable tradition from Rome, or did they take a snapshot of a varying tradition? By the late ninth century, the time of our earliest notated manuscripts, the melodic tradition had probably gained a degree of consistency. David Hughes has demonstrated the near uniformity of early written sources with respect to contour.[36] Although Leo Treitler has argued that this concordance may reflect the influence of writing rather than oral transmission, he concurs that the tradition was consistent in many essentials by the time it was written down.[37] Emma Hornby has demonstrated variability among early sources with respect to performance practices, characterizing the early written state of the repertory as one of compatibility rather than uniformity.[38] Her conclusions,

---

36. David Hughes, "Evidence for the Traditional View of the Transmission of Gregorian Chant," *Journal of the American Musicological Society* 40 (1987): 377–404.

37. Treitler's view is articulated most thoroughly in *With Voice and Pen: Coming to Know Medieval Song and How It Was Made* (New York: Oxford University Press, 2003), 136–44.

38. Emma Hornby, "The Transmission of Western Chant in the Eighth and Ninth Centuries: Evaluating Kenneth Levy's Reading of the Evidence," *Journal of Musicology* 21 (2004): 418–57.

however, do not change the impression of a tradition that had settled somewhat by the time it was committed to notation. The offertory verses are no exception. As the comparative manuscript studies summarized at the companion Web site show, the pitched sources do reflect points of melodic instability, but only in very specific places. The eleventh-century Roman manuscripts make a similar impression.[39] A case for melodic instability of the verses at the time of the Frankish reception is not bolstered by the written sources and would rest mainly on the lack of similarity between the Gregorian and Roman versions and the liturgical context.

As compelling as evidence for a compatible melodic tradition at the time of writing may be, it does not tell us how variable the tradition was a century earlier, when the Franks received the Roman chant. I doubt we will ever know the answer to this question. In reflecting on it, it is important to keep in mind Peter Jeffery's caveat that the transmission of the tradition to the Franks was not a one-time event; it was a series of events that took place at different times and in different places.[40] As Jeffery and Treitler have each emphasized, it is unlikely that medieval singers shared our conceptions of uniformity. The heterogeneity of pre-Carolingian liturgies and repertories, considered in chapter 2, reinforces the impression that the goal of liturgical unity often attributed to the Carolingian era was something of a novelty. Recent work on liturgical manuscripts, moreover, calls for a revision of the very assumption that Carolingian liturgical practice was indeed "unified." Liturgical uniformity may have been an ideal, but it was not a reality. Noting that the Frankish liturgical sources present a picture of compatibility rather than uniformity, Rosamund McKitterick is skeptical that the melodic tradition was fixed when the liturgy was not.[41] An especially forceful challenge to the notion of liturgical uniformity comes in recent work of Daniel DiCenso, who examines the sacramentaries attached to the Mass antiphoners indexed in Hesbert's *Antiphonale Missarum Sextuplex*. The differences between these books are fundamental. Some of the antiphoners are bound with sacramentaries of Gregorian tradition, others with various redactions of the Gelasian tradition, and others with sacramentaries reflecting a mixture of the two. Hesbert's side-by-side placement of festivals and chants, DiCenso argues, obscures important differences between these books and the liturgical practices they represent. The "eccentricities" attributed to the Rheinau gradual, for example, are reflected in its redaction of the Gelasian sacramentary. In the absence of a liturgical norm, the characterization of the Mass

---

39. I discuss exceptions in chapter 6 and, in greater detail, in the individual commentary each offertory at the companion Web site. See also Steiner, "On the Verses of the Offertory *Elegerunt*."
40. Peter Jeffery, "Rome and Jerusalem: From Oral Tradition to Written Repertory," in Boone, *Essays on Medieval Music in Honor of David G. Hughes*, 234–36.
41. Rosamund McKitterick, review of *Gregorian Chant and the Carolingians*, by Kenneth Levy, *Early Music History* 19 (2000): 283–85. "Although a remarkable degree of consistency may have been achieved by the tenth century, parallel liturgical and textual evidence would suggest that harmony rather than uniformity prevailed before that" (284).

antiphoner as "eccentric" loses its validity.[42] Given this variety of Carolingian liturgical practice, it is unlikely that the eighth-century melodic tradition was uniform in the modern sense. It follows that the written sources will never fully reveal the chant of the Roman *schola* or that of early Frankish practice. What they can offer is insight into the processes of transmitting and transforming melodies in two distinct cultures that did not know musical notation and only later came to value uniformity.

42. DiCenso's doctoral thesis, "Charlemagne's Song: Gregorian Chant and the 'Romanization' of an Empire," is in progress at Magdalene College, Cambridge. Preliminary results, "The Carolingian Liturgical Reforms: How Sacramentaries May Change Our Understanding of Chant 'Transmission,'" presented at the annual meeting of the American Musicological Society in Quebec City, November 2007. I thank Dr. DiCenso for sharing work in progress and clarifying points in subsequent correspondence.

6

THE OFFERTORIES IN MANUSCRIPTS
An Introduction to the Edition

Recent work on the editing of music has emphasized its critical nature. An edition reflects choices and judgments made at many junctures, from the selection of sources and the representation of specific neumes to the methodology employed in determining representative readings.[1] In this introduction to the edition, I outline the premises that underlie these choices, describe the sources employed, and illustrate the types of variants encountered.

This study aims not to present a detailed study of variants within a single regional tradition but to ascertain, through comparative transcription, the extent of variation in the broader tradition and determine which manuscripts best represent a majority or preferred version. I have incorporated a core group of representative manuscripts that includes selected Beneventan and Aquitanian sources, as well as Montpellier 159. Additional manuscripts, serving a secondary role, include sources from northern and central Italy, Francia, and German-speaking areas. (The manuscripts and their sigla are listed in appendix 2.) This work builds on and complements several existing partial editions of the repertory, based primarily on Aquitanian sources.[2]

In the downloadable PDF files at the companion Web site, the Gregorian and Roman versions may be viewed in side-by-side transcriptions. The "Gregorian" version is represented by a single manuscript chosen from the core group of sources; this reading functions as a basis for stylistic assessment, comparison with other Gregorian manuscripts, and comparison with the Roman version. Because modal emendation is so widespread in the offertories, the base version given in the transcription is selected with the criterion that it exhibit minimal editing or emendation. For reasons that will become clear, a Beneventan version

---

1. See James Grier, *The Critical Editing of Music: History, Method, and Practice* (Cambridge: Cambridge University Press, 1996), 8–37.
2. See Hubert Sidler, "Studien zu den alten Offertorien mit ihren Versen," (Ph.D. diss., University of Fribourg, 1939); Grover Allen Pittman, "The Lenten Offertories of the Aquitanian Manuscripts" (Ph.D. diss., Catholic University of America, 1973); Cheryl Crawford Frasch, "Notation as a Guide to Modality in the Offertories of Paris, B.N. lat. 903" (Ph.D. diss., Ohio State University, 1986); Dean Richard Justmann, "Mode-One Offertories: A Critical Edition with Analysis" (Ph.D. diss., Northwestern University, 1988); and Roman Hankeln, *Die Offertoriumsprosuln der aquitanischen Handschriften:Voruntersuchungen zur Edition des aquitanischen Offertoriumscorpus und seiner Erweiterungen* (Tutzing: Hans Schneider, 1999).

often serves as the base reading, except in cases where the Beneventan sources reflect emendation. Like most recent plainsong editions, this one incorporates minimal editorial intervention and avoids composite readings where possible. Typically the transcription presents the melody and words as they occur in one manuscript.

This approach reflects the emphasis of modern chant scholarship on the oral origins and transmission of the repertory. While comparative transcription allows us to establish majority readings and determine where scribal emendations have taken place, it is unfeasible to establish a single "authentic" or "original" version of this repertory. Even if the melodies originated as single, authoritative versions—a questionable proposition—the written sources provide only an indirect witness to that tradition. The manuscripts offer our best record of how the melodies were understood and performed in the specific times and places they represent. Readers may gain a broader picture of transmission for each chant in the commentary of appendix 3, where the results of the comparative transcriptions are summarized and analyzed.

CORE AND PERIPHERAL SOURCES

Beneventan manuscripts play an especially important role in this study. The importance of the Beneventan tradition was established long ago by René-Jean Hesbert, who noted distinctive and anachronistic features of its liturgy, melodies, and notation. Hesbert argued that, despite their eleventh-century copying date, the Beneventan sources are witnesses to a much older chant tradition.[3] Various types of evidence point to an early reception of Gregorian chant in Benevento, followed by a period of relative isolation. One such index is the transition from Old Beneventan to Gregorian melodies in newly added festivals. The Feast of the Twelve Brothers, instituted in 760, is the last with Old Beneventan proper items. There are no Old Beneventan chants for St. Mercurius, whose relics were brought to Benevento in 768, or for St. Bartholomew, added in 838, whose Mass employs contrafacts of Gregorian melodies. Clearly Gregorian chant had arrived in Benevento by this time.[4] Later Frankish additions to the calendar, however, are

3. René-Jean Hesbert, *Le codex 10 673 de la Bibliothèque Vaticane fonds latin (xie siècle)*, Paleographie musicale vol. 14 ([Solesmes, France]: Abbaye Saint Pierre de Solesmes, 1931), 97–196.
4. Thomas Forrest Kelly, *The Beneventan Chant* (Cambridge: Cambridge University Press, 1989), 11–13, 28. The 838 date is contested in Mathias Bielitz, *Zum Bezeichneten der Neumen, insbesondere der Liqueszenz: Ein Hypothesenansatz zum Verhältnis von Musik und Sprache, zur diatonischen Rationalität, zur Bewegungs-und Raum Analogie, zur Entstehung der Neumenschrift und zur Rezeption des Gregorianischen Chorals in Benevent.* (Neckargemünd: Männeles Verlag, 1998). Pfisterer, however, presents a compelling argument that the feast could not have been instituted after c. 1000. See Andreas Pfisterer, *Cantilena Romana: Untersuchungen zur Überlieferung des gregorianischen Chorals* (Tützing: Hans Schneider, 2002): 81–82.

either lacking in Beneventan manuscripts or supplied with formularies unique to
Benevento. These include the seventh Sunday after Pentecost, the second Sunday
of Lent, Saturday of Passion Week, and Saturday after Ash Wednesday. Some
Beneventan manuscripts also reflect an older usage in providing two graduals for
Saturday of the fourth week in Lent.[5]

Other indices of early reception include the texts of the Beneventan chant
manuscripts, which are heavily dependent on the PsR. Although the Gallican
psalter began to exert an influence in Benevento in the tenth and eleventh
centuries, the chant manuscripts copied during this time show few traces of its
influence. As Thomas Kelly has argued, the prominence of the PsR in the
Beneventan MSS suggests that Gregorian chant arrived in Benevento prior to
the PsG's influence in the north.[6] Melodic evidence for early reception resides in
the preference for b rather than c as a repercussive pitch, evident especially in
deuterus chants. The independence of the Beneventan melodic tradition is further
demonstrated by a comparative study of the offertories, which exhibit variants
unique to Benevento. As Hesbert has suggested, the distinctive notation and
melodic variants render improbable a substantial later influence of northern
practice.[7]

Another reason for the primacy of Beneventan manuscripts lies in this study's
focus on the relationship between the Gregorian and Roman melodies. As is widely
known, the Roman tradition transmits isolated Gregorian melodies such as the
Easter Vigil canticle tracts, indicating that the Roman tradition was influenced
by Gregorian chant between the eighth and late eleventh centuries. Much of
this contact probably occurred through Beneventan and Montecassinese
channels. Desiderius, abbot of Montecassino, served as the cardinal priest of
St. Cecilia in Trastevere in the late eleventh century, when Bodmer 74 was copied
(in 1071).[8] A direct Montecassinese influence on the musical practice of St. Cecilia
in Trastevere is evident in a repertory of distinctive alleluias with prosulas found
only in Beneventan manuscripts and in Bod 74.[9] Emma Hornby has shown that
the Gregorian Easter Vigil Tracts in the Roman manuscripts exhibit the closest
correspondence to those of Beneventan manuscripts, suggesting that they reached

5. These features were first noted by Hesbert, *Le codex 10 673*; and are also summarized in Kelly,
   Beneventan Chant, 18–22.
6. Kelly, *Beneventan Chant*, 19.
7. Hesbert, *Le codex 10 673*. Pfisterer has challenged some aspects of Hesbert's argument, particularly
   as they concern the relevance of liturgical evidence for melodic transmission. Pfisterer nevertheless
   places the reception of Gregorian chant in Benevento before the mid–ninth century, concurring
   that a later large-scale transmission is unlikely. Pfisterer, *Cantilena*, 81–82.
8. Herbert E. J. Cowdrey, *The Age of Abbot Desiderius: Montecassino, the Papacy, and the Normans in
   the Eleventh and Early Twelfth Centuries* (Oxford: Oxford University Press, 1983).
9. Alejandro Planchart, "Proses in the Sources of Old Roman Chant, and Their Alleluias," in
   The Study of Medieval Chant: Paths and Bridges, East and West, ed. Peter Jeffrey (Cambridge:
   Boydell and Brewer, 2001), 313–39.

Rome through Montecassinese channels.[10] Further Beneventan influence on Rome is evident in the similarities between Roman and Beneventan notation. As Hornby has argued, the use of a Beneventan source as a basis for comparison with the Roman tradition places the comparative study of the two versions in a context where contact between them is documented. A comparison of Benevento 34 and Bodmer 74 allows us to rule out, as far as possible, the possibility of Gregorian influence on the Roman melodies.[11] In *Gressus meos* (33) and *Tollite portas* (6), for example, the Beneventan manuscripts transmit distinctive versions of the closing melismas. In both cases, the corresponding Roman melisma differs substantially from both the Beneventan one and the more common international one. Thus we can exclude the possibility that the Roman version of this melisma was influenced by "seepage" of Gregorian melodies through Beneventan channels. Beneventan sources present peculiar readings of melismas in several other pieces, including *Benedictus qui venit* (54), *Domine deus salutis* (24), and *Super flumina* (66). These melismas are either lacking or very different in the Roman version.

For these reasons, I have often adopted a Beneventan reading, usually that of Ben 34, as a base version, except in some cases where the Beneventan version shows evidence of modal emendation. I have also incorporated three incomplete Beneventan sources from the eleventh century. The earliest, Ben 40, possibly from Santa Sofia, preserves the Post-Paschal and Post-Pentecost offertories, along with much of the sanctorale. This manuscript lacks lines and clefs and is not fully consistent in its heightening. Ben 38, a diastematic source with added lines, begins at Septuagesima, with a lacuna in the third week of Lent. Ben 39, from the convent of St. Peter, begins with Monday of Passion Week. The twelfth-century Ben 35, nearly complete, begins with Epiphany. These manuscripts present a largely unified melodic tradition, differing primarily in their use of "ornamental" neumes. The quilisma, for example, appears frequently in Ben 40 but is absent in Ben 34. The later Beneventan sources, however, show a greater variety of liquescent forms. The Beneventan manuscripts also vary occasionally in their approach to modal emendation, a trend illustrated on a case-by-case basis.

While the independence of the Beneventan tradition underscores its importance as a witness, it also raises the likelihood that melodic changes entered the tradition between the ninth and eleventh centuries. The distinctive renditions of certain melismas in Benevento, mentioned earlier, support the theory that an independent melodic tradition developed in Benevento subsequent to the repertory's reception there. To gain the clearest possible picture of the melodies' early transmission, then, Beneventan manuscripts must be examined in combination with sources from other regional traditions. A wider sampling of manuscripts is also

---

10. Hornby, *Gregorian and Old Roman Eighth-Mode Tracts: A Case Study in the Transmission of Western Chant* (Aldershot, England: Ashgate, 2002), 50–53.
11. Ibid., 54.

crucial in addressing the problems of emendation. The Beneventan scribes exhibit a penchant for modal emendation that is lacking in Montpellier 159 and in some Aquitanian manuscripts. In this respect, the offertories are an exception to the often-cited melodic similarities between Beneventan and Aquitanian manuscripts.[12]

Montpellier H 159 (Mo 159), the famous manuscript from Dijon copied in the early eleventh century, is the first source of the Mass proper repertory to unequivocally indicate pitch.[13] Mo 159 has been employed as a primary source in previous editions of offertories, particularly as a basis for comparison with Aquitanian sources. The entire manuscript has been transcribed and carefully studied by Finn Egeland Hansen.[14] Although scholars have noted some idiosyncratic features of Mo 159's melodic tradition, the manuscript remains a witness of universally acknowledged importance.

Two Aquitanian manuscripts hold particular importance for this study: Paris 1121, a troper and offertoriale from St. Martial, and Paris 776, a gradual from Gaillac. As James Grier has shown, Pa 1121 was copied at St. Martial by Adémar of Chabannes in 1027–28.[15] Along with Mo 159, it is our earliest diastematic witness to the offertory repertory. Pa 776, copied in the late eleventh century, is of particular value for this repertory. Because of their modal ambiguity and use of nondiatonic pitches, the offertories are especially susceptible to variants in pitch level. As Roman Hankeln and Rupert Fischer have shown, the scribe of Pa 776 often presents "unemended" versions of the melodies, notating problematic passages at the pitch level at which they were most likely sung.[16] The manuscript is an essential tool in sorting through the problems of modal structure in the offertories. Other Aquitanian sources in the core group include Pa 780 from Narbonne and Lo 4951 from Toulouse. Of these four core Aquitanian sources, Lo 4951 most frequently departs from the others in exhibiting melodic peculiarities. In specific problematic passages where a preferred reading is difficult to establish, I have incorporated other Aquitanian manuscripts, including several offertoriales from St. Martial, Pa 1133, 1134, 1135, 1136, and 1137, all direct or indirect descendants

---

12. See the discussion in Hornby, *Gregorian and Old Roman Eighth-Mode Tracts*, 14–54.
13. On the origin and date, see Michel Huglo, "Le Tonaire de Saint-Bénigne de Dijon," *Annales musicologiques* 4 (1956): 7–18; For the questions about Mo 159's status as a representative manuscript, see Huglo, review of *The Grammar of Gregorian Tonality: An Investigation Based on the Repertory in Codex H 159, Montpellier*, by Finn Egeland Hansen, *Journal of the American Musicological Society* 37 (1984): 421–24.
14. Finn Egeland Hansen, *H 159 Montpellier* (Copenhagen: Dan Fog, 1974).
15. James Grier, "The Musical Autographs of Adémar de Chabannes (989–1034)," *Early Music History* 24 (2005): 125–67. For a penetrating study of the context surrounding this important source and Adémar's scribal practices, see Grier, *The Musical World of a Medieval Monk: Adémar de Chabannes in Eleventh-Century Aquitaine* (Cambridge: Cambridge University Press, 2007), 1–96.
16. Hankeln, *Offertoriumsprosuln*, 1:86–94; Rupert Fischer, "Die Bedeutung des Codex Paris, B.N. lat. 776 (Albi) und des Codex St.Gallen, Stiftsbibliothek 381 (Versikular) für die Rekonstruktion gregorianischer Melodien," *Beiträge zur Gregorianik* 22 (1996): 43–73.

of Pa 1121;[17] the later St. Martial gradual Pa 1132; and Pa 903 from St. Yrieix. Although the latter manuscript is widely available and commonly employed in comparative studies, it is not included among the core sources because of its propensity for melodic editing.[18]

As noted, a Beneventan reading is employed as the base reading for the majority of pieces in the edition. The decision of whether a given variant is significant enough to warrant the use of a manuscript representing another tradition as the base version is a judgment made and explained on a case-by-case basis, depending on the degree of Beneventan distinctiveness and the nature of the variant readings. When the Beneventan peculiarity is a question of melodic variance, I have often retained the Beneventan version and noted its differences in the commentary. In the previously mentioned final melisma of *Gressus meos*, for example, the Beneventan sources present a reading that differs in structure from that of all other regional traditions. Ben 34 as a whole, however, is consistent with the international tradition, and I have employed it as a base version, providing a more common reading of the final melisma, transcribed from Mo 159, in the supplemental examples. When I have selected another reading as a base version, it is typically because the Beneventan sources reflect emendations made either to circumvent nondiatonic pitches or to create a modal consistency. In *Erit vobis* (53), for example, the Beneventan sources present a sixth-mode version of the melody that contrasts with the *tetrardus* structure found in most other manuscripts. In this case, the use of a Beneventan source for the primary reading would give an impression of the melody that reflects extensive emendation. Because the Aquitanian sources are more broadly representative, I have adopted one as the base version, indicating where the Beneventan readings differ in the notes and supplemental musical examples in appendix 3.

Many offertories are stable in transmission, with few, if any, significant variants. In these cases, the core group of sources presents a largely unified tradition.[19] Pitched manuscripts from other regional traditions may nevertheless yield valuable insight into certain problem spots. The peripheral sources in this study speak to two important issues. The first, involving transposition and modal emendation, is such a pervasive feature of the offertory that it becomes central to any study of the genre. Examining a wide range of sources helps to shed light on the reasons for the variants and to establish a preferred version. To this end, I have examined

17. See Grier, "Musical Autographs."
18. Nicholas Stuart, "Melodic Editing in an Eleventh-Century Gradual (Paris, B.N. lat. 903)," *Journal of the Plainsong and Medieval Music Society* 2 (1979): 2–10.
19. These findings are consistent with those of Andreas Pfisterer in his broader study of the Mass proper. Pfisterer has argued that a clear picture of the earliest written transmission can be gained on the basis of a few sources, including the early adiastematic manuscripts and the core group employed here. See *Cantilena*, 11–76; 235–42.

additional manuscripts that were available to me in facsimile or microfilm. These peripheral sources also address an issue of secondary importance in this study: the extent to which local significant variants and unique readings entered into the tradition. Among peripheral sources, cadential formulas are occasionally exchanged for other familiar ones, and melismas may be shortened or otherwise altered. As I explain below, I have not given extensive consideration to minor variants such as passing tones, the number of note repetitions, and differences around the half steps E-F or b-c.

In relatively rare passages where the core group of pitched sources show significant variants in contour or melismatic density, I have employed four early adiastematic sources, La 239, Ch 47, SG 339, and Ei 121, to help determine a preferred reading. The choice of pitched manuscripts for the peripheral group was guided by the criterion that they include verses, confining the choices to a relatively narrow time frame between the eleventh and thirteenth centuries, when offertory verses fell out of use in most places. Although the sampling is by no means exhaustive, it does give a good overview of the genre's international transmission. From the northern and central Italian traditions I have incorporated three principal sources: the eleventh- or twelfth-century Mod 7, from Forlimpopoli, near Ravenna; the eleventh- or twelfth-century Pst 120; and RoV 52 from Arezzo. I have consulted three additional Italian manuscripts in specific problem spots: the twelfth-century To 18 from Bobbio; Pad 47, an early twelfth-century source from Ravenna; and the thirteenth-century Pia 65. When these manuscripts depart from the majority reading, they often do so in similar ways, illustrating that variants have entered the Italian tradition at an earlier stage. The Italian sources, for example, present a variant, elaborate reading of *Deus laudem*, a verse of *Domine fac mecum* (31). To 18 is often distinct from other Italian sources in its treatment of longer melismas, which are sometimes shortened or suppressed altogether.

From German-speaking areas, where pitched notation is a later arrival, I have employed Be 40078, a twelfth-century source from Quedlinburg in the Hamburg-Bremen diocese, and the twelfth-century Gr 807 from St. Florian.[20] Three additional sources have been consulted in specific cases: the thirteenth-century Tri 2254 and two fragmentary manuscripts, Mü 10086 from Prüfening outside of Regensburg, which preserves Christmas Day through the second week of Lent; and Rei 264, which contains the latter part of the temporale and much of the sanctorale. Although they are consistent in many respects with the core Aquitanian and Beneventan group, the German sources do exhibit small variants particular to

20. Rudolph Flotzinger argues persuasively for an origin at St. Florian rather than Klosterneuberg in "Zu Herkunft und Datierung der Gradualien Gr 807 und Wien 13314," *Studia musicologica* 31 (1989): 57–80.

that tradition. These include the "German chant dialect," the raising of b to c, a custom sometimes found at the fifth below (E to F) and fourth above (high e to f). In this respect, Be 40078 shows the most extensive "German" influence, often avoiding E and b altogether except at the final cadences of *deuterus* chants. The sampling also includes Pa 1235 from Nevers and Cai 61 from Lille, which exemplify the filtering of small variants into the tradition. In rare cases where these two manuscripts differ significantly from the others, they sometimes agree with one another. In the following pages, I survey the types of variant that occur among primary and secondary sources, clarify the distinction between major and minor variants, and explain the methodology for .establishing preferred readings. I follow with a summary of approaches to transcribing particular neumes.

MINOR VARIANTS

Among the core group of sources, most variant readings fall into the categories of "trivial variants" defined by David Hughes: the use of "ornamental" neumes such as the quilisma and oriscus; the number of note repetitions, usually on F or c; the use of passing tones; and differences at the two semitone points, E-F and b-c.[21] To the broad category of minor variants I would add differences in the approach to the focal pitch F or c. Although these types of variants are ubiquitous, they perhaps stand out most prominently in passages of the offertories that adopt a "recitational" style focused on F or c. The sources show small differences in their ways of moving around the pitches a and c or G and c and their equivalents a fifth lower. The first verse of *Miserere mihi* (26), example 6.1, illustrates these types of variant. This short verse is built from a vocabulary of small melodic segments and cadential patterns that occur often in offertories of modes 3 and 8, and, at the lower level of transposition, modes 2 and 4. Example 6.1 shows three readings from early adiastematic sources, three from the core group, and two from peripheral manuscripts. The versions are distinguished by small variants, such as the use of b or c and the number of repetitions of c. On the final syllable of "quoniam," for example, the figure c-d-c in Ben 34 appears as c-d-c-c in Mo 159 and Pa 776 and as c-d-b-c in Gr 807. At the cadential pattern on "agnosco," Gr 807 adopts c rather than b as the top note, reflecting the German chant dialect. On the accented syllables of "delictum" and "meum," the figure G-b-d-c in Ben 34 is G-c-d-c in Pa 776 and a-c-d-c in Pa 1235. Another variant point is the treatment of unaccented syllables in the approach to the focal pitch c, as on the second and third syllables of

21. David Hughes, "Evidence for the Traditional View of the Transmission of Gregorian Chant," *Journal of the American Musicological Society* 40 (1987): 377–404.

EXAMPLE 6.1 *Quoniam iniquitatem*

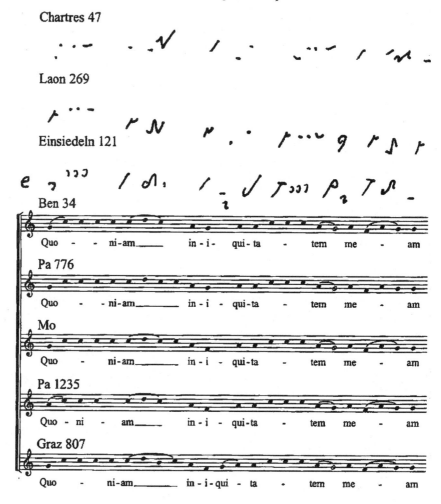

"iniquitatem" and "delictum." To some degree, similar variants are evident in the earliest manuscripts. On the third syllable of "iniquitatem," for example, La 239 has a single note, consistent with the three core sources, but Ei 121 has a pes, also found in Gr 807. Although these small variants attest to regional differences in the delivery of passages in the recitational style, this verse nevertheless exemplifies a consistency within the adiastematic sources that is characteristic of the repertory as a whole. For example, Ei 121 and La 239 indicate lengthening in many of the same places, with the altered forms of neumes and sometimes with the letter "t" ("trahere"): on the accent of "iniqui*ta*tem," the first c of and last syllable of "agnosco," and the first note of "me." Because these variants are not central to the issues addressed in this study, they do not receive extensive consideration in the commentary.

EXAMPLE 6.1 (*continued*)

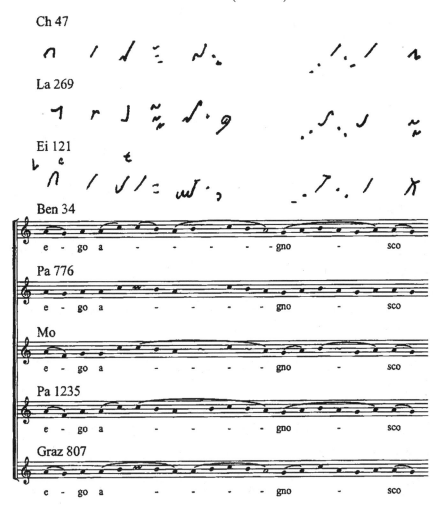

SIGNIFICANT VARIANTS

Significant variants are defined as differences in pitch level, modality, contour, or interval content that involve a passage of more than three or four notes. In terms of melodic contour, many offertories exhibit the same stability in transmission that has been observed in other genres of the core Mass proper repertory. The offertories, however, do include some important exceptions to this trend, particularly in the long melismas, which occasionally exhibit variants in length, contour, or passing differences in pitch level. I discuss these points of significant variance in the commentary of appendix 3.

The most common type of significant variant in the offertories involves partial transposition, a phenomenon already given extensive consideration in the work of

EXAMPLE 6.1 *(continued)*

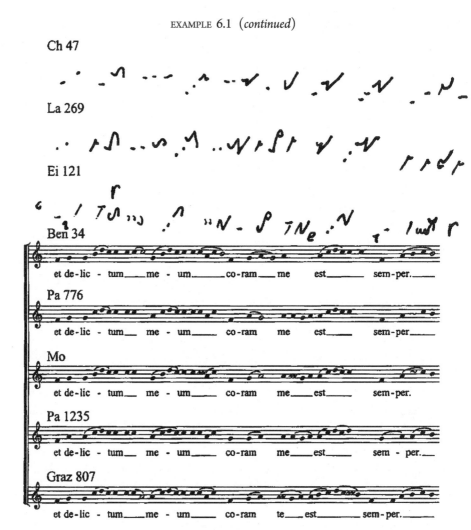

Hubert Sidler, Grover Pitman, Cheryl Frasch, Dean Justmann, and Roman Han-keln.[22] As demonstrated in early studies of the issue by Dominique Delalande, Gustav Jacobsthal, and Urbanus Bomm, and more recently by Theodore Karp, pitch-level variants can often be attributed to the use of nondiatonic pitches.[23] Created long before the codification of the modes, the chant repertory was not fully consistent with

22. See note 2.

23. Gustav Jacobsthal, *Die chromatische Alteration im liturgischen Gesang der abendländischen Kirche* (Berlin: J. Springer, 1897; reprint, Hildesheim: Olms, 1970). *Urbanus Bomm, Der Wechel der Modalitätbestimmung in der Tradition der Meßgesänge im IX. bis XIII. Jahrhundert und sein Einfluß auf der Tradition ihrer Melodien* (Einsiedeln, 1929; reprint, Hildesheim: Olms, 1975); Dominique Delalande, *Vers la version authentique du Graduel grégorien: Le Graduel des Prêcheurs, Bibliothèque d'histoire Dominicaine* (Paris: Éditions Cerf, 1949); Theodore Karp, *Aspects of Orality and Formularity in Gregorian Chant* (Evanston, Ill.: Northwestern University Press, 1998): 181–224.

TABLE 6.1 The *Enchiriadis* Tone-System

Graves	Finales	Superiores	Excellentes
ΓA B-flat C	D E F G	a b c d	E f-sharp g aa

the diatonic eight-mode system later imposed on it. The diatonic system permitted chromatic alteration at only one point in the scale, b/b-flat. The studies cited above have revealed in some chants a rich tonal spectrum that lies outside this diatonic framework. Corroboration of the manuscript evidence for nondiatonic practice is found in some of the earliest theoretical writings. The *Enchiriadis* tradition, for example, transmits a system of tone-semitone-tone tetrachords in a disjunct arrangement distinct from the diatonic system later associated with plainchant (see table 6.1). Each note of the tetrachord has a different quality, *protus*, *deuterus*, *tritus*, or *tetrardus*, distinguished by its intervallic environment. Nancy Phillips and Calvin Bower have emphasized its practical significance for plainsong. Bower characterizes the system as an outgrowth of a practical *cantus* tradition that had not yet found harmony with the quantitative tradition inherited from ancient Greece. The *Enchiriadis* treatises were the most widely copied musical texts during the ninth and tenth centuries, and Bower speculates that the fundamentals of the *Enchiriadis* tone-system have their origin in the cantor's art of the late eighth or early ninth century.[24]

The author of *Scolica enchiriadis* provides a flexible system of accommodating pitches outside of the tetrachord system through alteration of the *deuterus* and *tritus* notes of the *finales* tetrachord. The *deuterus* note could be lowered a semitone and the *tritus* note raised a semitone, thereby providing E-flat and F-sharp. These alterations changed not only the pitch in question but also its intervallic environment and modal quality. Although the author describes these pitches as *vitia*, defects or imperfections, he acknowledges that they are necessary in the performance of chant, comparable to solecisms in metric poetry.[25]

Karp's important study places the nondiatonic notes in the context of the later "coniunctae" of the Anonymous Berkeley manuscript.

24. Nancy C. Phillips, "Musica and Scolica enchiriadis: The Literary, Theoretical, and Musical Sources," (Ph.D. diss., New York University, 1985), 473–480; and "Notationen und Notationslehren von Boethius bis zum 12. Jahrhundert," in *Geschichte der Musiktheorie*, vol. 4, ed. Michel Huglo et. al. (Darmstadt: Wissenschaftliche Buchgellschaft, 2000), 591–602. Calvin M. Bower, "'Adhuc ex parte et in enigmate cernimus . . . ': Reflections on the Closing Chapters of *Musica enchiriadis*," in *Music in the Mirror: Reflections on the History of Music Theory and Literature for the Twenty-First Century*, ed. Andreas Giger and Thomas Mathiesen (Lincoln: University of Nebraska Press, 2002), 21–44, and "The Transmission of Ancient Music Theory into the Middle Ages," in *The Cambridge History of Western Music Theory*, ed. Thomas Christensen (Cambridge: Cambridge University Press, 2002), 153–64.

25. "Vitia nimirum sunt, sed sicut barbarismi et soloecismi metris plerumque figuraliter intermiscentur, ita limmata interdum de industria cantibus inseruntur." Hans Schmid, ed., *Musica et Scolica Enchiriadis una cum aliquibus tractatulis adiunctis* (Munich: Bayerische Akademie der Wissenschaften, 1981), 70.

The dasia signs of the tradition provided for graphic representation of these vitia.[26]

In the late ninth century, another strand of theoretical thought sought to synthesize the chant tradition with the Greater and Lesser Perfect Systems inherited from the Greeks. The Greek system consists of tetrachords that descend by two tones and a semitone. In the Greater Perfect System, two sets of conjunct tetrachords on the upper and lower ends were separated by a disjunction in the middle. In the Lesser Perfect System, a conjunct synemmenon tetrachord was added. Writing between 885 and 889, Hucbald reformulated the Greek system, taking as a basis a tetrachord formed from the four finals of chant, D, E F, and G, and arranging the other tetrachords around it according to the Greek model: two conjunct tetrachords on each end, a disjunction in the middle, and a synemmenon tetrachord that provided for b-flat (see fig. 6.2). The diatonic system described by Hucbald became the basis of the standard medieval scale and the notational matrix of chant. This development fundamentally affected the written transmission of the repertory and, in some cases, I argue, its performance. Because the b-flat of the synemmenon tetrachord provided the only chromatic alteration possible in this system, chants with other nondiatonic notes had to be altered, at least in writing, to fit into the diatonic framework.

Pitches that were unavailable in the notational system were often accommodated by transposing the melody fully or partially to a new pitch level, most commonly to the fifth above the final, the position of the alternate finals known as sociales, affines, or affinales. Theorists pointed to a relationship of affinity between three of the four finals, D, E, F, and the notes a fifth above, a, b, and c, which have the same immediate intervallic environment. This value of these sociales as alternate finals is described by Hucbald and many later writers.[27] By transposing a chant to the affinal position, E-flat could be represented with b-flat. The Enchiriadis treatises describe a relationship of partial affinity with the tones

26. See the discussions in Jacobsthal, Die chromatische Alteration, 269–354; Charles Atkinson, "From Vitium to Tonus Acquisitus: On the Evolution of the Notational Matrix of Medieval Chant." In Cantus Planus: Papers Read at the Third Meeting, Tihany, Hungary, 19–24 September 1988, ed. László Dobszay (Budapest: Hungarian Academy of Sciences Institute for Musicology, 1990), 181–99; and idem, The Critical Nexus: Tone-System, Mode, and Notation in Early Medieval Music (New York: Oxford University Press, 2008), 128–34. A more detailed analysis of the relationship between the vitia and the extended nondiatonic practice of the offertories is given in Rebecca Maloy, "Scolica enchiriadis and 'non-diatonic' Plainsong Tradition," Early Music History 28 (2009), 61–96.
27. De harmonica institutione, in Scriptores ecclesiastici de musica sacra potissimum, ed. Martin Gerbert (St. Blaise: Typis San-Blasianis, 1784; reprint ed., Hildesheim: Olms, 1963) (GS), 1:119. ("quinta semper loca his quatour superiora quadam sibi connexionis unisone iunguntur, adeo, ut pleraque etiam in eis quasi regulariter mela inveniatur desinere"). For a thorough study of these passages, see Delores Pesce, The Affinities and Medieval Transposition (Bloomington: Indiana University Press, 1987) and the more recent discussion in Atkinson, The Critical Nexus, 160–61, 221–3; 226–8.

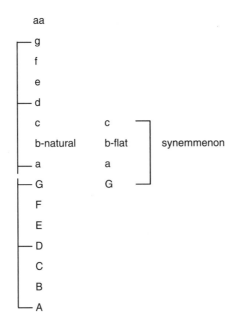

FIGURE 6.1 Hucbald's Reformulation of the Greater Perfect System

a fourth above the final, called *compares*.[28] In practical application, transposition of a fourth allowed F-sharp to be represented by b-natural at the higher position. Another transposition often found in the offertories is that of the whole tone, most often employed to represent nondiatonic pitches in the higher octave.

The manuscripts employed in this study adopt a variety of approaches to the treatment of nondiatonic pitches, at times resulting in a bewildering variety of readings. The offertories thus offer a wealth of opportunity to study the interaction between theory and practice and between the written and aural traditions. The early studies of "chromatic alterations" in chant focused on these variants as a means to restore the melodies to a putative authentic state. Bomm and Sidler thus sought the "Originallage" of the melodies. While valuable work with this objective continues to be undertaken, I have approached the problem without the assumption that there is a single original version. In many cases, however, it is nevertheless possible to form plausible hypotheses about which versions are emendations and which should be considered the "unemended" reading. An unemended or preferred reading often emerges through an analysis of several variables in the

---

28. See Schmid, *Musica et scolica enchiriadis*, 75–76. ("Altera est concordatio paulo minor, dum vel elevationis difficultatem mitigare volentes vel submissiorem gravitatem erigere aut in sursum aut in iusum quintana transpositione subjungimus," and "Sociales autem suos quisque sonus non solum quintis habet regionibus, sed et quartis locis alios sibi quaerit compares, qui tertiae simphoniae locus est.").

EXAMPLE 6.2 *Sanctificavit*, excerpt

manuscript tradition, including intervallic differences between various readings and the nature of the emendations. A broader understanding of style, what is typical and atypical in the chant tradition, also plays a role in determining preferred readings. The following example illustrates how these factors help to determine the most plausible unemended reading of a problem spot.

Sanctificavit (64) exemplifies the nondiatonic richness of the pretheoretical chant tradition. In chapter 3, this piece served as an example of the rhetorical treatment of the words in many Gregorian offertories. A look at this offertory in a wide range of sources suggests that these rhetorical effects were enhanced by "modulations": longer passages of the chant were displaced from the diatonic background scale. Example 6.2 shows several versions of a passage from *Sanctificavit*. The higher range at "adoravit dicens" marks the end of narration and sets up the subsequent dialogue. Beginning at "obsecro," the version of Pa 776 is written a tone below its level in Ben 34 and Mo 159. Without accidentals, the two readings differ in intervallic structure. Pa 776 is *tritus* in quality, articulating major third c-e, whereas Mo 159 and Ben 34 have a *protus* quality, articulating the minor third d-f. Both readings of the passage are well established in the manuscript tradition. As the majority Aquitanian version, the Pa 776 reading is found in a wide range of sources with no demonstrable scribal relationship, precluding the possibility that it is a scribal error. Outside of the Aquitanian tradition, however, the passage is usually notated at the level of the Ben 34. Mo 159 adopts a "hybrid" version, matching the Aquitanian reading on the final syllable of "Moyses" and the Beneventan reading beginning with "obsecro."

The different intervallic structure of the two versions at "obsecro" suggests one of two possible interpretations. If the *protus* character of Ben 34's reading represents the intended tonal structure of the passage, then an e-flat would be required to replicate this structure at the level of the Aquitanian version a whole tone lower. The other possibility is that the *tritus* structure of the Aquitanian version is intended; if so, an f-sharp would be required in the Beneventan reading. Either alternative is certainly possible. In judging which is more plausible, the general stylistic tendencies of the tradition come into consideration. The version of Ben 34 is more typical in intervallic content than the version of Pa 776: the gesture on the last syllable of "procidens," articulating the third a-c, occurs frequently at this position. At "adoravit dicens," a standard *protus* cadential pattern is projected an octave above its usual position on low D. On "obsecro domine," the *tritus* pitch high f serves a usual repercussive function, and the passage comes to a close with a typical *deuterus* cadential figure on "tui." Without nondiatonic alterations, the Aquitanian reading is less consistent with the typical tonal structures of chant. Although the cadential pattern on "dicens" occurs both in *protus* and *tritus* contexts, the following passage, beginning on "obsecro," is far more typical in the *protus* intervallic context of the Beneventan version, with the semitone below the repercussive pitch. Sung a tone lower without nondiatonic alterations, this passage is anomalous in intervallic structure. On the basis of stylistic norms, then, the more plausible explanation is that the Aquitanian manuscripts represent a tradition that employed e-flat at "obsecro domine dimitte" and b-flat on "tui." At "obsecro domine," a *protus* intervallic structure is projected onto a segment of the background scale that is not normally *protus* in quality.

This reading of the evidence receives some circumstantial support from the nature of the sources in question. As noted, Pa 776 serves as a valuable witness in determining nondiatonic pitches because of its tendency to notate problem spots in the "untransposed" range. The hybrid readings of the passage from *Sanctificavit*, however, illustrate the problems that arise in seeking to understand the transpositional differences. In Mo 159, the passage begins at the pitch level of Pa 776 but moves to the level of Ben 34 at "obsecro." Two geographically diverse sources in the sampling, Pa 1235 and Rei 264, transmit similar readings. These hybrid versions reinforce the impression that the unemended reading is that of the Aquitanian manuscripts: the hybrid versions maintain the untransposed range until a nondiatonic pitch is required, at "obsecro." The cadential pattern on "dicens," however, is a point of uncertainty. If e-flat was sung on "obsecro" in the Aquitanian version, can we assume that it was on "dicens" as well? This possibility is suggested by the Beneventan, the Italian, and most German sources, which have a *protus* cadence on "dicens." To maintain this intervallic structure at the level of the Aquitanian sources, an e-flat is required. It is unclear, then, why the three hybrid readings leave the passage at the lower level of transposition, with a c-*tritus* cadence. As this passage shows, the reasons for particular emendations and their implications for performance cannot always be ascertained.

The Aquitanian readings of this passage suggest that in the aural, pretheoretical tradition, the typical melodic vocabulary of the repertory could be sung in portions of the background scale that were inconsistent with the diatonic system. While the *vitia* of the *Enchiriadis* tradition provided a means of accommodating some of these passages, the standard medieval gamut did not. Because upward transpositions of a fifth or a fourth required displacing sections of a piece, they were not a always a practical solution for representing altered pitches, especially in the higher register. Perhaps for this reason, whole-tone transpositions such as those in *Sanctificavit* occur with some frequency in the offertories. While whole-tone transposition did not have the same theoretical grounding in the affinities that fourth and fifth transpositions did, the practice is described by the southern German theorist known as John of Afflighem, as a means of circumventing nondiatonic pitches in the communion *Beatus servus*.[29]

Nondiatonic pitches were not the only irregularities of the chant tradition that were subject to emendation. In *Sanctificavit* (ex. 6.2), melodic gestures normally associated with the *protus* pitches D and a, such as the figure on "procidens," are written at a different position in Pa 776 and Mo 159, beginning on the final syllable

---

29. "Sed et in communione Beatus servus levis error habetur, qui per unum podatum incongrue prolatum efficitur. Hunc autem quidam sic corrigunt, quod Dominus a trite diezeugmenon in mese cadere faciunt, et invenerit in parhypate meson incipiunt et super omnia in lichanos meson; alii autem ita emendant quod invenerit iuxta usum incipiunt, et penultimam eius in mese inchoantes in lichanos meson emittunt, et ultimam in hypate meson, incipientes in parhypate meson exire faciunt, super omnia secundum priores corrigunt." J. Smits van Waesberghe, ed., *Johannes Affligemensis, De musica cum tonario*, Corpus scriptorum de musica, vol. 1 ([Rome]: American Institute of Musicology, 1950), 137.

of "Moyses." The few sources in this group that distinguish between b and b-flat write b-flat here. The resulting intervallic structure is identical to that of Ben 34, but written a tone lower. Passages of this sort, in what I term the "G-*protus*" region, occur with some frequency in certain manuscripts of the core group, including Mo 159, Pa 776, and Pa 1121. The scribe of the late German source Be 40078 also notates most of these passages on G, with a b-flat. In Beneventan and Italian manuscripts, however, the same gestures are nearly always written a whole tone higher. In *Micrologus*, Guido of Arezzo describes the introduction of b-flat in some contexts as effecting a change in the usual qualities of pitches, creating a modal "transformation" in which "G sounds as *protus*, and a as *deuterus*, whereas b-flat itself sounds as *tritus*." Singers can avoid this transformation, he suggests, by making precisely the whole-tone transposition found in Ben 34: "If you wish not to have b-flat at all, simply alter the passages in which it occurs, so that instead of F G a and b-flat you have G a b (natural) c and d . . . it best avoids a sad confusion if one apportions such ascents and descents clear-sightedly between D E F and a b c."[30] The transformation described by Guido is perhaps especially evident in passages like "procidens" in Example 6.2, which consist of melodic figures more commonly placed in the traditionally *protus* parts of the background scale, D-F and a-c. Guido's view that these passages should be reworked reflects a commitment to a diatonic framework in which each scale step is consistently associated with a single modal quality.

The transpositional variants between sources sometimes exhibit general patterns according to regional tradition. Most Aquitanian readings of problematic passages in *Sanctificavit*, for example, are notated in the "untransposed" or "unemended" range. In other cases, however, the emendations differ among sources from the same regions. Readings that are unique within their manuscript group appear to reflect the preferences of individual scribes or cantors. In *Benedicite gentes* (36), for example, Ben 34 and Ben 35 differ in their notation of a problematic passage in the third verse, and in *Sanctificavit*, Ben 34 and Ben 39 adopt different ways of circumventing the nondiatonic pitches in the second verse. Some regional traditions show a progressive tendency to avoid the G-*protus*. The St. Martial offertoriales, for example, notate such a spot in the third verse of *Benedicite gentes* (phrases 17 and 18 in the transcriptions) on G, whereas the scribe of a later gradual from St. Martial, Paris 1132, writes the passage a tone higher, perhaps reflecting the encroaching influence of modal diatonicism on musical practice.

The pervasive use of transposition and modal emendation in the repertory naturally complicates the question of which manuscripts to use as base readings in

---

30. Translation is based on that of Warren Babb in Claude Palisca, ed., *Hucbald, Guido and John on Music: Three Medieval Treatises* (New Haven, Conn.: Yale University Press, 1978), 64. Guido appears to prohibit b-flat outright in *Regulae* and especially in the *Epistola*. See Dolores Pesce, ed., *Guido d'Arezzo's Regule Rithmice, Prologus in Antiphonarium, and Epistola ad Michahelem: A Critical Text and Translation* (Ottawa: Institute of Medieval Music, 1999), 348–49; 514–17.

the transcriptions. In the case of melodic variants, I have typically used a Beneventan version and described any peculiar features of the Beneventan tradition in
appendix 3. Modally problematic cases such as *Sanctificavit* and *Benedicite gentes*,
however, require a different approach. In these cases, I have determined a preferred
reading according to the criteria illustrated in the preceding discussion. For the
base version, I have chosen a manuscript that presents the problem spots at their
probable unemended pitch level and added parenthetical accidentals above the
notes in question. These accidentals are hypothetical, based on variant readings
among the manuscripts. I explain the reasoning behind them in appendix 3. In the
case of *Sanctificavit*, Pa 776 best represents an unemended reading, and I have
chosen it as the base version. As I have shown, Pa 776 is also a majority reading
among Aquitanian sources. In many of these problematic passages, however, the
unemended reading is *not* a majority or consensus reading. A problematic passage
in the third verse of *Benedicite gentes* (36) may serve as a brief illustration. Once
again, Pa 776 is the base reading. At the end of the G-*protus* passage described
above, I have hypothesized that an E-flat is required on "mea" (phrase 18 in the
transcriptions) if the passage is sung at the pitch level indicated in Pa 776. The
hypothesis rests on the intervallic differences between Pa 776 and other manuscripts. In the great majority of sources, however, the passage is transposed or
otherwise edited, precisely because the pretheoretical tradition employed a pitch
that was theoretically nonexistent. Pa 776, as noted, is valuable because of the
scribe's tendency to notate these passages at their unemended pitch level. In cases
of nondiatonic pitches, then, the preferred reading often differs from the consensus
or majority version.

Because of the variety among otherwise closely related manuscripts, sources
in the peripheral group can assume a special importance in ascertaining the
most plausible unemended readings. For *Oravi deum* (63), I have transcribed
the base version from Pa 1121. Beginning at "super" (phrase 3), this reading is
modally irregular. The typical *deuterus* melodic traits heard throughout the
beginning of the melody are now projected a whole tone lower. Although this
irregularity is found in only one other Aquitanian manuscript in the core
group, Pa 776, it is preserved in three unrelated peripheral sources, Cai 61,
Rei 264, and Be 40078. These manuscripts adopt the pitch-level profile of Pa
1121, notating the melody at the affinal position. In Rei 265 and Be 40078,
the chant begins in the normal transposed *deuterus* range but ends a whole
tone lower, on a, with notated b-flats. Cai 61 is similar to these sources but
gives an alternative final cadence on G. John of Afflighem, moreover, recommends that *Oravi deum* should be emended at "super," showing a version in
which this passage is a whole tone above its level in Pa 1121.[31] The same

---

31. "Sed et in Offertorio Oravi Deum meum in duobus locis emendatione indiget, scilicet in principio
et ubi est super, ut hic patet." Smits van Waesberghe, *Johannes Affligemensis*, 150.

solution is indicated in Frutolf's tonary and adopted in most manuscripts. Without the witnesses of John, Frutolf, and the late, unrelated practical sources, it would be tempting to view the versions of Pa 1121 and Pa 776 as scribal errors. Because of its presence in three geographically diverse late manuscripts, however, this reading emerges as the *lectio difficilior* and the probable unemended version.

Many of the transpositional variants in the offertories involve one discrete section, such as a single verse. The sources differ in their indication of the relative pitch level between the respond, verse, and repetendum. These variants underscore the importance of establishing a preferred version as a basis for stylistic assessment and comparison to the Roman versions. In the *Offertoriale Triplex*, for example, the final verses of the sixth-mode offertories *Domine in auxilium* (27), *Iustitiae* (29), and *In virtute* (70) are written in the corresponding authentic mode. Hankeln's edition of *Iustitiae*, however, clearly establishes a plagal version of the final verse as the preferred reading.[32] For reasons I explain in the commentary of appendix 3, the same applies to *Domine in auxilium* and *In virtute*. Although an expansion of range in the final verse is an important stylistic attribute of the genre, the plagal reading of the final verse emerges as both a majority and preferred reading of these particular offertories. As these examples illustrate, a full and accurate assessment of style can emerge only from establishing unemended readings.

In some cases, the pitch-level variants create problems for transcription. The notated pitch level of the repetendum cue sometimes differs from that of the corresponding passage in the respond, especially in Aquitanian sources. For Hankeln, these "incorrect" cues serve as a point of departure for drawing a distinction between "Notationslage" (notation level) and "Aufführungslage" (performance level). Arguing from the premise that the recurring music of the repetendum was sung at the same pitch level each time, Hankeln proposes that the repetendum cue can serve as a reliable guide to the relative pitch level between respond and verse in performance. When the pitch level of a verse is not clearly indicated in uncleffed Aquitanian sources, its performance level can be determined by reading the verse backward from its repetendum cue, deriving the pitches of the repetendum from the corresponding passage in the respond.[33] In most cases, Hankeln's hypothesis is indeed the most plausible explanation for these inconsistent repetendum cues, and I have often employed his method to determine pitch level in Aquitanian sources. In a few cases, however, I hypothesize that the repetendum was actually sung at a

---

32. Hankeln, *Die Offertoriumsprosuln*, 1: 104, and "'Was meint der Schreiber?'" Überlegungen zur Notation des Offertoriums *Tui Sunt Caeli* im Graduale Von St. Yrieix, Paris Bibliothèque Nationale, Fonds Latin 903," in *Cantus Planus: Papers Read at the Sixth Meeting, Eger, Hungary*, vol. 2, ed. László Dobszay (Budapest: Hungarian Academy of Sciences, 1995), 539–59.

33. Hankeln, *Offertoriumsprosuln*, 1:88–94. This phenomenon also occurs in office responsories. See Ike de Loos, "The Transmission of the *Responsoria Prolixa* According to the Manuscripts of St. Mary's Church, Utrecht," *Tijdschrift van de Koninklijke Vereniging voor Nederlandse Muziek Geschiedenis* 49 (1999): 5–32.

different pitch level from the corresponding passage in the respond, because of a
disparity in range between the respond and final verse.[34] In a few cases where
the meaning of the cues is especially uncertain, I have given both the notated
level and the hypothetical performance level in the transcription. I discuss the
problem on a case-by-case basis in the notes for individual offertories in the critical
commentary.

Although the distinction between notated level and performance level is
an important one, the evidence suggests that in some traditions, the transpositions changed the performance of the melody. Implications for performance
are especially compelling when transpositional variants are accompanied by
melodic editing that facilitates the transition to a new pitch level. In *In virtute*
(70), for example, the Aquitanian sources present a plagal reading of the
verse, as mentioned above. In certain adiastematic manuscripts from the
St. Gall tradition, moreover, the significative letter *i* (inferius) indicates that
the verse begins below the final, consistent with the plagal version. In other
manuscripts, however, the verse is written in the authentic range. In a few of
these authentic-range sources, such as Gr 807 and Mü 10086, the scribes alter
the final melisma of the verse, either to facilitate the transition to the
repetendum or to bring the verse to a close on the final F. Several different
versions of the melisma may be examined in appendix 3. This melodic editing
suggests that in these particular cases, variants in the notated pitch level have
implications for performance. Without emendation of the final melisma, the
transition to the repetendum would require a leap of more than an octave.
That modal emendation can change the performance of melodies is also
implied in some contemporaneous writings. The author of the *Dialogus de
musica*, for example, writing around 1000, describes modal emendations in the
context of sung practice.[35]

---

34. See, for example, the notes to *Vir erat* in appendix 3, where the repetendum is written too high in
many Aquitanian sources and in the Roman version. See also Rebecca Maloy, "Problems of Pitch
Level and Modal Structure in the Gregorian Offertories," in *The Offertory and Its Verses: Research,
Past, Present, and Future*, ed. Roman Hankeln (Trondheim: Tapir Academic Press, 2007), 67–88.
35. For example, "In maximum saepe errorem vulgares cantores labuntur, quia vim toni et semitonii,
aliarumque consonantiarum minime perpendunt. Nescientes, quod unius vocis dissimilitudo
modum mutare compellat, ut haec antiphona: O beatum pontificem, quae cum in principio et
fine secundi modi esset, propter illius tantum vocis elevationem, ubi dicitur: o Martine dulcedo in
primo tono a Domno Oddone curiosissime est emendata." *Scriptores ecclesiastici de musica sacra
potissimum*, GS, 1:256. "Medieval singers often fall into the greatest error because they scarcely
consider the qualities of tone and semitone and of the other consonances. . . . They do not know
that a dissimilarity of a single pitch forces a mode to change, as in the antiphon *O beatum
Pontificem*, which, although in the second mode from beginning to end, was most painstakingly
emended to the first mode by Dom Odo." *Source Readings in Music History*, vol. 2, *The Early
Christian Period and the Latin Middle Ages*, ed. and trans. James McKinnon (New York: Norton,
1998), 205–6. Pseudo-Odo's views on emendation are further discussed in Atkinson, *The Critical
Nexus*, 217–19.

Not all transpositional variants in the offertories are attributable to non-diatonic pitches. Hankeln has proposed two additional reasons for the variants: the modal ambiguity of offertories, particularly in their verses, which often contain few references to the final, and an aesthetic motivation, a desire to enhance or deemphasize the climactic expansion of range already present in many offertories. An additional reason, I have argued, is to make the melody more consistent with modal theory. The sixth-mode offertories such as *In virtute* and *Domine in auxilium* may serve again as an illustration. As noted, most sources in the core group notate the final verses in the plagal range. In several of the peripheral manuscripts, however, the second verse is marked by an expansion into the authentic range. If notated in the normal plagal range, the final verses would employ low B-flats and E-flats, pitches not available in the notational system. These problems, however, can be circumvented by notating the whole offertory, respond and both verses, in the transposed range, with the final on c. While this solution, implemented in many manuscripts, solves the notational problems presented by B-flat and E-flat, it does not address the modal irregularities of the unemended reading. These final verses are anomalous in tonal structure, with internal cadences on F, a fifth below the final c. The fifth F-c, characteristic of the *tritus* authentic, is projected a fifth below the final, reversing the usual relationship between plagal and authentic. In sources such as Gr 807, the responds and first verses are written in the untransposed plagal range, with a final of F, whereas the last verse is transposed up a fifth, appearing in the authentic range. This change regularizes the tonal structure of the melody as a whole: the second verse, with its cadences on F, appears as an authentic melody in relation to its plagal respond.

VARIANTS AMONG ROMAN MANUSCRIPTS

Of the three Roman sources for the Mass Proper, only two include offertory verses, Bod 74 from St. Cecilia in Trastevere, copied in 1071, and the twelfth-century Vat 5319, a gradual long thought to be from St. John Lateran but possibly made for the stational liturgy of the *schola cantorum*.[36] The thirteenth-century RoS 22, from St. Peter's, does not transmit verses. Bod 74 lacks several of the Post-Pentecost offertories that appear in Vat 5319, such as *Vir erat* and *Sanctificavit*, as well as a full set of verses for some offertories. I have normally employed Bod 74 as a base version, except when it does not present the full chant.

In most cases, these three manuscripts differ only in details such as passing tones and the use of the oriscus and liquescence. Bod 74 and Vat 5319, in fact, often show a marked similarity even in these details. Major variants, however,

36. Pfisterer, *Cantilena*, 107–8.

may occasionally be found in some of the longer melismas, as described on a case-by-case basis. The closing alleluias in the responds of the Easter Week offertories are also a point of significant variance.[37] Another type of variant occasionally found among the Roman manuscripts involves partial whole-tone transposition. At the beginning of *Populum humilem* (37), for example, Vat 5319 is written a whole tone below Bod 74, a reading also matched in RoS 22. In examining similar instances of whole-tone transposition, Carl Serpa has shown that the passages in question are often written with a b-flat in Vat 5319, leading to the hypothesis that the scribe employs b-flat to correct scribal errors.[38] For reasons that are unclear, a few Roman offertories, such as *Custodi me* (46) and *Eripe me . . . domine* (45), present more extensive transpositional variants.

OTHER EDITING AND TRANSCRIPTION ISSUES

In transcribing the base versions given in the edition, I have made few editorial emendations. In rare instances, however, I have corrected what I perceive to be scribal errors. These cases, usually short passages of three or four notes, are indicated with brackets in the transcription and described in appendix 3.

The following signs have been adopted to indicate special neumes: ⌿ for the oriscus; ∼ for the quilisma (not used in Ben 34); and open noteheads for liquescences. Some signs in the Roman and Beneventan manuscripts require special clarification. Beneventan manuscripts employ a great variety of signs to indicate liquescence, a trend that becomes increasingly pronounced in later manuscripts such as Ben 34 and 35. It is unclear whether this variety of signs represents subtly different approaches to singing liquescent syllables or whether they are simply "graphic ornaments," as John Boe has proposed in the case of the Beneventan apostrophus.[39] For the purposes of transcription, the most important question is whether the liquescence sign applies to the note to which it is attached or whether it signifies a second, added note. In a recent study of Ben 34, Rupert Fischer defines three "degrees" of liquescence.[40] The first, he argues, refers to the note to which it is attached, without an extra pitch. This interpretation is supported by contexts where the liquescent neume is followed by a repeated note. Here the scribe's intention can be clarified by the use of the punctum or virga or the two forms of the clivis. When a note following the liquescent is of the same pitch and is

37. See, for example, the notes on *Scapulis suis* (19), *Domine in auxilium* (27), and *Iustus ut palma* (71) in appendix 3.
38. Carl Serpa, "B-Flats in the Old Roman Mass Propers of Manuscript Rome, vat. lat. 5319," paper presented at the Midwest Chapter meeting of the American Musicological Society, October 1999.
39. John Boe, "The Beneventan Apostrophus in South Italian Notation, A.D. 1000–1100," *Early Music History* 3 (1983): 43–66.
40. Rupert Fischer, "Benevento, Biblioteca capitolare, cod. 34," *Beiträge zur Gregorianik* 22 (1996): 111–35.

a punctum, it suggests that the liquescence does not involve an additional note. For similar reasons, Fischer's third degree of liquescence seems clearly to indicate the presence of an additional note. When it is followed by a repeated note, it is represented as virga, suggesting that the liquescent refers to an additional, lower note. Fischer's second degree of liquescence, however, is somewhat ambiguous. He surmises that it does not involve an additional note. In all cases in the offertories where a liquescence of this second degree is followed by a note of the same pitch, however, the following note is written as either a virga or the form of the clivis that follows a lower note, clarifying that the liquescent note is the lower neighbor of the pitch that is indicated. Although the repeated-note context is a reliable guide to interpreting a liquescence sign in specific contexts, we cannot be absolutely sure that these signs have the same meaning each time they occur. The two alternatives are a neutral transcription that does not specify whether there should be an extra note and a consistent transcription of all liquescence types each time they occur. I have opted for the latter solution, based on the repeated-note context I have described: first-degree liquescences are interpreted as referring to the note to which it is attached, whereas second- and third-degree liquescences are interpreted as referring to a second note. When a single note occurs with a liquescence sign of the first degree, I have interpreted it as unison liquescence, transcribed with a single notehead tied to an open notehead. I have adopted a similar principle in transcribing the liquescences of Bod 74 and Vat 5319, employing instances of repeated notes and the use of the virga and special clivis form as guides for consistently transcribing the same sign.

Two other types of neumes that require commentary in Ben 34 are the apostrophus and the various compound neumes that involve an oriscus. Although the apostrophus looks like a liquescence, it is frequently employed outside of liquescence contexts. Its use and significance is the subject of a penetrating study by Boe.[41] In offertories and other Mass proper chants, the apostrophus is used for low, unaccented syllables at the beginnings of phrases. Boe shows that the apostrophus in earlier sources such as Ben 38 and 40 is not consistently maintained in later manuscripts such as Ben 34 and Ben 35, where it is often replaced with regular puncta. Ben 35 has a tendency to employ this neume only on liquescent syllables, whereas Ben 34, Boe argues, seems to retain the neume as a graphic ornament. In transcriptions from Ben 34, I have not distinguished the apostrophus from regular notes.

In the case of the oriscus, my transcriptions are consistent with Fischer's interpretations. In compound neumes of Ben 34, a wavy line is associated with certain melodic figures followed by a descending note. It often occurs, for example, as the first element of a clivis or in figures such as acaaG, with the wavy element on the penultimate note. In the case of the clivis, this form is clearly distinct from the

41. Boe, "Beneventan Apostrophus."

other two clivis forms, and its first element occurs in contexts where an oriscus would be expected. I have transcribed the first element of this clivis as an oriscus. Though common in Ben 34, this oriscus sign differs from the common oriscus form in earlier Beneventan sources, as well as Vat 5319 and Bod 74, which represent the oriscus with a distinctive hook-like figure. In Bod 74, the form of the clivis that follows a higher note is consistently written with a wavy line that resembles the special clivis of Ben 34. Because this is the normal form of the clivis that follows a higher note in Bodmer, I have transcribed it as a normal clivis.

In transcriptions of Mo 159, the use of special signs requires comment. In addition to its letter notation, Mo 159 employs well-known irregular pitch signs at the positions of the semitone, E, a (in proximity to b-flat), and b. The meaning of these signs has not been fully resolved. Gmelch proposed that they indicate microtonal inflections, an argument taken up again by Finn Egeland Hansen.[42] I have transcribed these notes with an open diamond figure. Finally, many central Italian manuscripts at times draw a long line where repeated notes occur in other manuscripts, usually at the position of F or C. Some sources use a variety of different lengths for this line. It is unclear whether these figures represent repeated notes, and if so, how many; or whether they indicate a change in performance practice in which formerly repeated notes were simply given a longer duration. Because of these ambiguities, I have transcribed them as single notes.

The use of the parenthetical accidentals in the transcriptions requires commentary. In transcriptions of the Gregorian repertory, I have employed two different types of parenthetical accidental, one beside the pitch in question and one above it. The first type is attributable simply to the lack of distinction between b-flat and b-natural in most of the core manuscripts. Only one manuscript employed for base transcriptions, Mo 159, consistently distinguishes between b-natural and b-flat, one of many reasons for its value. Indications of b-flat are lacking in Beneventan manuscripts and in most Aquitanian sources. The b-flats in Mo 159, however, are nearly always consistent with those in later manuscripts that do distinguish between b and b-flat. These later sources are primarily from German-speaking areas but also include the Aquitanian manuscript Pa 903, through its use of special neumes indicating the half step, and, inconsistently, Pa 1235, Cai 61, and Mod 7. When a b-flat consistently appears in sources that distinguish between b-natural and b-flat, I have added a parenthetical b-flat beside the note, generally once on each line, to the base transcription of the Gregorian reading. When a parenthetical b-flat appears beside a note, then, it reflects a choice made not on a theoretical or stylistic basis but rather on manuscript evidence. In some cases, Mo 159 indicates b-flats in passages where other manuscripts do not. These discrepancies, perhaps

42. Joseph Gmelch, *Die Viertelstonstufen im Messtonale von Montpellier* (Eichstätt: P. Brönnersche, 1911); Hansen, *H 159 Montpellier*.

reflecting different practices, are described in the commentary. The parenthetical accidentals written above the note in question are hypothetical, indicating places where the use of a nondiatonic pitch is probable.

In the Roman manuscripts, a sign for b-flat is employed very rarely in Vat 5319 and not at all in Bod 74. These sources present no direct evidence for when b-flat was used more generally. In the transcriptions, I have limited the indications of b-flat in the Roman reading to the few places where it is written in the manuscript. While it is of course very likely that a b-flat would have been sung in clear *tritus* contexts such as Formula B, I have not indicated that.[43] While a b-flat sign in Vat 5319 may have been used to correct scribal errors in some cases, it is also employed when melodic gestures involving b-flat occur outside their usual context. In *Vir erat*, for example, Vat 5319 employs b-flat in a passage where it serves as a repercussive pitch, similar to the *tritus* function normally served by c. The relationship to the Gregorian version, however, confirms the impression that the passage is written at the intended pitch level.

In the transcription of words I have sought to faithfully represent what is written on the page, be it an alternative reading or simply an error. Readers of the transcriptions will notice discrepancies between the Gregorian and Roman versions of the texts, many of which reflect differences in the psalter traditions discussed in chapter 2.

43. It is probable that low B-flat was sung in the respond *Dextera domini* (16).

APPENDIX 1

Textual Sources and Variants

Offertory	PsR Reading	Departures from PsR in the Roman Text	Departures from PsR in the Gregorian Text
1. Ad te domine	24:3 expectant domine	domine om. αβγδεη moz med Gall TQUVX	domine om. (all)
2. Deus tu convertens	84:7 convertens 84:3 plebis		conversus (Rh) Ga 84:3 plebi (La 239) α Babcd
3. Benedixisti	84:3 plebis		84:3 plebi (Cha 47 La 239 Co) αBabcd
6. Tollite portas	23:7 vestris	vestras η moz, Ga A2M2T2	vestras (all)
	23:7 introibit		introivit (Rh) γ
	23:1 universi	universis (Vat 5319)-	
	23:1 habitant in ea[1]		habitant in eo: (La 239 Cha 47 Ei 121) moz med Ga
	23:2 fundavit eam	fundavit ea α T2 f	fundavit eum Ga, med (La 239 Ei 121 Co)
	23:2 preparavit illam	preparavit eam αγη	preparavit eum Ga (La 239 Ei 121 Co) med Ga
8. Deus enim firmavit	92:2 sedis 91:1 fortitudinem 92:1 virtutem	sedes αδζσ moz med	sedes fortitudine (Ei 121)δ2Ga virtute (Cha 47 Ei 121 La 239 Co) δAHN2TBC2 DQ2R2fab GaBDPQUVX
	92:5 decent	decet αο moz med Ga SPQRV	dicet (Cha 47)– decet (Ben 34 Co)

234

Offertory	PsR Reading	Departures from PsR in the Roman Text	Departures from PsR in the Gregorian Text
	92:5 testimonia tua domine	testimoniam	domine om. (all) αγδ moz med Ga
	92:5 domui tuae	domine– (Vat 5319)	domum tuam (Cha 47 Ei 121 La 239 Co) α moz med
9. Tui sunt	88:15 iustitia	iustitiam (Bod 74) S	iustitiam (Cha 47 Ei 121)
	88:10 fluctuum	fluctum (Vat 5319) αγσMKP	fluctum (Ben 34)
	88:10 potastati	potestatem (Bod 74)δ2 mozNQ	potestatis (Cha 47 Ei 121) γσGaMC potestates (Co)–
10. Reges tharsis	71:11servient		serviunt (Co) moz
	71:2 in tua iustitia		cum iustitia (all) α
	71:3 colles iustitiam	71:3 colles iustitia α	
11. Iubilate deo omnis	99:3 quod	quia γ	quia (all)
12. Iubilate deo universa	65:1 omnis	universa–	universa (all)
	65:16 me	me om. α2 βγδεζ moz med Ga Aug S	me om. (all)
	65:16 vobis	nobis (Vat 5319)–	
	65:16 dominum	deum: α2γδ med Ga Aug KTPQRUX	deum (all except Rh)
14. Bonum est	91:12 et respexit	quia respexit–	quia respexit (all)
	91:12 oculus tuus		oculus meus (all) α moz med Ga2
15. Perfice gressus	16:7 facis	facit (Vat 5319)–	facit[3] (La 239)
	16:1 deprecationi meae	deprecationis meae Vat 5319)–	deprecationem meam (all) ζ moz med Ga AHM
	16:13 eripe animam meam		eripe domine (all) –
16. Benedictus es…in labiis[4]	118:32 dum		cum (Ei 121) αγδ moz med
	118:32 dilatares	dilataris (Bod)–	
17. Exaltabo te	29:8 bona		bona om. (all) αγδλ moz med Ga
18. Domine vivifica	118:108 beneplacita fac	fac mihi in beneplacito–oris tui (Vat 5319)–	fac mihi in beneplacito (all)
	118:108 oris mei		

(continued)

Offertory	PsR Reading	Departures from PsR in the Roman Text	Departures from PsR in the Gregorian Text
19. Scapulis suis[5]	90:4 obumbrabit	obumbravit αγδmozHMSBVX	obumbravit (La 239 Co Rh)
	90:6 sagitta volante	sagittem volantem (Vat 5319)	
	90:14 speravit		sperabit (Ben 34 La 239 Ei 121) δζ moz N
	90:14 et liberabo	et om. α moz med BCDPQRUVX	et om. (all)
20. Levabo[6]	118:18 revela	levabo–	levabo (all except Ei 121)
	118:33 viam	et viam–	
	118:77 mihi		super me (all)–[7]
	118:77 et viam	ut viam (moz, med)	
21. In te speravi	30:17 in tua misericordia	propter misericordiam tuam–[8]	propter misericordiam tuam (all)
	30: 15 tempora mea		temporam mean (Rh) –
	30:20 et perfecisti	et om. αβγδλ moz med Ga	et om.
22. Meditabor	118:47 meditabor		meditabar (La 239 Cha 47 Ben 34) αδη moz Ga N*ST2RVX
	118:47 nimis	valde αγ	valde (all)
	118:47 vehementer	vehementer om. moz Ga	vehementer om. (all)
	118:57 portio mea	pars mea αγ	pars mea (all)
	118:58 deprecatus		precatus α (all except Bl)
	118:58 faciem	vultum αγ med	vultum (all)
23. Benedic anima	102:1 dominum		domino (Cha 47 Ei 121 La 239 Bl Co Cr) moz, Ga D
	102:3 propitus	propitiatur med Ga BC	propitiatur (all)
	102:4 qui	et–[9]	et
	102:4 redemit	redemet αγζσ moz SBPQUVX	redemet (Ben 34 Cha 47 La 239 Co)
	102:18 faciant		facient (Co)

Offertory	PsR Reading	Departures from PsR in the Roman Text	Departures from PsR in the Gregorian Text
25. Benedicam	15:7 benedicam dominum		benedicam domino (Ei 121, Bl) δ moz Ga
	15:7 qui michi tribuit		qui tribuit michi (Rh) Ga
	15:8 providebam dominum	providebam deum–	providebam deum (Ben 34 Ei 121 Cr) providebam deo (Cha 47 Co) nec (Rh)–
	15:8 ne		
	15:6 dixi	ego dixi–	ego dixi (all)
	15:10 mihi fecisti		fecisti mihi (all) α
26. Miserere mihi	50:3 mei	mihi γδ	mihi (all)
	50:3 deus	domine δ	domine (all)
	50:5 agnosco		cognosco (Co) Ga
	50:6 sermonibus		miserationibus (Co)–
27. Domine in auxilium	39:15 simul	inimici mei η2 λ moz PQ2RUVXabcd	simul om. (all)–
28. Illumina oculos	12:4 illumina		inclina (Rh)–
	12:4 ne umquam		nequando (all)–[10]
	12:4 obdormiam		dormiam (Co, Ben 34)–
	12:4 mortem	morte βγ moz med S2 D	morte (all)
	12:2 consilium		consilia (Cha 47, La 239, Ei 121 Co) η, Ga, T
	12:2 animam meam	anima mea (Vat 5319) βη moz med Ga TBCDQX	anima mea (Ben 34 Ei 121 La 239)
29. Iustitiae	18:12 custodiet ea	custodiet eam (Vat 5319) α	custodiet eam (Ben 34) eas– (Ei 121) custodit (Rh)γδη moz med Ga
	18:10 timor domini	timor dei–	timor dei–(all)
	18:10 permanet		permanens (Cha 47 Ei 121 La 239 Co) αβγδζη moz Ga HMSKT
	18:10 iudicia dei		iudicia domini (all) αβδζη Ga TDf

(*continued*)

Offertory	PsR Reading	Departures from PsR in the Roman Text	Departures from PsR in the Gregorian Text
30. Exaudi deus[11]	54:3 conturbatus sunt		conturbata sunt (Bl)–
	54:17 dominum	deum αγmoz med Ga H	deum (all)
31. Domine fac mecum	108:4 diligerent me		me diligerent (La 239 Co)[12] γ med Ga
32. Intende voci	5:9 viam meam	vias meas (Vat 5319)–	vias meas (Co)
33. Gressus meos	118:130 dat parvulis	da parvulis (Vat 5319)–	da parvulis (Cha 47) dans parvulis (Ei 121 Co) R
34. Laudate dominum	134:3 dominus	dominus om.γ NBDRV	dominus om. (all except Rh)
	134:13 memoriale	memorialem (Vat 5319) αδHS	
	134:14 iudicabit	iudicavit αγη moz HMNSPQ	iudicavit (Ben 34)
35. Expectans expectavi[13]	39:6 quis	qui (Vat 5319) λ med Ga	
	39:11 iusticiam tuam		iusticiam meam (Cha 47 Ei 121 La 239) γ
	39:11 salutare	salutarem (Vat 5319) γ A	
	39:18 liberator	protector αβγδη med Ga	protector (all)
36. Benedicite gentes	65:8 deum nostrum		deo nostro (Ei 121) εζ moz
	65:8 vocem	voci ε med	
	65:8 laudis		laudi– Cha 47 La 239 Co
	65:2 laudi	laudis UV	
	65:3 multitudine	multitudinem (Vat 5319 only) γ	
	65:4 psallat	psallam (Vat 5319 only) α	
	65:5 videte	audite (Ps. 65:16)– (Vat 5319 only)	
	65:17 ad ipsum	ab ipso (Vat 5319 only)α2εζ	
	65:19 deprecationis meae		orationis meae (all) α2βγδ med Aug

Offertory	PsR Reading	Departures from PsR in the Roman Text	Departures from PsR in the Gregorian Text
	65:20 deprecationem		orationem (Rh) α2 moz med Ga
37. Populum humilem	17:48 dominus	dominus om. αβδη moz med Ga	dominus om. (all)
	17:49 et	et om. αβγδη	et om. (all)
38. Factus est dominus[14]	17:38 persequar		persequatur–(Co)
	17:40 virtute	virtutem αγδημoz SKTPQVXabcd	virtutem (Cha 47)
	17:40 bellum	bellum + et ζ	bellum+ et (all)
39. Confitebor tibi[15]	118:17 vivam	viam (Bod)–	
	118:36 avaritiam	avaritia med AHMNR	avaritia (Cha 47 Co)
	118:58 faciem	verse not in OR	vultum αγmed[16]
41. Sperent in te	9:13 orationem	orationes moz TBCPQUVX	orationes (Ben 34)
	9:5 qui	et–	
	9:6 periit	periet (Vat 5319) ASKT	periet (Ben 34)
42. Eripe me . . . deus	58:4 occupaverunt	captaverunt med	captaverunt (all)
	58:4 in me fortes	fortes in me–	fortes in me (all)
	58:17 susceptor	adiutor–	adiutor (all)
43. Benedictus es . . . et non tradas	118:121 ne tradas[17]		non tradas (all) γη med Ga
	118:121 persequentibus	calumniantibus η Ga[18]	calumniantibus (all)
	118:150 adpropiaverunt		appropinquaverunt αη Ga f
44. Improperium	68: 21 miseriam	miseria (Vat 5319) –	
	68: 21 mecum	mecum om. δε moz med Ga esca mea	mecum om. (all)
	68:22 escam meam	αδε moz	esca mea (Co)
	68:2 introierunt	intraverunt γδε Ga	intraverunt (all)
	62:13 adversum	adversus αPQRabcd	adversus (Bl)
45. Eripe me . . . domine[19]	142:10 tu es deus meus	deus meus es tu Ga[20]	deus meus es tu (all)
	142:2 et non		et ne intres (Ben 34 Ei

(continued)

Offertory	PsR Reading	Departures from PsR in the Roman Text	Departures from PsR in the Gregorian Text
	intres 142:2 iudicio	et ne intres α moz PQ[21]	121 La 239 Co) iudicium (Ben 34 Ei 121) med
46. Custodi	139:6 laqueos		laqueum (Cha 47 Co) γδ Ga
	139:5 qui 139:7 es tu	quia ζ es–	
47. Domine exaudi	101:3 ne avertas		non avertas (La 239 Co)
	101:14 see note[22]		
48. Terra tremuit	75:10 exsurgeret 75:10 iudicio	resurgeret β moz med PQUVabc	resurgeret (all) β moz med PQUVabc iudicium (Cha 47 La 239 Co Cr) δζ Ga
	75:4 cornua	cornu moz SPQRUVXab	cornu (all)
50. Intonuit	17:3 domine	dominus moz med Ga HBCDVabcd	
	17:48 dominus 17:49 et ab insurgentibus	dominus om. αβδη moz med Ga Cab et om. αβγδη moz med Ga SK	dominus om. (all) et om. (all)
51. Portas celi	77:23 ianuas 77:24 manducare 77:24 eis 77:1 populus	portas αγ moz ut ederent–[23] illis γ popule γ moz medBCXabcd	portas (all) ut ederent (all[24]) illis (all) popule (all except Co)
	77:1 legem		in legem (all except Ben 34 and Co) γ
54. Benedictus qui venit[25]	117:26 vos	factum η moz med KBCQRUVX	vobis η Ga (All except Ben 34)
	117:23 factus		factum (all)
	117:23 mirabilis	mirabile αη moz med Ga TCDQRUVX	mirabile (all)
55. Deus deus meus	62:7 factus es 62:8 exaltabo	exaltabor –(Vat 5319)	fuisti (Co) δ moz Ga
56. Lauda anima mea	145:7 facit		faciet (Ben 34 La 239) AH faciens (Ei 121)δ med
	145:7 soluit	solvet (Vat 5319) γ moz ANS	solvit– (La 239 Ei 121 Co)
	145:9 dominus custodit	custodit dominus–	custodit dominus (all)

Offertory	PsR Reading	Departures from PsR in the Roman Text	Departures from PsR in the Gregorian Text
	145:9 viam	vias (Bod) moz	vias (La Ei 121 Ben 34)
	145:9 regnabit	regnavit (Vat 5319)	regnavit (Ben 34 Co)
	145:9 exterminabit	αγδ HMNSQ exterminavit (Vat 5319) α ANSPQ	exterminavit (Ben 34)
57. Confitebor domino	108:31 adstetit	adstitit αγ moz BCD	adstitit (all)
	108:31 faceret		faciet (La 239)– faciat (Co) αγ
	108:27 haec est et tu	haec est om.–	est et omitted γ Ga[26]
	108:29 detrahunt	detrahebant–	detrahebant (all)–
	108:29 reverentiam	reverentia δ moz med H2 N2	reverentia (Ben 34 Ei 121 Co)
58. Ascendit deus	46:3 deus[27]		dominus (all) αη med Ga T
	46:3 omnes deos		omnem terram (all) αβδη moz Ga S
59. Emitte spiritum	103:31 saeculum	saecula–[28]	saecula (all)
	103:1 dominum		domino (Ca Ei 121 La 239 Co) δ moz Ga
	103:2 amictus	amictum–	
	103:2 lumine	lumen δ moz MSPQRUVX	lumen (Ben 34)
	103:3 tegis	tegit (Vat 5319 only) δ moz med TPQRU	tegit (Ben 34)
	103:3 ponit		ponis (Ei 121, La 239) α Ga U ponet (Co) δζHM
60. Confirma hoc	67:30 templo sancto		sancto om. (all) αγδεζ moz med Ga Aug.
	67:5 cantate deo	cantate domino γδ	cantate domino (all)
	67:27 dominum deum	deum dominum γ med Ga	deo domino (Ca Ei 121) α2
	67:34 super caelos		super om. (all)–
62. Immittit angelus[29]	33:8 inmittet		inmittit (Cha 47 Ei 121 Co) moz AHNKT emittet (Bl) ε
	33:8 angelum dominus		angelus domini (all except Co and La 239) γδε moz med Ga KTV
	33:3 audiant		audient (Cha 47) H2
	33:6 erubescent	33: 6 erubescant–	erubescant (Co)

(continued)

Offertory	PsR Reading	Departures from PsR in the Roman Text	Departures from PsR in the Gregorian Text
65. Si ambulavero	137:7 extendisti	extendis–	extendis (Cha 47 Co)– extendes (Cr Ei 121 La 239)–
	137:2 misericordiam tuam		misericordia tua (Ei 121) γη Ga BCDPQYXabcd
	137:2 veritatem tuam		veritate tua (Ei 121)αη Ga BCDPQUZabcd
66. Super flumina	136:3 quia	quoniam α	quoniam
	136:3 cantionium		canticorum α moz
	136:6 si non meminero tui	si non meminero tui (PsR) + si tui non meminero α	si tui non meminero α
69. De profundis[30]	129:3 iniquitates		iniquitatem (La 239 Cha 47) δ ζ moz med Ben 34
	12:3 observaveris		observaberis (Cha 47 La 239 Ei 121) ζηGa[31]
70. In virtute	20:2 exaltabit	exaltavit HMSKDUV	exaltavit (Cha 47)
71. Iustus ut palma	91:13 Libani	quae in Libano est	quae in Libano est (all except Rh)
	91:14 plantati... florebunt	γδσ[32] plantatus... florebit–	plantatus... florebit (all)
72. Anima nostra	123:5 aquam	aqua–	
	123:6 captionem	captione AHMNSK	captione (Cha 47 Co)
73. Inveni	88:21 servum meum		servo meo (Bl)
	88:21 in oleo	in om. moz med T2 PQRUVX	et in oleo γδ (all)
	88:22 confortabit		confortavit (Cha 47 Ben 34 Co) αδζ moz AHMS
74. Offerentur (minor)[33]	44:15 adducentur	offerentur αγδ moz med QR[34]	Offerentur (all)
	44:15 postea	post eam αγδ moz GaATBDPQRVUX	post eam (except for La 239)
	44:5 speciem tuam	specie tua δεηλ med GaN2 T2	specie tua
	44:5	pulcritudine tua	pulcritudine tua

Offertory	PsR Reading	Departures from PsR in the Roman Text	Departures from PsR in the Gregorian Text
	pulchritudinem tuam	γδεη moz med Ga N2 T2	
76. Veritas mea[35]	88:20 adiutorium		adiutorium meum (all except Co)–
77. Constitues eos[36]	44:17 erunt		ero (Co)
	44:18 generatione et progenie	progenie et generatione δ moz	progenie et generatione
	44:4 gladium tuum	gladio tua ε2 η moz Ga N2	gladio tua (all except Ben 34)
78. Filie regum[37]	44:10 adstetit	adstitit β moz A NTBD	
	44:10 circumamicta	circumdata η Ga	
79. Letamini	31:6 adproximabunt		proximabunt (Cha 47, Ei 121) γδη
82. Confitebuntur	88:2 pronuntiabo		adnuntiabo (all) α Ga
83. Repleti	89:14 misericordia tua	misericordiam tuam (Vat 5319) αγδ moz AHMNS	misericordiam tuam (Ei 121)
	89:14 exultavimus	exultabimus (Vat 5319) moz MVX	exultabimus (Ei 121 Cha 47)
	89:2 fierent montes		fierunt (Ei 121)– montes fierent (Co)αγ med Ga
	89:2 firmaretur	formaretur δζ moz Ga N2 S	formaretur (all)
	89:2 usque		usque om. δ moz med
84. Mirabilis	67:1 a facie eius qui oderunt eum	qui oderunt eum a facie eius α2βγδεGa Aug.	qui oderunt eum a facie eius (all)
85. Gloriabuntur	5:12 diligunt	noverunt (Vat 5319)–	
	5:13 iustum		iusto (Cha 47 La 239 Co Cr) Ga iustis (Ei 121)–
86. Michi autem[38]	138:3 semitam meam	semitas meas M	semitas meas (Ei 121 Ben 34)

1. Bodmer 74 lacks the verses for this offertory.
2. This reading is also transmitted in Ambrogio Amelli, *Liber psalmorum iuxta antiquissimam latinam versionem nunc primum ex Casinensi cod. 557 in lucem profertur* (Rome: F Pustet, 1912); and in citations of Augustine and Julianus of Eclanum. See *Vetus latina Database: The Bible Versions of the Latin Fathers* (Turnhout: Brepols, 2003).
3. Hesbert notes that in Co the original is "facis," but "facit" has been written in with a second hand. René-Jean Hesbert, *Antiphonale missarum sextuplex* (Brussels: Vromant, 1935), 47.

(continued)

4. The Gregorian and Roman versions differ in text repetition in v. 3: most Gregorian sources repeat "iudicia tua." In both Roman manuscripts, "non sum oblitus" is repeated.

5. The Gregorian and Roman versions have significant differences in v. 2. (See phrase 8 in the side-by-side transcriptions.) The Roman is an intact verse from the PsR, 90:11. The Gregorian is centonized from 90:11 and 90:12.

6. The Gregorian and Roman versions show significant differences in v. 2. (See the transcriptions, phrases 7, 8, and 9.) Both versions are centonized from 118:77.

7. "Super me" is cited in an oration text. See *Vetus latina Database.*

8. "Propter misericordiam tuam" is cited by Ambrose of Milan and in *Actae vel passiones vel vitae sanctorum.* See *Vetus latina Database.*

9. "Et redimet" appears in several citations, including Coelestin, Pseudo-Gennadius, and Jerome. See *Vetus latina Database.*

10. This reading is lacking in the sources used by Weber but may be an African reading. It is found in Amelli, *Liber psalmorum,* a codex preserving African characteristics.

11. Other differences are the result of text adjustment.

12. Co and La have "me diligerent me," a conflation of PsR and PsG.

13. The Roman sources lack the Gregorian's verse *Statuit super petram.*

14. Gregorian and Roman have significant differences in the structure of the text.

15. OR manuscripts lack two verses of the Gregorian.

16. Also cited by Augustine. See *Vetus latina Database.*

17. The Gregorian and Roman texts here have different centonizations. Gregorian sources have "a calumniantibus me superbis" ("superbi" is from Ps. 118:122). The Roman sources have "in me."

18. Also in Amelli, *Liber psalmorum.* Pseudo-Hieronymus cites a reading that matches the Gregorian version of the text for the whole of 118:121. See *Vetus latina Database.*

19. The Roman and Gregorian traditions have separate second verses here. The Roman (also found in Benevento and Milan) is the second half of Ps. 142:5, based on the PsR. Two different Gregorian verses are formed from 142:6 and142:7. Both verses are consistent with the Roman and Gallican psalters (which show no differences here).

20. The same version is cited by Cassiodorus. See *Vetus latina Database.*

21. Also in Amelli, *Liber psalmorum,* and some citations of Ambrose. See *Vetus latina Database.*

22. The Gregorian version has the PsG reading "quia tempus miserendi eius quia venit tempus." The Roman has the unknown reading "quia venit tempus quia tempus venit miserendi eius," matching the text of the companion tract. These differences are also mentioned in Andreas Pfisterer, *Cantilena Romana, Untersuchungen zur Überlieferung des gregorianischen Chorals* (Paderborn: Schö-ningh, 2001), 136.

23. Cited in the"Eusebius Gallicanus" collection. See *Vetus latina Database.*

24. Chartres has "ut ederem."

25. Vat 5319 presents a shortened version of the respond, omitting "Benediximus vobis de domo domini" (Bodmer 74 has the full verse).

26. Co presents a text that is different from the others.

27. Vat 5319 is missing second verse.

28. Also Amelli, *Liber psalmorum.* See *Vetus latina Database.*

29. Bodmer 74 is missing the final verse.

30. The verses are missing in the Old Roman tradition.

31. Prosper of Aquitaine cites a reading of 129:3 that is identical to the Gregorian version of the text.

32. Also in several citations, including Ambrose and Eucherius, bishop of Lyon. *Vetus latina Database.*

33. The Roman transmits the verse *Adducentur* (normally the second verse in Gregorian sources) as part of the respond and appends an additional verse, *Specie tua* (which circulates with *Diffusa est* in Gregorian sources).

34. Also in several citations, particularly Ambrose and Augustine. *Vetus latina Database.*

35. Bodmer lacks the verse *Posui adiutorium.*

36. For a summary of the different verse transmission in Gregorian and Roman versions and a hypothesis, see Pfisterer, *Cantilena Romana,* 167–69.

37. No verses are indicated in Vat 5319. In Bodmer 74, the verses *Eructavit* and *Specie* are cued.

38. The Gregorian verse *Domine probasti* is lacking in the Roman tradition. The verse is based on the PsR rather than the PsG.

APPENDIX 2
Manuscripts Cited

Be 40078   Berlin, Staatsbibliothek, Mus. ms. 40078. Gradual, twelfth century. From Quedlinburg.

Ben 34   Benevento, Biblioteca capitolare, 35. Gradual with tropes and proses, first half of twelfth century. From S. Sophia, Benevento. Facsimile: *Le Codex VI.34 de la Bibliothèque Capitulaire de Bénévent (XIe–XIIe siècle). Graduel de Bénévent avec prosaire et tropaire.* Berne: Éditions H. Lang, 1937, 1971. Paléographie Musicale 15.

Ben 35   Benevento, Biblioteca capitolare, 35. Gradual with tropes and proses, first half of twelfth century. From Benevento.

Ben 38   Benevento, Biblioteca capitolare, 38. Gradual with tropes and proses, before 1050. From Benevento.

Ben 39   Benevento, Biblioteca capitolare, 39. Gradual with tropes and proses, late eleventh century. Possibly from St. Peter's, Benevento.

Ben 40   Benevento, Biblioteca capitolare, 40. Gradual with tropes and proses, early eleventh century. Possibly from S. Sofia, Benevento. Facsimile: *Benevento Biblioteca Capitolare 40*, ed. Nino Albarosa and Alberto Turco. Padua: La Linea editrice, 1991.

Bod 74   Cologne-Geneva, Bibliotheca Bodmeriana, 74. Old Roman Gradual, 1071. From Santa Cecilia in Trastevere, Rome. Facsimile: *Das Graduale von Santa Cecilia in Trastevere (Cod. Bodmer 74).* 2 vols., ed. Max Lütolf. Cologny-Genève: Foundation Martin Bodmer, 1987.

Cai 61   Cambrai, Bibliotheque municipale, 61. Gradual with kyriale, sequences, and processional antiphons, early twelfth century. Possibly from Saint-Pierre de Lille.

Cha 47   Chartres, Bibliothèque Capitulaire, 47. Gradual, ninth—tenth century. From Bretagne.
Facsimile: *Antiphonale Missarum Sancti Gregorii. Xe siècle. Codex 47 de la Bibliothèque de Chartres.* Berne: Éditions H. Lang, 1912, 1972. Paléographie Musicale 11.

Ei 121   Einsiedeln, Stiftsbibliothek, 121. Gradual and sequentiary, tenth or eleventh century. From St. Gall, Muerbach or Einsiedeln.
Facsimile: *Le codex 121 de la Bibliothèque d' Einsiedeln (X–XI siècle): Antiphonale missarum sancti Gregorii.* Berne: éditions H. Lang, 1894, 1974. Paléographie Musicale 4.

Gr 807   Graz, Universitaetsbibliothek, 807. Gradual, twelfth century (after 1133). From Passau.
Facsimile: *Le manuscrit 807, Universitätsbibliothek Graz (XIIe siècle): Graduel de Klosterneuburg.* Berne: éditions H. Lang, 1974. Paléographie Musicale 19.

La 239   Laon, Bibliothèque Municapale, 239. Gradual, beginning of tenth century. From the region of Laon.
Facsimile: *Antiphonale Missarum Sancti Gregorii, IXe–Xe siècle, codex 239 de la Bibliothèque de Laon.* Berne: Éditions H. Lang, 1909, 1971. Paléographie Musicale 10.

Lo 4951   London, British Library, Harliean 4951. Gradual, eleventh century. From Toulouse.

Mod 7   Modena, Archivio capitolare, 0.I.7 Gradual with tropes and proses, late eleventh century. From Forlimpopoli, near Ravenna.

Mo 159   Montpellier, Faculte de Médicine H 159. Tonary, early eleventh century. From Dijon.
Facsimile: *Antiphonarium tonale missarum, XIe siècle, codex H. 159 de la Bibliothèque de l'école de médecine de Montpellier.* Berne: éditions H. Lang, 1901, 1972. Paléographie Musicale 7–8.

Mü 10086   Munich, Bayerische Staatsbibliothek, Clm. 10086, Gradual, twelfth—thirteenth century. From Prüfening.

Mü 14965b   Munich, Bayerische Staatsbibliothek, Clm. 14965b. Tonary, beginning of twelfth century. From southern Germany, possibly Bamberg or St. Emmeram.
Facsimile: *München, Bayerische Staatsbibliothek, Clm 14965b: The Tonary of Frutolf of Michelsberg.* Edited by Rebecca Maloy. Ottawa: Institute of Mediaeval Music, 2006.

Pad 47   Padua, Biblioteca capitolare, 47. Gradual with tropes and proses, early twelfth century. From Ravenna.

Pa 776   Paris, Bibliothèque nationale, lat. 776. Gradual, eleventh century. Probably from St. Michel-de-Gaillac, near Albi.
Facsimile: *Il cod. Paris Bibliothèque Nationale de France lat. 776: sec. XI: Graduale di Gaillac,* ed. Nino Albarosa et al. Padua: La Linea editrice, 2001.

Pa 903   Paris, Bibliothèque nationale, lat. 903. Gradual, troper, and proser, eleventh century. From St. Yrieix.
Facsimile: *Le codex 903 de la Bibliothèque nationale de Paris (XIe siècle). Graduel de Saint-Yrieix.* Berne: Éditions H. Lang, 1930, 1971. Paléographie Musicale 13/2.

Pa 1121   Paris, Bibliothèque nationale, lat. 1121. Troper and offertoriale, early eleventh century (ca. 1028). From St. Martial, Limoges.

Pa 1132   Paris, Bibliothèque nationale, lat. 1132. Gradual and sequentiary, late eleventh century (after 1063). From St. Martial, Limoges.

Pa 1133   Paris, Bibliothèque nationale, lat. 1133. Troper and offertoriale, eleventh century. From St. Martial, Limoges.

Pa 1134   Paris, Bibliothèque nationale, lat. 1134. Troper and offertoriale, eleventh century. From St. Martial, Limoges.

Pa 1135   Paris, Bibliothèque nationale, lat. 1135. Troper and offertoriale, eleventh century. From St. Martial, Limoges.

Pa 1136   Paris, Bibliothèque nationale, lat. 1136. Troper and offertoriale, eleventh century. From St. Martial, Limoges.

Pa 1137   Paris, Bibliothèque nationale, lat. 1137. Troper and offertoriale, eleventh century. From St. Martial, Limoges.

Pa 1235   Paris, Bibliotheque nationale, n.a. lat. 1235. Gradual with tropes and proses, twelfth century. From the Cathedral of St. Cyr, Nevers.

Pia 65   Piacenza, Biblioteca e archivio capitolare di San Antonio, 65. Antiphoner, tonary, calendar, hymnal, gradual, troper-proser, early thirteenth century (c. 1200). From Piacenza.

Pst 120   Pistoia, Biblioteca Capitolare, 120. Gradual with tropes and proses, early twelfth century. Possibly from Pistoia.

Rei 264   Reims, Bibliotheque municipale, 264. Gradual with kyriale and sequences, twelfth or thirteenth century. From St. Thierry, near Reims.

RoA 123   Rome, Biblioteca Angelica, 123. Gradual, trope, and proser, early eleventh century (before 1039). From Bologna.
Le codex 123 de la Bibliothèque angelica de Rome (XIe siècle). Graduel et Tropaire de Bologne. Berne: éditions H. Lang, 1969, Paléographie Musicale 18.

RoS 22   Rome, Archivio San Pietro, F 22. Old Roman gradual, thirteenth century. From St. Peter's, Rome.

RoV 52   Rome, Biblioteca Vallicelliana, 52. Gradual with tropes and proses. Eleventh-twelfth century. From Arezzo.

SG 339   St. Gall, Stiftsbibliothek. 339. Gradual and sequentiary, early eleventh century. From St. Gall. Facsimile: *Le codex 339 de la Bibliothèque de Saint-Gall (Xe siècle): Antiphonale Missarum Sancti Gregorii.* Berne: éditions H. Lang, 1889, 1974. Paléographie Musicale 1.

Tri 2254   Trier, Stadtbibliothek, 2254 (2197). Gradual, proser, and kyriale thirteenth century. Probably from Trier.

To 18   Turin, Biblioteca nazionale, 18. Gradual, processional, and kyriale, twelfth century. From Bobbio.

Vat 5319   Vatican City, Biblioteca Apostolica Vaticana, vat. lat. 5319. Old Roman gradual, proser, and kyriale, late eleventh or early twelfth century. From Rome, possibly St. John Lateran.

APPENDIX 3

Commentary on Edition

AD TE DOMINE LEVAVI (1)

The pitch-level variants and probable nondiatonic pitches in this offertory have been demonstrated by Sidler, Pitman, Frasch, and Hankeln.[1] In many sources, the respond and first verse are written at the affinal position, ending on a. Mo 159, for example, adopts a final of a and employs several pitches that cannot be written at the lower level in its notational system. As Sidler suggested, Mo's pitches D, F, and b-flat would be Γ, low-B-flat, and E-flat at the position of the regular final, D. Mo 159 employs a b-flat at "erubescam" (phrase 2), the source of the parenthetical E-flat in the base transcription of Ben 34. Mo 159 also implies an E-flat in v. 2 at "custodi animam" (phrase 9).

These two cases of nondiatonic practice are variously treated in later MSS. The first, "erubescam," is not reflected in many later MSS. Most peripheral sources notate the respond and first verse at the normal position, with a final of D and no nondiatonic indications. The nondiatonic practice, however, is preserved in Be 40078; the respond and first verse are written at the affinal position and employ the b-flat at "erubescam."

The opening of v. 2 is a point of variance in pitch level, probably reflecting the nondiatonic practice implied in Mo 159. The base version of Ben 34 presents a plagal reading of the verse, opening with the pitches A-D, a version matched in Pa 780 and Lo 4951. In other core MSS, including Pa 776 and Pa 1121, the verse opening is written a fifth higher; the opening pitches, D-a, are characteristic of mode 1. In Mo 159, the verse is designated as authentic by the tonary letters. The two versions join at "meam" (phrase 9), immediately after the problem spot at "custodi animam."

Although both versions of the second verse are found across a broad spectrum of MSS, I consider the plagal reading of the verse the more probable unemended version, consistent with Sidler's hypothesis. The status of the authentic reading as an emendation is supported by the nondiatonic pitches that would result at the lower level of transposition and the relationship to the Roman version, which remains in the plagal range. Among later MSS, the nondiatonic practice suggested by Mo 159 is evident in Be 40078 and Gr 807, which are notated a fifth above Ben 34 and have corresponding b-flats in v. 2 at "custodi animam."[2] The practice is further implied by a unique reading found in Pad 47, described below. Some early adiastematic MSS also suggest a performance at the plagal level. Ei 121, for example, has the letters "im" at the opening of v. 2, indicating that the verse begins below the final.

Pitch level of respond and v. 1 (in MSS that unequivocally indicate pitch):

= Ben 34: Pa 1235, Gr 807, Pad 47, Pst 120, RoV 52

---

1. Sidler (1939), 11, Pitman (1973), 82, Frasch (1986), 1:161, and Hankeln (1999), 1:94.
2. The corresponding note at "erubescam" in Gr 807 is not an E but a D.

5↑ Ben 34 (= Mo 159): Be 40078

v. 2 "Respice ... meam":

= Ben 34: Pa 780, Lo 4951, Pa 1235, To 18
5↑ Ben 34 (= Mo 159): Pa 776, Pa 1121, Pa 1132, Pa 1134–37, Be 40078, Cai 61, Pst 120, Gr 807

A unique reading in v. 2 in Pad 47 supports the hypothesis that an E-flat was sung at "custodi." The verse begins with the incipit D-G, remaining a fourth above Ben 34 until "custodi." On "custodi animam" the melodic segments where the hypothetical E-flat occurs (DEF in Ben 34) are written a tone higher, EFG, suggesting that interval between the first two notes is a semitone.

The MSS otherwise show very few melodic variants.

Pad 47: v. 2 "[invocavi] TE": the end the melisma differs from that of the majority version CF GF CD CF GFC FECD FFD

Roman sources: Vat 5319 is very similar in detail to Bod 74. Aside from differences in passing tones and the oriscus, it has the following small difference: v. 1 "et": melisma starts CE.

RoS 22 (slashes indicate syllable breaks):
"Animam": DC
"eruBESCAM": FGaGaGFE/FGaGFE
"IRRIDEANT": ED/FE/ED/DEFEDEDEDC
"NON": DFEDC
"CON/FUNdentur": DFEDC/EFGFGFEFD

DEUS TU CONVERTENS (2)

This offertory presents few major variants among the core group of sources. The small variants within the core group involve the number of pitch repetitions or the pitches b and c, with a greater focus on b in the Beneventan sources. The b's in the opening, on "deus" and "vivificabis," for example, are c's in Mo 159 and the Aquitanian sources.

More significant variants include the following: v.1 plebi/plebis tuae (phrase 7).

The reading of Ben 34 (the only Beneventan version of the verse) is anomalous here, closing with a *deuterus* cadence that imitates the verbally identical phrase of *Benedixisti* (3). Mo 159 and most Aquitanian sources have a shorter melisma and a verse ending on D, distributing the four syllables of "plebi tuae" as in Mo 159: aGaGFGa G FF FFFDED.

Most Aquitanian and German sources present a reading identical or very similar to that of Mo 159, as do all early adiastematic MSS in the sampling. The Italian sources, however, match Ben 34 in the cadential pattern on "tuae." The melisma on "plebi/plebis" is a point of variance in some MSS. Although most Aquitanian sources match Mo 159, Pa 780 has a longer form of the melisma, aGaGFGaGaGF.

Among some peripheral sources, there are other points of variance in melismas, as shown in the sample readings below. Spaces between note groups indicate neume groupings, and boldface indicates specific variant points.

v. 1 "terram": Cai 61 has bcd cdcb acedc acc ca G **acba cb** bc ded ec cb (Pa 1235 is identical in the bolded segment)

To 18 has a longer melisma, differing at the opening: **b cd ede cb** ac cc edc ac cc caG abcb abc cb bcd edec

v. 2 "et": Cai 61 acccaF **acba cb** bc ded ec cb

To 18: The last part of the melisma is repeated (perhaps an error): abcb bcd edec (repeat).

v. 2 "Caelo": To 18 has a different ending: ac ca cccaG aGaG GGe Ga

Be 40078: G c ca **b**caG c Ga c ca **b**caG bbab db caaGa cc ca cc caaG aFG **bcaG aca** (similar in other German sources)

Many MSS, including Ben 34, have a prosula at the end of the second verse. In Ben 34, the repetendum cue follows the prosula.

Roman sources: This offertory is lacking in Bod 74. There are very few variants between RoS 22 and Vat 5319, mostly involving the filling in of intervals with passing tones.

BENEDIXISTI DOMINE (3)

There are few major variants within the core group of sources. Most involve passing tones and variants at the points E-F and b-c. "Peccata" in v. 1 is a good example of the latter kind of variant. Ben 34 has Gba/bGcbc. The same version is found in Pa 776, and a similar one occurs in Lo 4951 (Gba/ba cbc). Pa 1121, however, has **aca**/**ca**cbc.

The Beneventan MSS exhibit several small differences from the others:

Respond "[terram] tuAM": all sources in the core group besides Ben 34 have **D**GFE

v. 2 "domiNE": Ben 34 presents a slightly shortened melisma. Pa 776 is typical of the Aquitanian sources: cccbaccdccd**aaG**. A similar reading is found in most peripheral sources.

v. 2 "saluTARE TUUM": The Beneventan MSS transmit an independent reading of the text underlay. Most MSS have a reading closer to that of Pa 776: aG/aGF/FGacacGE/FGFGFF ori. E

Individual MSS: v. 1 "operuisti": Mo 159 adopts G rather than F as a reciting pitch at "operuisti" and notates the first three syllables a tone above all other sources examined.

Pst 120: "[salutare] tuUM": aGaGFE

Pad 47:

v. 2 "ostende nobis do [mine]": This verse opening is written at various pitch levels in relation to the majority version (slashes indicate syllable divisions): E/aa/GF/aFE/FGa/a/a.

v. 2 "domiNE": cc cb a cc db cdaG

To 18:

respond, "benedixISti": FGE GaG FGFE (shorter melisma)

v. 1 "Omnia": bd edc dcb cc ca cdc (shorter melisma)

v. 1 "PECcata": FaG

v. 1 "Iram": aGaGE GFED Ga(different melisma)

v. 2 "NO/BIS": cb aG/abc

v. 2 "domiNE": cb abc dcb

v. "noBIS": cc cG acb cdca acb cdc bca ccaG acaFGF GcccGEGG acaG

Pa 1235: v. 1 "domiNE": cb ac c dc cda aG

The German MSS give a reading very close to that of the core group, with the expected raising of b to c.

Roman sources: There are no significant variants. RoS 22 has the following variant: "BenedixISti": Fa abGffed**F**GFEFE.

CONFORTAMINI (4)

The sources exhibit small variants in recitational style, mainly involving the pitches E and F or b and c.

Pitch-level variants: Most sources are notated at the same pitch level as Ben 34 throughout. There are three exceptions, however, among the MSS in the sampling. Mo 159 notates the whole offertory at the affinal position, closing on b, probably because of the need for low B-flat and a possible E-flat. Two sources, Gr 807 and Cai 61, notate the final verse a fifth above the majority reading. The upward transposition of the final verse in Cai 61 may be attributable to the introduction of low B-flat in the final verse. Gr 807, however, employs a notational sign for B-flat in other places, so its move into the authentic range for the final verse may have been made simply for aesthetic reasons.

1. Respond, opening passage: At the affinal position, Mo 159 employs a b-flat in the opening of the respond. In a contour that is duplicated in most Aquitanian sources, it opens with the pitches G a b-flat c. As Sidler proposed, the b-flats in the reading of Mo 159, written at the affinal position, suggest the use of the nondiatonic pitch E-flat at the lower level.[1] While this reading is implied in some Aquitanian sources, such as Pa 776 and Pa 780, it is not reflected in MSS from other regions. The Beneventan sources write a normal E. Most other MSS avoid E altogether. Because of the uncertainties surrounding this pitch, I have not included it in the transcription of Ben 34.

2. v. 2 "Praestat/praestatis certamen" (phrase 10): At the affinal position, Mo 159 employs an F here, implying the presence of low B-flat in the normal range. The internal cadence on "certamen" is treated in various ways in the sources:

Mo 159:	a	GacaFGF	F F ori G
Pa 780:	D	CDFDCDB	B
Pa 1121:	D	CDFDCDB	B B (ori.) C
Pa 776:	DC (liq.)	CDFDCD	A A (ori.) B
Ben 34:	C (liq.)	CDFDCDB	AB

On the final syllable, Pa 1121 and Pa 780 present a version similar to that of Mo 159, in which the B's are presumably B-flats. The other sources write the end of the cadential figure a tone lower.

Roman sources: Vat 5319 is the only source to transmit the verses of this offertory. Bod 74 and RoS 22 notate the offertory in the untransposed range, closing on E.
Respond, "tiMERE":

RoS 22: FGaGabaGFEF/FGFE.

Respond, "NOS":

Bod 74: GFGabaGFG
RoS 22: GFGabaGFGF

---

1. Sidler (1939), 23–25.

EXSULTA SATIS (5)

In most sources, this offertory closes on E, but in a few, such as Lo 4951, the respond ends on G.[1]

The second verse is a problem spot, with an extreme diversity among MSS. The modal ambiguity and pitch-level variants of the verse are addressed in studies by Sidler, Frasch, and Hankeln.[2] The peripheral sources I have incorporated are consistent with the diversity of the Aquitanian sources, demonstrated by Frasch and Hankeln, and unfortunately shed no new light on the reasons for the variants. Hankeln views Mo 159, chosen as a base version here, as representing the *Aufführungslage* and plausibly attributes the variants to a lack of modal clarity in the verse.[3] Because indications of b-flat are lacking in most Aquitanian MSS and in Beneventan MSS, it is not always possible to determine whether the various versions differ in intervallic structure.

The single Beneventan version, Ben 34, presents a reading not matched in any other source, with *tritus* characteristics (the other Beneventan MSS are incomplete, lacking this offertory). This version is probably best viewed simply as a different interpretation of the verse's modal properties.

v 2. "Quia ecce venio . . . omnipotens": Sidler considers Mo 159 the *lectio difficilior* in this passage and thus the more probable reading.[4] The interval of transposition between MSS changes several times, with the sources finally joining (temporarily) at "omnipotens."[5] The following summary disregards differences of less than three or four notes. With these small melodic variants in mind, a reading essentially matching that of Mo 159 is found in the geographically diverse sources Pa 776, Pa 1121, To 18, and Be 40078. Other sources may be summarized as follows.

a. "Quia ecce . . . medio tui": The following sources begin 2↑ Mo 159 and join at "venio": Pa 903, Pst 120, Pad 47 (a variant reading of "ecce": d cdedc cb ab/ba); Gr 807 (melodically variant at "habitabo"). There are no intervallic differences that would have prompted the transposition.

Pa 780 is 2↑ Mo 159 for most of the passage. Pa 1132 begins as Mo 159 but is 2↑ Mo 159 beginning at "venio." Lo 4951 has a variant opening and is alternately 2↑ or 3↑ beginning on the second syllable of "venio." Ben 34 begins 2↓ Mo 159 and joins at "venio. . . . in medio" (with a variant reading of "venio"). Pa 1235 begins 2↑ Mo 159 and is alternately 2↑ or 3↑ beginning at "venio."

b. "dicit dominus" ("dicit" is a point of melodic variance):

    = Mo 159: Pa 1132, Pa 776, Be 40078, Pa 1235, To 18
    2↓Mo 159: Gr 807
    2↑Mo 159: Ben 34, Pa 1132 (beginning at "dominus."); Pst 120 (at "dominus")

c. "omnipotens": all sources briefly join Mo 159.

2. "et confugient":

    = Mo 159 (with melodic variants): Pa 1235, Be 40078, Pad 47, Pst 120
    2↓ Mo 159: (with variants) Ben 34, Lo 4951

---

1. See Bomm (1929), 162–64; Frasch (1986), 1:207–8.
2. Sidler (1939), 28–31; Frasch (1986), 1: 207–8; 2:293–303; Hankeln (1999), 1:95–96; 2:135.
3. Hankeln (1999), 1:95–96.
4. Sidler (1939), 29.
5. Frasch (1986), 1:173–76.

3. "ad te in illa die":

    = Mo 159: Pa 776, 780, 903, Lo 4951, Pad 47, Pst 120

    2↓ Mo 159: Gr 807, Be 40078

    2↑ Mo 159: Ben 34

    3↓ Mo 159 at "ad te in illa": Pa 1121, 1132. The passage articulates the major third F-a rather than the minor third a-c.

    Pa 1235: starts at Mo 159 level, 2↓ at "illa."

    To 18: starts at Mo 159 level, variant reading at "die": aGFE FaG/G.

6. "omnes gentes":

    = Mo 159: all except Ben 34, which is 2↓.

    To 18 lacks the melisma on "plebe."

    Roman MSS: RoS 22 has a slightly varied melisma on "syon": GaG cdcdc bc abaGF GabaGaG.

TOLLITE PORTAS (6)

In terms of pitch level, *Tollite portas* has three variant points: the respond, specifically its ending, the beginning of the second verse, and the final melisma of the second verse. The Beneventan version provided in the transcriptions is an unproblematic second-mode melody with a final verse in the authentic range. A second version of *Tollite* is written at the affinal position, remaining a fifth above the Beneventan version until the end of the closing melisma on "gloriae," which suddenly shifts downward by a tone to articulate the third G-b-flat. This G-*protus* version is found in several key core sources, including Mo 159, Pa 776, and Pa 1121, as well as Be 40078 and Cai 61. The two different endings are shown in example 6.1.

Although this version is not reproduced in its entirety here, it may be studied in Hansen's transcription of Mo 159, as well as in Hankeln's edition (in the version of Pa 776).[1]

The D-*protus* version of Ben 34 has been chosen for the base transcription because it is the more common reading among the sources examined and thus representative of a wider general practice. The version closing on G, however, clearly represents an authentic early tradition. Its authority is attested by its presence in early sources and later appearances in Cai 61 and Be 40078. Bomm viewed the G-*protus* version as the "Originalfassung" and the D-protus version as an emendation.[2] Concurring with Bomm, Sidler noted that the b-flats at the close of the respond would be E-flats if the piece were written a fifth lower.[3] The sudden change in modal character at the close of the G-*protus* version is unusual, to say the least, and establishes the G-version as the *lectio difficilior*. With two exceptions (Pa 1135 and Pa 1235, discussed in the notes below), the D-*protus* versions present a nearly identical reading of the final melisma, which, coupled with its status as the majority reading, suggests that this version is an authentic alternative reading. The Roman version closes on D and has a

---

1. Hansen (1974), 420–21; Hankeln (1999), 3:18.
2. Bomm (1929), 175.
3. Sidler (1939), 45–46.

EXAMPLE AP 3 6.1

EXAMPLE AP 3 6.2

pitch-level profile similar to that of Ben 34. While the scribe of the tonary of Frutolf of Michelsberg opts for the D ending, his notation of the melisma indicates his awareness of it as a problem spot.

The differences at the close of the respond have implications for the pitch level of both verses. The versions that close on D are consistent in pitch level: the respond and first verse have typical second-mode characteristics, with internal cadences on the final and D and F as the most prominent pitches. The final verse is in the authentic range, focused on a. All sources with a G final notate the respond and the first verse a fifth above the level of the Beneventan version. In the majority of these sources, the second verse begins a fourth above the level of the Beneventan version, as shown in example 6.2. Here the verse is a *tetrardus* authentic melody focused on D, consistent with the G ending of the respond. Cai 61 presents a unique pitch-level profile. The respond, notated at the level of Mo 159, closes on G, whereas the two verses are in the same range as Ben 34. The repetendum is notated a fifth too low, implying a pitch-level profile identical to that of Ben 34, with the low C-*protus* ending.

Further variants in pitch level occur at the close of the second verse, as shown in example 6.3.

In most sources that notate the verse in the *tetrardus* authentic range, such as Mo 159, the interval of transposition relative to Ben 34 changes to a fifth at the end of the melisma. Sidler proposed that this apparent whole-tone transposition indicates a use of nondiatonic pitches and thus argued for a "retransposition" of this segment (cdedeede, etc.) down a whole tone to derive a b-natural, which would be F-sharp at the level of Ben 34.[4] Hankeln

4. Ibid.

EXAMPLE AP 3 6.3

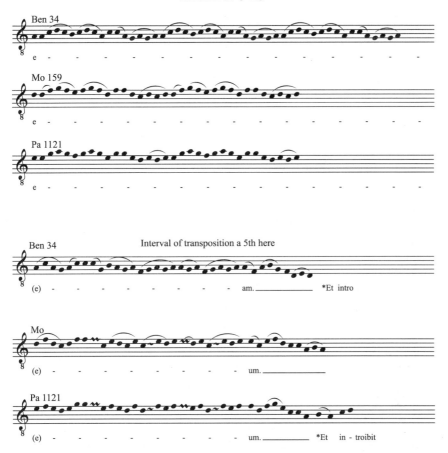

has more plausibly attributed this transposition to the modal ambiguity of the melody as whole, and posited the written level of 776 and Mo 159 as the *Aufführungslage*.[5] The downward transposition of this reading facilitates the transition to the repetendum, with the *protus* characteristics of its internal phrases. Pa 1121, line 3 in example 6.3, remains a fifth above the reading of Ben 34, consistent with its notation of the whole verse at this level.

A summary follows of pitch-level profile of the MSS relative to Ben 34. For the Aquitanian sources, I have read the base pitch level according to the "gloriae" melisma of the respond: those with the downward shift at the end of the melisma, matching the version of Mo 159, are interpreted as ending on G (rather than C, which is not a legitimate final), whereas those with a D-ending are interpreted as being in the normal (rather than transposed) plagal range, like Ben 34. In summarizing the pitch-level

---

5. Hankeln (1999), 1:100.

profile as a whole for the Aquitanian sources, I have followed Hankeln's methodology, using
the repetendum as a guide to reading the relative pitch level between the sections of an
offertory. In most Aquitanian sources, the placement of the repetendum suggests that the
intended pitch-level profile of the respond and two verses is that of Ben 34, since the
repetendum appears at the correct pitch level only if the pitch-level profile of Ben 34 is
assumed.[6]

1. Respond to "gloriae" melisma, and verse 1:

= Ben 34: [Lo 4951 Pa 780 Pa 1132] Gr 807, Pst 120, Pad 47, RoV 52, Mü 10086
5↑ Ben 34: Mo 159, Pa 776, Pa 1121, Cai 61, Be 40078, Pia 65, To 18

2. End of "gloriae" melisma:

= Ben 34, ending on D: 4951, Pa 780, Pa 1132, Gr 807, Pst 120, Pad 47, RoV 52, Mad
20–4, Bc 10086
4↑ Ben 34, ending on G: Mo 159, Pa 776, Pa 1121, Cai 61, Be 40078, Pia 65
5↑ Ben 34, ending on a: To 18

3. Verse 2 to the end of "eum" melisma:

= Ben 34: 4951, Pa 780, Pa 1132, Gr 807, Cai 61, Pst 120, Pad 47, RoV 52, Mad 20–4,
Mü 10086, To 18.
4↑ Ben 34: Mo 159, Pa 776, Be 40078, Pia 65
5↑ Ben 34: Pa 1121

4. End of "eum" melisma:

= Ben 34: Pa 780, Pa 903, Lo 4951, RoV 52, Pad 47, Mü 10086, To 18
5↑ Ben 34: Mo 159, Pa 776, Pa 1135, Be 40078, Pia 65
2↑ Ben 34: Pa 1121, 1132,[7] Pst 120, Cai 61

Beneventan distinctiveness in v. 2 at the "eum" melisma: Ben 34, the only Beneventan
version of this offertory with the verse, has a form of the melisma that is unique among the
sources examined, with an extra repetition of the opening material.

Individual MSS: Paris 1235 presents an unusual reading of the problematic end of the
melisma, where the change in transpositional level occurs. Where Ben 34 begins with
FGaGa, Pa 1235 has aFGaGaaGaGaGa.

The "gloriae" melisma" of respond: Pa 1135 presents a unique reading of the
final melisma, FFFDFGFFFDGFDDCFEECD. Although it appears to end on D, it
shares the change of reciting pitch with the G-protus sources. Pa 1235 has a shortened
form of the melisma, in which the problematic ending is simply eliminated:
FFFDFGFFFFDGFFD.

Roman MSS: The verses of this offertory are transmitted only Vat 5319. In the respond,
the three sources exhibit no significant variants.

---

6. See the summary in Hankeln (1999), 2:213.
7. Hankeln transcribes the end of the melisma at the level of Mo 159 and 776, but it seems to be
   written a tone higher, consistent with the repetendum on E. See Hankeln (1999), 3:72.

LAETENTUR CAELI (7)

Aside from variants around the pitches E and F, this piece shows very few differences between MSS on the Gregorian side. Small differences are found in the following MSS from the peripheral group.

Be 40078: respond, "terRA": DGFE FGEFD (same in verse endings, terRA in v. 1, eIUS in v. 2).

Pad 47:

> respond, "DO/MI/NI": FGaG/GF/FGaG
> v. 1 "cantiCUM": GEG
> v. 2 "[nomen] Eius": GaGFG
> v. 2 "benenunCIate": EGaG

RoV 52:

> respond "TERra": EaGaF GaG (ori.) (same in v. 1, TERra and v. 2 Eius)
> respond, "quoniam": bottom note is E rather than D
> v. 1 "benenunciA/TE": acG.acG

Roman MSS: Vat 5319 and Bodmer 74 show more variants than usual.

Vat 5319:

> respond "VEnit": FaGaGF aG GF Ga(ori.)GFGF
> v. 1 "domiNO" (first time): EFGaFE aGabaG
> v. 1 "noVUM": EG
> v. 1 "CAN/TA/TE" (second time): FEF/EDFED/EFD
> v. 2 "domiNO": EFGaFE aGabaG (as in v. 1)
> v. 2 "ET/BE/BE/DI/CI/TE": Gc dc cb/a/G/F/F/F F(ori.)EDC FGaGabaG

RoS 22:

> "exULtet": EFG
> "veNIT": EFGF aGFEFE

DEUS ENIM FIRMAVIT (8)

The MSS are inconsistent in their use of b-flat. In the respond, Mo 159 indicates flats at several points where they are not indicated in many other MSS: "firMAvit," "DEus" (phrase 2), "tunc," and in the final cadence. Only the b-flat on "firmavit" is witnessed in another MS, Pa 903 (through the use of the quilisma). The reading of Mo 159 thus has a G-*protus* quality throughout the respond. In the base transcription of Ben 34, I have given parenthetical b-flats only where they are found more widely.

There are a few significant variants between MSS of the core group. The opening passage, for example, is a point of variance among core MSS:

	De-us
Ben 34:	G FGF
Mo:	a aG
Pa 776:	G GF

Pa 1121 and Lo 4951 match Pa 776, whereas Pa 780 matches Mo 159. Ben 34's reading is a common one in the peripheral group, found in MSS such as RoV 52 and Be 40078.

v. 1 "DOminus"(verse opening): Lo 4951 has a shorted melisma: DFFG GF GF F(ori.)D GccaFG Gcca cd cd ccaFGa c c(ori.).

v. 1 "decorEM [induit]": Pa 1121 has a shorter version of the melisma, but gives more notes to the first syllable of "induit."

de-co-	rem	in	[duit]
Pa 1121:	acb caG ba bGF	acca cdcG cdc c(ori.)a	

v. 2 "domui tuae": Most Gregorian MSS (with the exception of Pa 776) have "do-mum tuam." Mo 159 and Pa 1121 have a different melodic reading on "doMUM," as in Mo 159: cdcc GaG. The version of Ben 34, however, is matched in the early adiastematic MSS Cha 47, La 239, and Ei 121, as well as in most Aquitanian sources. Outside the core group, he version of Mo 159 is found only in Pa 1235 and Cai 61.

v. 2 "diErum": The sources differ in the ways they close this melisma. Ben 34 (the only Beneventan MS to transmit this verse) gives a slightly shortened version of the melisma, with one fewer repetition of the figuration between D, G, a, and c. The same shortening is found in Lo 4951. Pa 776 gives a more typical reading (the boldface segment is missing in Ben 34): GE GabcccabaGb cccabaG aGFaaG ccG baGGE-GaG FGaccaG G(ori.)DEFFFD GaccaG DGaccaFG DGaccaccaGb **DGaccaccaGb** ab b (ori.)ab.

The longer version of the melisma is found in most core MSS, including Mo, Pa 1121, and Pa 780, and in most sources in the peripheral group.

The sources also differ in their adoption of E, D, or F as the bottom note of the melisma. In contrast to Ben 34, Mo 159 adopts D rather than E as the bottom note in the first part of the melisma, whereas Pa 1121 adopts F as the bottom note in the second half of the melisma.

Peripheral MSS:
Pst 120:

opening, "DE/US E/NIM": a/GaG/F/G

v. 2 "diErum" has a longer version of the melisma:

GD Gac cc ca baGccccabaG aGF aa ac ca baG GDG a aG DGaccaG GDF F FD GaccaG DGac ca ccaFG DGac ca ccaGa EGac ca ccaG cac c cac

RoV 52: v. 2 "DOmine" (phrase 11): melisma begins DG acGaGF.

Be 40078: v. 1 "DOminus" (verse opening): DEF G(ori.)F GEFDG G bcaFG Gc ca cdcG cdc dbcaF (etc.).

Roman MSS: In the verses there are several significant variants between Vat 5319 and Bod 74.

Vat 5319:

v. 1 "DOminus" (verse opening): Vat 5319 has a much longer melisma than Bod 74, with an internal repetition: c c(ori.)babaGFGaG Gac **cbaGGFGaGGacb**

v. 1 "domiNUS" (verse opening): acbaG (the more common cadential pattern)

v. 1 "[induit] doMInus": dcbc(ori.)ba

v. 1 "FORtitudinem": abaG Gc

v. 2 "testimonia tua": Vat 5319 has just "testimoniam"

"testimoNI/AM": c c(ori.)ba/aGa c c(ori.)ba aGa

RoS 22:

> "Enim": bcba
> "terRE": GcbabaG cabaGF GabaGaba
> "SE/DES": a different text underlay is suggested by the neume groupings:
> abaGcdc/cb

TUI SUNT CAELI (9)

The pitch-level variants in *Tui sunt caeli* have been discussed by Hankeln, Frasch, and Sidler. The base version of Ben 34 represents both the majority version and Hankeln's *Aufführungslage*. Several Aquitanian MSS in the sampling, however, do exhibit variants in pitch level. In Pa 776, Pa 780, and Pa 1121, some or all of the verses are written a fifth below their level in Ben 34, but, as Hankeln argued, the repetendum, written a fifth too low, suggests a performance level of Ben 34.[1] Outside of the Aquitanian tradition, these pitch-level variants are not found in the sampling incorporated into this study.

Melodic variants: There are very few major variants among core MSS.

Peripheral MSS have the following variants.

Cai 61:

> v. 1 "metuenDUS": Gca baG aG
> v. 1 "TUam": CF FD CD DFF DCD F FD FGFGG GFE

Pa 1235:

> Respond, "Eius": FF FEFED
> Respond, "pre/pa/ra/ti/o": E/EF/Ga/G/Gab-flatGF FEDED
> v. 1 "metuenDUS": aca baG aG
> v. 2 "faciEM": DCDF FDCD
> v. 2 "PLAcito": GaGa
> v. 2 "CORnu": melisma begins FFF FEGE aGF ba GaGE
> v. 3 "SIcut": DF FGF FED (liq.)
> v. 3 "DEXtera": melisma begins Ga cbc

Pad 47:

> respond "Eius": FF FD FF GE FF FE
> v. 1 "[circuitu] Eius": GaGFE FGaGFE FGaGFE
> v. 2 "CORnu": DF FF DGE FG aba GaGF acccaF **GaFE FGEC** (etc.)

Pst 120:

> respond "TERra": GFEaGF
> v. 1 "metuenDUS": acabaGaG
> v. 1 "[circuitu] Eius": GbaG FaGFE FaGF
> v. 2 "CORnu": DF FF FD GE FG aba GaGF accaF **GaGE** FG FGFDC (etc.)

---

1. See Hankeln (1999) 1:101–2; 2:137; 3:20–21; and Hankeln (1995), 539–60.

Be 40078:

Respond "IUstiticia": DaG
v. 2 "DEXtera": DF cbc c ca bcaG acGE G G bcaG acG etc.
Roman MSS: Bod 74 lacks the third verse. There are no significant melodic variants
     between Bod 74 and Vat 5319.

RoS 22:

"ceLI": EDEFGFEF
"TERrarum": FGaGbaGFGF
"iuSTI": aGaFGaGFGaGF(liq.)
"preparatiO": GaGFEDFE

REGES THARSIS (10)

Reges tharsis exhibits pitch-level variants that were discussed long ago by Sidler.[1] Pa 776 is
employed as the base reading because its scribe notates the problematic passages in their
probable unemended range. This MS, however, is somewhat anomalous in lacking a
repetendum cue after the first verse and giving a varied, written-out repetendum at the
end of the second verse. In many MSS, a repetendum to "omnes gentes" is indicated after
the first and final verses. The scribe of Pa 776 does not maintain a consistent horizontal
reference point between the first and second verses, but the custos at the end of the second
verse and the written-out repetendum at the end of the third verse confirm that the
intended pitch level is that of Mo 159 and the other MSS.

Pa 776 has one small difference from other MSS that is probably a scribal error. In
phrase 6, at "filio regis," Pa 776 has the notes gfff on the last two syllables of "filio," with an
unclear text underlay. I have emended it to the more common reading gf/f, eliminating the
extra f.

v. 1 "et iusticiam"—end of verse: At "iusticiam" (phrase 6), Pa 776 expands into the
upper part of the range and remains there through the end of the verse. This reading is
matched in two other key core MSS, Mo 159 and Pa 1121, and in Be 40078. In the majority
of MSS, however, this passage is written a fourth below Pa 776 beginning at "iusticiam,"
with a focal pitch of c. In Mo 159, moreover, the written-out repetendum to "omnes gentes"
is also written a fourth higher than its pitch level in other MSS. While this cue might imply
that the performance level was a fourth below the written level, Mo 159 consistently
employs b-flat here, resulting in an intervallic structure identical to that of the majority
version a fourth lower.

Perhaps the most likely reason for the transposition is the need for a nondiatonic pitch,
eb, on the word "iusticiam," which is indicated with a parenthetical e-flat in the base
transcription. The melodic gesture on "iusticiam," an upward leap of a fifth followed by a
half step, is a common one in the chant repertory, especially in first-mode melodies.
Typically, the leap is placed a fourth lower than it is here, from D to a, with a b-flat. To
replicate this intervallic structure at the level of Pa 776, an e-flat is required. Pa 1235, written
a fourth lower, does indicate a b-flat here. Mo 159, however, writes this segment in the
higher register and indicates an e-natural. While the reading of Mo 159 might cast doubt on

1. Sidler (1929), 60–65.

the nondiatonic practice here, I am inclined to view Mo's reading as a simple ad hoc solution to the problem. When the same melodic gesture is written at the lower level in Mo 159, it consistently employs the expected b-flat. (There are too many instances to list, but see the opening of the second verse of *Dextera domini* [13].) It seems improbable that the same gesture would be sung differently at the higher level of transposition, except as an emendation. In Be 40078, the e is raised to f, reflecting the German chant dialect.

The early adiastematic MSS reinforce the impression that the higher version of the melody found in Pa 776 is the preferred reading. In the MSS written at the lower level, the downward transposition begins on the word "et," which starts on either C or D. The scribe of Ei 121, however, writes tractuli on the final note of "da" and on "et" (phrases 5 and 6) with an "e" ("equaliter") between them, indicating that "et" should start on F, the final note of "da." This version is consistent with Pa 776 and the other higher readings, but not the lower versions.

Two of the German MSS in the sampling, Gr 807 and Be 10086, exemplify a phenomenon I have observed in other offertories. These MSS represent a tradition in which a nondiatonic practice was probably suppressed, but the problematic segment of the melody is nevertheless written in the "emended" range, perhaps out of custom. In both MSS, the note corresponding to the b-flat in Pa 1235 (and the e [flat] in Pa 776) is c, reflecting the German chant dialect. With this melodic change, the e-flat at the higher level would no longer be needed, because the corresponding note at the higher level would be f (as it is in Be 40078).

Although Lo 4951 is written a fourth lower, its melodic reading differs here. "Et iusticiam" reads F/F/aGab(quil.)ca, probably a scribal emendation that facilitates the transition to the lower level.

Pitch level at "iusticiam": =Pa 776: Mo 159, Pa 780 (joins the lower level at "filio"), Pa 1121, Pa 1132, Be 40078. A fourth lower: Lo 4951, Ben 34, Ben 35, Pa 1235, Cai 61, Gr 807, Mü 10086, RoV 52, Pad 47, Mod 7, Pst 120.

v. 3 "[suscipiant]MONtes" (phrase 9): This melisma varies at the point where Pa 776 recites on b (flat). The following sample readings begin with the first descent to D:

Pa 776:	D FG FFFFD	F babbbGbdc cccacdd (ori.) cdcd
Pa 1121:	D FGF FFF (ori).	D aba aa a(ori.)F bab bbb(ori.)G bccbcbc
Pa 780:	D FGF FFFD	F aG aa a(ori.)F a cb cc c(ori.)a cd d(ori.) c dcd
Lo 4951:	D FFGFFFFD	ac ccca acddcdcd (liq.)
Mo 159 (b's are flat):	D FGF FFFD	Gcb bbbG bdc ccca cddc dcd
Cai 61:	D FGF FF FD	FaG G GEF a aG a(liq.)
RoV 52:	D FGF FF FD	FaG GGGE Gcb c ca cd dcdcdc(liq.)
Pa 1235:	D FGF FF FD	FaG cc ca cc cac
Gr 807:	D FGF FFFD	cdc ccca cddc dcdc

The reciting pitch in the last part of the melisma is alternately c, b (flat), a, or even, in one case, G. Although there are intervallic differences between the versions, it is not possible to reconstruct an unemended reading. The variants may reflect a point of melodic instability rather than a non-diatonic practice.

v. 3 "Orietur...eius" (phrase 11): In Mo 159, this opening portion of the verse is written a fourth above its position in Pa 776. Mo 159 employs a b-natural on "eius," equivalent to f-sharp at the level of Pa 776. The same upward transposition is found in other core MSS, including Ben 34, and in the peripheral MS Pad 47. That "eius" is the source of the transposition is suggested by the variant treatment of the verse opening, especially on "eius," and the rejoining of most sources (in pitch level) beginning at "iusticia" (phrase 12). In some MSS, for example, the verse begins at the level of Pa 776 but is briefly written a fourth higher on "eius." This solution is found in Lo 4951, the south German MS Mü 10086, and, with a somewhat different melodic reading, Pst 120.

Although the great majority of MSS join the level of Pa 776 at "iusticia," two MSS included in the sampling, Pa 1235 and RoV 52, present reworked versions of the verse. Pa 1235 has a substantially different melody on "eius" and, beginning at "iusticia," is a fifth below Pa 776, joining at "et dominabitur." There are no intervallic differences that would suggest the use of a nondiatonic pitch. RoV 52 is a fifth below Pa 776 at "iusticia," and in the following passage presents a different version of the melody that is alternately a third and a fourth below Pa 776, joining at "luna."

Sample readings of "eius":

Pa 776:	GEF(-sharp)GaGabGGa	aGGEDDCD
Mo (b's are natural)	c ab cdcdeccd	bccaGGFG
Lo 4951:	cacd cdeccd	dcdccaGGF
Pa 1235:	GFFGFGaFFG	GFGF
RoV 52:	FDEFGFGaFFG	GFDCD
Pst 120:	cGabccdeccd	dcbaGa

Roman MSS:
Vat 5319:

v. 1 "iustiTIa": dedc
v. 2 "PAcem": dec
v. 2 verse ending, "iudiciO": a longer melisma matching that of v. 1: FGaG c c c(ori.)
   baGFGaG **c c c(ori.) baGcd**

RoS 22 has no significant variants.

IUBILATE DEO OMNIS (11)

The Roman version has a longer text than the Gregorian does, lacking the text repetition in the respond. To facilitate comparison with the Gregorian version, I have adopted the phrase numbering of the Roman version.

This piece has a complex transmission. It is unlikely that any the MSS in the sampling notates the entire offertory at an unemended pitch level. Pitch-level variants are found in both verses.

EXAMPLE AP 3 11.1

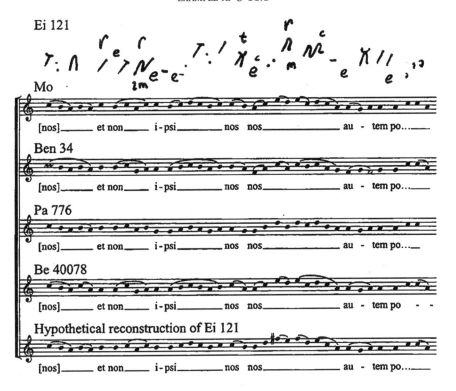

The first variant point occurs in v. 1, phrase 5, at "non ipsi nos":

	non	ip- si	nos	nos
Pa 776:[1]	bcab	G GabaGa	aG	Gbdbdcdba
Ben 34:	bcGa	a abcbab	ba	FacacbcaG
Mo 159:	bcac	c bcdcbc	cb	acedecdca
Pa 1121:	bcac	c bcdcbc	cb	cdfdfefed
Lo 4951:	acGa	F FGaGFG	GF	FacbcaG
Pa 1235:	GaGFG	G Gacab	aG	Gacbdcdcdca
Cai 61:	bcab	b bcdcd	cb	acedecdca
Gr 807:	acGa	a accbab	ca	cdfdfefdc
Mü 10086:	bcac	c accbab	cb	cdfdfefdc
Be 40078:	acGa	a abcbab	ca	aceecdca
Frutolf tonary:	acGa		[c]a	acedecdca
Mod 7:	ccac	c acdcbc	cb	cdedecdcb

---

1. In Pa 776, this passage marks a change in the value of the dry point line, indicated with an "equaliter" sign, probably because of lack of writing space. While the "e" does not function as it normally does here, the pitch level of the following passage (the second "nos") suggests a reading of this cadence on G, the solution adopted by Hankeln and Frasch. See Hankeln (1999), 3:23; and Frasch (1986), 2:338.

| Pad 47: | ccac | c acdcbc | cb | bcedecdcb |
| Pst 120 | abGa | a abcbab | ba | acdcdcdca |

Nearly all MSS join at "autem" or "populus" and remain at the same level throughout the verse. There are intervallic differences between the various versions at the cadential pattern on "ipsi nos" and the following passage on "nos." On "ipsi nos," Mo 159's cadence on b-natural, matched in several disparate MSS, revolves around the notes b-natural, c, and d, a semitone followed by a whole tone. The versions a tone lower, presumably sing with a b-natural, have a tone followed by a semitone, a-b-natural-c. The distinctive F-cadence in Lo 4951 has two whole tones, F-G-a. Intervallic differences are even more prominent at the second "nos," where there are melodic variants as well as pitch-level differences.

While I will not attempt to propose a single "original" version of this passage, the bewildering variety among the MSS suggests the presence of a nondiatonic pitch. In this rare case, an early adiastematic MS, Ei 121, offers enough information to help in a (very) hypothetical reconstruction. A few contrasting versions of the passage are presented in example 11.1. I have included the last few notes of the melisma on "nos" that precedes the problem spot. Since this melisma is uniform in the pitched sources, it is reasonable to suppose that the melisma ended on a in Ei 121. In Ei 121, the melisma is followed by a virga and the letter "s," indicating a higher pitch on "et," most likely b or c, followed by an "equaliter" sign indicating that "non" starts on the same pitch as "et." "Ipsi," in turn, begins on the same pitch as the closing note of "non." There is an "e" between the two "nos's," indicating that the second one starts on the closing pitch of the first one.

Each of the pitched readings in the sampling is contradicted by an indication in Ei 121 at some point. The most likely reading, as I have proposed with the solution in line 5 of example 11.1, is a version that is at the level of Mo 159 until the second "nos," where, according to the "equaliter" sign (matched in only one pitched MS, Pad 47) it is a tone higher. This reading would produce the nondiatonic pitch f-sharp. The variety of readings in the second "nos," summarized above, supports the hypothesis that the second "nos" is the source of the problem. With the exception of Ben 34, the core MSS begin the second "nos" with the equivalent of a minor triad, placed in portions of the scale where one is possible: a-c-e, G-b (flat?) d. If this minor third is a preferred reading, however, the Beneventan versions appear as reworkings of the passage, and Lo 4951 presents a similar reading. Because of the hypothetical status of this reconstruction, I have not incorporated it into the base transcription.

Verse 2: Although I have not been able to establish a definitive unemended reading of this verse, I can offer some hypotheses, building on previous work of Sidler, Pitman and Hankeln.[2] There are three variant points: the beginning of the verse, "et usque (phrase 10), . . ." and "veritas" (phrase 10). The pitch level in the three variant points is summarized below, followed by a discussion of each passage.

1. "Laudate nomen eius . . . misericordia eius" (phrases 7, 8 and 9):

   = Pa 776: Ben 34, Ben 35, Pa 780, Lo 4951 (?),[3] Pa 1235, Pad 47, Pst, 120
   4↑ Pa 776: Mo (third? at "dominus"), Cai 61
   5↓ Pa 776: Be 40078

2. Sidler (1939), 68–70; Pitman (1973), 264–69; Hankeln (1999), 1:102–3.
3. The pitch level of Lo 4951 is not clear because the verse starts on a new line without a custos. The verse proceeds in a way that suggests a beginning at the level of Pa 776.

Within this passage, "dominus" is a point of variance. The interval of transposition between Mo 159 and the other MSS changes to a third here, whereas Cai 61 remains mostly a fourth above the other MSS:

Mo (with b-flats):	cdegffec	/dcc(ori.)bc	/cb
Cai 61:	cdegegfe	/feecd	/dc
Pa 776:	Gacdbdcb	/cbbGa	/aG

Pa 1121, Pa 780, Ben 34 are the same in pitch level as Pa 776. The majority of peripheral MSS match Pa 776, with the exception of Pa 1235, which cadences on a.

2. "et usque in saeculum saeculi" (phrase 10):

=Pa 776: Pa 780, Pa 1121

Pa 1235 = Pa 776 at "et usque" then is a fourth higher (joining Mo 159) at "saeculi."

Pst 120 =Pa 776; interval of transposition changes to 2↑ at "saeculum saeculi."

4↑ Pa 776: Mo 159, Lo, 4951,Ben 34, Ben 35, Cai 61
5↓ Pa 776: Be 40078 (2↓ at "[sae]culum saeculi)

3. "veritas," final melisma (phrase 10):
=Pa 776: Pa 780, Pa 1121
3↑ Pa 776: all others

Passage 1: Mo 159 begins the verse a fourth higher than most other MSS do, with a referential pitch of f rather than c. Sidler argued long ago that Mo 159's reading was a transposition made to represent the pitch F-sharp on [suavis] "est" where Mo 159's b-natural corresponds to F-sharp a fourth lower. These intervallic differences suggest that level of Pa 776 is the preferred reading.

Passage 2: In the higher version of Mo 159, b-natural's occur on the second syllable of "saeculum" and again at the cadence on "seculi." Although most non-Aquitanian MSS are a fourth above Pa 776 by this point, two Aquitanian MSS in the core group are at the level of Pa 776, requiring an F-sharp to duplicate the intervallic structure of Mo 159.[4] The cadential figure on "saeculi," which revolves around c, b, and a, is equivalent to G, F-sharp, and E at this lower level. Two MSS included in the sampling, Pa 1235 and Pst 120, begin this passage ("et usque") at the level of Pa 776, moving to the higher register of Mo 159 at "saeculi."

In previous editions of this piece, the passage is treated in various ways. Pitman presents a consensus Aquitanian reading that matches the pitch level of Pa 776. Hankeln, however, notes that the repetendum cue is notated a third too high in some MSS, including Pa 776. He thus proposes a discrepancy between the written and notated levels at the end of the verse. Beginning with "in saeculum," he posits an *Aufführungslage* that is either at the level of Mo 159 or a tone lower, joining Mo 159 at "veritas." As Hankeln's two alternative suggestions imply, no solution to this problem is fully satisfactory. While each of Hankeln's hypotheses is plausible, I have opted for an unemended reading that is at the level of Pa 776

4. See Sidler (1939), 69.

through variant point 2. Several factors suggest that the version of Pa 776 is the preferred reading of this passage, including the nondiatonic pitches implied by the variants, the choice of the same pitch level in unrelated MSS such as Pa 1235 and Pst 120, and the variety of the other versions. On the second syllable of "saeculum," for example, where Mo 159 employs a b-natural that suggests an F-sharp at the level of Pa 776, Pst 120 suddenly shifts down a whole tone. The last two syllables of "saeculum" are FE/FFF DED, a tone below Pa 776, allowing the irregular semitone G/F-sharp to be represented with F/E. This reading of "saeculum" is matched in Be 40078, which has been a fifth below Pa 776 until "saeculum," where it is a whole tone lower. At the next problem spot, on "saeculi," Pst 120 and Pa 1235 join the level of Mo 159, a fourth higher, with brief transitional sections, and Be 40078 remains a whole tone below Pa 776:

		sae-	cu-	li
Pa 776:		EEDEGGG/EF(#)GFEF/F(#)E		
Mo (b's are natural):		a aGa ccc/ abcbab		ba
Pa 1235:		GGAGccc/abcbab		ba
Pst 120:		FGaaGaccc/abcbaGa		aG
Be 40078:		DDCDFFF/DEFEDE		FD

This variety implies the presence of a nondiatonic pitch at this point, most likely at the level of Pa 776 and the other Aquitanian MSS.

Passage 3: At final melisma on "veritas," the great majority of MSS are at the level of Mo 159, a fifth above Pa 776, but the three Aquitanian MSS write the passage a third lower, with some melodic variants. The preferred reading is not clear. I have given both the notated level of Pa 776 and the hypothetical performance level suggested by Hankeln, a third higher. Hankeln's suggestion is consistent with the repetendum cue and is the most probable solution. It is not clear, however, why this passage appears a third too low in a majority of Aquitanian MSS.

Other melodic variants: respond, first "TERra": Some MSS in the core group have a few extra notes:

Pa 776:	Fac edc ac bbG	babc GFGF
Lo 4951:	Fac edc ac bbG bbbG	babc GFGF
Ben 34:	Fac edc acbbG bb bG	babc GFGF

v. 1 "iPSE": Beneventan MSS present a distinctive and shorter reading of this melisma, as in Ben 34: cb decb dec c ca cc d dc dcd

Roman MSS: Vat 5319:

respond, "DOminus": cccdedcb
v. 1 "[fecit] NOS": cdcc(ori.)baGcd
v. 1 "[pascue] Eius": GcaGaGaF(liq.)/GaGF (mostly written a tone below Bod 74).

IUBILATE DEO UNIVERSA (12)

The sources show some variants in the longer melismas, particularly among MSS outside the core group.

1. v. 1 final syllable of "dixerunt": At the beginning of the melisma, some of the sources outside the core group differ in their use of the pitches a and c:

> Ben 34: GFaaGccaccacGF (etc.)
>
> Be 40078: GFaaGaaGccacGF (etc.)
>
> Pst 120: aGaaGaaGccabGF (etc.)
>
> Pad 47: baccaccaccacGF (etc.)

These differences are replicated when the melisma returns in v. 2, on the final syllable of "medullata."

2. End of v. 1 "labia" melisma: Three of the Italian sources in the sampling, Pad 47, Pst 120, and Mod 7, exhibit significant variants from the majority version in the first part of the melisma. Pst 120 transposes a segment of the melisma up a whole tone. Because this version is identical to the majority in intervallic structure, the reasons for the transpositions are unclear. A similar transposition, however, is found in Pa 1235; Justmann's transcriptions show a partially similar reading in Brussels 3823.[1]

> Pad 47:   ac cF abGF aG cba Gcba Gcbc ab-flatcbab GaGF (etc.)
>
> Pst 120:   ac cG abGF aG dc cb adccb adcd bcdcbc aba aG abc dcbaGaG

3. v. 2: Final melisma on "offeram": Sources outside the core group show some small variants, often particular to individual MSS. Near the end of the melisma, Mo 159 and several other MSS reach several times to d.

> Ben 34: GacccabaGaccc
>
> Mo 159: Gadcdcccc(ori.)Gcdc
>
> Pst120 begins the melisma slightly differently: caaGabGFGaGacaaGabGF...[2]
>
> Pad 47: at the end of the melisma, the notes aGF are stated only twice (not three times, as in other sources).

For reasons that are unclear, To 18 has a completely different ending of the second verse, beginning with "medullata." The melisma on "offeram" shares some material with the other readings, but begins differently and is truncated:

---

1. Justmann (1988), 2:1042–43.

2. Justmann s transcriptions show a similar reading in two other sources, Mod 13 and Ver 161. Justmann (1988), 1:492.

```
a        c(liq.)   cdede   cdadcdc
me-      dul-      la      ta
edecbbcdedeccccaGabGFGaGacccacdcccaGacaGaddcddcccaGFaaGcccaGFbaGGacc
of-
edc      dca       a
[of-]    fe-       ram
```

Roman MSS: Vat 5319 and RoS 22 show few significant differences from Bodmer 74, with one exception: In v. 2, Vat 5319 has the repeat of the words "locutus est os meum . . ." that are present in the Gregorian sources but lacking in Bodmer. The opening two notes of Vat 5319 are GG, contrasting with DD in Bodmer. In v. 2, Bodmer is missing the first note of "medullata" (or at least it is not visible on the facsimile). In Vat 5319, the corresponding note is F.

DEXTERA DOMINI (13)

This offertory has variant repetenda. In base version of Lo 4951 and in most Aquitanian, Italian, and Beneventan MSS, the cue directs the performer to the beginning of the respond, leaving open the question of whether the initial phrase "dextera ·domini fecit virtutem," constituted the repetendum or whether the whole respond was repeated. In Mo 159, the repetendum is to "non moriar."

There are two problems of pitch level in this offertory. The first involves the notated level of the respond and first verse. In Mo 159 and in a few other MSS, the respond and first verse are notated at the affinal position, undoubtedly because of the need for low B-flat, which is represented by F at the higher level of transposition. In a majority of MSS, however, the respond closes on D, without emending the passages with low B. Although a low B-flat is clearly intended, it is indicated only in a few later MSS that employ a notational sign for low B-flat, such as Gr 807.

A second problem arises in the final verse. In a great majority of MSS, the second verse is a first-mode melody, as it appears in the base transcription. The scribe of Pa 776, however, notates the second verse a fourth lower, a position confirmed by the repetendum cue. To replicate the intervallic structure of the majority version at the position of Pa 776, an f-sharp is required. A similar version is found in many MSS from St. Martial and in RoV 52.

With the principle that the *lectio difficilior* is the more powerful reading, the version of Pa 776 would emerge as the preferred pretheoretical version, and the majority version as the results of modal emendation. The presence of this reading in one Italian MS included in the sampling indicates that it was not limited to Aquitaine. The second verse is also modally irregular in the Roman tradition: melodic material typical of first-mode Roman melodies is projected a fifth below its usual pitch level. Given the uncertainties surrounding the performance of this version, I am hesitant to posit it at the single preferred version. The version in the normal first-mode range reflects the more common practice, and I have given it in the base transcription.

The lower version of the verse found in Pa 776 (Example 13.1) is modally irregular. In the second verse, melodic vocabulary typical of *protus* chants is projected a fourth below its usual position. The melodic activity of this verse is focused within two disjunct T-S-T tetrachords, A-B-C-D and E-F-sharp-G-a, with C, the *tritus* pitch of the first tetrachord,

EXAMPLE **13.1**A

EXAMPLE 3 13.1B

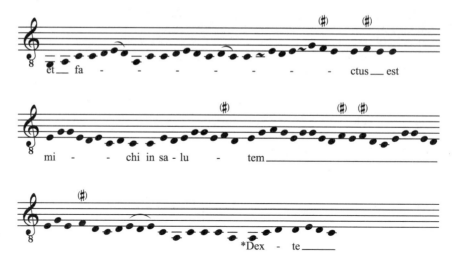

serving a repercussive function. The parenthetical F-sharps in the transcription are derived from the b-naturals that occur in the majority version a fourth higher, and are consistent with the typical melodic gestures of the chant repertory.

Pitch-level profile: =Lo 4951: Pa 780, Ben 34 (lacks second verse), Cai 61, Pa 1235, Gr 807, Be 40078, Mü 10086, Pad 47, Pst 120, Mod 7.

Respond and first verse at affinal position, second verse = Lo 4951: Mo 159.

Second verse 4 ↓ Lo 4951: Pa 776, Pa 1134 (according to rep.),[1] Pa 1136, Pa 1137 (no rep.), Pa 1135, Pa 1132 (according to rep.), RoV 52. (Pa 1121 lacks a notated repetendum.)

Individual MSS: In Pa 1121, the verse begins on a new line, with no repetendum cue. In Ben 35, the scribe alternates between F and c clefs, obscuring the intended pitch level. In Pa 780, the written level of the verse (relative to the first verse) matches that of Pa 776, but the repetendum cue begins on the next page, with no custos.

Other variants: There are very few significant variants among core or peripheral MSS. v. 2 "cadeREM" has a different reading in Beneventan MSS, as in Ben 34: FaGF FDF FDF FF.

Roman MSS: Respond, "narrabo opera": The text underlay, indicated by the placement of the text and the neume groupings, is a point of variance in the three Roman MSS. RoS 22 and Bodmer present similar readings, with a different version in Vat 5319:

	[narra] bo	o-	pe-	ra
Bod 74	DE	DFEDC	FGF	EFGFGFEF
RoS 22:	DE	DFEDCDF	GF	EFGFGFEF
Vat 5319:	DEDFEDC	FGF	[G]?	EFGFGFEF

In Landwehr-Melnicki's transcription of Vat 5319, a G is given over "pe" that is not visible on the microfilm.[2] Although the melody is not formulaic here, it does employ some standard melodic material, and Bod 74 and RoS 22 align the text and melody in a way that is

---

1. The notated level (in relation to the first verse) is that of Lo 4951.
2. Stäblein and Landwehr-Melnicki ed. (1970), 273.

atypical. The notes DFEDC that occur on the first syllable of "opera" in Bod 74 and RoS 22 are more commonly used as a cadential figure (especially in eighth-mode offertories, at the higher transposition), and the figure FGF would typically fall on the accented syllable, as it does in 5319. Despite its unusual alignment between melody and lyrics, however, the presence of a reading close to Bod 74's in the much later RoS 22 suggests that it is not a simple mistake.

Vat 5319:

> respond, "moRI/AR": GFE/EFEDCDC (liq.)
> respond, "VIvam": DEFEDCDCA
> v. 1, "es": **DF** FFEFEDCC(ori.)BACDE
> v. 2 "MI/CHI": BCDED/DCDEDCDC
> v. 2 "saLU/TEM": **D FGFGFF(ori.)**DCDEDC/ **DC** FFEFEDCC(ori.)BACDE
> v. 2 "et dominus suscepit": Vat 5319 lacks "et"

RoS 22:

> "dexteRA [domini fecit]": DCDEDEF FED
> "virTUtem": EEDCDE**FED**
> "exalTAvit": melisma begins FGaGFG (etc.)

BONUM EST (14)

The Gregorian and Roman versions show a structural difference in the respond and repetenda. The Roman respond ends with a repeat of the opening, "bonum est confiteri," that is lacking in the Gregorian, and this reprise is altered melodically to form a final cadence. It is probable that this repeat was sung as the repetendum in the Roman version, whereas the whole respond was probably sung as a repetendum in the Gregorian version.

Mo 159 indicates b-flats in several places where they do not occur in other MSS, resulting in a G-*protus* reading of the respond's opening phrases. In the respond, Mo 159 has b-flats in the following places: respond, "boNUM"; respond, "noMIni"; respond, "TUo" (matched in Pa 903; indicated with a quilisma); v. 3 "corNU" (matched in Pad 47); v. 3 "MEum."

Only two of these b-flats, then, are confirmed in another MS. For the other passages, there are no flats indicated in the following MSS that often indicate b-flat: Gr 807, Be 40078, Mü 10086,[1] and Mod 7. In the case of the German MSS, however, several of the notes corresponding to b-flat in Mo 159 are c's, reflecting the German chant dialect. Even though b-flats were undoubtedly sung at some times and places, it is not clear how widespread this practice was, and I have decided not to give these parenthetical b-flats in the transcription of Ben 34.

Aside from these differences in the use of b-flat, there are very few melodic variants among core or peripheral MSS:

> v. 3 "[cornu] ME/UM" and "[inimicos] ME/OS"
> Mo 159: cdc b-flat a/GaG

---

1. Mü 10086 indicates a b-flat as the top note on "confiteri" in the respond (corresponding to c in most other MSS), followed by a natural on "domino."

Verse endings in Lo 4951:

> v. 1 "tuE": GGa Ga G baG
> v. 2 "inquitaTEM": GGa Ga G baG
> v. 3 "tuA" (sic): cdccaG Ga Ga G baG

Among peripheral MSS, most differences involve variants in recitational style, with the following exception in the opening of the respond:

	Bo-	num	est
Pad 47:	FF	FaG	GE

Identical reading in Mod 7.
Roman MSS:
Vat 5319:

> [Bonum] "est": D EDEDCBDFEDFED (both times)
> v. 2, "iniMIci": EDCDE (whole tone above Bod. 74)

RoS 22:

> [Bonum] "est": DEDEDCB DFEDFED (both times).

PERFICE GRESSUS (15)

There is one point of melodic variance where the Beneventan MSS give an independent reading, on v. 2, at "ut pupillam oculi" (phrase 8). The following shows the passage in selected core MSS.

	o-	cu-	li
Ben 34:	acbc	cabG	G
Mo 159:	b acbG aE Gbab	FG	G
Pa 776:	b acbG aFG Gbab	EG	G
Lo 4951:	b acbG GFE Gbab	FG	G

All peripheral MSS present a reading closer to Mo 159 and the Aquitanian MSS, though there are further variants in some of these sources:

	o-	cu-	li
RoV 52:	a Gba GFGE Gc abc	G	G
Pad 47:	acba bG aGaG	Ga	a
Gr 807:	c acbG aFGcac	FG	G
Cai 61:	b ac bG aF acac	FG	G

Roman MSS: Bod 74 lacks the verse *Custodi me* and presents a shorter version of the verse *Exaudi domine*, missing the end of the verse, "auribus percipe orationem meam." At the end of the verse *Ego autem*, Vat 5319 lacks notation for the words "gloria tua." In the transcription, these notes are supplied from Bodmer. There are very few melodic variants between MSS. Bod 74: v. 2 opening of the verse "Ego": ab.

BENEDICTUS ES...IN LABIIS (16)

The transpositional variants in the second verse of this offertory were described long ago by Sidler and further addressed by Hankeln.[1] Based on the intervallic differences between MSS, both authors persuasively argue that the transpositions are attributable to the presence of the nondiatonic pitch high f-sharp. Ben 34 was chosen as the base version because its scribe notates this verse in the probable unemended range, corresponding to Hankeln's *Aufführungslage*. In this respect, this piece is a departure from this scribe's usual tendency toward emendation.

The first hypothetical f-sharp occurs at the repetition of the words "viam iniquitatis" (phrase 13) and the second at "de lege tua" (phrase 14), followed by a series of f-sharps in the same phrase. Mo 159 is written a whole tone below Ben 34, with a b-flat, so that the semitone e-f in Ben 34 is equivalent to the whole tone d-e in Mo. The third hypothetical f-sharp occurs in the final melisma.

Although the intervallic differences between the versions, especially Mo 159, certainly suggest the use of f-sharps in these passages, it is unclear how widespread and longstanding this practice was. Outside of Aquitaine and Benevento, most MSS place the verse a fifth below the reading of Ben 34, a transposition that would allow f-sharp to be represented with b-natural. Many sources, however, do not clearly distinguish between b-flat and b-natural. In Pa 1235 and Cai 61, the verse is notated a fifth below Ben 34. Where the first hypothetical f-sharp occurs, on "viam iniquitatis," the notes corresponding to the F-sharps are c's rather than b-naturals (a reading also found in German MSS). At "lege," the scribes of Pa 1235 and Cai 61 indicate a b-flat, equivalent to f-natural at the higher position. Although the b's that follow, on "tua" and "mei," are not indicated as either flat or natural, it seems probable the flat was intended to apply to the whole passage. If so, however, the reasons for writing the verse in the lower register are not clear. In Cai 61, all the remaining b's are indicated as flat, even in the final melisma, where two hypothetical f-sharps are suggested by Mo. In the final melisma, Pa 1235 indicates a b-flat corresponding to the second hypothetical f-sharp, but not the first. Cai 61 and Pa 1235, then, may represent a tradition in which the nondiatonic practice suggested by Mo 159 was suppressed but the verse was nevertheless written at the lower level of transposition. In other later MSS, such as Gr 807 and Be 40078, the b's on "lege," "tua," and "mei" can perhaps be assumed to be natural in the absence of a flat sign.

The question of how far-reaching the nondiatonic practice was also arises in the case of Ben 34. Given this scribe's theoretical awareness and tendency to transpose problem spots, can the notation of the verse in Hankeln's *Aufführungslage* be seen as a suppression of nondiatonic practice? While the answer is not clear, the scribe of Ben 35 writes the verse a fifth lower, indicating that this practice was known at some Beneventan institutions.

1. Sidler (1929), 44–47; Hankeln (1999), 1:103–5; 2:139, 3:31–33.

Another point of variance concerns the repetition of the words "iudicia tua" (phrase 16). This repetition is lacking in Ben 34, Ben 35, Compiègne, and the Roman MSS. While the circulation of the version without the repetition in these disparate sources may suggest that it is an alternative early reading, the text repetition is present in all other MSS, including the early notated sources in the sampling and Ben 38. In the transcription, this material is supplied from Ben 38.

As noted in Hankeln's summary of Aquitanian sources, the verse incipit is a point of variance. The following summarizes the pitch level at "domine" though the end of the verse:

= Ben 34: Pa 776 (according to repetendum); RoV 52
2↓Ben 34: Mo
5↓Ben 34: Lo 4951, Cai 61, Pa 1235, Gr 807, Be 40078, Pad 47

The pitch level of the second verse in some of the Aquitanian MSS is unclear. As noted in Hankeln's study, several Aquitanian sources appear to begin the verse on E, but the pitch level of the repetendum suggests that the scribe did not maintain a consistent axis between the two verses. With a reading of the pitch level derived from the repetendum, the verse incipit in Pa 776 is a tone above that of Ben 34, joining at "domine." The reasons for this discrepancy are unclear. The repetendum is lacking in Pa 780. As summarized by Hankeln, the St. Martial sources (with the exception of Pa 1132) seem to be written a third below the level of Ben 34, but the repetendum cues give conflicting information about the intended pitch level.[2]

The sources are inconsistent in verse division and repetenda, and the designation of five verses (with no repetenda until the end) in the Beneventan MSS is unusual. A more common practice is to divide the material into three verses, *Beati immaculati, In via testimoniorum,* and *Viam iniquitatis.* In the Beneventan and several Aquitanian MSS, the last verse closes with a cue to "aufer a plebe" (phrase 8), suggesting that perhaps the performance concluded at the end of this verse, resulting in a migration of final from E to the affinal b.

There are few significant melodic variants, either among core or peripheral MSS. Lo 4951:

respond, "omniA": cbca
v. 1 "[exquirunt] eam": ccc a cc edb ccc adcb

Cai 61: respond, "TUas" (2nd time): Gacc dec a cb cc cb

In verse 2, Ben 34 has a probable scribal error on the last syllable of "tua" (phrase 8), where it has a single e instead of e-d, as found in the other MSS. I have emended the transcription here.

Roman MSS: The Roman verses have first-mode characteristics, a trait that probably derives from the close verbal relationship between the first verse, *Beati immaculati,* and *Confitebor tibi* (39). In the Gregorian tradition, *Confitebor tibi* has a first verse, *Beati immaculati,* that is verbally identical to the first verse of *Benedictus es.* Although the Roman version of *Confitebor tibi* lacks this verse, the Roman verse of *Benedictus es* shows a compelling musical similarity to the Gregorian verse of *Confitebor tibi.* In Bod 74, there are several additional verse indications, at "aufer," "viam veritatis," and "viam mandatorum."

2. Hankeln (1999), 1:104; 2:139.

Because these seem to mark sections rather than complete verses, I have not indicated them. Vat 5319 lacks notation beginning with the verse *In via testimoniorum*. There are few significant variants among the sources.

Vat 5319:

- v. 1 "beAti": a slightly shorter version of the melisma, lacking the last 4 notes of Bodmer's melisma
- v. 1: Bodmer's reading "beati qui servantur" (Ps. 118:2) is probably a simple error. Vat 5319 has "scrutantur," the reading of all known psalters.
- v. 1 "AU/FER": a/aG
- v. 1 "obproBRIUM ET": recitation on c

EXALTABO TE (17)

The respond and first verse of this offertory are often written at the affinal position, undoubtedly because of the need for low B-flat in the respond. The transposition of the first two sections raises questions about the intended pitch level of the final verse, which, in most cases, is written in the normal first-mode range (in relation to the transposed plagal respond and first verse). The most likely preferred reading is that of Pa 776, given as the base version, where the respond and first verse are in the normal plagal range and the second verse is in the authentic range. The following summarizes the pitch-level profile of the sources.

There are very few significant variants among core or peripheral MSS. v. 2 "deCOri":

Ben 34: c bca ccG **aFa** (etc.)
Mod 7: c bca cca **aGa** (etc.)
Ben 34: v. 1 "aniMAM" (5↑)

Roman MSS: In Vat 5319 the whole offertory is notated at the affinal position. There are no significant variants between MSS.

DOMINE VIVIFICA (18)

This offertory exhibits few significant variants between MSS. The Beneventan tradition, however, does show some small differences from other core MSS, as evident in the summary below.

respond, "[eloquium] TU/UM": This is a point of variance:[1]

Mo 159: FGEFDED/D
Pa 776: FGFD/FFFDED
Pa 780: FGF/FED
Pa 1121: FGFF/DED (same in Lo 4951, Pa 1235, Cai 61; Pad 47 FGF/DED)
Be 40078: FGF/DFD
Gr 807: FGFE/DFD

---

1. I was not able to read the version of Mod 7 on the microfilm.

respond, "testimoniA": Pa 780: ccba bG abaGG
respond, "tuA": Pa 780: EGEF/FE

v. 1 "DOmine":

> Mo 159: Gcca ccaG **bdb**
> Pa 776: Gcca ccaG **cdc** (identical reading in Pa 780, Pa 1235, Cai 61, Pad 47)
> Lo 4951: Gcca ccaG **bdc**
> Be 40078: Gc ca bcaG adc
> Gr 807: G bca bcaG adc
> Mod 7: Gc ca cccaG acb (identical to Ben 34)

> v. 1 "[misericordiam] TUam": Mo 159: bdbc (identical reading in Pa 780)
> v. 2 "beneplaCIto": Mo 159: bdbc (same in Pa 780)
> Variants in individual MSS:
> Lo 4951: v. 2 "domiNE": melisma ends ccc a a(ori.) FGF (ori.) E

Pa 1235:

> v. 2 "mandaTA": cbcbced
> v. 2 "benePLAcito": ca dcdc ded

> Be 40078: respond "domiNE": ab(quil.)cdc bca aG adc
> Mod 7: v. 2 "benePLAcito": ca dcdc ded
> Pad 47: v. 2 "benePLAcito": cb cbcb ded

Roman MSS: Bod 74 lacks the second verse. Bod 74 and Vat 5319 exhibit a rare transpositional variant at the beginning of v. 1, where Bod 74 is written mostly a third lower than Vat, joining at "secundum." At the level of Bod 74, the verse opening is nearly identical to that of two other verses, in *Gressus meos* (v. *Cognovi domine*) and *Levabo oculos* (v. *Legem pone*). It is not clear, however, that the reading of Vat 5319 is in error here, since passages with figural similarities are sometimes written at different pitch levels. With only two MSS transmitting the Roman version of this verse, there is not enough information to establish a preferred reading. I have selected Vat 5319 as the base version simply because it is the only MS to contain the second verse.

SCAPULIS SUIS (19)

In the Gregorian tradition, there are only minor variants between MSS, as the following sampling shows.

Verse 1: "tiMOre": Most MSS begin the melisma with a, as in Mo 159: accc (ori.) ac; or Pa 776: acccabc.

Verse 2: a. In the Beneventan MSS, "UMquam" and "ofFENdas" are a literal repetition of "SUis" and "manDAvit." While the sources in the core group are nearly uniform at "suis" and "mandavit," they are variant when the material recurs, possibly because of the liquescent syllables.

"UMquam": Mo 159, Pa 1121, and Lo 4951: Faca b (flat) a G (liq.); Pa 776: F acacaaG (liq.)

"ofFENdas": Mo 159: Facab-flat a a (ori.) F (liq.); Pa 1121 and Lo 4951: FacacaaG (liq.); Pa 776: FacacaaG (liq.)

Verse ending, melisma on "TUam": Mo 159: acccFGaGaG. Also a point of variance outside the core group, i.e. Pa 1235: caGaGacaG; Gr 807: bcaFGacbcaFGF.

Verse 3: melisma on "eum": The following segments of the melisma take a number of slightly different forms:

Ben 34: f f (ori.) dd (ori.) cd fffdd (ori.)
Mo 159: ffefcdfff(ori.)efcd
Pa 1121: efdd(ori.) cdfefdd (ori.) cd
Mod 7: ffdecdfffdecd

There are minor variants toward the end of the melisma, for example:

Ben 34: ccc da G Gac dc ac dcd
Pa 776: ccccaFGacdcabc (quil.) dcd (similar reading in the other Aquitanian sources)
Gr 807: cc dca abc dcG abc

Individual sources:

Pa 1235: v. 3 "speraVIT": decdcbcb
Cai 61: v. 3 "tuUM": cc ca cbG aG ca Ga

To 18 v. 2 "eum" melisma: some segments near the beginning of the melisma adopt e rather than f as the top note. The melisma begins: dacdfffdc dcd ff gfdc efed dc eedcd eeecbc e ecdca (etc.).

Roman MSS:

Vat 5319: "NOCturno": bcecedcdc.

Verse 2 (major variant): Vat 5319 presents a much shorter version of the final melisma on the first syllable of "eum," lacking the repetition scheme of Bod 74's version. The entire melisma reads ededed cbcd d fedc cdc.

RoS 22:

"tiBI": GaGbaGFGF
"domiNUS": FEGFEFE

LEVABO OCULOS (20)

The parenthetical b-flats are derived primarily from their use in Mo. In many later MSS, the b-flats in passages such as "doceas" (phrase 2) are raised to c. The G-*protus* opening of v. 1, however, is maintained in some later MSS, with b-flats indicated in Gr 807 and Pa 1235. None of the sources examined undertakes a whole-tone transposition here, as might be expected.

The few points of variance are as follows.

End of respond, "domine": Mo 159 has "tua," with the cadential pattern altered for a two-syllable word: Ga(quil) cab/aG. Ben 34's version is found in La 239, Pa 776 and Pa

780, whereas Mo's version, the more common one, is found in Ch 47, Ei 121, Pa 1121, Lo 4951, Gr 807, Cai 61, Pa 1235, Pad 47, RoV 52, and Mod 7.

v. 2 "tuAE": The Aquitanian MSS match Ben 34 here, but Mo 159 has DFDD(ori.)C, a reading matched in most peripheral MSS.

Roman MSS:

Vat 5319:

v. 1 "Legem": These notes are mistakenly written a third too low but corrected with the custos that follows.

v. 1 "exQUIram": abcdcbab(ori.)aG

v. 2 "domiNE": This melisma is written a third too low in Vat 5319, but again corrected with the custos that follows.

v. 2 "LEX": ac dcd

v. 2 "meditatiO": two extra notes are appended to the end of the melisma, aG

RoS 22:

"doceAS": cdcba bcdcbabG
"[iustitia] tuA": aGbaGaG
"intellecTUM": aGFEFGFGbaGF
"MANdata": aGbaGF

IN TE SPERAVI (21)

There are no significant variants among the core group of sources and very few outside the core group. Individual sources:

To 18 v. 1 "TUam": CD FGFDC FGD FF FGF
Pa 1235 v. 1 "SERvum:" DF F FD EFDC CDFF aG (liq.)

The Roman sources also lack significant variants.

MEDITABOR (22)

The parenthetical B-flats indicated in the opening and at the final melisma on "dilexi" reflect a point of variance in the MS tradition and were probably not universally sung. In many MSS, this offertory is written at the affinal position and the corresponding notes are F's, clearly suggesting the use of low B-flat. These MSS include Ben 34, RoV 52, and Pad 47. In Mo 159, however, it is written in the normal plagal range, with the low B's left as is, and the same version is found in Cai 61, Pa 1235, Mod 7, Pst 120, and Be 40078.

The base version of Ben 35 contains one certain scribal error and other anomalies that are most likely errors. The penultimate line of the offertory, stretching from "[se]cundum" through "pedes [meos]," is written a third too high in Ben 35. The status of this passage as a scribal error is clearly indicated by the custos at the end of the line, between "pedes" and "meos," which serves as a correction of the cleffing. Another possible scribal error concerns "meAS" in phrase 2. The bracketed notes G-F are lacking in Ben 35 but occur in all other

MSS, including the Beneventan sources. In v. 2, Ben 35 is missing four notes over "conVERti" (phrase 6) that occur in all other sources. These are indicated with brackets. A fourth variant is the last two syllables on "dominus" in verse 1 (phrase 3). The two F's in this passage are G's in most other MSS.

Distinctive readings in Beneventan MSS: In v. 1, the text "pars mea dominus" is matched in Ben 34, but reads "pars mea domine" in other sources. V. 1 "[vultum] TUum": Ben 35's reading is matched in Ben 34, but most MSS have EFGFGFD.

Significant melodic variant: In some Aquitanian MSS, the second verse closes with a very long melisma on "conVERti." Among the core MSS, this melisma is found only in Pa 776 and Lo 4951.[1] The version of Pa 776 is aG aGFa DFDF FFFD aaaF GGEFG FG baGa FDE FF FF EG (quil.)aG aGFa DFDF FFFD aaaG GGE FG FG baG aFDE GaFE GaFE EFG GF GG EFGG Gc c(ori.)G aa Gc c(ori.)G aa Gaccccc caGF EFDC DE(quil.) FEF EFD EFG G(ori.) F FaGaG aFG(liq.).

Lo 4951:

> v. 1 "meO": DFDCD
> v. 2 "miseREre" is missing a segment of the melisma. The melisma reads FGGFGFEF DE(quil.)FE CD FG FGabG

Mod 7: A lacuna on the opening melisma of v. 1 ("pars").

Roman MSS: There are very few variants.
> Vat 5319: v. 2 "TU/UM": CDEDED/CBDFEDFE

> RoS 22: "TUa": FGFEGFEFDE

BENEDIC ANIMA MEA (23)

There are no significant variants in the respond and first verse. The second verse exhibits several pitch-level variants. Pa 776 was chosen as the base version because it presents the verse in its most probable unemended range.

In many sources, including Mo 159, Cai 61, Lo 4951, and Be 40078, the second verse begins a fourth above its position in Pa 776. Mo 159, Lo 4951, and Cai 61 join the level of Pa 776 at "omnium" (phrase 9), whereas the scribe of Be 40078 continues at the higher level for the whole verse.

An upward transposition of a fourth is often employed to represent the nondiatonic pitch F-sharp, equivalent to b-natural at the higher position. It is probable that this pitch was employed on the last syllable of "caelo" (phrase 9). At this point, Mo 159 uses the special semitone sign at the position of b. A b-natural at this level is equivalent to F-sharp at the position of Pa 776, a fourth lower. Although Cai 61 lacks a natural sign here, it does not indicate a b-flat, as it does for the rest of the b's in this verse. Other emendations of this passage support the hypothesis that an F-sharp is intended at "caeLO." Ben 34 and Gr 807, for example, start the verse at the level of Pa 776. Beginning at "caelo," however, both versions are written a whole tone below Pa 776, rejoining the level of Pa 776 at "omnium." Both sources thus have the half step F-E on "caelo," corresponding to the whole tone G-F in Pa 776. In Pst 120, the verse likewise starts at the level of Pa 776, but beginning on the final

---

1. According to Pitman (1973), 224, it is also found in Pa 1135.

syllable of "caelo," it is written a fourth higher, so that the whole tone G-F in Pa 776 is the semitone c-b in Pst 120. The hypothetical F-sharp on "caelo" occurs just before the temporary change of recitation pitch from c to G and temporarily creates a *tritus* quality for G.

The emended readings Mo 159, Cai 61, Lo 4951, and Pst 120 are written a fourth above Pa 776 until "omnium," thus lacking the shift of range at "omnium" that is found in Pa 776, Pa 1121, and other MSS. This shift of range, however, is suggested in the adiastematic MSS La 239 and Ei 121, which have the letter *s* (sursum) here, confirming the impression that Pa 776 represents the "unemended" pitch level at "in caelo . . . omnium."

A summary of pitch level in the sources:

= Pa 776 throughout: Pa 1121, Pa 780, Pa 1235.
Verse begins a fourth above Pa 776, joins at "omnium": Mo 159, Cai 61.
Entire verse a fourth above Pa 776: Be 40078, Mod 7.

Whole tone below Pa 776 beginning at "caelo," joining Pa 776 at "omnium": Ben 34 (transposition begins on the last two notes of "CAELo"), Gr 807 (transposition begins at "CAElo").
Fourth transposition beginning at "CAElo," joining Pa 776 at "omnium": Lo 4951 (last syllable of "caelo" is b [flat?] a), Pst 120.
Fourth transposition beginning at "paravit," joining Pa 776 at "omnium": RoV 52
In RoV 52 the last syllable of "lo" is G-F. This source shows no discernable evidence of nondiatonic practice in the verse, but the passage between "paravit" and "eius" is placed in a more common segment of the background scale.
Individual MSS:
Pad 47 presents a shortened version of the second verse, lacking "ut faciant ea . . . regnum eius." The verse closes with the words "omnibus dominabitur." The lengthy melisma on "omnibus" shares some material with that on "omnium" in the majority version but is not identical to it. The same shortening of the verse is not found in the other MS from Ravenna, Mod 7.
Mod 7: Differs in a segment of the final melisma on v. 2: "omniUM": fgfc df fgfd fa gaga ff gfd fefdc ededc dd cd ff fc**edcedc ec** cdff gafe.
Roman MSS: There are no significant variants.

DOMINE DEUS SALUTIS (24)

The Roman tradition lacks one of the three verses that circulate in Gregorian MSS. Here the phrases are given parallel numbers to facilitate comparison between the two versions.

This offertory shows two points of significant variance among the core group of MSS. The melisma on "mane" in the second verse (phrase 9) is shortened in the Beneventan MSS and in Lo 4951, lacking several of the internal notes that appear in most other MSS. The same melisma, with the same variant between MSS, occurs in the Easter Week offertory *Benedictus qui venit* (54). The early adiastematic MSS SG 339, Ei 121, La 239, and Cha 47 are consistent with the longer version. Some

sample readings of the melisma are given below, and more may be found in the notes to
Benedictus qui venit.

Ben 34:	cdcaGFG	FaGaG			babGF	FGaca FGaGa
Lo 4951:	cdccaGFG	FGaGaG			babGF	GacaFGaGa
Pa 776:	cdccaGFG	FGaGa accca ccdcaaF FGaGaG	babGF	Gaca	FGaGa
Gr 807:	cdbcaFG	FGaGaGa cc ca cc dc aaF FGaG aG	cacGF	GacaF	FGaGa

The other significant variant concerns the pitch level in the opening of the third verse. In
some MSS, "factus sum sicut homo" is written a fifth below its position in Ben 34. The pitch
level of Ben 34 is matched in most core sources, including Mo 159 and all Aquitanian MSS
except Pa 1121. The lower level is found in most MSS from St. Martial and a few unrelated
sources, such as Gr 807.[1] Since the two versions are identical in interval structure, the reason
for the lower notation in some MSS is unclear. Perhaps the downward transposition is made
by analogy to the second verse, whose incipit is otherwise melodically identical. In one MS in
the sampling, Mü 10086, the whole third verse is written a fifth below the level of Ben 34, a
reading also found in Pa 1133.[2] In Mü 10086, moreover, the second verse is also transposed
down a fifth, with the low B's indicated as flat, for unknown reasons.[3]

Pitch level of "factus sum sicut homo":

= Ben 34: Mo 159, Pa 776, Pa 780, Lo 4951, Pa 1235, Be 40078, Cai 61, Pad 47, Pst
120, Mod 7, RoV 52, To 18
5↓ Ben 34: Pa 1121, Pa 1133, Pa 1136, Pa 1137, Gr 807, Mü 10086

With the exceptions of Pa 1133 and Mü 10086, all MSS join Ben 34 at "sine."
    Transpositions in individual MSS:
    Mü 10086: The second verse is written a fifth lower than the majority reading
    Pa 1235 presents a unique version of the opening of the first verse, "inclina aurem tuam
ad precem meam domine," which is mostly a fourth below the majority reading, with the
cadence on "domine" falling on D rather than G.
    Other melodic variants: v. 2 "mea" (phrase 10): The Beneventan MSS transmit
distinctive readings of this verse ending, with a more elaborate cadential pattern. The
other sources in the core group have Ga/Ga.
    Aside from the melisma on "mane," most variants among core MSS involve differences
in recitational style. The figure G-b-d-c that occurs often in Ben 34, for example, is
consistently G-c-d-c in Pa 776 and in most other Aquitanian MSS. There are a few
significant variants in peripheral MSS, as follows:

v. 2 "preVEniet" in RoV 52: **GabGa** ced
v. 3 "mortuOS":

---

1. See the summaries in Hankeln 1 (1999), 105–6; 2, 139; and Pitman (1972), 107–8.
2. Hankeln 2 (1999), 139.
3. Mo 159 has one b-flat in this verse, on the last syllable of "perveniet," which would be E-flat at the
   position a fifth lower, but in Mü 10086, the corresponding note is F. Like most later German MSS,
   Be 40078 lacks repetendum cues.

Pa 1235: dcdbca aGa

Cai 61: dcda caaGa

Mod 7: cabaGa aG

v. 3 "[traditus] sum" in Be 40078: GaGF

v. 3 "egredieBAR": the final melisma exhibits variants among several MSS, which are highlighted in boldface.

Mod 7: cd cc ca ccc dc ccc ca cac cc cacGF GG Fac **GbaG** acca cccaG abcb c ca ccca F abGFG FGaGa **FGaGa** GacccaG ccadcb bd eca cbGa

Cai 61: bd cc ca cc cd ccc ca cac c ca caF **aa Ga** ccc dcb ac cb cc aGa bcb c cb **ccaF aca Ga** (etc.)

RoV 52: cd cc ca ccc dc cc ca cac c ca caF **F aa Ga** cc cdcb (etc.)

Pst 120: cdc cc dc **ccc dc** cc ca cac cc cac GF **FG G**ac c cdcb ac ca ccaG Gabcb c ca **cdca GbaGa** FGaGa **FGaGa** (etc.)

To 18 is missing the final melisma.

Individual MSS: RoV 52 indicates a verse division within v. 3, at "traditus."

Roman MSS:

Vat 5319:

respond: ME/E: The two "e" syllables were perhaps not distinguished in performance, but the neumes indicate the following: Gabcba/aGabaGaG

v. 1 diE: aG **cdc** cdcbdcbacba

v. 2 tradiTUS: a (ori.) GF

First verse lacks repetendum cue, second verse has a repetendum cue to "in."

RoS 22: "ME/AE": Gabcba/aGabaGaG

BENEDICAM DOMINUM (25)

The pitch level variants in the second verse of this offertory have been demonstrated by Pitman and Hankeln. The pitch-level profile of Ben 34, the base version, is matched in Mo 159 and in unrelated MSS such as Be 40078. In other MSS, however, the opening passage of v. 2, though "vias vitae" (phrase 7), is written either a whole tone higher or a fourth lower. Ben 34 has a rare notated b-flat in the verse opening, and Mo 159 indicates b-flats throughout the passage. The transpositions at levels a whole tone higher and a fourth lower, then, do not produce intervallic differences that would point to nondiatonic notes as the reason for the variants.

Some Aquitanian MSS, including Pa 776 and Pa 1121, have a written level for the second verse a fourth below Ben 34. In Pa 776, however, the repetendum cue suggests a performance level a fourth above the written level, at the position of Ben 34. Hankeln has accordingly posited the level of Mo (and Ben 34) as the *Aufführungslage* in Pa 776.[1] The variety among the other readings, summarized below, reinforces the impression that they are emendations, or in some cases reworkings of the melody, and that the level of Ben 34 is

---

1. Hankeln (1999), 1:105–6; 2:140. Most Aquitanian MSS appear to start the verse a fourth lower but lack clear repetendum cues.

the preferred reading.[2] One possible reason for the transpositions here is the G-*protus* quality of the opening passage, particularly at "fecisti mihi." The passage is notated a tone higher in the Italian MSS examined, consistent with the Guidonian recommendation for emending G-*protus* passages. In many of the MSS that begin the verse a fourth below Ben 34, the melisma on the second syllable of "vias" is reworked to create a transition between the two transpositional levels, joining the level of Ben 34 within the melisma or at "vitae."

Pitch level at "notas . . . vitae":

> = Ben 34: Mo 159, Pa 776 (according to repetendum), Pa 1121 (?),[3] Pa 780, Cai 61, Be 40078, Gr 807, Mü 10086

2↑ Ben 34:

> Pad 47 (joins Ben 34 during the melisma on "viAS": c bcb aba GGF FGaGaca)
> Pst 120 (joins Ben 34 during the melisma on "viAS": c bcb aba GGE GaG aca a c [liq.])
> Mod 7: same as Pad 47
> RoV 52 (joins Ben 34 temporarily during the melisma on viAS, then again at "ad implebis")
> Frutolf tonary

4↓ Ben 34:

> Lo 4951 is 4↓ Ben 34 until "VI/AS," with a highly reworked version of the melisma that reads: DE(quil.)FGF/FGacaGaGFGFD FGaGaca aaa
> Pa 1235 is 4↓ Ben 34 until the end of the melisma on "viAS," where the interval of transposition changes to a third (DFD) and then a second (EGE): The melisma reads: CD GFF/EFEF DFD CCA C DFD EGE(liq.).
> Most sources from St. Martial appear to notate the verse a fourth below the level of Ben 34, but lack repetendum cues to confirm this level.[4]

Melodic variants occur at the following points:

> respond, "QUO/NI/AM": Mod 7: DG/G abca /acb c FG
> respond, "[est] miCHI": Pa 776: ED

v. 1 "DOminus":

> Mo 159: melisma begins Fac
> Pa 776: melisma begins CDa. Same reading in Be 40078
> Pa 1121: melisma begins DFa
> Gr 807: melisma begins Da
> Mod 7: melisma begins FGa

v. 1 "meae" (verse ending). The Beneventan text underlay differs from that of other MSS. The majority reading places the last syllable on the last four notes.

---

2. In additional to the summary below, see Pitman's descriptions of the transitional "bridges" in other MSS. Pitman (1973), 77–81.
3. The repetendum in Pa 1121 suggests a performance level equal to Ben 34 and Pa 776. There is an "equaliter" sign functioning as a custos between verses, however, that suggests a performance a fourth lower. As Pitman suggests, this sign might be an error. Ibid.
4. See Hankeln (1999), 2:140.

v. 2 "NOtas": Ben 34's reading F-c is anomalous. Mo 159, most Aquitanian MSS, and German MSS have a whole tone (B-flat-c, c-d, or F-G) here. Italian MSS are a mixture: Mod 7 and Pad 47 have G-d.

v. 2 "viAS": besides the emended versions described above, there are the following variants:

Pa 776: baba GaGF FG(quil.)aGacaa (no descent to D)
Be 40078 (b's are flat): b b ba GbG F FD FG(quil.)aG acG\a
Gr 807 (b's are flat): b(ori.)a GbF EFD FGaG aca

v. 2 "fiNEM":

In the first two segments of the melisma, Mo 159 adopts c rather than d as the top note: a GbcbGa GbcbGa. Ben 34's version is matched in the Aquitanian MSS, but the version with c as the top note is found elsewhere:
Be 40078: melisma begins a Ga(quil.)c CGa Ga(quil.)c CGa
Gr 807: a GacbGa GacbGa
Mod 7: a GabcccbGa GabcccbGa (same in Pad 47 and Pist 120)
Gr 807 also differs in some other segments of the melisma following the Gacc segment: Gacc ca ca cG aa

Roman MSS:
Vat 5319:

v. 1 "E/GO": aGacba/Ga(ori.)GFG (written a whole tone higher than in Bodmer 74)

RoS 22:

"SEMper": GcaGaGaFG
"quoniAM": acaGF GbaGaG

MISERERE MIHI (26)

This offertory shows only minor variants between sources, mainly around the pitches b and c. The melodic figure Gbdc that occurs several times in Ben 24 (see v. 1 "delictum" and "meum") is realized in other sources from the core group, like Pa 776 and Pa 1121, as acdc.

v. 1 "me": Ben 34 has a single a here. Most other sources have a aGa.

Individual MSS:

Pa 1235: Respond, "miseriCORdiam": Pa 1235 has a more ornate alternative version, making it identical to the verbally parallel passage in *Domine fac mecum*: cccbacca(liq.)
Be 40078: Respond, "domine": Gc (ori.) cba cG
Gr 807:

v. 2, "FEci": f (ori.)eddefef
v. 2 "TUis": bc deb cd cd eb cd cd ecbaGa

Roman version: Bod 74 has a shortened version of the first verse: "Tibi soli peccavi et malum coram te feci."

DOMINE IN AUXILIUM (27)

The Gregorian *Domine in auxilium* exhibits few significant melodic variants among the core group of sources. The Beneventan reading employed as the base version is representative of the group as a whole. Two issues, however, require discussion. The first is structural. Some sources close with a cue to repeat the opening of the offertory, "domine in auxilium meum respice," which also serves as the repetendum cue in sources that indicate repetenda. Other MSS lack this cue, simply closing with "eam." These differences are consistent with the remarks of John of Afflighem: "Many end this offertory badly by avoiding the heptaphone that is at the end because it seems to them ill-sounding. Therefore in certain books they repeat at the end what occurs in its beginning."[1] The presence or absence of this reprise affects the offertory's modal assignment, an issue Bomm addresses.[2] The internal phrases of the respond and first verse are characteristic of mode 6, sharing material with other sixth-mode offertories. The sources with the reprise end unproblematically on F (or the affinal c) at "respice," a practice also reflected in the Roman version. The sources without the refrain, however, close variously on C or F (sometimes G if the offertory is written at the affinal position). Although this chant is lacking in most tonaries, it is classified as a *tritus* chant by Bern of Reichenau, Frutolf, Ugolino, and the Tonary of Munich, Bayerische Staatsbibliothek clm. 9921, an eleventh-century MS from Ottobeuren.[3]

Most sources in the core group lack a cue to the beginning of the offertory and close the respond on low C, as shown in Ben 34. Ben 38, however, does have a cue to return to the opening. It is doubtful that performances with verses actually ended on low C, which is not a legitimate final. Mo 159, for example, appears to close the respond on low C and lacks repetendum cues, but nonetheless classifies this piece among *tritus plagal* chants, perhaps implying that a repetendum was performed after the second verse. Most MSS with repetendum cues indicate "domine in auxilium," the beginning of the offertory, as the repetendum. We may speculate that the repetendum consisted not of the whole respond but of "domine in auxilium meum respice," thus coming to a conclusion on F. Ben 34 is unusual in indicating "confundantur" as the repetendum cue for the first verse and lacking a cue after the second verse.

To summarize the ending of the respond in the sources, a version matching the low C ending of Ben 34 is found in Mo 159, Pa, 780, Pa 776, Pa 1121, and Pa 1132. These sources lack a repeat of the opening at the end of the respond, but with the exception of Pa 776, they do have a repetendum cue at the end of the second verse (as do the other sources from St. Martial), suggesting that perhaps a performance with verses came to a conclusion on F, at "respice." The respond closes on low C, without repetendum cues, in Be 40078. In Pa 1235, which is written at affinal position, it closes on G. In many Italian sources, including

---

1. "Hoc offertorium plurimi male emittunt vitantes heptaphonum qui in fine est, quia eis absonus videtur. Unde et in quibusdam libris in principio eius invenitur et in fine repetunt." Johannes Afflighemensis, De musica cum tonario, ed. J. Smits van Waesberghe, Corpus scriptorum de musica, vol. 1 ([Rome]: American Institute of Musicology, 1950), 188. Translation is that of Warren Babb in Palisca, ed. (1978), 180.

2. Bomm (1929), 155–58.

3. See Alexander Rausch, *Die Musiktractate des Abtes Bern von Reichenau: Edition und Interpretation* (Tutzing: H. Schneider, 1999), 277; *Frutolfi Breviarium de Musica et Tonarius*, ed. Coelestin Vivell (Vienna: Akademie der Wissenschaften Sitzungberichte, 1919), 157; *Ugolini Urbevetanis Declaratio musicae disciplinae*, ed. Albert Seay, Corpus scriptorum de musica, vol. 7/1 ([Rome]: American Institute of Musicology, 1959), 168.

Mod 7, Pad 47, RoV 52, To 18, Pst 120, and Pia 65, the respond concludes with a cue to return to the beginning and repeat the first phrase of the respond. With the cue observed in performance, the respond would conclude unproblematically on F. Finally, a few sources in the sampling emend the melisma on "meam" to close on F, D, or, at the affinal position, a, as in the following sources:

> Tri 2254: CFDF
> Lo 4951: FFGG(ori.)F
> Frutolf tonary: CFCF
> Mü 10086: DFD

A second variant point is the relative pitch level between the respond and second verse. *Domine in auxilium* presents a pitch-level problem similar to most other sixth-mode offertories. In the Beneventan version, the verse is an unproblematic *tritus* authentic melody in relation to the plagal respond. In some versions, however, the second verse is written a fifth below the level of Ben 34. In the second verse, the typical characteristics of mode 5 are projected a fifth below the final. Most of the melody remains within the fifth B (flat)-F, and the cadence on "respexit me" is on low B (flat), a fifth below the final.

This latter version is the majority reading among Aquitanian sources and is also found (at the affinal position) in many Italian MSS. It is clear that the low B-flats and probable E-flats in this version of the final verse would have necessitated an upward transposition of the final verse. These problem spots, however, do not fully explain the differences in pitch-level profile; this version could be transmitted in staff notation by simply writing the whole offertory, respond and both verses, at the affinal position, a solution adopted in many sources. Given the theoretical awareness of the Aquitanian scribes, it is probable that the affinal position was their intention as well. In the version of Ben 34, however, the respond and second verse appear in a relationship that is more consistent with contemporaneous understandings of mode, since the second verse appears as an unproblematic *tritus authentic* melody in relation to the plagal respond.

To some extent, the pitch-level profile of the sources suggests a regional preference for one version or the other. In a few cases, however, variants in pitch-level profile can be found among sources that are otherwise closely related. The repetendum cue in Pa 1137, for example, indicates a pitch-level profile matching that of Ben 34, whereas the other sources from St. Martial match Pa 1121. These differences suggest that the pitch-level profile was, to some extent, the purview of individual scribes.

A summary of sources follows: Pitch-level profile of Ben 34: Mo 159, Pa 1137, Lo 4951, Pst 120, To 18, Pia 65, Tri 2254, Mü 10086, Be 40078, Gr 807. Final verse written a fifth below the level of Ben 34: Pa 776, Pa 780, Pa 1134, 1135, 1136, and 1132. At the affinal position: Pad 47, Mod 7, RoV 52, Madrid 20-4. Pa 1235: Respond is at the affinal position; verse 1 is in the untransposed range.

Roman MSS:

Bod 74 and Vat 5319 have the verses in the following order: (1). Expectans; (2) Avertantur. There are no significant melodic variants.

ILLUMINA OCULOS (28)

The Beneventan MSS are unusual in one respect: "dormiam" in the respond (phrase 1) reads "obdormiam" in most other MSS (with only Compiègne matching Beneventan MSS). The melodic reading typically matches that of Mo 159: "OB/DORmiam": E/GEGaG.

Other melodic variants:

respond, "eAM" Some MSS dip down to D:

Mo 159: FFF GaGD FFF aGF GF (quil.)E (same reading in Lo 4951 and Pa 776).

Pa 1121 and Pa 780 have the reading of Ben 34: FFF GaGF FFF aGF GFE.

Ben 34's reading is also found in the peripheral MSS RoV 52 and Be 40078.

Mo 159's reading is found in Cai 61, Pa 1235, Mod 7, Pad 47, and Pst 120.

respond, "IN [morte]": Pa 776 and Pa 1121 have Da(liq.).
v. 1 "domiNE": Pa 1121 and Lo 4951 are essentially identical to Ben 34, but Pa 776, Pa 780, and Mo 159 have a different reading:

Mo 159: cc cb(quil.)a cc dc cdaa(ori.)G

Pa 776: b cccba ccd ccd aaG

Pa 780: cccba ccd ccd aaG

Ben 34's version is matched in Cai 61. Mo 159's version is matched in the following peripheral MSS: Pa 1235, RoV 52, Mod 7, Pad 47, Pst 120, and Be 40078.

Variants in individual MSS:

Pa 776: v. 2 "boNA": bccaG aaG ccaaG ccGbaG (a truncated version of the melisma).
Pa 1121: v. 1 "CONsilium": EG.
Pa 780: v. 2 "exAUdi": cdc c(ori.)a cca ccaGa (longer version of the melisma).
Lo 4951: v. 1 "aniMA": abaGa.
Cai 61:

respond, "MEos" (all b's are flat): aG ba bGF FGa baG ba

v. 2 "cantabo": b-flats are indicated here, whereas they are not in other sources.

Be 40078: v. 1 "animam meam" (*sic*): indicates b-naturals rather than the b-flats found in most MSS that distinguish between b-natural and b-flat.
Gr 807:

respond, "morTE": cccGF GF GaGF GFE

respond, "ADversus": DFDF

Roman MSS: There are no significant variants. In phrase 6, the Roman reading concludes with a cadential pattern associated with the *protus* and *tetrardus* maneria, but written a tone lower. Vat 5319 employs a notated b-flat here. A similar cadence occurs in *Immittet* (69).

IUSTITIAE DOMINI (29)

This offertory exhibits significant variants at two points: the end of the respond—hence the modal assignment—and the relative pitch level between the respond and second verse.[1]

The *deuterus* ending of the respond in the base version of Pa 776 is the majority reading and is implied by the neumes in the early adiastematic MSS examined. In some MSS, however, the respond is emended to close on F. The alternative ending may be attributable to certain melodic characteristics this piece shares with the sixth-mode offertories (discussed in chapter 3). The following MSS have alternative endings on F:

Mo 159: FFF(ori.) C FFF aGF GFE/F
Lo 4951: E FFF D FFF aGF aGFGF/F
Ben 34: FFF DFFF aGF aGFGF/F(liq.) (same in Ben 35)

In this respect, Ben 34 and Ben 35 differ from the earlier Beneventan MSS, Ben 38 and 40, which have the ending on E.

Another variant concerns the relative pitch level of the respond and second verse. The reading of Pa 776 is the preferred version and the majority version among Aquitanian MSS. When the whole offertory is transcribed in the normal plagal range, with the final on E, several problems emerge in the second verse. This verse has the traits of the fifth mode, but projected a fifth below the normal fifth-mode range. At "conspectu tuo" (phrase 8) a caesura occurs on low B-flat, which is now heard as a temporary final, resulting in the need for a nondiatonic pitch, E-flat, in the final melisma. In pitch-specific MSS, these problems are addressed in two different ways. The group of MSS designated group 1 below preserves the pitch-level profile of Pa 776. In pitch-specific MSS, the entire offertory is simply transposed to the affinal position to close on b or c. This solution solves the notational problem of E-flats in the final melisma (allowing this note to be represented by b-flat) but preserves the modal irregularity of the second verse. Sources in group 2 indicate a shift in range between the two verses, creating a version more consistent with traditional conceptions of mode. In most cases, the respond and first verse are notated in the normal plagal range, closing on E or F, and the second verse is in the authentic range. A few MSS replicate this pitch-level profile at the affinal position.

The indications of E-flat and E-natural in the transcription of Pa 776 derive from the indications in Mo 159, where the verse is written a fifth higher and alternates between b-flat and b-natural.

Group 1, pitch-level profile of Pa 776: Pa 780, Pa 1121, Lo 4951, Ben 38, Pad 47 (affinal position), RoV 52 (affinal position), Mod 7 (affinal position)

Group 2, second verse 5↑ Pa 776: Ben 34 (at affinal position), Ben 35, Cai 61, Pa 1235, Pst 120, Gr 807, Be 40078

Melodic variants: The MSS differ in their indication of text underlay at "custodi*et ea/ eam*." Most MSS in the sampling follow the underlay indicated in Pa 776, but the following MSS vary:

Mo 159: "ET/E [am]": F/FF F(ori.) C (etc.)
Ben 34: F/FFF (etc.)

v.2: Some MSS more consistently adopt low B-flat (rather than C) as the bottom note (or, at the higher level of transposition, F rather than G). Mo 159, for example, has F's on "et [erunt]" and "ut [complaceant]," which would be low B-flats at the level of Pa 776. Pa

---

1. On the problem of modal assignment, see Bomm (1929), 169–71. Both problems are also discussed in Frasch (1986), 1:189; and Hankeln (1999), 1:108.

1121 adopts B (flat) as the bottom note at the end of the melisma on "complaceant," corresponding to the final c of the melisma in Pa 776.

v. 2 "comPLAceant":

>Lo 4951: DFGFGFGFGa FFFDC FFG FG FGFGaFFFDC FDF **FDC FD F(ORI.) DC FDB** FDE(QUIL.)FG
>
>Pa 1235: melisma ends cdaG caG aG
>
>Cai 61: melisma ends daG caG caF cacd

v. 2 "SEMper":

>Pa 1121: FGFD ECB DF aGF FFF FabG F F(ori.) D **FFD GF DD(ori.)B BDF** (etc.)
>
>Lo 4951: Ending of the melisma is FFF FG FG(quil.)a G FGF
>
>Pa 1235: cdca baG ac edc ccc ce fdc caccc **cdc ca ccadc aF Fac** (etc.).

The ending of v. 2 ("semPER") is a point of variance in a few MSS (though Pa 776 reflects the reading in most peripheral MSS examined):

>Mo 159: cc cba ca FG
>
>Pa 1121: FFFED EC BB(ori.) C
>
>Lo 4951: F (following the altered version of the melisma on the first syllable)
>
>Ben 34: cccbacG FG
>
>RoV 52: cccbaca

Roman MSS:
>Vat 5319:

>respond, "RECte": FGaGaGa(ori.) GF
>
>respond, "cusTOdiet": aGF FGaGbaG
>
>v. 1 "preCEPtum": baGaGFG FGF acGaGFGF EFE **DFEDC** DFFF GaGaGFGE FGaGaGF
>
>v. 1 "VEra": Vat 5319 has the longer version of the melisma's ending: FacGaG FGF EFEDFEDE(ori.)DC DFF GaGaG**FGE GaGaGF**

>RoS 22:

>"IUstitite": aG
>
>"dulciOra": aFGaGaGF
>
>"serVUS": GEFEDC

EXAUDI DEUS (30)

This offertory has few significant variants between sources.

1. Respond, "MEam": In several sources outside the core group, notes 6, 7, and 8 of the melisma are Fga (rather than Fac): These include Gr 807 and the Italian sources.

Individual MSS:

Pa 1235: respond "exAUdi" [me]: ccbG aG acbG aba (liq.); v. 2. "retribuENdo": d dc deda deda dedcba c cd ff gfgf fgf gag (liq.)

To 18: v. 2, "retribuENdo" (major variant): dedc dc cc ca bcbaG bcba cc dcca Ga cc dcdc de cc cad

Roman sources: The only significant variant is at the end of the respond, "exaudi me." Bod 74 has what appear to be two alternative endings. The second is nearly identical to that of Vat 5319, closing on a. The first is more ornate:

Ex- au- di- me

Gc dc c cbcbabaG acbaba G GF acbabaG (liq.) GacbabaGa GF

The ending of RoS 22 is similar to that of 5319 and the second ending of Bod 74, closing on a.

DOMINE FAC MECUM (31)

This fourth-mode offertory is notated at the affinal position in most sources, undoubtedly because the low F in the respond would become B-flat at the lower level of transposition, a note unavailable in most notational systems. Only three sources included in the sampling, Pa 903, Gr 807 (which has a sign for B-flat), and Mo 159 notate the respond (along with the verses *Deus laudem* and *Pro eo*) in the untransposed range. In Pa 903 the passage is emended so that the B-flat is a C, and in Mo 159, the note is written as a B-natural.

Domine fac mecum exhibits a particular prominence of small variants around the pitches b and c. The Beneventan sources are the most consistently focused on b. Some change of tonal focus to c is evident already in the earliest pitch-readable sources, Mo 159 and Pa 1121. On the final syllable of "peccatoris" in verse 1, for example, the Beneventan sources have babca, whereas Pa 1121 has cabcb. The change of focus to c seems to distinguish the sources chronologically. A marked emphasis on c is evident not only in late German sources such as Be 40078 and Tri 2254 but also in the thirteenth-century Italian MS To 18. In most passages, these sources avoid b altogether, except at the final cadence; passages such as "deus laudem" in verse 1, for example, consist entirely of repetition of c rather than alternation between b and c.

Locuti sunt, the second verse in a majority of sources, contrasts modally and melodically with the rest of the offertory. The Italian sources included in the sampling present a distinctive reading of this verse, both in pitch level and melodic detail. These sources notate the beginning of the verse a fifth higher than it appears in Ben 34 and the other sources, joining at "circumdederunt me." The Italian MSS, moreover, exhibit several other departures from the majority version, as shown in example 31.1. A very similar version of the verse may be found without pitched notation in RoA 123, and in Mod 7, Pad 47, Pst 120, and Pia 65. To 18 exhibits some, but not all, of these characteristics.

EXAMPLE 31.1

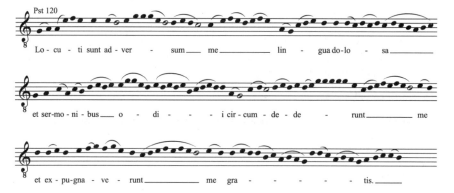

Roman sources: In Bod 74, the offertory is notated in the normal plagal range, ending on E. There are no major melodic variants.

INTENDE VOCI (32)

The parenthetical b-flats at "laetentur" (phrase 8) are derived from their use in Mo 159, but are also indicated in Tri 2254.

In its hypothetical unemended version, written at the pitch level of Pa 1121, this offertory employs one nondiatonic pitch, at "viam meam" (phrase 7).[1] In Mo 159 and most non-Aquitanian MSS, "meam" is written a whole tone higher. Ben 34 is unique among the sources examined in notating the passage a fourth lower. A second pitch-level variant occurs at "gloriabuntur" (phrase 9), described below.

Pitch level at "[viam] meam":

= Pa 1121: Pa 776, Pa 780, Pa 1136, Lo 4951, Be 40078 (note corresponding to Pa 1121's E [flat] is F), Gr 807 (note corresponding to Pa 1121's E [flat] is F)
2↑ Pa Pa 1121: Mo 159, Ben 35, Cai 61, Pa 1235, Pad 47, Pst 120, RoV 52, To 18, Tri 2254, Frutolf tonary
4↓ Pa 1121: Ben 34

Pitch level at "gloriabuntur": Many MSS notate this passage a whole tone above the level of Pa 1121. Mo 159 is a tone higher beginning on the second syllable of "aeternum," whereas most other MSS are a tone higher beginning on the first syllable of "gloriabuntur." All MSS join in the melisma on "gloria*buntur*" or at "qui diligunt," *except* for Pa 776. In Pa 776, the rest of the verse remains a tone above Pa 1121, including the repetendum to "quoniam," which is notated a tone too high.

Although the reasons for the variants are not clear, the variety of versions suggests that an emendation has taken place. The passage is written at the level of Pa 1121 in several later MSS that distinguish between b natural and b-flat. A b-flat is indicated in Tri 2254, Cai 61, and Ben 34 (one of the few notated b-flats in this MS). With a b-flat, Pa 1121 has the same intervallic structure as the majority version a tone higher. Either the reading of Pa 776 is a scribal error or it represents a pretheoretical tradition in which the tonal focus of the verse migrated from c to d (with the e's in the majority reading sung as f-sharp's) and the repetendum was also sung a tone higher. I have shown evidence for similar "modulations" in other offertories, such as *Oravi deum* and *Ave Maria*. In *Intende*, however, the evidence for this practice is limited to one MS included in the sampling and may well reflect an error. For this reason, I have opted for Pa 1121 as the base version.

Pitch level of "gloriabuntur":

= Pa 1121: Ben 34, Ben 39, Pa 780, Lo 4951, Tri 2254, Cai 61
2↑ Pa 1121: Pa 776, Pa 1136, Pa 1137, Pa 1132, Mo 159, Pst 120, Mod 7, Pad 47, To 18, RoV 52, Gr 807, Be 40078

On "gloriabuntur":

Ben 34: One of the very few places where this MS employs a notated b-flat: G/G/G/b-flat G bbcba bcdc (liq.)/ed

---

1. See also Pitman (1973), 103.

Pa 1121: G/G/G/bGbbcba bc(quil.)d/dc (very similar readings in Pa 780, Lo 4951, Cai 61, Trier 2254).

Melodic variants: Although there are very few major variants, small variants are found at several points around the pitches G and F. Melodic figures that revolve around the pitches c-a-G-a occasionally appear as c-a-F-a. These points of variance do not appear to be correlated with regional tradition or groups of MSS. One example is in the final melisma of the respond, on "DOmine." Pa 776 is anomalous among core sources in having F as the lowest note. In most MSS G is the lowest note:

Pa 1121: FG(quil.)aGa ccc dcdc c(ori.) G acbac (same reading in Lo 4951)
Mo 159: FG(quil.)aGa ccc dc dcc(ori.)G Gcbac (same reading in Ben 34)

Pa 776's reading, however, is matched in some unrelated MSS such as Pad 47.

Another example occurs on "oRAbo" in the respond, where Ben 34 and Ben 35 start with Fac instead of Gac.

v. 2 "in conspeCTU": Ben 34: GFa
v. 2 "aeTER/NUM": Mo 159: cd/ded ede

Roman MSS:

Respond, "[orationis] meae": The neume groupings seem to indicate a different text underlay in Bod 74, Vat 5319, and RoS 22, perhaps because the two "e" sounds were not distinguished in performance.

Vat 5319:

v. 1: "VER/BA": deded(liq.)/dedc

RoS 22:

"inTENde": babcbcba
"ME/E": Gabcba/aGabaGaG

GRESSUS MEOS (33)

In both the Gregorian and Roman traditions, *Gressus meos* has an unusual structure in which a complete repetendum is written out after the second verse, with a long added melisma. As Kenneth Levy has shown, the melisma of the Gregorian version has several other functions in the chant repertory, including a use as the basis for an Italian sequence.[1]

Gressus meos exhibits several points of variance among the sources. The Beneventan reading presented as the base version is consistent with Mo 159 and Aquitanian MSS, except at the closing melisma, as described below. The major melodic and pitch-level variants are as follows:

1. The opening pitches. The respond starts variously with D-ED (Pa 776), D-DF (RoV 52), E-EG (Pia 65), EGF (Pa 780), or F-FG (Mo 159, Beneventan MSS, Lo 4951, Pa 1121); and even G-Ga (To 18).[2]

---

1. Levy (1971), 40–61.
2. Hankeln (1999), 2:224.

EXAMPLE 33.1

2. Respond, "secundum" melisma: Most Aquitanian sources present a reading similar to Ben 34, differing only in the number of repeated notes and the use of the oriscus. Mo 159, however, adopts a more literal repetition of the opening notes: cccaGG (ori.) FGacccaG G (ori.) FG (quil.) ab-flat aG (liq.). A similar version is found in two of the Italian sources, To 18 and RoV 52.

3. Respond and repetendum, "ut non dominetur omnis": The Italian sources have "ut non dominetur *mei* omnis." The extra syllables are accommodated with notes from the melisma on "dominetur."

4. Verse 1, "dat/dans": The Italian sources present a shortened form of this melisma, omitting its last two notes.

5. Second verse, "cognovi domine"

In pitch level, Ben 34 represents the majority reading, found in Mo 159, Pa 776, several other Aquitanian sources, and the German MSS. The pitch level variants among a few of the Aquitanian sources in this passage are discussed by Hankeln, who notes that Pa 1133 begins a fourth below Mo 159 and several other sources.[3] The passage is also variant among Italian sources. The scribe of Pad 47 begins "cognovi" a fourth above its usual position, joining with the majority version on "domine." A very similar reading is found in two of the other Italian sources, Mod 7 and Pia 65. Pst 120 and To 18 begin like these MSS, a fourth above Ben 34, but subsequently place the melisma on "domine" a whole tone above its usual position. The reasons for the upward transposition of a fourth are unclear.

Two sources from German-speaking areas have a slightly longer melisma on the final syllable of "domine," as in Tri 2254 (with the b-flat applying to the whole passage): Ga (quil.)b-flat GbbabaGbG.

6. Second verse, "iustitia" melisma (ex. 33.1): The Beneventan version of this melisma, found in Ben 34, 35, and 38, differs from the others in its repetition scheme. The version of Mo 159, shown in example 33.1, is representative of a broad international tradition.

Notes on specific sources: v. 1, "dans" In Lo 4951 this melisma is lengthened to create a standard cadential pattern, with the following notes: Gccbab (quil.)cba.

Roman sources: The version of Vat 5319 is nearly identical to that of Bod 74 except for the "iustitia" melisma, where Vat 5319 omits a few passing notes toward the end of the melisma. The last seventeen notes of the melisma: FGaGFGFbacbabcbab. RoS 22 exhibits the following small differences from Bod 74:

"MEos": Ga
"seCUNdum": ccbabab
"oMNIS": FEFGFEDFG
"IUstitias" (sic): aG
"IustitiAS" (sic): GaGacbcbabcbab

3. Ben 34 and 35 move to the higher register on "iusticiam"; ci/am is a/Ge(liq.).

LAUDATE DOMINUM (34)

In most MSS, this offertory is notated at the affinal position, undoubtedly because of the low B-flat required at "populum" (phrase 10).

Aside from small differences in recitational style, there are very few variants among core and peripheral MSS.

The Beneventan MSS have the following very small differences from most other MSS:

respond: "EST," and v. 2: "benediciTE": Most MSS lack the second D in the Beneventan version, as in the following:

Mo 159 (at affinal position): Ga(quil.)cb(quil.)Da ca
Pa 1121: DE(quil.)FDCED

v. 1 "staTIS": Most MSS have GFFD FGF
v. 2 "SE/CU/LA": Most MSS have F/D/FD
Lo 4951: v. 3, "ierusaLEM" (final melisma): bottom note is B rather than A
RoV 52 (at affinal position): v. 2 "doMI/NUS": cbGa/aG

Roman MSS:

Vat 5319: v. 2 "hierusaLEM": This final melisma is transposed up a fifth, perhaps because of the need for low B-flat. There are no significant variants in RoS 22.

EXSPECTANS EXPECTAVI (35)

As Pitman persuasively argued, this offertory has a variant point related to the use of the nondiatonic pitch high f–sharp in v. 2.[1] In many sources, including Mo 159, the passage beginning "benenuntiavi" (phrase 8) is written a tone below Pa 776, remaining there until "magna" at the end of the verse; Mo 159 indicates a b–flat. The whole tone d–e in Mo 159, which occurs on "tuam" and in the melisma on "ecclesia," is equivalent to e–f in Pa 776. To duplicate Mo 159's intervallic structure at the level of Pa 776, an f–sharp is required. The nondiatonic pitch is also suggested by Be 40078, where this verse is notated a fourth above Pa 776 and employs both b–flat and b–natural, equivalent to f and f–sharp at the level of Pa 776. Other sources, including Ben 34, Ben 35, Pa 1235 and most Italian MSS in the sampling, write the passage at the same level as Pa 776, evidently eliminating the non-diatonic pitch and changing the intervallic structure. Pa 776 was chosen as the base version because it places this passage in its "unemended" range.

Summary of pitch level of v 1:

1. At the level of Pa 776 throughout: Pa 1121, Ben 34, Ben 35, Pa 1235, RoV 52, Pst 120, Mod 7
2. The entire verse written a fourth above Pa 776: Be 40078, Cai 61
3. A whole tone below Pa 776 at "benenunciavi," joining again at "magna": Mo 159
4. A whole tone below Pa 776 beginning at "tuam" through the end of the verse: To 18
5. Individual solutions:

---

1. Pitman (1973), 269–72, 339–41.

a. Tri 2254 is a tone below Pa 776 beginning on the third syllable of "iusticiam" and joins Pa 776 at "magna."

b. Lo 4951 is a fourth below Pa 776 beginning at "iusticiam" and a fifth below beginning on the last syllable of "iusticiam," thereby representing the f–sharp with a b–natural.

c. The Frutolf tonary indicates that "benenuntiavi" should begin on F, a fifth below the level of Pa 776, also allowing the f–sharp to be represented with b–natural.

Other significant variants:

v. 2 "ecCLESia" melisma: In addition to the whole–tone transposition, several sources in the core group differ from Pa 776 in one segment of this melisma:

Pa 776: . . . ggged **egef(#)dc** cdedecb . . .

Mo 159 (all b's are flat): . . . fffdc **dedecb**   cdc cba bca . . . A reading similar to Mo 159 is found in Beneventan MSS and in many Italian and German sources.

Lo 4951 has a slightly shortened melisma (written a fifth below Pa 776): accaG cccaG abab GFGa cde c.

v. 3 "iusticiam tuam" (or "meam") "non abscondi" (phrase 9): This passage is a point of variance, possibly because of the awkwardness created by the leap of a seventh, D–c, in Pa 776. There are variants among core and peripheral MSS as follows. All MSS except Pa 1121 join Pa 776 at some point in the passage that immediately follows, on "in corde."

	me/tu	am	non	ab-	scon
Pa 776:	GaGE	EGEED	cd	c	cd(liq.) etc.
Mo 159:	GaGE	EGFFE	bc	b	bc(liq.)
Pa 1121:	FGFD	DFDDC	cd	d	cd^2
Pa 1137:	abaF	GaGGF	cd	c	cd
Pa 1136:	GaGE	EGEED	bc	b	bc
Lo 4951:	GaGE	EGFFE	bc	b	bc
Ben 34:	cdca	acaaG	cd	c (liq.)	cd (liq.)[3] (also in Ben 35)
T 2254:	FGFFD	DFDDC	c	c	c^4 (also in Cai 61, Ber 40078, Frutolf)
Pa 1235:	ab–flat aG	GaGGF	cc	c	bc

---

2. Pa 1121 exhibits some differences leading up to this passage, very similar to Trier 2254 described below. Beginning within the melisma on "iuSTIciam'," it is a whole tone below Pa 776, with recitation on b–flat at "iuSTIciam'" and ci/am is F/DF. "Non abscondi" begins on a new line and is preceded by a custos ("following "tuam") that places "non abscondi" and the rest of the verse a whole tone higher than the other readings. This is probably to be regarded as an error.

3. Ben 34 and 35 move to the higher register on "iusticiam"; ci/am is a/Gc(liq.).

4. Trier 2254 also shows some differences leading up to this passage, with recitation on b–flat at "iusticiam"; ci/am is F/DF.

RoV 52:	GaGF	FGFE	cc	c	cd (liq.)
Pst 120:	GaGE	FGEFD	Gc	c	bc(liq.)
Pad 47:	GaGE	FEFD	cd	c	cd
Mod 7:	GaGE	FGFE	cd	c	c

The greatest point of variance between the MSS is the final syllable of "tuam/meam," which ends variously on E, D, F, G, and C. While the intervallic differences between versions such as Mo 159 and Pa 776 on the last syllable of "meam/tuam" may suggest a nondiatonic pitch, other readings, such as Pa 1121 (matched in Trier 2254) are intervallically identical to Pa 776. I am inclined to attribute the different readings simply to the modal ambiguity inherent in the melody as a whole, which contains few references to the final, and to the awkwardness of the leap of a seventh (from "tuam" to "non") in Pa 776. With this reasoning, Pa 776 emerges as the *lectio difficilior*.

Roman MSS: The Roman tradition lacks the first verse found widely in Gregorian MSS. Vat 5319 is written at the affinal position and shows the following variants:

respond, "CANticum": ccdcbacbaba
v. 1: "mulTA": ba
v. 2: "FE/CISti": Ga/a

In the verses, Vat 5319 is more standard in its use of Formula A. Bod 74 alternates in its recitation between the standard torculus EFD and the single note F. All of the corresponding places are torculi in Vat 5319:

v. 1: "Deus"; "mirabiLIa"; "cogiTIoNIbus"; "QUIS"
v. 2: "MEo"; "VEriTAtem"; "MEus"

In Vat 5319, the start of a new verse is indicated at "benenuntiavi."

RoS 22 shows the typical differences from Bod 74 and Vat 5319 in its use of Formula B. The last segment is dedcbcd (rather than dcbcd): "domiNUM", "ME", "meAM"

Other variants in F22:

"CANticum": cdcbacbaba
"Ymnum": bdcb

BENEDICITE GENTES (36)

The respond and first two verses of *Benedicite gentes* exhibit no major variants, aside from minor differences in recitational style. In v. 3, however, the sources differ in pitch level, producing several different readings.[1] The variants begin at "ad ipsum" (phrase 17). Pa 776 was chosen as base version because its reading of this passage is the most probable preferred reading; it is also the majority version among Aquitanian sources.

Example 36.1 presents several different versions of the passage. In Pa 776 (line 1), a common referential interval of mode 1, a-c, is projected a tone lower, with the pitches G-b-

---

1. This passage is discussed in Hankeln (1999), 1:108; and 2:1434–4.

EXAMPLE **36.1**A

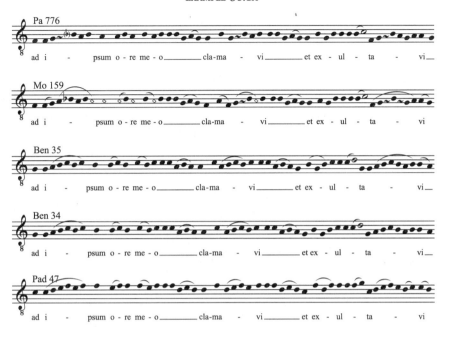

EXAMPLE **36.1**B

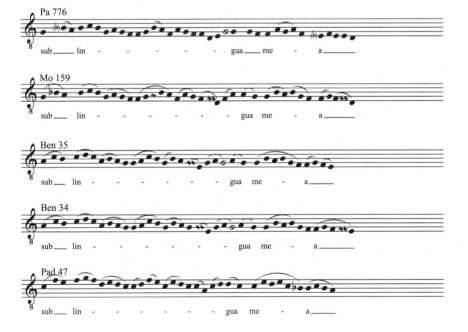

EXAMPLE 36.1c

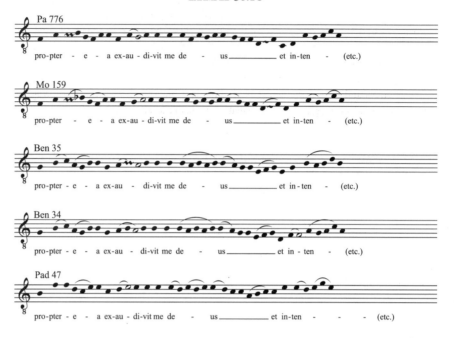

flat. This reading is found in Mo 159 and in several Aquitanian sources, including Pa 1121, Pa 780, and Lo 4951. In Ben 34 and Ben 35, lines 3 and 4, the passage is notated a tone higher, a range more consistent with the characteristics of the first mode. This reading of the passage is adopted in sources from a wide geographical spectrum, as summarized below.

The second variant point occurs between the melisma on "lingua" and the cadence on "mea." Several of the G-*protus* sources, including Mo 159, join the pitch level of Ben 34.

These sources move to the upper range at different places, but generally on the last syllable of "lingua." Mo 159's reading of the melodic figure on the last syllable of "mea" thus differs intervallically from that of Pa 776. Without chromatic inflections, the semitone F-E in Mo 159 is the whole tone E-D in Pa 776. I would hypothesize that this upward transposition was made to represent the semitone D-E-flat at the level of Pa 776. This hypothesis is supported by the reading of Pad 47 (line 5), which is a fifth higher than Pa 776 and notates a b-flat here.

It is doubtful that the nondiatonic pitch on "mea" is the only cause of the variant readings of this passage. The readings that match Ben 34 at the beginning of the passage articulate the third a-c and are based in the diazeugmenon tetrachord; the lower version is based in the synemmenon tetrachord. Like several other passages in the offertories, this one exhibits the characteristic of modal "transformation" described by Guido, in which G and b-flat, used in close proximity, create a G-*protus* sound. The whole-tone transposition in the other sources is recommended by Guido as a solution. It is worthy of note that Mo 159 adopts the ambiguous sign here that may indicate microtonal inflections, as indicated by the diamond in the transcription.

Most of the sources included in the sampling join at or before "propterea." The majority version of this passage, shown in five of the six sources in the example, is marked by a normal first-mode structure centered on the pitch a. Two sources, Ben 35 (line 3) and Gr 807, however, remain a whole tone above the others. Gr 807 (not shown in the example) joins at "et intende" and Ben 35 in the final melisma of the verse. These sources present a different intervallic structure from the others at the cadential figure on "deus," which is EFG in Ben 35 and DEF in the majority reading. It is unclear whether this transposition represents a nondiatonic pitch, such as E-flat at the lower level.

1. "Ad ipsum":

= Pa 776: Mo 159, Pa 903, Pa 4951, Pa 780, Be 40078, Pa 1121, Pa 1135, Pa 1136, Pa 1137, Pia 65
2↑ Pa 776: Ben 34, Ben 35, Pa 1134, Pa 1132, Pa 1235, Cai 61, Gr 807, Pst 120, RoV 52
5↑ Pa 776: Pad 47, Mod 7

2. Final syllable of "mea":
2↑ Pa 776: all except
= Pa 776: Pa 1121, Pa 1136, Pa 780, Lo 4951
5↑ Pa 776: Pad 47, Mod 7

3. "propterea":
= Pa 776: all except
2↑Pa 776: Ben 35, Gr 807, Pa 1132
5↑ Pa 776: Pad 47, Mod 7

4. "Et intende":
5↑ Pa 776: Pad 47, Mod 7
= Pa 776: all others except Pa 1132

Notes on specific sources:
Pa 776: In the final alleluia of the respond (phrase 7), the text has been erased.
Several Italian sources assume the same register profile as Paris 776, but notate the entire offertory a fifth higher.

Pst 120 lacks the third verse.
To 18 lacks notation in the third verse.
v. 3 cadence on "mea": Pa 1235 has DDFDDC; Be 40078 has DFDC.
v. 3 melisma on "lingua" in Pia 65: abaGaGFFGaGFaGFFEFa/aaG.

Roman MSS: Bodmer C74 has the verses in the following order: (1) *In multitudine*; (2) *Iubilate*; (3) *Venite*. The first two verses in the transcriptions have been reversed to facilitate comparison with Pa 776.

There are very few significant variants.
Respond, "DOminus": Vat 5319 and RoS 22 have FGFE
Melisma on final syllable of "alleluia": RoS 22 has a more elaborate melisma:
DFEDFEFDCD
v. 3 "Ipso": Vat 5319 FGaGaF; et [exultavit]: G ori. FEaG liq.

POPULUM HUMILEM (37)

The sources exhibit variants in several of the long melismas in the second verse.

v. 2 melisma on "MEus": Sources in the core group exhibit some small points of variance, as exemplified by the following (significant differences from Mo 159 are shown in bold): Pa 776: **bbb** GFGaFG **bbb** GFGa cdec a a (ori.) Ga ccacb cdcdcca cb c dcdcc aFGFa **a (ori.) Ga** cdccaG. The Beneventan sources have an abbreviated version, as in Ben 34: aa aGFGa FGaaaGFGa c dec aa(ori.)G a c cacb cdcc(ori)acb cdcdccaG.

v. 2 "exalTAbis": Although sources in the core group show only small variants, some sources in the peripheral group have different versions of the melisma, particularly in Italian sources. The segments that reflect significant differences are shown in bold.

Ben 34 (minor differences from Mo 159): acc ccc abc dc **Fac** ccc abc dc ac dc ac e ed ce ec edc **ac ca** dcb GacccaGF acccaGF ac cc abc

Pad 47: acccc abc dcFa cc ccc abc dc ac dc ac d eed **c e ecdcb a d dcedc bc e ecedc bceeecbacccaGFG** ccccc abc d (similar version in Mod 7)

RoV 52: acccc abc dc Fga ccccc abc dc ac dc ac d e ed **fe g gdfe bd db dcb bc eeecba bc eeecbaeee**

To 18: an abbreviated melisma, acc ca abc dc ac d dc **cf ecedc Gacc** aGFacc abc (The melisma of Pst 120 is much closer to those of the core group.)

Pa 1235: ac cccc cac cdc FGa cccc ca cdc ac dc ac **de ed df fcedc** cd dc dcb Ga cbcaGF acbc aGF ca c cac

Variants in individual sources:

Gr 807: v. 2, "MEus": differs in contour in the later part of the melisma, where the c-d oscillation begins: acb db ca cb adc ebc (etc.)

Pa 1235: v. 2, "MEus": differs in contour in the later part of the melisma, where the c-d oscillation begins: adcdc ca cb adcdbc a (etc.)

Roman version: The beginning of the respond, through "populum humilem," is written a whole tone lower both in Vat 5319 and RoS 22, presumably necessitating the use of b-flat.

FACTUS EST DOMINUS (38)

Factus est dominus is one of the few offertories with substantial verbal differences between the Gregorian and Roman versions. The Roman respond begins as the Gregorian does, but continues differently. The lyrics of the Gregorian respond are found transmitted as the first verse of the Roman. The reason for the longer text of the Roman version is not clear. Since it is not found in any Gregorian MSS, it may reflect a change that took place after the transmission of the tradition to the Franks. In the base transcription, the two versions are aligned in the places where they have matching lyrics. To facilitate comparison of the two versions, the phrases are numbered according to the longer Roman version. Neither version has repetenda indicated.

The modal instability of this chant was discussed long ago by Bomm. The chant ends variously on F, E, or D.[1] Mo 159 and the Aquitanian MSS close the chant on E, whereas the

---

1. Bomm (1929), 163–64.

Beneventan MSS close it on D. The endings are further discussed below, with other melodic variants.

Factus est dominus also presents a problem of pitch level and modal consistency at the end of the second verse, beginning with "inimicorum meorum" (phrase 14). The base reading of Pa 776 represents the majority Aquitanian version and the probable unemended pitch level. Similar readings are found in Pa 1121 and Pa 780. To some extent, the passage is G-*protus* in quality: a b-flat is employed in Mo 159 and implied by the sources that notate the passage, fully or partially, a whole tone higher, with c as the focal pitch. By the passage at "dedisti mihi" (phrase 15), most non-Aquitanian MSS are a whole tone above Pa 776. On "mihi," the interval F-E in Pa 776 appears in these sources at the whole tone G-F. To duplicate the intervallic structure of these versions, an E-flat is required at the level of Pa 776. The MSS that are a tone higher move to this position at different points in the melody, a variety that suggests they are emendations.

= Pa 776: Pa 1121, Pa 780, Gr 807

2↑ Pa 776 (Unless otherwise noted, the whole-tone transposition continues through the end of the verse):

Mo 159 (beginning at "et inimicorum")

Ben 34 and 35 (beginning on the second note of "dedisti," returning to level of Pa 776 at "odientes")

Pa 1235 (beginning in the melisma on "subplanTASti":"subplanTAS/TI" is: cc adcd ceded fff/ded)

Cai 61: (beginning at "et inimicorum")

Tri 2254: (beginning at "subplanTASti")

Mod 7 (beginning at "inimicos meos")

Pad 47 (beginning at "subplanTASti")

Pst 120 (beginning at "et" [subplantasti])

RoV 52 (beginning at "et" [subplantasti])

Three MSS included in the sampling adopt different solutions to the problem. In Be 40078, the verse is written a fifth above its level in Pa 776, and the E-flat at "mihi" at the level of Pa 776 is confirmed by a notated b-flat in Be 40078, which also occurs on the first syllable of "dedisti." The scribe of Lo 4951 notates the passage, beginning at "ad bellum," a fourth below Pa 776 (and an octave below Be 40078), presumably representing the problematic E-flat with a low B-flat. Gr 807 is notated at the level of Pa 776, and the note corresponding to an E-flat on "mihi" is a D.

Melodic variants:

respond, "eum":

Mo 159 opens the melisma differently: a aGG(ori.)F EFDC DFF (etc.)

respond, final cadence:

As mentioned, the closing three or four notes are a point of variance. The sources incorporated into this study, however, do not differ to the extent of those studied by Bomm; there is a clear majority ending on E:

closing notes GFE/E: Pa 776, Mo 159, Pa 1121, Pa 780, Cai 61, Pa 1235, Be 40078, Gr 807, Mod 7, Pst 120, Pad 47, RoV 52

Lo 4951: FGGF/D

Ben 34, 35: GFD/D

v. 1 "meOS": Ben 34: DFDD(ori.)C (Ben 35 same without oriscus)

v. 1 "COM/PREhendos" (small variant):

> Mo 159 and Beneventan MSS: FGF/GaG
> Pa 780: FGF/aGa
> Pa 1121: FGF/aG (etc.)
> Lo 4951: as in Pa 776

v. 1 "non" (small variant):

> Mo 159: DG FG(quil.) a b-flat
> Ben 34, 35: DE DEab
> Pa 780: FG FG(quil)ab

v. 1 "defiClant": Ben 34 (and other Ben MSS): FGaG

v. 2 "ME/US": Ben 34: bbb/GaG (Ben 35 has the usual reading)

v. 2 "SUB/TUS": Ben 34 and 35 Gb(liq.)/bcd

v. 2 "inimicorum": Pa 776 is the majority Aquitanian version and found in Beneventan sources, Pa 1235, and the Italian MSS; Mo 159 and several other MSS have a different reading, departing from the literal repetition of the previous phrase that is found in Pa 776:

	et in-i- mi- co-rum me-o- rum
Mo 159 (2↑ Pa 776):	G/ac/[b]c/ba/bc/c/ c/c[b]cba/ba
Gr 807 (= Pa 776, b's are flat):	F/Gb/b /b /b/ b/b/ cbaG/bG

Roman MSS: As mentioned, the version of Bod 74 and Vat 5319 has a longer text than the Gregorian does. The Roman version transmits a different respond text, with three verses; the text of the first "verse" is identical to that of the Gregorian respond.[2] Although this section is designated as a verse in both Bod 74 and Vat 5319, it closes with a cadence normally reserved for the ends of responds in sixth-mode offertories. The verses, moreover, close with a repetendum to "et liberator," which is in the middle of the first "verse." This section, then, is atypical of a verse both in its closing cadence and in serving as the source for the repetendum. These features may suggest that the respond and the section designated as the first verse may be alternate responds, as Peter Jeffery has suggested.[3] How these sections were performed is not clear. RoS 22, which lacks verses, transmits only the portion indicated as the respond in Bod 74 and Vat 5319.

Vat 5319 shows a significant difference from Bod 74 in one passage: the beginning of the third verse, *Precinxisti*, is written a tone above Bod 74 until the final syllable of "virtutem." This melisma occurs numerous times in the repertory, and in all other cases it is a tone lower. This variant is probably best viewed as a simple error.

RoS 22 has the following variants:

2. Possible explanations for the textual variants are proposed in Helmut Hucke, "Zur Aufzeichnung," 300–302; Jeffery (1992), 29; and Dyer, (1998), 26–29. Hucke proposed that the compiler of the Old Roman sources used Gregorian sources in copying, an argument echoed by Leo Treitler. Jeffery suggested that the Roman respond and first verse were intended as alternate responds. On the basis of the close correspondence of the Roman respond with the Verona psalter and other Old Latin witnesses, Dyer proposed that the respond was discarded in the Gregorian tradition because the psalm translation was "archaic and unfamiliar."

3. See note 2.

"DOminus": aca GbaG

The alternate version of the final cadential segment in Formula B (common in RoS 22 but not found in the other MSS): GaGFEFG (rather than GFEFG) on "meUS," "feCIT," "potentiBUS."

A different version of the final cadence, "hodeRUNT ME": FGaGbaGFGa/GaGFEF

CONFITEBOR TIBI (39)

The Roman version of this offertory lacks two of the verses that circulate with it in the Gregorian tradition, *Beati immaculati* and *Deprecatus sum*. For purposes of comparing the two versions, the phrases in the transcriptions are labeled according to the longer Gregorian version.

The first verse of the Gregorian version, *Beati immaculati*, is verbally identical to that of the *deuterus* offertory *Benedictus es . . . in labiis* (16) but has a different melody. The Roman tradition lacks a corresponding verse in *Confitebor tibi*. In the Roman tradition, however, the first verse of *Benedictus es . . . in labiis* has a melody similar to that of the Gregorian version of the corresponding verse in *Confitebor tibi*, with first-mode characteristics. The verse melody is clearly common to the two traditions, but at some point became associated with two different responds.

In both traditions, *Confitebor tibi* shares melodic material with other first-mode offertories. The melisma that opens the Gregorian first verse also opens the first verse of *Laetamini*, also on the word "beati." The lengthy melisma that opens the corresponding Roman verse, in *Benedictus es . . . in labiis*, is also found in *Laetamini* (79) and *Gloria et honore* (74).

In most Gregorian MSS, the verse that begins "deprecatus sum" (phrase 13) is transmitted as part of the second verse, but in Ben 34 and Be 40078 it marks the beginning of a new verse. In Lo 4951, "inclina" (phrase 10) marks the beginning of a new verse.

Beneventan distinctiveness: The Beneventan tradition has an independent reading of the cadence on "domini" in phrase 4. The other MSS have the traditional *protus* cadential pattern on the last two syllables of "domini": DEFEDE/ED. V. 1 "eUM": Beneventan MSS have a distinctive reading of this verse ending. The other MSS have DFDCD.

Other melodic variants: The melisma on "ioCUNda" (phrase 12) is a point of variance. Ben 34's reading is matched in the other core MSS. German MSS present a reading close to that of the core group. The Italian MSS, Pa 1235, and Cai 61, however, transmit variant readings:

RoV 52: FF GFD FFF GFD FaGaG c caca **F FD FGFa** GaG FGFD FF FD FFF

Pst 120: FFF **GFF** D FF **FGFFD** FaGaG ccac**GFGF** FGF a GaG FGFD FF FD FFF

Pad 47: FFF FGFD FF GFD FaG aG cca cG FD FaGa FaGF FFFDFFF

Pa 1235: FFF GF FD FFF GF FD FaGaG c caca **F FD F FE** FGE aGaG FGFD FFFD FFFD

Cai 61: FFF GF FC FFF GF FC FaGaG c cG **ba G GE F FE** FGFa GaG FGFD FF FD FF FE(liq.)

Individual MSS:

Lo 4951: respond "VERbum": FacaG aGFGFD
Pa 780: v. 3 "[legem] TUam": a cca bcaG

Gr 807:

    v. 1 "testimoNI/A": G/GaG
    v. 1 "Eius": FG aG aGF (liq.)
    v. 2 "ioCUNda": the bottom note of the melisma is C (rather than D)
    v. 3 "leGEM": differs in the parts of the melisma in boldface: aGc cc cabaGa Gabcba
        Gabcba Gc cc ca bcaGa **bcda bcd** cd ec bca bcaG cca(liq.)

Be 40078:

    v. 2 "ioCUNda": the bottom note of the melisma is C (rather than D)
    v. 3 "leGEM", differs in the parts of the melisma in boldface: aGc cc cabaGa Gabcba
        Gabcba Gc cc ca bcaGa **ccda ccd** cd ec bca bcaG cca(liq.)

RoV 52:

    v. 1 "[testimonia] Eius": FGaGFG
    v. 3 "leGEM", missing the last few notes of the melisma: aGc cc ca cccaGa Gabcba
        Gabcba Ga c ca ccaGc cc ca cd cdec ca bcaG cc

Pa 1235: respond, "DOmine": aGa bcba

Roman MSS:
  Vat 5319:

    respond "TIbi": a ccc(ori.) ba
    respond "ME": FabcaG
    v. 1 "leGEM": ba(liq.)
    v. 1 "cusTOdiam": FGaba
    v. 2 "viVI/FI/CA": a (ori.) c/c (ori.)/GFGF FE

RoS 22:

  "viVIfica": ac cb
  "seCUNdum": FFEDEDEDC

DOMINE CONVERTERE (40)

This sixth-mode offertory presents no major variants until the expansion into the authentic range in v. 2, at "sana me domine" (phrase 7), a point of variance in pitch level.[1] There are at least five different readings of this passage among the sources examined. In the majority reading of the verse, found in Ben 34, Mo 159, Pa 776, and many peripheral MSS, the entire passage has a focal pitch of c. In these sources, the final melisma is written a tone higher than it is in Pa 1121, the base reading of the edition. In a second group, represented by Pa 1121, the passage is at the level of Mo 159 and Ben 34 until the final melisma on "ossa,"

---

1. See Pitman (1973), 194–98; and Hankeln (1999), 1:108–9.

which is a tone lower. In many of the MSS from St. Martial, the whole passage, beginning at "sana me," is written a tone below the level of Mo 159, remaining there until the end of the verse.[2] In two MSS, Pa 1235 and To 18, the respond, first, v. 1, and beginning of v. 2 are notated at the affinal position, with a final of c, but these MSS join the level of Mo 159 at "sana me domine." Finally, in some sources, such as RoV 52, the pitch level of Pa 1235 is replicated a fifth lower.

Hankeln hypothesizes that the pitch level of Pa 1121, with its lower notation of the final melisma, is the *Aufführungslage*, and that a discrepancy exists between the notated and performance levels in Pa 776.[3] The repetendum cue in Pa 776 is written a tone lower than the corresponding passage in the respond, suggesting a performance level a tone below the written level. A performance at the level of Pa 1121 requires the use of the nondiatonic pitch e-flat, equivalent to b-flat in the versions written a fourth lower. In the versions written a tone higher, the interval c-e-flat may be represented with d-f. I find Hankeln's hypothesis plausible and accordingly I have adopted Pa 1121 as the base version and the most probable unemended reading. In this case, the preferred reading differs from the majority reading. As shown in the following summary, most MSS write the close of the second verse a tone above Pa 1121.

1. "Miserere"(beginning of v. 2):

   = Pa 1121: all except
   5↑ Pa 1121: To 18, Pa 1235

2. "Sana me domine":

   = Pa 1121: all except
   2↓ Pa 1121: Pa 1132, 1133–36

3. "ossa mea":
   = Pa 1121: Pa 1132, 1133, 1134, 1135, 1136
   2↑ Pa 1121: Ben 34, Ben 35, Ben 39, Mo 159, Pa 776, Pa 1235, Cai 61, Be 40078, Gr 807, Pst 120, To 18
   4↓ Pa 1121: Lo 4951, RoV 52

Roman sources: In many passages, Vat 5319, Bod 74, and RoS 22 agree in striking detail in their use of Formula B. There are the following differences:

"Respond [misericordiam] TUam": Vat 5319 has a more common and much less ornate form of this precadential segment, simply GaF, creating more literal repetition within the respond. Bod 74, by contrast, distinguishes the final cadence from the others with the special ornate form. RoS 22 is closer to Bod 74: FGaGaGF.

v. 1 "arguAS": Vat 5319 has FgaGaGaGF (liq.) (more ornate than Bod 74)
v. 2 "miseREre": Vat 5319 has a shorter form of the standard sixth-mode melisma than Bod 74 does. In the first thirty notes, through the repeated F's, Vat 5319 is identical to Bod 74, then the melisma closes with GaGaGF.

Structural differences: RoS 22 closes with a repeat of the opening words, "domine convertere et eripe," that is lacking in the other two Roman MSS, perhaps by analogy to

2. See Hankeln (1999), 2:142.
3. Ibid., 108–9.

Domine in auxilium and *Desiderium*. Vat 5319 has a repetendum after the first verse that is lacking in Bod 74.

SPERENT IN TE (41)

The repetenda in *Sperent in te* are a point of variance. The base reading of Ben 34 has "quoniam" as the repetendum, whereas other MSS, including Mo and the Aquitanian MSS, have "psallite," matching the Roman reading.

This offertory shows very few variants between MSS.

Lo 4951 verse endings:

v. 1 "PAU/PE/RUM": E/EGFE/E

v. 2 "deUS": E GFGF F(ori.)E

Pad 47:

"iudiCAS": aca aGa

v. 2 "domiNUS": ba

v. 2 "iudiCI/A": aG/GGGF Gaba

Pst 120: v. 2 "iudiciA": melisma begins GGGE
Mo 159: v. 2 "iudiciA": melisma begins GGGE

Be 40078: v. 2 "domiNUS": ca
Gr 807: respond, "TU/UM", a different syllable distribution: cadcb/b

Roman MSS:

Vat 5319: v. 1 "pauPErum": GaGF
RoS 22 shows its standard differences in the use of Formula B. Where Vat 5319 and Bod 74 have GFEFG, RoS 22 has GaGFEFG on oMNES.

"doMIne": GaGF

"DEreLINquis": FGF/ GFEDEFGFEDEDC (same at oblLItus)

"querenTES/TE": FGaGaF/GaGF

ERIPE ME . . . DEUS MEUS (42)

Ben 34, adopted as the base version, is missing four notes in a melisma on "FORtes" (phrase 5), a probable scribal error. These are shown in brackets in the transcription.

In the pretheoretical tradition, this offertory probably employed nondiatonic pitches at two places in the verse *Quia factus es*: the melisma on "meus" (phrase 6) and the final melisma of the verse, on "meae." The scribe of Mo 159 writes the opening of the verse a fourth above the level of Ben 34, joining at "et refugium." In the melisma on "meum," Mo 159 indicates b-naturals, equivalent to F-sharp at the level of Ben 34. This nondiatonic practice is also reflected in Pa 1235 and in two sources written a fifth below Ben 34, Be

EXAMPLE **42.1**A

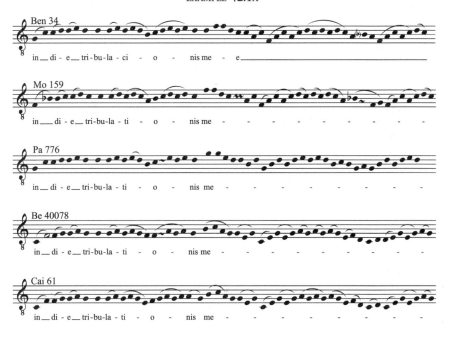

EXAMPLE **42.1**B

40078, and Cai 61; the latter two MSS employ low B-naturals, equivalent to F-sharp at the level of Ben 34. It is unclear, however, how widespread this nondiatonic practice was. The pitch level of Ben 34 represents the majority reading, and the lack of transpositions in other MSS raises the possibility that the nondiatonic practice was suppressed in many traditions. This melisma is also a point of melodic variance, as described below. The pitch level at the beginning of the verse for the sources in the sampling can be summarized as follows (the transposition continues through phrase 7, unless otherwise indicated):

   = Ben 34: Ben 38, Ben 39, Ben 35, Pa 776, Pa 780, Pa 1121, Lo 4951, Pad 47, Pst 120, RoV 52, To 18
   4↑ Ben 34: Mo 159 (joining at Ben 34 "et refugium"), Pa 1235 (joining Ben 34 at "in die")
   5↓ Ben 34: Cai 61, Be 40078

The second problem spot is the end of v. 2, at the melisma on "meae." Although the pitch level of Ben 34 is found in a great majority of other MSS, the nature of the variants among a few of the core and peripheral MSS suggests that the majority version may reflect an emendation. The pitch-level profile of the MSS at "in die" and "meae" can be summarized as follows.

v. 2 "in die tribulationis":

   = Ben 34: All except Mo 159, Cai 61, and Be 40078
   2↓ Ben 34: Mo 159
   5↓ Ben 34: Cai 61, Be 40078

v. 2 meae:

   = Ben 34: All except Pa 776, RoV 52, Cai 61, and Be 40078
   2↑ Ben 34: Pa 776, RoV 52, Gr 807
   4↓ Ben 34: Cai 61 (with melodic variants), Be 40078. In both MSS, the interval of transposition changes to a fifth at the end of the melisma.

Mo 159 presents a reading that is unique among the MSS examined: "in die tribulationis" is a tone below the level of Ben 34. It is doubtful that this whole-tone transposition reflects a nondiatonic pitch at "in die tribulationibus"; Mo 159 consistently uses b-flat, thereby retaining the same intervallic structure as Ben 34. The lower notation of Mo 159, however, does suggest a deliberate emendation on the part of the scribe, perhaps reflecting the need for a nondiatonic pitch further on. At "meae," Mo 159 joins Ben 34 and the majority of other MSS. Pa 776, however, remains a tone above these MSS. Although Pa 776 is unique among the Aquitanian MSS examined, it is doubtful that its reading of this passage is a scribal error: it is matched in the unrelated MSS Gr 807 and RoV 52. Pa 776's pitch-level profile is also confirmed by the two later MSS, Be 40078 and Cai 61. These MSS duplicate the pitch-level profile of Pa 776 a fifth lower until the very end of the melisma, where the interval of transposition changes to a sixth.

Several different readings of the passage are presented in example 42.1. To replicate the intervallic structure of the majority version (Ben 34) at the level of Pa 776, a c-sharp is required at the end of the passage. This point is precisely where the lower readings, Cai 61 and Be 40078, change in their intervallic relationship to the other MSS, presumably because an F-sharp would be needed at the position a fifth below Pa 776. The half step b-c in Ben 34 is equivalent to c (sharp)-d in Pa 776 and E-F in Be 40078. The nature of the relationship between these MSS leads to a tentative hypothesis that Pa 776 represents the unemended version in pitch level and that the pretheoretical tradition employed a c-sharp.

Melodic variants: The independence of the Beneventan tradition is evident in several brief passages: respond "MEis" (a point of slight variance):

Ben 34: ad ecc dcdcdc (same reading in Ben 35, Ben 39)
Mo 159: de cc dc dc dc (same reading in Pa 780, Lo 4951)
Pa 776: de cc dcdc

MSS in the peripheral group present a reading closer to that of Mo 159 and Pa 776.

v. *Quia factus es*, "MEus": As mentioned, this melisma is a point of variance among core MSS, particularly at the segment in boldface. Pa 776 has a shortened version that is not found in other MSS included in the sampling.

Ben 34: bcdedcbcaG**ccbdc bcaG** bGGG FGaFG FGED GG FababaGa
Mo 159 (4↑): efgagfefdc **fc ffcgfefd** cecc bcdcc abaG cc bdededcd
Pa 776: bcded bcaG cGG FGaFG EFED GG GababaGa
Pa 1121: bcdedcbcaG **caccbdc bcaG bGG GGaGaGG** FGED GG GababaGa
Pa 780: bcdedcbcaG **cG ccbdccdaG** cGG FGaGG EFEED GG GababaGa
Lo 4951: bcdedc bcaG bG ccbdcbcaG bGG FGaFG EFED GababaGa

Sources outside the core group exhibit further variance, as the following sample readings show:

Gr 807: bc dedc bcaG cG ccb dc cccaG GEF FGEF DFDC FFE FGaGaGFG
RoV 52: bcdedc bcaG cac cb dc bcaG bG FGaGa GaGF GababaGa
Pst 120: bcdedcbcaG cac cdcbcaG GEF EFGF EFDC GG GabcabaGa
Mod 7: bcdedcbcaG bGa cb dcbcaG bGa bc dc bcaG aaG GabcabaGa
Cai 61 (5↓): EFGaGF EFDC FC F FE GF EFDC FCC BCDC ABAΓ CCB
    DEDEDCD
Pa 1235 (4↑): efg agf efdc fcffeg fefdc dcc ac dcc abaG ccb dededcd

Variants in individual MSS:
Verse endings in Lo 4951:

v. *Quia factus es:* cfffffdcdcbabaaG
v. *Quia ecce:* dffdcdcba ccdcb abaaG
v. *Quia ecce*, "FORtes": Lo 4951 is missing four notes of the melisma, the figure cdcb.

Pa 1121: E (rather than F) is the top note in the melismas on "captaVErunt", "FORtes", and "[tribulationis] MEae".

Roman MSS: Respond, "domiNE": Vat 5319 and RoS 22 have a melisma on the final syllable of "domine" that is lacking in Bod 74. The melisma is varied repetition of the one that occurs on the first syllable of "domine":

Vat 5319: Gb dedcb dedcb cbabG bacbaGa aG
RoS 22: Gb dedcb dedcbcbabG bacbaGaG

v. *Quia factus*, "QUI/A": Vat 5319 has a less ornate opening: G/cb

v. *Quia factus*, "[refugium] MEum": Vat 5319: c c(ori.)baG cbc

BENEDICTUS ES ... ET NON TRADAS (43)

The Roman version of this offertory has a text repetition in the respond that is lacking in the Gregorian, a difference probably attributable to the verbal and melodic similarities to *Benedictus es ... in labiis* (16), which begins with identical words and music, and where the text repetition is present in both versions.

The opening of the second verse, "Adpropiaverunt ... confundantur," exhibits complex variants in pitch level that are most likely attributable to nondiatonic practice. Because of the intervallic inconsistencies between readings and the lack of repetendum cues in some key Aquitanian MSS, however, I have not been able to establish an unemended version of the second verse with any degree of certainty. For this reason, I have given Mo 159, the majority reading, as the base version.

Example 43.1 presents five different readings of the verse opening. Because the opening pitches of the various versions do not necessarily correlate with their eventual pitch level, 1 will discuss pitch level beginning with "persequentes." Here Mo 159 (line 1) represents the pitch level found in a majority of MSS, as summarized below. Ben 34 (line 2) is written a tone lower, a reading also found in Pa 1235. Pa 776 (line 3) is a fourth lower, a reading matched in Pa 1121 (line 4) and several other Aquitanian MSS. Be 40078 (line 5) is the only MS that presents the passage a fifth below Mo 159. Intervallic differences between these readings are evident at the ends of the short melisma on "me" and the melisma on "iniqui." Mo 159 and Be 40078 have a semitone (c-b-natural and F-E), Ben 34 has a-b (flat?), and Pa 776 has G-F. The semitone in the majority version of Mo 159 suggests that

EXAMPLE 43.1A

EXAMPLE 43.1B

2   Example

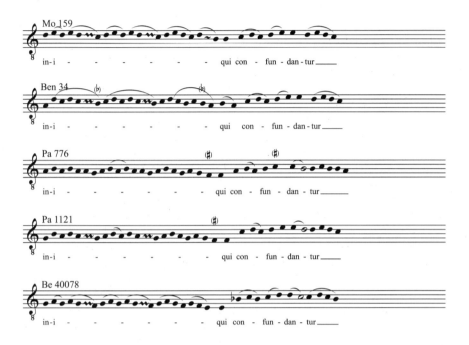

perhaps an F-sharp is intended at the level of Pa 776 and Pa 1121, both at "me" and "iniqui."
The same solution is suggested by Pitman.[1]

While the intervallic differences between the versions support a hypothesis that the
level of Pa 776 and Pa 1121 is the unemended pitch level at "persequentes me iniqui," it is
unclear how a hypothetical unemended version of the chant would proceed at "iniqui
confundantur" and through the rest of the verse. Nearly all non-Aquitanian MSS, along with
Pa 1121 and Lo 4951, join the level of Mo 159 here. The only exception is Be 40078, where
the passage is positioned a whole tone below Mo 159 through the end of the verse. In the
Aquitanian tradition, Pa 776, Pa 780, Pa 1136, and Pa 1135 remain a third below Mo 159
throughout the verse. These Aquitanian MSS, however, lack repetendum cues to confirm
that the notated level is indeed the performance level (though Pa 1135 and 1136 do have a
custos between the first and second verses).

Regarding the intervallic structure at "confundantur," it is worth noting that the same
melody and words occur elsewhere in the repertory, suggesting that the intervallic structure
of the majority reading is the intended one.[2] Because the reading of Pa 776 is found in
several other Aquitanian MSS, however, I am hesitant to dismiss it as an error. If the level of
Pa 776, a third below the majority reading, is considered the unemended version at
"confundantur," a c-sharp would be required to replicate the intervallic structure of the

---

1. Pitman (1973), 295–96.
2. See *Domine in auxilium.*

majority version. With a hypothesis that Pa 776 is the preferred reading at "persequentes" and the majority reading is the unemended reading at "confundantur," however, the transition between the two sections is problematic. Assuming that an F-sharp was sung as the final note of "iniqui," the transition between the two sections would require the improbable leap of a diminished fifth, as suggested by Pa 1121.[3]

To summarize, the base reading of Mo 159 is probably emended at "persequentes me iniqui." I would cautiously surmise that Pa 776, with F-sharp and c-sharp, represents the unemended version of the verse as a whole. In this version, the melody is displaced in relation to the diatonic background scale and never gets back "on track." Because the evidence for this supposition is not conclusive, however, I have adopted the majority version of Mo 159 as the base reading.

There are few significant melodic variants between MSS. These are as follows:

v. 1 "faciES":

> Pa 776: cdcbcbaGaG
> Pa 1121: cdbcaGa

v. 1 "IU/DI/CI/UM":

> Lo 4951: ccbab(quil.)cba/aG/Ga(quil.)bab/aG
> On the syllable "ci" Gr 807 has the version of this common figure found throughout this MS: bdbc.

v. 2 "inIqui": This is a point of variance; most Aquitanian MSS match Mo 159, but several
   sources have shorter melismas:
   Pa 1235 has a shortened melisma: dedc dedc dcb
   Ben 39: eded dcd edcdcb
"inIUste": The Aquitanian and Beneventan MSS have a different reading:
Lo 4951: cccaG b(ori.)aGa
Pa 776: cccaGbaGa
Ben 39: cc ca Gca Ga

This reading is matched in MSS from German-speaking areas, such as Gr 807: cc ca GcaGa; and in Italian MSS such as Mod 7.

v. 2 "IN ME": Lo 4951 Ga(quil.)bab/aG
Roman MSS:

Vat 5319: "iustificatioNES": (first time): c cbcabaGF ab(ori.)aGFGF

RoS 22: "iustificatioNES": (first time): c cbca baGFGF

IMPROPERIUM (44)

The MSS that indicate b-flat are inconsistent in the places they do so. Mo 159 uses b-flats in several places where they would not be automatically expected in the context and do not occur in other MSS: in the respond on "expectavit," [cor] "meum," and "aceto," in v. 1 on "usque," and in v. 2 on "in me." I have indicated b-flats only in the places where they are

---

3. As in Pitman's consensus reading of the Aquitanian MSS. Ibid.

both implied by the context and are consistently indicated in the MSS that distinguish between b-flat and b-natural.

In many MSS, including Ben 34, this offertory is an unproblematic eighth-mode melody, with some passages expanding into the authentic range. Several sources, however, notate the final verse (beginning in phrase 14) a fifth below the regular eighth-mode position, adopting F, rather than c, as the repercussive pitch. To some extent, the two approaches to notating the verse are regionally correlated: the normal eighth mode range is preferred in the Italian and Beneventan sources, whereas most sources from both eastern and western Frankish areas notate the verse a fifth lower. The Aquitanian sources, however, are a mixture: the lower level is implied in most of the St. Martial sources, whereas Pa 776, Pa 780, and Lo 4951 notate the verse in the normal eighth-mode range.

In many of the MSS that begin a fifth below Ben 34, the interval of transposition changes to a fourth near the end of the verse, on the third syllable of "beneplaciti." Although this reading is reflected in a majority of the MSS that notate the verse at this lower level, a few sources remain a fifth below the eighth-mode readings.

The reasons for the lower notation of the second verse in some MSS are unclear. The four early adiastematic sources examined, La 239, Cha 47, SG 339, and Ei 121, begin v. 3 with upward motion, consistent with the higher, eighth-mode reading of the verse. In the first part of the verse, Mo 159 consistently employs b-flat, as do the other sources that distinguish between b-natural and b-flat, producing a reading that is identical in intervallic structure to Ben 34. At "beneplaciti," where the interval of transposition changes to a fourth, Mo 159 adopts G as a repercussive pitch, showing an intervallic difference with Pa 1132, which remains a fifth below Ben 34. On "beneplacti" and the final syllable of "misericordiae," Mo 159 employs F, the whole tone below the repercussive pitch, which would be an E-flat at the level of Pa 1132 and a b-flat at the level of Ben 34. While this difference in intervallic structure may explain the change in transpositional level at "beneplaciti," however, the reasons for the initial downward transposition of a fifth are unclear.

Several of the Aquitanian sources, including Pa 1121, 1134, 1136, and 1137, lack notated repetendum cues at the end of the verse, making it difficult or impossible to establish the intended pitch level of the verse. In several of these cases, the notated level of the verse appears much lower than that of the second verse, suggesting that the level of Mo 159 is intended, but in view of the lack of consistent horizontal alignment between verses, this level is hypothetical. These cases are indicated with brackets in the summary below.

1. v. 2 "Ego vero":

= Ben 34: Ben 38, Ben 39, Ben 35, Pa 776, Pa 780, Pa 1135, Pa 903, Pa 1235, Lo 4951, Mod 7, To 18, Pia 65, Pst 120, RoV 52

5↓ Ben 34: Mo 159, 1132, [Pa 1121, 1134, Pa 1136, Pa 1137], Gr 807, Be 40078, Tri 2254,

2. [bene]placiti:

= Ben 34: Pa 776, Pa 780, Pa 1135, Pa 1235 (with melodic variants), Lo 4951, Mod 7, To 18, Pia 65, Pst 120, RoV 52

4↓ Ben 34: Mo 159, Gr 807, Be 40078, Tri 2254, 1, [Pa 1121, Pa 1134]

5↓ Ben 34: Pa 1132 [Pa 1136, Pa 1137], Mad 20-4

Pitch level in Aquitanian sources:

Pa 1121: The third verse begins on a new line and has no repetendum cue.

Pa 1134: The third verse has no repetendum cue, but appears to be notated at the level of Mo 159.

Pa 1136: Relative to the second verse, the third verse appears to be a fourth below Ben, perhaps indicating that the level of Mo 159 is intended.

Pa 1135: The repetendum cue indicates that the intended level is that of Ben 34.

Pa 1137: Relative to the second verse, the third verse appears to be a fourth below Ben, perhaps indicating that the level of Mo 159 is intended.

Pa 1132: The third verse starts on a new line, but the repetendum cue indicates that the intended level is that of Mo 159.

Other melodic variants: There are few major variants among the core group of Aquitanian and Beneventan sources and Mo 159. These are as follows.

Many sources outside Benevento and Aquitaine begin the offertory on F rather than D, as in Mo 159: FGEFE. Beneventan sources are atypical at the cadential pattern on "miserIAM": The Beneventan reading abcGG contrasts with a more elaborate cadential pattern found in most sources, as exemplified by the reading of Pa 776: ab (quil)cbaGa/aG. Mo 159 departs from the reading of the Aquitanian and Beneventan MSS in several places:

v. 1 "MEam": cdc db caG G(ori.)F GF cc dcdb caG G(ori.)F GcaGaGFG (The Aquitanian MSS present a reading close to that of Ben 34.)

v. 3 "[ad te] DO/MI/NE": Gba(quil)G/G (The Aquitanian MSS present a reading close to that of Ben 34.)

Lo 4951:

"quaesiVI": aG
"potaveRUNT": GFGababaaG liq.
v. 1"MEam": shortened melisma: cdcdccaGGFGcaGaGFG

To 18:

v. 1 "Aquae": shortened melisma: FabaGacaGabbcbccbabaGa
v. 2 "psallebant": FFFEF/Ga/acccaG/Ga
v. 2 "VInum": acdcaGbaGGFacaGaGFG

Pa 1235: v. 3 "oratiOnem": edcbcaGcccaGccdfffdccaGacccedc Roman MSS: Bod 74 lacks the third verse and has the following variants:

"expecTA/VIT": cdc c(ori.)ba/abaGaG
aceTO: GacbaGa aG.

RoS 22:

"NON": dcdedfedcdc
"IN/I/STI ME/A": A slightly varying melody, with a longer melisma on MEa: cba/cdeded/cd cdcbabcdcbabG/acbaG
"a/CE/TO": cdcdcbcaGaG cdcdcbcba bcbabaG/ G acbaGa aG

ERIPE ME...DOMINE (45)

The three Holy Week offertories are characterized by an inconsistency of verse transmission. For *Eripe me...domine*, the *Antiphonale Missarum Sextuplex* MSS and the four early notated MSS included in the sampling (La 239, Cha 47, Ei 121, and SG 339) lack a second verse, which suggests that the early Gregorian tradition had only one verse, *Exaudi me*. A second verse is also lacking in all German and Italian MSS included in the sampling. Three different second verses are found in Mo 159, the Aquitanian MSS, and the Beneventan MSS. *In factis* serves as a second verse at both Rome and Benevento; for the purposes of comparing the Roman and "Gregorian" readings, a Beneventan version has been employed as the base version for the transcription. Many Aquitanian MSS have *Expandi manus meas* as a second verse, and Mo 159 has the second verse *Velociter exaudi*. The added Aquitanian verse, shown in example 45.1, is an individual melody, whereas Mo 159's second verse, *Velociter exaudi*, is melodically based on the first verse, *Exaudi me*.

Expandi manus and *Velociter exaudi* are based on Ps. 142:6 and 142:7. Both lyrics are consistent with the Roman and Gallican psalters, which are identical here.

Pitch-level variants in the respond: In the respond, the pitch-level profile of Ben 39 is the majority reading, matched in all MSS except the following.

1. Ben 34 is a fifth below the majority version beginning at "doce me" (phrase 3), so that it closes on the regular final E rather than b.

2. Pad 47: The opening of the respond, "eripe me," is written a fifth above the majority version, joining at "domine."

These readings of Ben 34 and Pad 47, unique among the sampling, may reflect attempts to correct a disparity of range between the beginning and end of the respond. The majority version of the respond, shown in the base transcription of Ben 39, is modally anomalous, beginning as a regular *deuterus* melody but migrating upward to close on b.

Pitch-level variants in the verse *Exaudi me*: Most MSS match Ben 39 in pitch level throughout. The following are exceptional readings:

1. Mo 159 is briefly a whole tone above Ben 39 at "ne intres," with b-flats. Mo 159 joins Ben 39 at the fifth note of "inTRES"; inTRES begins b-flat b-flat (ori.) Ga caG (etc.).

2. Lo 4951 is a fifth above Ben 39 beginning at "in tua iusticia" and remains there through the end of the verse.

EXAMPLE 45.1

Pitch-level variants in the Beneventan verse *In factis:* Ben 34 and Ben 38 are a fifth below Ben 39 beginning at "meditabor." Ben 35 lacks this verse. The reasons for this variant are unclear.

Melodic variants: There is some inconsistency in the use of b-flat between Mo 159 and later MSS. In the respond, Pa 1235 uses b-flat on "domine," whereas other MSS do not. I have placed parenthetical b-flats only in the passages where they occur in the majority of sources.

The Beneventan MSS have an independent reading of the opening of v. 1, "exAUdi," transmitting a much shorter version of this melisma than that found in the broader international tradition. The first twelve notes are omitted, as the following comparison shows:

Mo 159: Ga cc caG aaG aa Ga cc deed fed ec(quil.)b
Ben 39: Gac c de ed fedec c(ori.)b

Small melodic variants in core MSS: v. *Exaudi,* "IN [iudicio]": Some MSS, including Pa 780 and Lo 4951, have DG.

Roman MSS: Vat 5319 has some missing notes at the beginning of the melisma on "exAUdi" (v. 1). The notes cannot be supplied from Bod 74, whose melodic reading differs here.

There are rare significant melodic differences among Roman MSS, including a transpositional variant in the respond. Bod 74 begins at the same pitch level as Vat 5319, has a different melodic reading on the last syllable of "voluntatem" (phrase 3), and is a fifth lower than Vat 5319 beginning at "tuam." The latter part of the respond and the two verses, then, are notated a fifth below their position in Vat 5319, reflecting a type of variant also found among Gregorian sources. The reasons for these variants are unclear. RoS 22, which transmits only the respond, has the pitch-level profile of Vat 5319. The reading of Bod 74 may be a correction to the perceived inconsistency of range between the beginning of the respond, in the *deuterus* plagal range, and end of the respond, on the affinal b. Vat 5319 was chosen as the base version in part because its reading is the majority among the three Roman MSS. Its overall range, beginning at the normal *deuterus* plagal position but closing on b, corresponds to that of the majority Gregorian version.

A second significant variant occurs at the beginning of the verse *Exaudi me,* where Bod 74 has a different melisma. In Bod 74, the opening of the melisma is similar to that of the verse *In factis,* whereas the closing of the melisma matches the one in Vat 5319:

Bod 74, "exAUdi" (at the lower transposition): aGaG (liq.) E (ori.) DC
  FGaGaGFGaGF GaGFEF(liq.)
Bod 74, "FACtis": aGaG (liq.) E(ori.)DC FGaGaGF GaGFEFD

Other melodic variants:

Bod 74:

respond, "volunTAtem": a(ori.) GFG

v. 1 "IUsticia": EFGFaGFG
RoS 22: "DE": DC

CUSTODI ME (46)

Like the other Holy Week offertories, *Custodi me* has an inconsistency of verse transmission. Roman MSS lack the first verse of the Gregorian version, *Eripe me*. It is not clear, however, that this verse is a Frankish addition, because the text matches the PsR against the PsG.[1] The Roman MSS have a verse, *Dominus virtus*, that is lacking in Gregorian MSS. In the base transcription, the Roman verses are given in the order that they occur in Gregorian MSS in order to facilitate comparison between the two versions.

Although the Roman MSS have a corresponding verse, it appears that the verse *Dixi domino* (beginning in phrase 6) was not a consistent part of the early dissemination of the repertory in Francia. This verse is absent in most sources indexed in *Antiphonale missarum sextuplex*, with the exception of Silvanectensis, and in all early notated MSS incorporated

EXAMPLE 46.1

Benevento 34 f. 113

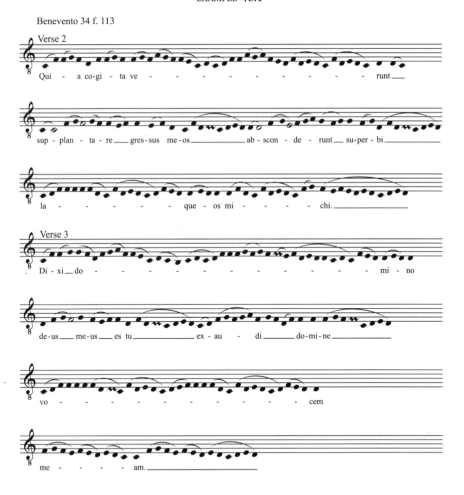

---

1. In Ps. 139:2, the PsG has "libera me" instead of "eripe me."

into the sampling, including La 239, SG 339, Cha 47, Ei 121, and RoA 123. The verse is also absent in the four MSS from German-speaking areas included in the sampling (Gr 807, Be 40078, Rei 264, and Trier 2254). It is present, however, in some Aquitanian MSS (Pa 776, Lo 4951, and Pa 903), in Mo 159, in the Beneventan MSS, and in the five Italian MSS examined.

The instability of melodic transmission in *Custodi me* is illustrated in Justmann's transcriptions.[2] The second and third verses, *Qui cogitaverunt* and *Dixi domino*, exhibit an unusual degree of melodic variance, with a completely different melody in Beneventan sources and yet a third melody in To 18. As Justmann's transcriptions show, To 18's version of *Qui cogitaverunt* is partially matched in Provins 12.[3] Although Mo 159 and the Aquitanian sources have essentially the same melody for these verses, there are variants in the melisma that occurs on "cogitaVErunt" (v. 2) and "DOmino" (v. 3). The melisma has an AAB form in some MSS and no repetition in other sources. The part of the melisma shown in boldface below is lacking in Mo 159.

Mo 159: cdcb cdca FG(quil.)aGa aa(ori.)Ga   cdc dca b-flat
Pa 776: cdcb cdca FG(quil.)aGa aa   Ga **cdcb cdca FG(quil.)aGa**   cdc dca b

The version of Mo 159, without the repetition, is implied in the early MSS, SG 339, Ei 121, La 239, and Cha 47. Mo 159 was chosen as a base version because it best represents this earlier tradition of the melody. The longer version of the melisma, with the repetition, is found in all Aquitanian MSS included in the sampling, except for Pa 1121 and the other sources from St. Martial. The longer version is also found in RoA 123 and most MSS in the peripheral group. The only exception, RoV 52, has the shorter version of the melisma in the verse *Qui cogitaverunt* and the longer version in the verse *Dixi domino*.[4]

A Beneventan reading of the last two verses is provided as example 46.1. In the Beneventan tradition the third verse, *Dixi domino*, employs much of the same melodic material as the verse *Qui cogitaverunt*. There is one significant melodic variant among Beneventan MSS in the verse *Dixi domino*. Ben 39 and Ben 40 have a longer version of the melisma on DOmino, with an internal repetition:

Ben 34: GFD F GaF FEC DCB CDCD   FFF GFG (etc.)
Ben 39: GFD F GaFFFEC DCB CDCD FGFFDC DCB CDCD   FFF FGF (etc.)

Other melodic variants among core MSS: The last two verses exhibit more variance than usual among the core group of Aquitanian sources and Mo 159, as well as further variants in the peripheral MSS.

v. *Qui cogitaverunt*, "meOS": Pa 776: DFDDC (same in Lo 4951)
v. *Qui cogitaverunt*, "absconDErunt":

Pa 776: DFGa
Lo 4951: FGa
v. *Dixi domino*, "ES": Pa 776: DFDCDED (same in Lo 4951)

2. Justmann (1988), 409–27; 688–705; 970–1006; 1274–91; and 1558–70.
3. According to Justmann's transcriptions, the two versions of the verse *Qui dixerunt* part ways toward the end of the verse, at "super laqueos mihi." Provins 12 lacks the verse *Dixi domino*.
4. Justmann's transcriptions show the same reading in Modena (Mod) 0.1.3. Justmann (1988), 417–18; 423–24.

Significant variants in the peripheral group:

Qui cogitaverunt, "cogitaVErunt": Gr 807: cdcb cdca **FaG**

v. *Qui cogitaverunt*, "meOS":

> Pst 120: DFDC
> RoV 52 (at higher transposition): acaG
> Cai 61: DFDCD

> v. *Qui cogitaverunt*, "absconDErunt": Italian MSS have FGa (matching Lo 4951 above),
> except for Pad 47, which has FGa .FGa.
> v. *Qui cogitaverunt*, "laQUEos": Cai 61: DFG G FGa FF FD
> v. *Dixi domino*, "DI/XI": Cai 61: Da/a
> v. *Dixi domino*, "DOmino": Cai 61 is unique among the MSS examined in indicating b-
> flats in this melisma.

v. *Dixi domino*, "VOcem":

> Cai 61: DF GG FGa FFD FGGG FGa FF FD CD EFEDE
> Pst 120: DFG GFG FFFC DF FF FGa FFFDC CDEF FEDE
> Mod 7: DF G GFG FFD DFFF GFE FFF GFE FD DEF FEDE
> Pad 47: DF GGF GF FD DFFF FaccccaFaF Gab baGa (cadences on G)

Pitch-level variants:

> RoV 52: The entire offertory is written at the affinal position.
> Be 40078: The verse *Qui cogitaverunt* is written at the affinal position.

Roman MSS: In the respond, the Roman sources show complex transpositional variants that are very rare in the repertory. Bod 74 begins a fifth above Vat 5319, but the interval of transposition changes several times before the two versions join on the second syllable of "hominibus." Bod 74's relationship to Vat 5319 can be summarized as follows:

> "Custodi me": 5↑ Vat 5319
> "domine de manu": 2↑ Vat 5319 (melodically variant on DOmine: Gabacba bcaG bab;
> and "maNU": cbcd)
> "peccatoris": 5↑ Vat 5319
> "et ab ho [minibus]": 2↑ Vat 5319 ("hoMInibus": bG bcaGa)
> "[ho] minibus":= Vat 5319

Vat 5319's pitch level is matched in RoS 22. There is unfortunately too little information to posit one version or the other as a preferred reading. The differences between the two versions seem to reflect a confusion about the "modality" of the chant (in pretheoretical terms), a change in practice, or a difference in the melody as it was sung at different institutions. Although there is little melodic correspondence with the Gregorian version, the opening of Vat 5319 exhibits the *protus* characteristics of the Gregorian. In several cases, however, material in the melody occurs outside of its usual modal context. The verse *Dixi domino*, for example, begins with a gesture more typical of sixth-mode verses but notated a tone higher.

DOMINE EXAUDI (47)

Like the other two Holy Week offertories, *Domine exaudi* shows an inconsistency of verse transmission. Cha 47 and the Beneventan MSS have only one verse for this offertory, *Ne avertas*. The most complete Gregorian MSS have three verses, *Ne avertas, Quia oblitus sum,* and *Tu exurgens*. The order of the latter two verses is occasionally reversed. *Quia oblitus sum* is lacking in the Roman MSS, the sources indexed in *Antiphonale Missarum Sextuplex,* and, with the exception of SG 339 and Ei 121, the sampling of early notated MSS. While these factors may suggest that the verse *Quia oblitus* is a Frankish addition, its textual basis is the Roman psalter and not the Gallican psalter.[1]

The verse *Tu exurgens* might also be a later addition. The Gregorian *Tu exurgens* has the PsG reading "quia tempus miserendi eius quia venit tempus," contrasting with the PsR-based Gregorian tract sung on the same day. The Roman version has a text repetition that is also found in the tract for the same day, "quia venit tempus quia tempus venit miserendi eius."

Among Gregorian MSS, there are two distinct melodic versions of *Tu exurgens,* a situation very unusual among core offertories. These patterns raise the possibility that the verse *Tu exurgens* was not a part of the core repertory disseminated in Francia but subsequently added on each side of the Alps. Because of their complexity of transmission, variants in these two verses are discussed separately. In the Roman MSS, *Ne avertas* is not designated as a verse.

Melodic variants in respond and first verse: [ad] "TE" [perveniat]: Pa 776 presents a unique reading here. The bracketed notes in the transcription do not appear other MSS. All core and peripheral MSS have shorter version of the melisma:

Mo 159: acaa(ori.)Ga

EXAMPLE 47.1A

---

1. The PsG has "commedere" instead of "manducare" in Ps. 101:5.

EXAMPLE 47.1B

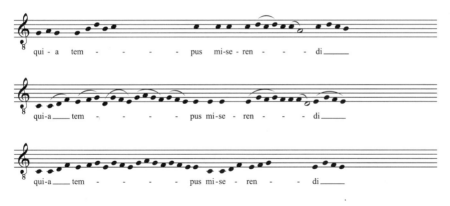

There is an identical reading in all Aquitanian MSS, a similar version in the Beneventan MSS (aca aGa), and the neumes in early adiastematic sources are also consistent with this reading.

Transpositional variants in v. *Quia oblitus:*

    = Pa 776: Pad 47, Mod 7
    5↓ Pa 776: Mo 159, Pst 120, RoV 52
    2↓ Pa 776: Be 40078

Pitch level uncertain: Pa 1121, Pa 1137, Pa 1136
Melodic variants in v. *Quia oblitus:*

a. Core MSS and German sources: Mo 159, Aquitanian, and German sources present a unified melodic tradition, with the few significant variants as follows: "quiA": Pa 1121 (assuming the lower level of transposition): FEFEDCDC. This reading is also matched in Gr 807.

EXAMPLE 47.1C

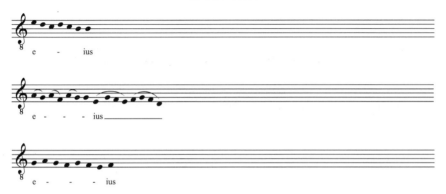

EXAMPLE 47.1D

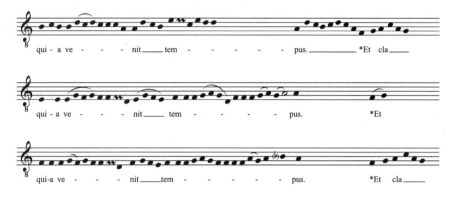

b. Italian MSS: There are more significant melodic variants among the Italian sources
that transmit this verse:

"manduCA/RE":

> Mod 7 and Pad 47: abaG/aG
> Pst 120: FGFE/ED

RoV 52: EFED/ED
"PA/NEM":

> Mod 7 and Pad 47: Fa/c
> Pst 120: DF/F
> RoV 52: CD/ EGG
> "ME/AM":

> Mod 7: dcdc cbab cc dca cbGa Ga bc dc cbaG/ acab
> Pad 47: dc dcb ab cc dcaba FG Gabc dcba /acab
> Pst 120: aGaGaGEF aa ba aF GFEF DEFGaGFE/DFDE
> RoV 52: aGaGaGFEF aaaFGEFEDE DEFGaGFED/DFDE

Melodic variants in v. *Tu exurgens:* As mentioned above, there are two distinct versions of
this melody in the core MSS. The melody of Pa 776, in line 1 of example 47.1, matches that
of La 239, thus representing the earliest extant version of the melody. This version is found
in most Aquitanian MSS and in one peripheral MS, Rei 264. The second version is best
represented by Pa 780 in line 3 of example 47.1. This version also has early witnesses,
including Ei 121 and SG 339, and is found in most peripheral MSS. Mo 159, transcribed in
line 2, is more consistent with the version of Pa 780 but departs from it at "miserendi,"
where it matches Pa 776, and especially at "eius," where it has a reading not found in any of
the other MSS examined.

The version of SG 339, Ei 121, and Pa 780 is found in all Italian MSS examined, in Gr
807, and in Be 40078. The four Italian MSS included in the sampling vary in the pitch level
of the incipit: Mod 7 and Pad 47 begin a fourth above Pa 780, on c, and join Mo 159 at
"misereberis." Pst 120 and RoV 52 begin at the level of Pa 780, on F.

Pa 776's version occurs only in one MS outside the Aquitanian sphere, Rei 264. The choice of melodic version is correlated with the pitch level—the versions that match Pa 780 are a fifth lower than the reading of Pa 776—except at the incipit of the verse, which is a point of variance.

Note on the transcription of Pa 776: In Pa 776, the pitch axis is consistently maintained throughout the respond and both verses. The third verse begins on a new line but is preceded by a custos, a departure from usual practice. The repetendum, however, appears to be notated a tone too high. In this case, I have given preference to the custodes rather than the repetendum as an indicator of pitch, thus deriving a reading similar to the other MSS that have this version of the verse *Tu exurgens*. To avoid confusion in the transcription, I have emended the repetendum cue at the end of v. 3 accordingly. Variants in Roman MSS: There are no significant variants (and few variants of any sort) between Bod 74 and Vat 5319.

Variants in RoS 22:

"exAUdi": cbcabaGF acbabaG(liq.)
"TUam": cdedfdcbc
"ME" (greatly shortened melisma): Gac cbca GaG EFGFEFE

TERRA TREMUIT (48)

Although *Terra tremuit* shows few significant melodic differences between MSS, two issues require comment. The first is structural. The base version of Pa 776 is somewhat atypical in lacking repetendum cues after verses 1 and 2, though the same format is found in Lo 4951. In Pa 776, there are two alleluia melodies, one that closes the respond and another that follows the final verse. Although both melodies are found in all sources, the MSS differ in their indications of repetendum cues to these alleluias. In some MSS, the alleluia that is indicated at the close of v. 3 in Pa 776 occurs at the end of each verse, a format followed in Be 40078 and Pa 1235. In other sources, this "verse" alleluia occurs at the end of the first two verses, but the last verse closes with a cue to the alleluia that was heard in the respond. This structural format is found among several sources in the core group, including Pa 1121 and Ben 34. In other MSS, such as Mo 159, the repetenda are not notated.

The opening of the third verse is a problem spot. Several MSS, including Mo 159 and Cai 61, present a reading very similar to that of Pa 776. Mo 159 indicates a b-natural on "ibi." In other MSS, however, most of the passage is notated a tone higher. The passage variously begins with the fifth D-a, the fourth E-a, or the fifth E-b. All MSS join with Pa 776 at the melisma on the final syllable of "confregit." The following sampling of MSS at "ibi confregit" illustrates this variety.

	I- bi con-	fre-	git
Pa 1121:	bd/decde/abG (liq.)	adcbcbb(ori.)	aGacc (etc.)
Lo 4951:	Da/acabc/Ga	acbabaaG	aGacc (etc.)
Ben 39:	Da/acabc/GaF (liq.)	acbabaa(ori)F (liq.)	GFacc (etc.)
Rei 264:	Gc/cdbcd/acb (liq.)	cdcbcbb (ori.)	aGacc (etc.)
Tri 2254:	Eb/bdbcd/ab(quil.)ca	bdcccb(liq.)	aGacc (etc.)

RoV 52:   Ea/abaab/GaG(liq.)   cdcbcbG(liq.)   aGacc (etc.)

Lo 4951 and Ben 39 present a similar reading that is also matched in sources as diverse as Be 40078, Pa 1235, Pst 120, and Pad 47. Ben 34 erroneously begins the verse on D and notates the melisma on the last syllable of "confregit" a third below its usual position. That this reading is a scribal error is suggested by the custos at the end of the line, which is also written a third lower than the beginning of the next line, where Ben 34 joins the other MSS. The intention of the scribe at the beginning of the verse, however, is not clear.

The variety of different versions suggests a lack of compatibility between the aural tradition and the notational system at the opening of the melody. While it is likely that a nondiatonic pitch was employed, an unemended reading is difficult to construct. In the version of Ben 39 and Lo 4951, beginning with D-a, the mode-1 quality conforms to that of the other verses and the opening passage is placed in a more normal position on the background scale. The version of Pa 776 and Mo 159 reflects the tendency toward melodic repetition in this offertory, because the melodic material at "ibi" is echoed at "illuminans" (phrase 10).

Variants in individual sources: With the exception of the opening of v. 3, there are few significant variants among core sources. Most peripheral MSS present a reading very close to that of the core group, with a few exceptions:

Be 40078: The third verse is written a fourth above its level in the other MSS and employs b-natural once, in the melisma on "confregit," suggesting an f-sharp at the lower level. This nondiatonic practice is not preserved in the other MSS examined.

Pa 1235:

v. 1 "IUdea": D-a (creating a more literal repetition of "notus")
v. 1 "in" [israhel]: Cd GF
v. 1 "IsraHEL": FGaG GaF FFF GaG
v. 2 "habitatiO": GFaGE
v. 3 "miraBIliter": FGFE FGFGFE FGE FGa cdc caG
v. 3 "eTERrnus": FGE GbaG aG (liq.)
To 18: This MS is unusual in having tropes inserted between verses.
v. 1 "IsraHEL": shortened melisma, FGaGE Ga aG
v. 2 "syON": lacks the melisma
v. 3: "arCHUM": shortened melisma, cccaG abc dccb
Roman MSS:

Vat 5319 varies slightly in the boldface segment of the melisma on "alLEluia": aGaGF aGaGF aG GF **Ga(ori.)GFG.**

Vat 5319 dum: DF GF(liq.).
RoS 22:

"iudiciO": Ga aaGF GabaGFGF
"alleluIA": EFGFaGFEFE

ANGELUS DOMINI (49)

The repetenda in this offertory are a point of variance among core MSS. After verse 1, the base version of Ben 39 has a melodically varied, written-out version of the repetendum "sicit dixit alleluia," and this alleluia melody is also cued following the second verse. Although a similar version is found in Mo 159, many MSS, including Pa 776, have this more ornate version of the repetendum only at the end of v. 2, often following a prosula on the "videte" melisma. In these sources, v. 1 either closes without repetendum or is followed by a repetendum cue to the end of the respond.

Two of the Beneventan MSS, Ben 34 and 35, are anomalous in one passage at the end of v. 2. The end of the melisma on "videte" is written a fifth below its position in all other MSS: Ben 34 aGabaG cG abaG **FG aGa c cacGG/G.**

There is no discernable indication of a nondiatonic pitch here. I have chosen Ben 39 as the base version because it is representative of a broader international tradition in this passage.

There are two probable scribal errors in Ben 39. At the end of the respond (phrase 3), Ben 39 omits the words "sicut dixit." Instead, these notes are included as part of the "alleluia" that follows. The presence of these words in all other MSS, coupled with the liquescence that should appear on the last syllable of "sicut" (which is in the middle of a melisma in Ben 39) suggests that this is a scribal error. I have provided the words "sicut dixit" in brackets and given the usual text underlay for "alleluia." In the melisma on the second "alleluia," at the end of v. 1 (phrase 4), Ben 39 omits two notes that appear in all other sources. In the transcription I have shown them in brackets.

Some Beneventan MSS have an additional verse, *Surrexit dominus*, that is not found in other traditions and is not given in the transcription. In Ben 39 it serves as the second verse, and in Ben 34 as the first verse. Its melodic material is derived from that of the respond and first verse.

Aquitanian MSS present a slightly different version of the varied repetendum, as in the version of Pa 776: v. 2 "alLEluia": a dcdcbG ac bcaG G dcd G dcd cbG ac abG (similar version in the other Aquitanian MSS).
Individual MSS:

Pa 1121: In several passages, Pa 1121 has stepwise motion where other MSS have leaps and repeated notes:

respond, "desCENdit": ca a(ori.)F GaGF FD EC **CDEFGa** caG G(ori.)FG(liq.)
v. 1 "Euntes" FG G bbbGF FD **DEFGa** (etc.)
v. 1 "alLEluia" (the varied repetendum): a dcdcbG ac bcaG G dcd G dcdcbF ac abG

Pa 1235:

v. 1 "Eius": The first seven notes of this short melisma are mistakenly written a third too low but are corrected by the custos at the end of the line.
v. 1 "galiLEam": cc cc ca bcd edec cb

Pad 47:

v. 1 "VI/DE/BItis": acb/c acbc (etc.)
v. 1 "alLEluia" (second repetendum): d adcdcbG ac bc aG adcd adcdcbG ac bcG

Pst 120:

The order of the two verses is reversed; the numbering below reflects their usual order.

v. 1 "E/UNtes": CD/Da cdca bGF (etc.)
v. 1 VIdebitis: adc
v. 2, opening: The melisma is divided into three segments, each followed by a prosula. The melisma on "videte" is also prosulated.

RoV 52:

v. 1 "eUNtes": c is the top note of the melisma.
v. 1 "Eius": acb cdba **Gb babG**
v. 1 "VI/DEbitis": acb c acbc (etc.)
v. 1 "alLEluia": cdcdcbG **Gb acba** adcd cdcdcbG Gb acG
v. 2 "Vi/DEte": Gb/bG (etc.)

Be 40078: The order of the verses is reversed.

Roman MSS:
respond, "CElo": The three Roman MSS exhibit melodic variants at the end of the melisma and a transpositional variant in the middle. Much of the melodic figuration in this melisma is shared with the melisma common to sixth mode offertories. In Bod 74, the middle part of the melisma is written at the same position as it is in the sixth-mode offertories, whereas in Vat 5319 and RoS 22 it is written a tone higher, a position more consistent with the eighth-mode structure of this piece.
respond, "CElo":

Bod 74: cbab(ori.)aGaG acba dcdcbcaFGF EFEDFEDEDCDFFF ababaGaF acbF
Vat 5319: cbabaGaG acba dcdcba **GaG FGFEGFEFED EG GG(ori.) ababaGaF** acbG
RoS 22: cbabaGaG acba dcdb cba**GbaGF GFEGFEFEDE GababG aGF** acbG

A very similar melisma, with similar transpositional variants, occurs at the end of the respond on "alleluia."

Vat 5319:

v. 1 "Eius": Gaba babG(liq.)
v. 1 is followed by a repetendum to "sicut dixit," lacking in Bodmer.
v. 2 On "STEtit," a much shorter version of the melisma: babaGaG acba dcdc ababaGaF acbG
v. 2 "ET": FaGFG

INTONUIT DE CAELO (50)

In most MSS, the second verse of this *deuterus* plagal piece has an expansion to the authentic range, with a change of focal pitch from F to c, matching the base version of Ben 34. In a few sources, however, the whole offertory, respond and both verses, is notated in the transposed plagal range, with a final of b and a focal pitch of c; these MSS lack the contrast in range between respond and second verse.

Because the comparative study did not produce a clear unemended reading, a Beneventan MS representing the majority version was chosen for the base transcription. The transpositional variants, however, may attest to a nondiatonic tradition in the second verse.

Mo 159 employs a b-flat on "eripies" (phrase 11), equal to E-flat at the lower level of transposition. This pitch may be found in all sources that distinguish between b-natural and b-flat; it is indicated with a parenthetical b-flat in the base reading of Ben 34. The F's that appear on "eripes," moreover, would be low B-flats if written a fifth lower. For the scribe of Mo 159, a notation of the whole offertory at the affinal position is not an option because the first verse uses a b-natural on "liberator" (phrase 8), which would be an f-sharp at the higher position.

Although a preferred reading of this offertory was not possible to establish with certainty, the move into the authentic range for the second verse may be an emendation made in response to the nondiatonic pitch at the end of the verse. If so, the plagal reading of the second verse would be the preferred one. In many diverse later MSS, such as Pa 1235 and RoV 52, the respond and both verses are written in the transposed plagal range. The Beneventan and Aquitanian sources, however, attest to the inconsistencies and perhaps ad hoc nature of the notation. In two early sources, Ben 38 and 40, the second verse appears to be written as the same pitch level as the first verse. In Ben 34 and Ben 39, the respond and first verse are in the untransposed plagal range, whereas the second verse is in the authentic range, a pitch-level profile confirmed by the repetendum cue. The scribe of Ben 35, the latest of these sources, undertakes a unique emendation, in which the second verse begins in the plagal range but joins the majority reading before the problem spot at the end of the verse, with a transition in which the melody is briefly a third below the majority reading (on "[insuren] tibus me") and joins on "exaltabis." Although the unique reading of Ben 35 supports a hypothesis that the higher reading of the verse is an emendation, the transitional bridge attests to a concern for the actual sound of the melody, suggesting that the scribe's ad hoc solution to the notational problem in the second verse had implications for performance.

Among Aquitanian MSS, the repetendum cues are inconsistent and may attest to a variety of practice. In Lo 4951, Pa 780, Pa 1134 and Pa 1135, the cue suggests a performance in the authentic range, whereas in Pa 1132, a later MS from St. Martial, it points to a performance level in the plagal range. A few Aquitanian MSS hint at a further nondiatonic practice in the pretheoretical tradition, one that is not possible to reconstruct securely. If Pa 776 is interpreted as beginning the second verse in the authentic range, the repetendum cue appears to be notated a tone too high, beginning on G rather than F. For several other offertories, such as *Oravi deum* and *Domine convertere*, I and others have hypothesized that similar evidence in Pa 776 implies a performance of the verse a tone below its written level.[1]

The variety of versions points to the problems inherent in the assumption that there is always a single authentic version of the melody that can be reconstructed.

While a plagal reading of the verse emerges as the most probable unemended reading in the Beneventan sources, an authentic-range performance of the verse is strongly implied in many Aquitanian MSS, including Lo 4951 and Pa 780. For these reasons, selecting a source to serve as a base reading for *Intonuit de caelo* is especially difficult. Given the inconsistencies among MSS from the same regional tradition, one wonders whether a higher or lower performance of the verse or its ending was the choice of individual cantors. A move into the authentic range for the final verse may have been undertaken not only in response to the need for emendation but also for aesthetic reasons, since it is stylistically consistent with the genre as a whole.

---

1. On *Domine convertere*, see also Hankeln (1999), 108–9.

Second verse in authentic range: Mo 159, Pa 780 (confirmed by repetendum), Lo 4951 (confirmed by repetendum), Pa 1134 (confirmed by repetendum), Ben 34, Ben 39, Mod 7, Pst 120, Pad 47, Cai 61, Be 40078, Tri 2254, Rei 264, Gr 807.

Second verse in plagal range (or whole offertory in transposed plagal range): Ben 38, Pa 1132 (confirmed by repetendum), Pa 1136 (written level; no repetendum), Pa 1121 (written level; repetendum starts on new line with no custos), Pa 1235, RoV 52.

Other melodic variants: Like other *deuterus* chants, *Intonuit* exhibits many variants around the pitches E and F, and in the second verse, b and c. The Beneventan tradition differs from the majority international reading in the following places.

1. respond, "alleluia": In most non-Beneventan MSS, the segments of the melisma in boldface below are notated a tone higher, as in the reading of Mo 159: "alLEluia": E FaGFF(ori.) **EG (quil.) aGa FG (quil.) aG aF GE** aGG(ori.)F GaG.

2. v. 1 "[refugium] MEum": most core MSS have a reading very similar to that of Mo 159: FF GF GFF DF(quil.)GF(quil.)E. Some peripheral MSS exhibit further variants, as indicated below.

3. "iraCUNdis": This melisma is a point of variance. In most traditions, it is slightly shorter than in the Beneventan sources:

Mo 159: Gc dcc(ori.)G cdc db cba(liq.)
Pa 776: acdcca cdccba(liq.)

4. v. 2 "genTI/BUS": Mo 159: a/aba
Individual MSS:

Lo 4951:

respond, "alLEluia": shortened melisma. The second statement of EFGFG is omitted.
v, 2 "inIquo": ca cb

Pa 1235 (respond and v. 1 are a fifth higher):

respond, "alTISsime": ded de
respond, "alLEluia": c bcedc cb cdede cdedec d dc ed dc ded
v. 1 "reFUgium": c cc dfed db cdededcd

Cai 61: respond, "intonuit . . . dominus": Cai 61 is unique among the MSS examined in notating the opening, "intonuit de ce[lo]," a fourth below the majority reading, and "[ce]lo dominus" a whole tone below. The reasons for this transposition are not clear. The whole-tone transposition at "dominus" results in intervallic differences. In MSS that specify b-flat, a b-flat is indicated, resulting in a passage that articulates the minor third G-b-flat. In Cai 61, the referential interval is the major third F-a. It is not clear whether this unique reading points to a nondiatonic practice.

respond, "alTISsimus": GaG Ga
respond, "alLEluia": E GaGF EG aGa FGaG aFGE aG GF GaG
v. 1 "reFUGium": FF G b-flat aG GE F GaG a
v. 2 "iraCUNdis": ccc Gc dc cGc dccb cba(liq.)

Be 40078:

respond, "CElo": GaG GEFED
respond, "alTISsimus": GaGa
respond, "alLEluia": FE FaGF FF FG(quil)aGa FG(quil)aGa aF GF aGGF aGaG
v. 1 [refugium] "MEum": DF GF GFFD DGFEF

Gr 807:

> respond, "ET" [altissimus]: a
> respond, "alLEluia": FacaGFEF F FGaGa FGaGaF G (ori.)FE aGF aGa
> v, 1 "reFUGium": FF F(ori.)E GaGaGF
> v. 1 [refugium] "MEum": DG aG aE FD DF GFEF
> v. 2 "GENtibus": cd cdc c(ori.)bG bab cc ca ca c cdc(liq.)

In Italian MSS, G-*protus* passages are often written a whole tone higher, consistent with the Guidonian recommendation for emending them. The sources, however, undertake this emendation in different places, as the variants below show.

RoV 52 (respond and v. 1 are written a fifth higher):

> respond, "alLEluia": bcedc ca Gacbc cdedecdc eddc ded
> v. 1 "diLIgam" (a longer version of the melisma): bcbGa cc ca cccaG abcb **abcb** cdededcd
> v. 2 "GEntibus": melisma begins: cd cdcbcbaba (etc.)

Pad 47:

> respond, "alTISsimus": GaG Ga
> respond, "alLEluia": The segments equivalent to EFGFG EFGFG EFD in Ben 34 are a tone higher with a melodic variant at the end, FGaGa FGaG aFGF.
> v. 1 "firmaMENtum": G DGF
> v. 1 [refugium] "MEum": FF GF GF DEF GFE
> v. 2 "ME/US": melisma ends cdededcd/dc
> v. 2 "GENtibus": cdc bcb GaG a cc ca ba abc
> v. 2 "iraCUNdis": ac dc a cdc db cbG (liq.)
> v. 2 "VIro": a c b-flat
> v. 2 "E/RI/PI/ES": aGaG/abcb/abcb/cG Gaba FaFa.

Mod 7 (has many of the same variants as Pad 47 above):

> respond, "CElo": GbabG FED
> respond, "alTIS/SImus" [sic]: GaG Ga/FGF
> respond "alLEluia": F aba G GE FGaGa FGaG aFGF aGF GaG
> v. 1 "domiNE": FF FE DFEDE
> v. 1 "firmaNENtum": FF DGF
> v. 1 [refugium] "MEum": FF DF GFGF DEF GFE
> v. 2 "ME/US": melisma ends cdededcd/dc
> v. 2 "VIro": a c b-flat
> v. 2 "inIquo": acbaG

Roman MSS: In v. 1, Bod 74 lacks the phrase "et refugium meum," which is found in Vat 5319. The omission of this phrase is probably a simple error, and it is supplied from Vat 5319 in the transcription. In Vat 5319 and RoS 22, the whole offertory is notated at the affinal position. Following the second verse, Vat 5319 has a repetendum cue to "et," which Bodmer lacks.

The only other significant difference between Roman MSS is the final alleluia, a point of variance in several of the Easter Week offertories. Bod 74 employs a *deuterus* alleluia melodically identical to that of Bod 74's *In die sollemnitatis*, which also shares material with the closing melisma of *Terra tremuit*. Vat 5319 and RoS 22 close with a *tetrardus*

alleluia, which is similar but not identical to that of *Benedictus qui venit*. Vat 5319: "AL/LE/
LU/IA": cb(liq.)/dcdcdcc (ori.) baGaG cdcdc bcba bcbab/ba(liq.)/GacbaG aG

RoS 22: "AL/LE/LU/IA": d/dcdcdbaGaG cdcdcbcba bcbab/bb(liq.)/GacbaGa aG.
RoS 22 exhibits two other small variants:

"CElo": cdcb
"deDIT": ccl.

PORTAS CAELI (51)

There is one point of Beneventan distinctiveness in v. 1. Most Gregorian sources have "*in
legem*," accommodating the extra syllable with one or two c's.

In v. 2 there are small differences in the melisma on "meum" among both core and
peripheral sources, as shown in the sampling below (differences from Ben 34 in
boldface):.

Pa 776: cdcb ac **b dcaGa** cba baGa/aG

Mo 159: **cedc bcb dcba(quil.)Ga** cb(quil.)a baGa/aGa

Pa 1121: cdcb a cb dc **baGa** cba baGa/aG

RoV 52: bdcb acb **edcaG** acbabaGa/aG

Mod 7: cdcb **cdcdcbaGa** cbabaGa/aG (very similar in To 18)

Gr 807: cdcb **c(ori.)a CaG** aGFG cba caGa/aG

In v. 2, there are minor differences in the "loquar" melisma:

Mo is nearly identical to Ben 34

Pa 776: **E**GbaG **E**GacaaG **FGa**ccaccaG G(ori)F GacaGFG (quil.)abaGa/aG

Pa 1121 is nearly identical to Pa 776

Be 40078: DGcaG DGacaaG DGa c ca bcaF acba cG/G (shortened melisma)

Lo 4951 presents a different reading in many passages:

v. 1 Shortened melisma on "MEam": GFGaaccd ccd aGGFG(quil.)a b

v. 1 "oris mei": acd cdcc(ori.)/ ba/ GaG/G

v. 2 "paraBOLIS": dfffdc cd(quil.)eddc

v. 2: [os] "MEum": shorter melisma: cdcbacbcbaGa/aG

v. 2 On "loquar," Lo 4951 has a shorter melisma that presents problems because the
horizontal alignment is not maintained between the melisma and the previous passage.
Using the repetendum as a guide, the melisma reads: EGbaG EGacaaG FgG (quil.)ab

Mod 7: "ORIS": acdcdc/cb

Gr 807:

Respond, "HOMO": a cdc db c (ori.) a cba caGa/aG

v. 1 "aPERiam": melisma has top note of f: Ga bc dc dbc dfc dfd

Roman MSS: There are very few differences between Vat 5319 and Bod 74.

Vat 5319:

respond, "APparuit": DG

v. 2 "secuLI": cbcdcbc

RoS 22: "alLEluia": cdededc ededc cbdcbacbabaGa ced cdcba dcdcbcbacbab

IN DIE SOLLEMNITATIS (52)

The modal and pitch-level variance in this offertory was illustrated in Justmann's dissertation.[1] In an essay by Theodore Karp, *In die* is employed as an example of methodology in dealing with difficult chants.[2] The south German theorist known as John of Afflighem describes this chant as "much disordered" (*multi confusi*), and suggests that it can be more easily emended at the affinal position.[3] In addition to the core and peripheral MSS used in this study, this discussion of the piece draws on Justmann's fifty-five transcriptions of the respond.

Although this chant has a variety of closing pitches, most versions are *protus*, ending either on D or at the affinal position, on a. Karp's study analyzes the many small melodic variants between the different readings, undoubtedly resulting from the modal ambiguity of the chant and the need for emendation. In larger terms, however, the sources can be classified into two groups, represented by the two readings of the respond given in the transcription. In terms of overall pitch-level profile, Mo represents the *lectio difficilior*, and Pa 776, here transcribed with a final of D, represents the majority version (though it is more often written at the affinal position). After "vestrae dicit" (phrase 1), Pa 776 proceeds unproblematically as a first-mode melody. Mo begins and ends the respond at the affinal position, a fifth above Pa 776. The internal part of the chant, however, is written a fourth above Pa 776 and consistently employs a b-flat, beginning with "dicit dominus" (phrase 1). The interval of transposition returns to a fifth within the final melisma, on "alleluia" (on the twelfth note).

At the position of the normal *protus* range, a fifth lower, the b-flats in Mo would be E-flats. Although the reading of Mo is a minority version, it is found in several Frankish sources and geographically disparate MSS, including Be 40078 and the thirteenth-century Italian MS Rossi 76. I would cautiously hypothesize that Mo's pitch-level profile reflects that of the unemended reading, simply notated at the affinal position. In the majority version, matching the pitch-level profile of Pa 776, there is little sign of the "great disorder" described by John except on the final syllable a "sollemnitatis," a problem spot discussed below.

---

1. Justmann (1988), 447–53; 725–31; 1007–13; 1311–17; 1590–96.
2. Karp (1995), 151–64.
3. "Si autem multum sunt confusi et in affinibus facilius possunt emendari, eo dirigantur, quemadmodum illud offertorium." Smits van Waesberghe (1950), 148. See the translation in Palisca, ed. (1978), 155. "If, however, they are much disordered and can be emended more easily in the kindred range, let them be rearranged there, as in this offertory."

The nondiatonic pitch E-flat implied in the version of Mo points to the modal ambiguity of the melody, which reflects a mixture of *protus* and *deuterus* characteristics. Typical *deuterus* melodic gestures include the figure on the last two syllables of "dominus," that on "vos," and, to a lesser extent, on "in terram." In Pa 776, these melodic figures are written at the normal *deuterus* position, employing the semitone between E and F. In Mo 159, they employ the semitone between b-flat and a; the latter pitch also serves as the final of the *protus* chant. Mo 159, then, evidently reflects a tradition in which these *deuterus* melodic figures were sung a whole tone below their usual position, with a semitone between D and E-flat.

In some MSS, final cadence is altered to close on E or, at the affinal position, G or b. These altered endings are probably attributable to the modal ambiguity of the melody. The *deuterus* characteristics of many internal phrases evidently led to an alteration of the final cadence to close on E or b, the most common alternate finals.

I would argue that the melodic variants in the respond, documented in Karp's and Justmann's studies, occur at specific places and are almost always related to the need for emendation. By way of illustration, I would like to consider the first problem spot, on the last syllable of "sollemnitatis." As noted, Pa 776 employs a common solution to the overall "modal disorder" of the melody, writing the problematic melodic figures involving E-flat and D a tone higher, in their normal *deuterus* position, beginning at "dicit dominus." In these versions, however, one problem remains. On the last syllable of "sollemnitatis" (phrase 1), Mo has a b-flat, equivalent to E-flat at the position of Pa 776. The melodic variants that arise here are clearly attempts to circumvent the E-flat of the unemended reading. Pa 776's reading, E (flat)-F, is matched in Pa 780 and Lo 4951. Pa 1121 and 1132 simply have two F's here. The scribe of Pa 903 recomposes the passage: the previous syllable, "sollemniTAtis," is transposed up a whole tone, ac abc, and "tis" is Ga. According to Justmann's transcriptions, a similar solution is taken in Avignon 181; Madrid 51 and Madrid 18 match Pa 776 at "ta" but have Ga, a transposition of a third, on "tis." Following this passage, the Aquitanian MSS present a largely unified tradition. Some of the French MSS in Justmann's transcriptions adopt other solutions. Angers 96, Angers 97, and Leningrad 6, written at the affinal position, have a-c on "tis," equivalent to D-F at the lower level. This solution is also found in many German MSS, including Gr 807 and others in Justmann's large sampling. Orleans 119 has FG on "tis," a reading a whole tone above Pa 776, and remains a whole tone above Pa 776 through "vestrae," joining on "dicit" (a version also found in Beneventan MSS and others summarized below).

The clear association of variants with nondiatonic pitches suggests that the varied transmission of this offertory is attributable to nondiatonic pitches rather than melodic instability per se. The scribes introduced small melodic variants by necessity, as ad hoc solutions to the problem of notating the chant within the diatonic framework. Among certain late German and Italian MSS in Justmann's large sampling, such as Munich 2541 and Salzburg 20, the final melisma on "alleluia" is also altered, followed by a reworked final cadence. These more extensive reworkings contrast with the consistent readings of the final melisma found in earlier MSS. In some sources, the melisma on "fluentem" is altered as a way of circumventing low B-flat. In some Italian MSS, for example, the notes of the final melisma corresponding to Pa 776's F-D-C-B(flat) are F-E-D-C (Modena 0.1.3) or G-F-D-C (Vercelli 162). In Beneventan MSS, by contrast, the b is simply left as is.

The pitch-level profile of the sources is summarized below. Because the problem spots of this offertory are primarily in the respond rather than the verses, many more sources can be examined in a study of the problem spots. To give a broader picture beyond the MSS normally used in this study, the following summary of pitch-level in the respond incorporates selected MSS transcribed by Justmann, based on his transcriptions.

1. Pitch-level profile of Pa 776, at the affinal position: Ben 34 (2↑ at [sollemnita] "tis vestrae"), Provins 12 (2↑ at [sollemnita] "tis vestrae"), RoV 52, Pst 120, Cai 61, Rei 264, Trier 2254 (2↓ briefly at "lac"), Pa 17310, Angers 96 and 97, Pst 119, Vercelli 161, Rossi 231, Wolfenbüttel 40 (2↑ at [sollemnita] "tis vestrae"), Namur 515.

2. Pitch-level profile of Pa 776, at the normal plagal position (ending on D): [Pa 780, Pa 1121], Ben 39 (2↑ at [sollemnita] tis vestrae], Gr 807, Pa 903 (2↑ and 3↑ at [solemni]tatis), Brussels 3823, Orleans 116 (2↑ at [solelmnita]"tis vestrae"), Pa 1890, Modena 0.1.3, Vercelli 162, Milan S 74, Melk 109.

3. Pitch-level profile of Pa 776, with an altered final cadence:

   a. Pa 1132 (affinal position): on G; last syllable of "alleluia" is changed to aG (also in Graz 1655).
   b. Lo 4951, Madrid 18, and Madrid 5: on E; written a whole tone above Pa 776 beginning with the ten notes of the melisma on "alLEuia".
   c. Ben 39: On E; last syllable of "alleluia" is changed to ED.
   d. To 18 (affinal position): on G, with a substantially different melisma on "alleluia."
   e. Pa 1669 (affinal position): on b; written a whole tone above the majority reading beginning with the last fifteen notes of the melisma on "alLEluia."
   f. In Justmann's transcriptions, Munich 2541 and Salzburg 20 have similar *deuterus* endings, preceded by shortened and greatly varied melismas on "alleluia."

4. Pitch-level profile of Mo 159: Paris 904, Brussels 3824, Angers 96 and 97, Be 40078, Reims 224, Rossi 76.

5. Unique reading: Leningrad 6, at the level of Mo until the last syllable of "inducam," presents a variant reading of "vos," a whole tone higher.

Roman MSS: Bod 74 lacks the second verse for this offertory. The respond and first verse show no significant variants from Vat 5319. RoS 22:

"VEstre": EGFEGFE
"TERram": FEFEDC (etc.)

ERIT VOBIS (53)

A first illustrated by Bomm, this offertory exhibits a great variety of modal characteristics.[1] Its diversity of transmission is probably attributable to a mixture of factors, including nondiatonic pitches, modal ambiguity, and perhaps a resulting lack of clarity in the aural tradition. I have not been able to determine a single preferred reading or propose explanations for all the variants. The commentary that follows and the supplemental examples provide several possible solutions to the problems.

Because MSS in the core group show such diversity of pitch level in the respond, selecting a base version for the transcription proved especially difficult. The ending on G in the transcription of Pa 780 is matched in most pitched MSS. The Beneventan sources

1. Bomm (1929), 160–62.

EXAMPLE 53.1

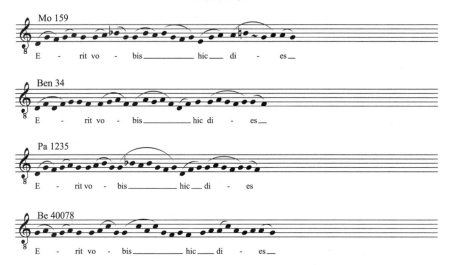

present a highly emended *tritus* version of the respond that is matched in two German MSS, Gr 807 and Be 40078. In Mo 159, a lengthy passage of the respond is probably emended. As described below, two of the Aquitanian sources in the core group, Pa 776 and Pa 1121, exhibit too many inconsistencies with the other MSS to provide a reliable reading. Pa 780, chosen as the base version, presents most of the respond and first verse at the probable unemended pitch level, closing on G. As described below, the variants imply that F-sharps were employed in phrase 3.

1. The opening passage, "erit vobis hic dies": Four versions of the opening passage are shown in example 53.1. With the assumption that the intended starting pitch in the Aquitanian MSS is D or E, as in most pitched MSS, all Aquitanian MSS present a reading similar to that of Mo 159. I have used this majority reading as a guide to determining the opening pitches of Pa 780 in the transcription. Although similar readings of "erit vobis" are found in most MSS (except in Benevento), variants begin at "hic dies." The alternate use of b-natural and b-flat in Mo 159 (line 1) exemplifies the problematic modality of this offertory. The b-flats in the opening passage are matched in the other MSS that distinguish between b-natural and b-flat. The result is a mixture of G-*protus* and *tetrardus* characteristics. In the Beneventan manuscripts, represented by Ben 34 (line 2), the passage is *tritus* in quality throughout, cadencing on F. Pa 1235 (line 3) presents a hybrid version, with an opening that matches Pa 780 and Mo 159, but an F-*tritus* cadence on "dies." A similar reading is found in Cai 61.

Since Mo 159 employs a b-natural on "dies," the *tritus* and *tetrardus* versions of the end of the passage are intervallically identical. The Beneventan version, however, differs intervallically from the majority reading on the opening "erit vobis," articulating a major third, F-a, rather than the minor third, G-b-flat, found in Mo and most MSS. It is possible that the difference in intervallic structure points to the use of a nondiatonic pitch, perhaps a-flat at the level of Ben 34. The hybrid readings of the passage, such as that found in Pa 1235, would perhaps support this hypothesis. The variants, however, may also simply reflect the modal ambiguity of the piece as a whole. Since the *tritus* reading of the opening is confined to Beneventan MSS, perhaps the opening is simply an adaptation that brings the opening of the melody into conformity with the *tritus* ending in the Beneventan sources

EXAMPLE 53.2A

(see example 53.2). Be 40078 (line 4) gives an alternate reading of the opening passage that is matched in Rei 264, Tri 2254, To 18, and Mod 7.

2. Cadence on the first "alleluia" (phrase 1): This cadence is melodically variant. Pa 780's reading FGaGF/GF is the majority reading. Mo 159, Pa 1235, and Cai 61 have FGa/GF.

3. Cadence on "domino" (phrase 2): The *deuterus* cadence of Pa 780 is matched in all Aquitanian sources, all Beneventan sources, Pa 1235, Cai 61, Pst 120, and all German sources except for Be 40078. "Domino" concludes on F in Be 40078, Mod 7, RoV 52, and To 18.

4. "In progenies" (phrase 3) to the end of the respond: Here the sources show an extraordinary diversity in their choice of F or G as a focal pitch, beginning with "vestris/vestras." A selection of various readings is given in example 53.2. The sources in the example

EXAMPLE 53.2B

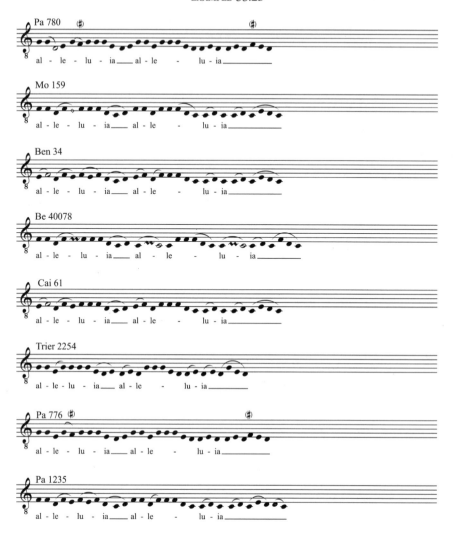

were chosen to illustrate the very different approaches to emendation. Pa 780 adopts G as a focal pitch throughout, a reading also matched in Lo 4951. The Beneventan sources, by contrast, give a *tritus* reading, consistently adopting F as a focal pitch; this version of the ending is consistent with the *tritus* characteristics of the opening in Beneventan sources. This *tritus* reading is matched in some German sources, such as Rei 264. Most other MSS in the example alternate between F and G, moving between them at different points.

    The pitch-level variants are probably attributable, at least in part, to the use of a nondiatonic pitch. The *tritus* and *tetrardus* versions differ in the pitch below the final, which is the semitone in *tritus* and whole tone in *tetrardus*. In this passage, the semitone below the recitation pitch appears on "diem" and in the first and second "alleluia." If the version on G is taken as the "unemended" pitch level, the downward transposition to F

EXAMPLE 53.2c

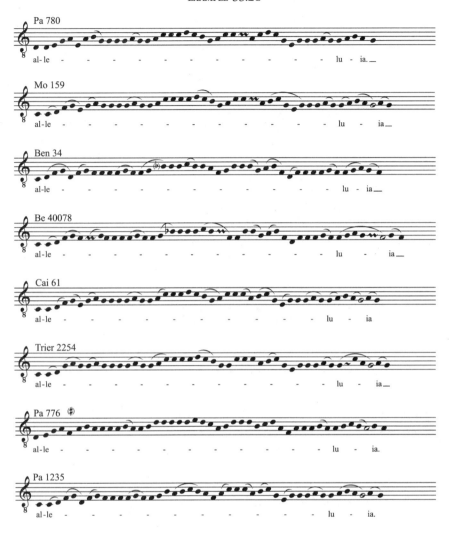

would suggest that an F-sharp is required at this point, indicated parenthetically in the transcription of Pa 780. If the version on F is taken as the "correct" pitch level, an upward transposition to G would suggest that an E-flat is intended at the lower level. The first alternative is more plausible for several reasons. The respond closes on G in the great majority of sources. With the exception of Be 40078 and Gr 807 (which end on F) and Rei 264 (which closes on E), most non-Beneventan sources close on G. These sources move the referential pitch from G to F and back to G at various points. Mo (line 2), for example, moves to F at "legitimum," whereas Cai 61 (line 5) moves on "sempiternum." Nearly all MSS join on G in the last "alleluia," where the hypothetical F-sharp is no longer required. The general stylistic traits of the chant repertory further argue in favor of the version on G with an F-sharp. This passage consists of melodic material that is typical of the chant repertory. Normally it is placed between the pitches F and D or a and c, with a semitone below the recitational pitch. The placement of this material a tone higher than usual in *Erit vobis,* between the pitches E and G, suggests that an F-sharp is required. The reading of Tri 2254 (line 6) is instructive: the focal pitch is G throughout, except for a downward transposition at "diem," where the irregular semitone is required. In the first and second "alleluias," where the irregular semitone occurs at the level of Pa 780, the pitch F (sharp) appears as G in Tri 2254, reflecting the German chant dialect. An emendation similar to that of Tri 2254 is suggested in the Frutolf tonary. While the need for F-sharp is probably the primary reason for the diverse versions, the variants may also reflect inconsistencies in the aural tradition, attributable to a lack of modal clarity throughout the respond and verses.

Although the latter solution is reflected in the base transcription, I would like to explore yet a third possible solution to the problem. One key MSS in the core group, Pa 776, presents a reading not found in the other sources, with the possible exception of Pa 1121, which is difficult to decipher because of inconsistent heightening at the place in question.[2] With the assumption that the starting pitch of the respond is D or E, these two versions close on a. Pa 776 is shown in the line 7 of example 53.1. The last "alleluia" is marked by a shift of recitation pitch from G to a. This reading of the passage follows the pitch-level profile of Mo a whole tone higher, with the same upward shift of focal pitch for the last "alleluia." Without chromatic alteration, however, an ending on the *protus* pitch a would result in an intervallic structure different from that of other MSS. The ending of nearly all MSS on G, without a b-flat, argues against a *protus* quality for the closing passage and in favor of a *tetrardus* ending. Another possible solution, then, would be to assume a closing pitch of G and transcribe this version down a whole tone *in toto*. This reading would result in an opening passage that partly matches Ben 34 and partly Pa 1235. On balance, however, Pa 780 seems the more likely preferred reading.

1. Pitch level at "in progenies vestras":

   = Pa 780: Pa 776, Pa 1121 (?), Lo 4951, Pa 1235, Cai 61, Tri 2254, Rei 264, Gr 807
   2↓ Pa 780: Mo 159, Ben 34, Ben 35, Ben 39, Pa 1132, Be 40078, Pad 47, Mod 7, Pst 120, To 18, RoV 52

2. Pitch level at "legitimum":

   = Pa 780: Pa 776, Pa 1121 (?), Lo 4951, Cai 61, Gr 807 (starting on the third syllable)
   2↓ Pa 780: Mo 159, Ben 34, Ben 35, Ben 39, Be 40078, Tri 2254, Pad 47, Mod 7, Pst 120, To 18, RoV 52

3. Pitch level at "sempiternum diem":

   = Pa 780: Lo 4951, Tri 2254 (2↓ at "diem"),
   2↓ Pa 780: Mo 159, Ben 34, Ben 35, Ben 39, Be 40078, Rei 264, Cai 61, Pa 1235, Pad 47, Mod 7, Pst 120, To 18, RoV 52

4. Pitch level at "alleluia" 1 and 2:

   = Pa 780: Pa 776, Pa 1121 (?), Lo 4951, Tri 2254
   2↓ Pa 780: Mo 159, Ben 34, Ben 35, Ben 39, Be 40078, Rei 264, Gr 807, Pa 1235, Cai 61, Pad 47, Pst 120, To 18, RoV 52

2. The problem spot is "in progeniis vestras." In the respond, "in progenies" begins on low C and the following notes are either DFDF or EGEG. In both repetendum cues, the first two notes of "in progenies" appear to be CD, which would produce a reading like that of Pa 776.

5. Pitch level at "alleluia" 3:

= Pa 780: Mo 159, Lo 4951, Cai 61, Tri 2254, Rei 264, Pa 1235 (joins within the melisma on the second syllable of "alleluia," when the melisma reaches c), Pad 47 (reading similar to Pa 1235), To 18 (reading similar to Pa 1235), Mod 7 (also joins within the melisma on the second syllable of "alleluia," but earlier, on the eighth note), Pst 120 (same reading as Mod 7), RoV 52 (same as Pad 47).
2↓ Pa 780: Ben 34, Ben 35, Ben 39, Be 40078
2↑ Pa 780: Pa 776, Pa 1121 (?)

The verses present further problems in pitch level. The Aquitanian MSS differ in the order of the verses, and most include a repetendum cue only after the final verse. Although the Aquitanian MSS present no large-scale partial transpositions in relation to Mo 159, the repetendum cues, when present, give conflicting information about the intended pitch level of the verses in relation to the respond. Outside the Aquitanian tradition, moreover, partial transpositions may be found in several sources.

In the transcription of Pa 780, I have derived the pitch level of the second verse, *In mente*, from the repetendum cue, resulting in a reading a fourth below the pitch level of Mo 159. (The written level is relation to the second verse is a fifth below Mo 159). Several F-sharps are required to replicate the interval structure of Mo at this position. It is not clear, however, that this version is the preferred reading. In Ei 121, the scribe writes the letters "lm" at the verse opening, indicating a moderate heightening of pitch consistent with the majority reading of Mo but not with Pa 780. In the transcription, I have provided the version of Mo as an alternative. Because the verse *Dixit dominus* lacks a repetendum cue and because its relationship to the second verse is not always a reliable guide, its intended pitch level is unclear. I have tentatively transcribed it at the level of Mo 159, the majority reading. The summaries of pitch level below are provided in relation to Mo 159.

Beginning of v. *Dixit Moyses*: In the majority of MSS examined, the verse is notated at the same pitch level as Pa 780. These include the late German MSS, along with Cai 61 and Pa 1235. As mentioned, however, the repetendum cues in Aquitanian MSS, when present, give conflicting information about the intended pitch level of the verse. Three of the four Italian sources in the sampling, moreover, transmit different readings, joining the majority reading of Mo in pitch level at "estote." These differences in the Italian MSS may be attributable simply to the modal ambiguity of the piece as a whole.

Pitch level of the verse *Dixit dominus* in relation to Mo/780:

= Mo 159: Ben 34, Cai 61, Pa 1235, Pst 120, Gr 807, Tri 2254, Be 40078
4↓ Mo 159: Pa 1121 (according to repetendum)

Distinctive or unclear readings:

Mod 7: Verse begins 3↓ Mo 159, joins at "estote"; the words "bono animo" are missing.
RoV 52: Verse begins 3↓ Mo 159, presents a melodically variant reading of "animo estote," joins at "veniet vobis."
Pad 47: Verse begins 2↑ Mo 159, presents a melodically variant reading of "animo estote." The passage that begins "et veniet vobis" is 3↑ Mo (like To 18 below), joining "deo."
To 18: For reasons that are unclear, To 18 presents the passage that begins "et veniet vobis" 3↑ Mo 159, joining in the melisma on "deo."

Pa 776: The written and performance levels are unclear because of the problematic ending of the respond and because verse lacks a repetendum cue.

Lo 4951: The written level throughout is a 2↑ Mo 159, but there is no repetendum cue to confirm the written level.

Position of *In mente* verse in relation to Mo 159 (with variants at "de terra et de domo"):

2↓ Mo 159: Pa 776 (according to repetendum)

4↓ Mo 159: Pa 1121, Pa 780 (3↓ at "de domo")

5↓ Mo 159: Pa 1235 (mostly); Mod 7 (joins Mo at "in quo existis")

= Mo 159: Lo 4951, Ben 34 (2↓ Mo at "de terra"; joins at "manu"), Ben 39 (same as Ben 34) Cai 61, Gr 807, Re 264, Be 40078 Tri 2254

= Pa 780: Pa 1121, Ben 35, Pa 1235

4↑ Pa 780: Ben 34, Mo 159, Pa 776, Lo 4951, Cai 61, Gr 807, Be 40078, Rei 264, Pst 120, To 18

Emended and distinctive versions: Tri 2254 is 6↑ Pa 780, until the melisma on the final syllable of "istum," where the interval of transposition changes to a fifth. Mod 7 begins at the level of Pa 780 but is a fifth higher beginning at "in quo existis" (where the low B-flat would be required). RoV 52 begins at the level of Pa 780 but departs from it at "in qua [*sic*] existis." The pitch-level relationship to Pa 780 is as follows: In qua 5↑; existis 3↑; egypti 4↑; in manu 3↑; potenti 4↑.

From after the initial phrase, these four sources diverge. Beginning with "in quo existis," Tri 2254 joins at "in quo," whereas Pa 1235 and Pa 780 remain a fifth below Mo 159 throughout.

Melodic variants: Melisma on "deo": In sources from German-speaking areas, the fourth note of the melisma is b-flat rather than b-natural, as in Mo 159.

Roman version: Bod 74 is the only Roman source to transmit the verses of *Erit vobis*. Vat 5319 and RoS 22, notated at the affinal position, are nearly identical to Bod 74 until the closing alleluias, where they show a rare significant difference. Vat 5319 and RoS 22 present a version more florid than Bod 74's. Their version is nearly identical to the closing "alleluia" melisma of *Benedictus qui venit* (54), thus closing on G rather than E. While the variants in the Roman tradition could reflect practices at the different institutions they represent, it is also possible that they attest to further melodic stereotyping in the tradition that took place between the copying of Bod 74 and Vat 5319.

RoS 22: "AL/LE/LU/IA": G/aG/cd cdcdccbaGaG cdcdcb acbab/bb (liq.)/Gacba-GaG. RoS 22 shows some variants from the others in the last cadential segment of Formula B. The segment GFEFG in 5319 and Bodmer is consistently GaGFEFG in RoS 22: on the first "alleluiA," "celebrabiTIS," and "domiNO."

BENEDICTUS QUI VENIT (54)

In most MSS the order of the two verses is 1. Lapidem 2. Haec dies. Beneventan and Roman sources have the two verses in the opposite order.

b-flats: The MSS that indicate b-flats do not do so in the same places, perhaps indicating an inconsistency of practice. The parenthetical b-flats in the base transcription are derived from their use in Mo 159. Later MSS are not always in agreement with Mo or with one another. Be 40078 indicates a b-flat at "rePRObaverunt" that is lacking in Mo 159. Cai 61 employs b-flats at "haec dies" in v. 1. The later MSS, however, do not indicate b-flat on "domiNI" in the respond.

Editorial emendation: In the melisma stated twice on "exulTEmus" and "laeTEmur," a small segment of the melisma, indicated with brackets in the base transcription, is written incorrectly the first time in Ben 34. Beginning with the fifth note, the scribe writes babG instead of cbca. The status of this passage as a scribal error is evident from the other Beneventan sources and from the second statement of the melisma, where it is written correctly. I have emended this passage in the transcription.

Beneventan distinctiveness: respond, "vos": Most MSS have "vobis" instead of "vos," a Gallican psalter adaptation, with a melodically identical reading. The syllables of "vobis" are distributed FG/acaGa.

The Beneventan sources show small differences from the majority of other MSS in several of the melismas. In the following passages, Mo presents a more common reading. Some of the more significant differences are shown in boldface.

v. 1 "edifiCANntes": Mo 159: eg de (quil.)f gd fff(ori.)d **ff gdc de(quil.)f**

v. 1 "anGUli": Mo 159: de(Quil.)f ge fdc

v. 1 "exulTEmus" and "laeTEmur":

Beneventan MSS present a shortened version of the melisma, which is also found in Lo 4951. The same melisma, with the same variant, occurs in the second verse of *Domine deus salutis*. All Beneventan sources omit a section of the melisma that is shown in boldface in the sample readings below. With the exception of Lo 4951, the Aquitanian, French, German, and Italian sources present very similar readings of the melisma, as shown in the sampling below (differences from Ben 34 are shown in boldface). The early adiastematic sources in the sampling also transmit the majority version. The reasons for the isolated presence of this shorter form of the melisma at Benevento and Toulouse (Lo 4951) are unclear.

Pa 776: cdca cbcaFG FG(quil.)aGaG a **ccca ccdc aaF FG(quil.)aGaG** babGF GacaF FG(quil.)aGa

Be 40078: cdcG cbcaFG FG(quil)aG aGa **cc ca cc dca aF FG(quil.)aG aG** ca caF GacaF FG(quil)aGa

Pa 1235: ac dca cbcaFG FGaGaG **ac ccacbdc a aF FGaGaG** babGF GacaGF GaGa

Mod 7: cdca **ababG**FG FGaGaG **acc ca cc dc aF FGaGaG** babGF Fa ca FGaGa

Cai 61: Gc db G cbcGGFG FGaGaG **acc ca cc dc a aF FGaGaG babaF** Ga caGF GaGa

As mentioned, the second verse in Mo 159 is written a fourth above its position in most MSS. Mo 159 employs a b-natural in the second statement of the melisma, suggesting an F-sharp at the lower level. This pitch, however, is indicated only in the second statement of the melisma. The two statements are otherwise identical. I am nevertheless hesitant to attribute the difference to an error, since the higher notation of the verse, not found in most sources, suggests the presence of a chromatic inflection.

Mo 159, "ExulTEmus": (all b's are flat unless indicated): fgfc fe fdbc bc(quil.)dc dc **dfff (ori.)d ff gfdd(ori.)** bc(quil.)dc dc ed ecb cd fd (ori.) bc(quil.)dcd

"LaeTEmur": fgfc fe fdbc bc(quil.)dc dc **dfff(ori.)d ff gfdd(ori.)** b-**natural!** (quil.)dc dc ed ecb cd fdd(ori.) bc(quil.)dcd

Individual MSS: Other than those described above, there are very few variants among core MSS. The Italian MSS present a reading close to that of the core group. Small variants in peripheral MSS include the following.

Be 40078:

> v. 2 "rePRObaverunt": b-flat
> v. 2 "Edificantes": dc c adc ed cc aca
> v. 2 "CAput": d cdede
> Gr 807: v. 1 "DIes": FGaGaGF

Pa 1235:

> respond, "domiNI": no b-flat indicated
> v. 1 "DI/ES": FGaGaGFG/GF
> v. 1 "exulTEmus": see above
> v. 2 "edifiCANtes": df fdf fd fffed f fe(liq.)

Cai 61:

> respond, "domiNI": no b-flat indicated
> v. 1 "ea": melisma begins ac caG caG GF (etc.)
> v. 2 "Edificantes": dcc cdc edc cba ba
> v. 2 "edifiCANtes": fgd fgd ff fd c de fe(liq.)

Pst 120: v. 1 "reprobaveRUNT": cfed

Roman sources: Vat 5319 presents a much shorter version of the respond text, lacking "benediximus vos de domo domini." RoS 22 has a slightly less ornate version of the final melisma: "AL/LE/LU/IA": aGcdcb/acbab/bb/GacbaGaGG.

DEUS DEUS MEUS (55)

The Beneventan sources exhibit two small differences from the majority of other sources. In a segment of the final melisma of v. 2, the Beneventan version is missing the notes in boldface:

> Mo 159: cca **FG ab**(quil.) **cb**(quil.) a FGbaG EF aGF etc.
> Ben 34: cca FG baG EF aGF etc.

The Beneventan MSS also differ here: v. 2 "quia [factus es]": Mo has DEF FGEF.

The final melisma is subject to small variants in some peripheral MSS, as listed below. There are otherwise very few significant variants.

Pa 1121: v. 2 "tuA/RUM": acaGacaGba/b
Gr 807:

> respond, "ET" [in nomine]: CFE
> v. 1 "TUam": FFFD CFDCD FFFD FGF GDEFD
> v. 2 "QUIa": DCFGaG
> v. 2 "tuArum": GaGF acaG ccc

Pst 120:

v. 2 "exulTAbo": ac ca aGaF Gac ca aGaF GabcaGa FaG c ca FGa baG GabaGEF aGFEF FGaGa (etc.)

Mod 7:

v. 2 opening, "INMa/TU": Ga/F/G

v. 2 "exulTAbo": ac ca aGaF Ga c ca aGaF abcbaGa FaG c ca aGF cba FG baG EF aGE F (etc.)

Pad 47:

v. 2 opening, "INMa/TU": Ga/F/G

v. 2 "exulTAbo": c ccaaFaF FG c cabGaF Ga caFa FaG cca FabaG EF aGF EF aG DF FGaGa caG (etc.)

To 18: This MS presents some variants not found among the other Italian sources in the sampling:

respond, "VI/GIlo": DEDC/DEDC
respond, "alLEluia" : CFFGFGFCD FFFE FGFG

v. 2 "quia factus es adiutor": This section migrates upward and is mostly a third above the majority reading of Ben 34, joining again at "meus."

v. 2 "exulTAbor": Shortened and varied melisma: acbcaG GF Ga cbcaFG FaG abGF ac c c ca FGa cba FG baG EF aGF

Roman MSS: The Roman version of this offertory is unusual in corresponding most to the Gregorian version in its final verse. In both traditions, the final verse has the traits of mode 1. In typical fashion, however, the Roman melody as a whole is more uniform than the Gregorian. The two verses are nearly identical, beginning with a typical first-mode gesture and continuing with repeated statements of the formula associated with mode 1. The first verse contrasts with the second-mode characteristics of the Gregorian, lacking melodic resemblance.

Aside from the use of liquescences and the oriscus, there are very few variants between Vat 5319 and Bod 74. RoS 22 shows some minor variant readings and a substantial variant in the final melisma. In RoS 22, the ending of this melisma is very similar to that of the final alleluia in *Terra Tremuit* (48). In Bod 74 and Vat 5319, by contrast, the *Deus deus* melisma begins as the *Terra tremuit* melisma but continues differently. The greater similarity between the two melismas in the latest MS, RoS 22, may reflect further melodic stereotyping that has taken place in the tradition between the copying of the earlier sources and the copying of RoS 22.

Vat 5319: respond, "meAS": FaGFEFF(ori.)ED

RoS 22:

"DEus": EFD
"te": ED
"luCE": GF aGabaGFGF
"alLE/LU/IA": GF FaGaGF aGaGF aGF GabaGFG/GG/EFGFaGFEFE

LAUDA ANIMA (56)

This piece exhibits very few significant variants between MSS. In a pattern evident in most *deuterus* pieces, variants at the semitone E-F are prevalent. The Beneventan reading employs E to a greater extent than other MSS do. In a similar sort of variant, the Beneventan base version departs from other MSS in one small variant in the opening syllable: "LAUda" is CDGE in Ben 34 and CEGE in most other MSS.

   v. 2 "Tuus": The text underlay indicated in Ben 34, though matched in other Beneventan MSS, differs from other core and peripheral MSS. The majority reading gives the first eight notes of the melisma to the first syllable.

   v. 2 "Sion": The Beneventan MSS have a different text underlay from other sources. In most MSS, only the first four notes are given to the first syllable.

Lo 4951:

   v. 1 "FAciet": CEGFG
   v. 2 "saeCU/LI": EGFE/EGFGFFE

Cai 61: The two verses have written-out repetenda to "alleluia."

Pa 1235:

   respond, "AL/LEluia": DF GF/FD FFF(etc.)
   v. 1 "IN" [seculum] FGFGF FD GaG

Mod 7:

   v. 1 "IN" [seculum]: FF GF aGF GaG
   v. 1 "DAT": FG aGa

RoV 52:

   respond, "DEo": FGFE
   respond, "DIuero": EFG aG GF

   v. 1 "cuSTOdi": EFG
   v. 1 "DAT" GaGa
   v. 2 "deus TU" (rather than "tuus")

Pad 47

   v.1 "IN" [saeculum] FF GF aGF GaG
   v. 1 "DAT": FG GFG
   v. 2 "SAEculum": A different text underlay, with melodic differences indicated in boldface: ca c ca ccaGb Ga c ca ccaGb **acdc** bc dcb ca c ca acaG Ga cbG a c cacba/c cac GFE/FGFE

Be 40078:

   respond, "meA"
   "alleLU/IA": EGEF/FE
   v. 2 "SAEculi": melisma ends bcaG acGE GbcaG Gc ca cGE

Gr 807:

respond, "alleLU/IA": EGEF/FE (same at v. 1, "saeculum")

v. 2 "SAEculi": c c(ori.)a bcaG cGa bca bcaG c Gc dc **ccedc** cc cc ca bcaG **acbG Ga cbG Ga bcacGE**

Roman MSS:

In Vat 5319, the whole offertory is written at the affinal position. There are otherwise no significant variants in RoS 22 and Vat 5319.

CONFITEBOR DOMINO (57)

Although *Confitebor domino* has very few significant variants among core or peripheral MSS, there is one passage where the Beneventan MSS differ from other traditions: in the melisma on the final syllable of "letabitur" (phrase 11). This melisma, which echoes "pauperis" in the respond (phrase 3), is found in all Beneventan sources but not in other traditions, where the final syllable of "letabitur" is accommodated with a single note, G.

Variants in individual MSS:

Pa 1121: v. 2 "eam": The end of the melisma appears to be written a tone below the majority version: Facbdc aa(ori.)Ga **abaG bGE FGE FGF bbbGF Gb**. This reading is not matched in the other MSS from St. Martial.

Pa 1235:

v. 2 "DOmine": ac dcd

v. 2 "salvum me": recitation note G

v. 2 "haec": Ga cdc

Cai 61: v. 2 "SERvus": top note of f rather than g: aG a cc de fe ec de fe (also in Be 40078)

Pad 47 v. 2 "SERvus": aGaccdeged cde gege

To 18:

v. 1 "MEus": cdedc cba dc

v. 1 "Eam": Fga dcdcaG aGa acba caFG aF GaGaGFG cccaGa

Roman MSS:

Vat 5319:

v. 1 [manus] "TUa": ad dedcdc

RoS 22:

"confiTEbor": abG

"DO/MIno": cbacba/GbaGFG

"meO": aGbaGaG

"MEdio": aGaba

"PAU/pe/RIS": acbacba/Gacba cbaGF GbaGaG

"alLEluia": aGaG cdcdcbaGaG cdcdcbcba bcba**baG**

ASCENDIT DEUS (58)

In addition to the base transcription from Ben 34, I have included an alternative reading of the ending of v. 1 (phrase 5), for reasons described below.

This offertory exhibits several variants in pitch level. The base version of Ben 34 represents the relative pitch level between sections found in the great majority of MSS.

In Mo 159, the second and third verses are notated twice. Version 1 in Mo matches the level of Ben 34 until the verse endings, which are written a whole tone lower than Ben 34 (at "super omnem" in v. 2 and "sub pedibus" in v. 3). In version 2, the second and third verses are notated a fifth below Ben 34 until the verse endings, where the pitch level joins that of Ben 34. There are small melodic differences between Mo 159's two versions, attributable in part to the need for pitches unavailable in Mo 159's notation system that would be required to write the verses at the lower level.[1] In terms of pitch level, both versions that appear in Mo 159 are unique among the sources examined. While neither of Mo's versions is fully matched in any other MS, however, several MSS do correspond to Mo 159 in specific places. The pitch level at these variant points can be summarized as follows.

1. End of v. 1, "in voce exultationis":= Ben 34: All MSS in the sampling except: 2↓ Ben 34: Mo 159, Pa 1121, Ben 38, Cai 61, Gr 807, Be 40078, Rei 264.

2. beginning of v. 2, "Quoniam dominus" through "magnus":

   = Ben 34: All except Mo 159, version 2
   5↓ Ben 34: Mo 159, version 2

3. End of v. 2, "super omnem terram":

   = Ben 34: all except Mo 159, version 1, and Rei 264
   2↓ Ben 34: Mo version 1, and Rei 264

4. Pitch level at beginning of v. 3, "subiecit" through "gentes":= Ben 34: All except:
   5↓ Ben 34: Mo 159, version 2, Pa 780 (written level), Pa 1121 (written level; repetendum not notated), and Pa 903

5. Pitch level at end of verse 3, "sub pedibus nostris":= Ben 34: All except: 2↓ Ben 34: Mo 159, version 1, Rei 264

Pa 780 presents an unusual reading in which the written level of the third verse begins a fifth below Ben 34 but joins Ben 34 at "sub pedibus." The repetendum, however, is written a fifth too high, and the scribe's intention is not clear. If the verse is read with the assumption that the repetendum closes on D, however, the result is a reading that is not matched in other MSS. A similar pitch-level profile of the verse itself is found in Pa 1134, but this source lacks a notated repetendum cue to confirm the written level at the beginning of the verse. The early adiastematic MS Ei 121 shows a verse opening consistent with the higher reading, with a virga and the letter *l* (levate). All versions that begin at a confirmable level a fifth below Ben 34 join Ben 34 at "sub pedibus." The reading of Ei 121 has the letter *i* here, consistent with the majority version of Ben 34 rather than that of Mo 159, version 2. Although these factors suggest that the majority reading of Ben 34 is the preferred and unemended version, the reasons for writing this section of the third verse a fifth lower are not clear. There are no intervallic differences in this passage that would suggest

---

1. The F's in the majority version of Ben 34, for example would be low B-flats at the level of Mo 159 version 2. In Mo 159 version 2, they appear as C's on, for example, "terribilis" in v. 2.

the presence of a nondiatonic pitch. Perhaps the two versions simply represent performance alternatives.

As the foregoing summary shows, the verse endings are another point of variance. The three verses of *Ascendit* end with essentially the same melodic material, on "exultationis" (v. 1), "super omnem terram" (v. 2), and "[sub]pedibus nostris" (v. 3). In Mo 159, version 1, each statement of this material is written a whole tone lower than it is in most MSS, with a focal pitch of b-flat rather than c, joining the majority reading for the last seven notes. For v. 1, Mo's reading is found in several unrelated MSS: Ben 38, Pa 1121, Cai 61, and the three German sources, Gr 807, Be 40078, and Rei 264. In the second and third verses, however, Mo's reading is matched only in Rei 264.

The intervallic differences between the two versions may point to a nondiatonic pitch, as the following comparisons show:

v. 1, last twelve notes:

Mo (b's are flat):	bbb FDF FGE [flat?]	FGF
Pa 776:	ccc GEG GaF [sharp?]	GaG
Ben 34:	ccc GDF GaE	EGa

Without accidentals, the two versions are different intervallically: The whole tone F-G in Pa 776 occurs at the same position as the semitone E-F in Mo 159. If Mo represents the unemended pitch level here, then the reading of Pa 776 (the majority version) could be an emendation to represent E-flat. If Pa 776 is the unemended pitch level, an F-sharp would be required to duplicate the intervallic structure of Mo 159. In other versions, however, the note corresponding to Mo's E is an F:

Pa 1121:	bbb FDF FGF FGF (identical readings in Gr 807, Be 40078, and
Rei 264)	
Lo 4951:	cc aFG GaF FGF F(ori.) DED

The problems in establishing a preferred version of this passage are complicated by the melodic similarities between the three verse endings. As mentioned, the scribes of Mo and Rei 264 write all three statements of this material a whole tone below Ben 34. In Pa 1121, Ben 38, Gr 807, and Be 40078, however, the ending of v. 1 is a tone lower than the corresponding passage in verses 2 and 3.

In v. 1, the passage immediately preceding this verse ending is also a point of variance. In Ben 34, the cadence on "deo" (phrase 4) is G-a-b(-flat) G/G, a reading matched in Mo and Pa 776. In many other MSS, however, it is a tone higher: pitch level at v. 1, "deo":

= Ben 34: Ben 38, Mo 159, Pa 776, Pa 1121, Cai 61, Gr 807, Be 40078, Rei 264, To 18
2↑ Ben 34: Ben 39, Lo 4951, Pa 780, Pa 903, Pa 1235, RoV 52, Pst 120, Mod 7, Pad 47

To summarize, the lower reading of the verse ending in v. 2 and 3 is found only in Mo (version 1) and one other source, Rei 264. In verse 1, however, the lower reading of the verse ending is found in all three German MSS and the unrelated sources Ben 38, Pa 1121, and Cai 61. In verse 1, then, this reading cannot be dismissed as a peculiarity

of Mo 159. The majority reading of Ben 34 is certainly the more regular in tonal
structure and the lower reading the *lectio difficilior*. I would cautiously surmise that the
unemended reading of the ending of v. 1 is at the level of Mo and Ben 38, with a b-flat
and E-flat, while the endings of verses 2 and 3 were sung a tone higher. In most MSS
that adopt the lower pitch level of this passage, the hypothetical E-flat is either left as
is or written as an F (as in Pa 1121 above). With this scenario, the minority verse
endings of verses 2 and 3 in Mo and Rei 264 can perhaps be explained as adaptations to make
the second and third verse endings conform to that of the first verse. This hypothetical
unemended reading, however, is preserved only in Ben 38 and Pa 1121. While I have not
adopted Ben 38 as the base reading simply because of the uncertainties surrounding this
passage, I have included it as an alternative reading in the transcription.

Transcription issues: In phrase 4, Ben 34 has a scribal error that is corrected by a custos
at the end of the line. At [iubila]te deo (v. 1), an erroneous F clef occurs, corrected by the
custos on D at the end of the line. I have emended the transcription accordingly. A similar
error occurs at the end of v. 2 (phrase 7), where the close of the verse and repetendum are
written a whole tone too high.

Beneventan independence: Beneventan MSS transmit a shortened and varied version of
the melisma on "terribiLIS" (v. 2, phrase 6). The other MSS transmit a reading similar to
that of Pa 776:

a Fac Fac Fac aGFG FFDDC D FFF C DFDC CDFF aGFG FF DGE FFF.

Other melodic variants: v. 3 "subjeCIT": The melisma is a point of slight variance
among core MSS. Benevenan MSS lack a threefold repetition of a that appears in Mo 159,
Aquitanian MSS, and most peripheral MSS:

Mo (version 1): db dc dc c(ori.) a accc(ori.)a Gba aaa
Pa 1121: dc db ca a(ori.) Ga cc c(ori.)G aca aaa
Pa 776 gives shorter version of melisma: db dc caaG aca aaa

German MSS give a reading similar to that of Mo 159.
Italian MSS also have a variant reading of this melisma:

Pst 120: dcdc dcca acc ca cdc ccc
RoV 52: dc dc ca aG a c ca dec ccc
Mod 7 is closer to Mo 159: dcdc dc aaG a ccc ca Gba aaa
v. 3 is lacking in Pad 47

v. 3 "populos nobis et gentes": Cai 61:The scribe appears to write this section of v. 3 a third
too high, perhaps a scribal error.
Roman MSS:
Vat 5319:

respond, "DOminus": shorter version of the melisma, FaGabGF
v. 1 "exultatioNIS": FEFGFE (the less ornate version of this figure)
Vat 5319 lacks v. 2

RoS 22:

"iubilatiO/NE": G ababaG/abaG
"alleluIA": E FGFaGFEFE

EMITTE SPIRITUM (59)

This offertory has very few significant variants between sources, especially in the core group. The minor differences between Ben 34 and the non-Beneventan MSS are as follows:

respond "TUum":

  Mo 159: FGaaG

  Pa 776: FGaG

  (similar in other core and peripheral MSS)

  respond "seCUla": Mo 159: GacGG(ori.)FG (other sources in the core group are identical to Ben 34).

  v. 1 "magnifiCAtus": Most non-Beneventan MSS have a reading identical to that of Mo 159: Gc ccc dc dcc.

  v. 2 "veheMENter": Mo 159: melisma opens G cdc **abaG** (similar reading in the Aquitanian MSS).

  v. 2 "aMIC/TUS": Mo 159: FaG/G

  v. 2, "vestiMENtum": Mo 159: melisma opens G cdc **abaG** (as in "vehementer" above)

  v. 3 "QUI": Mo 159: FG aG (same in other core sources)

  v. 3 "Aquis":

  Mo 159: FG b-flat GF b-flat a

  v. 3 QUI/POnis DF/FaG

Individual sources:

  Lo 4951: v. 3 "aQUIS": acc accc acc ab GFG

Cai 61:

  respond "eMITte": F

  respond "creaBUNtur": cccaGF GabaG(liq.)

  respond "gloriA": decc(ori.)Ga bcb

  v. 1 "MEus": Gcc ca ccaG acb a

  v. 2 "PELlem": G aca G GF Ga

Pa 1235:

  respond "eMITte": F

  respond "TU/UM": F GaG ac cc/c (different text underlay indicated)

  respond "creaBUNtur": cbcaGF GabaG(liq.) (similar to Cai 61)

  v. 1 "MEus": Gc ca bcaG ac aGca

  v. 2 "conFES/SI/Onem": ae/ed/dedb cdca ced

  v. 3 "EX/TEN/DENS": a/Ga cb ba(liq.)/baba aca aG

  v. 3 "PELlem": Gacba G GF GaG(liq.) (similar to Cai 61)

  Pst 120 is very close to the core group.

RoV C 52:

  respond "alLEluia": cccc cabaGa ccbabcba

  v. 2 "Amictus": Fa

To 18:

respond "TU/UM": FGaGac/ccc
respond "FAciem": Fa cdc
respond "seCUla": abcbG
v. 1 "magniFIcatus": aG
verses 2 and 3 not notated

Pad 47:

v. 1 "MEum": slightly longer melisma that begins **cdca**cdcdc (etc.)
v. 3 "extenDENS": aGa babG ababG

Gr 807:

v. 2 "EX/TENdens": F/FG aGa
v. 2 "Aquis": FGaGFa
v. 2 "POnis": FaG
v. 2 "TUum": cc ca cbcaG aGF G aca cGa
Be 40078 presents a reading very close to that of the core group.

Roman sources:
Vat 5319:

respond "spiriTUM": aG (liq.)
respond "alLEluia": a transpositional variant in the middle part of the melisma, in
boldface: cdcbababa GaG ababa GaG ac dcdc bca **GaGFGFE GFEFED EG GG** abab
(etc.)
RoS 2: "alLEluia"is similar, but not identical, to Vat 5319: cdccba baba GaG ababaGaG
ac**ba** dcdcbca **GaGFG FEGFEFEDF GaG** baba (etc.)

CONFIRMA HOC (60)

In terms of pitch level, Ben 34 presents an unusual reading of this offertory; a few of its
peculiarities also occur in Ben 35. Ben 39, chosen as the base version, presents a reading
consistent with other core sources, except in one passage, described under (3) below.

1. Opening passage, "confirma hoc": For reasons that are unclear, the scribes of Ben 34
and Ben 35 begin the offertory a fourth below the majority reading represented by Ben 39.
On the last syllable of "confirma," there are further variants. The reasons for the variant
readings in this problem spot are difficult to ascertain, as the following sampling shows.

[Confir]	ma	hoc
Ben 39:	FGa	abG babGaG (liq.)
Mo (b's are natural):	Gac	b b(ori.)cG ba bGa
Pa 1121:	GGG	GaF babGa
Lo 4951:	EFG	GaF babGa
Pa 780:	GGa	abG cbcab
Pa 776:	EFG	GaF babGa
Cai 61:	FGa	acG cbcab

Be 40078:   Ga   acG ca cGa (same in Gr 807)

Mod 7:   Gac   c ca cbbab (same in Pad 47)

Pst 120:   Gab   abG cbcGa

Most of the sources join in the second part of the short melisma on "hoc." On the last syllable of "confirma," there are intervallic differences between MSS. In Mo and Ben 39, the neumes consist of two successive whole tones, perhaps suggesting that an E-flat was required at the level of Pa 776. In Pa 776, the first five notes are mistakenly written a third too low and corrected with letter notation, which may attest to some uncertainty on the part of the scribe about the opening of the melody.

2. "DEO": Ben 34 is a whole tone above the other MSS here, with a different intervallic structure. The reasons for the different reading are not clear.

3. v. 2 "dominum de fontibus": The scribe of Ben 39 writes this passage a whole tone lower than it appears in all other MSS of the core group. The passage is indicated with brackets in the transcription. I consider Ben 39's reading an error and have provided the more common reading in the edition.

The other sources included in the sampling match Mo here, joining with Ben 39 at "de."

4. v. 2 "IsraHEL": Where brackets are indicated in the base transcription, Ben 39 has a scribal error, writing a segment of the melisma a tone too low. The status of this reading as an error becomes evident with a comparison of the closing melisma of the final verse, on "orientem." The two melismas differ in their opening notes but are otherwise nearly identical. In v. 3, Ben 39 matches the other sources in this segment. I have emended this segment in the base transcription.

5. v. 3 "cantate deo":

a. "cantate": The low B on "cantate" was likely sung as flat, a pitch not theoretically available in most notation systems. In most MSS, however, this B is left as is, matching Ben 39, with the following exceptions:

Pa 1235, Pa 780, RoV 52: The last three notes of "cantate" are DDC.
Pad 47 and Mod 7: The beginning of the verse is notated at the affinal position, joining the majority version at "psallite."
Tri 2254: The whole verse is written at the affinal position.
Cai 61 and Gr 807 have a notated low B-flat.
In Ben 34, all of "cantate deo" is notated a tone above the majority version, producing some differences in intervallic structure.

b. "DEo": Some sources in the core group have FDF instead of CDCD (as in Ben 39).

CDCD: Mo 159, Ben 34, Ben 35, Pst 120
FDF Pa 776, Pa 780
DFDF: Pa 1121, Pa 1235, Cai 61, Be 40078
DFEF: Gr 807
DCD Lo 4951
DEDE: RoV 52
GaGa (at affinal position): Mod 7

Pad 47 preserves a possible nondiatonic practice in this passage. The beginning of the passage is written at the affinal position, and "DEo" is written as G-b-flat G-b-flat, equivalent to E-flat at the lower level.

6. v. 3 "PSALlite": Beneventan MSS present a very small difference in this melisma, omitting the notes indicated in boldface, as in Mo 159: DG acaGF **FFF** **a**GF GFF DGF EFD (etc.).

Variants in individual MSS:

Verse endings in Lo 4951: The slightly altered verse endings create a more exact "melodic rhyme" between verses:

v. 1 "ilLI": DF FFF FGFG FF(ori.)E
v. 2 "israHEL" and v. 3 oriENtem: melisma ends FGFGF F(ori.)E

Cai 61:

v. 2 "DOmino": DFa
v. 2 "israHEL": melisma has the additional notes FGFGEF at the end

Be 40078:

v. 2 "DEo": FaGF FD GF GE FD CGFG F FD FGF aGF GFE

"DOmino": DGa
   Gr 807: v. 1 "asCENdit": aG ca cGF (liq.)
Mod 7:

respond, "EST" GaGaFE
v. 1 "diciTE": FaGF
v. 1 "NOmini": FGF
v. 1 "DOminus": FGaGa
v. 1 "NOmen": FGaGa
v. 2 "DEo": melisma ends baG aGF
v. 2 "DOminum": EFGa

Pst 120: v. 1 "Eius": FGFG
   Roman MSS:

Vat 5319:
   respond, "TUo": aGa(ori.)GFEF
   v. 1 "EST": EFGFGa(ori.)GFGF
   v. 2 "israHEL": melisma begins abaGaGF**EFE** GaGFGFE (etc.)
   v. 3 "oriENtem": same variants as v. 2 above

RoS 22:

"operaTUS": GGFEFD
"HIErusaLEM": aaGFGabaGFG/EF
"muneRA": FGaGbaG

PRECATUS EST MOYSES (61)

In phrase 1, the base reading of Pa 1121 lacks a first statement of the words "et dixit," which are found in a majority of MSS. The passage (which uses melodic material also found in *Angelus domini*) is supplied from Pa 776.

The problem spots in *Precatus est Moyses* have been addressed in studies by Frasch and Hankeln.[1] As Hankeln discusses, there are probable scribal errors in several of the Aquitanian MSS, complicating the process of establishing a preferred reading. In Theinred of Dover's treatise, *Precatus est* is given as an example of an offertory that has three relocations of the semitones, implying that it uses low B-flat, E-flat, and F-sharp.[2]

The problems in the respond begin with the passage "et placatus factus est" (phrase 6). I have provided the Pa 780 version as an alternative reading. Although Pa 1121's reading is matched in Mo 159 and in the majority of peripheral MSS, most Aquitanian MSS notate this passage a whole tone lower, at the position of Pa 780. The intervallic differences between the two versions suggest that one of two nondiatonic pitches was employed in the pretheoretical tradition. If Pa 1121 represents the intended interval structure of the passage, an e-flat would be required to reproduce this structure at the level of Pa 780. In Pa 1121, f-sharp would be required to replicate this intervallic structure of Pa 780. Either alternative is possible. Given the tendency of Pa 776 and other Aquitanian MSS to notate passages in their unemended range, however, the first alternative seems more plausible.
Pitch level at "et placatus factus est dominus":

= Pa 1121: Mo 159, Ben 34, Ben 35, Gr 807, Be 40078, Tri 2254, RoV 52
2↓ Pa 1121: Pa 776, Pa 780, Lo 4951, Pa 1235, Pad 47, Mod 7, Pst 120

Most MSS join Pa 1121 at "de malignitate." Pa 776 continues a whole tone below Pa 1121 for the remainder of the verse, a probable error. Pa 1235 joins within "dominus" (with a slightly different melodic reading).

Pitch level of verse 1: The MSS exhibit many pitch-level variants here, as summarized below. At "invenisti" (phrase 8), Mo 159 and most non-Aquitanian MSS are written a fifth above the base version of Pa 1121, then a fourth above beginning at "et scio" (phrase 9) and continuing to the end of the verse. Pa 1121, however, represents the majority notated level among Aquitanian MSS.[3] Hankeln sees a discrepancy between the written and performance levels of the verse in the Aquitanian MSS, beginning at "invenisti," and proposes an *Aufführungslage* for the whole verse equivalent to that of Mo 159. Most Aquitanian MSS, however, lack a notated repetendum cue after this verse that would offer a confirmation of the performance level. Although Pa 1121 lacks a notated repetendum cue after the verse, there is a rare "equaliter" sign between the respond and first verse that confirms the intended pitch level of the verse.

I have opted for the lower version of the verse, found in Pa 1121, as the preferred reading for several reasons. First, Mo 159's shift of range between "Moysen" and "invenisti" is a minority reading, found only in two other sources examined, Pa 1235 and RoV 52. Mo 159's minority status here may suggest that its reading of this passage is an emendation. The

---

1. See Frasch (1986), 1:197–202; 2: 408-21; Hankeln (1999), 1:106–107 and 2:141.
2. See Snyder (2006), 99–106.
3. In Pa 1121 the verse begins with an equaliter sign. Here I have interpreted the sign as indicating that the horizontal axis is maintained between sections, and that the verse begins on a. The interpretation of the pitch level thus differs from that of Hankeln 2 (1999), 141.

significative letters in Ei 121, moreover, are consistent with the reading of Pa 1121, but not with Mo or the versions a fourth higher. In Ei 121 the verse begins with an "equaliter" sign, suggesting that the opening pitch is G, inconsistent with the readings that begin on high c or d. Ei 121 has another "equaliter" between "Moysen" and "invenisti," which contradicts the register shift of Mo's minority reading but is consistent with Pa 1121. Finally, the non-diatonic tradition for this offertory mentioned by Theinred of Dover is not discernable at the pitch level of Mo or the peripheral MSS. At the level of the majority Aquitanian reading of Pa 1121, however, F-sharps are required to replicate the intervallic structure of Mo beginning in phrase 9. In this version, "invenisti gratiam" has *protus* characteristics (such as excursions into the lower tetrachord, G-D, which are not uncommon in eighth-mode melodies). In phrase 9, the *tetrardus* characteristics heard in the respond and the beginning of the second verse are projected a fourth lower, possibly to distinguish the voice of God from the voice of the narrator heard throughout the respond and the opening of the verse. The other readings place these passages in the traditionally *tetrardus* part of the background scale.

Pitch level of v. 1:

1. Verse opening, "dixit dominus":

    = Pa 1121: Mo 159, Pa 776, Pa 780, Pa 1134, Pa 1136, Lo 4951, Ben 34, Ben 35, Pa 1235 (cadence is on G), RoV 52, Gr 807, Frutolf tonary
    4↑ Pa 1121: Mod 7
    5↑ Pa 1121: Tri 2254
    5↓ Pa 1121: Pst 120

2. "ad Moysen":

    = Pa 1121: Mo 159, Pa 776, Pa 780, Pa 1134, Pa 1136, Lo 4951, Pa 1235 (cadence is on E), Gr 807
    5↑ Pa 1121: Tri 2254
    4↑ Pa 1121: Ben 34, Mod 7
    2↓ Pa 1121: Pst 120 (joins at "moySEN")

3. "[Invenisti] gratiam in conspectu meo": Most non-Aquitanian MSS begin this passage at 4↑ Pa 1121 on "invenisti," switching to 5↑ at "gratiam." This difference is not reflected in the summary.
    = Pa 1121: Pa 776, Pa 1134, Pa 1136, Pa 780, Gr 807, Frutolf tonary
    5↑ Pa 1121: Mo 159, Lo 4951, RoV 52, Mod 7, Pa 1235 (changes to 4↑ at "meo")
    Unique reading: Pst 120 (beginning= Pa 1121; grati [am] is 3↑; conspectu is 5↑)

4. "Et scio": 4↑ Pa 1121: all except:= Pa 1121: Pa 776, Pa 780, Pa 1134, Pa 1136.

    Melodic variants: The Beneventan reading is very similar to that of the core Aquitanian MSS. A few significant variants are found in Lo 4951 and in some peripheral MSS.

    Pa 776: respond, "in conspectu" (both times): Pa 776 notates this passage a tone higher than Pa 1121. The reading of Pa 1121 is the majority reading among core MSS (the reading of Pa 776 is also found in several Italian MSS).

Lo 4951:

respond, "et dixit" (both times): D/DFFDEFGaG/G (the first statement is shorter and written a fifth lower than the majority reading. The second statement is the same as the majority reading melodically but written a fifth lower).

respond, "aBRAM": cd(quil.)edc

v. 1 "peccaTA": shortened melisma: efffdcbcdecc ddcd(quil.) edccd fffdcbcdeccdd cd (quil.)edcd(quil.)ec

Pa 1235:

respond, [populo] TUo: GF abaGa

v. 1 "peccaTA": small variants in final melisma: fefdcb cdeb cd dc ded c cd fefdcb cdeb cd dc **dededc** fgf fdc fefdc dfe (etc.)

v. 2 "acCEdite": GE GaGF GF FFFECD DF GaG

Be 40078: v. 1 "Omnibus": FacGE FDCD FF GaG cc caa(ori.)G aFG ac cc ccc

  Gr 807: respond, "populO": db ca cccbG aca caF Ga ccba bcba

Pad 47:

respond, [lac] "ET": G abca ca (etc.)

respond, "PopuLO": dca cc cc cG acacGF Ga cccbabcba (slightly shortened melisma)

v. 1 "moY/SEN": dca cdedc/cbdcb

v. 1 "peccaTA": fffdcb cde cc d dc c defd cdf fff dcb cde cc d dc cdefd dc f fgfdcd fffdc dfe fged ededc dca c defd fd fffd cca

Mod 7:

respond, "in conspectu" (both times): whole tone above Pa 1121

respond, [lac] "ET": G abca ca (etc.)

respond, [placatus factus est] "DO/MI/NUS": cded/dcdede/ed

v. 1 "peccaTA": reading very similar to that of Pad 47

Pst 120:

respond, "[con] spectu do [mini]" (both times): Written a whole tone above Pa 1121

v. 1 "peccaTA": ffd c cb cded ccd dc ded ccd f fd c ca cded cc d dc ded cdf fedf dc dff db dfe fgdc ededc dca cdfd fd fffd c ca

v. 2 "moySES (second time)": melisma ends CDC

RoV 52:

respond, "in conspectu" (both times): Written a whole tone above Pa 1121

v. 1 "peccaTA": cccaGF FGa FF G GF GaG FFG cccaGF FGa FF G GF GaG Fa c cdcaG accaG acb cdba babaGaGF Ga caca cc caG GE Ga (similar to Pst 120 above, but written a fourth lower)

lacks the second verse

Roman MSS: In the verse *Dixit Moyses*, the final cadence, on the last two syllables of "tempore," is written a whole tone below its normal position. This apparent irregularity (which occurs a few other times in the repertory) is also present in Vat 5319.

Vat 5319:

respond "DIxit" (second time), a shorter and varied version of the melisma: Gac cbcba G GF acGF F(ori.)EDC FacbaG GF acbabG respond, "FLUENTEM": ba/G/ac

verse *Dixit dominus*, "TERra": GababG(liq.)

verse *Dixit dominus*, "PEC/CA/ta": neume groupings suggest a different text underlay:
c/cc(ori.)b cba abcdcbaG

verse *Dixit Moyses* has "populorum israhel" instead of "filiorum israhel" (same melody)

RoS 22:

"DIxit" (first time): G ac cbcbaG acbG

"DIxit" (second time): GacbcaG aGaGF ac **GGFED** acbaGF acbabaG

"A/BRA/HAM": defedefd/cb/ded

"FLU/ENtem": ba/G

IMMITTET (62)

The base version of Ben 34 is atypical in a few very brief passages:

Respond, "viDEte": In most MSS, this melisma is very similar to "TEMpore" in v. 1, as in the sample readings of Mo and Pa 776:

Pa 776: c dcd ccba **ccbac**

Mo: cdc db caG   **ccb(quil.)ac**

Beneventan MSS have a shorter version of the melisma, without the repeated notes and passing tone: cdcdccaG **cac**

v. 3 "eruBEScant": Ben 34 has a slightly shortened version of this melisma, different from most core MSS in lacking the notes in boldface:

Mo: ccb (quil.) a **Gb (quil.) c cba** Gb (quil.) cb (quil.) a b (quil.) aGa

Pa 776: cc cbG **ab(quil.)**   c   **cbG** ab(quil.) cba   baGa

The longer version of the melisma is found in Ben 38, Ben 35, Pa 1121 and Pa 780. Of the MSS in the core group, only Lo 4951 has a reading nearly identical to that of Ben 34: cc cbG ab(quil.)cba baGa. A similar reading is found in Pad 47: ccbG G abcba cbGa.

There are very few variants between MSS. Other melodic variants:

Pa 776: v. 2 "INvicem", a shorter version of the melisma: c dcd ccbab(quil.)cba.

Peripheral MSS show a tendency to add or omit passing tones, as in Cai 61, respond, DO/MIni: ac cbaG/ac cbaG.

Other variants in peripheral MSS:

Cai 61: v. 3 "eruBEScant": cb cbGa bcb c bGa bcbabaga.

A few MSS differ from the norm in their verse indications. Pa 780, for example, indicates only one verse, at "benedicam" (though it presents the full music and lyrics). Pst 120 has a new verse beginning at "iste pauper clamavi."

Roman MSS: Bod 74 lacks the final verse of this offertory. One anomaly that occurs in both Vat 5319 and Bodmer is the cadence at the end of the second verse, on "invicem." For reasons that are unclear, this typical *tetrardus* cadential pattern is written a tone below its usual position, closing on F in both MSS. A similar cadence occurs in *Illumina oculos* (28) in phrase 6, with a notated b-flat in Vat 5319.

Bod 74: v. 2 "laudaBI/TUR": cba/b (written a tone lower than Vat 5319).

RoS 22:

"IM/Mitet": Gaba baGF
"Eum": abaG
"DOmine": melisma begins cdcdccaGF

ORAVI DEUM MEUM (63)

Oravi deum has a complex and varied transmission, undoubtedly because nondiatonic pitches were employed in the pretheoretical tradition. I have adopted Pa 1121 as a base reading because it represents the most probable unemended version. *Oravi* begins as a *deuterus* melody and, in a great majority of sources, closes on E. In the pretheoretical

EXAMPLE 63.1A

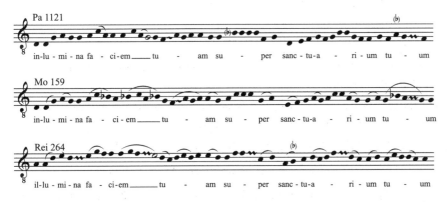

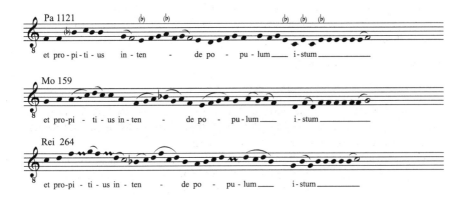

EXAMPLE 63.1B

2   Example 63.1

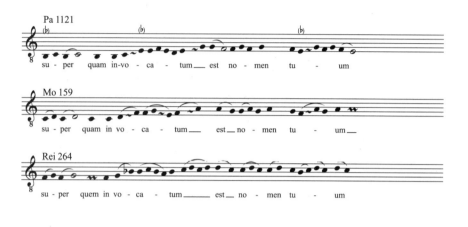

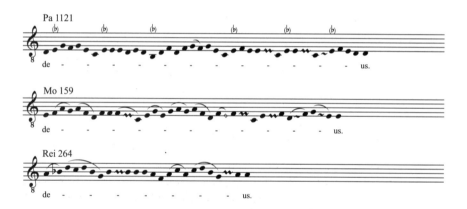

tradition, however, it most likely closed on D, with a *deuterus* E-flat. Each problem spot is discussed separately.

1. Respond, opening "Oravi." John of Afflighem mentions that *Oravi deum* requires emendation at two places in the respond, namely the beginning and at "super."[1] The opening passage is indeed a point of melodic variance. Several versions, including Pa 1121, incorporate a low B, on the second syllable of "oravi," which was undoubtedly sung as B-flat, a pitch that was theoretically nonexistent:

Pa 1121: EE(ori.) FDGFFFFD B(flat) DFD B(flat)DFDEF.

Rei 264, notated at the affinal position, employs F, equivalent to B-flat at the lower level, and b-flat, equivalent to E-flat at the lower level: bc adc c cbG a b-flat aG aca b-natural c.

---

1. Palisca (1978), 156.

In other sources, the b-flat is avoided by means of melodic variants, as in the following: Mo 159: E E(ori.)F DGF FF FDC DFDC DFD EF (very similar readings in many other sources, including Pa 776 and Pa 1132).

2. Respond, "super sanctua[rium]" (phrase 3) to end: According to John, this passage requires an emendation so that "super" begins on c. This emendation is shown in Frutolf's tonary and found in the great majority of MSS. A few sources, however, give clues to the pretheoretical tradition. Example 63.1 shows three different versions. Beginning with "super," Pa 1121 (line 1) adopts b-flat as a focal pitch. The majority version, represented by Mo 159 (line 2), is written a tone higher through the end of the respond. In Pa 1121, typical melodic gestures of the chant tradition are positioned a tone below their usual position. At this lower position, several nondiatonic pitches are required to replicate the intervallic structure of Mo 159's majority reading, including low B-flat, E-flat, and a-flat. The respond ends on D, with an E-flat that results in a *deuterus* tonal structure. Singing "super" on b-flat, then, evidently resulted in a modulation of sorts, in which the *deuterus* melodic characteristics heard in the first half of the melody were projected a tone lower; E-*deuterus* becomes D-*deuterus*.

Despite its irregularity, this reading cannot be dismissed as a scribal error; it is also found in Pa 776 and is preserved in three late geographically diverse sources, Cai 61, Rei 264, and Be 40078. These versions are notated a fifth higher, at the affinal position, and replicate the pitch-level profile of Pa 1121. Be 40078 and Rei 264 begin as regular *deuterus* melodies notated at the affinal position but close on a, with a b-flat. Cai 61 is similar to these versions but has a modified ending on G. The version of Rei 264 is shown in line 3 of example 63.1. Several of the b-flats in Mo 159 would result in a-flats at the level of Pa 776 and e-flats at the level of Rei 264. Rei 264 avoids the latter pitch by either writing a regular e, as on" [sanctuarium] tuum", or an f, as on "intende."

Two sources in the core group, Lo 4951 and Pa 780, adopt distinctive emendations of the passage that begins at "super." Both match Pa 1121 at "super." Lo 4951, however, joins the level of Mo 159 on the first syllable of "sanctuarium," and Pa 780 joins the level of Mo 159 on the third syllable of "propicius." In Lo 4951, the starting pitch of each line in the respond is indicated with letters in a later hand, probably attesting to the problematic pitch level of the respond.

Near the beginning of this problem spot, on [sanctuarium] "tuum," Mo 159, written a tone higher, has a b-flat, the source of the parenthetical a-flat in the transcription of Pa 1121. In other sources, a b-flat is not specified.

= Pa 1121: Pa 776, Lo 4951 (2↑ beginning at "sanctuarium"), and Pa 780 (2 ↑ beginning at "propicius")

5↑ Pa 1121: Be 40078, Rei 264, Cai 61 (Both sources begin the offertory at this level and remain there throughout).

2↑ Pa 1121: Mo 159, Ben 34, Ben 35, Ben 39, Pa 1132, Pa 1235, Pst 120, Pia 65, Tri 2254, Gr 807

The verses: In the pretheoretical tradition, the problematic ending of the respond may have had implications for the performance level of the verses. I have transcribed the verses of Pa 1121 both at their written level, which matches that of most MSS in the core group, and at their hypothetical performance level. The written level of Pa 1121 matches that of most MSS, including Mo 159, which consistently indicates b-flat here. In Pa 1121, however, the repetendum cue after v. 1, to "super quem," is notated a tone too high, beginning on C rather than B-flat. Pa 776 presents a similar situation: if Pa 776 is read with the assumption that the verse begins at the level of the majority version, then the repetendum cue to "super quem," which follows the second verse, is notated a tone too high, beginning on C.

There are two possible explanations for this situation. The first, according to Hankeln's theory about the meaning of the "incorrect" repetendum cues, is that the cue attests to a performance tradition in which the verses were performed a tone below their written level, consistent with the lower ending of the respond. A performance level of the verses a whole tone below the level of Mo 159 would result in a nondiatonic melody. The opening of verse 1 would adopt ab as a focal pitch. With an emendation of the respond at "super," so that it closes on E, the verses proceed unproblematically. A second possibility is that the verses were sung at their notated level, matching the majority reading, but that the repetendum was performed a tone above its original position, consistent with the emended version found in most MSS.

The inconsistency between the respond and repetendum is certainly related to the problematic ending of the respond. If the unemended version of the respond involves a downward shift of the *deuterus* structure by a whole tone, when did the chant get back "on track?" The notated level of the verses in Pa 1121 suggests a return to a diatonic position at the start of the first verse. This alternative, however, creates a problem in the transition to the repetendum. A performance of the respond at the notated level and the repetendum in its original, unemended range involves a rather sudden shift back to the D-*deuterus* tonal area. If the repetendum is taken as a guide to the correct pitch level of the verses, the result is the hypothetical performance level shown in the transcription. In this version, the dislocation of the melody in the respond continues in both verses, and the chant never gets back on track.

In the two verses, most sources present a pitch-level profile similar to that of Mo 159. Rei 264, Be 40078, and Cai 61, for example, join the level of Mo 159 at the beginning of v. 1 and remain there throughout. There are, however, two problem spots within the verses, both relating to the G-*protus* characteristics of certain passages. At its written level, Pa 1121 alternately adopts b (flat) and c as focal pitches, a reading matched in Mo 159. The b-flat is heard at the beginning of verse 1 ("Adhuc . . . orantes") and at "Michael" in v. 2. In many other MSS, however, these places are written a whole tone higher, so that c is the focal pitch throughout. These readings are perhaps best viewed as emendations made in response to the G-*protus* quality of these passages. I have shown that certain MSS exhibit a propensity for whole-tone transposition of G-*protus* passages, in other pieces such as *Sanctificavit* and *Benedicite gentes*.

v. 1: "Adhuc . . . orantes":

= Pa 1121 (written level): Pa 776, Pa 780, Mo 159, Be 40078, Cai 61, Tri 2254, Rei 264
2↑Pa 1121: Ben 34, Ben 35, Ben 39, Lo 4951, Pa 1235, Pst 120, Pia 65, Gr 807

v. 2: "Michael":

= Pa 1121: Pa 780, Ben 34, Ben 35, Ben 39, Pa 1235, Cai 61, Be 40078 (without indicating a b-flat), Rei 264, Tri 2254, Piacenza 65
2↑ Pa 1121: Lo 4951, Pst 120, Ben 39, Gr 807

Other melodic variants: v. 2 "PO/PU/LI": The version of Pa 1121 is matched in the Aquitanian and Beneventan MSS, as well as most peripheral sources. Mo 159 has a different reading and text underlay: G/Gab(quil.)cb(quil.)a/aG.
Roman MSS: Bod 74 lacks this offertory. RoS 22 has the following variants:

"israHEL": GF GaGabaGFGF
"doMIne": GbaGFEF
"serVI": GaGbaGFGF
"inTENde": FGaGbaGFEF

Significant variant in the final cadence on "DE/US": EFGFE/FE (lacks the long melisma of Vat 5319)

SANCTIFICAVIT (64)

In most Gregorian sources, the last verse ends with the words "tunc Moyses," which provide a transition to the repetendum, "fecit." These words, however, are probably a late addition, and they are a point of melodic variance. Some MSS have a more elaborate transition to the repetendum than the base version of Pa 776 does. Mo 159, for example, has a long melisma on "Moyses":

Mo y- ses
Gab(quil.)cb(quil.)aG FE(quil.)D Gab(quil.)cb(quil.)aG FE(quil.)D FG Ga a(ori.)G

This melisma, however, is lacking in most Aquitanian MSS, in the Beneventan sources, and in most early notated MSS.[1] The Roman version takes "in conspectu" as a repetendum.

Sanctificavit has an extraordinarily varied transmission in terms of pitch level, reflecting many instances of nondiatonic practice. Theinred of Dover, writing in the mid–twelfth century, describes this chant as having three relocations of the semitones, implying that it employs E-flat, low B-flat, and F-sharp.[2] Although the comparative transcriptions produced evidence for the use of all three pitches, as well as eb in the higher octave, the evidence for F-sharp (at "illud" in the respond) is very tentative.

Pa 776 was chosen as the base reading because of its minimal tendency toward modal emendation. There are no less than twelve significant pitch-level variants among the sources. Whole-tone transpositions are particularly prominent. Although most sources fall into a few distinct groups in their treatment of the nondiatonic pitches, highly individual readings may be found in certain MSS such as Lo 4951.

1. Respond, "illud": Mo 159 presents a minority reading of this passage that is notated a whole tone lower than Pa 776 and has a different intervallic structure:

Mo 159: aGFFFF (ori.) EFaG
Pa 776: aGGGG (ori)FGbaa

The version of Pa 776 is matched in the great majority of sources. Only one other MS in the sampling, Pst 120, notates the passage at the level of Mo 159.

Snyder sees the version of Mo 159 as the unemended pitch level and suggests that an E-flat was sung here.[3] Another option, however, is that Pa 776 represents the unemended pitch level of the passage and that the version of Mo is the transposed version. An F-sharp would be required at the level of Pa 776 to replicate the intervallic structure of Mo 159. This passage, in fact, is the most plausible instance of the F# mentioned by Theinred. In some

---

1. Ei 121, La 239, and SG 339 simply have an unnotated "tunc" or "tunc moyses."
2. Snyder (2006), 99–106.
3. Ibid.

sources at the level of Pa 776, the note corresponding to the hypothetical F-sharp is written as an E, as exemplified in Cai 61: aGGGGEGbaa.

The evidence for nondiatonic practice here, however, is not conclusive. The variant may instead reflect a point of melodic instability. If the variant does reflect a nondiatonic practice, I see F-sharp (rather than E-flat) as the more likely alternative, given the tendency of Pa 776 to write passages in the unemended range, the tendency of Mo 159 to give the correct intervallic structure of problem spots at an "emended" pitch level, and the status of Pa 776's pitch level as a majority reading. In practice, however, an F-sharp is admittedly aurally disconcerting. If an F-sharp was indeed sung at one time, it may have been simply suppressed in most MSS. If performers choose not to sing the F-sharp, a b-flat (rather than b-natural) should follow.

2. End of respond, "israhel": Two German sources, Gr 807 and Be 40078, close the melody on E rather than F, as exemplified in the following version of the melisma on "Israhel": Gr 807: GabcaGEFFDFGEGGE.

3. v. 1: "aSCENdit" melisma: Although Mo and the other Aquitanian sources present a reading very similar to that of Pa 776, Ben 34 notates the boldface parts of the melisma a tone higher:

Pa 776: cff**cdedcdcb**[flat]**cb**[flat]**c**(quil.)**dcdcd**fffdffgf
Ben 34: dff**defededcdcedede**fffdffgf

The other Beneventan sources present a reading closer to that of Pa 776. One source in the sampling, RoV 52, presents a unique reading of the melisma: cccccabaGaGFaaGaaa-Gacdc.

4. v. 1: "Moyses procidens": The variant starts on second syllable of "Moyses." This problem spot, discussed in chapter 6, is best considered in the three parts "Moyses procidens," "adoravit dicens," and "obsecro . . . populi tui," shown below. In "Moyses procidens," the reading of Pa 776 matches Mo 159 and the other Aquitanian sources, but the passage is transposed up a whole tone in many other sources, including the Beneventan MSS. While the upward transposition is probably attributable in part to the G-*protus* characteristics of the passage and the wish to avoid b-flat in close proximity to G, the subsequent passages reflect the introduction of nondiatonic pitches.

a. "Moyses procidens":

= Pa 776: Ben 39, Mo 159, Lo 4951, Pa 780, Pa 1121, Pa 1132, Pa 903, Pa 1235, Gr 807, Rei 264
2↑ Pa 776: Ben 34, Ben 35, Be 40078, Cai 61, Tri 2254, Mod 7, RoV 52, Pst 120, To 18

b. "adoravit dicens":

= Pa 776: Ben 39, Mo 159, Lo 4951, Pa 780, Pa 1121, Pa 1132, Pa 903, Pa 1235, Rei 264
2↑ Pa 776: Ben 34, Ben 35, Be 40078, Cai 61, Pa 1235, Gr 807, Tri 2254, Mod 7, RoV 52, Pst 120, To 18

c. "obsecro . . . populi tui":

= Pa 776: Ben 39, Lo 4951, Pa 780, Pa 1121, Pa 1132, Pa 903
2↑ Pa 776: Mo 159, Ben 34, Ben 35, Be 40078, Pa 1235, Cai 61, Pa 1235, Rei 264, Gr 807, Tr 2254, Mod 7, RoV 52, Pst 120, To 18

This passage is given as Example 6.2 in chapter 6. Although most non-Aquitanian sources match the pitch level of Ben 34 at "obsecro," the Aquitanian sources, represented by

Pa 776 in line 1, are united in writing the passage a tone below its pitch level in the other readings, a version also found in Ben 39. Without accidentals, the two readings differ in interval content: the Aquitanian sources articulate the major third c-e, in contrast to the minor third d-f found in Ben 34 and the other sources. These differences in intervallic structure suggest the use of a nondiatonic pitch. One possibility is that the major third of the Aquitanian sources is intended. If so, an f-sharp would be required in the Ben 34 and Mo 159. The other, more likely, possibility is that the Aquitanian sources transmit the preferred pitch level, but that an e-flat was sung.

The melodic characteristics shed some light on the question of which is the more likely alternative. The version of Ben 34 is unproblematic, adopting melodic vocabulary typical of the chant repertory in general: high f is the repercussive pitch, and the cadential pattern on "tui" is a typical *deuterus* cadential pattern. In the Aquitanian/Ben 39 version, these figures do not occur in their normal intervallic environment and sound foreign. With the Aquitanian reading as the *lectio difficilior*, it is probable that these sources preserve an authentic early reading, sung with an e-flat, a nondiatonic note represented by whole-tone transposition in the other versions.

5: end of v. 1: "[domi] us faciam secundum verbum tuum": All MSS in the core group match the pitch level of Pa 776, as do most Italian MSS. The six German and French sources in the sampling, however, notate this passage a tone higher, so that the verse concludes on G: Gr 807, Be 40078, Pa 1235, Cai 61, Tri 2254, and Rei 264. The same reading is also found in the late Italian MS To 18. Because the passage is identical intervallically at the two transpositions, it is probable that this variant reflects the modal ambiguity of the verse rather than a nondiatonic pitch.

6. Beginning of v. 2 "Oravit moyses":

= Pa 776: Ben 39, Lo 4951
5↑ Pa 776: all others

Most MSS notate this passage a fifth above the level Pa 776 until "dum pertransiero" (with the interval changing to a fourth in some spots). Several factors, however, suggest that the lower level of Pa 776 is the unemended reading. In Ei 121, the verse begins with an *i*, consistent only with the lower, minority reading of the verse. The probable nondiatonic pitches discussed below, moreover, preclude the verse from being notated at the lower level without emendation. In all MSS, the verse closes at the level of Pa 776. The sources, however, join Pa 776 at different points. This variety reinforces the impression that Pa 776 is the preferred version.

7: "et dixit si" (phrase 15): Mo employs a b-flat here, implying an E-flat at the level of Pa 776. In one MS, Ben 34, the melodic segment in question is written a tone higher.

Mo (all b's are b-flats): dcdcabcdcd/dc
Ben 34: dcdcac**dede**/dc

8. "si inveni gratiam in con [spectu]" (phrase 16):

= Pa 776: Lo 4951
2↑ Pa 776: Ben 39
5↑ Pa 776: Mo 159, Pa 1121, Pa 1235, Rei 264 (with melodic variants), Cai 61, Gr 807, Be 40078, To 18
6↑ Pa 776: Ben 34, Pa 903

Ben 34 and Pa 903 are a tone above the majority reading, a change reflected at the lower level in Ben 39, which is a whole tone above Pa 776 here. This version differs intervallically from the others on the final syllable of "gratiam," ending with the semitone e-f in Ben 34 and the whole tone in the other sources.

Pa 776: b(flat)GaG
Mo 159: fded
Ben 34: gefe

9. "ostende michi te ipsum" (phrase 17):

5↑ Pa 776: all except Ben 39 (Lo 4951 joins the level of Mo and the other sources).

10: "manifeste" (phrase 17):
5↑ Pa 776: all except:
= Pa 776: Ben 39
4↑ Pa 776: Ben 34, Lo 4951

The majority of MSS are a fifth above Pa 776. Those that distinguish between b-natural and b-flat write b-flat at the cadential passage on "ut videam te," suggesting that an E-flat is intended at the level of Pa 776 and Ben 39.

Ben 34 and Lo 4951 write most of the passage a tone below the other sources, joining (briefly) at "ut videam te."

11. "et locutus est . . . lapidis" (phrases 18-20):

= Pa 776: Ben 39, Lo 4951
4↑ Pa 776: Mo 159, Pa 1121
5↑ Pa 776: Ben 34, Pa 1134, Pa 903, Be 40078, Cai 61, Be 40078, Mod 7, Rei 264,
    Gr 807

Mo 159 is a fourth above Pa 776, adopting b-flat as a temporary final, with an internal cadence on b-flat at "potest." This reading is matched in other MSS in the core group, but most sources outside the core group are a tone above Mo here, notating the passage with c as the cadential pitch. The reason for the change of transpositional level in Mo to a fourth above Pa 776 is not clear. Mo consistently employs b-flats, resulting in an intervallic structure identical to that of Pa 776

12. "et protegat te" (phrase 20): 5↑ 776: all except Ben 39.

13. "donec pertranseam" (phrase 20): Here Ben 39, which has followed the level of Pa 776 until this point, is temporarily a tone above Pa 776, undoubtedly because the low B's in Pa 776 were sung as B-flats. At the position a fifth higher, this pitch is represented as F. In Ben 39, these B-flats are sung as C's, with no intervallic differences.

14. "dum pertransiero" (phrase 21):

= Pa 776: all except:
4↑ Pa 776: Pa 1235 (joining with Pa 776 at "meam")
5↑ Pa 776: Ben 34, Mod 7

Most sources have a downward motion here, contradicting the readings of Pa 776 and Ben 39. Ei 121, however, has the letter *l* here, consistent with Pa 776 and Ben 39.

The joining of the other sources with Pa 776 here reinforces the status of Pa 776 as a preferred reading, since nondiatonic pitches were evidently no longer required at this point in the verse. Pa 1235 is a unique reading that remains a fourth above Pa 776 until "auferam" and then, after a transitional passage on "auferam manum," joins with Pa 776 at "meam." Pa 1235 is inconsistent in its use of a sign for b-flat. Without a b-flat, the intervallic structure of the passage differs considerably from that of the other readings. Ben 34 is unusual in remaining in the higher register, a fifth above Pa 776, through the end of the verse.

Roman MSS: Bod 74 lacks this offertory. RoS 22 has the following variants:

"SANCtificavit": FGFEFGFEDFEDED
"OFferens": aGacba
"offerRENS": GaGFEFG
"ILlud": GF aGa
"holLOcaustum": aGacaG
"vicTI/MAS": The notes accommodating the final syllables are grouped differently and suggest a different text underlay: cbcd ededc/dedc.

SI AMBULAVERO (65)

Although there are very few significant variants among the sources, the Beneventan MSS exhibit some small variants from the others.

Respond, "ME": The Aquitanian MSS and most peripheral MSS adopt F as the lowest note (rather than the G in the Beneventan reading) as in Pa 776: c bcabGF bccbab (qui.) cba. Mo 159, however, matches Ben 34.

v. 1 "DIe": The other MSS in the core group and the peripheral MSS have an extra 4 notes at the end of the melisma that are lacking in Beneventan MSS (the segment in boldface):

Pa 776: . . .　　　　　caF GaGF Ga(quil.)ba **baGa**

Lo 4951: melisma ends . . . caF Ga(quil.)b abaGa

v. 2 "DOmine": There is a slight variant among MSS in the beginning of the melisma. Ben 34 has D as the bottom note, whereas other core MSS have F or E:

Pa 776: Melisma begins Gcca**bGF** accaGabGF . . .

Lo 4951: Melisma begins GccaGaFE accaGaGF

Verse endings in Lo 4951:

v. 1 "TU/AM": cccacaaGaG/G

v. 2 "TU/AM": ab(quil.)cbaGa/aG

Variants among peripheral MSS:

RoV 52: v. 2 "DOmine": a major variant in the beginning of the melisma: **bcaG GccaG aGF** accaG abGFacbc acccaGF Gabcdcbabcba.

The other Italian MSS present readings consistent with the core group:

v. 2 "TU/AM": abcbaGa/aG (same as Lo 4951)

Variants in Roman MSS:

Vat 5319:

   respond, "MEdio": Gac cbc

   respond, "meOrum": melisma begins aGaGF . . .

RoS 22:

   "tribulatiOnis": Fac abaGFacbG

   "ET": GabaGaGaG

   "meOrum": aaGFGFGaGFEFED Fac abaGF acbG

   "TUa": ac dc bcabaGF acGaGF acbcba cabaGF acbabaga

SUPER FLUMINA (66)

In v. 3, the Roman version has a longer text than the Gregorian does, reflecting either a Frankish abbreviation or an addition made in Rome subsequent to the repertory's transmission north.

In Gregorian MSS, the repetenda are a point of variance and confusion. In verses 2 and 3, the words "qui dixerunt" serve as an introduction to a melodically variant repetendum that brings the performance back to the beginning of the respond. As Pfisterer has suggested, it seems likely that the repetenda for the second and third verses, though written out, function as an introductory element, and that the whole respond was to be sung.[1] One possible reason for the variant repetenda is the modal contrast between the first-mode respond and the verses, which have the traits of mode 7.

The MSS differ in the pitch level of the second and third verses, as shown in the work of Justmann, Frasch, and Hankeln.[2] Most Aquitanian MSS, including Pa 776, notate these verses a tone above the level of Mo 159, with a focal pitch of c. A few other sources place the verse a fifth above Mo 159, with a focal pitch of high f, or fourth below, with a focal pitch of low F. In all cases, the second and third verses are marked by a move away from the *protus* structure of the respond, creating a problematic transition to the repetendum. Pfisterer notes the resemblance of a passage in the third verse to the seventh-mode alleluia *Te decet* and parts of the respond to two first-mode graduals.[3]

In his edition of the Aquitanian version, Hankeln posits the level of Mo 159 as the preferred version, a hypothesis based partially on the pitch level of the repetenda.[4] The second and third verses have melodically variant repetenda, and neither is melodically identical to the corresponding place in the respond, undoubtedly because of the need to provide a transition between the two modal areas. In Mo 159, the cadence

---

1. Pfisterer (2007), 42–43.
2. Frasch (1986), 445–57; Justmann (1988); Hankeln (1999), 2:109–11.
3. Pfisterer (2007), 44–45.
4. Hankeln (1999), 2:109–11.

of the repetendum on "babylonis" is on F, matching the corresponding place in the respond. Assuming that the repetendum is an instruction to repeat the full respond, Mo's reading of the repetendum would allow for the performance to conclude on its original final, D. In Pa 776 and many other Aquitanian MSS, however, the repetendum is written a tone above its level in Mo 159, corresponding to the higher notation of the last two verses; at this level, a full repeat of the respond would result in an ending in a different mode, a tone higher. As a solution to this problem, Hankeln transcribes the second and third verses of Pa 776 at the level of Mo 159, a whole tone below their written level.[5]

While I cannot propose a definite a reason for the variants, I can offer some relevant observations. The pitch level of the majority Aquitanian version is matched in two of the Italian MSS included in the sampling, Pst 120 and RoV 52, and in two of the Beneventan MSS. The Italian MSS have the same repetendum as the Aquitanian sources do, and both notate the repetendum at the "correct" pitch level relative to the respond. The notation of these verses at the higher level, then, is not merely an irregularity of Aquitanian sources. There are intervallic differences between Mo and the version notated a whole tone higher, on "dextera mea" and "qui dixerunt," where Mo has an E-natural. At the higher level of Pa 776 and other Aquitanian MSS, an F-sharp would be required to replicate the intervallic structure of Mo 159. At the level of Mo 159, an E-flat would be needed to replicate the intervallic structure of Pa 776. Several of the MSS at the higher level periodically join Mo 159. In Lo 4951, for example, most of the verse is written at the higher level, but this version matches Mo at "dextera mea," where the irregular semitone would be required, and again at both verse endings, so that the repetendum is placed at the normal position. Two other MSS, Pa 780 and To 18, join Mo 159 at "meminero." The variety of the versions at the higher position perhaps suggests that they are emendations. Another possible reason for writing the verses at different positions in the background scale is a desire to avoid the G-*protus* characteristics of Mo 159 throughout the last two verses. The tendency of some Aquitanian MSS, especially Pa 776, to notate G-*protus* passages at their unemended pitch level, however, speaks against this hypothesis. Although the whole-tone transposition is a common way to emend G-*protus* passages, moreover, the verses of *Super flumina* also appear at other positions, as summarized below. This offertory illustrates well the sometimes ad hoc nature of scribal emendations and the possibility of fluidity in the performance tradition.

Pitch level of v. 2:

= Mo 159: Gr 807, Be 40078
2↑ Mo 159: Pa 776, Pa 780 (joins Mo at "meminero"), Lo 4951, Ben 35, Ben 39, Pa 1235, Pst 120, RoV52, To 18 (joins Mo at "meminero")
5↑ Mo 159: Pad 47 (= Mo at "qui dixerunt")
4↓ Mo 159: Ben 34, Mod 7

Pitch level of v. 3:

= Mo 159: Pa 780, Gr 807, Be 40078

5. Hankeln (1999), 3:49–50.

2↑ Mo 159: Pa 776, Lo 4951 (joins Mo briefly at "Ierusalem"), Ben 38, Ben 39, Pa 1235, Pst 120, RoV 52
5↑ Mo 159: Pad 47
4↓Mo 159: Ben 34

Melodic variants in Beneventan MSS: The independence of the Beneventan MSS is especially apparent in the long melismas of *Super flumina*, which can be summarized as follows:

v. 1, "susPENdimus": Beneventan MSS have a greatly shortened melisma, as in Ben 34: D CDF F Ga aGa FacGF FGD CD C DFF G abcba.

v. 1, "interogaVERrunt": variant reading in Beneventan MSS, as in Ben 34: aFGE FGF FGDEDCD CDF F Ga aGa a Gac cccc dca.

v. 1, "alieNA": Ben 34: D FF FD FGF FGDE D D(ori.)C (similar in other Ben MSS).

v. 2, "memineRO": Near the middle of this melisma, corresponding to the last twenty-seven notes of Mo's melisma, most sources have a repetition, as in Mo 159: Fa (quil.) b-flat a (quil.) FG Fa (quil.) b-flat a (quil.) FG. Ben 34 lacks this repetition, but it is present in the other Beneventan MSS.

v. 3, "hierusaLEM": Beneventan sources present a different reading of the melisma, as in Ben 39 (written a whole tone above Mo 159): aE GF Ga aaG ab abaE a baG ccc abaa cdca c caG c caa c cGbaG GF G acaca cc caGG DEFG.

Other melodic variants:

Respond, "siON": This melisma is a point of variance. The early adiastematic sources examined present a consistent reading, but Lo 4951 presents a shortened version of this melisma, omitting the internal repetition: FD FGaGa caGa FD FG FG FG FF DED. According to Justmann's transcriptions, some of the same notes are omitted not only in two other Aquitanian MSS, Ma 18 and Ma 51, but also in three Italian MSS.[6] The three Italian MSS, in fact, present a reading of the melisma nearly identical to that of Lo 4951, suggesting that this variant entered the tradition at an early date.

v. 1, "interogaVErunt": Aquitanian MSS begin this melisma slightly differently from Mo 159. The Aquitanian version is similar to the Beneventan reading at the start of the melisma, as in Pa 776:

Mo 159: aFGFDCD FFDCD
Pa 776: aF GE FG FF GDCD
Ben 34: aFGE FGF FGEFEDCD

Lo 4951 presents a longer reading of the end of this melisma, where the first part is repeated. The added portion of the melisma is indicated in boldface: aFG DFG FFG DCD CDFFG a a (ori.)G aa Gacc dcaFa **GaG FGFD FECD CDFFG a a(ori.) G aaG accdca**.

To 18 is missing a section of this melisma, corresponding to notes 51–60 of Mo 159.

v. 1 "cantiCOrum": Lo 4951: aFG DEDCD
v. 2 "alieNA": To 18 D FF GDCD
v. 2 "memineRO": To 18 is missing the last 23 notes
v. 3 "IerusaLEM": Lo 4951 leaves out one segment of the melisma: G(ori.) D Ga FGFD GaGFacccaba [missing segment here] acdca ccaG (etc.)

6. The Italian MSS are Pistoia 199, Florence 44, and Milan S. 74. See Justmann (1988), 559, 1143.

Roman MSS:

Vat 5319:

respond, "organa nostra": This passage appears to be written a third too high, but a custos after "nostra" corrects the error.

v. 1 "cantiCUM": FGFEFD

RoS 22:

"tuI": G

"syON": DC DFEF aGaGEFGF **GaGFED** FFEDFED

VIR ERAT (67)

In most MSS, *Vir erat* is notated in the transposed second-mode range, with a final of a, reflecting the use of nondiatonic pitches in the verses. Three sources in the sampling, Ben 34, Ben 39, and Rei 264, begin the respond in the normal plagal range and later move to the

EXAMPLE 67.1A

Pa 776 (transcribed at affinal position)

for-ti-tu do_____ me - - - a__

Be 40078 (written at affinal position)

for-ti-tu do_____ me - - - - a__

Mo 159 (written at affinal position)

for-ti - tu-do_____ me - - - a__

Ben 34 (written at affinal position)

for-ti-tu-do_____ me - - - a__

Pa 1121 (transcribed at affinal position)

for-ti - tu - do_____ me - - a__

Pa 1235 (written at affinal position)

for - ti-tu - do_____ me - - - a__

Pa 776 (transcribed in normal plagal range)

for-ti - tu do_____ me - - a__

EXAMPLE 67.1B

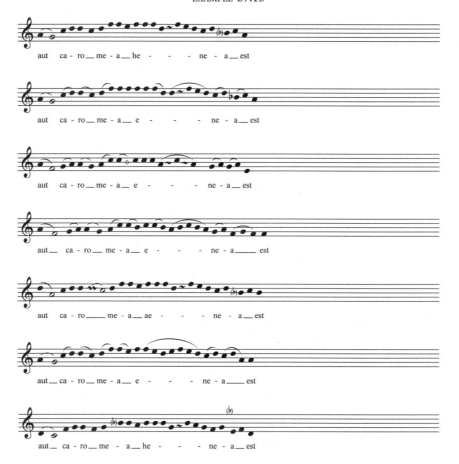

transposed range (Ben 34 and 39 at the beginning of v. 1 and Rei at the beginning of v. 2). In Ben 39 and Rei, however, the repetendum cue begins at the affinal position, a fifth above the level of the corresponding passage in the respond. This discrepancy may suggest that the respond and first three verses were sung at the same pitch level, reflecting the notated level of other MSS, and that the move to the affinal position does not reflect the pitch level in performance.

Vir erat presents two problem spots: the close of v. 3 and the nine repetitions of "ut videat bona" in v. 4. In the transcriptions, Pa 776 serves as the base Gregorian reading and is transcribed in the normal second-mode range, with a final of D. This transcription facilitates comparison to the Roman version, which is also notated with a D final. In the supplementary examples below, however, Pa 776 is transcribed at the affinal position to facilitate comparison with other Gregorian sources.

Verse 3: [lapidum est] "fortitudo" (phrase 15) to the end of the verse: Several readings of this problem spot are shown in example 67.1 In many MSS, including Mo 159, most of this passage is written a fourth below the level of Pa 776, but the interval of transposition is briefly a third at "fortitudo mea." As shown in example 67.1, this passage is also a point of

EXAMPLE 67.2A

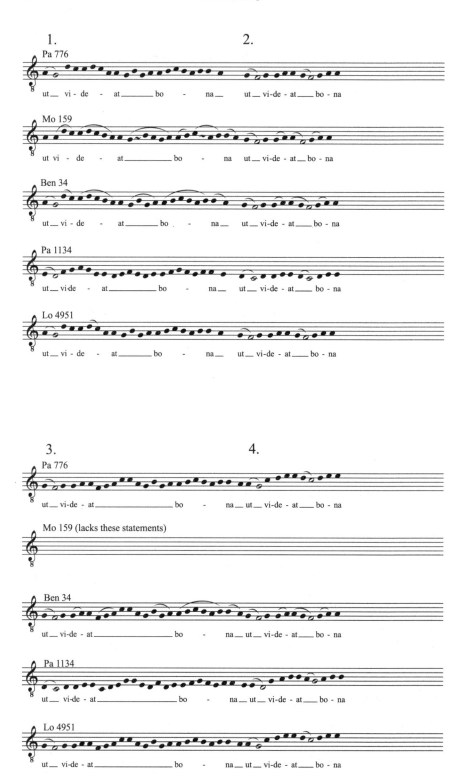

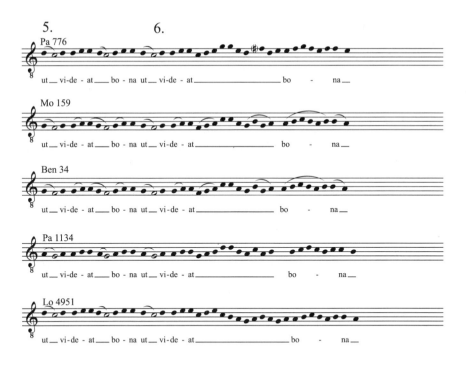

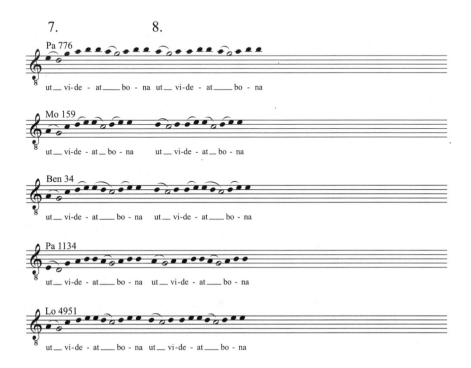

9.

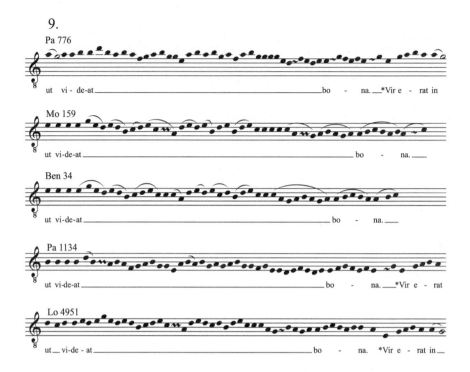

melodic variance, particularly on "mea." Pa 1121 (line 5) presents an alternative reading of the melisma that differs from that of Pa 776, Mo 159, and Ben 34, but ultimately joins the pitch level of Pa 776. Pa 1235 (line 6) gives a reading of the melisma on "mea" similar to that of Pa 1121 but written a tone lower, with a different intervallic structure.

The reasons for the variants are unclear. The various versions differ intervallically on "fortitudo mea," as is evident in a comparison of Pa 776 (line 1) and Mo 159 (line 3). On "mea," there are two intervallic differences. On the final syllable, semitone f-e in Pa 776 appears as the whole tone d-c in Mo and Ben 34, and as the whole tone e-d in Pa 1235. The melodic differences between Pa 776 and Mo 159 also result in an intervallic difference at the melisma on the first syllable. In Pa 776 the last four notes of the melisma *on mea* are defe, whereas Mo has b (natural) cdc, implying the use of a nondiatonic pitch. If the reading of Mo and Ben 34 is taken as the preferred intervallic structure, then an eb would be required to replicate this structure at the level of Pa 776. In several MSS, however, the passage is notated at the level of Pa 776 and simply written with an e-natural, as shown in the reading of Be 40078 (line 2). The hypothetical e-flat in Pa 776, however, is equivalent to an a-flat in the normal plagal range, a nondiatonic pitch that is implied infrequently in the chant repertory.

With the next passage, "aut caro mea . . . " the two versions are a fourth apart and remain so through the end of the verse. Be 40078 employs a b-flat at "enea," which is given as a parenthetical b-flat in Pa 776 and a parenthetical E-flat in the base transcription.

pitch level= Mo (with melodic variants): Pa 903, Lo 4951, Ben 34, Ben 34, Ben 38, Pst 120, RoV 52, Mod 7 pitch level= Pa 776 (with melodic variants): Pa 1121, Pa 780, Be 40078, Rei 264, Pa 1235

Verse 4, "ut videat/am bona" (phrase 19) to the end: The passage that consists of nine statements of "ut videat/am bona" is among the most variant spots in the repertory, with several distinct versions. Transcriptions of v. 4 are provided in examples 67.2a and b. Example 67.2a shows variants among some of the core sources and additional Aquitanian MSS. Example 67.2b shows variants among selected peripheral sources. In terms of pitch level, many of the core sources match either Pa 776 or Ben 34. Pa 1121, for example, presents a reading similar to that of Pa 776. The pitch-level profile of Ben 34 is matched in the other Beneventan sources and, in a shortened version, Mo 159. As described in chapter 3, Pa 776 and the Roman version are very similar in their pitch-level profiles.

Before considering the reasons for the variants, some transcription problems warrant consideration. Some Aquitanian sources present a problem I have not been able to fully solve. In the transcription of Pa 776, I have determined the starting pitch level of v. 4 based on the end of v. 3. The resulting transcription matches the pitch-level profile of the Old Roman version and other diverse sources, such as Pa 1121 and Gr 807. Pa 776, however, exemplifies a persistent problem in the offertories: an inconsistency between the notated level of verse and repetendum cue. In most Aquitanian sources, the final verse is followed by a cue to "vir erat," the beginning of the respond. In Pa 776, the repetendum cue is notated an octave above the level of the corresponding place in the respond, as shown in line 1 of example 67.2a. When Pa 776 is transcribed at the affinal position, it starts on low E. The repetendum, however, starts on high e. The same inconsistency is found in other MSS, including Pa 1121, Paris 909, and Pa 1137.

I see two possible explanations for the incompatible repetendum cue. One is that the notated level of the fourth verse represents the intended pitch level and that the repeat of the respond was really sung an octave higher than its original pitch level. If so, perhaps the higher notation is attributable to the dramatic expansion of range in the final verse. The disparity of range between the opening of the respond and the close of the v. 4 may have created a practical problem for the singers in the transition to the repetendum. If the repetendum was sung at its original pitch level, it would have required a sudden downward shift of more than an octave. As a solution, the repetendum may have been sung an octave above its original pitch level. A second possibility, consistent with Hankeln's theory about the "incorrect" repetendum cues, is that the verse was sung an octave below its original level, and that the repetendum cue is correctly notated.

I consider the first alternative more likely in this case. A performance of the final verse an octave below its written level seems counterintuitive, simply because it would be so anticlimactic and incongruous with the range of the piece as a whole. The Roman version, discussed below, attests to a tradition in which the repetendum was performed at a position a fifth higher than the corresponding passage in the respond, with the performance concluding on the affinal a. The notation of the repetendum cue in Pa 776 and 1121 suggests that a similar tradition prevailed in Aquitaine, with the repetendum sung an octave higher. While I find Hankeln's theory generally persuasive, then, I think it more likely in this case that the repetendum was simply sung an octave higher and that the performance concluded on high d, in keeping with the climactic effect of the final verse. The ending on high d, which has no theoretical grounding, is reminiscent of some early sequences. In the edition, I have transcribed the verse and repetendum in Pa 776 at their written level.

Two other Aquitanian sources, Pa 1134 and Lo 4951, have been included in example 67.2a to illustrate the variants in the Aquitanian tradition. In the case of Pa 1134, the pitch

EXAMPLE 67.2B

1.   2.

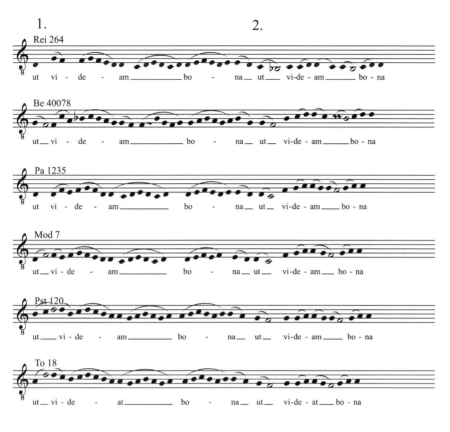

Vir erat, final verse

3.   4.

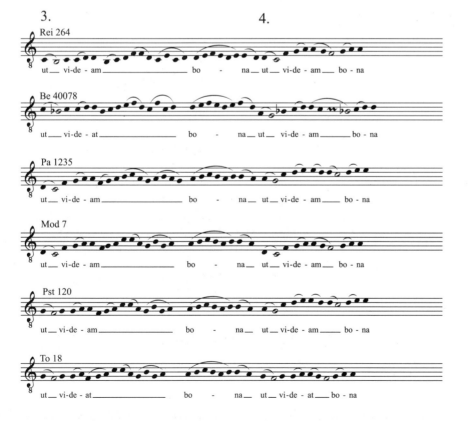

Vir erat, final verse

level again presents problems I have not been able to fully resolve, and the transcription is in part hypothetical. I have included it simply to illustrate the problems inherent in the tradition. The verse begins on a new line. I have transcribed it with the premise that the repetendum was sung at the same pitch level as beginning of the respond and that the starting notes of the repetendum (at the affinal position) are thus E-G-a-b. The resulting transcription produces a reading that is a fourth below Pa 776 until the seventh statement of "ut videat..." where it is an octave lower. In performance, this reading would require several nondiatonic pitches to derive the correct interval structure. On the third statement of "ut videat bona," for example, the D-F interval on the last syllable of "videat" is equivalent to G-b (natural) in 776 and Ben 34, requiring an F-sharp. The corresponding passage in the sixth statement has the notes a-c-a, corresponding to G-b-natural-G in Mo 159. If Pa 1134 is transcribed with the assumption that the repetendum was sung an octave higher, however, the resulting version of the verse would be an octave lower than it is written here, an even less probable reading. Similarly surprising versions, however, are found among the sources transcribed in example 67.2b, which are unambiguous with respect to pitch.

These shifts in pitch level most likely reflect the need for nondiatonic pitches. The transcription of Pa 776 at two different levels, the normal plagal range in the base

Vir erat, final verse

transcription and the affinal position in the example 67.2a, illustrates the problems that arise at both positions. As I have shown, the end of the third verse, if notated in the normal plagal range, requires an E-flat. The final verse, moreover, requires low B-flat, represented as F at the higher level. For these reasons, the whole offertory is typically written at the affinal position. At the affinal position, however, new problems arise. The reading of Pa 776, transcribed at the affinal position in line 1 of example 67.2a, differs intervallically from the others in the sixth statement of "ut videat bona," where it has the pitches d-f-d-e. In Mo 159 (line 2) and many other sources, this passage is written a fifth lower, with the pitches G-b-natural-G-F. The use of b-natural rather than b-flat in Mo implies that an F-sharp would be required at the level of Pa 776, here and at the subsequent cadence on "bona." This impression is reinforced by the Italian source Pst 120 (example 67.2.b, line 5), which matches Pa 776 until this point. The passage in question, however, is a whole tone below Pa 776, with the pitches c-e-c-d, again implying an f-sharp at the level of Pa 776. Pst 120 remains a tone below Pa 776 for the rest of the verse. The difficulties of writing the offertory at both the normal and affinal position are undoubtedly the primary reason for the diversity of versions.

An additional reason for the variants may be the previously mentioned transition to the repetendum. In many sources, the final verse closes in a range much higher than that of the

Vir erat, final verse

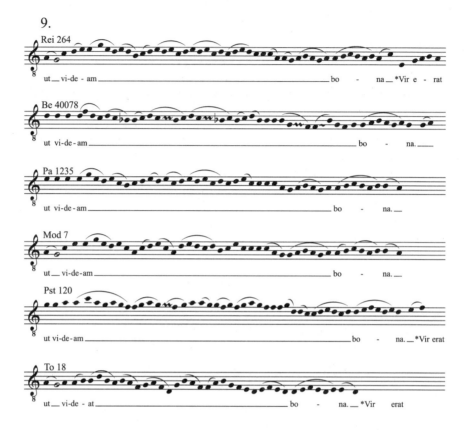

respond. If the repetendum was sung at the same pitch level as the respond, the transition may have posed a problem for singers. In Pst 120 (example 67.2b, line 5), for example, the respond is notated at the affinal position, beginning with the notes E-G-a-b. The final verse, however, closes in the higher octave, with the third d-e-f. The transition to the repetendum, then, would have required a leap of a ninth. Although Pst 120 has a repetendum, the cue has no notation, and it is unclear how the singers would have resolved the problem. Several other readings of the verse, however, conclude in a range and tonal area more congruous with that of the respond. Mo 159, for example, closes the verse with the third a-b-c, consistent with the transposed second-mode range of the respond.

A third reason for the variety of versions may lie in a simple desire to normalize the melody's extraordinary range. The diversity of range among the sources is indeed striking. In Pa 776 the verse spans nearly two octaves. Ben 34 and Mo 159, by contrast, have a range from F to g, just over an octave (lines 2 and 3 of example 67.2a). Perhaps the most interesting emendation of range is that of To 18 (example 67.2b, line 6), which begins in the range of Ben 34 and Mo but closes a fifth lower, perhaps to facilitate the transition to the repetendum. This reading lacks all traces of the climactic expansion of range found in the other versions.

With these observations, we may hypothesize that the striking diversity of readings in the sources results from a combination of factors: pitches that were unavailable on the gamut, an irregular modal structure, and an extraordinary range and resulting problematic transition to the repetendum. While the extent to which the different versions reflect actual performance is difficult to ascertain, the problematic transition to the repetendum probably did result in a diversity of performance traditions, perhaps dependent on the preferences and voice ranges of individual soloists. Some of the transcriptions provided in the examples, however, present problems whose solutions are elusive. For reasons that are unclear, the scribe of Be 40078 (example 67.2b, line 2) sets much of the verse in the G-*protus* tonal area. A few sources depart from the norm in their repeat structure. Mo 159, for example, has only seven statements of "ut videat bona." In the seventh and eighth statements of "ut videat bona," To 18 presents a reading that is unique among the sources examined: both statements are set to the more elaborate melody of the sixth statement. Lo 4951 (example 67.2a, line 5) differs from the other sources in the sixth statement of "ut videat bona": most sources repeat the melodic material of the third statement at a higher pitch level, but Lo 4951 has different material here.

The Roman version: Bodmer 74 lacks this offertory. Several features of the version in Vat 5319 warrant comment. First, the letter *v*, normally used to mark verse divisions, occurs at most points of text repetition in the verses (i.e. in phrase 18: V. Quoniam V. Quoniam V. Quoniam). These seem to simply serve as a visual marker of text repetitions. I have not included these in the transcription, but rather followed the verse division of the Gregorian reading. The offertory is written in the normal plagal range. It is likely that the low B's at the end of verse 2 on "agam" were sung as B-flats, just as they clearly were in the Gregorian version. The final verse has a pitch-level profile similar to that of Pa 776. The repetendum is written a fifth above the level of the corresponding place in the respond. The melody of the repetendum, moreover, differs from its initial statement, appearing in a much more florid version and coming to a close on the affinal a. The melodic differences suggest a special performance practice, with a melodically varied repetendum that lacks an equivalent in the Gregorian reading.

The horizontal alignment is briefly lost at several points, especially at the ends of lines. At "carnem quoque eius" (phrase 6), the cadential figure on "eius" is incorrectly written a tone too high. The mistake is evident both from the melodic figuration (the cadential pattern, on C, occurs many times in *Vir erat* and, in many other offertories, on G) and in the custos that follows "eius," a D that is indicated at the correct level and not the written level. The alignment is corrected at the beginning of the following line. I have transcribed the passage a tone lower than written, and the transcription differs from that of MMMA. A very similar situation is found at the first "quae est enim" (phrase 12) and the first syllable of "numquid" (phrase 15), which is written a third too low. Each time the mistake is corrected by the custos that follows, and I have used that custos as the guide in transcription.

The final verse presents two different readings of the text, "videam" (common in German sources) and "videat" (the majority reading elsewhere in Gregorian sources). The use of the b-flat sign in the verses on "calamitas" (verse 1) and the parallel passage on "est" (verse 2) is very rare in the Roman MSS.

RECORDARE MEI (68)

This offertory is the only one with two distinct melodic and textual versions, which have been discussed by Justmann, Maiani, and Steiner.[1] The version given in the base transcription, which I shall call version 1, is found in the Roman, Beneventan, Aquitanian, and many French MSS; it also circulates as a Gregorian and Roman responsory. A second version, found in most German and Italian MSS, as well as some French sources, is melodically distinct from the first and shows some textual differences. Mo 159 is unique among MSS examined (and also among Justmann's larger sampling) in transmitting both versions.

The Roman version of the offertory has no verses. In each Gregorian version, there are differences in verse transmission. Version 1 has *Recordare quod steterim* as a first verse in some Aquitanian and French MSS and *Memento domine et ostende* as a second verse in some Aquitanian MSS. Yet another verse, *Memento nostri domine*, circulates in some Beneventan MSS. In version 2, the part of version 1 that begins "everte cor eius" is transmitted as a verse, and one MS cited by Justmann has *Recordare quod steterim* as a second verse.[2] The status of these verses as later additions is evident from the regional variation and their absence in the Roman tradition.[3]

As Justmann, Steiner, and Maiani have argued, version 1 appears to be earlier than version 2; version 1 is found not only in the Roman tradition but also in Mont-Blandin and Corbie. Steiner has argued persuasively that the second version of *Recordare mei* was created after the piece was adopted as a responsory, in order to distinguish the two liturgical uses.[4] Another factor consistent with the chronological priority of version 1 is its melodic correspondence to the Roman version. Although version 2 appears to be based melodically on version 1, it has a long melisma at the end of the section designated as a respond.

Melodic variants among core MSS in version 1:

opening, "RE/COR/DA/RE": Pa 776, Lo 4951: F/aG (liq.)/a/aG

Although the rest of the respond is at the same level as Ben 34 among core MSS, Hankeln notes that the part beginning "nos autem" is written a fifth lower in Pa 903, Pa 1135, and Mo.[5]

Final cadence: Mo 159: [recordare] "ME/I": G/G (a less ornate version than the majority reading).

Mo 159 classifies this chant as a *tetrardus* melody with a final cadence on G. The final syllable of "aeternum" is simply aG rather than ba.

Roman MSS: Bodmer 74 lacks this offertory. There few variants between RoS 22 and Vat 5319.

RoS 22:

[hos] "MEum": cdcba bcdcbabG
"eTERnum": end of melisma: cbcbabG cbcd

---

1. Justman (1988), 1115–31; Maiani (1996), 216–17; Steiner (2007), 57–66.
2. Justmann (1988), 121–23. Two MSS, Mo and Pa 904, transmit *Recordare quod steterim* as a separate chant.
3. Variants in the Aquitanian verses are illustrated by Hankeln. Particularly notable are the differences in pitch level and melisma length in the Aquitanian second verse. See Hankeln (1999), 3:194–96.
4. Steiner (2007), 67–88.
5. See the summary in Hankeln (1999), 2:145.

DE PROFUNDIS (69)

Although the Roman MSS lack verses for this offertory, they are present in the earliest Gregorian MSS. Mont-Blandin, however, has a different second verse indicated, "Quia apud te qui propiciato est" (Ps. 129:4).

Mo presents a reading of *De profundis* that is unique among the MSS included in the sampling. It is notated a fourth above the reading of Ben 34, with a final of G. Despite the G final, the scribe of Mo includes *De profundis* with the *protus* chants. Although most passages are *protus* in quality, with a b-flat, Mo does employ a b-natural twice: on the second syllable of "clamavi" in the opening and at the ending of the first verse, where the b on the second syllable of "tui" is a b-natural. These notes are equivalent to F-sharp at the majority lower level of Ben 34. If Mo's intervallic structure were replicated at the level of Ben 34, "claMAvi" would read C-D-E-F-sharp-E, and "tuI" (phrase 3) would be D-F-sharp-D. The second b-natural in Mo is not matched when the same melodic material returns at the end of the second verse, on "sustineBIT" (phrase 5). Here all b's are flat. Because this possible nondiatonic practice is witnessed in only one MS included in the sampling, Mo 159, I have not shown it in the base transcription of Ben 34.

Because of the close proximity to F, it is likely that the low B in the opening of Ben 34 was sung as a B-flat. In most MSS, the first note is A rather than B.

Variants among core MSS: There are very few melodic variants in either core or peripheral MSS. The Aquitanian MSS and Mo 159 differ from other MSS in v. 1, at the cadence on "tue." Most MSS in the core group have the standard cadential pattern DEFEF/ED. Italian and German MSS have DEFEFEDE/ED, a reading closer to Ben 34, and this version is also found in Pa 1121). Ben 34 exhibits another small difference from the majority of sources in the respond at "ad" (phrase 1). Most MSS have the reading of Pa 776, FEFD.

Mo 159:

respond, "AD": b-flat a b-flat G
respond, "MEam" (all b's are flat): Gbb FaG Gba bcaG aG aGF GF(quil.)D

Pa 776:

respond, "meAM": melisma begins DFFFDED D FEFG ED

Pa 1121:

respond, "meAM": melisma begins DFF F(oei.)DCED

Peripheral MSS:

Pa 1235:

v. 1 "TU/E": DEFEFEDE/ED
v. 1 "intenDENtes": CF GFCD F FED F FD(liq.)
v. 1 "TUi" (significant variant): D DCDA DF EFD **DCDA** DFEFDCD **FGa** FD EFDC FFFED.

When this melodic material returns in v. 2, Pa 1235 has some of the same variants, but not all: v. 2 "domiNE": DDCDA DFE FDCD FGaFD EFDC FFFED.

RoV 52: v. 2 "TU/AM": DEFEFEDE/ED
Pst 120:v. 2 "TU/AM": D EFEFEDE/ED

Be 40078:

respond, "MEam": melisma begins FF FC FD DFE
v. 1 "TU/AM": DE(quil.)FEFEDE/FD
v. 1 "intenDENtes": FGFFCD FF FED F F FD(liq.)
v. 2 "oratiOnem": DED FF FED FEF

Roman MSS: Bod 74 74 lacks this offertory. RoS 22 has the following small variants:

"exAUdi": c cbca bagF acbabaG
"oratiOnem": c
"meAM": GcaGbaGFGa

IN VIRTUTE (70)

This offertory exhibits several pitch-level variants. The differences in its overall pitch-level profile are similar to those of *Desiderium* (89), *Domine in auxilium* (27), and *Iustitiae* (29): the sources differ in their indication of the relative pitch level between the respond and second verse. In Ben 34, the respond and first verse are notated at the affinal position, with a final of c, and second verse is in the *tritus* authentic range. In a few MSS, however, the respond and first verse are notated in the normal plagal range a fifth below Ben 34, closing on F, and the second verse is written at the level of Ben 34.

The variants in pitch level arise from problematic pitches in at least three places. In the opening phrase of the respond, Mo 159, notated at the affinal position, employs b-flats (given as a parenthetical b-flat in the transcription of Ben 34). A b-flat is also found in most other sources that employ a sign for it, such as Be 40078 and Rei 264. At the lower level of transposition, this pitch would be E-flat. Mo 159 also employs some passing b-flats in the first verse; in Ben 34, these pitches are simply c's.[1] In the final verse, Mo uses b-flat and F, which would be E-flat and low B-flat at the lower level. In Ben 34, a corresponding b (flat) occurs before the cadence on "impones."

In its indication of the relative pitch level between the respond and two verses, Ben 34 is clearly the preferred reading, as suggested by its presence in the majority of sources and the nondiatonic pitches that would result if the piece were written in the untransposed plagal range. With the preferred status of Ben 34 in mind, other possible nondiatonic pitches occur in the final melisma of the second verse, which is a point of variance among the sources. Several different versions are shown in example 70.1. In Mo 159 (line 2), most of the final melisma is written a whole tone below that of Ben 34 (line 1) and employs both b-natural and b-flat. If the reading of Ben 34 is considered to be a fifth above the normal plagal range, as seems likely, then Mo's reading, a whole-tone below Ben 34, represents a shift in the transpositional level to a fourth above the untransposed range. A downward transposition of Mo's final melisma by a fourth would result in an F-sharp at the beginning of the melisma. In view of the proximity of f and the b-flats that immediately follow, however, this b-natural is dubious and may be a scribal error.[2] A more likely candidate for a nondiatonic pitch is the

---

1. On the past two syllables on "petiit" and on the second syllable of "saeculi."
2. As Steiner showed, Ott "retransposes" the final melisma of Mo incorrectly, producing F-sharp's that correspond to the b-flats of Mo 159. See Steiner (1966), 166–68.

EXAMPLE 70.1

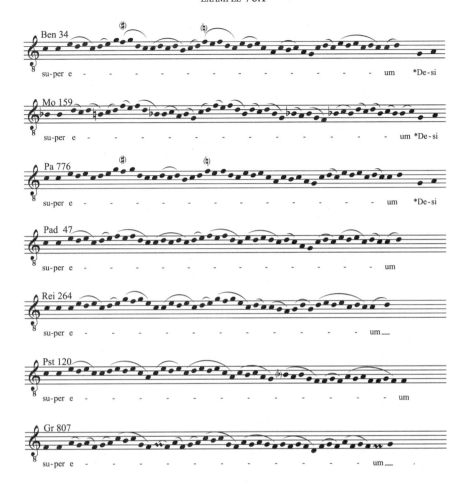

interval between the seventh and eighth notes of the melisma. The whole-tone g-f in Ben 34 and Pa 776 appears as the semitone f-e in Mo 159 and many other sources.

Most sources in the core group, including Pa 776, present a reading of the final melisma very similar to that of Ben 34. In Pa 1121, however, this melisma is written a whole tone lower, matching the level of Mo 159, with some melodic variants. Outside the core group of sources, the final melisma exhibits melodic variants that result in brief shifts of transpositional level, as shown in the readings of Pad 47 (line 4) and Rei 264 (line 5). Although these readings mostly match the level of Ben 34, certain segments deviate from it by a whole tone.

In some sources included in the sampling, including Gr 807 and Mü 10086, the modal structure of the offertory as a whole is normalized: the respond and first verse are written in the untransposed plagal range, a fifth below Ben 34, and the second verse is written at the level of Ben 34, in the authentic range. These sources, however, require an adjustment to circumvent the nondiatonic pitch E-flat at the beginning of the offertory, the notes equivalent to the b-flats in Mo 159 (given parenthetically in the transcription of Ben 34).

In Pst 120, the whole opening passage, "in virtute tua domine," is written a tone above its normal position, allowing the problematic interval C-E-flat to be written as D-F. In Mü 10086, it is simply written as a normal E. The downward transposition of the respond and second verse regularizes the modal structure of the offertory: the second verse appears unproblematically as a *tritus* authentic melody in relation to the plagal respond. These sources, however, present an additional problem: the new disparity of range between the respond and second verse and the transition to the repetendum. In all three sources, the final melisma of the second verse is altered, presumably either to facilitate the transition to the repetendum or, in performances without a repetendum, to bring the offertory to a close on the final F. The scribe of Pst 120 (line 6 of example 70.1) extensively alters the melisma so that it concludes on F. In Mü 10086 and Gr 807, the melisma is simply transposed down a fifth, as shown in Gr 807 (line 7), producing an ending on F.

Respond and v. 1= Ben 34 (final of c): Mo 159, Pa 776, Pa 1121, Pa 1132, Pa 780, Pad 47, Mod 7, RoV 52, Pia 65, To 18, Rei 264, Be 40078, Tri 2254.

Respond and v. 1 5↓ Ben 34 (final of F): Gr 807, Mü 10086, Pst 120.

Verse 2, final melisma (beginning with "super"):

= Ben 34 (sometimes with melodic variants): Pa 776, Pa 1136, Pa 1137, Lo 4951, Pa 1132, Pad, 47, RoV 52, Mod 7, Pia 65, Rei 264, Be 40078, Tri 2254

2↓ Ben 34 (with melodic variants): Mo 159, Pa 1121

5↓ Ben 34: Mü 10086, Gr 807, Cai 61.

Notes on individual sources:

Pa 780: final melisma of second verse: The starting pitch of the final melisma is not visible on the microfilm.

Cai 61: The respond is written in the transposed plagal range, v. 1 in the untransposed range.

Roman version: In the Roman tradition, this offertory lacks the second verse that circulates in Gregorian MSS. Vat 5319 shows some significant variants from Bodmer, as follows. Differences are indicated in boldface.

Vat 5319 is written in the normal plagal range, closing on F, a fifth below Bod 74.

Respond, "super salutARE": **a**ccc(**ori**)ba/**G**ccc(**ori.**)baG.

In the verse, Vat 5319 has a shorter form of the melisma on "diErum":

baGaGFGFEFEDFEDEDCDFFFGaGaGFGFEFGaGF.

melisma on "SEculi": In Vat 5319, the last thirteen notes of the melisma are **Ga-GaGFGFE**GaGaG. The boldface segment shows a change in the interval of transposition from a fifth to a sixth. In transposed plagal range, the passage would be written a tone lower than the corresponding passage in Bod 74.

RoS 22:

"saluTA/RE": egfe/dgfed
"vehemenTER": dedcbcd

IUSTUS UT PALMA (71)

Following the second verse, many Gregorian MSS have a melodically varied repetendum to "sicut caedrus" that is lacking in the base reading of Ben 34 and in the Roman version.

Ben 34 is the only Beneventan source in the sampling to transmit this offertory with its verses. This MS, selected as the base version, presents a shortened version of the final melisma in the second verse. The reading of Mo 159 is more typical (the notes in boldface are lacking in Ben 34):

Mo 159, v. 2 "floreBIT": aa(ori.)G cccaa(ori.)F GFE FG(quil.)aG aFD FF EG(quil.)aG aa(ori.)G ccaa(ori.)F GFE FG(quil.)aG aFD FC EG FGF GF GFE FGFEDC **DE(quil.)FE FGFEDCD** FGFGFEF.

Two other very minor points of Beneventan independence occur in v. 2, on "domiNI," where most MSS have the reading FGFE rather than EGE of Ben 34, and on "atriis," where a more typical reading of the first two syllables is that of Mo 159: GaGa/aaGa.

This offertory otherwise shows few significant melodic variants between MSS. Most MSS in the core group present readings very similar to that of Ben 34.

Mo 159:

v. 1 "maNE": DFDF

v. 2 "in atriIS": caG aFE **FGFF(ori.)E**

v. 2 "miseriCORdiam": G FFFG FFF(ori.)D GaFF(ori.)EF

Pa 1121: v. 2 "miseriCORdiam": G FF FG FF F(ori.)D Ga FF(ori.)EF

Pa 780: v. 3 "atriIS": aaGa caG aF **EF(quil.)GFE**

RoV 52: v. 2 "miseriCORdiam": GFFGFF GFD GaFEF

The varied repetendum at the end of v. 2 differs from Mo 159 and the Aquitanian MSS at the end of the melisma on "CAEdrus": abc dca GabaGa cccGbaG aca ccc **cdededcbaGa**.

Pad 47:

v. 2 "maNE": FGFDED

v. 1 "boNUM": GFGF FD FF FD **FGFE**

v. 2 "miseriCORdiam": GFFFG FF FD GEG

v. 2 "Et veritatem" (words and music) is missing

v. 3 "doMI/ni": GEG

v. 3 "atTRIIS": a different text underlay is indicated, with the longer melisma on the second syllable.

v. 3 "floreBIT": a aG ccca FE GFGFE FGaGaFEF FGaGa aG GGEG GFE FGaGaFE FD EG FGF GFGFE (etc.)

Pst 120:

v. 1 "maNE": FGFF CDC

v. 2 "miseriCORdiam": G FFG FF FG GaF FEF

v. 3 "atriIS": caG aFE FGFE

Pa 1235: v. 1 "boNUM": GFGF FD FF FD **FGFE**

Cai 61:

v. 1 "boNUM": GE GF FD FF FD **FGFE**

v. 3 "plantatus": indicates a different text underlay, with the long melisma on the last syllable.

Be 40078:

v. 1 "tuO": FGF F(ori.)

v. 2 "miseriCORdiam": GFF FG FF FD GaF FF(ori.)

Roman MSS: In Vat 5319, the order of verses 2 and 3 is reversed. There is one significant variant between Bod 74 and Vat 5319, in the final melisma of the verse *Plantatus.* Vat 5319 presents a much longer (and slightly varied) version of the melisma. The notes in boldface are lacking in Bod 74.

"floreBIT": aGaGbaG baGaGFGFF(ori.)EDF aGaG EFDEDC FGFGFDE GFGFEDCDCD FGFEDaGbaG baG aGF GFEDF aGa GEF DEDC FGFG FDE GFGFEDCDCD **F FEDaGaGbaGF F(ori.)EDC DCD FGF F(ori.) GaGFEDEDFF**

Other variants in Vat 5319:

respond, "multipliCAbitur": end of melisma goes to a instead of b: GF Ga(ori.)GFG

v. 2 "BOnum": melisma ends GFGabaGFGF

RoS 22:

"floRE/BIT": GaFGF/DGFD

"QUAE": GaGaGFFEDC

"LI/BAno": GaGaGFFEDC FGa/aGaG c cbcbaGa

"multipliCAbitur": Fa ba GaGFGFE aGaGF GabaGFG

ANIMA NOSTRA (72)

This offertory exhibits variants in its notated pitch level and thus in the tonal structure of the piece as a whole.

Pa 776, transcribed with the final on D, represents the probable unemended version of the chant. The end of the second verse (phrase 8) employs two pitches that are unavailable on the gamut, low B-flat and the F below Γ. Phrase 8 is irregular in modal structure. Melodic material associated with the first and second modes is projected a fifth below its usual pitch level. The gesture on "nos," for example, often marks a caesura in first-mode offertories, and the figure on "in" is a typical opening phrase for first-mode pieces.

Despite the irregularity of this version, the MS evidence suggests that it is the preferred reading in the pretheoretical tradition. It is the majority reading among Aquitanian MSS, and most other MSS replicate the pitch-level profile of Pa 776 a fifth higher, at the affinal position. In a common minority version, found in Ben 34 and other MSS, the respond and first verse are written in the normal plagal range, with a final of D, and the second verse is written a fifth higher. A few MSS included in the sampling adopt distinctive emendations, moving to the higher register within the second verse, as summarized below.

The repetendum in Pa 776 is written a fifth too low. With other instances of this phenomenon, these "incorrect" repetendum cues seem to indicate a discrepancy between the written and notated levels of the verse, as Hankeln has suggested. In *Anima nostra*, however, I consider it more likely that the repetendum was actually sung at this lower level in the pretheoretical tradition. Because the closing of the second verse has moved into a new tonal area, singing the repetendum at its normal position (starting on F) would require a leap of a seventh between verse and repetendum.[1] The significative letters in Ei 121 support the hypothesis that the pitch-level profile of Pa 776 is the preferred version. The scribe places an *i* (inferius) at the beginning of the second verse, consistent with the majority version of Pa 776 but not with the emended version of Ben 34, where the second verse is written a fifth higher. This emendation corrects both the irregular tonal structure of the melody and the problematic transition to the repetendum.

Another notable feature of *Anima nostra* is the melodically variant repetendum, with an added melisma on the final syllable of "laqueus" and some other small variants. The varied repetendum is found in most other MSS from the core group.

Summary of pitch-level profile:

> = Pa 776: Pa 780, Lo 4951, Pa 1121, Cai 61, Be 40078 (at affinal position), Mo 159, Pist 120 (at affinal position),
> Second verse 5↑ Pa 776: Ben 34, Pa 1235, Gr 807, Rei 264, Mü 10086, Pad 47, Mod 7

Unique emendations: RoV 52 is written a fifth above Pa 776 beginning at "qui non dedit." Pa 903 is written a whole tone above Pa 776 on the last syllable of "captionem" and a fifth above Pa 776 on "eorum," with a transitional section at "dentibus."

Melodic variants:

> v. 1, "doMInus": Most core and peripheral MSS have FGF.
> "eO/RUM": This final melisma of the second verse is a point of variance, perhaps because of the theoretically nonexistent pitch F below Γ and the problematic transition to the repetendum. The following are sample readings:

> Pa 1121 (similar to Pa 776): DFD BBΓ CDCB CBF ΓBABA FΓ /FΓ
> Mo (at affinal position): G ca FF(ori.)D **GaGF** GFD FGF FE(quil.)DE/DF
> Ben 34 (at affinal position): G Gca FF(ori.)D FaGF GEC DFE FECD/CD
> Be 40078 (at affinal position): GcaF FF(ori.)D FaGF GFD FGEFEDE/DDE
> Pad 47 (at affinal position): Gba GGF FaG FGFD FGFE CD/CD

Roman MSS: There are no significant variants.

INVENI (73)

In both the Gregorian and Roman traditions, *Inveni* has an inconsistency of verse transmission. Gregorian MSS fall into two groups. In the first group, represented by Pa 776 in the transcription, the second verse begins with "veritas mea cum ipso in nomine meo exaltabitur

---

1. This argument is made in greater depth in Maloy (2007), 67–70.

cornu eius." The melody and text are the same as that of the offertory respond *Veritas mea* (76) but notated a fifth higher to correspond to the *tetrardus* modality of *Inveni*. The verse continues "et ponam in saeculum saeculi . . . " The second group transmits a truncated version of the verse, which begins with "et ponam." The two traditions have the same melody for the section beginning at "et ponam." The MSS may be summarized as follows.

Longer version of the verse, beginning with *Veritas mea*: Mt. Blandin, Silvanectensis, Lo 4951, Pa 776, Pa 780, Pa 1121, Ei 121, SG 339, Cha 47, Gr 807 (with many melodic variants.)[1]

Shorter version of the verse, beginning with *Et ponam:* Mo 159, Beneventan MSS, Compiègne, Cai 61, Pa 1235, Rei 264, Be 40078, Pad 47, Pst 120, RoV 52, Pad 47, Mod 7.

As the summary shows, both traditions are found in *Antiphonale Missarum Sextuplex* and early adiastematic MSS. Most later MSS, however, have the shorter version of the verse. Among pitch-readable MSS, Gr 807 is the only non-Aquitanian MS in the sampling to include the "veritas mea" material, and its melody differs substantially from that found in Aquitanian sources (and from the corresponding offertory respond *Veritas mea*). In the Roman tradition, Vat 5319 has a corresponding verse that begins with "veritas mea," using the same melody and text as the Roman version of the respond *Veritas mea* (76), notated in the second-mode range. The portion of the verse that begins "et ponam" is indicated as a separate, third verse and is not notated. Bod 74 presents only the material corresponding to the Gregorian first verse, *Potens es*, and divides it into two verses at "posui adiutorium."

Pa 776 and Vat 5319 were chosen as base versions because they present the fuller version of the second verse, thereby allowing for the most extensive comparisons between the Gregorian and Roman versions. Although the reason for the widely circulated shorter version is not clear, it is notable that Mt. Blandin and Vat 5319 give the same text for both verses, perhaps suggesting that the longer version should be regarded as the preferred reading and the shorter version as an abbreviation. The differences between Vat 5319 and Bod 74, however, may also reflect the practices of the different institutions they represent.

Melodic variants:

> respond, "brachium" (phrase 4): The text underlay Pa 776 is not the majority reading, though it is also found in Pa 1121. In Mo 159, Lo 4951, Beneventan MSS, and most peripheral sources, the ascent to c is placed on the second syllable of "brachium," as in Mo 159:
>
> "bra-chi-um:" G/Gab(quil.)cb/ c
>
> respond, "oleo sancto" (phrase 2): Pa 1235 has "sancto meo," accommodating the extra syllables with a repeat of the material on "sancto."
>
> v. 1 "circuito TUo" (phrase 5): Ben 34: aGFG cbabG
>
> v. 2 final melisma on "Eius" (variant portion in boldface): Pa 1235: ac dcdc cacc deca cd cdec cd **cdbcaF Fa acbc aGF ac c cbcaGF Fac** cd(liq.)

Pa 1121 lacks the second verse.
Gr 807:

---

1. *Inveni* is lacking in La 239.

v. 1 "SUper": Ga GaF Gcac

v. 2. As mentioned, Gr 807 is the only late non-Aquitanian MS to transmit the "veritas mea" part of v. 2. The melody appears to be related to the Aquitanian version at "misericordia mea" and "cornu," where it adopts standard recitational vocabulary, but differs from it substantially in the other passages.

"VE/RI/Tas": cc caG c ccc/aG/FG

"ME/A": GaFG cc ca cG/F

"ET" [misericordia]: Ga

"ET/IN/NO/MI/NE": cd/cdc/c/c/c

"ME/O": ca ccc/abc

"EX/AL/TA/BI/TUR": G/a/cd/dc/c/

"[cornu] E/IUS": acaG Gabca ca(liq.)/GF

Roman MSS: As previously mentioned, Bod 74 transmits only the first verse, divided into two verses at "posui." Vat 5319 lacks notation for a small portion of v. 1, "tu dixisiti" (phrase 6), and the notes are supplied from Bodmer in the transcription. There are otherwise no significant variants between Bod 74 and Vat 5319.

OFFERENTUR (*MINOR*) (74)

Like several other offertories based on Psalm 44, the Roman and Gregorian versions of *Offerentur* present complex variants. In the Gregorian tradition, there are two *Offerentur* offertories, traditionally referred to as "minor" and "maior." The texts may be compared in the following table.

Offerentur *maior, Gregorian*	Offerentur *minor,* Gregorian	Offerentur, Roman
Offerentur regi virgines proxime eius offerentur tibi adducentur in laeticia et exultacione adducentur in templo regi	Offerentur regi virgines post eam proxime eius offerentur tibi	Offerentur regi virgines post eam proxime eius offerentur tibi adducentur in laeticia et exultatione adducentur in templum regi offerentur regi virgines
V. 1 Eructavit cor meum verbum bonum eructavit cor meum verbum bonum dico ego opera mea regi lingua mea calamo scribe velociter scribentis adducentur	Eructavit cor meum verbum bonum dico ego opera mea regi	Eructavit cor meum verbum bonum dico ego opera mea regi
v. 2 Diffusa est gratia in labiis tuis propterea benedixit te deus in aeternum	Adducentur in laeticia et exultatione adducentur in templum regi	Specie tua et pulchritudine tua intende prospere procede et regna

Although the text of the Roman respond might appear on first glance to correspond more closely to *Offerentur* maior, the melodic relationships suggest that the Gregorian *Offerentur* minor is cognate with the Roman version. The lyrics shown in the table, however, are presented in a different order in the Gregorian and Roman readings. *Adducentur in laeticia* consistently serves as the second verse in the Gregorian *Offerentur minor*, whereas in the Roman version this material is simply incorporated into the respond. In the base transcription, the Gregorian verses are presented in reverse order (verse 2 followed by verse 1) to facilitate comparison to the Roman version.

In the Roman tradition, *Offerentur* has the same two verses, in text and music, as *Filiae regum* (78) and *Diffusa est* (80), *Eructavit* and *Specie tua*. Because the verse *Specie* is lacking in the Gregorian *Offerentur* but present in the Gregorian *Diffusa*, the Roman version is transcribed from *Diffusa est* (80).

The Roman version has a varied, written-out repetendum that is lacking in the Gregorian tradition.

Melodic variants in core MSS: There are only a few variants.

v. 2 "adducentur" [in templum] second time:

Mo 159: melisma begins aFaaGEDC FF . . .

v. 2 "REgi":

Mo 159 is missing notes 23–25 of the melisma.

In Pa 776, Pa 780, Lo 4951, E rather than D as the bottom note in the latter part of the melisma (corresponding to the second and third D's of Ben 34).

Variants in peripheral MSS: There are no specific points of instability in *Offerentur*. Variants entered the melodic tradition to varying degrees. Cai 61, Be 40078, and Gr 807, for example, present readings very close to that of the core group, whereas Pa 1235 and some of the Italian MSS reflect the filtering of small variants into the tradition.

Pa 1235:

respond, "tiBI": DCDF F FD FF FED ED
v. 1 "reGI": EF DEF FDFED EDF
v. 2 "adduCENtur" [in laeticia]: DF GFDF **CD Da** GabGF Gaca **DF** FFDC (etc.)
v. 2 "LAEticia": aFa GaFE **GFGF** EDCD FF
v. 2 "adduCENtur" [regi]: aFaGF **FED FEF**DCBCD (liq.)

RoV 52

v. 2 "adduCENtur" [in leticia]: DF GFDF DF aa GabGF Gaca DFFFDCFGG FGa cc
aGFa**GF GF Ga**
v. 2 "adduCENtur" [in templum]: aF aGF **DC** FFF DCB CD

Pad 47:

v. 1 "BO/NUM": FGaF/F
v. 2 "reGIS": The entire end of the verse is notated a third lower than the other versions, possibly a scribal error.

Roman MSS: Vat 5319: The entire offertory is written at the affinal position. There are no significant melodic variants. RoS 22: "reGIS": DFDFED.

GLORIA ET HONORE (75)

The Gregorian and Roman versions of this offertory share melodic material with others of the first mode. The opening melisma of the first verse in the Gregorian tradition also occurs in *Repleti sumus* (82). The corresponding Roman melisma is found in *Laetamini* (79) and the *deuterus Benedictus es . . . in labiis* (16), a verse that probably originally circulated with *Confitebor tibi* (39).

There are some inconsistencies between Mo 159 and later MSS in their use of b-flat, perhaps reflecting a change in practice. The parenthetical b-flats in the base transcription are found in Mo 159 and later MSS; some later MSS such as Gr 807 and Be 40078 also indicate flats at "noster" (phrase 3).

Beneventan MSS show a small difference from others at the end of v. 1. In Mo 159 and Aquitanian MSS, the notes over the two syllables of "caelos" are distributed as follows: Pa 776: aG baF FGaGa GbaFGF/F.

Variants among core MSS:

v. 1 "NOster": Aquitanian MSS have acc cba Gba

v. 2 "HOmo": There are small variants in this melisma:

Ben 34: FGa ccc cdcdaG acc cGF aG abc abca (same reading in Ben 35, Lo 4951)

Pa 776: FGac ccc cdc caG a accGF aG ab(quil.)c ab(quil.) ca (same reading in other Aquitanian MSS)

Mo 159: FGa ccc deb caG acc caG aG ab(quil.)ca b(quil)ca

Variants in individual MSS:

Pa 776: v. 2 "hoMInis": cdcd ccaGGF Gab(quil.) ca (slightly shortened melisma)

Pa 780: respond, "oPEra": DE(quil.)FEDCD

Lo 4951:

v. 1 "admiRAbile": cdcaG **ccca** cdca

v. 1 "NOmen": aGG (ori.) F **accc** dcab

v. 2 "Eum": slightly shortened melisma:

a a(ori.)Ga Faca aGa FacaG abaF GaGE FGFD FFDEC

Pa 1235:

respond, "Eum": GaF FD

v. 1 "QUOniam": Fac

v. 2 "HOmo": version of Mo 159 above

v. 2 "Eius": FGaGaG acaca G GF aG abca ac ccc dcdc(liq.)

v. 2 "hoMInis": cdcdb ac G GF FGa caca

Cai 61:

respond "Eum" (second time): Ga bcbaG GaFF(ori.)D

respond "domiNE": F FGFED

v. 1 "NOster": acccba

v. 2 "HOmo": FGa ccc cdc da Ga cc caG aG aca bca

Gr 807:

    v. 1 "NOster": acccb acccba Gca

    v. 1 "admiRAbile": cdcaG acaG

    v. 2 "HOmo": FGaccc **deb** caG (etc.)

    v. 2 "QUOniam": **D** abca

    v. 2 "VIsitas": acaaG

    v. 2 "Eius" (b's are flat): aaGa Faca aGa Fb baGb baF GaGE (etc.)

Be 40078:

    v. 1 "NOster": a cccba Gca

    v. 2 "Eius": a cdc da cdb caGGF aF **FGaGa** ccc cdc dc(liq.)

    v. 2 "VIsitas": acaaG

RoV 52:

    Respond, "DOmine": GaGGF FaGF FDF FFF GFGFG

    v. 1 "CAE/LOS": bGbaF FGaGa GbaFGF/FG

    v. 2 "HOmo": FGa ccc decaG acc daF GaG aca bca

    v. 2 "Eius": acdcda cdcdcdccaGGF Gaca a ccc cdcd

Pst 120:

    v. 1 "NOmen": aGaFG Ga dca

    v. 1 "uniVERsa": acba

    v. 2 "HOmo": FGa cc decaG GcccaF aG aca abca

    v. 2 "Eius": acdcca cdc aGF aG abca ccc cdcd

    v. 2 "hoMInis": cdcca cbcaGF Ga cabca

Roman MSS: There are no significant variants between Bod 74, Vat 5319, and RoS 22.

VERITAS MEA (76)

In the Gregorian tradition, there are very few significant melodic variants between sources. In Mo 159, the respond and first verse are written in the transposed plagal range, ending on a, and the second verse in the normal authentic range. Mo 159 employs several pitches that cannot be written at the lower level, including b-flat (at the quilisma on "miseriCORdia" in the respond), equivalent to E-flat a fifth lower, and D on "EXaltabitur," equivalent to Γ at the lower level. In its notation at the affinal position and the b-flat on "misericordia," Mo 159 differs from most pitched sources, which are written in the normal plagal range and use an E-natural.

    Small variants are found in the following MSS.

Gr 807:

    v. 1 "poTENtem": DFFEDE

    v. 1 "pleBE": DFDF

Pad 47:

    v. 1 "POtentem": DGFE

v. 2 "MEo": a different opening of the final melisma: FG aGF aGF Fa aF EG abb aaFa aGaF abaE EGaF (etc.)

Mod 7: v. 2 "MEo": a different opening of the final melisma: FabaF GFCD FFDF FD F CF Ga aa aGaaGaF abGE EG

RoV 52:

v. 2 "DIS/PERgam": FGa/ GaFG
v. 2 "MEam": in the middle of the melisma, a (rather than b-flat) is the top note: FabaF GFD DF FD DF **Ga a a aGa aGaF**

Pa 1235:

respond, "meO": ACA CD
v. 1 "pleBE": DFDF
v. 1 "MEa": CDF FGFE FGFG
v. 2 "MEo": FabaF GFD CF FD CD **Da a Ga Ga bGaF GaGE** FGaF (etc.)

Roman sources: Because Bod 74 lacks the verse *Posui*, the more complete reading of Vat 5319 is given as the base version. At the end of v. 2, however, the repetendum cue in Vat 5319 is notated a fifth too high, a problem found often in Gregorian MSS but very rarely in the Roman tradition. Bod 74 presents a substantially different reading of the final melisma that ends in the lower part of the range and is followed by a repetendum cue at the "correct" level. The melisma begins a fourth lower (starting on "conSPECtu"), is longer, and is melodically variant.

Other variants in Bod 74:
respond [misericordia] "ME/A": ED/DEFEDEFE
v. 2 "miseriCOR/DIa": FGaG(liq.)/ac c(ori.)ba

CONSTITUES EOS (77)

There are small variants among the core group of sources at the following places. Peripheral sources generally exhibit the same range of variance, and for these passages, only sample readings are provided from the peripheral group.

Respond, "MEmores":

Pa 776: FF FF(ori.)D **F aG**
Lo 4951: FF FFF **FaG**
Pa 1121: FFFFD **Fba**

respond, "PRO/GEnie": Mo 159:DG/Gc (also in Mod 7)
    respond, "generatioNE": The bracketed notes in the base transcription (phrase 3) are omitted from Ben 34, a probable scribal error. They occur in all other MSS. In the base transcription they are supplied from Ben 39.
    v. 1 "eructavit": The Beneventan version matches the Roman verbally, but most non-Beneventan MSS included in the sampling have "eructuavit," accommodating the extra syllable with a single G. The exceptions are the Italian sources Mod 7, Pad 47, and RoV 52.
    v. 1 "DIco" (like "memores" above):

Pa 776: FF FF(ori.)D **F aG**
Pa 1121: FFFFD **Fba**

v. 1 "eGO/Opera": some sources indicate a different text underlay, as in Mo 159:
FE/GabGa.

v. 2 "scriBE" is a point of variance:

Ben 39: a aGaGFGD GaGaD GaG
Pa 1121: same notes as Ben 39
Mo 159: melisma begins a a(ori.)G aGF GD (cont. like Ben 34)
Lo 4951: same notes as Ben 39
Pa 776: aaG aGFG C GaGa C GaG
Pa 1235: a aGaGF GE FGF FD FaG
Mod 7: a aGa GFGD GbabF GaG
RoV 52: a aGaGFGF GaGaF GaG
Gr 807: a aGaGF GD GaGGE GaG

v. 2 "SCRIbentis": Mo 159: D
v. 2 "speCI/Osus": Most Aquitanian, Italian, and German MSS match Ben 34 here, with
a leap of a sixth on the third syllable (a b-flat is indicated in Gr 807). Mo 159 has an
alternative reading, two successive fourth leaps:

Mo 159: DG/GcaG (etc.)
Pa 1235: DG/GbaG

v. 2 "fiLI/IS": The Beneventan reading is distinctive. Most MSS have a text underlay similar
to that of Mo 159: DFED/D.

v. 3 "eTERnum": Mo 159: melisma begins GF aGF GF(quil.)E.
Significant variants in peripheral MSS (there are very few):
v. 2 "tuIS": Variants within small segments of the melisma occur in some Italian sources:

Mod 7: cda cbcaG cb bdeca **cdca cbcaG** (etc.)
RoV 52: cda cbcaG cb cdeca c ca cc aG **cb bab (etc.)**

The tonal contrast of the final verse, with its repercussive pitch on F, is found in all MSS.
Pa 776 has a written level a fifth higher, but the repetendum suggests that the performance
level is that of Ben 34 and the other MSS.

Roman MSS: This offertory is lacking in Bod 74. Vat 5319, the only MS to transmit the
verses of this offertory, presents a shorter version of the first verse, lacking an equivalent of
the Gregorian phrase 5.

RoS 22 has the following variants:

"TERram": FGaGbaGFG
"TUi": dedcbcbabaG
"generatioNE": aaGF FGaG baGFEGFEFE (closes on E rather than F)

FILIAE REGUM (78)

The verses of *Filiae regum* and two other offertories based on Psalm 44, *Diffusa est* (80) and *Offerentur* (74), present a complex picture of transmission between Rome and Francia. In the Roman tradition, the three offertories have the same verses, in text and melody: *Eructavit* and *Specie tua*. In Bod 74, these verses are notated once, for *Offerentur* (f. 3v), and cued in the other two cases. Vat 5319 has the same cues in *Diffusa est* but lacks verse cues for *Filiae regum*. In most Gregorian MSS, these three offertories have different sets of verses. *Filiae regum* normally circulates with the verses *Eructavit* and *Virga recta est*, the latter verse lacking an equivalent in Roman MSS. In Mont-Blandin, however, *Filiae regum* circulates with the same two verses as in the Roman graduals, *Eructavit* and *Specie* (with only incipits provided), suggesting that perhaps the verse *Virga recta* is a Frankish addition. *Specie*, moreover, is also the second verse in two peripheral MSS included in the sampling, Mod 7 and Pad 47, with the same melody as the *Specie* verse for *Diffusa est*. The other Italian MSS have *Virga recta* as the second verse. If *Virga recta* is a Frankish addition, it dates from a early period, since it is found in Compiègne, the later Silvanectensis, as well as Cha 47 and Ei 121.[1] Textually, the verse corresponds to the PsR rather than the PsG.[2]

There are several small melodic variants in this offertory, including the final cadence of the respond and resulting modal assignment. The ending on F in the Beneventan version is a minority reading. In many other MSS, the final cadence is on E, as the following sampling shows:

Mo 159: G GaG aGE
Pa 776: GFaGE
Mod 7: GFaGE
Pad 47: FaGE
Pst 120: GFaGFE
Cai 61: GFaG G (ori.)E
Be 40078: G GaGE

Cadences on F:

Lo 4951: GFaGF
Pa 1235: GFaG GF
RoV 52: G GaGF

Other melodic variants:

respond "reGUM": The Beneventan reading aca at the beginning of the melisma is distinctive. In most sources the melisma begins with cdc and continues as in Ben 34.
v. 1 "cor meUM": Unlike Ben 34, most MSS have cccaG**c**
v. 1 "BOnum": The Beneventan version is anomalous in notes 8–14, and this passage is also a point of variance between Mo 159 and the Aquitanian MSS:
Mo 159: melisma begins G acaGa **Fb-flat-aG a-b-flat-aG b-natural dc**
Pa 776: melisma begins GabaGa **F aGF abaG cdc (etc.)**
Lo 4951: GacaGa **FaGF acaG** cdc (etc.)

---

1. The Compiègne version has one significant textual variant, with an incipit "virga tua est" rather than "virga recta est."
2. Both verses also correspond to the Gaulois Psalter η as the respond does.

The readings of Pa 776 and Lo 4961 are also found in the following: Pa 780, Pa 1235.
Cai 61: G aca Ga **F b-flat GF acaG**
Mod 7: FacaGa **FGFE** aacaG (same in Pad 47)
RoV 52 GacaGa **GaGFacaG**

v. 1 "BOnum": The Beneventan reading differs from others in the last four or five notes
of the melisma. The other sources have a reading closer to Mo 159 and Pa 776.

Ben 34: FGaGa **abaG**
Mo 159: FG(qui.)aGa **cb(qui.)aG**
Pa 776: FG (qui.) aG ab(qui.) cba

v. 2 [deus] "TU/US": Mo 159: ad ecba/c
v. 2 verse ending "tuIS":

Lo 4951: GaF
Pa 1235: cdcba/acac

Among peripheral MSS, there are differences in recitational style. In the passage of v. 2,
"unxit te deus deus," for example, Pa 1235 adopts c rather than d as the highest note.

Variants in individual MSS:

Cai 61:

respond, [dextris] "TU/IS": cdcba/abca a(ori.)G
v. 1 "operA MEa": ccc edc cba**G/GcaGa**

Mod 7: v. 1 "verBUM": acaGa
RoV 52:

v. 1 "verBUM": acbac
v. 2 "iniquitaTEM": acaG

Be 40078: v1. "reGI": G
Roman MSS:

Vat 5319: This offertory has no verses cued. The respond is written at the affinal
position, with the following small variants:

"tuO": cbcd
"regNA": aG
"A" [dextris]: cde

RoS 22:

"tuO": FEFGFE
"tuIS": GaGFEFG
"inVESti": GaG
"circumDA/TA": FaGFFED/DFDEDCB DFED FGFF

LAETAMINI (79)

This offertory exhibits few variants. Core MSS:

v. 2 "temporRE": Most MSS have a slightly different reading, as in Pa 776: GFG FF DED.

Lo 4951: respond, "CORde": FG FFGFED(liq.)

Pa 780:

v. 2 "TE": DE(quil.)F GF F(ori.)D GFGFEC DFD DDD

v. 2 "SANCtus": FG

v. 2 "muTArum": acGF acaG ccccc

Most peripheral MSS present a reading very close to that of the core group, with the following exceptions.

Be 40078: respond, "CORde": F FG EFG EFGFE

Gr 807: v. 1 "peccaTA": DEFEDCD

RoV 52: respond, "IUsti": DF FFF GaGaFED

Cai 61:

respond, "ET": Da baG

v. 2 "SANCtus": FG

v. 2 "diluVIo": dcbcbaG

Roman MSS:

Vat 5319:

v. 1 "beaTI": FG

v. 2 "verumTAmen": FGababa

v. 2 "diLU/VIo": c cdcdc dc c(ori.) aGa/baG

RoS 22: "corDE": FFED FFEDFED (shortened melisma)

DIFFUSA EST GRATIA (80)

In the Roman tradition, this offertory has the same verses, in text and melody, as *Offerentur* (74) and *Filiae regum* (78). In Vat 5319 and Bod 74, the verses *Eructavit* and *Specie tua* are written out for *Offerentur* and merely cued in the other two offertories. In early Gregorian MSS, *Diffusa* circulates with the same two verses. The first, *Eructavit*, is cued in most sources, with neumes that indicate the melody of the corresponding verse in *Filiae regum* (not that of *Offerentur*, which uses a different melody). In most later Gregorian MSS, however, *Diffusa* circulates with only one verse, *Specie tua*. In Ben 34 and in the base transcription, only *Specie tua* is provided. For the Roman verse *Eructavit*, see the transcriptions of *Offerentur* and *Filiae regum*.

Melodic variants:

respond, "difFUSa": This syllable is a point of variance within the core MSS. Most peripheral MSS match the Aquitanian readings.

Ben 34: FGa b bab bab
Pa 1121: FG a a(ori.) G a a(ori.) G a
Pa 776: EFGa a(ori.) G aaGa (same reading in Cai 61)
Pa 780: FGaaG aaGa (same reading in Be 40078, RoV 52, Pad 47)
Mo 159: Ga b c c (ori.)b c c (ori.) b c
Mod 7: FGa abaa aaaa

respond, "IN" [aeternum]: Most MSS have a reading identical to Ben 34. Pa 776 has cccGa **cdec.**

    v. 1 "REGna": In Mo 159, the latter part of this melisma is notated a tone higher than it is in other MSS: cdecc a cca ccaa(ori.)FG FG(quil) aGa Ga(quil.)bab ab **dd dbaG bdd dbaG bdba bdba ab/G.** A different reading at the opening of the melisma is found in several of the Italian MSS, as in RoV 52: **cdecd cdeca** c caGFG FGaGa (etc.).
Individual MSS:
RoV 52:

    v. 1 "SPEcie": DF G aG baG GF Ga cdcb dcdca cc ca cc **dec**
    v. 1 "inTENde": This melisma is written a tone below the majority reading of Ben 34 and most MSS. That this is a scribal error, however, is suggested by the custos at the end of the line, followed by the final segment of the melisma notated at the correct level.

Cai 61: respond, "IN" [aeternun]: cc cG ac **dec** (like Pa 776 above)
  Mod 7

    The verse *Specie* is cued in *Diffusa* and written out as the second verse of *Filiae regum*
    v. 1 "TUa": acaaG
    v. "REGna": melisma begins **cd ecd cd eca** cccaG GFG (similar to RoV 52 above)

Pad 47:

    The verse *Specie* is cued in *Diffusa* and written out as the second verse of *Filiae regum*
    v. 1 v. 1 "TUa": acaG
    v. "REGna": The beginning of the melisma has the reading found in several of the other Italian sources; it is also variant in the second segment in boldface: **cd ecd cd eca** cccaG GFG aGa FGaGa **FGaGa** etc.

Roman MSS: There are only a few small variants.
  Vat 5319:

    respond, "SEculi": cdcdc bcba(ori.)GF GFGFGaG acbcba bcaG GFacbaG
    The verse *Specie*, written out in *Offerentur* and merely cued in *Diffusa*, is written at the affinal position, like the respond and first verse of *Offerentur*.
RoS 22: "SEculum": c dcdc bcbaGF GFGFGaG Fac cbcba bcbabaGF acbaG.

AVE MARIA (81)

The pitch level variants in this piece have been illustrated and discussed by Hankeln and Sidler.[1] Sidler proposed that *Ave Maria* was originally a *protus* melody, based partially on the first-mode characteristics of the final verse. Hankeln, however, notes the consistent *tetrardus*

---

1. Sidler (1939), 32–42: Hankeln (1999), 1:96–97.

EXAMPLE 81.1A

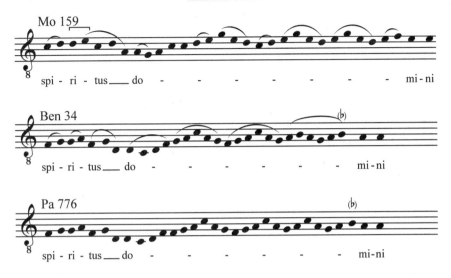

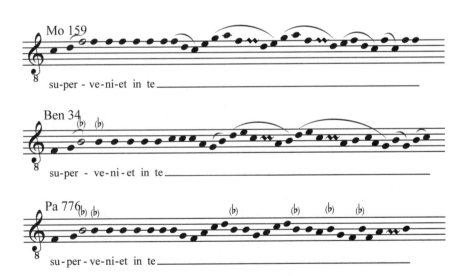

character of this chant in the Aquitanian MSS, and the sources included in the sampling present a similar picture. Although the melody does exhibit a mixture of modal traits, there is little evidence that it was ever consistently *protus*.

The passage "spiritus domini superveniet in te" (phrase 8) is a problem spot. Based on the transpositional variants, Hankeln persuasively posits an *Aufführungslage* that is equivalent to Pa 776 here.[2] Three different versions of the passage are shown in example 81.1. In

2. Hankeln (1999), 1:97.

EXAMPLE 81.1B

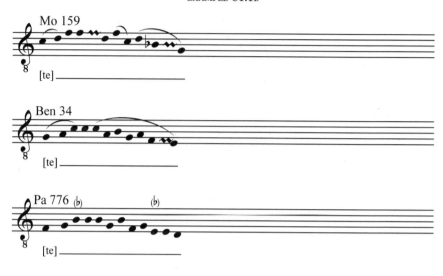

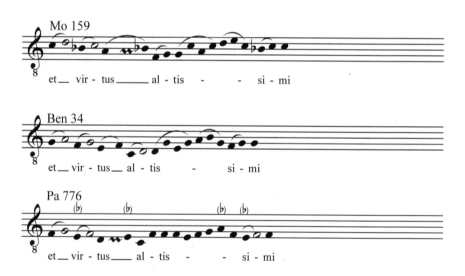

Mo 159 (line 1), this passage is marked by a move into the higher register, with high f as the repercussive pitch at "superveniet." A similar reading is found in several other MSS, as summarized below. In Pa 776 (line 3), however, the passage is written a fifth lower. In this version, "superveniet in te" is marked by a modulation of sorts, in which typical *tetrardus* melodic characteristics are projected a tone below their usual position: b [flat] (equivalent to high f in Mo 159) serves as the recitational pitch, and a hypothetical E-flat (equivalent to b-flat in Mo 159) is introduced at the end of the melisma on "te."

EXAMPLE 81.1C

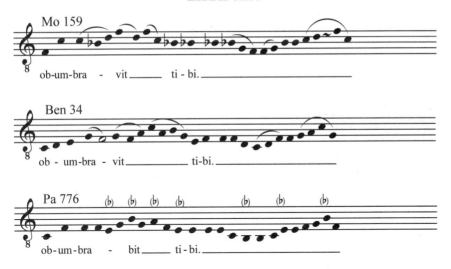

Hankeln's hypothesis that Pa 776 is the preferred reading of this passage receives support from a group of sources that notate the passage a whole tone above the level of Pa 776. Ben 34 (line 2), for example, writes the passage a tone higher than Pa 776 does, beginning with the melisma on "te." This transposition places the passage in the normal eighth-mode segment of the background scale and allows the irregular semitone at the end of the melisma, E-flat-D, to be represented with F-E. Although a similar transposition is found in Lo 4951, Gr 807, and in most Italian MSS in the sampling, these sources begin the transposition at different places, as summarized below. The variety of versions among this group suggests that the transpositions are emendations made in response to the irregularity of the passage and the need for E-flat. With this hypothesis, Pa 776 and Pa 780 are the only MSS in the sampling that notate this passage in its unemended range.[3]

The final passage of the verse, "et virtus altissimi obumbravit tibi" (phrase 9), presents a problem I have not been able to fully solve. As shown in example 81.1, Pa 776 continues at an interval a fifth below Mo 159 and a whole tone below Ben 34, a reading unique among the MSS examined. Hankeln considers the written level of Pa 776 at the end of the verse a scribal error, and in his edition he has placed it a whole tone higher. One reason for positing a scribal error lies in the two prosulas that follow the first verse in Pa 776, based on the "quomodo" melisma. After the move into the new tonal area at "super veniet," the version of Pa 776 never rejoins the level of Ben 34 or Mo 159; the two prosulas are thus written a whole tone lower than the melisma itself. With the premises that the prosulas were sung at the same level as the source melisma and that the pitch level between verse and prosula is accurately indicated in the MS, one must posit a scribal error somewhere earlier on. The problem of the written level in Pa 776 continues with the second verse and repetendum: the second verse is written a tone below its usual level, and the repetendum is a tone lower than the corresponding place in the respond.

This problem spot in *Ave Maria* is reminiscent of a similar passage in *Oravi deum*. In respond of *Oravi deum*, Pa 776 and 1121 present a reading that contains a modulation of

3. And Pa 780 is unique among the sources examined in beginning the transposition earlier, at "quae virum," where it is a fourth below Mo 159. See the summary in Hankeln (1999), 2:136.

sorts. Beginning in the middle of the respond, *deuterus* melodic passages are projected a tone below their usual position. In the case of *Oravi deum*, this reading is confirmed in some unrelated MSS that notate the passage at the affinal position: the chant starts as a regular b-*deuterus* chant and ends as an a-*deuterus* chant (with b-flats). The same questions are raised about the continuation of the chant in the verses: when, if ever, did it get back "on track?" In the case of *Oravi deum*, I have cautiously hypothesized that in Pa 1121 and Pa 776, the answer is never. In *Oravi deum*, this hypothesis is supported by a repetendum cue in Pa 1121. In *Ave Maria*, however, the repetendum is written a tone below its position in the respond, perhaps suggesting an *Aufführungslage* a tone higher. Hankeln's proposed solution to the problem, that "et virtus" is a scribal error and should be written a tone higher, is found in only one MS, Pa 780. This MS matches Pa 776 at "spiritus domini" but is a tone higher beginning at "et virtus," thereby returning to the normal eighth-mode range. The relative pitch level between the two sections ("spiritus domini . . . " and "et virtus . . . "), as it is notated in Pa 776, is duplicated in a great majority of sources: the interval between the end of the melisma on "te" and "et [virtus]" is a third, not a fourth, as it is in Pa 780 and in Hankeln's proposed correction of Pa 776. The relative pitch level between these two sections as they appear in Pa 776 is found in all MSS except Pa 780: at a position a fifth higher in Mo 159 and a whole tone higher in Ben 34, Gr 807, and most Italian sources. Either all sources except Pa 780 are emended versions in this particular passage or the level of Pa 776 represents the unemended pitch level, as it does in the earlier passage.

I consider the second possibility more likely and am thus hesitant to regard Pa 776's reading of the end of the verse as a scribal error. It is more probable that the whole-tone downward "modulation" that occurs in Pa 776 was maintained throughout the verse. The variety of the other versions, summarized below, reinforces the impression that they are emendations. The other versions move to a level a whole tone above Pa 776 at different points. In the edition, I have transcribed this passage in Pa 776 at its written level. At this level, several nondiatonic pitches, including low b-flat, E-flat, and a-flat, are required to duplicate the intervallic structure of the melody as it appears in Mo 159 and Ben 34. The three versions may be compared by examining the last system of example 81.1. With this hypothesis, the intended pitch level of the prosulas and second verse remains an unresolved problem: it is unclear when, if ever, the chant got back "on track." If such an adjustment was made, it was likely done at the beginning of the prosula or at the beginning of the second verse. In the transcription, I have given the end of v. 1 at its notated level and the second verse, hypothetically, at the level of the majority reading, a tone above its written level.

A few MSS notate v. 2 a fourth above the majority reading: Mo 159 and Pa 1121 and the other MSS from St. Martial. All other MSS match the majority reading given in the transcription, with the first-mode incipit C-D-D-a. Mo 159 employs a b-natural on the last syllable of "ideoque," which would be equivalent to F-sharp at the lower level. This nondiatonic practice, however, is not preserved in other traditions. In Pa 776 and many other MSS, the corresponding note is a. Ben 34 is the only Beneventan MS with verses to transmit this piece (because of lacunae in the other MSS), and it lacks the second verse.

Pitch level at "spiritus domine superveniet in te":

5↑ Pa 776: Mo 159, Cai 61, Pa 1121, Be 40078
2↑ Pa 776: Lo 4951 (at "superveniet"), Ben 34 (at "te"), Pad 47 (at "spiritus"), To 18 (at "superveniet"), Pia 65 (at "spiritus"), Gr 807 (on the third syllable of "superveniet": the

first two syllables are G and a), Frutolf tonary (on the third syllable of "superveniet"—same as Gr 807), Pa 780 (at "et virtus")

Editorial emendation: Pa 776 presents one small transcription problem. In the respond, "mulieribus" is the last word on the page, followed by a custos on pitch a. The a, however, is missing on the next page, which is probably a scribal error, since it is present in all other MSS. I have supplied it in the transcription and indicated it with brackets.

Individual MSS: Pa 780 is a fourth below Pa 776 at "quae virum," joining at "spiritus domini." Gr 807 moves to the lower register during the melisma on "virum"" ccb cGG(ori.) G EF Ga FFD(liq.).

Melodic variants: *Ave Maria* has an unusual number of melodic variants, even among the core MSS. In the earliest MSS, this offertory lacks the words "dominus tecum" (phrase 3), which, as Hesbert suggested, appear to be a later addition, made separately in the Gregorian and Roman traditions.[4] The passage is lacking in Mont-Blandin, Compiègne, Corbie, and Ei 121. These added words are accommodated with familiar melodic material: the melisma on "dominus" also occurs in *Angelus domini*.

Given the later addition of this material, the melodic variants here are not surprising. La 269 indicates a shorter melisma on "dominus" (without the repetition of material), a reading also found in Lo 4951 and Pa 780. Other sources, such as Pa 1235, lack the melisma on "dominus" altogether.

Some sources present a variant reading of "tecum," with a short melisma:

	te-	cum
Pa 1121:	G GGG aGF GD	acab/aG
Ben 34:	GaGFGD Gbab	/aG
Gr 807:	GG aGF GD Gcac	/aG
Be 40078:	GG GED EGaGF	/G
Pst 120:	GGG FaGFGD	Gcab/aG

Both versions, with and without the short melisma on "tecum," are found across a broad regional and chronological spectrum. The melisma is lacking in Mo 159, Pa 780, Lo 4951, Pa 1235, Pad 47.

v. 1 "VIrum":

Pa 1121: c c(ori.) bc G G (ori.)FG ccde
Be 40078: c cb cG G(ori.) FG cc de
Pst 120: cc cbca aFG Gc de

v. 1 "DOmini":

Gr 807: DCD EF Ga caG FG acaGF c
Pst 120: aGa cc de ged efg cde g edefedef

v. 2 "NA/SCE/TUR": The reading of Pa 776 is found in the Aquitanian MSS, with exception of Pa 780, and also matched in Pa 1235 and Cai 61. Mo 159 and many other MSS have a different reading:

4. Hesbert (1935), xxxix.

Mo 159 (at higher pitch level): dfed/dc/cedc

Pa 780: acba/aG/GbaG

Gr 807: acba/aG/G b-flat aG

Be 40078: acba/aG/G c aG (similar reading in Pst 120 and Pad 47)

v. 2 "DEi": Pa 776 is the Aquitanian version, also found in Pa 1235, but many MSS have a more elaborate version of this melisma, as found in Mo 159:

Mo 159 (at higher level of transposition, and all b's are flat): ccc(ori.) cdbaG Gabc cc (ori.) cdbaG Gabc dd(ori.)c

Gr 807: GaFED D EF Ga FED DEF Ga(ori.)G

Pst 120: GaFED DEFGa FED DEFGa aG G

Versions very similar to Gr 807 and Pst 120 found in Cai 61, Be 40078, and Pad 47.

Roman MSS: In the Roman tradition, v. 1 consists largely of material from the respond; v. 2 has *protus* characteristics, a trait that ties it to the Gregorian version. There is one significant variant between Bodmer and Vat 5319 in the melisma that occurs at the end of v. 1. The part in boldface is written a whole tone lower in Vat 5319: aGaG **baG GF** aGaG ababaGaG.

Other variants:

Vat 5319: v. 1 "naSCEtur": ba

RoS 22:

"maRIa": c cbcabaGF acbG

"gratiA": GFG FG

"beneDICta": cba

"beneDICtus": cba bcdcbabG

CONFITEBUNTUR CAELI (82)

In the opening passage, on "confitebuntur," Pa 776 differs from all other MSS. On the last two syllables, the scribe writes b/bdc. In all other MSS, these neumes are reversed: bdc/b. This is certainly a scribal error, and I have undertaken an editorial emendation of it.

There are also some differences between MSS in repetendum structure. In most MSS, the second verse closes with a repetendum to the first "alleluia" of the respond, indicating that the both alleluias were sung and that the performance came to a conclusion on G. In Pa 776, the verse closes with a written out repetendum of this "alleluia," with two tiny variants. Although it is not clear from the MS whether this repetendum is an instruction to close the melody here, on F, or to proceed to the final alleluia, it is likely that the performance was concluded on the original final G, requiring the singers to sing the second alleluia. In Mo 159, the repetendum cue is to the final "alleluia" of the respond.

Pitch-level variants in v. 2, *Quoniam*: Pa 776 was chosen as the base reading because it presents the most probable unemended version of the second verse. This verse presents complex transpositional variants, with several distinct versions. In most MSS, the verse begins a fourth below the reading of Pa 776. With the exception of Mo 159, which remains a fourth below Pa 776 throughout, all of these MSS join the level of Pa 776 before the end of the verse. The transition to the higher level, however, occurs at different times and in different ways, as summarized below.

While it was not possible to determine a preferred reading with certainty, various circumstantial factors point to the pitch-level profile of Pa 776 as a preferred reading: the ending of the verse at this position in a majority of MSS, the diversity of readings in the sources that begin a fourth lower, and the tendency evident in Pa 776 to notate problematic passages in their "unemended" range. A downward transposition of a fourth would typically be employed to represent the nondiatonic pitch high eb, with a b-flat. A b-flat is indicated only once in Mo 159, on the penultimate note of "erit" (phrase 10). I have indicated this spot with a parenthetical e-flat at the corresponding place in the transcription of Pa 776. It is doubtful, however, that this hypothetical e-flat is the sole cause of the different readings. Several sources included in the sampling move to the position of Pa 776 before the problem spot on "erit" (phrase 10), hinting at a possible nondiatonic pitch earlier on in the verse. The following intervallic differences with Pa 776 are evident in individual MSS, suggesting nondiatonic pitches.

1. "aequabitur" (phrase 9): A possible nondiatonic pitch is suggested here in some sources. Ben 34, 35, and 39 begin the verse at the level of Mo 159, a fourth below Pa 776. On the first syllable of "aequitabitur" (phrase 9), some MSS are a tone below Pa 776. The notes fgfg in Pa 776 appear as a semitone, efef, in the Beneventan sources, possibly attesting to a nondiatonic practice at this point. Pa 1132 also has this reading, but it is not found in other MSS from St. Martial. At the level of Pa 776, an f-sharp would be required to duplicate this intervallic structure.

Pa 776: fgefgfg
Ben 34: dfdefef
Pa 1132: dfdefef

The other sources match either Pa 776 here or are written a fifth lower, with no trace of a nondiatonic pitch. Because the problem seems particular to a small group of sources, I have not included accidentals in the transcriptions.

2. "filiOS" (phrase 10): This passage follows the problem spot on "erit deo." On the last syllable of "filios," Mo 159 is briefly written a fifth below Pa 776 rather than a fourth below. In Ben 34, this passage is part of a lengthy section that is written a whole tone below the level of Pa 776. The three versions may be compared as follows:

Pa 776: defed
Mo 159: Gabcb
Ben 34: cdededc

The minor third d-f in Pa 776 is the major third G-b-natural in Mo 159 and the major third c-e in Ben 34. An f-sharp would be required to replicate this intervallic structure at the level of Pa 776. On "dei," the interval of transposition between Mo 159 and Pa 776 changes back to a fourth, and Mo 159's motion around the pitches a, b, and c is intervallically identical to the motion around d, e, and f in Pa 776. Ben 34, however, places the passage on "dei" between c and e, equivalent to f-sharp at the level of Pa 776.

In most MSS there is no trace of this hypothetical nondiatonic practice. Many MSS, including Lo 4951, Tri 2254, Cai 61, and the MSS from St. Martial, for example, are identical in pitch level to Pa 776 here. Because of the inconsistency of transmission of this passage, I have not indicated any nondiatonic notes in the transcription.

Pitch level in individual MSS:

1. Pa 780 and Cai 61 are at the level of Pa 776 throughout.

2. Tri 2254 is at the level of Pa 776 throughout, except for "aut quis si [milis]," where it is a tone below. In this MS, the e-flat on "erit" is circumvented by simply reworking the melisma: df gf fff dcdfff.

3. The following MSS begin 4↓ Pa 776 and join it at various points: Pa 1121, Pa 1235, and Pst 120 join Pa 776 on "aequabitur." Pa 1132 joins on the second syllable of "aequabitur." Lo 4951 joins Pa 776 at "deo," with a transition during the melisma on "erit." Mod 7 and Be 40078 join Pa 776 at "deus." Pad 47 joins Pa 776 at "dei." Ben 39 joins on the third syllable of "aequitabitur," and is a second below Pa 776 on the last syllable of "filios." Ben 34 presents a highly emended reading of the verse that differs from the other sources in several passages. It is variously a fourth, a third, and a whole tone below Pa 776.

At verse opening: 4↓ 776

"aequabitur domino": 2↓ 776

"aut quis similis erit": at various invervals of transposition, with a different melodic readings.

Other significant variants: v. 1 "TU/AS" (phrase 5) is a point of variance among core and peripheral sources, as the following sample readings show:

Lo 4951: identical to Pa 776
Mo 159: dg ag aged/de(quil.)f ge
Pa 1235: dg agagd/dgf fd ced
Ben 34: df gfgfd/fgff (ori.)d ced
Mod 7: dg afed/decacded

v. 2 "DEus" (phrase 11): variant reading in Beneventan MSS: Ben 34: d ec c(ori.)d edec c (ori)d ff.

Roman MSS:

Vat 5319: respond, final "alleluia": The second half of the melisma on "le" and the final two syllables of "alleluia" are not notated. The melisma on "le" reads as follows:

cdededc ededc c (ori.) cbdcbacbaGaGF
v. 1 "in": bacbG
v. 1 "meO": cd
v. 1 concludes with a slightly varied written-out repetendum to the first "alleluia," with a modified cadence:

                                        al- le- lu-ia.

dc (liq.)/ dcd cdc c(ori.)baGaG cdcdcbcbabcbab ba(liq.)/ GacbaGa/ aG

v. 2, "deus" (signifcant variant): For reasons that are unclear, most of this melisma is notated a fifth below that of Bod 74:

De-   us
GGG aG FEFG GG aG FEFG G **cbaG**/cdc cbcd

For the last four notes of the melisma, in boldface, the interval of transposition changes to a third.

Vat 5319 indicates no repetendum at the end of v. 2.
RoS 22:

"conFItebuntur": GabdcG

"sancTOrum": edc

first "alLEluia": RoS 22 has a slightly shorter version of the melisma:
dcdcdccbaGaG cdcdcbabcbab

REPLETI SUMUS (83)

The Roman version has a longer text than the Gregorian does, as well as a written-out repetendum that is lacking in Gregorian MSS.

This piece exhibits almost no significant variants among the MSS included in the sampling.

Lo 4951: v. 1 "reFUgium": aca Gba

RoV 52: respond, "alLEluia": abaGFF GaGF GF FD FGF **GbaG GF** GFGF

 Roman MSS:

Vat 5319: respond, "noSTRIS": EGFF (ori) GFEDEDF FE (same at "progeniE" in v. 1)

RoS 22 is written at the affinal position and has the following variants:

"oMNI/BUS": bcba/bc

"noSTRIS": bdcdcbababcb

MIRABILIS (84)

Mirabilis exhibits one variant in pitch level. In some MSS, including Mo 159, the beginning of v. 2 is written a fifth above its level in Ben 34, joining at "aepulentur." The reading of Ben 34 is found among all core Aquitanian MSS, Pa 1235, and Cai 61, whereas Mo 159's version is matched in all Italian and German MSS. Because the two versions are intervallically identical, it is doubtful that the variants are attributable to nondiatonic pitches. The two versions may simply represent performance alternatives.

Pitch level a v. 2, "Pereant peccatores . . . iusti":

 = Ben 34: Ben 35, Pa 776, Pa 780, Pa 1121, Lo 4951, Cai 61, Pa 1235
 5↑ Ben 34: Mo 159, Mod 7, Pad 47, Pst 120, RoV 52, Be 40078, Gr 807

Other melodic variants:

respond, "PLEbi": Most MSS have the reading of Mo 159: aG cdc
verse endings:
v. 1 "eIUS"
v. 2 "leticiA"

Some MSS have a slightly shorter version of this melisma, as in Mo 159: GaGF acb cca FG; or Pa 1121: GaGF acb bcaFG. Pa 780, however, presents a reading similar to Ben 34: GaGF acb cca caFG.

Pa 776: "disSIpentur": acdc
Lo 4951: v. 2: missing "qui" [epulentur]

Pa 780:

> respond, "alleluIA": Gca aGGF
> v. 2: missing "qui" [epulentur]

Pa 1235:

> respond ends at "deus," omitting the "alleluia."
> respond, "SUis": ac dcdcba
> respond, "DEus": melisma begins cdcdbca (etc.)
> v. 1 "EXurgat": DG
> v. 1 "dissiPENtur": cc adc
> v. 1 "ET" [fugiant]: DG
> v. 1 "QUI": Faca
> v. 2 [facie] "DEi": FGFE
> v. 2 "EXultent": DG
> v. 2 "IN": Faca

Cai 61:

> respond ends at "deus," omitting the "alleluia."
> respond, "SUis": ac dc dcba
> v. 1 "EXurgat": DF
> v. 1 "dissiPENtur": c ca cdc

Mod 7:

> respond, "israHEL": FGa baG
> respond, "SANCtis": ac dcbaG
> respond, "alleluIA": melisma ends abaGF
> v. 2: missing "qui" [epulentur]
> v. 2 "epulentur": ac ccc dcd

Pad 47:

> respond, "israHEL": Fa baG
> respond, "VIRtutem": abcb(liq.)
> respond, "SANCtis": ac dcbaG
> respond, "alleluIA": melisma ends abaGF
> v. 1 "inImici": acb
> v. 1 "QUI": abca
> v. 1 [facie] "Eius": melisma begins EFGF
> v. 2: missing "qui" [epulentur]
> v. 2 "epulentur": ac ccc dcd

Pst 120:

> respond, "israHEL": Fa ba aG
> respond, "VIRtutem": abcb(liq.)
> v. 2: missing "qui" [epulentur]

RoV 52:

> respond, "israHEL": Fa baaG
> respond, "VIRtutem": abcb(liq.)

v. 2: missing "qui" [epulentur]

Be 40078:

v. 2: missing "qui" [epulentur]

Roman MSS:

Vat. 5319: v. 2 "qui epulentur": Vat 5319, like many Gregorian MSS, lacks the "qui." As a result, the text underlay in this passage is different: "E/PU/LEN": aG/aGa/a(ori.)GF Gaba babaG(liq.).

RoS 22: "DEus": last 12 notes are bcabaGF acbaG.

GLORIABUNTUR IN TE (85)

In the Gregorian tradition, the first verse of this offertory is identical, verbally and musically, to that of *Intende voci* (23). In most MSS, the verse is simply cued. The Roman melody, however, differs from that of the corresponding verse in *Intende voci*, instead adopting Formula B. To facilitate comparison between the Gregorian and Roman versions, I have transcribed the first verse from Ben 34 as it appears in *Intende*.

While Ben 34's normal *tritus* version is found among a great majority of MSS, two sources in the core group, Pa 776 and Pa 1121, hint at possible modal irregularities in the pretheoretical tradition. In three of the core Aquitanian MSS (Pa 776, Pa 780, and Pa 1121) the written level of the cue to the first verse, *Verba mea*, as well as the entire second verse, is a fifth below their position in Ben 34 and the great majority of other MSS. In Pa 780, the repetendum cue after the second verse, to "domine," implies a performance level for the verse equal to that of Ben 34. In Pa 776, however, the repetendum cue suggests a performance level a fourth below the level of Ben 34. Although Pa 776 is the only pitched source in the sampling to imply a lower performance level for the verse, this reading is consistent with Ei 121, which has the letter *i* (inferius) at the beginning of the verse, suggesting that it begins below the final. A similar pitch-level profile is found in two geographically diverse later versions, Tri 2254 and Pad 47. In both MSS, the respond is written at the affinal position, ending on c, and the second verse is in the normal authentic range, lacking a repetendum cue after the second verse. In the case of Tri 2254, this transposition of the respond may have been undertaken to represent low B-flat, as described below. In Ben 34 and most core sources, the corresponding note is c.

Pa 1121 and most MSS from St. Martial lack repetendum cues. For the second verse, a performance level identical to that of Ben 34 is implied by the repetendum cues in Pa 1134 and 1136. In Pa 1121, however, the end of the verse is notated a whole tone lower than it is in other MSS, beginning with "domine." To replicate the intervallic structure of the other versions at this level would require a high eb, corresponding to the high f in the other MSS.

Although Pa 776 and Pa 1121 suggest possible nondiatonic practices, their readings are inconsistent with one another. The other pitched MSS give too little information to posit either of these distinctive readings as a preferred version. For this reason, I have adopted the majority reading of Ben 34 as the base version.

There are very few melodic variants. The Aquitanian MSS provide a distinctive reading of one passage, in the second occurrence of "quoniam" in v. 2, as described below.

Mo 159:

> v. 2 "oraBO" (second time): Mo 159 employs a b-flat here, whereas most MSS that distinguish between b-flat and b-natural indicate a natural.
>
> v. 2 "TE" (second time), a different opening of the melisma: dcc(ori.)a cb adcc(ori.)a cb **Ga** cb(quil.)a (etc.).

Pa 776: v. 2 "quoNIam"(second time): cdc ab(quil.)c abcb

Pa 780:

> v. 2 "quoNIam" (second time): cdc ab(quil.)c abcb

Lo 4951:

> respond "diLI/GUNT": DEFEDE/ED
>
> v. 1, *Verba mea*, is written out
>
> v. 2 "quoNIam" (second time): cdc ab(quil.)cbcdc

Cai 61:

> respond, "gloriaBUNtur": BD c cdc c cdc
>
> v. 2: Cai 61 presents a shorter version of this verse, with the text repetition omitted.

> RoV 52: v. 2 "MA/NE": FGaGFG/GF (replaced with a more common cadential pattern)

Mod 7: has a lacuna here

Pst 120:

> v. 1, *Verba mea*, is written out
>
> v. 2 "TE" (second time): dcdcca GdcdcG acba
>
> v. 2: The word "mane" and its music are omitted
>
> v. 2 "MEam": cac cac ca ccc ac cac ca ccc dc ca c ca ccc dfffffdc dfffffdcdc **dedc dcdc** (etc.)

Pad 47:

> v. 2 "TE" (second time): dcca cb deccacb acba
>
> v. 2 "MEam": cac cac cca ac cac cca ccc dca cca ccc d fff ffffdc ff ff ffffdc **dc deca cb** (etc.)

Be 40078: transmits the second verse only. The respond and verse are notated at unusual positions on the background scale, the respond an octave above its position in Ben 34 and the second verse a fourth higher. In the case of the respond, the reason may lie in a melodic variant that requires a b-flat on the third syllable of "gloriabuntur," b-flat d ff gf ff gf. The scribe may have written the respond an octave higher because the low B-flat was not part of the notational system. The same melodic reading of "gloriabuntur" is found at the normal position in Cai 61 above, but without an accidental indicated, and in Tri 2254, where the whole respond is written at the affinal position.

Roman MSS:

Vat 5319:

> respond, "TE": FGaGbaGF
>
> respond, "doMIne": Ga(ori.)GF
>
> verses: Vat 5319 has no verse division indicated between the first and second verses, and lacks the text repetition of "quoniam ad te orabo."

v. [2]: "doMIne": Ga(ori.)GF

RoS 22 has the cadential variant in Formula B is that is used consistently in this MS: GaGFEFG rather than GFEFG (as in Bod 74 and Vat 5319): This variant occurs on "omNES" and "tuE."

"doMIne": GFED
"IUsto" [*sic*]: FGaGaGF
"coronaSTI": F GaGbaGFGa

MIHI AUTEM (86)

This piece exhibits numerous melodic variants and, in the final verse, pitch-level variants. The base version of Pa 776 presents a pitch-level profile of the third verse that reflects the most probable unemended version. Pa 776, however, is anomalous among core sources in two passages, namely the melisma on "meam" in v. 1 (phrase 4) and its repetition in v. 2 (phrase 7). Although this melisma is a point of variance, especially in peripheral MSS, most sources have a reading closer to that of Mo 159: DF GFF (ori) EDCD FFD CGE GF GE FGDC D FF F(ori.) D FGF GF GF(quil.) E.

For this melisma, the version of Mo 159 is implied in the neumes of the three early adiastematic MSS examined, including Cha 47, Ei 121, and La 239. Several MSS in the peripheral group, however, present a version closer to that of Pa 776, including Gr 807, which has the same internal descent to D and c: Gr 807: CFGFDCD EFD FGF GE FD CFDCD FFD FGF GFGFE. This latter reading is also implied by the neumes in SG 339, suggesting that an alternative reading of this passage was a part of the early melodic tradition.

The parenthetical b-flats in the base transcription are derived from the indications in Mo 159. In a great majority of cases, the b-flats in the three verses are matched in later MSS that employ a sign for b-flat. Pa 1235 and Cai 61, however, also indicate a b-flat in the opening of the respond, on the second syllable of "mihi," and at "sunt" and "eorum" in the respond. At "eorum" a b-flat is also indicated in Be 40078.

Pitch-level variants: In Mo 159 and most Aquitanian MSS, the final verse (phrase 8) is followed by a varied, written-out repetendum to "nimis confortatus est," with a different melody for "nimis confortatus." In the base reading Pa 776, the repetendum is notated through the first two syllables of "principatus," indicating that the full repetendum was to be sung following the melodically variant "nimis confortatus est." In Pa 776, the cue to the repetendum is notated a fifth above the expected level; at the notated level, the ending of the second verse and repetendum extend well beyond the *deuterus* range of the respond and first two verses; a full repetendum at the written level would conclude on the affinal b rather than the original final, E. The pitch-level profile of Pa 776, with the same inconsistency of repetendum, is found in other Aquitanian MSS, including Pa 1121, Pa 1134, and Pa 1137.[1] In most MSS, however, the verse is written a fifth below Pa 776 beginning at "tu formasti." In the majority reading, the second verse ends a fifth below the written level of Pa 776 and the repetendum concludes on E.

There are two possible ways to interpret the notation in Pa 776. The first is that the "incorrect" repetendum indicates a discrepancy between the notated and performance levels of the verse and that the whole verse should be sung a fifth lower. This hypothesis

---

1. Pa 1137 lacks the melodically variant repetendum and instead includes a cue to "nimis" that is identical to the corresponding place in the respond, except written a fifth too high.

rests on the assumption that the melodic material of the repetendum was sung at the same pitch level each time it occurs. The second possibility is that the notated level reflects actual performance, and the expansion into the higher part of the range at the end of the verse resulted in a migration of the final from E to b. I have provided both versions in the transcription, labeled "written level" and "hypothetical performance level."

I would cautiously hypothesize that the lower reading, the hypothetical performance level, is the intended one. Among the adiastematic MSS examined, only Ei 121 gives a clue to the performance level. The third verse, which immediately follows the second verse (with no repetendum), begins with an "im," indicating that the verse begins at a pitch lower than the end of the second verse. This reading is consistent only with Pa 776 at its hypothetical performance level. This evidence, coupled with the usual meaning of the "incorrect" repetendum cues, suggests that the lower reading is the preferred one.

The evidence for this hypothesis is strengthened by the variant readings in other MSS. At the end of the verse, beginning with "et posuisti" (phrase 10), most versions are a fifth below the written level of Pa 776, with notated b-flats in Mo 159. The various versions, however, move to this lower level at different points. The variety of readings suggests that an emendation has taken place in response to the presence of nondiatonic pitches. At the beginning of the verse, the nondiatonic pitches low-B-flat and E-flat would be required to reproduce the intervallic structure of the majority reading at the hypothetical performance level suggested by Pa 776 and others like it. By the close of the verse, most MSS have moved to the hypothetical performance level, a fifth below the written level of Pa 776, at a point when nondiatonic pitches are no longer required.

The hypothetical a-flat at "formasti" (phrase 9) is suggested by the intervallic relationship to Mo 159. Just before this point, at "tu," Mo 159 moves from the written level of Pa 776 to position a whole tone lower, a reading unique among the MSS in the sampling. At "formasti," Mo 159 is briefly a fourth below the written level of Pa 776 and employs a b-flat, equivalent to an e-flat at the written level of Pa 776 and, by extension, an a-flat at the hypothetical performance level. This hypothetical practice, however, is not reflected in most MSS. Most sources notate this passage a fifth below the written level of Pa 776 with no partial transpositions. The pitch in question is written as a regular a, suggesting that this nondiatonic practice was either confined to Dijon or suppressed in other areas.

In most MSS, the transpositional variants begin at "tu formasti."[2] In relation to the *written* level of Pa 776, these variants may be summarized as follows:

1. Pitch level at verse opening, "ecce":= Pa 776: all except the Beneventan MSS, which have partial transpositions here. Ben 34 and 38 are 2↓ Pa 776, with a notated b-flat. Both join Pa 776, on the final syllable of "domine." Ben 35 begins as Pa 776, but is 2↑ Pa 776 on "[domi]ne cognovisti," rejoining at "omnia."

2. Pitch level at "tu" (phrase 9):

= Pa 776: Pa 780, Pa 1121, Pa 1137, Pa 1134, Pa 1137, Pa 1235
2↓ Pa 776: Mo 159

---

2. Ben 38 presents an exceptional reading here. At its written level, it appears to be a fourth below the written level of Pa 776, but this reading would be inconsistent with the end of the verse and repetendum to "nimis," which are a fifth below the written level of Pa 776. This adjustment suggests that a scribal error has been made earlier on in the verse. Because of this lack of clarity, I have not included Ben 38 in the pitch-level summary.

5↓ Pa 776: Lo 4951, Ben 34, Ben 35, Cai 61, Gr 807, Be 40078, Rei 264, Mod 7, RoV 52, Pst 120 (beginning within the melisma; the melisma reads DG acaG aFE FFFD etc.)

3. Pitch level at "formasti" (phrase 9):

= Pa 776: Pa 780, Pa 1121, Pa 1134, Pa 1137, Pa 1235

5↓ Pa 776: Mo 159 (interval of transposition changes briefly to a fourth on the second syllable of "formasti": aG b-flat-a-b-flat), Ben 34, Ben 35, Pa 1235, Lo 4951, Cai 61, Rms 264, Gr 807, Be 40078, Mod 7, RoV 52, Pst 120.

4. Pitch level at "et posuisti":

= Pa 776: Pa 1121, Pa 1134, Pa 1137

5↓ Pa 776: Pa 780, Mo 159, Ben 34, Ben 35, Pa 1235, Lo 4951, Cai 61, Rei 264, Gr 807, Be 40078, Mod 7, Rov 52, Pst 120

Melodic variants: There are several points of variance in this offertory, among both core and peripheral MSS. The following summary gives the distinctive Beneventan variants first, followed by a listing of variant points, then a list of variants particular to individual peripheral MSS.

Beneventan distinctiveness: The following gives the readings of Ben 34. There are very similar readings in Ben 38 and Ben 35.

Ben 34: v. 2 "LONge," shortened melisma: aG G(ori.)F a baG aGE G aGF GFD FF FD FGaGaG babG (liq.)

v. 3 "Omnia": FGFD FGaGaG a cc ca a (liq. ori.) (Lo 4951 has similar shortened melisma)

Beneventan MSS lack the melodically varied repetendum that appears in Mo 159 and the Aquitanian MSS.

Other melodic variants in core MSS:

respond, "AUtem": Lo 4951: DDG

v. 1 [cognovisti] "ME": Lo 4951: CD FF aGFF(ori.)D GF DD(ori.) C GFGFF(ori.)D CFDC CDFF aGFG FF(ori.)D CGEFFF

v. 1 "cognoVI/STI" [sessionem]: Lo 4951: abGF/FED

v. 2 "investiGAsti": At the beginning of the melisma, E (rather than D) is the bottom note of the melisma in several core and peripheral MSS, including Pa 1121 and Pa 1235.

v. 3 "cognoVI/STI": Mo 159: Da/G b-flat AG

There is an identical reading in Lo 4951 and several peripheral MSS, including Pst 120 and Be 40078.

v. 3 "Omnia" has several smaller variants in the first half of the melisma:

Mo 159: GaGE FG(quil.)aGa G b-flat aE FG(quil.)aGa etc.
Pa 1121: GaFE FG(quil.)aGa Ga FE FG(quil.)aGa
Pa 780: identical to Mo 159

Lo 4951 presents a shorted form. The entire melisma reads: GaGE FG(quil.) aGaG ccc a aG(liq.). The text scribe, however, has left room for a longer melisma.

Ben 34 and Ben 35 have a shortened form very similar to that of Lo 4951.

Variants in peripheral MSS:
Pa 1235:

v. 1 "DOmine": FF FaGE FGacbc ac c cGaF babGa

v. 1 [cognovisti] "ME": a shorter form of the melisma with melodic variants:
CDFF aGF D FEDC GFGF FD DEDC CDFF FaGF GFF DGF

v. 1 [sessionem] "MEam" (identical at v. 2 [directionem] Meam):
DF GF EDCD F FD FGFGE FD DEDC CDF FD FGFGF GFE

v. 2"noVISsima": FGa **b-flat a** aG cccac

v. 3 "Omnia": **FGFD** FGaGa **FGFD** FGaGaG ccac

v. 2 "TU": melisma begins EG caG aFE ac (etc.)

Be 40078: v. 1 "[sessionem] MEam" (identical at v. 2 "[directionem] MEam"):
DFGFEDCD F FD FGF GE FD CFDCD FF FD FGF GFG FF

Gr 807: v. 1 [sessionem] "MEam" (identical at v. 2 [directionem] MEam): CFGFDCD
FFD FGF GE FD CFDCD FFD FGF GFGFE

Mod 7:

v. 1 "DOmine": FGaba FGaba cccG aFbaGa

v. 1 "cognoviSTI"[me]: DEDC

v. 1 "ressurectiOnem": Gba**GGD** FGa Ga bcba

v. 3 "cognoVI/STI": Fa/abaG

v. 3 "Omnia": GaFE FGaGa GaFE FGaGaG (etc.)

Pst 120:

v. 1 "DOmine": EFG aGF EFG aGGG cc (etc.)

v. 1 "MEam" (same in v. 2): DEFEDCD F FD FGFGF EDEDC D FFFD
FGFGF GFE

RoV 52: The far right side of the microfilm on the first page (the respond and beginning of
v. 1) was not possible to read clearly.

respond, "SUNT": FaGFG

v. 1 "ME": CD FFaGF FD GF **E EC** GFGFFD GFGFFD (etc.)

v. 1 [sessionem] "MEam" (same in v. 2, MEam): DF GFEDCD FF FD DGFGFFD
CEDC DFF FD FGFGFE. (This version of the melisma is closer to Pa 776 than to the
majority reading of Mo 159.)

v. 3 "Omnia": GaGF FGaGa **GaFE** FGaGaG (etc.)

Roman MSS: Bod 74 lacks this offertory. The Roman version lacks the second verse of
the Gregorian, *Intellexisti*. In the respond, RoS 22 has the following variants:

"auTEM": Gcb
"NImis": acbaba
"SUNT": aGFEFG
"deUS": EGF GaGFEDEDF
"princiPAtus": FGaGbaGF

ORATIO MEA (87)

This piece exhibits very few variants. The Beneventan MSS transmit an independent
reading in two passages. In the respond, the words "in eternum" read "in excelsis" in
most sources, with the same melody. "In eternum," however, is found in Compiègne, Cha

47, and all Beneventan MSS, suggesting that this variant entered the tradition early on. In the verse, on the final syllable of "custodivi," all non-Beneventan MSS have a short melisma, as in Mo 159: G FG(quil.)aG ab-flat a.

Lo 4951 presents a very different reading on "AU/RUM": de ccd ede ccd **aGa b(quil.) cd accca ccca Gab(quil.)c/bc abaG aG**.

 Cai 61: respond, "loCUS": a bcbaG
 Pa 1235:

 respond, "loCUS": aba/aG
 respond, "ME/A": cac cdaG GaGF ac dcdc cac cac caG aba aG
 verse, "PRO/BAvit": Ga/cd

Be 40078: verse, "PRO/BAvit": Fa/cd
Gr 807:

 respond, "MEa": ca cc daG
 verse, "AUrum": deb cd eb cddc def ge ff fd fffdcb cde fd(liq.)

Roman MSS: This offertory is lacking in Bod 74. RoS 22 has the following variants:

 "et": cdc
 "ME/US": FGaGbaGFEF/FGFE
 "exCELso": cdc bcbabcba Gacba **Gacba** bcdcbabG (5319 is missing the notes in boldface)
 "aSCENdat": Gac
 "domiNUM": GabaG
 "meA": ba cabaG abaG aGFGaG FaG cdcb **GbaGF bacbaG**

CONFESSIO ET PULCHRITUDO (88)

This offertory is sung with the *Cantate domino* verses of the Christmas offertory *Laetentur caeli* (7). In most MSS, the verses are simply cued.

 There are no significant variants among core MSS. They may be found only in the following sources:

Pa 1235: "conSPECtu": FF FDGF

Cai 61: "Eius": GaGa

Pst 120:

 "conSPECtu": FF FD FGF

 "Eius": GaGa

RoV 52: The whole offertory appears to be written a fourth below its usual position, with a final of low B. The reasons for the notation at this position are unclear. At "PULchritudo," a b-natural was probably employed at the level of Ben 34 (as it is indicated in Mo 159). At the position a fourth lower, there is no equivalent of this pitch (it would be F-sharp). There is otherwise only one significant variant: "magnificenTIa": CDECD.

 Roman MSS: This offertory is lacking in Bod 74. RoS 22 has no significant variants.

DESIDERIUM (89)

This offertory shows variants in pitch level that arise from an irregular tonal structure and the need for low B-flat in the final verse. Pa 776, transcribed at the affinal position, was chosen as the base version because its pitch-level profile, with all verses in the same (transposed) plagal range, is clearly the preferred reading. If this version were transcribed in the untransposed range, the low F's in the final verse would be B-flats. In the final melisma, moreover, it is likely that the b's were intended to be sung as b-flats, the equivalent of E-flat at the lower position.

The final verse of the offertory, with its cadence on F, has a fifth-mode melodic structure. This offertory thus presents a problem of modal structure similar to that of other sixth-mode offertories: a structure typical of the mode 5 is projected a fifth below the final c. A few sources included in the sampling present a structure more consistent with a traditional understanding of the modes: the respond and first two verses are notated in the untransposed range, closing on F, and the second verse is written in the normal authentic range. This version, however, is clearly an emendation, as evidenced by the status of Pa 776 as the majority version and the presence of the singular readings discussed below.

Pitch-level profile: = Pa 776: Pa 780, Pa 1134, 1135, 1137, 1137, Pst 120, Mod 7, RoV 52, Gr 807. (In Pa 1135, Pa 1136, and Pa 780, the pitch-level profile of Pa 776 is confirmed by a notated repetendum cue to "posuisti," which begins on c in the untransposed range. In Pa 1121, the verse starts on a new line and lacks a repetendum cue.)

The following sources notate the respond and first two verses in the untransposed plagal range, with F as the final. The final verse (*Inveniatur*), however, is written in the normal authentic range, with the tonal focus on c: Mo 159, To 18, Rei 264, Cai 61.

Several sources present distinctive readings of the final verse: Ben 34, Lo 4951, Pa 1235, Be 40078. These sources require some explanation. In Ben 34, the respond and verses are notated in the untransposed range until the word "tuis," where the low B-flat first appears. A new line starts on the final syllable of "tuis." While a custos indicates that the syllable "is" will begin on C, implying that the next note is low B-flat, a new F clef is introduced in the next line that moves the range of the verse up a fifth on the last syllable of "tuis." It is doubtful that the new clef indicates a sudden transposition in performance and more likely that it reflects a "correction" of the clefing, a retrospective decision that the whole offertory should be written at the affinal position. This impression is confirmed by the repetendum cue to "posuisti," which is notated to begin on c rather than F (its position in the respond).

In Lo 4951, both the final verse and repetendum cue begin on new lines. The final melisma of the verse, however, is written a fifth lower than its position in the other sources (relative to the rest of the verse), beginning at the same pitch as the cadence on "oderunt."

In Be 40078, the transposition to the higher register begins at v. 1, *Vitam petiit*.

Pa 1235 notates the offertory in the untransposed range until the latter part of the final verse. It presents a unique reading of the final verse, in which a transposition to the higher register is made gradually and transitionally in the course of the third verse. By the cadence on "oderunt," the verse is in the authentic range, so that the cadence falls on F.

There are very few significant melodic variants among Mo 159, the core group of Aquitanian and Beneventan sources, and MSS from German-speaking areas. Some Italian MSS, however, present a shortened version of the final melisma of v. 3. Pst 120, for example, closes the melisma with the figure acccabaFacdcc, lacking equivalents for the last thirteen notes of Pa 776. To 18 presents an even shorter form of the melisma: accdcdededcdcccde-decccedccca.

Roman MSS: This offertory, without verses, is found in two of the three Roman MSS, Vat 5319 and RoS 22. The version of Vat 5319 closes with a repetition of the opening words that is lacking in the Gregorian, along with an apparent cue to a verse, *Vitam,* with a melodic incipit that is not recognizable as the beginning of a sixth-mode offertory verse. Hucke identified the incipit as a reference to introit and communion psalmody. The reasons for its appearance here are unclear, and it is not been included in the transcription of Vat 5319.[1]

RoS 22 is notated in the untransposed range rather than the affinal position and exhibits some minor differences from Vat 5319 in its use of Formula B, particularly its final cadential segment, where it shows a typical preference for the longer form: GaGFEFG occurs in the place of Vat 5319's GFEFG several times. RoS 22 also has the following variants:

"ei": GaF-GaGFEFG
"eiUS": GaGFEFG
"eUM": GaGFEFG
"pretioSO": GaGFEFG

DOMINE DEUS IN SIMPLICITATE (90)

In phrase 6, Pa 776 has no note to accommodate the second syllable of "filii," a probable scribal error. I have supplied the F from the other Aquitanian MSS and indicated it with brackets in the transcription.

The variant modal assignment of *Domine deus in simplicitate* was addressed long ago by Bomm.[1] The internal phrases of the melody suggest the sixth mode. This melody is, in fact, similar to offertories in the sixth-mode family.[2] In many MSS of the core group, however, the respond closes on low C, as in the base reading of Pa 776. In Mo 159, the respond is written a fifth higher than it is in Pa 776 as I have transcribed it, closing on G. In Mo 159, however, the repetendum after the second verse, to "deus israhel," is written a fifth too low, starting on a rather than e, which implies that the respond was intended to be sung a fifth lower and close on low C. The notated level of the repetendum in Mo 159 implies that the Aquitanian sources should be transcribed to close on low C, rather than G, in order to maintain the intended relative pitch level between the respond and verses. The repetenda in the Aquitanian sources confirm this impression.

Low C, of course, is not a legitimate final. This inconsistency with modal theory explains the higher notation of the respond in Mo 159 and, in part, the variant endings in other sources. In some MSS, the end of the respond is emended to close on F, or, less frequently, D. In other cases, it closes with a cue to repeat the opening of the respond, "domine deus," which brings the respond to a close on F. The latter practice is mentioned by John of Afflighem, who disparages it.[3] The wide variety of endings in the respond can be summarized as follows:

---

1. Hucke (1980), "Zur Aufzeichnung," 300.
1. Bomm (1929), 158–60.
2. The common traits are described in chapter 3. In addition, the verse *Fecit salomon* shares substantial material, including the final melisma, with the verse *Exspectans* in *Domine in auxilium* (27).
3. "Hoc offertorium [Domine in auxilium] plurimi male emittunt vitantes heptaphonum qui in fine est, quia eis absonus videtur. Unde et in quibusdam libris in principio eius invenitur et in fine repetunt. Similiter in offertorio Domine deus in." Smits van Waesberghe (1950), 188. For a translation see Palisca, ed. (1978), 180.

Ending on G, without return to opening: Mo 159 (notated a fifth above the other MSS)
Ending on low C, without return to opening: [Pa 776, Pa 1121, Pa 780] Pa 1235, Cai 61

Ending on F, without return to opening:

Lo 4951: "voluntaTEM" is FacaGbaGF
Be 40078: "voluntaTEM" is acGF GFD DDF
Pa 1132: "voluntaTEM" is FacGFGFDCFF
To 18: "voluntaTEM" is FabaGF GaGaFED FFF
RoV 52: FacGFGFEDF
Frutolf tonary: Fac[G]F G[FD]CF

Ending with return to opening "domine deus" (thus on F): Ben 34, Ben 35, Ben 39, Mod 7, Pst 120, Pad 47, RoV 52 (crossed out by a later hand).
Ending on D: Tri 2254: "voluntaTEM" is FacGFED
Given the sixth mode traits of the melody, the C-ending in Aquitanian MSS (and the G ending in Mo 159) comes as something of a surprise and is probably to be regarded as the *lectio difficilior*. In contrast to the melodic consistency of the sources ending on C, the sources that close on F do so in different ways, suggesting that they are emendations made to close the respond on a legitimate final and perhaps also to bring the ending of the melody into conformity with the melodic traits of its internal phrases. The C-ending is thus the preferred reading, and Pa 776 was accordingly chosen as the base version. The repetendum in Pa 776, "dicentes," probably was intended to lead back to "deus israhel," as indicated in the Roman version.

Other significant variants: There are few consequential variants, with the following exceptions.

1. The order of the verses varies.
2. The relationship between the closing melismas of the two verses. In Pa 776, the verse *Fecit* closes with an extended version of the melisma that closes the verse *Maiestas*, with the added notes acaG acaGa. The same reading is found in the other Aquitanian MSS examined and most MSS outside the core group, with the Italian exception mentioned below. This reading is also consistent with the adiastematic MSS La 239 and Ei 121. In the Beneventan tradition, the melisma in the *Fecit* verse is nearly identical to the Aquitanian one, but Beneventan MSS have a shortened version of the final melisma in the verse *Maiestas* (on "dominum").
Ben 39: c dc ccc dc ca cbc ccbGaG cbcda FGFGF FGa c ca.
RoV 52 v. *Maiestas*, "DOminum": cdc ccc dca cb cdaGc dc ccc dca cb ccbGa cb cdaF GFGF FGac caG acaG acaGa (same melisma in v. *Fecit*)
3. v. *Maiestas*, "DOmini" (phrase 5): Different reading in Mo 159 and Pa 1235:
Mo 159: FG aG Ga
Pa 1235: FGaGa

Roman MSS:
Bod 74 lacks this offertory. In Vat 5319, the respond and both verses are written at the affinal position, with traits typical of other sixth-mode offertories, which attests to a broad tonal continuity with the Gregorian version.
The Roman respond closes with a cue to the beginning of the respond, "domine deus." It is unlikely, however, that the melody concluded at "deus," as it did in Beneventan and many Italian MSS, because "deus" occurs in the middle of a statement of Formula B. The performance is more likely to have ended at the cadence on "simplicitate."

RoS 22, notated at the regular *tritus* position, with the final on F, has the following variants:

"LEtus": FGaGbaG
"POpulus": FGaGaGF
"est": GaGFEFG
"gauDIo": GaGF
"cusTOdis": FEFG

MEMOR SIT DOMINUS (91)

With an original assignment to the Mass for the ordination of a bishop, this offertory is found in few of the MSS examined. In some later MSS it appears as part of the common of saints for a bishop or confessor. The offertory is transmitted, without verses, in Vat 5319. Outside of the Aquitanian tradition, *Memor sit* is found in only in two other MSS included in the sampling, Mod 7 and Pad 47, in a distinctly variant version. A fuller examination of these variants, however, is outside the scope of this study.

DOMINE IESU CHRISTE (92)

It is doubtful that the Requiem Mass formed a part of the core repertory transmitted from Rome to Francia in the eighth century. It is lacking in the early sources indexed in *Antiphonale Missarum Sextuplex,* appearing for the first time in La 239. *Domine Iesu Christe,* then, is one of the few demonstrable instances of reverse, Frankish-to-Roman transmission in the offertory repertory. This piece is not consistently present in Gregorian MSS, some of which transmit *Domine convertere* as the offertory for the Requiem Mass.

Given the late introduction of this piece into the repertory, it is not surprising to find a varied melodic and textual tradition among Gregorian MSS. Although all versions examined employ a simple second-mode recitation formula, the versions differ in the lyrics of the opening of the respond and in melodic details. The Aquitanian version, for example, lacks the words "de sancto tui" at the opening of the respond, has a different melody for the verse *Hostias,* and has three additional verses. A full examination of these variants, however, is outside the scope of this project.

STETIT ANGELUS (93)

Although *Stetit angelus* is not part of the core repertory, its shares a partial text, in the first verse, with the Roman St. Michael offertory, *In conspectu,* a piece also given as the Michael offertory in Mont-Blandin. As discussed in chapter 2, it is not clear whether the two versions are cognates. Both Michael offertories are included here, with the corresponding passages provided in side-by-side transcription.

Aside from some pitch-level variants among Italian sources, *Stetit angelus* exhibits few variants between MSS. The Beneventan MSS present a reading very close to that of Mo 159 and the Aquitanian sources, with the following very small exceptions:

v. "in conspecTU": In most MSS, the end of the melisma has a C that is lacking in the Beneventan MSS.

respond, "iuxta aram": Most MSS have a different text underlay, with the first three notes of "aram," DGF, given to the last syllable of "iuxta."

v. "ANgelorum": Mo 159 and most other MSS have CD.

v. "doMI/NE": The text underlay indicated in the transcription is strongly suggested by the placement and grouping of the neumes, but in most sources the underlay is cabc/aG.

Some Aquitanian MSS, including Pa 776 and Lo 4951 in the core group, have an additional verse, *Factum est silentium,* which is based to some extent on melodic material from the first verse.

Gr 807: Many of the b-flats in Ben 34 are c's, at "habens," "ascendit," "conspectu."

"Thurbilem" is written a whole tone lower than it is in other MSS, beginning on the second syllable.

Be 40078: respond, "alleluia" (words and music) omitted

Pa 1235:

respond, "iuxta aram": same text underlay as Ben 34.

respond, "ascendit": No b-flats indicated.

Cai 61: The verse is written a fourth below the majority reading of Ben 34, joining at "et confitebor." Because the b's in the majority version are usually indicated as flats (matching the version of Mo 159) the two readings are intervallically identical.

Italian MSS: For reasons that are unclear, many Italian MSS notate the respond and both verses at the affinal position. A fuller sampling of Italian MSS is presented in Justmann's dissertation.[1] In one version transcribed by Justmann, Rossi 76, the respond is notated with the final on G, retaining *protus* characteristics with the consistent use of b-flat. Further variants occur at the end of the verse, beginning with "sanctum tuum"; the Italian sources in his transcriptions end the verse variously on high g, a, D, or low G. These endings hint at a possible nondiatonic practice in the Italian tradition. In most MSS, the melodic figure on "tuum" articulates a minor third, G-b-flat (a flat is indicated in all MSS with a sign for it). In several of Justmann's MSS, however, the interval articulated is a major third, f-a in RoV 52, and c-e in Vercelli 161 and Vercelli 162.

RoV 52: The whole offertory is written at the affinal position, a fifth above the majority version of Ben 34.

respond: text reads "super" in place of "iuxta."

respond "aSCENdit" (5↑Ben 34): melisma begins ae dee gge (etc.)

v. "domine": text underlay is the same as the Beneventan MSS, contrasting with most other MSS. At the end of the verse, the transpositional level changes to an octave plus a third above the majority reading.

1. Justmann (1988), 541–54.

Pst 120:

"turiBUlem": ecdbaGa. The whole offertory is written at the affinal position, a fifth above the majority version of Ben 34.

v. "domine": text underlay is the same as the Beneventan MSS, contrasting with most other MSS.

Roman MSS: Bodmer 74 lacks *In conspectu angelorum*. RoS 22 has the usual variant in the cadential segment of Formula B: GFEFG in 5319 is GaGFEFG in RoS 22 on tiBI and tuUM.

"temPLUM": FEFG

"doMIni": FGaGaGFG

BEATUS ES SIMON (94)

As discussed in chapter 2, this offertory was probably added to the Roman repertory after the transmission of the tradition to the Franks. Although it is not part of the standard Gregorian repertory, it is found in two Beneventan MSS, Ben 39 and Ben 35. The Beneventan version is a contrafact of *Angelus domini*, and the two MSS exhibit a pitch-level variant at the end of the verse that is also found in the Beneventan tradition of *Angelus domini*. The end of the melisma on "Christus" is written a fifth lower in Ben 35. In the case of *Angelus domini*, the version of Ben 35 is an anomaly, whereas that of Ben 39 is found in all MSS outside of the Beneventan sphere.

In phrase 5, the bracketed notes over "filium" are not visible on the microfilm of Ben 39 and are supplied from Ben 35.

Roman MSS: The text underlay in Vat 5319 is unclear at "Petre." The syllable "tre" is written under last four notes of the melisma on "pet." I consider this to be an error because of the usual cadential function of the notes acbaG, and have emended the transcription accordingly. RoS 22 has the expected underlay.

Bod 74 lacks this offertory. RoS 22 shows the following variants from Vat 5319:

On "PETre": varied reading of the melisma: cbabaG aGacba dcdbcba GbaGF GFEFG-FEFEDE (etc.)

"SANguis": G ac cbcabaGF acbabG
"revalaVIT": aaGFaGFG
"PAter": Gabac
"EST": G acabaGF GbaGaG
"CElis": cbabaGaG acba dcdbcba GbaG FGFEFGFEFEDE G ababaGaF acbabaGa

SELECTED BIBLIOGRAPHY

Agustoni, Luigi. "Ein Vergleich zwischen dem Gregorianischen und dem Ambrosianischen Choral-einige Aspekte." In *Cantando praedicare: Godejard Joppich zum 60. Geburtstag*, ed. Stefan Klöckner, 13–28. Regensburg: Gustav Bosse, 1992.

Albarosa, Nino. "Offertorium Deus, tu convertens." *Muzyka* 34 (1989): 47–55.

Amelli, Ambrogio. *Liber psalmorum iuxta antiquissimam latinam versionem nunc primum ex Casinensi cod. 557 in lucem profertur.* Rome: F. Pustet, 1912.

Amiet, R. "La tradition manuscrite du missel ambrosien." *Scriptorium* 14 (1960): 16–60.

Andrieu, Michel. *Les Ordines Romani Du Haut Moyen Âge.* Louvain: Spicilegium sacrum lovaniense administration, 1951.

Apel, Willi. *Gregorian Chant.* Bloomington: Indiana University Press, 1958.

Atkinson, Charles M. "Das Tonsystem des Chorals im Spiegel mittelalterlicher Musiktraktate." In *Geschichte der Musiktheorie*, vol. 4, ed. Michel Huglo, 28–33. Darmstadt: Wissenschaftliche Buchgellschaft, 2000.

———. "*De accentibus toni oritur nota quae dicitur neuma*: Prosodic Accents, the Accent Theory, and the Paleo-Frankish Script." In *Essays on Medieval Music in Honor of David G. Hughes*, ed. Graeme Boone, 17–42. Cambridge, Mass.: Harvard University Press, 1995.

———. "From *Vitium* to *Tonus Acquisitus*: On the Evolution of the Notational Matrix of Medieval Chant." In *Cantus Planus: Papers Read at the Third Meeting, Tihany, Hungary, 19–24 September 1988*, ed. László Dobszay, 181–99. Budapest: Hungarian Academy of Sciences Institute for Musicology, 1990.

Augustine. *Sancti Aurelii Augustini Retractationum libri.* Edited by Almut Mutzenbecher. Corpus Christianorum: Series Latina, vol. 57. Turnholt: Brepols, 1984.

Bailey, Terence. *The Transitoria of the Ambrosian Mass: Compositional Process in Ecclesiastical Chant.* Ottawa: Institute of Mediaeval Music, 2003.

———. "Ambrosian Chant." In *New Grove Dictionary of Music and Musicians.* 2nd ed. New York: Grove, 2001.

———. "The Development and Chronology of the Ambrosian Sanctorale: The Evidence of the Antiphon Texts." In *The Divine Office in the Latin Middle Ages*, ed. Margot E. Fassler and Rebecca A. Baltzer, 257–76. New York: Oxford University Press, 2000.

———. "Milanese Melodic Tropes." *Journal of the Plainsong and Mediaeval Music Society* 11 (1988): 1–12.

———. "Ambrosian Chant in Southern Italy." *Journal of the Plainsong and Mediaeval Music Society* 6 (1983): 173–95.

———. *The Ambrosian Alleluias.* Englefield Green, England: Plainsong and Mediaeval Music Society, 1983.

Baroffio, Giacomo. "The Melismas in the Gregorian Offertories: A Checklist." In *The Offertory and Its Verses: Research, Past, Present, and Future*, ed. Roman Hankeln, 89–94. Trondheim: Tapir Academic Press, 2007.

————. "Iter Liturgicum Ambrosianum: Inventario Sommario Di Libri Liturgici Ambrosiani." *Aevum* 74 (2000): 583–603.

————. *"Die mailändische Überlieferung des Offertoriums Sanctificavit."* In *Festschrift Bruno Stablein zum 70 Geburtstag,* ed. Martin Ruhnke, 1–8. Kassel: Barenreiter, 1967.

————. "Die Offertorien der ambrosianischen Kirche: Vorstudie zur kritischen Ausgabeder mailändischen Gesänge." Ph.D. diss., Cologne University, 1964.

Bartlett, F. C. *Remembering: A Study in Experimental and Social Psychology.* London: Cambridge University Press, 1932.

Bede. *Historia ecclesiastica gentis anglorum.* 2 vols. Edited by J. E. King. Cambridge, Mass.: Harvard University Press, 1963.

Beisel, Fritz. *Studien zu den fränkisch-römischen Beziehungen: Von ihren Anfängen bis zum Ausgang des 6. Jahrhunderts.* Idstein: Ullrich-Schulz-Kirchner, 1987.

Bellingham, Jane, and Michel Huglo. "Gallican Chant." *New Grove Dictionary of Music and Musicians, 2nd ed.* New York: Grove, 2001.

Bernard, Philippe. "La schola cantorum romaine et les échanges liturgiques avec la Gaule au sixième siècle." *Études Grégoriennes* 37 (1999): 61–120.

————. *Du chant romain au chant gregorien (IVe–xIIIe siecle).* Paris: Cerf, 1996.

————. "Les variantes textuelles entre 'vieux-romain' et 'gregorien': Quelques resultats." In *Requirentes modos musicos: Melanges offerts à Dom Jean Claire à l'occasion de son 75e-anniversaire, de ses 50 ans de profession monastique, et de ses 25 ans comme maitre de choeur à Solesmes,* ed. Daniel Sailnier, 63–82. Sable-sur-Sarthe: Abbaye Saint-Pierre de Solesmes, 1996.

————. "Les versets des alléluias et des offertoires: Témoins et l'histoire de la culture à Rome entre 560 to 742." *Musica e Storia* 3 (1995): 5–40.

————. "Bilan historiographique de la question des rapports entre les chants 'vieux-romain' et 'gregorien.'" *Ecclesia Orans* 11 (1994): 7–35.

Bielitz, Mathias. *Zum Bezeichneten der Neumen, insbesondere der Liqueszenz: Ein Hypothesenansatz zum Verhältnis von Musik und Sprache, zur diatonischen Rationalität, zur Bewegungs-und Raum Analogie, zur Entstehung der Neumenschrift und zur Rezeption des Gregorianischen Chorals in Benevent.* Neckargemünd: Männeles Verlag, 1998.

Boe, John. "Deus Israel and Roman Introits." *Plainsong and Medieval Music* 14 (2005): 125–67.

————. "The Roman Missa Sponsalicia." *Plainsong and Medieval Music* 11 (2002): 127–66.

————. "Old Roman Votive-Mass Chants in Florence, Biblioteca Riccardiana, MSS 299 and 300, and Vatican City, Biblioteca Apostolica Vaticana, Archivio San Pietro F11: A Source Study." In *Western Plainchant in the First Millennium: Studies in the Medieval Liturgy and its Music,* ed. Sean Gallagher et al., 261–318. Aldershot, England: Ashgate, 2003.

————. "Music Notation in Archivio San Pietro C 105 and in the Farfa Breviary, Chigi C.VI.177." *Early Music History* 18 (1999): 1–45.

————. "Chant Notation in Eleventh-Century Roman Manuscripts before 1071." In *Essays on Medieval Music in Honor of David G. Hughes,* ed. Graeme Boone, 43–57. Cambridge, Mass.: Harvard University Press, 1995.

————. "The Beneventan Apostrophus in South Italian Notation, A.D. 1000–1100." *Early Music History* 3 (1983): 43–66.

————. "Old Beneventan Chant at Montecassino: Gloriosus Confessor Domini Benedictus." *Acta Musicologica* 55 (1983): 69–73.

————. "A New Source for Old Beneventan Chant: The Santa Sophia Maundy in MS Ottoboni Lat. 145." *Acta Musicologica* 52 (1980): 122–33.

Bogaert, Pierre-Maurice. "Le psautier latin des origines au xiie siècle: Essai d'histoire."
      In *Der Septuaginta-Psalter and seine Tocherübersetzungen: Symposium in Göttingen 1997*,
      ed. Anneli Aejmelaeus and Udo Quast, 51–81. Göttingen: Vandenhoeck und Ruprecht,
      2000.
————. "La Bible latine des origines au moyen âge." *Revue théologique de Louvain* 19
      (1988): 293–95.
Bomm, Urbanus. *Der Wechel der Modalitätbestimmung in der Tradition der Meßgesänge im
      IX. bis XIII. Jahrhundert und sein Einfluß auf der Tradition ihrer Melodien.* Einsiedeln,
      1929. Reprint, Hildesheim: Olms, 1975.
Booth, G. J. "The Offertory Rite in the Ordo Romanus Primus: A Study of Its Bearing on the
      So-Called 'Offertory Procession.'" Ph.D. diss., Catholic University of America, 1948.
Borders, James M. "The Northern Italian Antiphons *ante evangelium* and the Gallican
      Connection." *Journal of Musicological Research* 8 (1988): 1–53.
Borella, Pietro. "Influssi carolingi e monastici sul Messale Ambrosiano." In *Miscellanea li-
      turgica in honorem L. Cuniberti Mohlberg*, 1:73–115. Rome: Edizioni Liturgiche, 1948.
Boretius, Alfred, ed. *Monumenta germaniae historica Capitularia regum francorum.*
      Hannover: Hahn, 1883.
Bower, Calvin M. "The Transmission of Ancient Music Theory into the Middle Ages."
      In *The Cambridge History of Western Music Theory*, ed. Thomas Christensen, 136–67.
      Cambridge: Cambridge University Press, 2002.
————. "'Adhuc ex parte et in enigmate cernimus . . .': Reflections on the Closing
      Chapters of *Musica enchiriadis*." In *Music in the Mirror: Reflections on the History of Music
      Theory and Literature for the Twenty-First Century*, ed. Andreas Giger and Thomas
      Mathiesen, 21–44. Lincoln: University of Nebraska Press, 2002.
————. "The Grammatical Model of Musical Understanding in the Middle Ages." In
      Hermenutics and Medieval Culture, ed. Patrick Gallacher and Helen Damico, 133–45.
      Albany: State University of New York Press, 1989.
Boynton, Susan. *Liturgy and History at the Imperial Abbey of Farfa.* Ithaca, N.Y.: Cornell
      University Press, 2006.
Bradshaw, Paul F. *The Search for the Origins of Christian Worship: Sources and Methods for the
      Study of Early Liturgy.* London: Oxford University Press, 2002.
Brinktrine, I. "De orgine offertorii in Missa Romana." *Ephemerides Liturgicae* 15 (1926):
      15–20.
Brou, Louis, and José Vives. *Antifonario Visigótico Mozárabe de la Catedral de Léon.*
      Barcelona: CSIC (Inst P Enrique Flórez), 1959.
Bullough, Donald A. *Alcuin: Achievement and Reputation.* Leiden: Brill, 2004.
Busse Berger, Anna Maria. *Medieval Music and the Art of Memory.* Berkeley: University of
      California Press, 2005.
Callevaert, C. "De offerenda et oblatione in missa." *Periodica de re morali* 33 (1944): 61–94.
Calouri, Eleanor. "The Roman Offertory." Ph.D. diss., Brandeis University, 1958.
Capelle, B. "E'élément africain dans le Psalterium Casinense." *Revue Bénédictine* 32 (1920):
      113–31.
Carruthers, Mary. *The Book of Memory: A Study of Memory in Medieval Culture.* Cambridge:
      Cambridge University Press, 1990.
Clark, Alan. *The Origin and Development of the Offertory Rite and Its Function in the Mass.*
      Rome: Polyglottis Vaticanus, 1950.
————. "The Function of the Offertory Rite in the Mass." *Ephemerides liturgicae* 63(1950):
      309–44.

———. "The Offertory Rite: A Recent Study." *Ephemerides liturgicae* 67 (1953): 242–47.

Cohen, David E. "Notes, Modes, and Scales in the Earlier Middle Ages." In *The Cambridge History of Western Music Theory*, ed. Thomas Christensen, 307–63. Cambridge: Cambridge University Press, 2002.

Connolly, Thomas. "The Graduale of S. Cecilia in Trastevere and the Old Roman Tradition." *Journal of the American Musicological Society* 28 (1975): 413–58.

———. "The Introits of the Old Roman Chant." Ph.D. diss., Harvard University, 1972.

———. "Introits and Archetypes: Some Archaisms of the Old Roman Chant." *Journal of the American Musicological Society* 25 (1972): 157–74.

Cowdrey, Herbert E. J. *The Age of Abbot Desiderius: Montecassino, the Papacy, and the Normans in the Eleventh and Early Twelfth Centuries*. Oxford: Oxford University Press, 1983.

Crocker, Richard. "Gregorian Studies in the Twenty-First Century." *Plainsong and Medieval Music* 4 (1995): 1–35.

Cubitt, Catherine. "Unity and Diversity in the Early Anglo-Saxon Liturgy." In *Unity and Diversity in the Church: Papers Read at the 1994 Summer Meeting, and the 1995 Winter Meeting of the Ecclesiastical History Society*, ed. R. N. Swanson, 45–59. Cambridge, Mass.: Blackwell, 1996.

Cullin, Olivier. "Une pièce Gallicane conservée par la liturgie de Galliac. L'Offertoire Salvator Mundi pour les défunts." *Cahiers de fanjaeux* 17 (1982): 287–96.

Cutter, Paul. *Musical Sources of the Old-Roman Mass: An Inventory of MS Rome, St. Cecilia Gradual 1071; MS Rome, Vaticanum Latinum 5319; MSS Rome, SanPietro F 22 and F 11*. Stuttgart-Neuhausen: Hänssler, 1979.

———. "Oral Transmission of the Old Roman Responsories?" *Musical Quarterly* 62 (1976): 182–94.

———. "The Question of the Old Roman Chant: A Reappraisal." *Acta Musicologica* 39 (1967): 2–20.

———. "The Old Roman Chant Tradition: Oral or Written?" *Journal of the American Musicological Society* 20 (1967): 167–81.

Daur, Klaus. "Einleitung." In *Arnobii Iunoris Commentarii in Psalmos*. Turnholt: Brepols, 1990.

De Bruyne, Donatien. "Le problème du psautier romain." *Revue Bénédictine* 42 (1930): 101–26.

———. "La reconstitution du psautier hexaplaire latin." *Revue Bénédictine* 41 (1929): 97–324.

———. "Études sur les origines de la Vulgate en Espagne." *Revue Bénédictine* 31(1914): 373–401.

Delalande, Dominique. *Vers la version authentique du Graduel grégorien: Le Graduel des Prêcheurs, Bibliothèque d'histoire Dominicaine*. Paris: Cerf, 1949.

Dijk, S. J. P. van. "The Urban and Papal Rites in Seventh- and Eighth-Century Rome." *Sacris erudiri* 8 (1956): 76–142.

———. "Papal Schola versus Charlemagne." In *Organicae Voces: Festschrift Joseph Smits van Waesberghe angeboten anlässlich seines 60. Geburtstages*, 21–30. Amsterdam: Instituut voor Middeleeuwse Muziekwetenschap, 1963.

Dold, Alban. *Getilgte Paulus- und Psalmtexte unter getilgten Ambrosianischen Liturgiestücken aus cod. Sangall. 908*. Texte und Arbeiten 14. Beuron, Germany: Kunstschule der Erzabtei, 1928.

Duchesne, L., ed. *Le Liber pontificalis*. 3 vols. Paris: Éditions de Boccard, 1955–57.

Dyer, Joseph. "The Roman Offertory: An Introduction and Some Hypotheses." In *The Offertory and Its Verses: Research, Past, Present, and Future*, ed. Roman Hankeln, 15–40. Trondheim: Tapir Academic Press, 2007.

———. Review of *The Advent Project: The Later Seventh-Century Creation of the Roman Mass Proper*, by James McKinnon. *Early Music History* 20 (2001): 279–308.

———. "The Introit and Communion Psalmody of Old Roman Chant." In *Chant and Its Peripheries: Essays in Honour of Terence Bailey*, ed. Bryan Gillingham and Paul Merkley, 110–42. Ottawa: Institute of Medieval Music, 1998.

———. "'*Tropis semper variantibus*': Compositional' Strategies in the Offertories of the Old Roman Chant." *Early Music History* 17 (1998): 1–69.

———. "Roman Singers of the Later Middle Ages." In *Cantus Planus: Papers Read at the Sixth Meeting, Eger, Hungary, 1993*, vol. 1, ed. László Dobszay, 45–64. Budapest: Hungarian Academy of Sciences Institute for Musicology, 1995.

———. "Prolegomena to a History of Music and Liturgy at Rome in the Middle Ages." In *Essays on Medieval Music in Honor of David G. Hughes*, ed. Graeme Boone, 87–116. Cambridge, Mass.: Harvard University Press, 1995.

———. "The Schola Cantorum and Its Roman Milieu in the Early Middle Ages." In *De Musica et Cantu: Studien zur Geschichte der Kirchenmusik und der Oper: Helmut Hucke zum 60. Geburtstag*, ed. Peter Kahn and Anne-Katrin Heimer, 19–50. Hildesheim: Georg Olms, 1993.

———. "The Singing of Psalms in the Early-Medieval Office." *Speculum* 64 (1989): 535–78.

———. "Monastic Psalmody of the Middle Ages." *Revue Bénédictine* 99 (1989): 41–74.

———. "Psalmody and the Roman Mass." *Studies in Music* 10 (1985): 1–24.

———. "Latin Psalters, Old Roman and Gregorian Chants." *Kirchenmusikalisches Jahrbuch* 68 (1984): 11–30.

———. "The Offertory Chant of the Roman Liturgy and Its Musical Form." *Studi musicali* 11 (1982): 3–30.

———. "Augustine and the 'Hymni ante oblationum:' The Earliest Offertory Chants?" *Revue des études augustiniennes* 27 (1981): 85–99.

———. "The Offertories of Old-Roman Chant: A Musico-Liturgical Investigation." Ph.D. diss., Boston University, 1971.

Fassler, Margot. "Sermons, Sacramentaries, and Early Sources for the Office in the Latin West: The Example of Advent." In *The Divine Office in the Latin Middle Ages: Methodology and Source Studies, Regional Developments, Hagiography*, ed. Margot E. Fassler and Rebecca A. Baltzer, 15–47. New York: Oxford University Press, 2000.

Fernández De La Cuesta González, Ismael. "El Canto Viejo-Hispánico y el Canto Viejo-Galicano." *Revista De Musicología* 16 (1993): 438–56.

Ferrari, Guy. *Early Roman Monasteries: Notes for the History of Monasteries at Rome from the Fifth through the Tenth Century*. Vatican City: Pontifico Istituto de Archeologia Christiana, 1957.

Fischer, Bonifatius. *Beiträge Zur Geschichte Der Lateinischen Bibeltexte*. Freiburg: Herder, 1986.

———. "Zur Überlieferung altlateinischer Bibeltexte im Mittelalter." *Nederlands Archief voor Kerkgeschiedenis* 56 (1975): 19–33.

———. "Die Texte." In *Der Stuttgarter Bilderpsalter Bibl. fol. 23 Württembergische Landesbibliothek Stuttgart*, 2:223–88. Stuttgart: E. Schreiber Graphische Kunstanstalten, 1968.

Fischer, Rupert. "Die Bedeutung des Codex Paris, B.N. lat.776 (Albi) und des Codex St. Gallen, Stiftsbibliothek 381 (Versikular) für die Rekonstruktion gregorianischer Melodien." *Beiträge zur Gregorianik* 22 (1996): 43–73.

———. "Benevento, Biblioteca capitolare, cod. 34." *Beiträge zur Gregorianik* 22 (1996): 111–35.

Flotzinger, Rudolph. "Zu Herkunft und Datierung der Gradualien Graz 807 und Wien 13314." *Studia musicologica* 31 (1989): 57–80.

Frasch, Cheryl Crawford. "Notation as a Guide to Modality in the Offertories of Paris, B.N. lat. 903." Ph.D. diss., Ohio State University, 1986.

Frei, Judith. *Das ambrosianische Sakramentar D 3-3 aus dem mailändischen Metropolitankapitel: Ein textkritische und redaktionsgeschichtliche Untersuchung der mailändischen Sakramentartradition*. Achendorff: Münster Westfalen, 1974.

Ganshof, François Louis. *The Carolingians and the Frankish Monarchy*, trans. Janet Sondheimer. Ithaca, N.Y.: Cornell University Press, 1971.

Gmelch, Joseph. *Die viertelstonstufen im Messtonale von Montpellier*. Eichstätt: P. Brönnersche, 1911.

Gregory the Great. *Moralia in Iob*. Edited by Marci Adriaen. Corpus Christianorum: Series Latina, vol. 143. Turnholt: Brepols, 1979.

Gregory of Tours. *Liber miraculorum*. In *Patrologia Latina* 81 (Paris: J. P. Migne).

———. *Sermo in parochiis necessarius*. Edited by Germain Morin. Corpus Christianorum: Series Latina, vol. 103. Turnholt: Brepols, 1970.

Gretsch, Mechthild. "The Roman Psalter, Its Old English Glosses, and the English Benedictine Reform." In *The Liturgy of the Late Anglo-Saxon Church*, ed. Helen Gittos and M. Bradford Bedingfield, 13–28. London: Boydell Press, 2005.

Gribomont, Jean. "Le texte biblique de Grégoire." In *Grégoire le Grand (Colloque de Chantilly, 1982)*, ed. Jacques Fontaine et al., 467–75. Paris: CNRS, 1986.

———. "Les plus anciennes traductions latins." In *Le monde latin antique et la Bible*, ed. Jacques Fontaine and Charles Pietri, 56–57. Paris: Editions Beauchesne, 1985.

———. "La règle et la Bible." In *Atti de 7 congresso internazionale di studi sull'alto Medioevo*, 355–88 Spoleto: Presso la sede del Centro studi, 1982.

———. "La transmission des textes bibliques in Italie." In *La cultura in Italia fra tardo antico e alto medioevo: Atti del convegno tenuto a Roma, Consiglio Nazionale delle Ricerche, dal 12 al 16 novembre 1979*, 2:731–412. Rome: Herder, 1981.

———. "L'eglise et les versions bibliques." *La maison-dieu* 62 (1960): 41–68.

Gribomont, Jean, and Francesca Merlo. *Il Salterio di Rufino*. Rome: Abbey of St. Girolamo, 1972.

Grier, James. *The Musical World of a Medieval Monk: Adémar de Chabannes in Eleventh-Century Aquitaine*. Cambridge: Cambridge University Press, 2007.

———. "The Musical Autographs of Adémar de Chabannes (989–1034)." *Early Music History* 24 (2005): 125–67.

———. "Adémar de Chabannes, Carolingian Musical Practices, and Nota Romana." *Journal of the American Musicological Society* 56 (2003): 43–98.

———. "The Divine Office of St. Martial in the Early Eleventh Century." In *The Divine Office in the Latin Middle Ages*, ed. Margot Fassler and Rebecca Baltzer, 179–204. New York: Oxford University Press, 2000.

———. *The Critical Editing of Music: History, Method, and Practice*. Cambridge: Cambridge University Press, 1996.

Gryson, Roger, ed. *Apocalypsis Iohannis*. Vol. 26, 2,*Vetus latina: Die Reste der Altlateinischen Bible* (Freiburg: Herder, 2000).

Guillaume Durand. *Rationale Divinorum Officiorum*, ed. G. H. Buijssen. Assen: Van Gorcum, 1983.

Gushee, Lawrence A. "The *Musica diciplina* of Aurelian of Réôme: a Critical Text and Commentary." Ph.D. diss., Yale University, 1963.

Haas, Max. Review of *Cantilena Romana: Untersuchungen Zur Überlieferung Des Gregorianischen Chorals*, by Andreas Pfisterer. *Die Musikforschung* 58 (2005): 433.

———. *Mündliche Überlieferung und Altrömischer Choral: Historische und Analytische Computergestützte Untersuchunge*. Bern: Lang, 1997.

Hankeln, Roman, ed. *The Offertory and Its Verses: Research, Past, Present, and Future.* Trondheim: Tapir Academic Press, 2007.

———. "What Does the Prosula Tell? Aquitanian Offertory-Prosulas and Significance for the History of Offertory Melismas." In *The Offertory and Its Verses: Research, Past, Present, and Future*, ed. Roman Hankeln, 111–22. Trondheim: Tapir Academic Press, 2007.

———. *Die Offertoriumsprosuln der aquitanischen Handschriften: Voruntersuchungen zur Edition des aquitanischen Offertoriumscorpus und seiner Erweiterungen.* 3 vols. Tutzing: Hans Schneider, 1999.

———. "'Was Meint Der Schreiber?' Überlegungen zur Notation des Offertoriums *Tui Sunt Celi* im Graduale von St. Yrieix, Paris Bibliothèque Nationale, Fonds Latin 903." In *Cantus Planus: Papers Read at the Sixth Meeting, Eger, Hungary*, vol. 2, ed. László Dobszay, 539–60. Budapest: Hungarian Academy of Sciences, 1995.

Hansen, Finn Egeland. *H 159 Montpellier*. Copenhagen: Dan Fog, 1974.

———. *The Grammar of Gregorian Tonality.* 2 vols. Copenhagen: Dan Fog, 1979.

Hanssens, Jean-Michael. *Amalarii episcopi opera liturgica omnia.* 3 vols. *Studi e testi* 138–40. Vatican City: Biblioteca Apostolica Vaticana, 1950.

Hatten, Robert. *Musical Meaning in Beethoven: Markedness, Correlation, and Interpretation.* Bloomington: Indiana University Press, 1994.

Hawkes, Terence. *Structuralism and Semiotics.* Berkeley: University of California Press, 1977.

Heiming, P. Odilo. "Die mailändischen seiben Votivemessen für die einzelnen Tage der Woche und der Liber Sacramentorum des sel. Alkuin." In *Miscellanea liturgica in honorem L. Cuniberti Mohlberg*, 2:317–40. Rome: Edizioni Liturgiche, 1949.

———. "Vorgregorianisch-römische Offertorien in der mailändischen Liturgie." *Liturgisches Leben* 5 (1938): 72–79.

Helsen, Kate Eve. "The Great Responsories of the Divine Office: Aspects of Structure and Transmission." Ph.D. diss., Universität Regensburg, 2008.

Hen, Yitzhak. "Rome, Anglo-Saxon England and the Formation of the Frankish Liturgy." *Revue Bénédictine* 112 (2002): 301–22.

———. "The Liturgy of St Willibrord." *Anglo-Saxon England* 26 (1997): 41–62.

———. "Unity in Diversity: The Liturgy of Frankish Gaul before the Carolingians." In *Unity and Diversity in the Church: Papers Read at the 1994 Summer Meeting, and the 1995 Winter Meeting of the Ecclesiastical History Society*, ed. R. N. Swanson, 19–30. Cambridge, Mass.: Blackwell, 1996.

———. *Culture and Religion in Merovingian Gaul, AD 481–751.* Leiden: Brill, 1995.

Hesbert, René-Jean, ed. *Antiphonale Missarum Sextuplex.* Brussels: Vromant, 1935. Reprint, Rome: Herder, 1975.

———. "Un antique offertoire de la Pentecôte: 'Factus est repente.'" In *Organicae voces: Festschrift Joseph Smits van Waesberghe*, 59–69. Amsterdam: Instituut voor Middeleeuwse Muziekwetenschap, 1963.

Hiley, David. *Western Plainchant: A Handbook*. Oxford: Clarendon Press, 1993.

Hornby, Emma. "Reading the Bible: Rhetoric and Exegesis in Gregorian Chant." In *Cantus Planus: Papers Read at the Twelfth Meeding, Lillafüred, 2004*, ed. László Dobszay, 285–301. Budapest: Hungarian Academy of Sciences, 2006.

———. "The Transmission of Western Chant in the Eighth and Ninth Centuries: Evaluating Kenneth Levy's Reading of the Evidence." *Journal of Musicology* 21 (2004): 418–57.

———. *Gregorian and Old Roman Eighth-Mode Tracts: A Case Study in the Transmission of Western Chant*. Aldershot, England: Ashgate, 2002.

———. "Two Expressions of a Single Idea: Using the Eighth-Mode Tracts to Describe the Relationship between Old Roman and Gregorian Chant." In *Cantus Planus: Papers Read at the Ninth Meeting, Visegrad, Hungary, 1998*, ed. László Dobszay, 415–29. Budapest: Hungarian Academy of Sciences, 2001.

———. "The Origins of the Eighth-Mode Tracts: What Kept the Oral Transmission Stable?" *Études grégoriennes* 26 (1998): 135–62.

Hucke, Helmut. "Die Entstehung des Gregorianischen Gesangs." In *Neue Musik und Tradition: Festschrift Rudolf Stephan Zum 65. Geburtstag*, 11–23. Laaber: Laaber-Verlag, 1990.

———. "Gregorianische Fragen." *Die Musikforschung* 41 (1988): 304–30.

———. "Die Übergang von mündlicher zu schriftlicher Musiküberlieferung im Mittlealter." In *International Musicological Society: Report, Berkeley 1977*, ed. Daniel Heartz and Bonnie Wade, 180–91. Kassel: Barenreiter, 1981.

———. "Toward a New Historical View of Gregorian Chant." *Journal of the American Musicological Society* 33 (1980): 437–67.

———."Zur Aufzeichnung der altrömischen Offertorien." In *Ut Mens Concordet Voce: Festschrift Eugene Cardine*, ed. J. B. Göschl, 296–313. St. Ottilien, Germany: EOS Verlag, 1980.

———. "Karolingische Renaissance und Gregorianischer Gesang." *Die Musikforschung* 28 (1975): 4–13.

———. "Die Texte der Offertorien." In *Speculum Musicae Artis: Festgabe für Heinrich Husmann zum 60 Geburtstag*, ed. Heinz Becker and Reinhard Gerlach, 193–97. Munich: W. Fink, 1970.

———. "Zu Einigen Problemen der Choralforschung." *Die Musikforschung* 11 (1958): 385–414.

———. "Die Gregorianische Gradualeweise des 2. Tons und ihre ambrosianischen Parallelen: Ein Beitrag zur Erforschung des Ambrosianischen Gesangs." *Archiv für Musikwissenschaft* 13 (1956): 285–314.

———. "Gregorianischer Gesang in altrömischer und fränkischer Uberlieferung." *Archiv für Musikwissenschaft* 12 (1955): 74–87.

———. "Die Einführung des Gregorianischen Gesangs im Frankenreich." *Römische Quartalschrift* 49 (1954): 147–94.

Hughes, David G. "From the Advent Project to the Late Middle Ages: Some Issues of Transmission." In *Western Plainchant in the First Millennium: Studies in the Medieval Liturgy and Its Music*, ed. Sean Gallagher et al., 181–98. Aldershot, England: Ashgate, 2003.

———. "Guido's Tritus: An Aspect of Chant Style." In *The Study of Medieval Chant: Paths and Bridges, East and West: In Honor of Kenneth Levy*, ed. Peter Jeffery, 211–26. Woodbridge, England: Boydell and Brewer, 2001.

————. "The Alleluias Dies Sanctificatus and Vidimus Stellam as Examples of Late Chant Transmission." *Plainsong and Medieval Music* 7 (1998): 101–28.

————. "The Implications of Variants for Chant Transmission." In *De Musica et Cantu: Studien zur Geschichte der Kirchenmusik und der Oper: Helmut Hucke zum 60. Geburstag*, ed. Peter Kahn and Anne-Katrin Heimer, 65–74. Hildesheim: Georg Olms, 1993.

————. "Evidence for the Traditional View of the Transmission of Gregorian Chant." *Journal of the American Musicological Society* 40 (1987): 377–404.

Huglo, Michel. Review of *The Grammar of Gregorian Tonality: An Investigation Based on the Repertory in Codex H 159, Montpellier*, by Finn Egeland Hansen. *Journal of the American Musicological Society* 37 (1984): 416–24.

————. "Altgallikanische Liturgie." In *Geschichte der katholischen Kirchenmusik, 1, Von den Anfängen bis zum Tridentinum*, ed. Karl Gustav Fellerer, 219–33. Kassel: Bärenreiter, 1972.

————. *Fonti e paleografia del canto ambrosiano.* Milan: Archivio Ambrosiano, 1956.

————. "Le Tonaire de Saint-Bénigne de Dijon." *Annales musicologiques* 4 (1956): 7–18.

————. "Le chant vieux-romain: Manuscrits et témoins indirects." *Sacris erudiri* 6 (1954): 96–124.

Jacobsthal, Gustav. *Die chromatische Alteration im liturgischen Gesang der abendländischen Kirche.* Berlin: J. Springer, 1897. Reprint, Hildesheim: Olms, 1970.

Jeffery, Peter. "Monastic Reading and the Emerging Roman Chant Repertory." In *Western Plainchant in the First Millennium: Studies in the Medieval Liturgy and Its Music*, ed. Sean Gallagher et al., 45–104. Aldershot, England: Ashgate, 2003.

————. Review of *The Advent Project: The Later Seventh-Century Creation of the Roman Mass Proper*, by James McKinnon. *Journal of the American Musicological Society* 56 (2003): 169–78.

————. "Rome and Jerusalem: From Oral Tradition to Written Repertory in Two Ancient Liturgical Centers." In *Essays on Medieval Music in Honor of David G. Hughes*, ed. Graeme Boone, 207–48. Cambridge, Mass.: Harvard University Press, 1995.

————. *Re-envisioning Past Musical Cultures: Ethnomusicology in the Study of Gregorian Chant.* Chicago: University of Chicago, 1992.

————. "The Introduction of Psalmody into the Roman Mass by Pope Celestine I (422–432): Reinterpreting a Passage in the Liber Pontificalis." *Archiv Für Liturgiewissenschaft* 26 (1984): 147–65.

Jungmann, Joseph. *The Mass of the Roman Rite.* New York: Benziger, 1951.

Justmann, Dean Richard. "Mode-One Offertories: A Critical Edition with Analysis." Ph.D. diss., Northwestern University, 1988.

Kähmer, Inge. "Die Offertoriums-Überlieferung in Rom. Vat. Lat 5319." Ph.D. diss., University of Cologne, 1971.

Karp, Theodore C. *Aspects of Orality and Formularity in Gregorian Chant.* Evanston, Ill.: Northwestern University Press, 1998.

————. "The Offertory In die sollemnitatis." In *Laborare fratres in unum: Festschrift László Dobszay zum 60. Geburtstag*, ed. Janka Szendrei and David Hiley, 151–64. Hildesheim: Olms, 1995.

————. "Some Interrelationships between Gregorian and Old Roman Chant." In *Cantus Planus: Papers Read at the Fifth Meeting, 1992*, ed. László Dobszay, 187–203. Budapest: Hungarian Academy of Sciences Institute for Musicology, 1992.

Kelly, Thomas Forrest. "Old-Roman Chant and the Responsories of Noah: New Evidence from Sutri." *Early Music History* 26 (2007): 91–121.

————. "New Evidence of the Old Beneventan Chant." *Plainsong and Medieval Music* 9 (2000): 81–93.

————. "A Beneventan Borrowing in the Saint Cecilia Gradual." In *Max Lütolf zum 60. Geburtstag: Festschrift*, ed. Bernard Hangartner and Urs Fischer, 11–20. Basel: Wiese, 1994.

————. *The Beneventan Chant*. Cambridge: Cambridge University Press, 1989.

————. "Beneventan and Milanese Chant." *Journal of the Royal Musical Association* 112 (1987): 173–95.

————. "Non-Gregorian Music in an Antiphoner of Benevento." *Journal of Musicology* 5 (1987): 478–97.

————. "Montecassino and the Old Beneventan Chant." *Early Music History* 5 (1985): 53–83.

Kennedy, V. L. "The Offertory Rite." *Orate Fratres* 12 (1937–38): 193–98.

King, Archdale A. *Liturgies of the Primatial Sees*. Milwaukee: Bruce, 1957.

Klauser, Theodor. "Die liturgischen Austauschbeziegungen zwichen der römischen und der fränkisch-deutschen Kirche vom achten bis zum elften Jahrhundert." *Historisches Jahrbuch* 55 (1933): 169–77.

————. *A Short History of the Western Liturgy*. Translated by John Halliburton. New York: Oxford University Press, 1979.

Levy, Kenneth. "Gregorian Chant and the Romans." *Journal of the American Musicological Society* 56 (2003): 5–41.

————. *Tollite Portas*: An Ante-Evangelium Reclaimed?" In *Western Plainchant in the First Millennium: Studies in the Medieval Liturgy and Its Music*, ed. Sean Gallagher et al., 231–41. Aldershot, England: Ashgate, 2003.

————. "A New Look at Old Roman Chant II." *Early Music History* 20 (2001): 173–97.

————. "A New Look at Old Roman Chant I." *Early Music History: Studies in Medieval and Early Modern Music* 19 (2000): 81–104.

————. *Gregorian Chant and the Carolingians*. Princeton, N.J.: Princeton University Press, 1998.

————. "Gregorian Chant and Oral Transmission." In *Essays on Medieval Music in Honor of David G. Hughes*, ed. Graeme Boone, 277–86. Cambridge: Harvard University Press, 1995.

————. "Abbot Helisachar's Antiphoner." *Journal of the American Musicological Society* 48 (1995): 171–86.

————. "The Iberian Peninsula and the Formation of Early Western Chant." *Acta Musicologica* 63 (1991): 23–24.

————. "On Gregorian Orality." *Journal of the American Musicological Society* 43 (1990): 185–227.

————. "Charlemagne's Archetype of Gregorian Chant." *Journal of the American Musicological Society* 15 (1987): 1–30.

————. "Toledo, Rome, and the Legacy of Gaul." *Early Music History* 4 (1984): 51–101.

————. "Lux de Luce: The Origin of an Italian Sequence." *Musical Quarterly* 57 (1971): 40–61.

————. "The Italian Neophytes' Chants." *Journal of the American Musicological Society* 23 (1970): 181–227.

————. "The Byzantine Sanctus and Its Modal Tradition in East and West." *Annales musicologiques* 6 (1958): 7–67.

Lidov, David. "Lamento di Tristano." In *Music before 1600*, ed. Mark Everist, 93–113. Oxford: Blackwell, 1992.

Lipphardt, Walther. "Gregor der Grosse und sein Anteil an römischen Antiphonar." In *Actes du congrès internationale de musique sacrée* (1950): 248–54.

Loewe, Raphael. "The Medieval History of the Latin Vulgate." In *The Cambridge History of the Bible*, 2:102–54. Cambridge: Cambridge University Press, 1969.

Loos, Ike de. "The Transmission of the *Responsoria Prolixa* According to the Manuscripts of St. Mary's Church, Utrecht." *Tijdschrift van de Koninklijke Vereniging voor Nederlandse Muziek Geschied enis* 49 (1999): 5–32.

Lütolf, Max, ed. *Das Graduale von Santa Cecilia in Trastevere (Cod. Bodmer 74)*. 2 vols. Cologny-Genève: Foundation Martin Bodmer, 1987.

Magistretti, Marco, ed. *Manuale Ambrosianum ex codice saec. xi olim in usum canonicae Vallis Travaliae*. Milan: U Hoepli, 1904–1905.

Maiani, Brad. "Approaching the Communion Melodies." *Journal of the American Musicological Society* 53 (2000): 209–90.

———. "Readings and Responsories: The Eighth-Century Night Office Lectionary and the Responsoria Prolixa." *Journal of Musicology* 16 (1998): 254–82.

Maiani, Bradford Charles. "The Responsory-Communions: Toward a Chronology of Selected Proper Chants." Ph.D. diss., University of North Carolina, Chapel Hill, 1996.

Maloy, Rebecca. "Problems of Pitch Level and Modal Structure in Some Gregorian Offertories." In *The Offertory and Its Verses: Research, Past, Present, and Future*, ed. Roman Hankeln, 67–88. Trondheim: Tapir Academic Press, 2007.

———, ed. *München, Bayerische Staatsbibliothek, Clm 14965b: The Tonary of Frutolf of Michelsberg*. Ottawa: Institute of Mediaeval Music, 2006.

———. "The Word-Music Relationship in the Gregorian and Old Roman Offertories," *Studia Musicologica* 57 (2004): 131–48.

———. "The Roles of Notation in Frutolf of Michelsberg's Tonary." *Journal of Musicology* 19 (2002): 641–93.

———. "The Offertory Chant: Aspect of Chronology and Transmission." Ph.D. diss., University of Cincinnati, 2001.

Mansi, Giovan Domenico, and Philippe Labbe. *Sacrorum conciliorum, nova et amplissima collectio*. Graz: Akademische Druck und Verlagsanstalt, 1960.

Marsden, Richard. *The Text of the Old Testament in Anglo-Saxon England*. Cambridge: Cambridge University Press, 1995.

Mckinnon, James W. *The Advent Project: The Later-Seventh-Century Creation of the Roman Mass Proper*. Berkeley: University of California Press, 2000.

———. "Compositional Planning in the Roman Mass Proper." *Studia Musicologica Academiae Scientiarum Hungaricae* 3 (1998): 241–45.

———. "Festival, Text and Melody: Chronological Stages in the Life of a Chant?" In *Chant and Its Peripheries: Essays in Honour of Terence Bailey*, ed. Bryan Gillingham, 1–11. Ottawa: Institute of Mediaeval Music, 1998.

———. "The Gregorian Canticle Tracts of the Old Roman Easter Vigil." In *Festschrift Walter Wiora Zum 90. Geburtstag (30. Dezember 1996)*, ed. Christoph-Hellmut Mahling and Ruth Seiberts, 354–29. Tutzing: Schneider, 1997.

———. "Preface to the Study of the Alleluia." *Early Music History* 15 (1996): 213–49.

———. "Lector Chant versus Schola Chant: A Question of Historical Plausibility." In *Laborare fratres in unum: Festschrift László Dobszay zum 60. Geburtstag*, ed. Janka Szendrei and David Hiley, 201–11. Hildesheim: Olms, 1995.

———. "Properization: the Roman Mass." In *Cantus Planus: Papers Read at the Sixth Meeting, Eger, Hungary, 1993*, vol. 1, ed. László Dobszay, 15–22. Budapest: Hungarian Academy of Sciences Institute for Musicology, 1995.

———. "The Eighth-Century Frankish-Roman Communion Cycle." *Journal of the American Musicological Society* 45 (1992): 179–227.

McKitterick, Rosamond. Review of *Gregorian Chant and the Carolingians*, by Kenneth Levy. *Early Music History* 19 (2000): 278–87.

———. "Carolingian Bible Production: The Tours Anomaly." In *The Early Medieval Bible: Its Production, Decoration, and Use*, ed. Richard Gameson, 63–77. Cambridge: Cambridge University Press, 1994.

———. "Unity and Diversity in the Carolingian Church." In *Unity and Diversity in the Church: Papers Read at the 1994 Summer Meeting, and the 1995 Winter Meeting of the Ecclesiastical History Society*, ed. R. N. Swanson, 59–82. Cambridge, Mass.: Blackwell, 1996.

———. *Carolingian Culture: Emulation and Innovation*. Cambridge: Cambridge University Press, 1993.

———. *The Uses of Literacy in Early Mediaeval Europe*. Cambridge: Cambridge University Press, 1990.

———. *The Carolingians and the Written Word*. Cambridge: Cambridge University Press, 1989.

———. *The Frankish Kingdoms under the Carolingians, 751–987*. New York: Longman, 1983.

Metzger, Bruce M. *The Early Versions of the New Testament: Their Origin, Transmission, and Limitations*. Oxford, Clarendon, 1977.

Mohlberg, Cunibert, et al., eds. *Liber sacramentorum Romanae aeclessiae ordinis anni circuli*. Rerum Ecclesiasticarum Documenta. Rome: Herder, 1960.

Morin, Germain, ed. *Liber comicus, sive, Lectionarius missae quo Toletana Ecclesia ante annos mille et ducentos utebatur*. Maredsoli: Monasterio S. Benedicti, 1987.

Murphy, Joseph Michael. "The Communions of the Old Roman Chant." Ph.D. diss., University of Pennsylvania, 1977.

Nardini, Luisa. "Aliens in Disguise: Byzantine and Gallican Chants in the Latin Liturgy." *Plainsong and Medieval Music* 13 (2007): 145–72.

———. "Il Repertorio Neo-Gregoriano del Proprium Missae in Area Beneventana." Ph.D. diss., Università degli Studi di Roma, La Sapienza, 2001.

Netzer, N. *L'introduction de messe romaine en France sous les Carolingiens*. Paris: Picard, 1910.

Nickl, Georg. *Der Anteil des Volkes an der Messliturgie im Frankenreich*. Innsbruck: F. Rausch, 1930.

Noble, Thomas F. X. *The Republic of St. Peter: The Birth of the Papal State, 680–825*. Philadelphia: University of Pennsylvania Press, 1984.

Nowacki, Edward. "Reading the Melodies of the Old Roman Mass Proper: A Hypothesis Defended." In *Western Plainchant in the First Millennium: Studies in the Medieval Liturgy and Its Music*, ed. Sean Gallagher et al., 319–30. Aldershot, England: Ashgate, 2003.

———. "The Modes of the Old Roman Mass Proper: What Kind of Glue?" In *Cantus Planus: Papers Read at the Ninth Meeting, Esztergom, Visegrád, 1998*, ed. László Dobszay, 431–48. Budapest: Hungarian Academy of Sciences Institute for Musicology, 2001.

———. "Chant Research at the Turn of the Century and the Analytical Programme of Helmut Hucke." *Plainsong and Medieval Music* 7 (1998): 47–71.

———. "Constantinople-Aachen-Rome: The Transmission of *Veterem Hominem*." In *De Musica et Cantu: Studien zur Geschichte der Kirchenmusik und der Oper: Helmut Hucke zum 60. Geburtstag*, ed. Peter Kahn and Anne-Katrin Heimer, 95–115. Hildesheim: Georg Olms, 1993.

———. "Text Declamation as a Determinant of Melodic Form in the Old Roman Eighth-Mode Tracts." *Early Music History* 6 (1986): 193–226.

———. "The Gregorian Office Antiphons and the Comparative Method." *Journal of Musicology* 4 (1985): 243–75.

———. "The Syntactical Analysis of Plainchant." In *International Musicological Society: Report, Berkeley 1977*, ed. Daniel Heartz and Bonnie Wade, 191–201. Kassel: Bärenreiter, 1981.

———. "Studies on the Office Antiphons of the Old Roman Manuscripts." Ph.D. diss., Brandeis University, 1980.

Ott, Karl. "I versetti ambrosiani e gregoriani dell'offertorio." *Rassegna Gregoriana* 10 (1911): 345–60.

———. *Offertoriale sive versus offertoriorum*. Tournai: Typis Societatis S. Joannis Evangelistae, 1935).

———. *Offertoriale triplex cum versiculis*. Solesmes: Sablé-sur-Sarthe: Abbaye Saint-Pierre de Solesmes, 1985.

Palisca, Claude, ed. *Hucbald, Guido and John on Music: Three Medieval Treatises*. New Haven, Conn.: Yale University Press, 1978.

Pesce, Dolores. *The Affinities and Medieval Transposition*. Bloomington: Indiana University Press, 1987.

Pfisterer, Andreas. "*Super flumina Babylonis*: On the Prehistory of a Roman Offertory." In *The Offertory and Its Verses: Research, Past, Present, and Future*, ed. Roman Hankeln, 41–56. Trondheim: Tapir Academic Press, 2007.

———. "Remarks on Roman and Non-Roman Offertories." *Plainsong and Medieval Music* 14 (2005): 169–81.

———. "James McKinnon und die Datierung des gregorianischen Chorals." *Kirchenmusikalisches Jahrbuch* 85 (2002): 31–53.

———. *Cantilena Romana: Untersuchungen zur Überlieferung des gregorianischen Chorals*. Paderborn: Schöningh, 2001.

Phillips, Nancy. "Notationen und Notationslehren von Boethius bis zum 12. Jahrhundert." In *Geschichte der Musiktheorie*, vol. 4, ed. Michel Huglo, 591–602. Darmstadt: Wissenschaftliche Buchgellschaft, 2000.

Phillips, Nancy Catherine. "Musica and Scolica enchiriadis: The Literary, Theoretical, and Musical Sources." Ph.D. diss., New York University, 1985.

Pietschmann, Petrus. "Die nicht aus dem Psalter entnommenen Meßgesangstückeauf ihre Textgestalt untersucht." *Jahrbuch für Liturgiewissenschaft* 12 (1932): 87–144.

Pinell, Jordi. "Repertorio del 'sacrificium' (canto ofertorial del rito hispánico) para el ciclo dominical 'de quotidiano.'" *Ecclesia orans* 1 (1984): 57–111.

Pitman, Grover Allen. "The Lenten Offertories of the Aquitanian Manuscripts." Ph.D. diss., Catholic University of America, 1973.

Planchart, Alejandro Enrique. "Proses in the Sources of Roman Chant, and Their Alleluias." In *The Study of Medieval Chant: Paths and Bridges, East and West: In Honor of Kenneth Levy*, ed. Peter Jeffery, 313–39. Woodbridge, England: Boydell and Brewer, 2001.

Ponte, Joseph. "Aurelianus Reomensis Musica disciplina: A Critical Edition and Commentary." Ph.D. diss., Brandeis University, 1961.

Porter, W. S. "Studies in the Mozarabic Office." *Journal of Theological Studies* 35 (1934): 266–86.

Pothier, Dom Joseph. "Offertoire 'Beata es.'" *Revue du chant grégorien* 7 (1898): 17–20.

———. "L'offertoire 'Felix namque es.'" *Revue du chant grégorien* 15 (1907): 105–14.

———. "Exemples d'offertoires empruntés à d'anciens versets." *Revue du chant grégorien* 4 (1895–96): 160–69.

Powers, Harold. "Language Models and Music Analysis." *Ethnomusicology* 24 (1980): 1–60.

Praßl, Franz Karl. "Chromatische Veränderungen von Choralmelodien in Theorie und Praxis." In *Cantando praedicare: Godejard Joppich zum 60. Geburtstag*, ed. Stefan Klöckner, 157–68. Regensburg: Gustav Bosse, 1992.

Quasten, Johannes. "Oriental Influence in the Gallican Liturgy." *Traditio* 1 (1943).

Radcliffe, Edward. *Expositio antiquae liturgiae Gallicanae*. London: Larry Bradshaw Society, 1971.

Radice, Mark A. "Form, Style, and Structure in the Offertory Chants of the Tonary of St. Benigne of Dijon, H.159, Montpellier." *Ars musica Denver* 2 (1989): 16–23.

Randel, Don Michael. "The Old Hispanic Rite as Evidence for the Earliest Forms of the Western Christian Liturgies." *Revista De Musicología* 16 (1993): 491–96.

———. *An Index to Chants of the Mozarabic Rite*. Princeton, N.J.: Princeton University Press, 1973.

Rankin, Susan. Review of *The Advent Project: The Later-Seventh-Century Creation of the Roman Mass Proper*, by James McKinnon. *Plainsong and Medieval Music* 11 (2002): 73.

———. "Carolingian Music." In *Carolingian Culture: Emulation and Innovation*, ed. Rosamond McKitterick, 274–317. Cambridge: Cambridge University Press, 1994.

Ropa, Giampaolo. "Il culto della vergine a Bologna nel Medioevo." In *Codex Angelicus 123: Studi sul graduale-tropario Bolognese del secolo XI e sui manoscritti 0 collegati*, ed. Maria Teresa Rosa-Barezzani and Giampaolo Ropa, 3–32. Cremona: Una cosa rara, 1996.

Rose, Els. "Liturgical Commeration of the Saints in the *Missale Gothicum* (vat. reg. lat. 317): New Approaches to the Liturgy of Early Medieval Gaul." *Vigiliae Christianae* 58 (2004): 75–97.

Rubin, David. *Memory in Oral Traditions: The Cognitive Psychology of Epics, Ballads, and Counting-Out Rhymes*. Oxford: Clarendon Press, 1995.

Sabaino, Daniele. "Reminiscenze ambrosiane nella creatività liturgica di Angelica 123?" Elementi e ipotesi di rilettura." In *Codex Angelicus 123: Studi sul graduale-tropario Bolognese del secolo XI e sui manoscritti collegati*, ed. Maria Teresa Rosa-Barezzani and Giampaolo Ropa, 67–116. Cremona: Una cosa rara, 1996.

Salmon, Pierre, ed. *Le Lectionnaire de Luxeuil (Paris, ms. lat. 9427)*. Collectanea Biblica Latina 7. Rome: Abbaye Saint-Jérôme, 1944.

Schmid, Hans, ed. *Musica et Scolica Enchiriadis una cum aliquibus tractatulis adiunctis*. Munich: Bayerische Akademie der Wissenschaften, 1981.

Sidler, Hubert. "Studien zu den alten Offertorien mit ihren Versen." Ph.D. diss., University of Fribourg, 1939.

Smits van Waesberghe, Joseph, ed. *Johannes Affligemensis, De musica cum tonario*. Corpus scriptorum de musica, vol. 1. [Rome]: American Institute of Musicology, 1950.

———. "Neues über die Schola cantorum zu Rom." In *Internationaler Kongress für katholische Kirchenmusik*, 111–19. Vienna, 1955.

Snyder, John L. *Theinred of Dover's "De legitimus ordinibus pentachordorum et tetrachordorum": A Critical Text and Translation, with an Introduction, Annotations, and Indices*. Ottawa: Institute of Mediaeval Music, 2006.

————. "Non-diatonic Tones in Plainsong: Theinred of Dover versus Guido d'Arezzo." In *La Musique et la rite: Sacrè et profane: Actes du XIIIe Congrès de la Société internationale de musicologie*, 48–67. Strasbourg: Association de Publications près les Universités de Strasbourg, 1986.

Stäblein, Bruno, and Margareta Landwehr-Melnicki, eds. *Die Gesänge des altrömischen Graduale Vat. lat. 5319*. Monumenta Monodica Medii Aevi 2. Kassel: Bärenreiter, 1970.

Stäblein, Bruno. "Nochmals zur angeblichen Entstehung des gregorianischen Chorals." *Archiv für Musikwissenschaft* 37 (1970): 110–21.

————. "Kann der gregorianischen Choral in Frankenreich entstanden sein?" *Archiv für Musikwissenschaft* 35 (1968): 153–69.

————. "Zur Entstehung der gregorianischen Melodien." *Kirchenmusikalisches Jahrbuch* 35 (1955): 5–9.

Steiner, Ruth. "The Offertory-Responsory *Recordare mei Domine*." In *The Offertory and Its Verses: Research, Past, Present, and Future*, ed. Roman Hankeln, 57–66. Trondheim: Tapir Academic Press, 2007.

————. "On the Verses of the Offertory *Elegerunt*." In *The Study of Medieval Chant: Paths and Bridges, East and West: In Honor of Kenneth Levy*, ed. Peter Jeffery, 283–303. Woodbridge, England: Boydell and Brewer, 2001.

————. *Studies in Gregorian Chant*. Aldershot, England: Ashgate, 1999.

————. "Holocausta Medullata: An Offertory for St. Saturninus." In *De Musica et Cantu: Studien zur Geschichte der Kirchenmusik und der Oper: Helmut Hucke zum 60. Geburtstag*, ed. Peter Kahn and Anne-Katrin Heimer, 263–74. Hildesheim: Georg Olms, 1993.

————. "Some Questions about the Gregorian Offertories and Their Verses." *Journal of the American Musicological Society* 19 (1966): 177–81.

————. "Some Melismas for Office Responsories." *Journal of the American Musicological Society* 26 (1973): 108–31.

Strunk, Oliver, et al. *Source Readings in Music History*. New York: Norton, 1998.

Stuart, Nicholas. "Melodic Editing in an Eleventh-Century Gradual (Paris, B.N. lat. 903)." *Journal of the Plainsong and Medieval Music Society* 2 (1979): 2–10.

Sullivan, Richard E. "The Carolingian Age: Reflections on Its Place in the History of the Middle Ages." *Speculum* 64 (1989): 267–306.

Thurn, Hans. *Comes Romanus Wirziburgensis: Facsimile Edition of Codex M.p.th.f. 62 of the University Library of Würzburg*. Graz: Akademische Druck und Verlagsanstalt, 1968.

Tietze, Christoph. *Hymn Introits for the Liturgical Year*. Chicago: Hillenbrand, 2005.

Tirot, Paul. *Histoire des prières d'offertoire dans la liturgie romaine du VIIe au XVIe siècle*. Rome: Edizioni Liturgische, 1985.

Treitler, Leo. *With Voice and Pen: Coming to Know Medieval Song and How It Was Made*. New York: Oxford University Press, 2003.

————. "The 'Unwritten' and 'Written Transmission' of Medieval Chant and the Start-Up of Musical Notation." *Journal of Musicology* 10 (1992): 131–91.

————. "The Beginnings of Music Writing in the West: Historical and Semiotic Aspects." *Language and Communication* 9 (1989): 193.

————. "Communication." *Journal of the American Musicological Society* 41 (1988): 566–75.

————. "Reading and Singing: On the Genesis of Occidental Music-Writing." *Early Music History* 4 (1984): 135–208.

————. "Orality and Literacy in the Music of the Middle Ages." *Paragon* 2 (1984): 143–74.

―――. "Orality and Literacy in the Music of the European Middle Ages." In *The Oral and Literate in Music*, ed. Tokumaru Yosihiko and Yamaguti Osamu, 36–56. Toyko: Academia Music, 1986.

―――. "The Early History of Music Writing in the West." *Journal of the American Musicological Society* 35 (1982): 237–79.

―――. "Oral, Written, and Literate Process in the Transmission of Medieval Music." *Speculum* 56 (1981): 471–91.

―――. "Transmission and the Study of Music History." In *International Musicological Society: Report, Berkeley 1977*, ed. Daniel Heartz and Bonnie Wade, 202–11. Kassel: Barenreiter, 1981.

―――. "'Centonate' Chant: Übles Flickwerk or E Pluribus Unus?" *Journal of the American Musicological Society* 28 (1975): 1–23.

―――. "Homer and Gregory: The Transmission of Epic Poetry and Plainchant." *Musical Quarterly* 60 (1974): 333–72.

―――. "Music Syntax in the Middle Ages: Background to an Aesthetic Problem." *Perspectives of New Music* 4 (1965): 75–85.

Turco, Alberto. "Les tons des versets d'offertoires 'vieux romain.'" In *Requirentes modos musicos: Melanges offerts à Dom Jean Claire à l'occasion de son 75e- anniversaire, de ses 50 ans de profession monastique, et de ses 25 ans comme maitre de choeur à Solesmes*. Sable-sur-Sarthe: Abbaye Saint-Pierre de Solesmes, 1996.

Vaccari, Alberto. "I salteri de S. Girolamo e di S. Agostino." In *Scritti di erudizione e di filologia*, 207–55. Rome: Edizioni di storia e letteratura, 1952.

van der Mensbrugghe, A. "Pseudo-Germanus Reconsidered." *Studia Patristica* 5 (1962): 172–84.

―――. *The Emergence of Gregorian Chant*. Rochester, N.Y.: 1983.

van der Werf, Hendrick. "Communication." *Journal of the American Musicological Society* 42 (1989): 432–32.

Van Deusen, Nancy. "Formula or Formulation? Old Roman Chant and Italianate Melodic Style." In *Max Lütolf Zum 60. Geburtstag: Festschrift*, ed. Bernhard Hangartner and Urs Fischer, 21–30. Basel: Wiese, 1994.

―――. "An Historical and Stylistic Comparison of the Graduals of Gregorian and Old Roman Chant." Ph.D. diss., Indiana University, 1972.

Van Dijk, Stephen J. P. "The Papal Schola versus Charlemagne." In *Organicae voces: Festschrift Joseph Smits van Waesberghe*, 21–30. Amsterdam: Instituut voor Middeleeuwse Muziekwetenschap, 1963.

Vives, J., ed. *Oracional visigótico*. Monumenta hispaniae sacra, Serie litúrgica. Barcelona: Consejo Superior de Investigaciones Científicas, Escuela de Estudios Medievales, Sección de Barcelona, Balmesiana: Biblioteca Balmes, 1946.

Vogel, Cyrille. *Medieval Liturgy: An Introduction to the Sources*. Revised and translated by William Storey and Niels Rasmussen. Washington, D.C.: Pastoral Press, 1986.

―――. "Le réforme liturgique sous Charlemagne." In *Karl der Grosse: Lebenswerk und Nachleben*, ed. Wolfgang Braunfels, 217–32. Dusseldorf: Schwann, 1968.

―――. "La réforme cultuelle sous Pépin le Bref et sous Charlemagne." In *Die karolingische Renaissance*, ed. Erna Patzelt, 171–242. Graz: Akademische Druck und Verlagsanstalt, 1965.

―――. "Les échanges liturgiques entre Rome et les pays Francs jusqu'a l'époque de Charlemagne." In *Settimane de studie del centri italiano de studi sull'alto medioevo VII*, 185–95. Spoleto: Presso la Sede del Centro, 1960.

Wagner, Peter. *Einführung in die gregorianischem Melodien I.* Leipzig: Breitkopf und Härtel, 1911.

Wallace-Hadrill, John Michael. *The Frankish Church.* Oxford: Clarendon Press, 1984.

Weber, Robert. *Le Psautier romain et les autres anciens psautiers latins.* Rome: Abbaye St-Jerome, 1953.

Uldaric of Cluny. *Antiquiores consuetudines Cluniacensis monasterii.* In *Patrologia Latina* (Paris: J. P. Migne), 149.

Yates, Frances. *The Art of Memory.* New York: Routledge, 1999.

Zak, Sabine. "Sollemnis oblatio: Studien zum Offertorium im Mittelalter." *Kirchenmusikalisches Jahrbuch* 72 (1988): 27–51.

Zijlstra, A., Marcel J., and Hendrik Van Der Werf. "On Abbot Helischar's Antiphoner by Kenneth Levy, Summer 1995." *Journal of the American Musicological Society* 50 (1997): 238.

INDEX OF CHANTS

GENERAL INDEX